Enduring Issues in Mass Communication

The West Series in Mass Communication

Consulting Editors:
Everette E. Dennis • Arnold H. Ismach • Donald M. Gillmor
University of Minnesota

Enduring Issues in Mass Communication

Edited by

Everette E. Dennis
Arnold H. Ismach
Donald M. Gillmor

University of Minnesota

West Publishing Company • St. Paul • New York • Los Angeles • San Francisco

COPYRIGHT © 1978 By WEST PUBLISHING CO.
  50 West Kellogg Boulevard
  P. O. Box 3526
  St. Paul, Minnesota 55165

Printed in the United States of America

Library of Congress Cataloging in Publication Data

Main entry under title:

Enduring issues in mass communication.
  (The West series in mass communication)
  Includes bibliographies and index.
  1. Mass media—Addresses, essays, lectures.
I. Dennis, Everette E.   II. Ismach, Arnold.
III. Gillmor, Donald M.
P91.25.E5   301.16'1   77-19058
ISBN 0-8299-0173-6

Contents

v

Part Two

Part Three

Enduring Issues in Mass Communication

*

Preview

Generations of social and political philosophers have looked at journalism from a fundamental, and often unstated, premise: that the press is essential to the functioning of democratic society.[1] Without access to the full range of information about their world, this premise holds, citizens cannot fulfill their roles, and democracy will wither. Thus the press is regarded as democracy's life line, the glue that holds the system together.

This bias toward journalism, assigning it a central role in modern society, is acknowledged by critics and supporters alike.[2] Complaints about the mass media tend to focus on their performance and not on the assumption that they are vital parts of the democratic machinery. If democracy depends on an informed and active citizenry, the press is considered the vehicle to assure this condition.

It is not surprising, therefore, that most efforts to appraise the media assign functions to them that center on their informational role. Harold Lasswell, the political scientist, suggested thirty years ago a model for functional analysis of the media that still guides thinking on the subject today. The media, he wrote, provide surveillance of the environment, correlation of the components of society in responding to the environment, and transmission of the social heritage.[3]

Others have since translated Lasswell's formulation into more felicitous prose. In the process they have added other functions, such as satisfying the entertainment and other personal needs of audiences, enhancing the operation of commerce, and providing a vehicle for profit.[4] But at their core, attempts to specify mass media functions follow the Lasswellian model: the media should monitor society, help people to understand the world around them, and serve as a socializing force. The media are expected to create a sense of community and identity in their consumers, to mold speech and thought patterns, to provide models for living.

Over the years, mass communication has been examined and judged on the basis of these assumed functions. Do the news media adequately provide information about the environment? Are they effective in making

3

this information coherent and useful? Do they help shape the beliefs and values of their audiences? Is the vision of a democratic society, with the press as catalyst, being realized? If not, what changes are required of the media?

These are the enduring questions about mass communication. They remain issues—matters of disagreement and argument—today as they have been for decades. They provide the rationale for the selection of readings in this collection.

These articles, essays, and studies were chosen for their constancy and for their relevance to the enduring issues in mass communication and not for their correspondence to current topics that may be of passing interest. Some are classics, as pertinent today as when they were written. Others, including those specially written for this volume, synthesize a field of inquiry or integrate related topics. As a group, the articles examine the mass media in the context of society and not as isolated entities.

We live in an age of pervasive mass communication. The "information explosion" has become a cliché. Increasing literacy, greater affluence and discretionary time, and advances in communications technology have converged to bring mass media within the reach of every segment of society. One result of this change in the social equation has been growing concern about the effects of media on people. How well do the media serve Lasswell's injunction to transmit the social heritage and correlate the components of society?

Part One traces the transition in perspectives on media impact as they have evolved through three stages. The first stage was the development of the modern concept of public opinion and its corollary that propaganda is an all-powerful and dangerous force. Next was a stage in which empirical investigation raised doubts about the mass media's power to significantly influence public opinion or behavior—the "minimal effects" school. Finally, in the past decade, a third stage has been reached: the reemergence of the "powerful media" position.

The likelihood that media will fulfill their assigned functions depends to a great degree on the content of printed messages and broadcast programs. If journalists fail to monitor the environment effectively, then news consumers will suffer accordingly. The forces that shape news media content are examined in Part Two.

First among these forces are the professional norms that govern the structure and practice of journalism. Disagreement about what is news, and what should be news, is one of the more enduring issues in journalism. Next, the characteristics of journalists and the methods through which they approach their work are considered as a second locus from which to explain media content. A third factor has its origin in a distinguishing characteristic of mass media in America: they are almost exclusively privately controlled and operated for profit. The economics of the mass media thus suggests another source for the determination of content.

The widespread belief in the impact of mass media, and the resulting concern about content, has produced strong crosscurrents in society for reform, change, and control. Another force for change, more impersonal, has appeared in the form of technological advances. Most of the contemporary issues involving mass communication originate from one or more of these factors. Part Three examines the principal issues that dominate media discussion today.

The Constitution of the United States was shaped by the then-radical notion that the people should control their governors. To enable the press to inform the people about the activities of their governors, the First Amendment prohibited government from making any laws abridging freedom of the press. As it was then, this structure continues to be a source of perplexity and debate. The constitutional issues that affect media-society relations open this section.

Changes in the systems that deliver messages may have a profound impact on all other mass media issues. The advent of commercial television after World War II was one such change. Others with as great a potential for change are now on the drawing boards or awaiting economic feasibility. These innovations and their prospects are considered next.

Finally, there is the explosive question of who shall control the channels of communication. Access to the press by different elements of society is perhaps the principal public issue concerning mass media today. The several forms of access they seek are examined in the concluding readings.

Taken together, this collection of readings presents the fundamental concepts that have guided discourse about mass communication for the past fifty years. They should provide students with a useful foundation from which to view other issues about the mass media as they appear and fade with the passage of time.

Critics of initial drafts of this book suggested that all articles be edited into a homogenized style to sound as if they had been written by the same author.

"Students won't understand research reports."
"Law review articles are too difficult."
"Intellectual essays are beyond the reach of college students."

We heard these and other complaints. We disagree. We feel that it is important to present the flavor of the original work. We have, of course, edited for readability and consistency, but the idea of reducing an empirical research report to a bland summary of findings strikes us as insulting to students.

Research on mass communication in America falls into many different categories. Some of it is historical, some is social-scientific, some employs the methods of the literary critic or the legal scholar. We believe that it is important for students to delve into a wide range of scholarly materials in their search for learning and the advancement of knowledge. It is therefore important to look at work that employs different research methods.

But some things are common to all research. The student reading this book should examine the author's initial premises, whether stated formally or woven into descriptive prose. What does the author set out to do? What are the parameters of the research project or the analytical essay? What hypotheses are suggested? What methods of gathering data are used? Are they the most appropriate ones? How much can one generalize from that particular method? How far does the researcher carry it? What of the findings? Do they answer the questions originally posed?

Finally, what of the researcher's analysis? Does it stay within the bounds of the data (evidence, whether quantitative or qualitative), or does it go beyond? What are the implications of the article? How does it relate to earlier research? What unresolved questions does it leave?

It is crucial that the student remember that most research is somewhat fragmentary in the scheme of things. It must be linked with earlier observations and studies. Carefully examining the foundations of a particular study, the construction of the research process itself, and the extension of the findings is something the student should do with regularity, whether in mass communication or in psychology or political science.

In this book we call on the best efforts of students. The articles presented here demand that you think about what is said. No one of them has a corner on the truth, but all of them taken together present a rich basis for understanding mass communication in American society. Reflected in the articles are issues that have persisted in the literature for many years. There are no easy answers and researchers can only try to find their way through this most complex of fields.

NOTES

1. See, for example, William Rivers and Wilbur Schramm, *Responsibility in Mass Communication* (New York: Harper & Row, 1969); and Commission on Freedom of the Press, *A Free and Responsible Press* (Chicago: University of Chicago Press, 1947).

2. One of the few voices raised against this view is that of the French philosopher Jacques Ellul, who contends that not only is the press not essential to the proper functioning of society, but that it works against democracy. See his treatise, *The Political Illusion,* trans. Konrad Kellen (New York: Knopf, 1967), pp. 57-78; and Clifford G. Christians, *Jacques Ellul and Democracy's "Vital Information" Premise,* Journalism Monographs, No. 45 (Lexington, Ky.: Association for Education in Journalism), 1976.

3. Harold D. Lasswell, "The Structure and Function of Communication in Society," in L. Bryson (ed.), *The Communication of Ideas* (New York: Harper, 1948).

4. See, for example, Wilbur Schramm, *The Process and Effects of Mass Communication* (Urbana, Ill.: University of Illinois Press, 1954; rev. ed., with Donald F. Roberts, 1971); and Charles R. Wright, *Mass Communication: A Sociological Perspective* (New York: Random House, 1959; 2nd ed., 1975).

Part One

The Impact of Media on Society

Topics

Introduction

The notion that the press is powerful and has considerable influence on the individual and on institutions in society is deeply imbedded in our consciousness. Popular literature is replete with references to a powerful press. "The pen is mightier than the sword," goes one ancient aphorism. Buttressing this are the public statements of public people who have often spoken of the strength of the press. Napoleon, for example, was quoted as saying that "three hostile newspapers are more to be feared than a thousand bayonets."

In spite of the generally agreed-upon idea that the press had power, could sway opinions, and could change behavior, there was little systematic scholarly attention to the press or to mass communication generally until this century. It all began with the fierce propaganda battle that was waged as a part of World War I. The British and Germans, in the days before the United States' entry into the war, tried to sway opinions with a wide range of pamphlets, posters, and other materials. After the war the study of propaganda and its impact on men's minds became commonplace. The implicit assumption of the propaganda researchers and their followers was that communication messages delivered by mass media could not only provide information to the public but could also change opinions and move people to action. Mass media in this view had an important, if not central, role in society.

The importance of mass communication in shaping people's perceptions of the world was pointed up by Walter Lippmann in his important 1922 book *Public Opinion*. In this seminal work Lippmann introduced the idea of stereotypes, which he said were "pictures inside our heads." Society, Lippmann observed, had grown too large, too complex for the individual to cope with it without help. A good deal of that help—though by no means all—could come from the press. "The world that we have to deal with politically," he wrote, "is out of reach, out of sight, out of mind. It has to be explored, reported, and imagined." Enter the press (and later other means of mass communication), which helps the individual make "for himself a trustworthy picture inside his head of the world beyond his reach." Lippmann never doubted the importance of the press, and he commented that it had not yet been the subject of serious, scholarly inquiry. Still, he recognized the limitations of the press and the nature of its interactions with the rest of society when he wrote:

The press is no substitute for institutions. It is like the beam of a searchlight that moves restlessly about, bringing one episode and then another out of darkness into vision. Men cannot do the work of the world by this light alone. They cannot govern society by episodes, incidents, and eruptions. It is only when they work by a steady light of their own, that the press, when it is turned upon them reveals a situation intelligible enough for a popular decision. The trouble lies deeper than the press, and so does the remedy.[1]

If Lippmann qualified the role of the press, other commentators did not. Looking back on World War I and the growing reach of radio and film, many writers and commentators conjured up a vision of an all-powerful press, controlled by powerful persons, from which the individual could hardly escape. One high point in this period was Orson Welles's famous 1937 radio dramatization of H. G. Wells's "War of the Worlds." So real was the broadcast dramatizing Martians landing on earth that thousands of people fled their homes in fear. Didn't this prove the power of the media?

In the scholarly literature, the powerful-media concept was shaken by a 1940 study of voters and voting behavior in Erie County, Ohio. Instead of swaying voters and marshaling change, the press was seen as more of a reinforcing influence. Scholars began to doubt the influence of the media as change agents in communication. Study after study reinforced the 1940 research and its results. By 1960 Joseph Klapper, in a superb synthesis of the results of two decades of effects studies, could write, "Mass communication does not ordinarily serve as a necessary and sufficient cause of audience effects, but rather functions between and among and through a nexus of mediating factors and influences."[2]

At the same time that social scientists were sharply limiting the impact of mass media, critics of popular culture were taking a quite different view. Popular-culture scholars who came from the world of literary criticism saw the mass media as a monumental influence on the individual and society. They regarded the popular press as an instrument that was watering down, if not destroying, high culture. They saw the individual as being pushed toward a mindless and totalitarian mass society and the media as largely responsible for this dilemma. The eventual impact of social science on popular culture led to a sharp modification of this view by the 1970s, when media influence was viewed in a more dispassionate, objective light.

By the late 1960s, the traditional social science view of media influence also began to shift. Recognizing that media effects could be broken down into *cognitive, affective,* and *behavioral* components, researchers began to ask different questions about media impact.[3] Some were interested in informational learning rather than in the persuasive role of media. Perhaps, said media researchers F. Gerald Kline and Peter Clarke, we've been asking the wrong questions, concerning ourselves with measurements of *media use* instead of asking how the individual actually *discriminates* the message, what he makes of it. New questions brought new answers, and by the late 1970s, researchers spoke of a return to the notion of a powerful media. True, the media's role was more carefully defined than it once had been, but still the relative impact of the press was recognized as highly significant.

Thus there have been several stages in scholarly perceptions of media influence, impact, and effect. Part One presents some essays that reflect the main currents of these different stages. The attempt here is to present strong representative studies and views of each of the four strains of thought about media influence.

Understanding the role and impact of mass media in society has been the product of considerable development and refinement of thinking among scholars. The historic "powerful press" view was a logical explanation at the time it was advanced. The rules of evidence employed at the time seemed to support such an explanation. Later, new techniques of social analysis yielded different explanations. And still later, new questions and ever more sophisticated methods of research brought more refined (and qualified) answers.

It must be remembered as one looks at differing explanations of media effects that sometimes different levels of analysis are employed. Some researchers are concerned about individual effects, others about societal effects. Of course, evidence derived at one level of analysis does not necessarily have any application to a higher or lower level.

In the first essay, Wesley C. Clark clearly supports the notion of a powerful mass media. Clark says that media have been given less than adequate credit for massive social changes in America. Especially with regard to social legislation for labor standards, and for antitrust and security regulation, the media can proudly accept significant responsibility, he says. Clark uses the documentary methods of the social historian in building his case, an approach that contrasts markedly to other essays in this collection.

Political scientist Harold D. Lasswell expands on Lippmann's thinking in his essay, "The Manipulation of Representations." Lasswell sees the pictures in men's minds as being altered by manipulative propaganda. Human beings are relatively powerless in this interpretation.

The essays by Bernard Berelson and W. Phillips Davison attempt to qualify the role of the media in public opinion by relying on the understated findings of social science. Both suggest that variables influencing opinion change should be sorted out carefully and that the role of the media should not be overplayed.

A view quite opposite to the quiet scientific stance of Berelson and Davison is seen in the outspoken essay by Ernest van den Haag. A social philosopher, Van den Haag makes a broad societal assessment and concludes that the media are stripping people of personal experience. Overreliance on the media is a habit as overreliance on drugs is a habit, he concludes.

The essays by Don Dodson and Herbert Gans are contemporary examinations of the popular culture-mass culture debate. Dodson reviews the literature of this intellectual argument effectively, then presents a case study to demonstrate how one can differentiate popular culture from mass culture. Gans tries to determine the relevance of the debate and speculates on its future. The Gans essay is a brief excerpt from his book, *Popular Culture and High Culture*.

If the popular-culture scholars once struck broad, societal themes, decrying what they regarded as the devastating effect of media on society in general and high culture in particular, popular-culture study had taken a more optimistic turn by the mid-1960s. An upbeat view of media and its impact began with the writings of Herbert Marshall McLuhan, the Canadian media commentator and critic. McLuhan saw mass media as a central theme in the development of civilization and modern electronic media (especially television) and as a force bringing individuals and institutions closer together again. He posited that print media have placed man in a rigid mold—reading from left to right, thinking in Western-style logic—but that television, which calls on all the senses at once (in McLuhan's interpretation), energizes the individual and enhances communication between and among people. Reprinting an excerpt from McLuhan's work seems to us to beg the question, and we recommend that students read his *Understanding Media* for a more comprehensive view of the media guru and his work. It is also fair to point out that McLuhan's theories, which were largely speculative and sometimes fanciful, had lost favor among scholars by the early and mid-1970s. McLuhan did raise the question of media effects in a highly visible manner, however, and the several books by and about him attest to his role in placing media impact squarely on the public agenda.

An alternative to the popular-culture approach not included here is suggested by psychologist William Stephenson in *Play Theory of Communication*. Looking at the individual (rather than societal) functions of communication, Stephenson did not find a bleak prospect at all. Rather than concentrating on purposeful communication designed to bring about a change in behavior, he studied communication between and among individuals that is aimed at nothing more than a sense of satisfaction and well-being. Stephenson distinguished communication activity along two lines—work and play. Of play, he wrote:

Playing is pretending, a stepping outside the world of duty and responsibility. Play is an interlude in the day. It is not ordinary or real. It is voluntary and not a task or a moral duty. It is in some sense disinterested, providing temporary satisfaction...Play is secluded, taking place in a particular place set off for the purpose in time or space. The child goes into a corner to play house. And play is a free activity, yet it absorbs the players completely.[4]

The media, Stephenson says, have both work and play communication. Far from viewing the "escapist" entertainment fare of the media with alarm, he sees it as healthy—something that provides people with pleasure and a better life. The student will note that this view is light-years away from Van den Haag's lament and warning.

Another broad-based view of communication influence and effects is found in the cultural approach of communication researcher James Carey. To Carey, the popular-culture scholars buy into the "transmission" approach, wherein the media transmit messages to a quivering and helpless public. Carey offers a contrary view, which he calls a "cultural or ritual" view of communication. As he puts it:

...in a ritual definition, communication is linked to terms such as sharing, participation, association, fellowship and possession of a common faith. This definition exploits the ancient identity and common roots of the terms commonness, communion, community and communication. A ritual view of communication is not directed toward the extension of messages in space but the maintenance of society in time; not the act of imparting information but the representation of shared beliefs.[5]

This analysis, like Stephenson's, shows how contemporary scholars have modified the more negative and fearful interpretation of the popular-culture commentators.

As the concept of minimal media effects was solidified in social science studies during the 1940s, 1950s, and 1960s, the emphasis of the researcher was largely on attitude change. But the evidence that mass media messages had great impact in changing people's attitudes, especially with regard to politics, was not very persuasive. In recent years, however, a number of important communication researchers and scholars have begun to ask new questions, and they have found different answers.

Elisabeth Noelle-Neumann, a German public opinion researcher, makes a carefully qualified, but quite persuasive case for the return to a concept of a powerful mass media. She says that researchers have paid too little attention to three decisive factors of media. The media message is everywhere, she says, and it is difficult to escape it. Further, there is the cumulation of messages. Often researchers consider only a fragment of a message that may be reinforced over time.

Finally, the amazing agreement among journalists gives the media message a sameness that strengthens its influence. We quote only a portion of Noelle-Neumann's quite lengthy article, which first appeared in a Japanese communication journal, but she goes to great lengths to support her assumptions with hard data from studies in several countries.

Voter behavior studies by John P. Robinson have been an exciting chapter in a reinterpretation of media effects. Beginning with the presidential election of 1968, Robinson gathered data that demonstrated the strength of newspaper editorial endorsements in influencing voter behavior. In the article presented here, Robinson reports his findings from five elections and concludes that, even when other factors are taken into account, voters' choices are related to endorsements by the newspapers to which they are exposed. Robinson makes no wild claim about massive conversion as a result of newspaper editorial endorsements but points up the significant impact they can have on a small segment of voters, which can sometimes make the difference in a close election. Robinson expands on the minimal-effects literature, not by claiming that media outdistance interpersonal influences in voter behavior, but by pointing up the clear role that mass communication does play.

The Robinson article is, of course, an empirical study. In this, as in all studies where data is collected and later interpreted to answer a particular question or set of questions, the student should exercise particular caution. Does Robinson say, for example, how independent voters were actually selected? Were they self-selected? Robinson says cautiously that his evidence suggests that the press *does* affect behavior after all. However, how do we know that the press does not *follow* popular sentiment in endorsing candidates? Does Robinson seem to say that the press endorses and the public is thereby influenced? What do you think is a reasonable explanation?

Not surprisingly, researchers who studied political socialization (that is, how people, especially the young, learn their political behavior) have ignored the possible influence of the mass media. Sidney Kraus tries to correct this in his comprehensive article, "Mass Communication and Political Socialization." For years there was no evidence about the role of media in political socialization, because media were not even studied as a variable. Now this is being corrected, says Kraus, and although the evidence is still fragmentary, it is clear that media influence is worthy of further study.

In their zeal to find direct assaults of media on public attitudes, media researchers have often ignored the *informational learning* or cognitive influence of media, say Maxwell McCombs and Donald L. Shaw in their article, "The Agenda-Setting Function of the Press." Agenda-setting research, which explores the role of the media in influencing what the public thinks is important, has mostly focused on the role of the press in election campaigns, although a broader approach to this research was in evidence at the time this book was edited.

Some of McCombs and Shaw's subsequent findings are reported in L. John Martin's excellent synthesis, "Recent Political Theory on Mass Media Potential in Political Campaigns." Martin discusses new research findings related to the information-seeking and "uses and gratifications" roles of the media. Along with McCombs and Shaw and others, he concludes that the mass media not only tell people what to think about but are also a powerful determinant of the relative importance of issues they wish to discuss.

Finally, Elihu Katz, Jay G. Blumler, and Michael Gurevitch discuss "Utilization of Mass Communication by the Individual." This is an excellent summary of the "uses and gratifications" approach to mass media "consumption."

The articles in the last section of Part One demonstrate that through careful scholarship and precisely posited questions and research designs illuminating new data about media and media influence can be developed. Much of this research is quite new, and it may take years of study and experimentation to develop solid conclusions from it about the overall impact and influence of media. But one thing is sure. Many researchers are mining data in this area, and the impact, influence, and effects of media promise to be enduring issues in mass communication for some time to come.

The impact of media is not, as the student will recognize, simply a scholarly debate among social scientists interested in methodological tools but a very real issue in the society at large. Advertising generally, political campaigns specifically, and hundreds of other concerns are centrally tied to the notion of media impact and influence. Often public policy must also draw on such findings. Witness, for example, the work of the Surgeon General's office in the early 1970s in studying television and social behavior with special attention to the impact of television violence on children. To be sure, media influence is a very real issue for the American people, and scholars of various disciplines will no doubt continue to contribute to public understanding about it.

NOTES

1. Walter Lippmann, *Public Opinion* (New York: Macmillan, 1922), p. 229.

2. Joseph Klapper, *The Effects of Mass Communication* (New York: Free Press, 1960), p. 8.

3. In isolating the three components, psychologists and other researchers suggest that "an attitude...is a continuing set of interlocking components—including beliefs and evaluations (the cognitive component), feelings and emotions (the affective component), and the behavioral readiness (the action component)—concerning some social object." See Reed H. Blake and Edwin O. Haroldsen, *A Taxonomy of Concepts in Communication* (New York: Hastings House, 1975), p. 69.

4. William Stephenson, *The Play Theory of Communication* (Chicago: University of Chicago Press, 1967), p. 46.

5. James Carey, "A Cultural Approach to Communication," *Communication*, Vol. 2, pp. 1-22, Gordon and Breach. Science Publishers, Ltd., 1975.

FURTHER READING

Davison, W. Phillips; Boylan, James; and Yu, Frederick T.C. *Mass Media: Systems and Effects.* New York: Praeger, 1976.

DeFleur, Melvin L., and Ball-Rokeach, Sandra. *Theories of Mass Communication.* 3rd ed. New York: McKay, 1975.

Dennis, Everette E. *The Media Society: Evidence About Mass Communication in America.* Dubuque, Iowa: William C. Brown, 1978.

Schramm, Wilbur. *Men, Messages and Media: A Look at Human Communication.* New York: Harper & Row, 1973.

Wright, Charles R. *Mass Communication: A Sociological Perspective.* 2nd ed. New York: Random House, 1975.

Part One

Early Perspectives:
A Powerful Press

THE IMPACT OF MASS COMMUNICATIONS IN AMERICA

Wesley C. Clark

Most of the sins of America today are charged to mass communications. In fact, whole academic disciplines have been built on this assumption. The fact is that most of the sins credited to the mass media have been committed by others and the real sins of the mass media, like their accomplishments, have gone unheralded. Let me explain.

The impact of mass communications in America has been persistent, consistent, and with us for more than one hundred years now. The mass media have changed the face of America, in some ways for the better and in some ways for the worse, some obvious and some not so obvious. The mass media have been given some credit for a great many of these changes, but some are hardly credited to them at all, and yet it is they—the mass media—who are largely responsible for much of the social legislation which now affects your lives and mine.

THE IMPACT OF MASS MEDIA IN THE PAST

When people speak today of mass communications and of the mass media, they think of audiences in terms of hundreds, and perhaps even thousands, of millions. But one hundred years ago, when this country was more sparsely populated, circulations of newspapers were not in the millions. Nevertheless, the great newspapers and magazines which existed in those days were, by almost any standards, mass media,

Reprinted from "The Impact of Mass Communications in America" by Wesley C. Clark, in volume no. 378 of THE ANNALS *of the American Academy of Political and Social Science. Copyright© 1968, by the American Academy of Political and Social Science. Reprinted by permission.*

engaged in mass communications. They were directed to the masses. They were read by the masses, and, presumably, they had some effect on the masses.

For instance, Horace Greeley's *Tribune* never had a circulation of 300,000. But it was read throughout the United States, and the admonitions of Mr. Greeley were listened to and debated throughout the United States.

The mass media of those days were responsible for crystallizing the nation's opinions about the abolition of slavery and about the kinds of amendments to the Constitution which grew out of Abraham Lincoln's statement that all men are created equal. Without the newspaper's presentation of this point of view for ten or fifteen years, it is inconceivable that Lincoln would have made such a statement, and unlikely that the Civil War would have occurred when it did—and perhaps it might not have happened at all.

This is not to attribute to today's mass media and to the newspapers and magazines of the late nineteenth century all of the political and social changes which have come about in the American scene. The pulpit, the Chautauqua—that early-day version of television—and all of the other means of communication which were available in those days helped to create this atmosphere. Nevertheless, no serious historian of the times can deny the important role of the mass media in changing America.

With this in mind, a look at history reveals a number of other things for which the mass media were largely responsible. The muckrakers of the late nineteenth and early twentieth century—public figures such as Ida Tarbell, Lincoln Steffens, and others—were aided and abetted by newspapers and magazines across the land, and thus were largely responsible for the first early restrictions imposed upon business in this country. No Judge Landis could have come to the conclusion that the great monopoly of the Standard Oil Company should be broken up, had he not been so conditioned and so impressed by the press that such a decision was made easily possible. Nor can we deny the place of the nation's press in building the pressure which made it possible for the

Congress of the United States to adopt the kind of legislation which eventually resulted in the Standard Oil cases getting into the courts. To be sure, Teddy Roosevelt and others were trustbusters in those days, but these were men who were coursing a sea of sentiment created by mass magazine and mass newspaper stories over a period of twenty or thirty years.

Although it is fashionable today for educators to pick on editors and newspapers and publishers as being opponents of the schools, such statements are merely self-serving defenses for academic politicians eager to get their hands on the public money. The fact is that not only during the last half of the nineteenth century and during this century, but back to the very beginnings of the press in this country, newspapers have consistently supported education. They have made possible the system of public education in this country. No reputable newspaper in the land at any time has been opposed to good education. They have, of course, been opposed to abuses which educationists have imposed upon this system. They have been opposed to two Cadillacs for every superintendent of schools, and they have been opposed to the kind of under-the-table operations which go on in a great many school systems when it comes to purchasing school buildings and school furnishings.

The newspapers and magazines as protagonists of the schools have not acted out of sheer philanthropy. They had a serious purpose in this. They wanted educated people—people who could read and write—so that they would have more customers for their newspapers. And, in many instances, the newspaper has been the medium by which the young, the disadvantaged, and the illiterate have learned to read. Thus, the involvement of so many Negroes in athletics has made reading the sports pages in the newspapers a must for the young Negro. He wants to learn to read so that he can find out what his heroes, Wilt Chamberlain, Jim Brown, and Willy Mays, are doing. And this gives him a far higher motivation than can be given by any school teacher fresh out of a school of education. The fact is that, for more than two hundred years, newspapers, the basic mass media of the country, have pushed education to higher and higher levels.

CONTEMPORARY MASS MEDIA EFFECTS ON SOCIETY

This, perhaps, is ancient history. What are the mass media doing now, and what have they done recently, to change the face of America, or have they rather been merely carping critics of the changes which have come about?

One of the massive changes in the American scene has been the rise of the labor unions to positions of power. It is now apparent that the restrictions imposed upon business by various laws, and by the courts, have resulted in business' having little real power in the American political scene. It is also apparent that while government has risen to new heights of power and control, the only serious challenge to these powers is provided by the labor unions, who defy the government again and again, even when laws and sanctions have been reduced to a minimum.

How did this come about? It came about because for more than fifty years the press of this country, largely the newspapers, pleaded the cause of labor in a multitude of ways. They gave publicity to Sacco and Vanzetti, to Tom Moody, to all of the complaints against the crimes of management. They made folk heroes out of labor union leaders such as John L. Lewis of the United Mine Workers, Walter Reuther of the Congress of Industrial Organizations, Samuel Gompers of the American Federation of Labor, Eugene Debs of the American Railway Union, and a host of others. They created a climate which made it possible for legislators to pass, and for executive branches to approve, legislation favoring labor. This is apparent in the laws of both the federal and state governments. It is apparent in the executive branch of the government, and it is even apparent in the

judicial branch of the government. There is no need to cite the host of administrative rules or the flux of Supreme Court decisions which bear out this point.

But, in a sense, these are the obvious things which grew out of the creation by the mass media of a climate of opinion favorable to social change in America. There are many obvious changes in which the mass media played a decisive, although unheralded, role.

Social historians of the present and recent American scene give little or no credit to the role of the mass media in making possible the Social Security Act. But then the fashionable social historian these days is one who apparently prefers a political point of view to a scholarly and serious approach to history. At any rate, in my reading of the histories of the last thirty or forty years in America, the impression comes through clear and strong that the Social Security Act and all its benefits and aids to mankind were the invention of the New Deal, of President Franklin D. Roosevelt and the little group of brain trusters who surrounded him. This is nonsense.

Franklin D. Roosevelt and the New Deal were merely the mechanism which put into being an American dream which had been sold to the American people for some seventy-five years by the great insurance companies; for during that time, insurance companies had preached the necessity for security in old age. "Make sure you have enough insurance to take care of your family." "Take out an annuity to take care of your old age." These are not new slogans; these are not Social Security slogans; these have been the slogans of insurance companies ever since life insurance and annuity insurance began to play a role in the United States.

Where was this message published? How did it come to the attention of the people? It came to the attention of the people through the advertisements of the Metropolitan Life Insurance Company and the other great insurance companies in the great mass media.

Again, Medicaid and Medicare are the result, not of the wild-eyed dreams of some politician, but of the mass propaganda of various insurance businesses, told through the media of the newspapers, the magazines, radio, and television, and drummed into the American people for the last twenty years.

With all of this propaganda, these persuasive methods, and with the climate of opinion thereby created, it would be incredible if politicians had not seized upon these slogans or ideas and incorporated them into their platforms and then into law.

There are a number of other areas in which the mass media have changed the face of America with the aid and active participation of politicians. Thus, for instance, the jewel in the crown of the Kennedy administration—the Peace Corps—is a direct development of the widespread interest of the mass communicators in the missionaries of America. For more than one hundred years, the role of the missionaries in bettering the lot of people in the underdeveloped areas was the subject of a great many articles and of books. The principal criticism of the missionaries came from the fact that they were engaged in selling Christianity abroad. And we have such plays as Somerset Maugham's "Rain" and the like which sharpened this criticism considerably. But there was no question in many people's minds that the missionaries had done a considerable amount of good in alleviating the ills of mankind in foreign countries. The Peace Corps, thus, was something that was difficult for any politician to deny, once the idea of a missionary society without God, or with a multitude of gods, was conceived.

Again, the mass media's gilding of the glories of private charity, in all of its aspects, made it difficult for any politician to deny that an increase in the scope of public welfare was necessary.

THE IMPACT OF SOCIAL CHANGE ON THE MASS MEDIA

The great media of mass communications do not stand alone, untouched by the other forces which are changing our society. They not only shape our society; they are shaped by it. And as society changes the mass media, so it, in turn, is changed by them.

The factors which have had the most effect in changing the nation are its increasing population, its increasing mobility, and the almost astronomical increase in the area of the public interest.

As more and more people have come to populate the nation and as their mobility has increased tremendously, the public interest has, of necessity, widened and broadened. Where once the disposal of waste was a private matter—the head of the household buried the waste in the backyard or fed it to the pigs—now waste is no longer a private matter, nor solely the concern of a town or a county, but has become a federal concern. Again, where once the wage contract between the employer and the employee was a private arrangement, now the federal government has stepped in and regulates such arrangements.

Confronted with these increases in population and in mobility and the consequent enormous increase in the areas of public interest, the media of mass communication have been swamped with an increase in news. For wherever the citizen and the public interest meet—in crime, in zoning, in food regulations, in labor matters, and in thousands of other places where the law and the people meet—these events must be reported if the people of the nation are to have the kind of information that they need in order to govern themselves properly.

In the face of the enormous and increasing need for news, the media of mass communications find themselves limited by the mind of man himself. It becomes a question of just how much time and attention he will devote to finding out about his environment through the mass media.

Newspapers find that generally a man will devote thirty or forty minutes a day to reading the newspaper. Radio and television find that fifteen, or at most thirty, minutes comprise the outer limit of listening to or watching Huntley and Brinkley. In thirty or forty minutes, a man can read fifteen thousand to forty thousand words. In the same thirty minutes, he can listen to three thousand words, or about four newspaper columns.

This very fact tends to limit the amount of news which is published in the great newspapers and magazines, and limits even more severely the amount of news which is available through radio and television.

HIGHER THRESHOLDS OF ATTENTION, SECRECY, AND POLITICAL CENTRALIZATION

Thus, newspapers everywhere have tended to raise the thresholds of their attention. Even so, thresholds of radio and television are even higher, and of necessity must be higher.

That this rise in the thresholds of attention of the mass communicators has had a profound influence on the structure of our government is suggested by two illustrations—one concerned with the courts, and the other concerned with the legislative and executive branches of the government.

A recent study of a county containing more than 400,000 people indicated that in a single month there were two thousand court cases of all kinds—federal, state, county, and municipal—all of them available for reporting by the mass media. The same study showed that the two daily newspapers which serve the county printed stories about less than sixty of these cases. In more populous areas, the figures would be even more astounding.

That the press does not report more court cases is due to the constant pressure to raise the thresholds of their attention. Thus, for most people, we have established an unofficial system of secret courts. The courts, the bar associations, and the legislatures are now trying to provide a court system whose secrecy is offically instead of unofficially sanctioned. And this is despite the fact that if the history of civilization proves nothing else, it proves that where secrecy cloaks the use of power it also cloaks the abuse of power. The consequence of this judicial secrecy, official and unofficial, is a growing distrust by people everywhere of the courts, the judiciary, the legal profession, and the mass media.

The impact of the rising thresholds of attention of the mass media upon the legislative and executive branches of the government is best illustrated by the great metropolitan area of New York City, where some twenty congressmen are elected every two years. These are United States Congressmen—not dog wardens or local constables—but twenty members of that august body which enacts the laws of the United States. Yet, in campaign after campaign, the New York City papers in years past, and I suspect even in this year, devote, in the six weeks preceding an election, as few as five hundred words to each congressional candidate and, unless the congressional candidate is a John Lindsay, hardly more than that. As a matter of fact, most New Yorkers are unaware of the congressional district in which they live or of the congressman who, presumably, represents them.

In these circumstances, it is not important to be an outstanding congressman or to represent a particular district well. But it is important to be a member of a winning political party and to ride on the coattails of that party. Thus, more and more, for the metropolitan congressmen, the question of survival depends, not upon their own efforts, but upon the efforts and the image presented by the leader of the party—in short, the President of the United States, or the governor of the state.

The concentration of political power in the hands of a few, coupled with an increase in secrecy, both official and unofficial, has set the stage for the greatest era of palace intrigue and political chicanery since Machiavelli wrote *The Prince*.

And as the arena of meaningful political action moves more and more toward Washington, and as secrecy cloaks the actions of more and more areas of government, the political man in America becomes more and more frustrated and tempted to forgo political action. Many men, for instance, express a fleeting interest in Elizabeth Taylor, or would express an interest in a woman of comparable dimensional beauty. But few devote hours each day to studying Miss Taylor. The reason is clear: they know there is no real possibility of persuading Miss Taylor to their way of thinking. And, of course, the Miss Taylors whom they do not know about engage their interest even less. To ask a political man to be informed through the mass media about government in depth and in detail when he has little or no chance to use the information to change the course of government is to ask too much.

By raising the thresholds of their attention to unprecedented heights, the mass media of communications have both simplified and complicated American life. They have simplified it by making it easy to concentrate upon a few great political leaders. They have complicated it by making it impossible for many individuals to be heard when the mechanisms of society impinge abrasively upon their rights and their lives. They have also complicated it to the extent that if individuals or groups have problems which need to be brought to the attention of the public, they must hire public relations counsel to make sure that the things that they need are brought to the attention of the public, or they must create some kind of disturbance to make their needs known to the great mass media—or perhaps they must do both: hire public relations counsel to organize riots.

SUMMARY

To summarize, then: mass communications and the mass media have played a major role in changing the face of America; they are playing a major role; they will continue to do so.

The mass media, by their very nature, by the limitations imposed upon them by man and by a changing society, are challenging the basic assumptions upon which this government was erected.

They have given us instant nationwide fashions and modes, and perhaps instant heroes, or nonheroes, both political and nonpolitical.

They have contributed substantially to the frustrations, political and otherwise, which beset the American populace.

But they have also, and in this lies the hope of America, paved the way for the great pieces of social legislation which have made this nation a better place in which to live.

They are, in fact, a somewhat paraphrased and modern version of the cadets of Gascogne: "the supporters of new homes, new names, and new splendors."

THE MANIPULATION OF REPRESENTATIONS

Harold D. Lasswell

Propaganda in the broadest sense is the technique of influencing human action by the manipulation of representations. These representations may take spoken, written, pictorial, or musical form. The expected disproportion between the specific consequence and the general reaction which is behind some political assassination justifies the category "propaganda of the deed." Many official acts of legislation and administration derive their significance from the general as distinguished from the circumscribed results anticipated; these are the propaganda aspects of public policy. Both advertising and publicity fall within the field of propaganda....

It is true that techniques have value implications, even though values do not necessarily depend upon technique. Nevertheless, the processes by which such techniques as those of spelling, letter forming, piano playing, lathe handling, and dialectic are transmitted may be called education; while those by which value dispositions (hatred or respect toward a person, group, or policy) are organized may be called propaganda. The inculcation of traditional value attitudes is generally called education, while the term *propaganda* is reserved for the spreading of the subversive, debatable, or merely novel attitudes. If deliberation implies the consideration of a problem without predisposition to promote any particular situation, propaganda is concerned with eliciting such predispositions.

"Propaganda" by Harold D. Lasswell. Reprinted with permission of the publisher from the Encyclopedia of the Social Sciences, *Seligman and Johnson, editors. Volume 12, pp. 521-522. Copyright 1934, 1962 by Macmillan Publishing Co., Inc.*

Part One

A Minimal
Effect of Media

COMMUNICATIONS
AND PUBLIC OPINION

Bernard Berelson

Of the importance of this topic it is hardly necessary to speak. If the defenses of peace and prosperity, not to mention other desirable political conditions, are to be constructed in men's minds, then the critical position of communication and public opinion for that defense is evident. What is not so evident, perhaps, is why social scientists have given so little systematic attention to problems of the formation of public opinion with special reference to the role of the media of communication in that process. It was not evident to a "classical" writer on public opinion twenty-five years ago,[1] and it may be even less so today.

In any case, the field of interest is now developing and the line of development is reasonably clear. The political scientists's concern with political parties was generalized to a concern with the role of pressure groups in political life. The concern with pressure groups led directly into concern with propaganda, and that into concern with public opinion and the effect of propaganda upon it. At about this time, technicians began to develop scientific instruments by which to measure public opinion; a new medium of communication with great potentialities for popular influence came vigorously upon the scene; in a series of presidential elections people voted strongly for one candidate while their newspapers voted strongly for his opponent; and a World War made more visible as well as more urgent the battle for men's minds. Thus the background of academic interest was prepared just when dramatic events highlighted the urgency of the problem and when technical developments provided means for at least some solutions. As a result, interest in communication and public opinion is now at an all-time high.

From Communications in Modern Society, *pp. 527-543. Edited by Wilbur Schramm. Copyright © 1948 by the University of Illinois Press. Reprinted by permission.*

The purpose of this paper is to discuss the relationship between communication and public opinion. "Discuss" here means to report on some (illustrative) research findings in the area and to propose relevant (and again illustrative) hypotheses for investigation. By communication is meant the transmission of symbols via the major media of mass communication—radio, newspaper, film, magazine, book—and the major medium of private communication—personal conversation. By public opinion is meant people's response (that is, approval, disapproval, or indifference) to controversial political and social issues of general attention, such as international relations, domestic policy, election candidates, ethnic relations.

The paper is organized into two parts because the relationship between communication and public opinion is twofold. The first section deals with the effect of public opinion upon communication and the second with the effect of communication upon public opinion. The second section is traditional, and there is more to say about it; the first is usually neglected.

EFFECT OF PUBLIC OPINION UPON COMMUNICATION

This problem is usually neglected in analyses of the relationship because it is not so obvious as the other and perhaps because it is more difficult to study. The problem deals with the extent to which, and the ways in which, communication content is determined to harmonize with the actual or presumed opinions of the actual or potential audience. It is clear that one factor, among others, that conditions what the media of communications say on social and political issues is the desire or expectation of the readers-listeners-seers to be told certain things and not others. The reporter or commentator or editor or producer may know or may think he knows "what his public wants" on a given issue, and to the extent that such knowledge affects what he communicates, to that extent public opinion becomes a determinant of communications. This aspect of the relationship between communication and public opinion is not always admitted, or even recognized, because of the immorality of suggesting that anything but "truth" or "justice" contributes to the character of communication content.[2] However, everyone knows that communication channels of various kinds tell people what they want to hear. In such cases, public opinion sets limits upon the nature of what is typically communicated.

This determination (or really, partial determination, since this is, of course, not the only factor responsible for communication content any more than communication content is the only factor responsible for public opinion) can operate in two ways, once the communication channel (newspaper, magazine, political writer, radio commentator, and so forth) has attracted to itself a distinguishable audience. The two ways are themselves interrelated and can coexist. First, it can operate through conscious and deliberate and calculated manipulation of the content in order to coincide with the dominant audience opinion. Sometimes this operates by rule of thumb, as when someone on the production line in the communication process decides that "our public won't take this, or won't like it." Sometimes it operates through elaborate machinery organized precisely for the purpose, as when thousands of research dollars and hours are spent in finding out what kinds of people the audience is composed of and what kinds of opinions they hold on controversial issues. Whether the decision to conform to audience predispositions is taken on the front line or in the front office is for the moment immaterial; so is the question of why it happens, e.g., the desire or need for constant and large audiences for economic reasons. The important point is that overt consideration of audience opinion does (help to) shape the social and political content of the mass media. Everyone recalls the story of the foreign correspondent who cabled a thoroughgoing analysis of a relatively obscure Hungarian crisis to the home office only to be told: "We do not think it advisable to print it because it does not reflect Midwestern opinion on this point."[3]

The other method by which public opinion can affect communications is implicit, through the sincere and more or less nonconscious correspondence of ideology between producers and consumers. The two groups often see the world through the same colored glasses. The correspondence is achieved through a two-way process: the audience selects the communications which it finds most congenial and the producers select people with "the right viewpoint" to prepare communications for other people with "the right viewpoint." Although this latter process also occurs through deliberate decision, it also happens through the most laudable and honest motives that people of the same general persuasion as their audience are found in influential positions in particular communication agencies. This is all the more true in specialized enterprises like trade papers or magazines like *Fortune* or *The Nation*. In such cases, producers react to new issues and events like the modal members of their audience; and their communications fit audience predispositions, not through a process of tailoring, but through correspondence in outlook. "The daily re-election of the editor" serves to make the editor quite sensitive to the wishes of the electors. Here again the economic necessity to hold an audience and the political desire to do so are relevant factors, as well as the "correctness" of outlook. The point is that the nature of one's audience places certain limits upon what one can say to it—and still have an audience. The need of the audience is not only to be informed but also to be satisfied, and the latter is sometimes evaluated more highly than the former.

It is important to take account of this direction in the flow of influence between communication and public opinion in order to appreciate the reciprocal nature of that influence, i.e., to recognize that it is not all a one-way process. It is also important to note that the total effect of this reciprocal process is probably to stabilize and "conservatize" opinion since ideologies are constantly in process of reinforcement thereby. The over-all picture, then, is that of like begetting like begetting like.

THE EFFECT OF COMMUNICATION ON PUBLIC OPINION

But the effect of communication on public opinion needs to be examined much more closely and directly than that. To speak roughly, in the 1920s, propaganda was considered all-powerful—"it got us into the war"—and thus communication was thought to determine public opinion practically by itself. In the 1930s the Roosevelt campaigns "proved" that the newspaper had lost its influence and that a "golden voice" on the radio could sway men in almost any direction. Now, a body of empirical research is accumulating which provides some refined knowledge about the effect of communication on public opinion and promises to provide a good deal more in the next years.

What has such research contributed to the problem? By and large, do communications influence public opinion? By and large, of course, the answer is yes. But by-and-large questions and answers are not sufficient for a scientific theory of communication and public opinion. The proper answer to the general question, the answer which constitutes a useful formulation for research purposes, is this:

Some kinds of communication *on some kinds of* issues, *brought to the attention of some kinds of* people *under some kinds of* conditions, *have some kinds of* effects.

This formulation identifies five central factors (or rather groups of factors) which are involved in the process, and it is the interrelationship of these variables which represents the subject matter of theory in this field. At present, students can fill out only part of the total picture—a small part—but the development of major variables and the formulation of hypotheses and generalizations concerning them are steps in the right direction. Theoretical integration in any full sense is not as yet possible, but descriptions of some ways in which these factors operate can be usefully made. Each set of factors will be discussed illustratively (*not* completely) in an effort to demonstrate how each of them conditions the total effect of communication on public opinion and thus contributes to the formulation of a general theory.

KINDS OF COMMUNICATION

The effectiveness of communications as an influence upon public opinion varies with the nature of the communication.

First let us deal with the effect of certain media characteristics. The more personal the medium, the more effective it is in converting opinions. This means (other things being equal) that personal conversation is more effective than a radio speech, and that a radio speech is more effective than a newspaper account of it. The greater the amount of "personalism" the communication act contains, the more effective it presumably is. Recent analyses have confirmed the critical importance in opinion formation of personal contact between the individual and his fellows. The individual's opinions are formed in the context of his formal and informal group associations. College students become more liberal in political opinion over the period of their college attendance largely through the influence of the liberality of the college community, that is, the older students and the instructional staff.[4] Intensive case studies of current opinion toward the USSR held by adult men reveal the powerful influence of personal contacts: "The need to conform in one's opinion to the opinions of one's associates and of members of favored groups is an important motivational factor."[5] This effect operated in two ways: directly through the process of conformity as such and indirectly through the sharing of common values and information. The formation of political opinion during a presidential campaign was dependent upon personal influence to a large extent; the political homogeneity of social groups was strikingly high. "In comparison with the formal media of communication, personal relationships are potentially more influential for two reasons: their coverage is greater and they have certain psychological advantages over the formal media."[6] Personal contacts are more casual and nonpurposive than the formal media, they are more flexible in countering resistance, they can provide more desirable rewards for compliance, they offer reliance and trust in an intimate source, and they can persuade without convincing.[7]

The greater effectiveness of radio over newspapers derives to some extent from its greater "personalism." The radio speaks "to you" more than the newspaper does; it more closely approximates a personal conversation and can thus be more persuasive. The listener can "get a feel" of the speaker's personality, and this is often more effective a factor making for conversion of opinion than the content of the argument itself. The dominant characteristic which enabled Kate Smith to sell nearly $40,000,000 worth of war bonds in one day was the listener's image and evaluation of her personality established over a period of time.[8] In other areas, too, the (radio) personality of such influencers of public opinion as Raymond Gram Swing or Gabriel Heatter or Franklin Delano Roosevelt contributed to their influence.

This discussion of the role of personal contact in opinion formation would not be complete without mention of the relationship between personal conversation and the formal media of communication. This relationship introduces the notion of the "opinion leader" or "opinion transmitter" who takes material from the formal media and passes it on, with or without distortion or effect, to associates who do not use the formal media so frequently in the particular area of concern. There are such people in all social groups and for all social topics, from politics to sports and fashions. This "two-step flow of communication" has been identified and is currently being studied intensively.[9] The concept is of central importance for the formation of a general theory of communication and public opinion.

Within a medium of communication, the particular channels specialized to the subject's predispositions are more effective in converting his opinion than the generalized channels. "The specialized magazine already has a foot in the door, so to speak, because it is accepted by the reader as a reliable spokesman for some cause or group in which he is greatly interested and with which he identifies himself. The general magazine tries to speak to everyone at once and as a result is less able to aim its shots directly at a particular target....In Erie County in 1940,

the *Farm Journal* was mentioned as a concrete influence upon changes in vote intention as frequently as *Colliers,* despite their great difference in circulation, and the Townsend publication as frequently as *Life* or the *Saturday Evening Post.*"[10] Similarly farm programs on the air are probably more effective in influencing farmers' opinions than general radio programs dealing with the same issues.[11] Although there is little direct evidence on this point, it is at least a plausible hypothesis that the specialized communication, per unit of exposure, is more effective in promoting opinion changes than the generalized communication. In a sense, then, this is an obstacle to the homogenizing influence of the mass channels in the mass media.

These are a few ways in which the distinctions among the media themselves are involved in the effect of communication upon opinion. What about communication content? Obviously it has a central position in this process. Perhaps the primary distinction in communication content as a factor affecting public opinion is the most primitive, namely, the distinction between the reportorial content and the editorial or interpretive content. Too often discussions of the general problem of the effect of communications upon public opinion is restricted to the latter kind of content. Yet the former is probably more effective in converting opinion. The events reported through the media presumably change more minds—or solidify more—than the comments of editorial writers, columnists, and commentators. "It was Sherman and Sheridan, and not Greeley and Raymond, who had elected him (Lincoln in 1864)."[12] And again, "Opinion is generally determined more by events than by words—unless those words are themselves interpreted as an 'event.'"[13] In addition events tend to solidify opinion changes produced by words, changes which otherwise would be short-lived; and the *fait accompli* crystallizes opinion in favor of the event even though words had not previously been able to do so.[14] Thus the reportorial content of the media is probably more influential than the interpretive.

However, it is necessary to make two remarks here. First, the distinction between "events" and "words" is not easy to make. Is a major speech by the President of the United States an "event" or just "propaganda"? Or a report issued by a pressure group? Or an investigation by a congressional committee? Or a tour of inspection? What about "propaganda of the deed"? Although the distinction is useful, the borderline is not always crystal-clear. And secondly, many events exercise influence not in and of themselves, but with active assistance from "words." Thus, for example, the relatively sharp changes in opinion on the interventionist-isolationist issue which occurred at the time of the fall of France in June, 1940, are often attributed to the event itself. However, it must be recognized that this event was strongly interpreted in one way (i.e., pro-interventionism) by most newspapers and radio commentators and by the pronouncements of the national administration. What if most communication channels and the official administration had taken another view of the event? At the least one might suppose that the effect of "the event" would have been different. More recently, the event represented by people's experience in the meat crisis in the fall of 1946 was sometimes credited with the Republican congressional victory at that time. Yet it must be remembered that the communication media gave that event a dominant interpretation (i.e., anti-administration) even though another was possible. In short, the interrelationship of "events" and "words" must be recognized in this connection. The fact is that the communication media are most effective when their reportorial and interpretive contents are in congruence.

Finally, to illustrate this aspect of the process, there is the hypothesis that emotional content of the media is more effective in converting opinions than rational content. There is some evidence for this.

Votes for a Socialist candidate were increased more by "emotional" leaflets than by "rational" ones.[15] The highly effective bond broadcasts by Kate Smith even omitted two "rational" themes in favor of emphasis upon various "emotional" ones.[16] In the case of this distinction, of course, the need is not so much to test the finding as to refine it, especially for different population groups.

KINDS OF ISSUES

The effectiveness of communications as an influence upon public opinion varies with the nature of the issue.

Communication content is more effective in influencing public opinion on new or unstructured issues, i.e., those not particularly correlated with existing attitude clusters. The closer the opinion situation is to the *tabula rasa*, the easier it is for the communication media to write their own ticket. "Verbal statements and outlines of courses of action have maximum importance when opinion is unstructured..."[17] Again, with reference to opinion toward the USSR: "The object of the attitude is remote, the facts are ambiguous, and a person may fashion his own picture of Russia or fall in with the prevailing stereotypes"[18]—which are provided predominantly by the formal media.

Communication content is more effective in influencing opinion on peripheral issues than on crucial issues. That is, it is easier for the media to shape opinion on what to do about local courts than what to do about organized labor; and it is probably easier for them to shape opinion toward organized labor than on ethnic relations. The "relevance-quotient" or "intensity-quotient" of this issue is inversely correlated with the capacity of communication content to change minds.

Finally, communications are probably more effective in influencing opinion on "personalities" than on "issues." In the first place, Americans are an individualistic people. They like to have heroes; and the communications media do their best to supply heroes of various kinds to various groups in the population.[19] Secondly, Americans do not like to believe that there are deep-cutting political issues which have the potentiality of "class-ifying" the public so that they tend to resist the acceptance or even the recognition of some basic issues. As a result, the media probably can sway more people with "personality" arguments than with "issue" arguments.[20]

KINDS OF PEOPLE

The effectiveness of communications as an influence upon public opinion varies with the nature of the people.

In the first place, varying proportions of people simply do not read or see or listen to the different media. So far as direct effect of the media is concerned (and omitting considerations of indirect effects through such a process as opinion leadership), two-thirds of the adult population is not influenced by books, about one-half is not influenced by motion pictures, and so on. Direct effects of the media upon public opinion can be exercised only upon that part of the public which attends to the different media (and to different parts of them)—and that rules out distinguishable groups at the outset.

On one side of the coin is the distinction between peripheral and central issues; on the other side is the distinction between strong and weak predispositions. The stronger predispositions are on the issue, the more difficult it is for the media to convert opinions. Strong predispositions "compel" an opinion which the media only help to rationalize and reinforce; in recent presidential elections very few people of high income, rural residence, and Protestant religion were *converted* to a Republican vote by the media of communication. Strong predispositions make for greater interest in the issue, an earlier decision on it, and fewer changes afterwards. All this is clear enough. What may or may not be so clear, however, is that the

strongly predisposed on an issue actually manage not only to avoid contrary communication material, so that it just does not come to their attention, but also that they manage to misunderstand the material (which objectively is straightforward) when confronted by it. This has been particularly demonstrated in connection with communication material on ethnic relations, a topic on which predispositions run strong. Prejudiced people find several ways in which to evade the message of pro-tolerance propaganda: they avoid the intended identifications, they invalidate the message, they change the frame of reference, they "just don't get it."[21]

The less informed people are on an issue, the more susceptible they are to opinion conversion through the influence of the communication media. This means that the less informed are more mercurial in their opinions; the base of data upon which stable opinion is more securely founded[22] is simply absent from them, and the media (or more frequently, personal contacts) can more readily move them in different directions. "The compulsion of (media-supplied and other) stereotypes is great, particularly for persons with meager informational backgrounds."[23]

KINDS OF CONDITIONS

The effectiveness of communications as an influence upon public opinion varies with the nature of the conditions.

Many mass communications on controversial issues in this country have to make their way in a competitive situation, i.e., under conditions in which alternative proposals are also available in the media. In some areas, such as the desirability of professing religious beliefs, this is not true: there is a virtual pro-religious monopoly on communications available to large audiences in America today. But it is the case in most areas of political and social concern, although here too various minority groups, e.g., the Communists, feel that their point of view is not given fair or proper attention in the mass media. It is necessary to recognize that the effect of communications upon public opinion must usually be exercised in this context of competing communication content and not in a context of monopoly. This is of central importance: communication has effects upon converting opinion under conditions of monopoly which are much greater than its effects under conditions of competition (even though that competition might be quite uneven). However, the effectiveness of formal communications is not unlimited; there are suggestions that the virtual monopoly exercised by the Nazis over communication content did not succeed in converting some large groups of Germans to their political philosophy.

That is one point—the greater but not absolute effectiveness of communication monopoly. Another deals with the problem of "balance" within competition. What does "balance" mean in the mass media? Does it mean a fifty-fifty division between pro and anti-content? What is a "fair" distribution of attention to the different sides on a public controversy? One approach to this matter is to consider what might be called "functional balance" in the media, i.e., the proportionate distribution of content which enables partisans on an issue to read or see or listen to their own side with reasonably equal facility. This does not necessitate an automatic fifty-fifty division of the content. In one presidential campaign, for example, the Republicans and Democrats in a community read and heard their own side about equally, even though there was about a two-to-one disproportion of content favoring the Republicans.[24] In any case, the effect of the communication media upon public opinion is a function of the degree of competition on the issue within the media.

Another condition of communication exposure which affects opinion conversions is the purposiveness or non-purposiveness of the exposure. There is some slight evidence to suggest that non-purposive (or accidental) reading and listening is more effective in changing opinions than purposive (or deliberate).[25] In the first place, people see and hear more congenial material through deliberate communication exposure, and accidental reading and listening is more likely to bring diverse viewpoints to their attention. Secondly, in such exposure, defenses against new ideas are presumably weaker because preconceptions are not so pervasively present. Finally, there may be other psychological advantages centering around the gratification of "overhearing" something "not meant for you," a consideration that also weakens the resistance to "propaganda" (since "it would not be propaganda if it wasn't intended for you"). This factor of accidental-and-deliberate communication exposure corresponds to the factor of indirect-and-direct communication content, and the same hypothesis probably holds.[26] Direct content attacks the issue head-on (e.g., an article urging fairer treatment of Negroes). Indirect content takes the roundabout approach (e.g., a story about Negro children without direct reference to the problem of race relations). The indirect content is more effective in converting opinions for much the same reasons which apply to accidental exposure.

KINDS OF EFFECTS

Finally, the media of communication have different kinds of effects upon public opinion.

First, a distinction should be made between the effect of the media upon the holding of certain opinions rather than others and their effect upon the holding of political opinions at all. Most attention has been given to the former problem, but the latter—the problem of the creation and maintenance of political interest or political apathy—is of considerable importance. The media have a major influence in producing an interest in public affairs by constantly bringing them to people's attention in a context of presumed citizenly concern. The more the media stress a political issue, the less indecision there is on the issue among the general public.[27] At the same time, however, the communication media may also be promoting in actuality, but without intention, a sense of political apathy among some of its audience. This can occur in at least two ways.

In the first place, it is at least a plausible hypothesis that the attractive substance and easy accessibility of the entertainment or recreational or diversionary content of the mass media operate to minimize political interest for some groups in the population. Comedians, dramatic sketches, and popular music on the air; light fiction of the adventure, mystery, or romantic variety in magazines and books; comics and comic strips; feature films of "straight entertainment"—such "non-serious" content of the media may well serve to divert attention from political affairs directly and also to recreate the audience so that it is under less compulsion to "face up" to the general political problems which confront it and which shape its life. This is said with complete recognition of the psychological relief provided by such communication materials for many people; at the same time, their effect in lowering political interest and attention seems equally clear.

Secondly, the media may increase political apathy simply through presentation of the magnitude, the diversity, and the complexity of the political issues on which the responsible citizen is supposed to be informed. Some readers and listeners, conscious of their inability to become informed other than superficially on more than a few public problems, retreat from the whole area. How can one know what should be done about the Palestine partition, about inflation, about the Greek guerillas and the Chinese Communists, about race relations in the United States, about the cold war with the USSR, about labor-management relations generally or the latest strike specifically, about "free enterprise" or "planning," about the atom—all at the same time? The media atmosphere of public responsibility for public actions may thus become a boomerang: the more the public is enjoined to exercise its

duty to become an "informed citizenry," the less it feels able to do so. And, overwhelmed by the presentation of issues and problems of a public nature, part of the audience may withdraw into the relative security of their private problems and their private lives.

In any discussion of the effect of the media upon the *kinds of* political opinions held by people, an initial distinction should be made between long-run and short-run effects. The importance of the former is inversely related to the research attention which has been given them. The fact that it is easier to study short-run changes in attitudes produced by the communication media—not that that is easy!—should not divert attention from the pervasive, subtle, and durable effects of the media over long periods of time. For example, motion pictures undoubtedly affect the political attention of their audiences over the long run by strengthening certain "basic" values in terms of which political issues are later decided. The influence is remote and indirect, but it is nonetheless present and active. Or again, the communication media affect public opinion over the long run by providing a set of definitions for key political terms (of an affective nature) which come to be accepted through lack of adequate challenge. Thus, "freedom" in this country has mainly been defined in the media in terms of the absence of governmental intervention; and when the value of "freedom" is invoked in a political argument, it usually carries this meaning into the attitudinal battle. Other definitions are possible, but not so current. When it is suggested that "freedom of the press" be defined in terms of the ability of various population groups to secure the kind of communication they want (or someone thinks they should have) rather than in terms of governmental control, the proposal is confronted by the established definition—established through repetition over a long period of time.

Now for the short-run effects of the media upon opinion. Most is known about this area of the general problem, but not much is known. At the least, distinctions should be made among the various kinds of effects which the communication media can have upon public opinion. Usually the term "effect" includes only the conversion of opinions (i.e.,

changes away from a predispositional position
or prior attitudes), but the (more frequent)
reinforcement and activation effects should
not be overlooked. The media are extremely
effective in providing partisans with the
deference and the rationalizations needed to
maintain their position (i.e., reinforcement):
"If the press follows a tenacious policy during
an economic crisis, it may be able to retard or
prevent shifts from one major party to
another."[28] And they are also effective in
bringing to visibility people's latent attitudes
(i.e., activation).[29]

More than that, the media are effective in
structuring political issues for their audiences.
For example, there is a tendency for partisans
on each side of a controversial matter to
agree with their own side's argument in the
order in which those arguments are
emphasized in mass communications. Thus,
the media set the political stage, so to speak,
for the ensuing debate. In addition, there is
some evidence that private discussions of
political matters take their cue from the
media's presentation of the issues; people talk
politics along the lines laid down in the
media.[30]

Finally, one thing must be made quite
clear in this discussion of the effects of the
media upon public opinion. That is that
effects upon the audience do not follow
directly from and in correspondence with the
intent of the communicator or the content of
the communication. The predispositions of
the reader or listener are deeply involved in
the situation, and may operate to block or
modify the intended effect or even to set up a
boomerang effect. This has been found time
and again in studies of the effectiveness of
materials promoting tolerance toward ethnic
groups, on which topic predispositions run
strong.[31] In another context—and under
relatively favorable conditions—Communist
propaganda provided a catharsis for its
subjects, inefficiently for its own objectives,
because its themes directly countered strong
feelings of individualism and nationalism held
by the audience.[32]

CONCLUSION

This brief discussion of communication and
public opinion has indicated the reciprocal
effects of the two major factors upon one
another, and has presented a categorization
in terms of which the effects of
communication upon public opinion can
usefully be investigated. In this latter analysis,
five sets of variables were identified:
communications, issues, people, conditions,
effects.

The interrelationships of these variables
constitute the subject-matter of a scientific
theory in this field. For example, illustrative
hypotheses can be suggested which deal with
these interrelationships:

The more specialized the media
(communication), the greater reinforcement
(effect).

The greater the competition in a
communication system (conditions), the
greater reinforcement (effect).

The "deeper" the predispositional affect
toward the issue (people), the more effective
the indirect content (communication) in
converting opinion (effect).

And so on, within the formulation: some kinds
of communication on some kinds of issues,
brought to the attention of some kinds of
people under some kinds of conditions, have
some kinds of effects.

It is hypotheses of this sort that should be
systematically explored as the next step in
research in this field. Whatever the method of
investigation (and some of these are better
than others)—historical (Mott), trend analysis
(Cantril), statistical correlation of ecological
and voting data (Gosnell), case study (Smith),
opinion survey and analysis (Cottrell),[33]
experimental (I. and E. Division),[34] panel
(Lazarsfeld, Berelson, and Gaudet)—this sort
of propositional organization should be
considered as the framework of study. In this
way, a scientific theory of communications
and public opinion can be developed for the
enrichment not only of the field of
communications research generally, but for
social science as well.

NOTES

1. Walter Lippmann, *Public Opinion* (New York: Macmillan, 1922), p. 243.

2. However, some circles frankly acknowledge the power of the public to participate thus indirectly in the construction of communication content. This position is usually rationalized in terms of the presumed democratic ethic in which "the public is entitled to what it wants."

3. Leo Rosten, *The Washington Correspondents* (New York: Harcourt, Brace, 1937), p. 231.

4. Theodore M. Newcomb, *Personality and Social Change: Attitude Formation in a Student Community* (New York: Dryden Press, 1943).

5. Mahlon Brewster Smith, "Functional and Descriptive Analysis of Public Opinion," Ph.D. dissertation, Harvard University, 1947, p. 500.

6. Paul Lazarsfeld, Bernard Berelson, and Hazel Gaudet, *The People's Choice: How the Voter Makes Up His Mind in a Presidential Campaign* (New York: Duell, Sloan and Pearce, 1944), p. 150.

7. For a full discussion of these factors, see Chapter 16 of Lazarsfeld, Berelson, and Gaudet, *People's Choice.*

8. Robert K. Merton, with Marjorie Fiske and Alberta Curtis, *Mass Persuasion: The Social Psychology of a War Bond Drive* (New York: Harper and Brothers, 1946).

9. See Lazarsfeld, Berelson, and Gaudet, *People's Choice,* pp. 49-51, 151-52; and Elihu Katz and Paul Lazarsfeld, *Personal Influence* (Glencoe, Ill.: Free Press, 1955).

10. Lazarsfeld, Berelson, and Gaudet, *People's Choice,* pp. 135-136.

11. Some indirect evidence for this is available in William S. Robinson, "Radio Comes to the Farmer," in *Radio Research, 1941,* ed. P. F. Lazarsfeld and F. N. Stanton (New York: Duell, Sloan and Pearce, 1941), pp. 224-294.

12. Frank Luther Mott, "Newspapers in Presidential Campaigns," *Public Opinion Quarterly* 8, (1944); 354.

13. Hadley Cantril, "The Use of Trends," in *Gauging Public Opinion,* ed. Hadley Cantril (Princeton, N.J.: Princeton University Press, 1944), p. 226.

14. See Cantril, "Use of Trends," pp. 227-228 for examples.

15. George W. Hartmann, "A Field Experiment on the Comparative Effectiveness of 'Emotional' and 'Rational' Political Leaflets in Determining Election Results," *Journal of Abnormal and Social Psychology* 31 (1936): 99-114.

16. See Merton, *Mass Persuasion,* pp. 45-69 ("The Bond Appeals: A Thematic Analysis").

17. Cantril, "Use of Trends," p. 226.

18. Smith, "Functional and Descriptive Analysis," p. 195.

19. For an example see Leo Lowenthal, "Biographies in Popular Magazines," in *Radio Research, 1942-43,* ed. P. F. Lazarsfeld and F. N. Stanton (New York: Duell, Sloan and Pearce, 1944), pp. 507-548.

20. For a specific instance in which this was the case, see Bernard Berelson, "The Effects of Print Upon Public Opinion," in *Print, Radio and Film in a Democracy,* ed. Waples (Chicago: University of Chicago Press, 1943), pp. 55-56.

21. Eunice Cooper and Marie Jahoda, "The Evasion of Propaganda: How Prejudiced People Respond to Anti-prejudice Propaganda," *Journal of Psychology* 23 (1947): 15-25.

22. Cantril, "The Use of Trends," p. 229.

23. Smith, "Functional and Descriptive Analysis," p. 195. In this connection, see also Herbert Hyman and Paul Sheatsley, "Some Reasons Why Information Campaigns Fail," *Public Opinion Quarterly* 11 (1947): 412-423.

24. Lazarsfeld, Berelson, and Gaudet, *People's Choice,* pp. 110-36.

25. Based upon an unpublished manuscript by Paul F. Lazarsfeld.

26. For recent discussions of other conditions affecting this relationship, see Samuel Flowerman, "Mass Propaganda in the War Against Bigotry," *Journal of Abnormal and Social Psychology* 42 (1947): 429-439; Ernst Kris and Nathan Leites, "Trends in 20th Century Propaganda," in *Psychoanalysis and the Social Sciences* (New York: International Universities Press, 1947), pp. 393-409.

27. Berelson, "Effects of Print," p. 53.

28. Harold F. Gosnell, *Machine Politics: Chicago Model* (Chicago: University of Chicago Press, 1937), p. 181.

29. For a fuller description of these effects, see Lazarsfeld, Berelson, and Gaudet, *People's Choice,* chapters 8-10.

30. For documentation of these points, see Berelson, "Effects of Print," p. 53.

31. For example, see Cooper and Jahoda, "Evasion of Propaganda," pp. 15-25.

32. Harold D. Lasswell and Dorothy Blumenstock, "The Influence of Propaganda," in *World Revolutionary Propaganda: A Chicago Study,* ed. Lazarsfeld and Blumenstock (New York: Knopf, 1939), pp. 257-358.

33. Leonard Cottrell, *American Opinion on World Affairs in the Atomic Age* (Princeton, N.J.: Princeton University Press, 1948).

34. Information and Education Division, U.S. War Department, "The Effects of Presenting 'One Side' vs. 'Both Sides' in Changing Opinions on a Controversial Subject," in *Readings in Social Psychology,* ed. Theodore Newcomb and Eugene Hartley (New York: Holt, 1947), pp. 566-579.

ON THE EFFECTS
OF COMMUNICATION

W. Phillips Davison

Quantitative studies conducted in recent years, many of them laboratory experiments, have made it possible to formulate an impressive number of propositions about the effects of communication. Progress has also been made in collecting and systematizing these propositions, and in putting them to work in education, public relations, advertising, and other fields.[1] The qualitative literature on the effects of communication has been less well explored. Much of it still lies unrecognized in historical treatises, biographies, and the writings of reporters in all eras. Attempts to systematize or derive propositions from the relatively small segment of qualitative experience that has been sifted have been made largely in the literature of rhetoric, political communication, and psychological warfare.[2]

While knowledge about communication effects has increased steadily, although unevenly, many of the insights gained have tended to remain discrete. It has proved difficult to relate propositions to each other, and to the larger body of knowledge about human behavior. Some of the effects produced by communication have been identified and found to be associated with certain characteristics of the audiences being studied, but it has less often been possible to specify why these relationships rather than other ones have existed. Nevertheless, several major steps in the direction of linking the accumulated knowledge about communication effects more closely to social and psychological theory have been taken recently by Festinger; Hovland, Janis, and Kelley; Katz and Lazarsfeld; and others.[3] The most comprehensive proposal for a theoretical structure—at least in the case of mass communication—has been made by Klapper, who accounts for many of the observed variations in response to identical communication stimuli by the role played by certain mediating factors, such as audience predispositions, group affiliation, and opinion leadership.[4]

The purpose of this article is to suggest another method of interpreting the existing body of knowledge about the effects of communication. According to this mode of interpretation, communications serve as a link between man and his environment, and their effects may be explained in terms of the role they play in enabling people to bring about more satisfying relationships between themselves and the world around them.

In order to introduce this approach to the study of communication effects it will be necessary to restate briefly some familiar, even though not uncontroversial, assumptions about the needs of man and the ways these needs are satisfied.

BEHAVIORAL "EFFECTS" AND THEIR CAUSES

Our first assumption is that all human actions and reactions, including changes in attitude and knowledge, are in some way directed toward the satisfaction of wants or needs. That is, whatever we do is in response to some conscious or subconscious requirement or purpose. This is not to say that the action in question is always the most appropriate one, or that actions taken to satisfy one need may not work against the satisfaction of another. Nevertheless, it can be maintained that all actions can be traced to needs, that these in turn can be related to more generalized needs, and so on.[5]

There have been many attempts to draw up lists of basic human needs and wants. The physical requirements for human existence—food, clothing, and shelter—are fairly well agreed upon. Lists of other

From Public Opinion Quarterly 24 (Fall 1959): 343-360.
Copyright © 1960 by Public Opinion Quarterly.
Reprinted by permission.

desiderata that people pursue vary widely in their degree of generality and in their terminology, but there is a heavy degree of overlapping when it comes to values such as power, security, love, and respect. Cooley, for instance, captured in a few words several of the most widespread forces motivating human action when he wrote: "Always and everywhere men seek honor and dread ridicule, defer to public opinion, cherish their goods and their children, and admire courage, generosity, and success.[6] Lasswell lists eight goals which he finds pursued in nearly all cultures, although some are emphasized more in one culture than in another: power, respect, affection, rectitude, well-being, wealth, enlightenment, and skill.[7] Festinger suggests that the existence of inharmonious attitudes or conflicting elements of knowledge within an individual (a state that he labels "dissonance") produces a striving for consistency on the part of that individual, and that dissonance is thus a motivating factor in its own right.[8] A large number of lists and observations concerning human wants and needs could be cited. Indeed, consideration of the forces motivating human action and (to view the other side of the coin) the qualities that people pursue has always been one of the most persistent interests of those who have studied man's behavior. These forces and qualities vary from individual to individual and from culture to culture, but nearly all students agree that they can be identified—at least on a descriptive level—and that they are useful in explaining human actions.

Our second basic assumption is that man's wants and needs are dependent for their satisfaction on his environment. Some requirements can be satisfied from within the individual in the first instance—for example, some tensions can be relieved by yawning or stretching—but our self-sufficiency is exhausted when we must satisfy the more fundamental desires of which these tensions are an expression. Most of our needs or wants can be satisfied only if we are able to manipulate parts of the world outside ourselves, or to adjust in some way to this environment. In the case of requirements for food or clothing the sources of satisfaction are in our physical environment; needs for affection, esteem, or even self-respect, can ordinarily be satisfied only by other people. Our desires for some other goals, such as security and power, can be met in part from our material and in part from our social surroundings. Actions thus occur when we attempt to satisfy needs by manipulating or adjusting to certain aspects of the environment.[9]

Just as it is possible to subdivide needs or motives almost infinitely, if one should wish to engage in this exercise, the content of the environment could be arranged and rearranged in an impressive number of categories. For our purposes, however, it may be most useful to mention four aspects of the environment, as it is experienced by human beings: the physical, the social, the expected, and the imagined. Some may object that the latter two categories are of a different order from the first two (and overlap the first two because expectations and imagery include content from the real environment). This objection can be conceded or it can be disputed; a decision either way makes no difference to the argument that follows.

Different kinds of people depend on each of these different aspects of the environment for the satisfaction of their needs to varying degrees. The farmer's requirements are filled to a larger degree from the physical realm than, say, those of the entertainer, who is as dependent for success on the approval of other people as the farmer is on the weather. The young student may live largely in the world of the future, the mystic in the realm of the supernatural. To some degree, all of us orient our activities toward environmental circumstances in all four categories.

The trend of recent research has been to stress increasingly the importance of the social environment for most people. Satisfaction of physical needs often turns out to be largely a means to the end of achieving a relationship with the social environment that will satisfy other needs. From Veblen to the motivation researchers, students have emphasized that in the process of obtaining food, clothing, and air-conditioned shelter we usually are attempting to bolster our status in the community or elicit approval from the neighbors, or are in some other way orienting our actions toward the social environment. The willingness of human beings to bind their feet, wear corsets, or observe stringent diets, where norms or customs provide that such behavior will be socially rewarded, seems once again to underline the importance of adjustment to the social environment at the expense of the physical.

Our third assumption is that human attention is highly selective.[10] From birth, people learn that satisfaction of their needs is dependent more on certain aspects of their environment than on other aspects. They therefore focus their attention on these aspects. As wants and needs become more complicated the important aspects of the environment become more numerous, but in view of the almost infinite complexity of the world the selective principle remains and becomes even more rigid. We don't often examine the pattern on the wallpaper, listen to the ticking of the clock, or notice what color socks one of our colleagues is wearing, because we don't need this information.[11]

In view of the importance of the social environment for the satisfaction of most people's needs, we would expect that this would occupy a heavy share of their attention and be involved in a large proportion of their actions. This seems to be the case, although reliable information about the quantitative division of attention is difficult to obtain. Nevertheless, indirect evidence is afforded by such indices as the prominence of the social environment in informal conversations and in the content of people's worries and problems.[12]

ATTITUDES AS GUIDES TO ACTION

A fourth assumption is that people gradually accumulate and carry around with them a substantial quantity of information about those aspects of the environment that are important to them. This information, in the form of habits, stereotypes, attitudes, maxims, generalizations, and facts, has been accumulated in the course of their experience. In the past it has helped them to satisfy some of their needs, or they may think that it will be useful in the future. With the aid of these stored impressions people are able to decide easily and quickly what actions are appropriate in most of the situations in which they find themselves.[13]

The existence of the various aspects of this internal picture of the world has often been noted. Habits take us up and down stairs in our own houses, guide us to our offices in the morning, and do much of the work of driving our cars, leaving our consciousness free for other things. Stereotypes, as Walter Lippmann has pointed out, are also useful in reducing the burden on our capacities of perception: "For the attempt to see all things freshly and in detail, rather than as types and generalities, is exhausting...."[14] Lippmann refers to these images as "pictures in our heads." Cantril mentions the "assumptive form world" that we build up on the basis of past experience. Festinger sees the body of our attitudes and beliefs as constituting a fairly accurate mirror or map of reality.[15]

An attitude is particularly important as a labor-saving device, since it usually provides some key to the behavior that is appropriate when we encounter the subject of the attitude or when it comes up in conversation.[16] If we regard another person as "a good man" or "a bad man" this gives us some crude but useful guidance as to how we should act toward him. Likes and dislikes regarding food provide an even more obvious guide to behavior. Very frequently, attitudes have little relevance to action toward the object of the attitude itself, but instead provide a key to the proper behavior in a given social group. Thus people may be for or against a given foreign country (or baseball team) because this is the attitude one should display in the group in which they move, although they have little idea of what the country (or team) in question is actually like.

When attitudes, stereotypes, and the other forms of information that we have internalized are based on little experience and serve a minor need they tend to be lightly held and easily changed. When they are based on extensive experience and and/or serve a deeply felt need, it is difficult to affect them. But if a person's needs change, or if his environment is altered, then he usually has to abandon at least some of his stored-up information, since this leads him to follow lines of action that are inefficient in gaining for him a satisfactory adjustment to his environment.[17]

Changing one's attitudes, stereotypes, and so on, is additionally complicated by the necessity of maintaining as much consistency as possible within this body of internalized information. If two stored-up cognitions indicate two inconsistent courses of action the resulting conflict may be painful. A not excessively painful conflict can be observed in the case of the man in the coffee advertisement, who snaps: "I love coffee, but it keeps me awake." He "snaps" because of the discomfort caused by the inconsistency between his attitude and his experience. Fortunately, his problem can be solved by drinking caffeine-free coffee. The position of the man who is persuaded of the virtues of Presidential Candidate A, while his family and friends continue to admire Candidate B, is likely to be more difficult. One set of attitudes leads him to support his candidate in conversations; another set impels him either to recognize that Candidate B has some virtues or to remain silent. Recent voting studies have found that persons subject to

these "cross-pressures" are most likely to shift their opinions during a campaign.[18] Changing one important attitude, stereotype, or piece of information may necessitate an exhausting process of adjustment in other cognitions and even patterns of action. Most people would like to avoid this and therefore make important changes only when forced to do so.[19]

COMMUNICATION AS A LINK TO THE ENVIRONMENT

Habits, attitudes, and an accumulated stock of knowledge about those aspects of the environment that concern us most go a long way toward shaping our actions, but this stored-up information must be supplemented by a flow of current data about the world around us. The more complicated our needs and the more shifting the environment, the greater our requirements for current information become.

We need this current information for several different reasons. Some of it tells us about changes in the physical or social environment that may require an immediate adjustment in our behavior (a colleague is annoyed; our house is on fire). Other incoming information is stored in one form or another as of possible utility in the expected environment (Main Street is going to be turned into a four-lane highway; a vacation always costs more than you expect). It is probable, however, that a large proportion of our current informational intake primarily serves the purpose of reassuring us that our existing action patterns, attitudes, stereotypes, and so on, are indeed correct—i.e., that they are likely to satisfy our wants and needs.

Most of this information can be acquired by direct observation or personal conversation. The immediate physical surroundings are subject to our scrutiny. In the family, in the neighborhood, and on the job we learn about the most important things by observing, by talking to people, or by overhearing others talk among themselves.But there is still some important information that cannot be acquired at first hand. If a person enters employment in any

skilled capacity, if he takes his citizenship
seriously, or if he seeks to broaden his
knowledge in almost any sphere, he tends to
pay at least some attention to the media of
mass communication. This attention to the
mass media does not necessarily diminish his
participation in personal conversation; on the
contrary, it may give him more to talk about. [20]

Our attention to the mass media, as to
other aspects of the world around us, is highly
selective. We scan the newspaper headlines
and select a few stories to sample further or
even to read in full. We can expose ourselves
to only a very small proportion of the
available radio fare, and when it comes to
magazines and books our attention must be
selective in the extreme.

All the information that we are exposed to
through personal experience or the mass
media can be divided into three categories
according to our behavior toward it: some we
seek out eagerly; some we attend to on the
chance that it may prove useful; some we
attempt to exclude because we have reason to
believe that it would make satisfaction of our
wants and needs more difficult. [21]

In this formidable task of sorting incoming
information we are assisted by habits and
attitudes, many of them culturally defined,
just as habits and attitudes assist us in other
aspects of our behavior. On the basis of past
experience (either our own or that of others
that has been handed on to us) we believe
that useful facts are most likely to come from
a particular person or group, or are to be
found in a given newspaper, in certain radio
programs, or in other specified information
sources. Conversely, we know, or sense, that
there are some sources of information that
are likely to make it more difficult for us to
satisfy our requirements, and we make
strenuous efforts to avoid exposure to these.
Students have often noted the tendency of
the listener to turn off his radio when a
speaker of a political party he opposes comes
on the air.

A related category of devices that help us
select for attention those communications
that are likely to contain useful information
might be called "indicators." We learn that (at
least in some newspapers) the more
important news is likely to be given larger
headlines than the less important news.

Certain tones of voice indicate urgency;
others indicate sincerity. Some colors and
symbols signify danger. These and many
other indicators help us to give our attention
to communications that are likely to be
important to us, although we not infrequently
find that a widely accepted indicator has been
used by someone who wants to direct our
attention to a message of very little
importance to us.

By these and other sorting processes, we
try to obtain useful information from the
stream of communications. For most of us,
information about our personal social
environment, or information that we can use
in this social environment, is important, and
we give particular attention to learning about
anything that may affect our relationship to
those with whom we live and work. Most of us
are particularly interested in knowing what
other people think about us and what they
think about each other. We also like to have
information about those aspects of the
physical environment that affect our needs, or
are likely to affect them, and information that
may be professionally useful, but for most of
us these categories, although important, are
in the second rank.

In connection with the relative attention
given "personally useful" as opposed to
"professionally useful" information, a small
experiment conducted by the author may
prove suggestive. Forty-nine government
officials concerned with foreign affairs, most
of them with about fifteen years' experience in
this area of activity, were exposed for twenty
seconds to a poster showing ten greatly
enlarged newspaper headlines, and were
asked to read these headlines over to
themselves. No reason for the request was
given. Immediately afterward, they were asked
to write down as many of the headlines, or
approximations of the headlines, as they
could remember. [22]

The original hypothesis behind this experiment was that the officials would be most likely to remember those headlines that referred to matters with which they had been professionally concerned. This was not the case. The headline that was remembered most often was a dramatic one of a type that would be likely to provide conversational material. The next two apparently had to do with personal interests of many of the respondents. Next came matters of professional interest, and at the bottom came matters that apparently were of little personal or professional interest to most of the men. These results are shown in Table 1.

TABLE 1
Frequency with Which Headlines Were Recalled by Forty-nine Officials Concerned with Foreign Affairs

Headlines	Number of Mentions
Fallen Jet Is Hit by Train on Coast	29
LSU Rated No. 1 in Football Polls	28
Stock Offerings Rose Last Month	25
UN to Withdraw Group in Lebanon	23
Tunisia Will Buy Arms from Reds	16
Easing of Tension over Berlin Seen	13
Soviet Asks Curb on Atomic Planes	7
Railroads Yield on Tax in Jersey	7
Transport Unity Urged as U.S. Need	7
West Tries to End Nuclear Impasse	5
	160

To summarize our thesis thus far, it may be said that communications provide a link between the individual and the world outside himself. But they do not link him with all aspects of his environment; this would be impossible in view of the limited capacity of the single human being for attention and action. Instead, each person must somehow select for attention those communications that deal with aspects of the environment that are most likely to affect his needs.[23] In this selection process he is aided by habits and attitudes, as well as by his ability to choose consciously. If it were possible to judge objectively whether a person's selection of environmental aspects about which to inform himself was "good" or "bad" from the point of view of satisfying his basic needs, it would probably be concluded that most people choose fairly well but that there is always room for improvement.

The fact that we tend to perceive and remember things that are important to us is neither startling nor novel. It underlies many psychological tests and its implications have been taken into account by social workers, students of public opinion interviewing, and psychotherapists. It is also taken into account, although not always consciously formulated, by practical politicians, teachers, and many others.[24] The reason for going over this familiar ground here is that, in the opinion of the author, it provides a useful link in the chain of relationships between communication and action.

COMMUNICATIONS AND BEHAVIOR

It has been maintained above that the explanation of most human actions, at least those of interest to the social scientist, should be sought in people's efforts to establish a relationship with their environment that is likely to satisfy their needs. According to this way of thinking, a communication cannot properly be said to produce behavioral effects itself, since it merely serves to link the individual to some aspect of his environment, thus enabling him to react to it or manipulate it.

One might express the environment-communication-action relationship in its simplest terms as follows: a given situation exists in the environment; this situation is reported by a communication that comes to the attention of the individual; the individual then adjusts his behavior in a manner calculated to help satisfy some want or need.

Or, to translate this formula into experiential terms, we come into our house alone on a dark night; we hear a voice growl "stick 'em up—I gotya covered"; we probably then do as advised or else try to escape. In taking this action we are reacting not directly to the communication but to the situation we think exists in the environment—i.e., a burglar with a gun. If we know that our eight-year-old son is home or that someone has left the television on, we will respond to an identical communication in a different manner.

Communications can lead to adjustive behavior in those exposed to them in at least three ways. First, they can report an actual or expected change in the environment, or a previously unknown fact about the environment, that is important to the person at the receiving end of the communication; a death in the family, the poor financial condition of a local bank, or the fact that a favorite clothing store will start its annual sale next Wednesday.

Tactical psychological warfare communications during World War II were often of this type. They attempted to influence the behavior of enemy personnel by telling them about developments (or developments to be anticipated) in the military situation: "You have been cut off"; "The units defending your flank have already surrendered"; "Stay away from rail junctions—they will all be bombed." Application of this principle in advertising is even more familiar: "Now for the first time you can buy Product A with a leather carrying case"; "Hurry and order your copy of Book B before the limited edition is exhausted."

A second way that communications can lead to behavioral adjustments is by pointing out an existing feature of the environment (not a change or a completely new fact) and reminding the individual that his needs would be served if he adjusted his behavior in a given manner. Much of the strategic propaganda in World War II was of this type: Axis personnel were told again and again about the overwhelming economic superiority of the Allied powers, and were advised to surrender to avoid senseless destruction.

Allied audiences, for their part, were reminded of the great victories that the Axis forces had already achieved, and were urged to give up—also to avoid further destruction. In some cases, these communications may have contained information that was new to recipients of the propaganda, but in most instances leaflets or broadcasts served merely to remind people of facts they knew already and of needs they had already experienced. Similarly, many consumer items have been used for a long time in substantially the same form, but this does not deter advertisers from calling attention to the virtues of these products and trying to persuade people that it is to their advantage to buy them.

Communications that serve as reminders—either about conditions in the environment or about needs—have been observed to lead to substantial behavioral responses. Election studies have shown that those who lean toward a particular political party are more likely to get out and vote if they are exposed to this party's propaganda. Reminders may also strengthen existing attitudes by providing information that is in accord with them. These phenomena of activation and reinforcement were observed, for instance, in the election study of Lazarsfeld, Berelson, and Gaudet in Erie County, Ohio.[25] They are also likely to come into play on any hot day when we see a sign showing a picture of an ice-cold beverage and telling us where it may be obtained.

The third way in which communications may cause a behavioral adjustment is by bringing to a person's attention a new way of patterning his relationships to the environment. Those who have experienced a religious conversion or adopted a new philosophy may see the same environment about them, but they interpret it differently. Their basic needs may not have changed, but they find that a new pattern of behavior will serve these needs better than the pattern they had followed previously, or the relative emphasis they place on different values may have changed. A similar reorganization of behavior is sometimes brought about by education. Such organizing principles do not, of course, have to be presented in toto by specific communications; they sometimes are worked out by the individual on the basis of exposure to many diverse communications.

In all three cases, assuming that the information in question is perceived as "useful," immediate behavioral adjustments may take place, or (when immediate action is not appropriate) the information contained in the communications may be stored in the form of attitudes or remembered facts to guide future behavior.

In some respects, a communication is thus analogous to a conductor of electricity, whose characteristics influence the work done by the electricity only insofar as the conductor is a good or a poor one. The "conductivity" of a communication seems to be influenced primarily by two factors: whether or not it is clearly organized, uses the language best understood by the audience, etc.; and whether or not it is set off by the proper "indicators" and takes advantage of the communication habits of the audience.

Most research results on the effects of communication can be translated into these terms, although it is usually necessary to supplement the reported data with unsupported assumptions and untested inferences in order to trace the steps of the hypothesized process. For instance, a recent study sponsored by the United States Information Agency in Greece found that those Greeks who were favorably predisposed toward the United States were more likely than those who were not so predisposed to notice and remember a series of United States-sponsored newspaper advertisements.[26] Furthermore, the advertisements, which dealt with basic human rights supported by both Americans and Greeks, appeared to have the effect of strengthening the pro-American attitudes of those who held such attitudes already.

To interpret these observations in accordance with the scheme suggested here, we would have to assume that those affected by the advertisements were people who had found that information about the principles of democracy or about Greek-American ties had tended to satisfy certain of their needs in the past. It may have reassured them of the correctness of their decision in voting for a party supporting Greece's NATO ties. Some of them may have had relatives in the United States. Similar information may previously have helped them to maintain good relations with those among their associates who had similar attitudes or to defend themselves against the arguments of those opposed. The number of possibilities is very large. In any event, their experience had taught them to be on the lookout for—or at least not to resist—information of the type offered in the advertisements.

We also have to assume that the communications habits of those who noticed the advertisements were such that they looked upon the newspaper as a valuable source of information, and that the advertisements were written in a manner that easily conveyed meaning to the readers.

Very similar observations were made as a result of a postwar information campaign to make Cincinnati United Nations conscious. After an intensive six months' effort to inform people in the area about the United Nations, it was found that the people reached by the campaign tended to be those who were already interested in and favorably disposed toward the world organization.[27] In this case, to follow the interpretation suggested here, we would have to assume that the population of Cincinnati could be divided into those who had some use for information about the United Nations and those who did not. Most of those for whom such information was useful had already assembled at least some information from sources available to them prior to the campaign, but the campaign enabled them to obtain a little more. Those who had no use for information about the United Nations, however, continued to have no use for it and therefore disregarded the campaign along with other content of the communication flow for which they had no use.

Studies reported in the large body of literature on experimental modification of attitudes through communications can also be interpreted in these terms. To take a very simple example, subjects are sometimes given attitude tests, then exposed to communications for or against an issue or a political figure, and finally retested. If the issue or the political figure is one that is relatively unknown to them, their attitude changes in the direction of the communication are likely to be great.[28] If, on the other hand, the subject of the communication is one with which they already are well acquainted their attitudes are likely to change little or not at all. In the former case, the communication may be the only link or the most important link with a sector of the environment that hitherto has been largely unknown to them. Therefore, when they are faced with the necessity of espressing an opinion about this subject, they are forced to rely on information from the experimental communication. Conversely, in the latter case, the communication is only one of several links with this aspect of the environment, and when it comes to expressing an opinion, information that has already been stored from other sources may be quite adequate.

That utility influences the retention and also forgetting of facts is indicated by two observations of widely varying nature. McKown at Stanford (in an as yet unpublished study) found that the ability of a reader to conjure up a personal image of the supposed writer of a research report correlated highly with his ability to recall the content of the report. In this instance, the possibility that the report's contents might be useful in social relations as well as in professional activities appeared to result in its making a stronger impression.

The other observation comes from the experience of an interviewer of Soviet military personnel who had been captured by the Nazis. Many of the Soviet soldiers reported that they had been in Poland when Russian forces occupied the Eastern half of that country in 1940 and had been amazed at the high standard of living they found. Then, when they returned to Poland during the Soviet advance in 1944-45, they again had been amazed at the high standard of living. When the interviewer expressed surprise at the fact that they reported being amazed twice, his respondents explained that it had been wise to forget what they had seen in 1940.

A small experiment was conducted by the author to contrast the effectiveness of a communication in influencing an attitude that had little basis in knowledge or experience with the almost total inability of a communication to influence an attitude that was rooted in a substantial body of knowledge or personal experience. Sixty-nine government officials with an average of fifteen years' experience in foreign affairs were given tests to establish their attitudes on a four-point scale toward the United States foreign service and toward two German politicians.[29] They were then exposed to a speech (purportedly by a retired foreign service officer) sharply criticizing the foreign service and also to a speech (by a political scientist) highly praising *one* of the German politicians but not mentioning the other.

The results of the experiment were as expected. On the "after" test designed to elicit attitudes toward the foreign service, only one respondent appears to have shifted his rating by one point on the scale. (The possibility of compensating changes exists, but is very slight.) Most of these officials had had personal experience with the foreign service over a period of years, and had built up attitudes of considerable stability. Even though the criticisms made in the speech were shared by many of them, these criticisms had already been taken into account in their thinking and consequently gave them insufficient reason to revise the image of the foreign service they had already formed.

Although not unexpected, the results regarding the two German politicians—von Brentano and Erhard—were more interesting. Responses on these questions were divided into two groups: those from men who had had experience with reference to Western Europe and those from men who reported no such experience. With regard to Erhard, about whom no communication was presented, the scale ratings on the "before" and "after" tests were identical (or there were compensating changes, which is unlikely). The results in the case of von Brentano showed a pronounced influence of the persuasive communication among those with no Western European experience, while it had almost no influence in the case of those who were European experts. These results are shown in Table 2.[30]

Experiments such as this offer certain difficulties of interpretation, since they make use of communication habits that do not play a role in other situations. When confronted with a communication in the classroom or laboratory, the subject usually makes the conscious or subconscious assumption that the instructor or experimenter wants him to pay attention to it. Furthermore, by the time he has reached high school or college he presumably has the habit of paying attention in the classroom. Therefore, he may assimilate information that in another context he would regard as not having sufficient utility to justify his attention. For instance, in the case reported in Table 2 it is unlikely that most of those who were not experts on Western Europe would have read the speech about von Brentano if they had not been specifically asked to do so. Another aspect of the classroom or experimental situation is that it does not ordinarily reward an individual for maintaining a consistent opinion (as is usually the case in other situations) or penalize him for changing his opinion. Indeed, the opposite may be the case. Emphasis on keeping an open mind may even predispose him toward exposure to information that he would otherwise ignore, and may encourage him to revise his opinions in the light of new data. In experimental situations where subjects have been rewarded in some way for maintaining a consistent opinion, observed changes have been considerably less. Finally, in experimental situations, the social setting of the respondent is often ignored. We usually pay little attention to his relations with the other respondents or with the experimenter; yet these relationships may exercise an important influence on his responses. To translate these remarks into the terms that have been used above, we might say that in the experimental situation a subject's needs are often different from those in other situations and therefore somewhat different habits, including communication habits, are appropriate to this situation.

TABLE 2
Evaluation by 69 Foreign Affairs Experts of the Choice of von Brentano as Foreign Minister of the German Federal Republic before and after Reading a Speech Praising Him.*

	Before	After
Those with Western European Experience:		
Excellent	12	14
Good	16	16
Satisfactory	4	4
Poor	2	1
No opinion	4	3
Those with no Western European experience:		
Excellent	5	18
Good	11	10
Satisfactory	5	1
Poor	0	0
No opinion	10	2

*The question was: "In 1955, Dr. Heinrich von Brentano was appointed Foreign Minister of the German Federal Republic. On the basis of what you know about Dr. von Brentano, would you say that this choice was excellent, good, satisfactory, or poor?"

SOME IMPLICATIONS
FOR PERSUASION

This way of looking at the effects of communication suggests that the communicator can influence attitudes or behavior only when he is able to convey information that may be utilized by members of his audience to satisfy their wants or needs. If he has control of some significant aspect of his audience's environment, his task may be an easy one. All he must do is tell people about some environmental change or expected change that is important to them. For example, he may offer a large sum of money to anyone who does a certain thing. If he is a merchant, he may sell a product at a very low cost. We all have control over an aspect of the environment that is significant for members of the primary groups to which we belong—our own behavior.

Most communicators are in a more difficult position when they are trying to effect persuasion outside their own group, since they do not control aspects of the environment that are significant to their audiences. Furthermore, they usually do not have a monopoly of the channels of information, and must ordinarily assume that people have already located sources of information about aspects of the environment that are important to them. To influence behavior under these conditions the communicator's information must be more accurate or otherwise more useful than information from competing sources. He can, it is true, sometimes build on tendencies toward action that are already present by reminding people of existing needs and of how they may be satisfied. But to bring about any basic behavorial changes is very difficult. Attitudes and behavior patterns that are based on extensive information or on personal experience are likely to have already proved their utility and to be tough and highly resistant to change. Furthermore, the capacity of people to disregard information that is not useful (either because it is irrelevant or because it conflicts with already established patterns of thought and action) appears to be almost unlimited.[31]

This approach to the study of communication effects also suggests that soundly based knowledge about the principles of persuasion will be attainable only as a result of basic advances within psychology and sociology. A better understanding of the way people perceive their social environment and how they adjust to it appears to be particularly important. The advances that can be made independently in the field usually labeled "communication" are likely to be limited and tentative.

Nevertheless, communication studies, while they cannot stand alone, contribute to our understanding of human needs and the way these are satisfied. A substantial quantity of information on the various ways communications are utilized by different people is already available but has not been systematically organized. For most Americans, for example, news carried in the press of a totalitarian country is not very useful because of its incompleteness and inaccuracy. But for the citizen of such a country this news may be vital to preferment or even survival, since it lets him know what the power holders *want* him to believe.[32] Similarly, it has frequently been observed (e.g., in studies of prejudice) that communications from within the group have more effect on attitudes than identical communications from outside the group. This seems to be true in cases where the utility of the information to the recipient is not in its objective content but in the fact that a member of his group believes it.

Finally, this approach emphasizes that the communicator's audience is not a passive recipient—it cannot be regarded as a lump of clay to be molded by the master propagandist. Rather, the audience is made up of individuals who demand something from the communications to which they are exposed, and who select those that are likely to be useful to them. In other words, they must get something from the manipulator if he is to get something from them. A bargain is involved. Sometimes, it is true, the manipulator is able to lead his audience in to a bad bargain by emphasizing one need at the expense of another or by representing a change in the significant environment as greater than it actually has been. But audiences, too, can drive a hard bargain. Many communicators who have been widely disregarded or misunderstood know that to their cost.

NOTES

1. One of the most comprehensive summaries is the chapter by Carl I. Hovland, "Effects of the Mass Media of Communication," in *Handbook of Social Psychology,* ed. Gardner Lindzey (Cambridge, Mass.: Addison-Wesley, 1954). Literature summarizing a greater or lesser portion of what is known about the effects of communication and applying this knowledge to a variety of problem areas is now so voluminous that only a few examples can be given: Erik Barnouw, *Mass Communications* (New York: Holt, 1956); W. L. Brembeck and W. S. Howell, *Persuasion – A Means of Social Control* (Englewood Cliffs, N.J.: Prentice-Hall, 1952); Rex F. Harlow, *Social Science in Public Relations* (New York: Harper, 1957); *Mass Communication and Education* (National Education Association, Educational Policies Commission, 1958).

2. Aristotle's *Rhetoric* is still a widely used text in courses on public opinion and communication. A brief summary of experience in psychological warfare is presented by John W. Riley, Jr., and Leonard S. Cottrell, Jr., "Research for Psychological Warfare," *Public Opinion Quarterly* 21 (1957): 147-158. The principal anthologies on political communication and psychological warfare also include collections of qualitative as well as quantitative data on effect: William E. Daugherty and Morris Janowitz, *A Psychological Warfare Casebook* (Baltimore: Johns Hopkins Press, 1958); Daniel Lerner, *Propaganda in War and Crisis* (New York: Stewart, 1951); Wilbur Schramm, *The Process and Effects of Mass Communication* (Urbana: University of Illinois Press, 1954).

3. Leon Festinger, *A Theory of Cognitive Dissonance* (New York: Harper, 1957); Carl I. Hovland, Irving L. Janis, and Harold H. Kelley, *Communications and Persuasion: Psychological Studies of Opinion Change* (New Haven, Conn.: Yale University Press,. 1953); Elihu Katz and Paul F. Lazarsfeld, *Personal Influence: The Part Played by People in the Flow of Mass Communication* (New York: Free Press, 1955).

4. Joseph T. Klapper, "What We Know about the Effects of Mass Communication: The Brink of Hope," *Public Opinion Quarterly* 21 (1957): 453-474.

5. The definition of needs or motives can, of course, easily be reduced to absurdity if one attempts to achieve extremes either of generality or of specificity. At one extreme, all actions can be explained as efforts to relieve some type of tension, or as ultimately traceable to one single "drive"; at the other extreme, the explanation refers only to the immediate object of the action: e.g., the reason I buy a magazine is because I want a magazine. Intermediate levels of description, at which categories of specific actions can be related to more generalized needs, seem to be the most fruitful for purposes of social inquiry. See Gardner Murphy, "Social Motivation," in Handbook of Social Psychology, ed. Gardner Lindzey (Cambridge, Mass.: Addison-Wesley, 1954), p. 608.

6. Charles Horton Cooley, *Social Organization* (New York: Free Press, 1956), p. 28.

7. Harold D. Lasswell, *Power and Personality* (New York: Norton, 1948); also Harold D. Lasswell and Abraham Kaplan, *Power and Society* (New Haven, Conn.: Yale University Press, 1950), especially pp. 55-58.

8. Festinger, *Cognitive Dissonance.*

9. Kornhauser and Lazarsfeld observe, in another context, that any action is determined on the one hand by the total make-up of the individual and on the other by the total situation in which he finds himself. Explanations must refer both to the objective and the subjective. See Arthur Kornhauser and Paul F. Lazarsfeld, "The Analysis of Consumer Actions," in ed. Paul F Lazarsfeld and Morris Rosenberg, *The Language of Social Research,* (New York: Free Press, 1955), p. 393.

10. William James refers to this "narrowness of consciousness" as one of the most extraordinary facts of our life. "Although we are besieged at every moment by impressions from our whole sensory surface, we notice so very small a part of them." William James, *Psychology-Briefer Course* (New York: Holt, 1892).

11. A familiar classroom illustration of the selectivity of perception is for the instructor, half-way through the period, to cover his necktie with a large handkerchief and then ask the students what color the tie is. Ordinarily, fewer than half the students will be able to name the color correctly. This is, of course, as it should be, since there is usually no reason why they should pay attention to the color.

12. See Samuel A. Stouffer, *Communism, Conformity, and Civil Liberties* (New York: Doubleday, 1955), especially pp. 58-71; also Jeanne Watson, Warren Breed, and Harry Posman, "A Study in Urban Conversation: Sample of 1001 Remarks Overheard in Manhattan," *Journal of Social Psychology* 28 (1948): 121-133.

13. See Hadley Cantril, *The "Why" of Man's Experience* (New York: Macmillan, 1950), pp. 66, 77.

14. Walter Lippmann, *Public Opinion* (Baltimore: Penguin, 1946), p. 66.

15. Cantril, *Man's Experience* pp. 103-104; Festinger, *Cognitive Dissonance* p. 10. An application of Cantril's approach in a study of policy makers in seven countries has been made recently by Lloyd A. Free, *Six Allies and a Neutral* (New York: Free Press, 1959).

16. M. Brewster Smith, in connection with an intensive study of opinions toward Soviet Russia, found one function of attitude to be that of providing a person with an evaluation of the salient aspects of his world. "The greater the extent to which this evaluation takes account of the important harms and benefits that he may expect from his surroundings, the more adequately will it serve his adjustment in the longest run." M. Brewster Smith, *Functional and Descriptive Analysis of Public Opinion,"* Ph.D. dissertation, Harvard University, 1947, p. 34.

17. In his autobiography, Benjamin Franklin reports that at one time he was a vegetarian and considered the taking of fish a kind of unprovoked murder. On a voyage from Boston to Philadelphia, however, his ship became becalmed off Block Island and the crew diverted themselves by catching cod. When the fish came out of the frying pan, they smelled "admirably well." "I balanced some time between principle and inclination till I recollected that when the fish were opened, I saw smaller fish taken out of their stomachs. 'Then,' thought I, 'if you eat one another, I don't see why we mayn't eat you.' So I dined upon cod very heartily...."

18. Bernard Berelson, Paul F. Lazarsfeld, and William M. McPhee, *Voting* (Chicago: University of Chicago, 1954).

19. See Smith, "Functional and Descriptive Analysis", pp. 37-38: "Since his attitudes are inextricably involved in his psychological economy,...(a person) cannot alter them without at the same time carrying out more or less complicated readjustments."

20. At least, this is the case with opinion leaders in many fields, who typically belong to more organizations, have more social contacts, and in general are more gregarious than others. They also are likely to follow the mass media appropriate to their sphere of interest. See Elihu Katz, "The Two-Step Flow of Communication," *Public Opinion Quarterly* 21 (1957): 61-78.

21. Principal mechanisms of exclusion appear to be nonperception (the small boy simply doesn't hear his mother tell him to keep his hands out of the cookie jar); distortion (we note that crime in our town is due mainly to visitors from outside); and, most commonly, forgetting (many people have trouble remembering how little money is left in their checking accounts). All these exclusion mechanisms have been described in connection with systematic studies: for example, Frederic C. Barlett, *Remembering* (New York: Cambridge University Press, 1932); Gordon W. Allport and Leo J. Postman, *The Psychology of Rumor* (New York: Holt, 1947); Eunice Cooper and Marie Jahoda, "The Evasion of Propaganda," *Journal of Psychology* 23 (1947): 15-25. Distortion is, however, not only a mechanism for excluding information. It can also be used to make some information more useful or more comprehensible.

22. The forty-nine responses were obtained from several smaller groups. This made it possible to vary the order in which the headlines were presented. With minor exceptions, the rank order of the headlines in each subgroup remained the same.

23. The same communications may be used in various ways to satisfy different needs. On the basis of a study of children's attention to comics and TV programs, the Rileys observed that "the same media materials appeared to be interpreted and used differently by children in different social positions." The principle of selectivity was also illustrated by this study. Peer group members, for example, appeared to select materials from the media which would in some way be immediately useful for group living. See Matilda White Riley and John W. Riley, Jr., "A Sociological Approach to Communications Research," *Public Opinion Quarterly* 15 (1951): 456. Similar observations were made by Merton in his study of Kate Smith's marathon drive to sell war bonds by radio. Listeners who perceived the same aspects of the broadcast sometimes "used" this information in different ways. In other cases people's attention to different aspects of the performance could be related to their psychological requirements. See Robert K. Merton, *Mass Persuasion* (New York: Harper, 1946)

24. The politician who mingles with the crowd, looking friendly and receptive but saying little, "just to see what people have on their minds," is practicing somewhat the same technique as the nondirective interviewer or the psychologist who administers a projective test.

25. Paul F. Lazarsfeld, Bernard Berelson, and Hazel Gaudet, *The People's Choice* (New York: Columbia University Press, 1948).

26. Leo Bogart, "Measuring the Effectivenes of an Overseas Information Campaign: A Case History," *Public Opinion Quarterly* 21 (1957): 475-498.

27. Shirley A. Starr and Helen MacGill Hughes, "Report on an Educational Campaign: The Cincinnati Plan for the United Nations," *American Journal of Sociology* 55, (1950): 389-400.

28. See A. D. Annis and Norman C. Meier, "The Induction of Opinion Through Suggestion by Means of Planted Content,'" *Journal of Social Psychology* 5 (1934): 65-81. In this experiment a pronounced change in attitude toward a little-known Australian prime minister was achieved through exposure to material about him "planted" in a campus newspaper. One must assume that a much smaller change would have been achieved if the individual concerned had been better known to the respondents.

29. The attitude tests were given in three groups and the responses totaled later.

30. The question used to divide respondents into experts and nonexperts on Western Europe did not discriminate perfectly, as the four "no opinion" responses of the experts in the "before" test indicate. If a more accurate division could have been obtained, the changes probably would have been even fewer among the experts and more pronounced among the nonexperts.

31. The communicator may be able, however, to *make* his information useful—the very fact that certain people are talking about a subject makes this subject relevant for others.

32. See Paul Kecskemeti, "Totalitarian Communications as a Means of Control," *Public Opinion Quarterly* 14 (1950): 224-234. Some case material that illustrates Kecskemeti's observations very well is presented by Alex Inkeles and Raymond A. Bauer, *The Soviet Citizen* (Cambridge, Mass.: Harvard University Press, 1959), p. 175.

Part One

The Popular Culture View

OF HAPPINESS AND OF DESPAIR WE HAVE NO MEASURE

Ernest van den Haag

All mass media in the end alienate people from personal experience and, though appearing to offset it, intensify their moral isolation from each other, from reality and from themselves. One may turn to the mass media when lonely or bored. But mass media, once they become a habit, impair the capacity for meaningful experience. Though more diffuse and not as gripping, the habit feeds on itself, establishing a vicious circle as addictions do.

The mass media do not physically replace individual activities and contacts—excursions, travel, parties, etc. But they impinge on all. The portable radio is taken everywhere—from seashore to mountaintop—and everywhere it isolates the bearer from his surroundings, from other people, and from himself. Most people escape being by themselves at any time by voluntarily tuning in on something or somebody. Anyway, it is nearly beyond the power of individuals to escape broadcasts. Music and public announcements are piped into restaurants, bars, shops, cafes, and lobbies, into public means of transportation, and even taxis. You can turn off your radio but not your neighbor's, nor can you silence his portable or the set at the restaurant. Fortunately, most persons do not seem to miss privacy, the cost of which is even more beyond the average income than the cost of individuality.

People are never quite in one place or group without at the same time, singly or collectively, gravitating somewhere else, abstracted, if not transported by the mass media. The incessant announcements, arpeggios, croonings, sobs, bellows, brayings and jingles draw to some faraway world at large and by weakening community with immediate surroundings make people lonely even when in a crowd and crowded even when alone.

We have already stressed that mass media must offer homogenized fare to meet an average of tastes. Further, whatever the quality of the offerings, the very fact that one after the other is absorbed continuously, indiscriminately and casually, trivializes all. Even the most profound of experiences, articulated too often on the same level, is reduced to cliché. The impact of each of the offerings of mass media is thus weakened by the next one. But the impact of the stream of all mass-media offerings is cumulative and strong. It lessens people's capacity to experience life itself.

Sometimes it is argued that the audience confuses actuality with mass-media fiction and reacts to the characters and situations that appear in soap operas or comic strips as though they were real. For instance, wedding presents are sent to fictional couples. It seems more likely, however, that the audience prefers to invest fiction with reality—as a person might prefer to dream—without actually confusing it with reality. After all, even the kids know that Hopalong Cassidy is an actor and the adults know that "I Love Lucy" is fiction. Both, however, may attempt to live the fiction because they prefer it to their own lives. The significant effect is not the (quite limited) investment of fiction with reality, but the de-realization of life lived in largely fictitious terms. Art can deepen the perception of reality. But popular culture veils it, diverts from it, and becomes an obstacle to experiencing it. It is not so much an escape from life but an invasion of life first, and ultimately evasion altogether.

Parents, well knowing that mass media can absorb energy, often lighten the strain that the attempts of their children to reach for activity and direct experience would impose; they allow some energy to be absorbed by the vicarious experience of the television screen.

Before television, the cradle was rocked, or poppy juice given, to inhibit the initiative and motility of small children. Television, unlike these physical sedatives, tranquilizes by means of substitute gratifications. Manufactured activities and plots are offered to still the child's hunger for experiencing life. They effectively neutralize initiative and channel imagination. But the early introduction of de-individualized characters and situations and early homogenization of taste on a diet of meaningless activity hardly foster development. Perhaps poppy juice, offering no models in which to cast the imagination, was better.

The homogenizing effect of comic books or television, the fact that they neither express nor appeal to individuality, seems far more injurious to the child's mind and character than the violence they feature, though it is the latter that is often blamed for juvenile delinquency. The blame is misplaced. Violence is not new to life or fiction. It waxed large in ancient fables, fairy tales, and in tragedies from Sophocles to Shakespeare.

Mom always knew that "her boy could not have thought of it," that the other boys must have seduced him. The belief that viewing or reading about violence persuades children to engage in it is Mom's ancient conviction disguised as psychiatry. Children are quite spontaneously bloodthirsty and need both direct and fantasy outlets for violence. What is wrong with the violence of mass media is not that it is violence, but that it is not art—that it is meaningless violence which thrills but does not gratify. The violence of the desire for life and meaning is displaced and appears as a desire for meaningless violence. But the violence which is ceaselessly supplied cannot ultimately gratify it because it does not meet the repressed desire....

The gist of any culture is an ethos which gives meaning to the lives of those who dwell in it. If this be the purport of popular culture, it is foiled. We have suggested how it comes to grief in various aspects. What makes popular culture as a whole so disconcerting is best set forth now by exploring the relationship among diversion, art and boredom.

Freud thought of art as a diversion, "an illusion in contrast to reality," a "substitute gratification" like a dream. In this he fully shared what was and still is the popular view of art. It is a correct view—of popular "art," of pseudo-art produced to meet the demand for diversion. But it is a mistaken, reductive definition of art.

Freud finds the "dreamwork" attempting to hide or disguise the dreamer's true wishes and fears so that they may not alarm his consciousness. The "substitute gratification" produced by the dreamwork, mainly by displacements, helps the dreamer continue sleeping. However, one major function of art is precisely to undo this dreamwork, to see through disguises, to reveal to our consciousness the true nature of our wishes and fears. The dreamwork covers, to protect sleep. Art discovers and attempts to awaken the sleeper. Whereas the dreamwork tries to aid repression, the work of art intensifies and deepens perception and experience of the world and of the self. It attempts to pluck the heart of the mystery, to show where "the action lies in its true nature."

Though dreams and art both may disregard literal reality, they do so to answer opposite needs. The dream may ignore reality to keep the sleeper's eyes closed. Art transcends immediate reality to encompass wider views, penetrate into deeper experience and lead to a fuller confrontation of man's predicament. The dreamwork even tries to cover upsetting basic impulses with harmless immediate reality. Art, in contrast, ignores the immediate only to uncover the essential. Artistic revelation need not be concerned with outer or with social reality. It may be purely aesthetic. But it can never be an illusion if it is art. Far from distracting from reality, art is a form of reality which strips life of the fortuitous to lay bare its essentials and permit us to experience them.

In popular culture, however, "art" is all that Freud said art is, and no more. Like the dreamwork, popular culture distorts human experience to draw "substitute gratifications" or reassurances from it. Like the dreamwork, it presents "an illusion in contrast to reality." For this reason, popular "art" falls short of satisfaction. And all of popular culture leaves one vaguely discontented because, like popular art, it is only a "substitute gratification"; like a dream, it distracts from life and from real gratification.

Substitute gratifications are uneconomic, as Freud often stressed. They do not in the end gratify as much, and they cost more psychologically than the real gratifications which they shut out. This is why sublimation and realistic control are to be preferred to substitution and repression. That is why reality is to be preferred to illusion, full experience to symptomatic displacements and defense mechanisms. Yet substitute gratifications, habitually resorted to, incapacitate the individual for real ones. In part they cause or strengthen internalized hindrances to real and gratifying experience; in part they are longed for because internal barriers have already blocked real gratification of the original impulses.

Though the specific role it plays varies with the influence of other formative factors in the life of each individual, popular culture must be counted among the baffling variety of causes and effects of defense mechanisms and repressions. It may do much damage, or do none at all, or be the only relief possible, however deficient. But whenever popular culture plays a major role in life significant repressions have taken (or are taking) place. Popular culture supplants those gratifications, which are no longer sought because of the repression of the original impulses. But it is a substitute and spurious. It founders and cannot succeed because neither desire nor gratification are true. "Nought's had, all's spent/ where desire is got without content."

It may seem paradoxical to describe popular culture in terms of repression. Far from repressed, it strikes one as uninhibited. Yet the seeming paradox disappears if we assume that the uproarious din, the raucous noise and the shouting are attempts to drown the shriek of unused capacities, of repressed individuality, as it is bent into futility.

Repression bars impulses from awareness without satisfying them. This damming up always generates a feeling of futility and apathy or, in defense against it, an agitated need for action. The former may be called listless, the latter restless boredom. They may alternate and they may enter consciousness only through anxiety and a sense of meaninglessness, fatigue and nonfulfillment. Sometimes there is such a general numbing of the eagerness too often turned aside that only a dull feeling of dreariness and emptiness remains. More often, there is an insatiable longing for things to happen. The external world is to supply these events to fill the emptiness. Yet the bored person cannot designate what would satisfy a craving as ceaseless as it is vague. It is not satisfied by any event supplied.

The yearning for diversion to which popular culture caters cannot be sated by diversion "whereof a little more than a little is by much too much," because no displaced craving can be satisfied by catering to it in its displaced form. Only when it becomes possible to experience the desire in its true form and to dispense with the internalized processes that balked and displaced it does actual gratification become possible. Diversion at most, through weariness and fatigue, can numb and distract anxiety.

For instance, in many popular movies the tear ducts are massaged and thrills are produced by mechanized assaults on the centers of sensation. We are diverted temporarily and in the end perhaps drained—but not gratified. Direct manipulation of sensations can produce increases and discharges of tension, as does masturbation, but it is a substitute. It does not involve the whole individual as an individual, it does not involve reality but counterfeits it.

Sensations directly stimulated and discharged without being intensified and completed through feelings sifted and acknowledged by the intellect are debasing because they do not involve the whole individual in his relation to reality. When one becomes inured to bypassing reality and individuality in favor of meaningless excitement, ultimate gratification becomes impossible.

Once fundamental impulses are thwarted beyond retrieving, once they are so deeply repressed that no awareness is left of their aims, once the desire for a meaningful life has been lost as well as the capacity to create it, only a void remains. Life fades into tedium when the barrier between impulses and aims is so high that neither penetrates into consciousness and no sublimation whatever takes place. Diversion, however frantic, can overwhelm temporarily but not ultimately relieve the boredom which oozes from nonfulfillment.

Though the bored person hungers for things to happen to him, the disheartening fact is that when they do he empties them of the very meaning he unconsciously yearns for by using them as distractions. In popular culture even the second coming would become just another barren "thrill" to be watched on television till Milton Berle comes on. No distraction can cure boredom, just as the company so unceasingly pursued cannot stave off loneliness. The bored person is lonely for himself, not, as he thinks, for others. He misses the individuality, the capacity for experience from which he is debarred. No distraction can restore it. Hence he goes unrelieved and insatiable.

The popular demand for "inside" stories, for vicarious sharing of the private lives of "personalities" rests on the craving for private life—even someone else's—of those who are dimly aware of having none whatever, or at least no life that holds their interest. The attempts to allay boredom are as assiduous as they are unavailing. Countless books pretend to teach by general rules and devices what cannot be learned by devices and rules.

Individual personalities cannot be mass produced (with happiness thrown in or your money back). Nevertheless, the message of much popular culture is "you, too, can be happy" if you only buy this car or that hair tonic; you will be thrilled, you will have adventure, romance, popularity—you will no longer be lonely and left out if you follow this formula. And success, happiness or at least freedom from anxiety is also the burden of popular religion, as unchristian in these its aims as it is in its means. From Dale Carnegie to Norman Vincent Peale to Harry and Bonaro Overstreet only the vocabulary changes. The principle remains the same. The formula is well illustrated in the following.

Warm Smile Is an Attribute of Charm

For this, train the upper lip by this method:

1. *Stretch the upper lip down over the teeth. Say "Mo-o-o-o."*
2. *Hold the lip between the teeth and smile.*
3. *Purse the lips, pull them downward and grin.*
4. *Let the lower jaw fall and try to touch your nose with your upper lip.*

Months of daily practice are necessary to eliminate strain from the new way of smiling, but it, too, can become as natural as all beguiling smiles must be.

Whatever the formula, nothing can be more tiresome than the tireless, cheerless pursuit of pleasure. Days go slowly when they are empty; one cannot tell one from the other. And yet the years go fast. When time is endlessly killed, one lives in an endless present until time ends without ever having passed, leaving a person who never lived to exclaim, "I wasted time and now doth time waste me."

To the Christian, despair is a sin not because there is anything to be hoped for in this life, but because to despair is to lack faith in redemption from it—in the life everlasting. As for the pleasures of this life, they are not worth pursuing. Lancelot Andrewes described them: "...though they fade not of themselves yet to us they fade. We are hungry and we eat. Eat we not till that fades and we are as

weary of our fulness as we were of our fasting? We are weary and we rest. Rest we not till that fades and we are as weary of our rest as ever we were of our weariness?" Our bodies and minds themselves fade as do their pleasures. The insults of time are spared to none of us. Such is the human predicament.

In *Civilization and Its Discontents,* Freud pointed to the additional burdens that civilization imposes on human beings. They, too, are inevitable, for civilization, despite its cost, eases the total burden we bear.

A little more than a hundred years ago, Henry David Thoreau wrote in *Walden:* "The mass of men lead lives of quiet desperation....A stereotyped but unconscious despair is concealed even under what are called the games and amusements of mankind." Despair, we find, is no longer quiet. Popular culture tries to exorcise it with much clanging and banging. Perhaps it takes more noise to drone it out. Perhaps we are less willing to face it. But whether wrapped in popular culture, we are less happy than our quieter ancestors, or the natives of Bali, must remain an open question despite all romanticizing. (Nor do we have a feasible alternative to popular culture. Besides, a proposal for "the mass of men" would be unlikely to affect the substance of popular culture. And counsel to individuals must be individual.)

There have been periods happier and others more desperate than ours. But we don't know which. And even an assertion as reasonable as this is a conjecture like any comparison of today's bliss with yesterday's. The happiness felt in disparate groups, in disparate periods and places cannot be measured and compared. Our contention is simply that by distracting from the human predicament and blocking individuation and experience, popular culture impoverishes life without leading to contentment. But whether "the mass of men" felt better or worse without the mass-production techniques of which popular culture is an ineluctable part, we shall never know. Of happiness and of despair, we have no measure.

DIFFERENTIATING POPULAR CULTURE AND MASS CULTURE

Don Dodson

The study of popular culture is a muddy field through which generations of scholars and critics have slogged. Its terrain is now well trampled but still poorly charted. Partly because they do not agree on its boundaries, those who have explored it have engaged in what Bernard Rosenberg calls "an interminable and ferocious debate" in which "protagonists lambaste anatagonists—who clobber neutralists—in an arena littered with faulty logic, shopworn analogies, dubious data and, over all, the unappetizing remains of a stale argument."[1] Horrified by the results, Kingsley Amis once grumbled, "I have only reached the stage of firmly opting for any straight hour's-worth of mass-culture to again being told about it."[2]

The problem of definition has stalemated the debate. Are disputants even talking about the same thing? It is hard to tell, because the literature on mass culture is strewn with different terms for the same concept and with different definitions—if any at all—for the same term. The confusion of terms is crystallized in the title of one of the best-known anthologies

Paper presented at the 58th annual meeting of the Association for Education in Journalism, Ottawa, Canada, 16-20 August 1975. Reprinted by permission of the author.

in the field: *Mass Culture: The Popular Arts in America.*[3] Use of "popular" and "mass" as synonyms is almost universal. Most writers who do see a difference stress tone rather than substance. In one of the most important recent contributions to the debate, *Popular Culture and High Culture,* Herbert J. Gans asserts:

The term mass culture *is obviously pejorative;* mass *suggests an undifferentiated collectivity, even a mob, rather than individuals or members of a group; and* mass culture, *that mob's lack of culture. This negative judgment can be counteracted by the use of more positive terms like* popular culture *or* popular arts....[4]

Other terms that have been interchanged are the "brutal culture" of Edward Shils, the "masscult" of Dwight Macdonald, the "lowbrow" culture of Van Wyck Brooks, and the "kitsch" of Clement Greenberg.[5]

When Paul F. Lazarsfeld writes that "one should not worry too much about the definition" of mass society, he implies that his nonchalance encompasses mass culture as well.[6] But the diversity of terminology and definition have so confused the mass culture debate that such indifference may be a disservice. Shils, whose own term shares the weakness he finds in others, has spotted the problem:

I have reservations about the use of the term "mass culture," because it refers simultaneously to the substantive and qualitative properties of the culture, to the social status of its consumers, and to the media by which it is transmitted. Because of this at least threefold reference, it tends to beg some important questions regarding the relations among the three variables.[7]

Actually, although explicit definitions are rare, at least six criteria for defining "popular" or "mass" culture are implicit in the literature:

1. *Aesthetics.* According to Abraham Kaplan, "The *kind* of taste that the popular arts satisfy, and not how widespread that taste is, is what distinguishes them."[8] Kitsch, in Greenberg's classic formulation, "predigests art for the spectator and spares him effort, provides him with a short cut to the pleasure of art that detours what is necessarily difficult in genuine art."[9] Aesthetic quality is a slippery guideline for defining a social phenomenon.

2. *Genres.* The organization of several studies into classificatory sections—"Movies," "Television," "Spy Fiction," "Comic Books"—implies that popular culture can be defined by the genres it comprises.[10] This suggests that all movies, from *The Singing Nun* to *The Seventh Seal,* are popular culture. Such labeling rivets particular media and forms in a rigid cultural stance.

3. *Audience.* The size or qualities of its audience may define popular culture. William M. Hammel writes:

   > Current usage defines "popular arts" as those arts that appeal to the masses and that do not require a high level of intellectual or cultural refinement....We could say that the popular arts are more "democratic" since they are accessible to larger numbers of people and that "high art" tends to be "aristocratic," the province of the more cultivated.[11]

   Russel Nye similarly defines "popular" as "generally dispersed and approved."[12]

4. *Functions.* Popular culture is sometimes defined in terms of the functions it serves. "In my opinion," writes Ernest van den Haag, "emphasis on cultural objects misses the point. A sociologist (and to analyze mass culture is a sociological enterprise) must focus on the function of such objects in people's lives...."[13] Functions commonly cited—frequently superciliously—are entertainment and escape. Quoting T. S. Eliot, Van den Haag disparages the "craving to be 'distracted from distraction by distraction.'"[14] This approach, though affiliated with the aesthetic one, seems even more puritanical. Whatever the functions of popular culture, they are often presumed rather than demonstrated.[15] Even if they were more than putative, to incorporate them in a definition would confound a potential independent variable (popular culture) with potential dependent variables (escape or "narcotization"). The variables should be formulated separately.

5. *Mode of Production.* Macdonald describes mass culture as a commodity that is "manufactured wholesale for the market" with no other purpose than to be "an article for mass consumption, like chewing gum." It is cranked out by assembly-line technicians who are so specialized that they are "as alienated from their brainwork as the industrial worker is from his handwork."[16] Mass culture, thus, is a mode of production.

6. *Role of the Artist.* Another consideration is how the artist relates with his audience. Seen this way, popular culture is a process of communication as well as a collection of artifacts. Stuart Hall and Paddy Whannel, like several other writers, take this approach. Their cultural typology—folk, popular, mass, and minority—is one of the rare attempts to differentiate popular from mass culture. Folk art is the simplest type. It is a traditional expression of an "organic" community in which the artist is typically anonymous. Popular art, on the other hand, is a commercial nexus in which the artist becomes individualized and the community becomes an audience But the popular artist is still closely attuned to his audience. The mass artist, who is less sensitive to the audience but more slavish toward it, turns conventions into formulas. The creator of minority art is less concerned with appeasing his audience than any of the former. He is more absorbed in expressing himself and in wrestling with his material.[17] Hall and Whannel, unfortunately, mix sociological and aesthetic criteria.

TYPOLOGY OF CULTURES

The framework outlined here is an attempt to separate aesthetic and evaluative criteria from definitions of cultural types. It does not preclude value judgments in the end. It is based on the assumption, however, that building value judgments into the definitions themselves thwarts clear debate and careful study.

Any culture is a social system as well as a collection of symbols. Types of culture differ on the basis of how major participants—artist, entrepreneur, audience, and critic—interact with one another.

The artist, whether a creator or a performer, is anyone who manipulates symbols for an aesthetic purpose.

The entrepreneur is anyone whose specialty is to transmit symbols from artist to audience through commercial practices involving some initiative and risk. Although some social scientists distinguish between entrepreneurs "who in a sense start from scratch and those who perform entrepreneurial functions within already established organizations," the term here covers both activities.[18] It may apply to subordinates as well as manager.

The audience comprises all persons who attend to the finished work of the artist.

The critic is anyone—a reviewer, a censor, a scholar, or another artist—who makes public judgments about the work.

Varying relationships among these participants generate the typology delineated in Figure 1.

FIGURE 1
Four Systems of Culture

Folk Culture
ARTIST-AUDIENCE

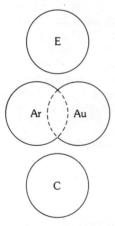

Elite Culture
ARTIST-CRITIC

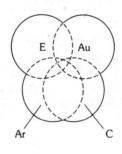

Popular Culture
ARTIST-entrepreneur-AUDIENCE

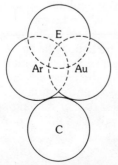

Mass Culture
artist-ENTREPRENEUR-audience

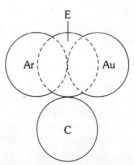

Ar = artist; Au = audience; E = entrepreneur; C = critic

Folk Culture

The relationship between artist and audience in folk culture is paramount. Neither entrepreneur nor critic has a role. The artist is a member of the audience and his role usually is not occupationally distinct. He is integrated into the community, and art is a community enterprise. Melville J. Herskovits has contrasted this type of culture with the modern approach to art:

> *The arts, in the conventions of Euroamerican culture, have been dissociated from the principal stream of life. Artistic creation is the function of the specialist; while the appreciation of what these specialists create is the privilege of those who at least command the leisure to pursue their avocation....The highest expression of the aesthetic experience is held to reside in objects that are not "profaned" by use....*
>
> *It can safely be said that there are no nonliterate societies where distinctions of this order prevail. Art is a part of life, not separated from it. This by no means implies that no specialization exists in such cultures; for wherever the creative drive comes into play, individuals are found to excel, or to be inept, in their performance.[19]*

An example of folk culture is the music of traditional societies such as the Igbo of Nigeria. Onuora Nzekwu, a prominent Nigerian writer, attributes the popularity of dancing among the Igbo to the lack of any distinction between professionals and amateurs: "None, not even the most accomplished dancer, dreamt of turning professional for that would as soon reduce him to an object of ridicule as would the confession: I can't dance, I do not know how to dance."[20] Supporting this appraisal, a Western scholar has reported:

> *Although music and expert musicianship are highly appreciated by the Igbo of Obimo, none of the inhabitants interviewed—musicians and non-musicians alike—viewed village musicians as an occupational class or profession. In fact, questions about this were often met with an incredulous look and remarks such as: "Music will not give us our food," and "It is no one's occupation, but if someone dies, a village musician will stop farming a while to play for the second burial ceremony."*

> *No one who played a musical instrument or performed as a lead singer or dancer identified his occupation as such. Most referred to themselves as farmers.[21]*

Traditional societies, contrary to a common misconception, are not the only preserves of folk culture. Almost everyone in North America has been a folk artist at one time or another. Who has never built a snowman or carved a jack-o-lantern or designed a Halloween costume or decorated a Christmas tree or done something similar? All these activities fit the definition of folk culture. The anonymous authors of graffiti are folk artists. So are the amateur painters whose colorful murals bring outdoor walls to life in cities from San Francisco to New York. Craftsmen still make handicrafts and paint motifs on barns in Pennsylvania Dutch country. Demonstrators paint their own placards, motorcycle clubs design their own regalia, and countless young people turn denim apparel into their own mosaics of embroidery or patchwork. Even if folk culture in North America has lost some of its vigor, the assembly line has not crushed it. Such collections as *Artists in Spite of Art, Twentieth-Century American Folk Art and Artists,* and *Ephemeral Folk Figures: Scarecrows, Harvest Figures, and Snowmen* attest its continuing life.[22]

Popular Culture

Popular culture is essentially a transmutation of folk culture wrought by modern technology and a money economy.The relationship between artist and audience is still dominant but is modified by the intervention of the entrepreneur.[23] The popular artist, unlike his folk counterpart, occupies a distinct though not necessarily full-time role as a professional entertainer. While he directs himself to the needs and wishes of a fairly homogeneous audience, he usually has broad leeway for personal expression. Popular culture, in short, individuates the artist despite the influence of audience and entrepreneur. Critics do not play a major role in shaping popular art except to publicize it.

One of the most striking examples of a popular culture in the United States was the San Francisco rock music scene in the 1960s.[24] It blossomed when the Family Dog, four "dropouts"with an idea, decided to become dance promoters in 1965. Renting the Longshore Hall for a dance concert featuring the Jefferson Airplane, the Marbles, the Great Society, and the Charlatans, they drew an ecstatic crowd, turned a profit, and inspired *San Francisco Chronicle* music columnist Ralph Gleason to describe it at the time as "a hippie happening which signified the linkage of the political and social hip movements."

"San Francisco can be the American Liverpool," Luria Castell of the Family Dog had said before the concert. "There's enough talent here, especially in the folk-music field." What was lacking, she said, was a place to dance. In his history of the San Francisco rock scene, Gleason continually stresses the importance of dancing. Reviewing a three-night "Trips Festival" three months after the first Longshore dance, he wrote:

The thing which provided all the paying customers is the fact that urban America is producing an increasing body of people who want to dance....We haven't had anything like it in over 20 years.

It is new. But new only to this class of people. Negroes have patronized dances right along. It is only the noncolored WASP population which has been so inhibited by the Gray Flannel Suit Age of Conformity that it could not dance. Now, this splinter group of creative people is dancing. These are the brave ones.

Despite Gleason's excesses of enthusiasm, his point is important. San Francisco rock was participatory. The bands, not yet controlled by business agents and record companies, had direct contact with their audience. Rock clubs like the Matrix, which the Jefferson Airplane operated, fostered close interaction. So did dance halls like the Fillmore Auditorium and the Avalon Ballroom. But the bands did not stop there. They gave free performances in parks throughout the city in 1966 and 1967.

The high point, a "Gathering of the Tribes" or "Human Be-In" in January 1967, drew 20,000 people to Golden Gate Park to parade their costumes, listen to poets like Allen Ginsberg and Gary Snyder, and dance to the music of such bands as the Grateful Dead, the Jefferson Airplane, and the Quicksilver Messenger Service.

By the summer of 1968, when Gleason compiled a list of San Francisco bands that had appeared in the past three years, he counted 387. The best of the bands wrote their own songs. Gleason describes them as "cooperative bands and usually bands that supported a whole hidden iceberg of other people—light shows, sound men, equipment handlers, wives, children, artists and what-not. Generally they lived together...and they all reached their decisions in a kind of committee action." Thus they were both mirrors and mouthpieces of a local bohemian tradition that took new form in "hippie" culture. Rock music helped give identity to the community that sustained it.

The sense of community began to unravel after the mass media spread the word and thousands of young people from all over the country poured into the Haight-Ashbury district for the "Summer of Love" in 1967. As promoter Bill Graham said, "When the music and the business hit *Life* and *Time* and your TV thing and Ed Sullivan had the heavy groups, then Joe Sophomore and Joe Straight and Joe Nine-to-Five became aware of the music." Spencer Dryden, the Jefferson Airplane's percussionist, remarked:

Haight/Ashbury used to be a thing of a bunch of people who knew where it was at [and] just happened to get together, you know. Now it's a place where a lot of people are looking for where it's at. Which is like the rest of the world, man, everybody's looking, the beautiful thing is when you get a bunch of people that have more or less come to some basic conclusions.

Heterogeneity, as much as drugs and violence, ushered in the decline of the San Francisco rock scene in the late 1960s.

Mass Culture

When social fragmentation and economic centralization concur, mass culture thrives. The relationship between artist and audience is disrupted by the entrepreneur, who becomes the pivotal figure. To maximize his profit, the entrepreneur shapes his product to the demands of a dispersed and heterogeneous market. He, rather than the artist, exercises ultimate control over the artistic work. The divorce of artist and audience diminishes direct feedback. Mass culture offers the critic a negligible role.

Differences between popular culture and mass culture leap into focus in the story of the Monkees.[25] "The teens have bought The Monkees," proclaimed an official of the agency that manufactured them. "They're the American Beatles." Were they? The Beatles had grown out of an insular working class culture that had spawned a dozen rock-'n'-roll clubs in Liverpool by the time the group formed in 1959. The habitués of these clubs

acquired a group consciousness that went beyond the fact that they appreciated the same music. The musicians were close to each other, but more important, the audiences and the musicians were friends. This was five years before the same syndrome of togetherness became evident in San Francisco, another city where groups had an opportunity to develop their music, because they were far removed from any recording studios and the clutches of the record company executives.[26]

Liverpool, like other cities isolated from the record industry in London, created its own distinctive style of rock-'n'-roll. Although the Beatles borrowed heavily from American singers like Chuck Berry and the Shirelles, they wrote most of their own songs. Their manager, Brian Epstein, tried to insulate them from business pressures.

The Monkees had no such roots. They were invented by two Hollywood producers, Robert Rafelson and Berton Schneider, who wanted to duplicate the success of the Beatle movies. Taking out ads in Hollywood trade papers in 1965, Rafelson and Schneider called for musicians to audition for a new TV series to star "4 insane boys, age 17-21." Four-hundred-thirty-seven applicants came. Rafelson and Schneider hired a research outfit to show screen tests of the eight finalists to random groups of youngsters. The four who survived had never worked together before. After months of coaching and rehearsals, they made their recording studio debut. "The boys didn't relate," said producer Donald Kirschner. "I was looking for a driving, exciting, frantic young sound. There was no sound to The Monkees." He produced the sound without them. His own studio musicians recorded prototype songs—"The boys can almost sing on top of them and they'll be hits"—and the Monkees completed an album and their first five TV shows within days. While RCA Victor spent $100,000 promoting the album, Screen Gems let contracts for the manufacture of fifty Monkee products ranging from Monkee chewing gum to Monkee wool caps. Jackie Cooper of Screen Gems summed it up: "The Monkees are not only in show business, they're in the advertising business."

The Monkees never disputed Cooper. Said Mickey Dolenz: "We're advertisers. We're selling a product. We're selling Monkees. It's gotta be that way."[27] And Mike Nesmith, who called the music "totally dishonest," told a reporter: "Maybe we were manufactured and put on the air strictly with a lot of hoopla. Tell the world that we're synthetic because, damn it, we are. Tell them The Monkees were wholly man-made overnight, that millions of dollars have been poured into this thing. Tell the world we don't record our own music." The Monkees were no American Beatles. They were the product of entrepreneurs.

Elite Culture

The term "elite culture" is unfortunate. Like "high" or "superior" culture, it points to social status rather than social relationships. It is not used here in that sense. Without a substitute that is both fitting and facile, the term will have to suffice.

The relationship between artist and critic is dominant in elite culture. While both entrepreneur and audience are important, neither controls the form or content of the art. These are molded by a set of aesthetic canons of which the critics are guardians. With these canons in mind, the artist keeps self-expression foremost. He may, as in much avant-garde art, reject the canons. But he is unlikely to be unaware of them. Only in elite culture could the notion of "art for art's sake" make any sense.

It has become a commonplace to note the alienation of the layman from the creations of contemporary artists—especially in music and the plastic arts—who work in elite culture. Not that most artists despise popularity when it comes to them. But many are unwilling to *aim* for a broad audience. They reserve the right to bore or to offend. Even Aaron Copland, who tried to balance public taste with his own creative integrity, warned that the artist "must never give up the right to be wrong, for the creator must forever be instinctive and spontaneous in his impulses, which means that he may learn as much from his miscalculations as from his successful achievements."[28] Such autonomy is stronger in elite culture than in any other kind.

Some creators pretend to be blithely unaware of the general public. Igor Stravinsky was once asked: "While composing do you ever think of an audience? Is there such a thing as a problem of communication?" He replied: "When I compose something, I cannot conceive that it should fail to be recognized for what it is, and understood. I use the language of music, and my statement in my grammar will be clear to the musician who has followed music up to where my contemporaries and I have brought it."[29] The language of contemporary music, however, sounds like arcane jargon to the average person. Its audience, apart from the musicians and critics who shape its grammar, is small and often ambivalent.

Another modern composer, Charles Wuorinen, has echoed Stravinsky in blunter terms:

...taking the "average" audience for major symphony concerts, and speaking personally, I can say that I care no more about them and their reactions than I do about the audience for juke boxes in bars. Indeed the latter are preferable because they really enjoy what they hear (I think), and in any case are not under the impression that their passive reception of "music" qualifies them for literate judgment.... There is, however, an audience about whom I care very much indeed.... This audience, made up mostly of composers, but increasingly of players and even non-musicians, is the one which has been exposed to enough twentieth-century music to accept it naturally.... This of course is not to say that their reactions could ever influence what I compose or the way I do it—but the way they feel does somehow influence my overall attitude to music. They are colleagues.[30]

Thus the artist in elite culture, like his counterparts in folk and popular culture, participates in a community of sorts. His community is not defined by social class as such—although that may be closely correlated—but by shared canons and tastes. Even within this community, however, the artist retains a strong measure of creative autonomy.

MASS OR POPULAR: DOES IT MAKE A DIFFERENCE?

The four cultures are "ideal types" that in reality form a continuum. Their boundaries, particularly folk-popular and popular-mass, may overlap. An individual may participate in all of them, and each type may coexist within a single society. While different societies frequently share a mass or a high culture, they more rarely share a folk or a popular culture. The typology undoubtedly simplifies real life. But does it oversimplify it?

Alfred Hitchcock tells the story of two men on an English train. "What's that package on the baggage rack over your head?" asks one. "Oh," says the other, "that's a MacGuffin." "Well, what is a MacGuffin?" "It's an apparatus for trapping lions in the Scottish highlands." Taken aback, the first man says, "But there are no lions in the Scottish highlands." The other replies: "Then that's no MacGuffin."[31] Like Englishmen on trains, scholars sometimes coin imaginary concepts.

Wide usage ratifies "folk culture" and "elite culture" as categories. But are "popular culture" and "mass culture"—as separate phenomena—really MacGuffins? Surely not. The Jefferson Airplane and the Monkees exemplify sharp differences. One group grew out of a close-knit community; the other rolled off an assembly line. One had creative autonomy; the other had none. One wrote its own songs; the other did not. Lumping the two under the same category, whether it is called "popular" or "mass," blurs real contrasts in the way they worked. Similar differences demarcate artists working in almost every genre of entertainment.

The term "mass" has a sociological meaning that cannot encompass the San Francisco rock scene between 1965 and 1967. Herbert Blumler has described four distinctive features of a mass: it comprises people from all walks of life; its members are anonymous; its members are physically separated and have little interaction; and it has meager social organization.[32] The bohemian community from which San Francisco rock sprang had none of these characteristics.

Since Eliot Freidson's seminal article on "Communication Research and the Concept of the Mass," communication researchers have tended to dismiss the utility of the "mass" concept as a description of the audience. But Freidson, who is concerned primarily with local audiences, concedes that the national audience is a mass in Blumler's sense. He adds:

However, while one can describe such an aggregate without reference to the organized groups that compose it, one cannot explain the behavior of its members except by reference to the local audiences to which they belong....If we are to consider the actual experience of members of the audience to determine their responses, then the concept of the mass has little relevance to that experience and is not appropriately used as the basis for explaining audience behavior.[33]

Freidson's point is important and valid within its context. Perhaps his view of audience responses, however, is too narrow. What do people respond *to* in a work of art: Content. Producers may tailor content—both form and them—to fit the audience. They know the mass has a lower "common denominator" than any homogeneous audience. Hence the concept of "mass" can be useful in explaining constraints on content. And content is certainly relevant to the way an audience responds. Several concepts may be useful.

Integration is the extent of direct contact between artist and audience. It is higher in popular culture than in mass culture.

Congruence is the accuracy with which content reflects the everyday environment—both physical and subjective—of audience members. The concept is obviously limited. It cannot apply to expressive forms such as melody and harmony that lack outside referents.

Escape is avoidance of the environment, especially to relieve tensions or evade problems, by audience members.

Orientation is an attempt to explore the environment and one's own role in it.

Two hypotheses seem reasonable:

1. Congruence will increase with integration. Popular culture will therefore be more congruent with the world of the audience than mass culture.

2. The functions of an art work will vary with its degree of congruence. While high congruence is likely to foster orientation, low congruence is more likely to abet escape. Thus mass culture would serve more of an escape function, and popular culture, more of an orientation function. This is not to say that the relationships are invariable. Just as popular culture may sometimes be a vehicle of escape, so mass culture may sometimes be a tool for orientation. All art, furthermore, surely serves a variety of functions.

If such hypotheses are at all fruitful, the typology of cultures should have theoretical value as well as descriptive utility. It is at least an instrument for highlighting cultural change. Paul Hemphill's *The Nashville Sound,* for example, conveys a vivid sense of how country music has changed. When we apply the typology of his impressionistic history, we can see how country music flourished as a folk culture when the people of Appalachia played homemade instruments and sang about everyday concerns; how it became a popular culture when the Grand Ole Opry gave it a commercial basis after 1925; and how it now verges on a mass culture as its audience disperses and its style melds with "pop" music in general. Hemphill writes:

…The country-music industry is in great shape. (Glen) Campbell, (Johnny) Cash, Buck Owens with weekly network television shows. (Bob) Dylan, Connie Francis, Dean Martin, Jimmy Dean singing "country" songs. European kids digging "country" music. Smiling Japanese cowboys in ten-gallon hats and rhinestoned outfits trying to sing "High Noon" like Tex Ritter, on the Japanese Grand Ole Opry. Close to $100 million a year for Nashville. Kids at Harvard saying they go for "country" music. Screen Gems sets up an office in Nashville so they'll be there for the day when musical sound tracks are recorded with the Nashville Sound. José Feliciano, a talented blind Puerto Rican who grew up in Spanish Harlem, doing "country" songs. Bill Monroe and the Bluegrass Boys making the scene at the Newport Folk Festival. The Opry moving out of the old house into air-conditioned quarters where there's more room for television crews. The industry is in great shape, yes. But you wonder about what is going to happen to the music—real Southern here's-how-it-is-down-home-folks country music—when all this is over. What happens to one of the few genuine forms of American music there ever was? Who cares?[34]

Hemphill cites many people who do. But it's hard to care unless one sees a difference, however intuitively, between popular culture and mass culture.

NOTES

1. Bernard Rosenberg, "Mass Culture Revisited," in
   Mass Culture Revisited, ed. Bernard Rosenberg and
   David Manning White (New York: Van Nostrand
   Reinhold, 1971), p.3.

2. Kingsley Amis, "Lone Voices: Views of the 'Fifties,'"
   Encounter 15 (July 1960): 6.

3. Bernard Rosenberg and David Manning White (eds.),
   Mass Culture: The Popular Arts in America (New
   York: Free Press, 1957).

4. Herbert J. Gans, *Popular Culture and High Culture:
   An Analysis and Evaluation of Taste* (New York:
   Basic Books, 1974), p. 10.

5. Van Wyck Brooks, "'Highbrow' and 'Lowbrow,'" in
   America's Coming of Age (Garden City, N.Y.:
   Doubleday, Anchor Books, 1958), pp. 1-19; Clement
   Greenberg, "Avant-Garde and Kitsch," in *Mass
   Culture,* ed. Rosenberg and White; Dwight
   Macdonald, "Masscult and Midcult," in *Against the
   American Gain* (New York: Random House, 1962),
   pp. 3-75; and Edward Shils, "Mass Society and Its
   Culture," in *Culture for the Millions?* ed. Norman
   Jacobs (Boston: Beacon Press, 1964).

6. Paul F. Lazarsfeld, "Mass Culture Today," in *Culture
   for the Millions?* ed. Norman Jacobs (Boston: Beacon
   Press, 1964), p. x.

7. Shils, "Mass Society," p. 400

8. Abraham Kaplan, "The Aesthetics of the Popular
   Arts," *The Journal of Aesthetics and Art Criticism* 24
   (Spring 1966): 352.

9. Greenberg, "Avant-Garde and Kitsch," p. 105.

10. William M. Hammel (ed.), *The Popular Arts in
    America: A Reader* (New York: Harcourt Brace
    Jovanovich, 1972); Rosenberg and White, *Mass
    Culture;* and Bernard Rosenberg and David Manning
    White (eds.) *Mass Culture Revisited* (New York: Van
    Nostrand Reinhold, 1971).

11. Hammel, *Popular Arts,* p. 1.

12. Russel Nye, *The Unembarrassed Muse: The Popular
    Arts in America* (New York: Dial Press, 1970), p. 1.

13. Ernest van den Haag, "A Dissent from the
    Consensual Society," in *Culture for the Millions?* ed.
    Norman Jacobs (Boston: Beacon Press, 1964), p. 53.

14. Ernest van den Haag, "Of Happiness and of Despair
    We Have No Measure," in *Mass Culture,* ed.
    Rosenberg and White, p. 505.

15. Exceptions to this generalization are the empirical
    "uses and gratifications" studies reviewed in Jay G.
    Blumler and Elihu Katz (eds.), *The Uses of Mass
    Communications: Current Perspectives on
    Gratifications Research,* in *Sage Annual Reviews of
    Communication Research,* vol. 3 (Beverly Hills,
    Calif.: Sage Publications, 1974); and Elihu Katz and
    David Foulkes, "On the Use of the Mass Media as
    'Escape': Clarification of a Concept," *Public Opinion
    Quarterly* 26 (Fall 1962): 377-388.

16. Macdonald, "Masscult and Midcult," pp. 3-75.

17. Stuart Hall and Paddy Whannel, *The Popular Arts*
    (Boston: Beacon Press, 1964); Oscar Handlin,
    "Comments on Mass and Popular Culture," in
    Culture for the Millions? ed. Norman Jacobs (Boston:
    Beacon Press, 1964), pp. 63-70; and Roy Harvey
    Pearce, "Mass Culture/Popular Culture: Notes for a
    Humanist's Primer," *College English* 23 (March
    1962): 417-432.

18. Orvis F. Collins, David G. Moore, and Darab B.
    Unwalls. *The Enterprising Man* (East Lansing, Mich.:
    MSU Business Studies, 1964), p. 19.

19. Melville J. Herskovits, *Man and His Works: The
    Science of Cultural Anthropology* (New York: Alfred
    A. Knopf, 1949), p. 379.

20. Onuora Nzekwu, "Igbo Dancing," *Nigeria Magazine*
    73 (June 1962): 35.

21. David Ames, "Professionals and Amateurs: The
    Musicians of Zaria and Obimo," *African Arts/Arts
    d'Afrique* 1 (Winter 1968): 80.

22. Ronald G. Carraher, *Artists in Spite of Art* (New
    York: Van Nostrand Reinhold, 1970); Herbert W.
    Hemphill, Jr., and Julia Weissman, *Twentieth-
    Century American Folk Art and Artists* (New York:
    Dutton, 1974); and Avon Neal, *Ephemeral Folk
    Figures: Scarecrows, Harvest Figures and Snowmen*
    (New York: Potter, 1969).

23. Sometimes the artist himself is an entrepreneur.
    Country singer Roy Acuff, for example, teamed up
    with songwriter Fred Rose in 1943 to found the
    lucrative Acuff-Rose Publications, Inc. Many other
    country stars have followed his example.

24. The material on San Francisco rock comes from
    Ralph Gleason, *The Jefferson Airplane and the San
    Francisco Sound* (New York: Ballantine Books,
    1969).

25. The material on the Monkees, except where
    otherwise noted, comes from Richard Warren Lewis,
    "When Four Nice Boys Go Ape!" *Saturday Evening
    Post,* 28 January 1967, pp. 74-78.

26. Peter McCabe and Robert D. Schonfeld, *Apple to the
    Core: The Unmaking of the Beatles* (London: Martin
    Brian & O'Keeffe, 1972), pp. 24-25.

27. "TV's Swinging Monkees," *Look,* 27 December
    1966, p. 96.

28. Arthur Berger, "Notes on the Flight of the American
    Composer," in *Culture for the Millions?* ed. Norman
    Jacobs (Boston: Beacon Press, 1964), p. 112.

29. Igor Stravinsky and Robert Craft, *Conversations with Igor Stravinsky* (Garden City, N.Y.: Doubleday, 1959), p. 14.

30. Charles Wuorinen, "An Interview with Barney Childs, 1962," in *Contemporary Composers on Contemporary Music*, ed. Elliott Schwartz and Barney Childs (New York: Holt, Rinehart and Winston, 1967), p. 369.

31. Alfred Hitchcock, "Rear Window," in *Focus on Hitchcock*, ed. Albert J. LaValley (Englewood Cliffs, N.J.: Prentice-Hall, 1972), pp. 43-44.

32. Herbert Blumler, "The Mass, the Public, and Public Opinion," in *Reader in Public Opinion and Communication,* 2nd ed., ed. Bernard Berelson and Morris Janowitz (New York: Free Press, 1966), p. 43.

33. Eliot Freidson, "Communications Research and the Concept of the Mass," in *The Process and Effects of Mass Communication*, rev. ed., ed. Wilbur Schramm and Donald F. Roberts (Urbana: University of Illinois Press, 1971), p. 207.

34. Paul Hemphill, *The Nashville Sound: Bright Lights and Country Music* (New York: Pocket Books, 1971), p. 166.

THE FUTURE OF THE MASS CULTURE CRITIQUE

Herbert Gans

The mass culture critique is endemic to urban-industrial society, and has existed ever since daily life became divided into periods of work and free time, particularly among the poor. In modern society, as Leo Lowenthal and Marjorie Fiske have shown, the critique originated in the eighteenth century with the beginnings of popular literature, a forerunner of today's mass media, and while even today it continues to emphasize symbolic culture, in print or on a screen, it also expanded to other spheres of life.[1] Since the nineteenth century, the critique has worried about leisure behavior in general, at least in America: at first about the popularity of alcohol and illicit sex, and later about the passivity of spectator sports and film or television viewing, the fear being that with increasing leisure time, the more intensified use of mass culture would lead to boredom, discontent, and possibly even social chaos. With respect to leisure facilities, in the nineteenth century and the early twentieth century, the critique emphasized the allegedly harmful effects of the music hall, the tavern, and the brothel; from about the 1920s to the 1950s, it focused on the movies, comic books, radio, and spectator sports. During the affluence of the 1950s, it expanded its concern to mass consumption in general, and to the suburban life-style in particular, but in the 1960s it narrowed again, centering now mainly on the negative effects of television viewing. The changing emphasis of the critique did not represent a change in the critique itself, however; rather, the critics chose to attack whatever then seemed most popular, or at least most visible or threatening to them in the off-work behavior of most Americans.

Since the late 1960s, however, the critique has undergone two substantial changes in direction. On the one hand, some of the critics dropped their attack on popular culture because they identified a new and greater enemy, the so-called youth culture, which they criticized for its political radicalism, hedonism, mysticism, and nihilism. The change of target was in part a response to the attack of youth culture spokesmen on high culture, for radicals such as Herbert Marcuse argued that high culture was sometimes as much the servant of an oppressive and antirevolutionary ruling class as mass culture, and Marcuse's argument was repeated with considerably less politeness by his younger colleagues. In a sense, the erstwhile critics of mass culture accepted the validity of

"The Future of the Mass Culture Critique," from Popular Culture and High Culture: An Analysis of Taste and Evaluation of Taste, *by Herbert J. Gans,* © *1974 by Basic Books, Inc., Publishers, New York.*

Marcuse's charge, for at least some now began to see positive features in mass culture's conservatism, perhaps with the hope, probably unconscious, that the defenders of mass culture would join with them to fight against the new, and as they saw it, common enemy.

The other change of direction has been even more drastic, suggesting at least by implication an end to the mass culture critique because high culture ideas had been accepted by and in popular culture. Thus, Nathan Glazer has written that:

Until the fifties, the distinction highbrow, middlebrow, and lowbrow was critical in discussing American culture. They have now quite disappeared...because highbrow ideas...have by now captured the old audience of the middlebrow.[2]

Daniel Bell went even farther, arguing that the old class conflict between high and mass culture had disappeared because, for a significant part of the population, cultural choices were no longer determined by class position:

Art [by which he means high culture art] has become increasingly autonomous, making the artist a powerful taste-maker in his own right; the "social location" of the individual (his social class or other position) no longer determines his life-style and his values....For the majority of the society...this general proposition may still hold true. But it is increasingly evident that for a significant proportion of the population, the relation of social position to cultural style, particularly if one thinks in gross dimensions such as working class, middle class and upper class—no longer holds.[3]

Glazer and Bell are quite correct to suggest that high culture standards and ideas have diffused more widely throughout the society, and have become more acceptable as well, at least in the upper-middle class. Even so, the distinction between high culture and popular culture has not disappeared; even a cursory look at an evening television program schedule or a magazine rack indicates that popular culture is still very different from high culture. Moreover, the youth culture of the 1960s has now declined, at least in public visibility, and no longer looks as threatening to the advocates of high culture as it did only a few years ago. Indeed, much of that youth culture is now being incorporated into commercial popular culture. The Rolling Stones may have replaced the Beatles and Elvis Presley in the pantheon of popular singers, but while their music and the cultural and political themes of their lyrics differ from those of their predecessors, they appeal to the same audience of young people and are handled by the same record companies. Thus, as the youth culture of the 1960s becomes part of the dominant popular culture of the 1970s, the differences between popular and high culture may once again widen, thus providing at least the raw material for a revival of the mass culture critique.

There is, however, a more important reason to suspect a revival of the critique. Actually, the existence of the critique has less to do with changes in high and popular culture than with the position of intellectuals in society, particularly those intellectuals who are or feel themselves to be part of the "Establishment"; over time, the critique has appeared when intellectuals have lost power and the status that goes with power, and it has virtually disappeared when intellectuals have gained power and status. Thus, the critique reached its apogee during the late 1940s and 1950s, not so much because of the rising affluence of that period and the dramatic expansion of consumer goods and other popular culture products which accompanied it, but because the affluence, status, and power of intellectuals during that period did not rise as well, and actually declined as a result of the "cultural apathy" of the Eisenhower era and Senator Joseph McCarthy's savage attacks on left-wing and liberal intellectuals. Conversely, the critique declined during the 1960s not only because of the flowering of youth culture, but also because intellectuals rose considerably in income, power, and status during the Kennedy and Johnson eras.

Two current trends in American society suggest, however, that another decline of intellectual status may be in the offing, and I suspect that the critique will soon return to a high position on the intellectual agenda. The first trend is the current academic depression, which struck the universities—where most practitioners of high culture are now to be found—during the Vietnam war, and which is now continuing partly because of the shrinkage of the university-age population cohort, and partly because of the federal government's economic and political policies. Not only are students, who are after all, the potential recruits for the next generation's high culture, losing their fellowships, but the Nixon Administration consciously tried to downgrade the influence of liberal and left-wing intellectuals—and other professionals—in American life even as it increased public subsidies for the arts. And if these Nixon administration policies continue . . . and more important, continue to have popular support in Middle America, intellectual criticism of Middle America's popular culture is likely to be resuscitated.

A second source of potential threat to the position of intellectuals comes from a very different political trend—the current revival of egalitarian ideas in America. Its impetus stems largely from nonintellectual sources: from students, women, blacks and other unequally treated populations, and from a rising dissatisfaction with economic inequality among Middle Americans whose expectations for a higher standard of living have been frustrated by the combined recession-inflation which began in the late 1960s.[4] Although some intellectuals are taking part in this revival, others, particularly humanist intellectuals, are opposing it, for they see more equality as a source of danger to high culture. Their view is by no means entirely irrational, for insofar as the economic vitality

of high culture depends on very rich people who are its customers and patrons, and who subsidize the magazines, museums, concerts, and other institutions which disseminate high culture, more economic equality might reduce their numbers, or at least reduce the amount of money they have to spend on and in behalf of high culture.[5] In addition, some defenders of high culture fear that greater equality would threaten the meritocratic basis on which high culture is said to be selected, and that other bases, including the recruitment of women and racial and ethnic minorities to institutions of high culture, would dilute the quality of high culture and the standards by which it is judged.[6]

Although both fears are understandable, I believe they will turn out to be groundless, for whatever changes the current demands for equality bring about in America, the users of high culture have sufficient prestige and power to protect their interests. For example, even if income redistribution reduced the spending power of the very rich, governmental and foundation subsidies for high culture would take up the slack; and even if the current meritocracy of *credentialism* were altered so that additional able women and racial and ethnic minority group members were hired by high culture institutions, the meritocracy of *performance* would not need to be violated, and the same combination of critical and audience judgment that now determines the standards and content of high culture would prevail. Nevertheless, the fears of high culture advocates are not likely to be stilled, and these fears may encourage some of them to be critical of egalitarian demands, and of the Middle Americans who make them. Thus, it is possible that the mass culture critique will be revived for use as an argument against the egalitarian trend.

Whatever the future ups and downs of the mass culture critique, however, this [discussion] is less concerned with the conflict between high and popular culture than with understanding them both. It is also concerned with the more fundamental question of what roles both high and popular culture play in American society, partly to arrive at policies which would replace cultural conflict with cultural coexistence—or pluralism—and would encourage greater creativity in all cultures, high and popular.

NOTES

1. The principal statements of the critique are presented in two books. The first is Bernard Rosenberg and David M. White, eds., *Mass Culture: The Popular Arts in America* (Glencoe, Ill.: The Free Press, 1957), particularly the articles by Bernard Rosenberg, Jose Ortega y Gasset, Leo Lowenthal, Dwight MacDonald, Clement Greenberg, T. W. Adorno, Marshall McLuhan, Irving Howe, Ernest van den Haag, Leslie Fiedler, and Melvin Tumin. The second book is Norman Jacobs, ed., *Culture for the Millions?* (Princeton, N.J.: Van Nostrand, 1961), particularly the articles by Hannah Arendt, Ernest van den Haag, Oscar Handlin, Randall Jarrell, and Stanley Edgar Hyman. See also T. S. Eliot, *Notes Towards the Definition of Culture* (New York: Harcourt, Brace, 1949), and the work of F. R. Leavis, for example, F. R. Leavis and Denys Thompson, *Culture and Environment* (London: Chatto and Windus, 1937).

2. The most pervasive, albeit implicit, rebuttal of the mass culture critique is to be found in David Riesman's sympathetic and empathic analysis of popular culture. See David Riesman, with Reuel Denney and Nathan Glazer, *The Lonely Crowd* (New Haven: Yale University Press, 1950) particularly chapters 4 and 5, and David Riesman, *Individualism Reconsidered* (Glencoe, Ill.: The Free Press, 1954) part 4. The best empirically based rebuttal of the charges against mass culture is Raymond A. Bauer and Alice H. Bauer, "American Mass Society and Mass Media," *Journal of Social Issues* 16, no. 3 (1960): 3-66. See also Joseph Klapper, *The Effects of Mass Communication* (New York: The Free Press of Glencoe, 1960); Wilbur Schramm, ed., *The Science of Communication* (New York: Basic Books, 1963); and Edward Shils, "The Mass Society and Its Culture," in Jacobs, *Culture for the Millions?*, pp. 1-27.

3. On this problem, see Paul Lazarsfeld, "Afterword," in Gary Steiner, *The People Look at Television* (New York: Alfred A. Knopf, 1963), pp. 409-422.

4. Leo Lowenthal, "Historical Perspectives of Popular Culture," in Rosenberg and White, *Mass Culture*, p. 55.

5. Dwight MacDonald, "A Theory of Mass Culture," in Rosenberg and White, *Mass Culture*, p. 55.

6. The implications of audience size are discussed by Rolf Myersohn, "A Critical Examination of Commerical Entertainment," in Robert W. Kleemeier, ed., *Aging and Leisure* (New York: Oxford University Press, 1961), pp. 243-272, especially pp. 254ff.

Part One

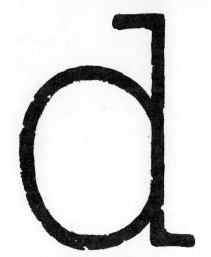

A Powerful
Media Revisited

RETURN TO THE CONCEPT OF POWERFUL MASS MEDIA

Elisabeth Noelle-Neumann

Laboratory experiment research into the effects of mass media on opinion formation leads to an underestimation of these effects owing to the fact that the decisive factors of mass media are not brought to bear in the traditional *laboratory experiment designs*. These effective factors are: cumulation, ubiquity, and the recently discovered tendency of journalists to produce an unrealistic consonance when reporting events. This results in extensive consonance throughout the media system, thus limiting the public's possibilities of forming an independent opinion and impeding selective perception with which the individual tries to keep his opinion from being influenced. This paper uses survey results proving strong selective perception among recipients. In presenting results of content analyses and surveys which show long-term attitude changes, it exemplifies a model of *effectiveness studies* which comprise the factors consonance, cumulation and omnipresence. An analysis of the phenomenon of public opinion supported by empirical data shows at what points these three factors can exert an especially strong influence on the formation of opinions.

Communication research: two steps forward, two steps back? Today, if I were to give an outline of the most important findings of 40 years of research into the effects of the mass media I would have to tell roughly the following: The effects of the mass media appear to be negligible. The well-known psychologist W. J. McGuire stated in his article entitled "Attitude and Attitude

Excerpts from Studies of Broadcasting. *Vol. 9, pp. 67-112. Tokyo: Nippon Hoso Kyokai, 1973.*

Change" published in 1969 that "the measured impact of the mass media as regards persuasiveness seems quite slight … A tremendous amount of applied research has been carried out to test the effectiveness of the mass media … The outcome has been quite embarrassing for proponents of the mass media, since there is little evidence of attitude change, much less change in gross behavior…"[1] The idea that the mass media help to form public opinion should be abandoned together with the concept of "public opinion". In an article entitled "Public Opinion" which appeared in the *International Encyclopedia of the Social Sciences* in 1968, W. Ph. Davison states—and he refers to Floyd H. Allport 1937—that there is "no entity of content…that can be discovered and then analyzed."[2]

There are several explanations for the unexpectedly slight impact of the mass media. In their compendium of empirical findings in the field of social research, Berelson and Steiner emphasize: The effect of mass media is less determined by their content than by the audience characteristics. "Here, perhaps more than elsewhere, the research findings can be organized into one broad generalization, dealing with the importance of audience characteristics in determining what people see, how they interpret it, and what effect it has upon them."[3]

The effectiveness of the mass media—I would continue the outline—is greatly reduced by the selective behavior of the recipients of mass communication, as discovered in the early 40s in the classic Erie County study.[4] The individual chooses from the overwhelming volume of material presented to him those pieces of information which support his own views, and he interprets and digests them selectively, again to suit his own convictions. This is explained by Festinger's theory of cognitive dissonance published in 1957, in which he asserts that the individual tends to shun inner uncertainty and conflict by picking out items which reinforce his convictions and decisions and by avoiding anything that could shake them.[5] From this is deduced one of the central arguments of communication research, namely, that "the mass media typically reinforce people in their attitude and practices but rarely convert them."[6]

However, I would have to continue that this selective perception theory has been given a sharp jolt in recent years by researchers like Sears and Freedman.[7] McGuire therefore sums up the position as follows: "We would suggest for an interim working hypothesis that the selective-avoidance postulate is a very poor predictor in laboratory situations and not much better in natural settings."[8] Thus we find ourselves more or less back where we started.

The same applies to the opinion leader thesis, the thesis of the two-step flow of communication, meaning in its first formulation that the mass media for the most part achieve their influence on the broad mass of the population not directly but rather through the vehicle of convincing personalities, the opinion leaders, who draw their arguments from the media and pass it on to persons of their own class whom they influence.[9] Research during the sixties in Germany and the U.S. did not come up with such opinion leaders under the conditions prevailing in Western industrialized countries.[10] Instead of the outstanding personality emitting information there emerged active persons who kept up an extensive exchange of views among themselves, the "givers and askers." As their counterpart were found not the expected "followership" of the opinion leaders, but "isolates," uninterested persons, without observable contacts to the givers and askers. A particularly intensive relationship with the mass media, as the hypothesis of the two-step flow of communication presupposes, was observed occasionally but it was by no means a regular phenomenon. So this, too, does not on the whole help to answer the question of the impact of the mass media.

I would complete my outline by stating that although the effect on the public, and especially the young, of brutality as presented by the mass media has been the subject of research for several decades, no answer has yet been provided. All that empirical research can proffer is that there is no clear indication of the impact of violence in this form.

What makes the situation particularly confusing is the instinctive tendency not to believe the many nil results, that the mass media have hardly any effect, or that there is no such thing as public opinion or opinion leaders, or that the presentation of brutality by the mass media does not leave any imprint on the public. Even the theory of selective exposure of persons to the mass media, and selective interpretation of the contents, and selective retention is so convincing that we are not prepared to abandon it without question.

The Discussion on Methods Should Be Reopened More recently the question has arisen as to where lie the difficulties of communication research, its strange failure in the face of central issues. Halloran, for instance, holds the view that far too much attention has been paid to methodology, with the result that theory has been neglected.[11] But let us examine this assumption against the background of the dissonance theory and selective avoidance which is meant to be explained by that theory. The theoretical concept seems to have been developed far enough to serve as a guide for empirical research, but those more than thirty empirical tests examined by the critics of the supportive selection theory by no means give unequivocal confirmation of the selectivity rule.[12] Nevertheless, nobody dares to conclude from this that selective exposure does not take place. Too clearly, too regularly it is proved that among recipients of partial communication there is a majority of party followers. One speaks of a "de facto selective exposure."[13] It could not be proved, however, that the audience's partiality is actually the result of an active search for, or preference of,

supportive communication, and not perhaps caused by other plausible factors. Should one not here entertain the possibility of inadequate method?....

A critic of present-day communication research recently said that the emphasis of many impact studies on short term effects gave the impression of someone trying to prove that smoking one cigarette leads to cancer.[14] It must surely be regarded as a combination of weak theory and weak method if, in many analyses in the field of communication research, the object whose effects are to be studied, that is the mass medium, is so inadequately defined that the research design excludes the decisive factors, which are ubiquity, and the cumulative effect as a consequence of periodicity. Consciousness of something being public and the cumulative element, both in the work of the communicators and in the impressions gained by the recipients, must at least be retained in the research design, otherwise the impact of communication may be analyzed, but not of mass communication.

The theory of selective perception is mainly criticized by arguing that no proof has been brought forward so far that dissonant communication is actively avoided....

The Effects of Mass Media Increase in Proportion to the Degree in Which Selective Perception Is Made Difficult Although the tendency to supportive selective perception can be empirically proved, provided suitable research techniques are applied, this does by no means justify the traditional conclusion that the impact of the mass media is slight, or that it at most strengthens attitudes but does not change them. Indeed, such confirmation should be followed by a systematic study of the conditions of the selective mechanism—under what conditions its effect is unimpeded, when it is limited, or when there is no effect at all. As regards the connection between selective perception and the effect of the mass media one can put forward the hypothesis that the more restricted the selection the less the reinforcement principle applies, in other words the greater the possibility of mass media of changing attitudes.[15]

We can see the extreme case where the selective possibility is ruled out in states with centrally controlled information systems. Here the facts and arguments proffered by the various media are very similar. Under such conditions there can hardly be any question whether the mass media effectively influence attitudes. Where there is a large extent of similarity in the presentation of certain material in all the media, we have a case of the selective mechanism being restricted or ruled out. Another case would be the situation of the "captive audience" in the laboratory experiment.

The strong impact obtained under such circumstances was a topic dealt with by Hovland in his famous study entitled "Reconciling Conflicting Results derived from Experimental and Survey Studies of Attitude Change."[16] Perhaps it is possible to show certain elements which restrict freedom of selection in the receptive situation of the televiewer.[17] Here we make only a passing reference to these possibilities. We are mostly concerned with the similarity factor on the assumption that it may constitute a major element in the impact of mass media. First, the question is whether such similarity, that is the consonance of facts and arguments, which does not ensue from the reality of the situation but occurs as a result of reporting and editorial selection, is to be found only where communication is government-controlled, or whether it also exists where the press has almost a free hand. Then we ask how widespread this artificial similarity is and how it comes about.

Research on this question must of necessity detach itself from the traditional method of observing only the recipients and turn its attention to the communicators whose professional behavior produces the similarity. In recent years Galtung and Halloran have concentrated their studies on the communicators and have come up with important points.[18] Galtung and Ruge drew up a catalogue of news values, the characteristics of news, according to which journalists decide whether or not they are to be published. They reach the conclusion that "the more consonant the signal is with the

mental image of what one expects to find, the more probable that it will recorded as worth listening to." And: "The more clear and unambiguous the signal (the less noise there is), the more probable that it will be recorded as worth listening to." And also: "If one signal has been tuned in to the more likely it will continue to be tuned in to as worth listening to."[19]

Following on from Galtung's catalogue, Halloran observed in a case study carried out over a period of two months in the autumn of 1968 how, in relation to a forthcoming event, a sort of "frame of reference" is at first formed almost by chance, a sort of perspective which shapes expectations of what is to happen, and how that framework has a cumulative effect in that it is further developed in subsequent weeks by newspapers of different orientation, and how, according to the criterion of consonance and clarity, everything that fits into the frame of reference fills the reports right up to the climax. Even if events take quite a different course than the one suggested by the frame of reference, the press, radio and television, showing an astonishing degree of similarity among themselves and common inconsistency with reality, still manage to produce consonance with their adopted starting position.

Consonance Eliminates Selective Perception and Increases the Effects of Mass Media. The News Value of Consonance Should Therefore Become a Major Topic of Communication Research At the 1969 UNESCO conference in Montreal, the existing doubts about the course of communication research were clearly expressed by inquiring: "Are we asking the right questions?"[20] We can now be more specific: Has the consonance factor, together with the characteristic factors of mass media effects, omnipresence and cumulation, received too little attention in research on the effects of the mass media?[21] In one particular context it does receive adequate consideration, that is, where the specific intention is to exercise influence through deliberately produced consonance in propaganda, suggestion, and brainwashing which is intensified by constant repetition.

The consonance phenomenon, which ought now to be the object of research, is produced in a different way even though the influencing effect may be the same as that of centrally controlled propaganda. It has been inconspicuous for so long because it is not primarily the result of deliberate distortion of reality but, and this is the basis of our assumption, of factors that are related to the personal charactertistics of journalists and their conditions of work.

The phenomenon was described clearly enough by Walter Lippmann in "Public Opinion," shortly before communication research began to be conducted on a more systematic basis in the early twenties. According to him, the reality of the "world outside" and the "pictures in our heads" do not coincide. Reality is too complex, too changeable and too remote from our personal experience, our sight and our grasp. Only by selecting but a few elements of reality, by considerably simplifying them and adapting them to those already known, is it possible to form pictures of reality and to communicate them to others. Thus there arises between man and his environment a pseudo-environment, pictures which may only contain a small portion of reality but are taken for the whole reality.[22] These pictures become more and more established, partly because what we have become accustomed to is recognized more easily in the environment or in reports dealing with that environment, and partly because, in view of the complexity of the world, we strive for intellectual economy and so there is a demand for stability, clarity and consistency in the pictures once obtained. There emerges the "stereotype," a word coined by Lippmann and an obvious choice to him as a journalist familiar with the technical process of stereotyping in rotation printing.

As is known, Lippmann's thinking on the relationship between reality and communication has been taken up by researchers only under one quite specific aspect. They have studied and criticized the connection between the stereotype, the similarity in the description of racial and ethnic minorities in the mass media, and prejudice against these sections of the population. As a result, however, the idea of the stereotype has also undergone a substantial change. It is now seen primarily as an instrument of propaganda for the forming or strengthening of prejudices, and not as Lippmann originally understood it as the result of the economy of perception and communication technique, or, in the words of N. Luhmann, as a technique of "reduction of the complexity (of reality)."[23] The stereotype of an event, an idea, a person, and consonance as the result of the journalists' conditions of work remained for the most part unresearched. It was not until Galtung and Halloran came along with their comparison of the "event as reality" and the "event as news" that the distinction between reality and "pictures in our heads", which was Lippmann's central theme, was again emphasized.[24]

Anticipating systematic research, one could say that the factors producing unrealistic consonance of news reporting, where freedom of the press and variety of mass communication exist, are:

1. Concurring assumptions and experiences of journalists of all levels and from all fields regarding the criteria for the acceptance of their material by the public which guide their style of reporting and their selection of material for "news values": priority for all elements appealing to the emotions, especially conflicts with an uncertain, or surprising outcome; priority for negative elements; priority for clarity, unambiguousness, easy comprehension, plausibility, and consonance with existing views: "news as olds", to use Galtung's expression.[25] And, finally, priority for texts and pictures of high technical and descriptive quality.

2. The common tendency of journalists to confirm their own opinions, to show that they have given the right interpretation of the situation and have correctly predicted what would happen (self-fulfilling prophecy).

3. Common dependence on certain sources, such as the wire news services.

4. Strong reciprocal influence in building up frames of reference: the newspaper reporter will follow the television program, and the television reporter will follow the papers.[26] Rival papers and TV programs are studied intensively.

5. Striving for approval from colleagues and superiors plays an important part in professional practice.

6. Greater uniformity of journalists' views in comparison to the population as a whole, owing to the frequency of certain demographic and psychological attributes in this profession....

With attention having long been concentrated on the deliberate distortion of reality by the mass media for propaganda purposes we now turn to the distortion resulting from the professional conflict between accuracy and news values, that is between conscientious, exact work and journalistic success. Halloran's thesis, which we must take as our basis, is that in the selection and presentation of news accuracy is not the main criterion, there being others more important.[27] In chronological order there are first the news values already mentioned which aim to arouse public response, then, as a situation develops or a person receives further "treatment", the preservation of consonance—partly in order to preserve the clarity which the public prefers and which television in particularly demands, and partly as the journalist's means of self-confirmation, of proving to himself that he has been right all along. Developing in this way, consonance tends not to remain confined to a single newspaper or television program but to spread through the whole media system.

This leads us to examine the effect of consonance (stereotype) on public opinion as asserted by Walter Lippmann, and at the same time to return to the question of the impact of the mass media on opinion formation.[28] Thus our hypothesis is: where consonance is highly developed there will be a strong influence on opinion formation because, among other things, the protective mechanism of selective perception is eliminated....

Public opinion as a process of interaction between individual attitudes and beliefs of individuals about majority opinion. By virtue of operating in public mass media influence the assessment of what is the majority opinion Let us now consider the third component which in our opinion has been neglected by researchers, namely the omnipresence of the mass media, the publicity factor, the element of operating in public. Hitherto, our approach to the subject of opinion formation and mass media has been as though we were dealing with isolated individuals on the recipients' end. But in fact the individuals are not isolated from each other; they show a great interest in their social environment, that is in other individuals and their perceptions and views of that environment. Especially their conceptions of prevailing opinions and attitudes have a considerable influence on them. We do not need to look for new terms with which to express the social-psychological phenomena resulting from these assessing and influencing processes. We have had them since the mid-17th and mid-18th centuries in "climate of opinion," "law of opinion," and "public opinion."[29] We also need these concepts to describe the factors governing the effects of the mass media: cumulation, journalistic striving for consonance, and publicity, in their mutual relationship and their socio-political significance.

Of course, there is, as we mentioned in the beginning, some doubt as to whether there exists such an entity as "public opinion" which can be discovered and then analyzed. Allport suggests to associate the term "public opinion" with a "process with a dimension of time", the origin, composition and functions of which should be studied with a view to formulating these on public opinion that permit of assessments within statistical tolerances and are empirically verifiable. [30]

The scope of this paper does not allow us a comprehensive study of the phenomenon "public opinion". However, it is necessary to examine it cursorily, because otherwise it would not be possible to gain an impression of the opinion-forming power of the mass media.

In theoretical discussion the topics and themes of "public opinion" have without justification been confined to the political sphere. A historical analysis shows that ever since this phrase was first coined in the 17th and 18th centuries and right up to the twenties and thirties, social-conventions, customs and norms have always been included in the domain of public opinion. [31] Public opinion imposes sanctions on individuals who offend against conventions—a process which Ross in a chapter on public opinion referred to as "social control." [32] But the fact that social control is a variant of the public opinion process (defence of prevailing conceptions), and that public opinion functions as an instrument of criticism not only against those in power but also against the individual member of society, became less and less appreciated through the use of this new term.—If the knowledge of the broad range of public opinion is revived, this means that the categories of persons participating in the process of opinion-formation cannot be narrowly confined, e.g., to persons interested in politics.—The historical argument has to be supplemented in due course by proof that the process of public opinion has the same attributes in both the political sphere and the sphere of social control.

These remarks only dispose of certain restrictions as to subject-matter and categories of persons, to enable us to give an adequately comprehensive description of the phenomenon "public opinion". On the other hand, we shall acknowledge certain limits in time and space, in other words, one of our theses on public opinion will be that its effectiveness cannot be limited to certain subjects and categories of persons but is limited to certain eras and areas. Expressions such as "Zeitgeist" or "spiritus loci" suggest that they contain elements of public opinion.

Let us return to those aspects we intend to examine in the context of public opinion: Prevailing opinions which those in power as well as ordinary individuals have to take into account, particularly the process by which these prevailing opinions emerge, the process of their assertion, and finally the process of the defence of their dominant position. We shall retain the word "opinion" so as not to stray too far away from the concept of public opinion, though in this connection we take opinion to mean also behavioral dispositions or attitudes.

Many observers have noticed that these prevailing opinions can be of widely differing character. They may be largely uniform and often long-standing (convention, stereotype, Tönnies speaks of "solid state of aggregation", Allport of "genetic ground work responses"), or they may be changeable, quickly appearing and quickly vanishing (Tönnies: "air-like stage of aggregation"), or having just become dominant after fierce conflict with other opinions and now establishing themselves for longer periods, cf. Tönnies: "generalization of a partial opinion"—"party opinion becomes public opinion." [33]

The controversial element differs according to the degree of unanimity and the origin of the opinion, but there is a common pressure towards conformism—Tocqueville refers to public opinion as being more of a compulsion towards conformity than a critical force—, in other words, that very claim to dominance with the effect of coercing the individual, challenging those in power, but integrating society. [34]

How does that demonstration of power which the individual member of society as well as the government regard as the "pressure of public opinion" occur? The mere fact that a majority of the population hold a particular opinion does not establish its dominance. What matters is the *concept* of majority as it takes shape in the mind of the individual member of society and of the politician from their observations of the world about them. In this context, the concept of majority can also be replaced by concepts of strength, determination, urgency or future prospects. When, from his observations, the individual member of society gains such an impression of strength, and if he agrees with that opinion, he will come forward assuredly and strongly with that opinion, otherwise he is discouraged and deems it better to remain silent.[35] Here one can use the simile of a helix, or spiral, as this attitude influences in turn the social environment's impression of opinion distribution and increases the dominance of whichever side is in the process of establishing itself as "public opinion".

The spiralling process of public opinion formation as it is assumed by this "hypothesis of silence" is described by Tocqueville in "L'Ancien Régime et la Révolution". There he recounts how contempt of religion had become a widespread and dominant passion with the 18th century French. An essential reason for this, he says, was the "falling silent" of the French church. "People still clinging to the old faith were afraid of being the only ones who did so, and as they were more frightened of isolation than of committing an error, they joined the masses, even if they did not agree with them. In this way the opinion of only part of the population seemed to be the opinion of all and everybody, and exactly for this reason seemed irresistible to those who were responsible for this deceptive illusion."[36] Today we can empirically observe this tendency of the weaker faction to remain silent, as will be shown below.

In connection with this "silence hypothesis" the significance of something being public emerges. If viewpoints are to influence assessments of the distribution of opinion, they must be expressed in public.

Indeed, here lies perhaps the original meaning and convincing power of the adjective "public" in the term "public opinion": opinions which one can voice in public without fear of sanctions, e.g., of isolation.[37] In recent times the term "silent majority" has been coined to express the impotence of a majority that does not voice its opinion.

Some authors, such as Allport, feel that the most disturbing feature of the term "public opinion" is that it encourages the tendency to personify a collectivity—for instance the "Volksseele" or "vox populi."[38] As an empirical scientist Allport emphasizes that public opinion consists of the opinions of individuals only. At the same time, however, he sees the link between individuals and the collectivity, the "social environment" when he stresses that the individual adopts attitudes which determine the processes of public opinion formation with an awareness of the attitudes of others: "They are frequently performed with an awareness that others are reacting in the same situation in a similar manner."[39] As soon as this link or interrelationship is understood, the collective element of public opinion loses its mystery. The interrelation can be easily operationalized for empirical research. Asch and Milgram have shown in laboratory experiments how the distribution of opinion in the environment influences the individual's public and private utterance of opinion.[40]

The first large-scale panel study, which was devoted to the observation of opinion formation—the Erie County Study of 1940—also quickly brought into view the interaction between the opinions of an individual member of society and the distribution of opinions in the environment.

Under the entry "Crystallization of Opinion" one can read how interaction of individuals—initiated by the propaganda of an election campaign, or by an important event, or by the necessity to make a decision, i.e., in an election—leads to a re-grouping of opinions.[41] Something new emerges which cannot be explained solely on the basis of the individual opinions as they existed before. The authors draw an analogy to the stabilization of price levels as a function of the interaction of supply and demand of a number of individuals. The price appears as a result of the interaction of one's own interest and the observation of the social environment....

Mass Media Effects Viewed Under the Aspect of Public Opinion Theory

It now becomes clear at what points the mass media can influence most effectively the formation of public opinion, in fact the more effectively, the more marked are consonance, cumulation and publicity or ubiquity.

1. One of these points is furnished by Luhmann's "thematization", the creation of attention for a certain topic or theme, which is given an aura of importance and urgency. Part of this process is to signal a crisis or to give a big resonance to a commentator of high status with a certain message.

2. How far demands and suggestions for solving problems can win preponderance in public opinion depends on how far they are seen to have a real chance of being realized or implemented. The mass media are able to form to a high degree judgments regarding such a chance.

3. Observation and perception of the social environment by individuals may be strongly influenced by the mass media: which opinions are dominant, which opinions are on the increase, which opinions one can utter in public without danger of becoming isolated. Thus the mass media would affect the spiralling process assumed by the silence hypothesis.

Are We Using the Right Methods? A Plea for Field Research

This paper started from the supposition that research on the effects of mass media suffers from certain methodological and theoretical weaknesses which are impeding satisfactory progress. We assume that it is justified to inquire: "Are we asking the right questions?" because research should explore new themes. Furthermore, the inquiry should be extended by asking: "Are we using the right methods?" Research designs seem to be unsatisfactory because—particularly in the prevailing laboratory experiments—factors are eliminated or but weakly simulated that are essential for the subject to be explored, i.e., the effects of *mass* media.

New thematic research objectives are suggested, viz.: the reality distorting consonance throughout the mass media as an effective factor and a fresh analysis of the phenomenon of public opinion with empirical methods. Combined with the latter, our thesis of the individual's assumptions about the social environment and about future developments together with the ensuing hypothesis of silence, should be tested as to their significance for the process of opinion formation. These hypotheses may allow better predictions about the trends of dominant opinions than were possible until now. Furthermore, it is quite possible that the exploration of the individual's assessment of his environment can be combined with the still necessary research on supportive selective perception, the degree of which could well depend on the individual's appraisal of the environment.

It is further proposed to use different methods, that is different from the usual laboratory experiments. Consonance across all the mass media is a most effective factor because it restricts or eliminates selective perception. It is especially important to investigate the *combination* of the three elements,—consonance, cumulation, ubiquity—as an effective factor of mass media. This presumably powerful combination can hardly be simulated realistically in a laboratory experiment. The study of media effectiveness therefore demands a shift in emphasis to field research. Some models for this kind of research have been described.

The aims of this paper made it necessary to conceive the subject quite broadly. Elaboration of certain parts and themes will follow as soon as possible.

CONCLUSION

The thesis that mass media do not change attitudes but only reinforce them cannot be upheld under conditions of consonance and cumulation. Our data point in this direction. It is true that there exists a tendency to protect attitudes through selective perception. Yet the more selective perception is being restricted—by consonance of reporting and editorial comment, reinforced by cumulation of periodical repetition in the media—the more attitudes can be influenced or molded by the mass media. Individual processes of opinion formation are then reinforced by the individual's observation of the social environment. We assume that the conceptions of which opinions *are* dominant in the environment, or which opinions are about to *become* dominant in the environment, are being influenced by the mass media. This process, we assume, is the more pronounced, the more people are reached, the more these opinions are public.

Individual tendencies, created or supported by the mass media, to express one's opinions in public or rather to keep silent, then influence in a spiralling process what has been called "climate of opinion" since the 17th century and, since the 18th century, "public opinion."

NOTES

1. William J. McGuire, "The Nature of Attitudes and Attitude Change," in *Handbook of Social Psychology*, vol. 3, 2nd ed., ed. Gardner Lindzey and Elliot Aronson (Reading, Mass.: Addison-Wesley, 1969), p. 229.

2. *International Encyclopedia of the Social Sciences*, 1968 ed., vol. 13, pp. 188-197, s.v. "Public Opinion," by W. Phillips Davison. He refers to Floyd H. Allport, "Toward a Science of Public Opinion," *Public Opinion Quarterly* 1 (1937): 7-23.

3. Bernard Berelson and Gary A. Steiner, *Human Behavior: An Inventory of Scientific Findings* (New York: Harcourt, Brace & World, 1964).

4. Paul F. Lazarsfeld, Bernard Berelson, and Hazel Gaudet, *The People's Choice: How the Voter Makes Up His Mind in a Presidential Campaign* (New York: Duell, Sloan and Pearce, 1944; 2nd ed., 1948; 3rd ed., New York: Columbia University Press, 1968).

5. Leon Festinger, *A Theory of Cognitive Dissonance* (Evanston, Ill.: Row Peterson, 1957).

6. Elihu Katz, "On Reopening the Question of Selectivity in Exposure to Mass Communication," in *Theories of Cognitive Consistency: A Sourcebook*, ed. Robert P. Abelson *et al.* (Chicago: Rand McNally, 1968), pp. 788-796.

7. See Jonathan L. Freedman and David O. Sears, abstract of "Voters' Preferences Among Types of Information," *American Psychologist* 18 (1963): 375; Jonathan L. Freedman and David O. Sears, "Selective Exposure," in *Advances in Experimental Social Psychology*, vol. 2, ed. Leonard Berkowitz (New York: Academic Press, 1965), pp. 57-97; Rüdiger Schulz, "Entscheidungsstrukturen der Redaktionsarbeit" (forthcoming); and David O. Sears and Jonathan L. Freedman, "Selective Exposure to Information: A Critical Review," *Public Opinion Quarterly* 31 (1967): 194-213.

8. McGuire, "Attitudes and Attitude Change," p. 221.

9. Lazarsfeld, Berelson, and Gaudet, *People's Choice*.

10. See Paul J. Deutschmann and Wayne A. Danielson, "Diffusion of Knowledge of the Major News Story," *Journalism Quarterly* 37 (Summer 1960): 345-355; Bradley S. Greenberg, "Person-to-Person Communication in the Diffusion of News Events," *Journalism Quarterly* 41 (1964): 489-494; Institut für Demoskopie Allensbach, "Meinungsbildnerinnen: Untersuchungen über persönliche Beeinflussungvorgänge zwischen Hausfrauen im Bereich der Haushaltspflege," *Allensbach Archive, IFD-Survey*, no. 1710 (September 1970); Elisabeth Noelle-Neumann, "Meinungsführer und Massenmedien," *Der Markenartikel*, 12 (1963); Elisabeth Noelle-Neumann, "Information und öffentliche Meinung," *Publizistik* 3/4 (Juli-Dezember 1966); and Verling C. Troldahl, "A Field Test of a Modified 'Two-Step Flow of Communication' Model," *Public Opinion Quarterly* 30 (1966): 609-623.

11. James D. Halloran, "The Impact of Violence in the Mass Media," paper prepared for UNESCO symposium on violence, June/July 1970.

12. See Freedman and Sears, "Selective Exposure"; Sears and Freedman, "Selective Exposure: Review"; and David O. Sears and Ronald P. Abeles, "Attitudes and Opinions," *Annual Review of Psychology* 20 (1969): 253-288.

13. Freedman and Sears, "Selective Exposure."

14. Jeremy Tunstall, introduction to *Media Sociology: A Reader,* ed. Jeremy Tunstall (London: Constable, 1970), p. 6.

15. Elisabeth Noelle, "Wirkung der Massenmedien," in *Publizistik: Das Fischer Lexicon,* ed. Elisabeth Noelle-Neumann and Winfried Schulz (Frankfurt/Main: Fischer Taschenbuch, 1971), pp. 316-350.

16. Carl I. Hovland, "Reconciling Conflicting Results Derived from Experimental and Survey Studies of Attitude Change," *American Psychologist* 14 (1959): 8-17.

17. Percy H. Tannenbaum, "Mündliche Mitteilung über Ergebnisse von Primatenforschung beim UNESCO—Seminar in Konstanz, September 1970: Forschung und Massenmedien."

18. Johan Galtung and Mari Holmboe Ruge, "The Structure of Foreign News: The Presentation of the Congo, Cuba and Cyprus Crisis in Four Norwegian Newspapers," *Journal of International Peace Research* 1 (1965): 64-90 (reprinted in Jeremy Tunstall (ed.) *Media Sociology: A Reader,* pp. 259-298); and James D. Halloran, Philip Elliot, and Graham Murdock, *Demonstrations and Communication: A Case Study* (Harmondsworth, England: Penguin, 1970).

19. Galtung and Ruge, "Structure of Foreign News," pp. 261-262 in Tunstall.

20. UNESCO, *Mass Media in Society: The Need of Research,* Reports and Papers on Mass Communication, no. 59 (Paris: UNESCO, 1970).

21. Another interesting factor which, even after many years of communication research appears to be completely new and apparently only became a research problem with the studies of Östgard and Galtung, is the "frequency effect," the significance of the time interval during which developments take place, for good and continuous or inadequate reporting. See Eina Östgard, "Factors Influencing the Flow of News," *Journal of International Peace Research,* no. 1 (1965); p. 39; and Galtung and Ruge, "Structure of Foreign News." On the other hand, the importance of the time of day at which an event becomes known has been examined in connection with research on the medium which first spreads a certain information. See Deutschmann and Danielson, "Diffusion of Knowledge"; and Greenberg, "Person-to-Person Communication."

22. Walter Lippman, *Public Opinion* (New York: Macmillan, 1922; paperback ed., 1960), p. 15.

23. Niklas Luhmann, "Öffentiche Meinung," in *Politische Planning: Aufsätze zur Soziologie von Politik und Verivaltung* (Opladen, West Germany: Westdeutscher, 1971), pp. 9-34.

24. Galtung and Ruge, "Structure of Foreign News"; and Halloran, Elliot, and Murdock, *Demonstrations and Communication.*

25. Galtung and Ruge, "Structure of Foreign News."

26. Halloran, Elliot, and Murdock, *Demonstrations and Communication;* and Elisabeth Noelle, "Die betriebliche Anpassung lokaler und regionaler Abonnementszeitungen an die durch intra—und intermediären Wettbewerb der Massenkommunikationsmittel ausgelösten Veränderungen der Leserbedürfnisse," in *Gutachten für das Presse- und Informationsamt der Bundesregierung* (Bonn: n.p., 1972).

27. Halloran, Elliot, and Murdock, *Demonstrations and Communication,* p. 300.

28. Lippmann, *Public Opinion.*

29. "Climate of opinion" was coined by Joseph Glanville, who was quoted in *Robert K. Merton, Social Theory and Social Structure* (Glencoe, Ill.: Free Press, 1964), p. 135, footnote 6; "law of opinion," by John Locke in "An Essay Concerning Human Understanding" (written 1671, published 1690); and "public opinion," by Jean Jacques Rousseau, *Discours sur les Arts et les Sciences* (Paris: n.p., 1750).

30. See Allport, "Toward a Science," p. 16: "When we try to find an object corresponding to the term public opinion, that is, when we regard it as an entity or a content to be discovered and then studied or analyzed, our efforts will meet with scant success." Davison, in the *International Encyclopedia of the Social Sciences,* refers to this too.

31. For example, see Allport, "Toward a Science," p. 18; James Bryce, *The American Commonwealth,* vols. 1 and 2 (New York: n.p., 1924), p. 271; and Ferdinand Tönnies, *Kritik der öffentlichen Meinung* (Berlin: Julius Springer, 1922), p. 231. See also Elisabeth Noelle, *Öffentliche Meinung und Soziale Kontrolle* (Tübingen, Germany: J.C.B. Mohr, Paul Siebeck, 1966), wherein are quoted at greater length Locke, "Concerning Human Understanding"; Franz von Holtzendorff, *Wesen und Wert der Öffentliche Meinung* (Munich: n.p., 1879-1880); Rudolf von Jhering, *Der Zweck in Recht,* vol. 2 (Leipzig, East Germany: Breitkopf & Härtel, 1883); and Edward A. Ross, *Social Control: A Survey of the Foundation of Order* (New York: Macmillan, 1901).

32. Ross, *Social Control.*

33. See Allport, "Toward a Science," p. 18; and Tönnies, *Kritik,* pp. 139-140.

34. Alexis de Tocqueville, *La Démocratie en Amérique,* vols. 1-4 (n.p., 1839-1840); this work is discussed in Noelle, *Öffentliche Meinung.*

35. Tönnies, on p. 232 of *Kritik,* sees "public opinion as the emerging power of common convictions." On p. 138, he says: "Public opinion always claims to be authoritative: it calls for approval and makes at least silence, the avoidance of contradiction a duty. With more or less success; the larger the degree of success, the more it proves itself to represent public opinion in spite of the more or less silenced opposition." Similarly Hermann Lübbe, *Hochschulreform und Gegenaufklärung: Analysen, Postulate, Polemik zur aktuellen Hochschul- und Wissenschaftspolitik,* Herderbücherei, vol. 418 (Freiburg, West Germany: Herder, 1972), who sees evidence of the "dominating opinion" in the fact that in conversation it remains unchallenged.

36. Alexis de Tocqueville, *Das alte Staatswesen und die Revolution* (Leipzig: Mendelssohn, 1857), p. 182 *(L'Ancien Régime et la Révolution,* 1856).

37. Interesting in this connection are observations in Werner Mangold, "Gruppendiskussionen," in *Handbuch der Empirischen Sozialforschung,* vol. 1, ed. René König (Stuttgart: Ferdinand Enke, 1962), pp. 209-225, during group discussions in which, depending on the participation of personalities who dominate the mood of the discussion, certain opinions were freely expressed whilst others were kept private. This suggests a distinction between "private opinion" and opinion publicly expressed. This was also the approach of Richard L. Schanck, "A Study of a Community and Its Groups and Institutions Conceived of as Behaviors of Individuals," *Psychological Monographs* 43, whole no. 195 (1932), who makes a distinction between "public" and "private" attitudes (quoted in Allport, "Toward a Science," p. 15).

38. Allport, "Toward a Science," pp. 7-8.

39. Allport, "Toward a Science," p. 13.

40. Solomon E. Asch, "Effects of Group Pressure upon the Modification and Distortion of Judgments," in *Groups, Leadership, and Men,* ed. H. Guetzkow (Pittsburgh: Carnegie Press, 1951) and in *Group Dynamics: Research and Theory,* ed. Dorwin Cartwright and Alvin Zander (Evanston, Ill.: Row Peterson, 1953), pp. 151-162; Stanley Milgram, "Nationality and Conformity," *Scientific American* 205 (December 1961): 45-51.

41. Lazarsfeld, Berelson, and Gaudet, *People's Choice,* preface to the 2nd ed., p. xxxvi.

THE PRESS AS KING-MAKER: WHAT SURVEYS FROM LAST FIVE CAMPAIGNS SHOW

John P. Robinson

This is, we are told, the age of television. No other technological innovation in this century has had more impact on how we spend our time. Estimates of the number of life-years spent in front of the television are used to speculate on the quality of life in our society. The public has become so dependent on television that they proclaim it their main news source. The developments in new media technology causing most excitement are adaptations of television—cable television, video cassettes, EVR.[1]

The impact of television is also central to recent debates about media coverage of politics. In the last 20 years dominant attention in books, review articles and journals has been given to topics like the packaging of candidates for television, campaign financing for electronic media coverage, equal time provisions for candidates and the impact of election projections on voting behavior.[2]

While there is good reason to study the impact of television on politics, because political decision-makers plan their strategy around television, considerable skepticism remains about television's impact on the voter.[3] In fact, little evidence exists which shows that television has a demonstrable impact on voting behavior.[4] Perhaps as Weiss appropriately notes, "the campaign period is of too short a duration and too filled with communication and countercommunication

*John P. Robinson, "The Press as King-Maker: What Surveys From Last Five Campaigns Show," * Journalism Quarterly, *vol. 51 (Winter 1974): 587-594, 606. Reprinted by permission.*

to permit much change." Prior to national election day, television transmits a continual glut of partisan campaign appeals. In contrast to the editorial endorsements of newspapers, however, television seldom offers its own message to the voters on how they ought to cast their ballots. The newspaper endorsement is a direct message, which appears to reduce objectively the confusing arguments of the campaign to a single conclusion. However, research has amply demonstrated that there are few regular readers of the editorial page in the newspaper, and certainly far fewer than the number who follow the election campaign on television, and who apparently regard television with greater credibility than they do newspaper accounts.[5]

That newspaper endorsements can and do influence voter decision in *local* elections seems a well-accepted part of conventional wisdom, and it also has received empirical support.[6] However, the classic research on voting behavior in *national* elections has so well documented the pervasive influences of personal factors, such as one's political party identification or the political orientations of one's peers,[7] that the likelihood of newspaper endorsements having any influence has been dismissed almost out of hand.

Nevertheless, research on the 1968 national election uncovered a curious and persistent relation between newspaper endorsements and voting behavior.[8] While voters were generally confused about or unaware of the partisan stands of reporting in television, radio or magazines, they accurately perceived where their favorite newspaper stood on the election. Moreover, these newspaper endorsements were clearly associated with how people reported they voted on election day, even after such

personal factors as party identification and pre-election vote intention were taken into account. However, the highly abnormal character of the 1968 election—with its third-party candidates, resignations and highly divisive internal conflict—made one cautious about generalizing too far from this particular election. The 1972 election, while not entirely free of these elements, might be seen as providing a more normal context in which to examine the possible influence of newspaper endorsements. Indeed, it may be argued that 1972 provided a rather unexciting presidential campaign, in which most matters were settled long before the newspapers made their endorsements.[9] Thus, the nature of the campaign could have minimized the possible impact of newspaper endorsements.

DATA BASES

As in our 1968 study, the data come from a national probability sample of American adults interviewed by the Center for Political Studies (CPS) of the University of Michigan after the election about their voting behavior and mass media usage *during* the campaign. Of this cross-section of 1,119 adults, which was also interviewed during the campaign about their political attitudes and vote intentions, a total of 501 reported both having voted and having followed the campaign in a newspaper. In general, this sample reported levels of mass media usage similar to that found in earlier CPS election studies,[10] indicating that, if in fact 1972 did provide a relatively unexciting campaign, attention to the media did not seem diminished by it.

In contrast to our 1968 study, respondents who read newspapers were not asked about their perceptions of where the newspapers stood but merely the name of the newspaper they read most closely about the campaign. The actual endorsements of these newspapers were then verified through listings in *Editor & Publisher*,[11] or by the CPS field staff in cases where a newspaper's endorsement was not reported in *Editor & Publisher*. By *Editor & Publisher's* calculations, some 93% of newspapers making endorsements in 1972 had endorsed Richard Nixon, with only 7% for George McGovern. Projected by circulation figures, 10 times as many Americans were exposed to a pro-Nixon as a pro-McGovern newspaper, with less than 15% of the readers being exposed to a paper that remained uncommitted.

TABLE 1

Percentages of Voters Voting for the Democratic Candidate by Newspaper Endorsement and Party Identification, 1972

Voter's Party	Newspaper Endorsement		
	Democratic Candidate (N = 53)	Neither Candidate (N = 197)	Republican Candidate (N = 251)
Democrat (N = 207)	71	61	46
Independent (N = 152)	50	34	26
Republican (N = 142)	0	6	5

RESULTS

The results, outlined in Table 1, indicate a basic replication of the results obtained for the 1968 study.[12] Independent voters exposed to a newspaper endorsing McGovern were twice as likely to vote for McGovern (50%) as independent voters exposed to a pro-Nixon newspaper (26%). However, this 24% differential in 1972 was matched by a 25% differential (71% vs. 46%) by newspaper endorsement among voters with Democratic party identification. In 1968, no such differential was found among Democrats, a

point which will be discussed in more detail below. Consistent with the 1968 results, no such differential was found among Republican party-identifiers in Table 1.

Table 1, of course, fails to take into account the several other factors beyond party identification that predict the vote and which may also lie behind the predictive power of exposure to newspapers of differing endorsements. Table 2 presents the voting differentials obtained after 12 such predictors are taken into account, predictors such as opinion giving, interest in the campaign, feelings of political efficacy, as well as age, education, region, urbanicity and sex. Also included *as a control variable* in Table 2 is vote intention expressed in the pre-election interview, a variable that may be considered an "overcontrol" since its correlation (.84) with actual reported vote in the post-election interview approaches unity. The combined statistical effects of these variables in Table 2 has been assessed by Multiple Classification Analysis (MCA), a computer program that provides estimates of the effects of single variables simultaneously controlled for the effects of several other variables.[13]

Table 2 indicates that introduction of these 12 variables does indeed substantially reduce the differentials in Table 1. Instead of 25% differentials, Table 2 indicates newspaper endorsements contribute a 7% difference (40% vs. 33%) in voting behavior after the other variables have been controlled. This is practically identical to the 6% differential found after a parallel MCA run was performed on the 1968 election data.[14] Such a finding is but one piece of evidence supporting the persistence of the newspaper endorsement effect that we shall encounter.

MCA is strictly a linear model and cannot detect differentials in which strong interaction effects among variables are present. We suspected a strong interaction effect would occur for the variable of region, particularly for the difference between voters in the South compared to those in the rest of the country.

Thus, the traditional Democratic loyalties of Nixon-voting Southerners (who were overwhelmingly exposed to pro-Nixon newspapers) might very well lie behind the differentials noted thus far. In other words, one might well expect Southerners to defect from the Democratic party candidate whether any stimulus from the mass media was present or not.

TABLE 2
Percentages of Voters Voting for the Democratic Candidate by Newspaper Endorsement, 1972 (after correction for 12 leading explanatory factors, including party identification)

	Newspaper Endorsement		
	Democratic Candidate	Neither Candidate	Republican Candidate
All voters (N = 501)	40	36	33
South (N = 140)	37	31	30
(Dems & Indeps only) (N = 102)	57	43	42
Non-South (N = 361)	45	38	35
(Dems & Indeps only) (N = 257)	69	63	60

However, the figures at the bottom of Table 2 show that the differential holds almost as well in the South as it does in the rest of the country. Moreover, among Democratic and Independent voters (for whom the differential is at a maximum in Table 1), the newspaper endorsement "effect" is even stronger in the South than elsewhere. This provides a second support for the presence of a real difference in voting behavior attributable simply to exposure to newspapers of different political orientation.

A third feature of the data in Tables 1 and 2 that bolsters confidence in this conclusion is the voting behavior of individuals exposed to uncommitted newspapers whose endorsement was unknown or could not be ascertained (i.e., the "neither" category of Table 1 and 2). To be consistent with the results thus far, these voters should exhibit voting behavior that falls somewhere between readers of pro-McGovern newspapers and readers of pro-Nixon newspapers. While voters exposed to uncommitted or unknown newspapers do not generally fall at the expected midway point in the Table 1 and Table 2 calculations (except for the most important row for all voters at the top of Table 2), their voting behavior does not fall outside the interval defined by readers of pro-McGovern and pro-Nixon newspapers.

Moreover, this middle position is maintained when the "neither" group is decomposed in Table 3, which contrasts readers exposed to an uncommitted newspaper with readers exposed to a newspaper whose allegiance was unknown or could not be ascertained. More powerful corroborative evidence is provided by the "non-readers" category in Table 3, which may be more akin to a "control group" than the neither group. As such, this group should also maintain a middle position. In fact, Table 3 shows their voting patterns to be practically identical to that of the total neither group.[15] In brief, the basic rank order of voting behavior, running from exposure to pro-McGovern endorsements to exposure to "neutral" or no messages to exposure to pro-Nixon endorsements, is impressively preserved when rather subtle distinctions are drawn within the middle of these three groups.

TABLE 3
Percentages of Voters in the 'Neither' Category of Table 1, and of Voters Who
Did Not Read Newspapers, Voting for the Democratic Candidate by Party Identification, 1972

Voter's Party ID	Readers in Neither Category			Non-readers
	Total Neither (N = 197)	Newspaper Uncommitted (N = 74)	Newspaper NA or DK (N = 123)	(N = 277)
Democrats (N = 87)	61	67	63	60
Independents (N = 61)	34	31	40	33
Republicans (N = 49)	6	5	0	8

TABLE 4
Percentages of Voters Voting for the Democratic Candidate by Newspaper Endorsement, 1956-1972

Year	Newspaper Endorsement			
	Democratic Candidate	Neither Candidate and Non-readers	Republican Candidate	Dem.-Rep. △ %
1956 (N = 969)	58	38	38	+20
1960 (N = 451)	60	46	45	+15
1964 (N = 972)	74	71	50	+24
1968 (N = 939)*	40	30	26	+14
1972 (N = 778)	45	36	27	+18

*Perceived newspaper endorsement, white voters only.

TABLE 5
Percentages of Voters Voting for the Democratic Presidential Candidate by Newspaper Endorsement
and by Party Identification, 1956-1972

Year	Democrats				Independents				Republicans			
	Newspaper Endorsement			Diff. D-R △ %	Newspaper Endorsement			Diff. D-R △ %	Newspaper Endorsement			Diff. D-R △ %
	Dem	Neither	Rep		Dem	Neither	Rep		Dem	Neither	Rep	
1956 (N = 969)	84	74	73	+11	27	22	28	− 1	0	4	5	− 5
1960 (N = 451)	79	79	80	− 1	61	−	48	+13	8	0	8	0
1964 (N = 972)	91	89	87	+ 4	70	71	35	+35	28	32	13	+15
1968 (N = 939*)	62	65	69	− 7	40	35	12	+28	12	4	8	+ 4
1972 (N = 778)	71	61	46	+25	50	34	26	+24	0	6	5	− 5

—Less than 10 respondents
*Perceived newspaper endorsement; white voters only

RESULTS IN
PREVIOUS ELECTIONS

One could get carried away with these results and perform the sort of statistical gerrymandering so popular in sports reporting by pointing out that in overall terms newspaper endorsements have predicted five out of the last six presidential elections. The only exception has been Kennedy's extremely close victory over Nixon in 1960, where Nixon was endorsed by more than four times as many newspapers as was Kennedy.

This argument of course fails to take into account the *margins* of victory in each campaign. Can, then, one predict the margin of electoral victory by some function of the proportion of newspapers endorsing the candidate? For the three presidential elections (1960, 1968, 1972) in which Richard Nixon was involved, the answer seems to be positive. In 1960 and 1968, when he received the endorsements of eight out of every 10 endorsing newspapers, the election was extremely close. In 1972, when he was endorsed at a nine out of 10 rate, he won by a landslide. On the other hand, Eisenhower won landslide victories in 1952 and 1956 with roughly the eight out of 10 ratio of support that Nixon enjoyed in 1960 and 1968. Moreover, it took a seven out of 10 support ratio for Johnson to win a landslide Democratic victory in 1964. And we have yet to consider the Roosevelt and Truman victories of the 1930s and 1940s in the face of overwhelming newspaper opposition. Thus, while there is some consistency in this pattern of victory margins and newspaper endorsements, it is hard to argue for anything resembling a lawful relation between the two.

This unpromising pattern of "ecological" correlations does not necessarily rule out the possibility of relations holding at the individual level of analysis that we have employed in Tables 1 and 2. Thus, we appear to have encountered a classic case of the "ecological fallacy" in the present data, as Table 4 confirms. Such a discrepancy, of course, has long been familiar in sociology.[16]

Table 4 indicates a highly consistent relation between individual voting behavior and exposure to newspaper endorsements over the last five national elections (which are as far back as University of Michigan election

study data on newspaper exposure are available). The overall voting differential between exposure to Democratic and Republican newspapers, as noted in the last column of Table 4, varies only between 14 percent and 24 percent, indicating a rather consistent and pervasive association. Those in the non-exposed or neutral endorsement categories continue to fall at some point between the two extremes (although not near the midpoints). As before, we are faced with a host of rival explanations of this set of results. In Table 4, not even the effects of party identification are controlled, and one would certainly expect the factor of selective exposure to be at work in Table 4. De facto selective exposure, the tendency for people to expose themselves to communications most congenial with their existing attitudes, is a well-known political phenomenon.[17] However, few Americans enjoy the luxury of choice in the matter of subscribing to newspapers which match their political loyalties. Nevertheless, some tendency does emerge in these national samples for Democrats to read more pro-Democratic newspapers and Republicans more pro-Republican newspapers. It is therefore necessary to introduce a control for party identification in Table 4, and this is provided in Table 5.

Table 5 presents a far more confusing picture than Table 4. In several cells, differentials by newspaper endorsement disappear or even take on negative values (indicating that readers of pro-Republican papers vote more Democratic than readers of pro-Democratic papers). Differences of the magnitude encountered in Tables 1 and 4 appear only in 1956 and 1972 for Democratic party identifiers, 1964 for Republican party identifiers and in 1960, 1964, and 1972 for Independents. The results of Table 5, at first glance then, do not fit into any simple pattern.

On closer inspection, however, two themes can be detected:

1. In close elections (1960 and 1968), voting differentials by newspaper endorsements are confined to Independents.
2. In landslide elections (1956, 1964, 1972), voting differentials by newspaper endorsement extend to members of the losing party as well as to Independents.

While there are exceptions to these two themes in Table 5 and the differentials vary more than one would need to proclaim these as lawful relations, they could provide convenient guidelines to examine the impact of newspapers in past and future elections.

SUMMARY AND CONCLUSIONS

In the climate of self-congratulation within the press following its exposure of the Watergate affair and consequent humbling of the powers of President Nixon, the other side of the coin has been forgotten. In the election of 1972, 93 percent of newspapers making endorsements had supported President Nixon's re-election bid.

Outside of the magnitude of the difference, the fact that newspapers overwhelmingly endorsed a Republican presidential candidate seems hardly noteworthy or even newsworthy. With the exception of 1964, newspapers historically have endorsed Republican presidential candidates. Moreover, research on the readership of editorial pages would hardly lead one to expect such content to have much impact on something as major as a presidential election.

Nevertheless, as in a parallel 1968 national survey, these endorsements were associated with clear differentials in voting behavior on the part of voters exposed to these endorsements. Confidence in the linkage between newspaper endorsements and presidential voting behavior was bolstered by the following empirical findings:

1. The differential remained after controls were applied for party identification.
2. The differential remained after controls were applied for 11 other predictors of voting behavior.
3. The differential remained after controls were applied for possible interaction effects due to region.
4. The differential after these controls were applied on the 1972 voting data was almost identical to the ± 3 percent differential obtained when a parallel analysis had been performed for 1968 voting data.
5. The voting behavior of individuals exposed to uncommitted newspapers, or newspapers for which endorsement information was not available, tended to fall between individuals exposed to pro-McGovern newspapers and pro-Nixon newspapers.
6. The voting behavior of individuals not exposed to newspapers tended to fall between individuals exposed to pro-McGovern newspapers and pro-Nixon newspapers.

While more elaborate tests are needed to establish firmer, or cause-and-effect, relations between newspaper endorsements and voting, on the whole these findings certainly provide sufficient reason to launch further inquiry which can test for such relations.[18]

These results, of course, do not square well with conventional wisdom or with other bodies of data. Several communities in which the newspaper took a Democratic stance can undoubtedly be found in which the aggregate vote was overwhelmingly pro-Republican, and vice versa. Nor have we found very convincing evidence in this paper for overall newspaper support to be predictive of the *margin* of victory in elections. Thus, reasonable explanations for these "ecological" discrepancies need to be advanced.

To the extent that these results do hold up under further scrutiny, they further the "return to the concept of the powerful mass media" that Noelle-Neumann has expressed. Reviewing the results of several field studies of media impact she conducted in West Germany and Switzerland, Noelle-Neumann concludes:

The thesis that mass media do not change attitudes but only reinforce them cannot be upheld under conditions of consonance and cumulation. Our data point in this direction. It is true there exists a tendency to protect attitudes through selective perception. Yet the more selective perception is being restricted—by consonance of reporting and editorial comment, reinforced by cumulation of periodical repetition in the media—the more attitudes can be influenced or molded by the mass media.[19]

The present results draw our research attention back to the printed media, which seem to have lost their glamor in the age of television. As in 1968, the voting differentials by newspaper dwarf those associated with television—a not surprising conclusion given television's reluctance to clearly endorse candidates.[20] Given the pervasive influences of the newspaper that have recently been isolated in the present data—and by Noelle-Neumann. Stempel, Stokes and Butler, and Mason[21] the time seems ripe for both research investigators and decision-makers to reconsider their disregard of the printed media.[22]

Future work ought to isolate the mechanisms of communications behavior at work in the present phenomenon. We have advanced the hypothesis that the newspaper per editorial is the one clear direct message emanating during the campaign. Is this in fact how the editorial is perceived by the audience? Do factors such as perceived partisanship or credibility of the newspaper affect in any way the reception of this message? Is information about the newspaper editorial stance conveyed directly or relayed by word-of-mouth through the community?

Investigations into the impact of newspapers should not be confined to voting behavior, despite the ideal behavioral criterion that elections provide to the researcher. The research of Noelle-Neumann and Stempel prompt several intriguing hypotheses about how the newspaper structures the public's view of the world. Our findings about the impact of differential editorial content raises the issue of whether these editorial stances may be further reflected in the newspaper's selection and placement of wire copy (the innovation initially associated with raised levels of newspaper objectivity).

Watergate has refocused the nation's attention on the role our press can play as a "king-breaker." However, following Noelle-Neumann, the question may be asked why there was not greater newspaper investigation and exposure of Watergate prior to the election. Could it be that McGovern's having been written off by the press (not only by "conservative" editors and publishers, but by the "liberal" Washington press corps) created an atmosphere within which Watergate was too uncomfortable or too threatening to report on more thoroughly? If so, the newspaper's role as king-maker extends well beyond the possible effects isolated in the present study; indeed, it becomes as significant as its role of king-breaker.

NOTES

1. See, for example, Walter Weiss, "Effects of the Mass Media of Communication," in *Handbook of Social Psychology,* vol. 5, (Boston: Addison-Wesley, 1970); Ben Bagdikian, *The Information Machines* (New York: Harper & Row, 1971).

2. See, for example, Weiss, "Effects of Mass Media"; also Harold Mendelsohn and Irving Crespi, *Polls, Television and the New Politics* (San Francisco: Chandler, 1970).

3. Angus Campbell, "Has Television Reshaped Politics?" *Columbia Journalism Review* 1 (1962): 10-13.

4. Weiss, "Effects of Mass Media," p. 176.

5. See, for example, Bagdikian, *Information Machines.*

6. See, for example, William Mason, "The Impact of Endorsements on Voting," *Sociological Methods and Research* 1 (May 1973): 463-95; Maxwell McCombs, "Editorial Endorsement: A Study of Influence," *Journalism Quarterly* 44 (Autumn 1967): 545-48.

7. Paul Lazarsfeld *et al., The People's Choice* (New York: Duell, Sloan and Pearce, 1944); Angus Campbell *et al., The American Voter* (New York: Wiley, 1960).

8. John Robinson, "Perceived Media Bias and the 1968 Election: Can the Media Affect Behavior After All?" *Journalism Quarterly* 49 (Summer 1972): 239-46.

9. Irving Crespi, "1972 and the American Voter," *Public Opinion Quarterly* 37 (Fall 1973): 441-442.

10. John Robinson *et al., Measures of Political Attitudes* (Ann Arbor, Mich: Survey Research Center, 1968), pp. 616-621.

11. *Editor & Publisher* 105 (4 November 1972): 9-12.

12. Robinson, "Perceived Media Bias." It must be noted that the data are not exactly comparable, since the 1968 data refer to the actual editorial stance of the newspaper. See Tables 4 and 5.

13. Frank Andrews *et al., Multiple Classification Analysis* (Ann Arbor, Mich.: Survey Research Center, 1967).

14. Robinson, "Perceived Media Bias," p. 244. To the extent that the pre-election intention does represent an "overcontrol," the reader may well feel more comfortable with a figure closer to the *overall* 15 percent differential in Table 1 than the 7 percent differential in Table 2 (or the 6 percent differential for 1968). The 15 percent differential does take into account the factor of party identification, which explains most of the variance in vote after the pre-election intention variable is taken into account.

15. The middle position of this group is also maintained after application of MCA.

16. W.S. Robinson, "Ecological Correlation and the Behavior of Individuals," *American Sociological Review* 15 (June 1950): 351-357. For a more recent attempt to explicate conditions under which the fallacy does or does not hold, see John Hammond, "Two Sources of Error in Ecological Correlations, *American Sociological Review* 38 (December 1973): 764-777.

17. Weiss, "Effects of Mass Media." For a more skeptical view of the prevalence of this phenomenon, see David Sears and Jonathan Freedman, "Selective Exposure to Information: A Critical Review," *Public Opinion Quarterly* 31 (Summer 1967): 194-213.

18. The question of the reverse flow of casuality, that is from the public to the newspaper, looks unsolvable at this time without an extremely sophisticated research design. While there can be little doubt that newspapers in many senses must conform to local norms in order to survive financially, mechanisms whereby public reaction can influence newspaper editorial endorsements for the race for the Presidency do not seem plausible. Moreover, the types of effects described here occur primarily within the undecided bloc of voters and it is even more implausible to suspect that these voters hold sway over newspaper editors in any direct sense. The remaining possibility is that both the voters and the editorial staffs are influenced by some as yet unspecified third variable; this seems the most plausible explanation given the lack of data, but the third variable in question would have to predict community-wide variation in voting. Our leaning toward newspaper endorsements as the causal agent rests in large degree on the voting behavior of those not exposed to newspaper endorsements in Table 3.

19. Elisabeth Noelle-Neumann, "Return to the Concept of Powerful Mass Media," in *Studies of Broadcasting,* Vol. 9, ed. H. Equchi and K. Sata (Tokyo: Nippon Hoso Kyokai, 1973), p. 109.

20. One comment is in order about those differential voting patterns by television exposure that *do* obtain in the 1972 campaign. In 1968, some tendency was found for voters with heavier exposure to television coverage of the campaign to vote Democratic. In contrast, heavier users of television for politics in 1972 were more likely to have voted Republican than were less frequent users of television. While the magnitude of these differences is too small to warrant extended speculation, it is interesting to note that they do favor the party in power.

21. Noelle-Neumann, "Powerful Mass Media"; Mason, "Impact of Endorsements." Guido H. Stempel, III, "Effects on Performance of a Cross-Media Monopoly," *Journalism Monographs* 29 (1973); Donald Stokes and David Butler, *Political Change in Britain* (New York: St. Martin's Press, 1969).

22. At the same time, several studies documenting various dimensions of the effects of the broadcast are emerging. See, for example, Thomas Patterson and Robert McClure, "Political Advertising, Voter Reaction," *Public Opinion Quarterly* 37 (Fall 1973): 447-448; John Robinson, "Rock Music and Drug Use," paper presented at the annual meeting of the American Psychological Association, September 1972; and Eli Rubinstein *et al., Television and Social Behavior* (Washington D.C.: National Institute of Mental Health, 1972).

MASS COMMUNICATION AND POLITICAL SOCIALIZATION

Sidney Kraus

It is especially appropriate today to examine what we think that we know about mass communication and political behavior. For in 1972 eleven million voters between eighteen and twenty years old were old enough to vote for President for the first time and forty-eight percent voted. They together with those twenty-four years old or under brought first voting to approximately thirteen million.[1]

These youthful voters have been bred on television. A dozen years ago it was noted by Schramm, Lyle, and Parker that "a child in his first sixteen years allocates to television's persuaders and entertainers as large a block of time as he allocates to his teachers in school."[2] At about the same time, Bailyn reported that the average viewing time for children between the ages of six to sixteen was twenty-two hours a week.[3] And Bronfenbrenner, studying changing patterns of childhood, recently concluded, "By the time the average child is sixteen he has watched from 12,000 to 15,000 hours of television. In other words, he has spent the equivalent of 15 to 20 solid months, 24 hours a day, before a television screen."[4]

It is difficult to provide evidence of television effects which all would agree to. The current controversy over television and violence is a case in point. Nevertheless, only those with tenacious biases would not

This article originally appeared in the Quarterly Journal of Speech, 59:4, (December, 1973). Copyright 1973 by the Quarterly Journal of Speech; used by permission. It was reprinted in Alan Wells, Mass Media and Society, Mayfield Publishing Co., 2nd edition, 1975, pp. 320-330. For an expanded version see Sidney Kraus and Dennis Davis, The Effects of Mass Communication on Political Behavior, Pennsylvania State University Press, 1976, Chapter 2.

concede that spending as much or more time with television than with school for twelve years is bound to influence some behavior. This discussion argues in favor of the view that television contributes to learning about politics and government, and that political behavior may be formed as a result of systematic television selection.

The television experience of youthful voters undoubtedly includes an unprecedented amount of foreign and domestic strife. Hollander, in his study of Adolescents and the War, begins with, "It is not difficult to conclude that the 'stories' to which the young of this country have listened are different from those of the generation before them."[5]

When they went to the polls the political "stories" they brought with them were undoubtedly television "stories." In this past decade television gave the viewer a running, visual history of a tragic war. It has recorded the killing of a campaigner seeking the presidential nomination of the Democratic Party. Most recently, another campaigner seeking a similar nomination was gunned down and television showed the sequence within hours of the shooting. Television showed these voters the killing of a Nobel peace prize civil rights leader. With each of these tragic shootings and killings, television covered the funerals and mournings and the subsequent interpretations of the meaning these events have on our national and international lives.

When these young voters went to the polls they also brought "stories" about other political institutions. For they have seen the killing of students by a state contingent of the National Guard; the destruction of government property; the burning of buildings in cities; and the rioting at a political convention with a Mayor of one of our largest cities swearing at the U.S. Senator of one of our smallest states. Their television included: protest speeches at the Supreme Court; civil rights demonstrations at Lincoln Memorial; the poor in tents before our government; presidents of universities meeting and not meeting demands and getting arrested; and, as an on-going interest, unbelievable moments on the moon.

In the past decade alone these new voters have been involved with the "Screening of America." It is the amount and kind of this screening that have escaped researchers as an important determinant in the formation of political attitudes and in voting behavior.

These screenings, of course, are of news events. They don't speak to the television fare of entertainment. We sorely lack any empirical evidence which gets at the effect a diet of television prime time or a diet of late afternoon programming has on the development of attitudes and values in children and adolescents, or in adults, for that matter. In 1960, Klapper concluded his widely used book on mass communication with the notion that

The role and effects of the media in the socialization of the child can perhaps no longer be accurately assessed, but some concept of its possible scope may be obtained by performing the mental experiment of imagining the process of socialization occuring in a society in which mass media did not exist. Our knowledge of primitive cultures and of pre-media years suggests that the present social system and the present culture are at least in part a product of the existence of mass communication, and may be dependent upon such communication for their continued existence.[6]

The unorthodox view of this article is that mass media, particularly television, play decisive roles in political socialization. There are a variety of reasons for this, not the least of which is the significant change in the way in which children grow up today. Other reasons are the growth and dominance of television in our daily lives and the increased technology in transmitting information.

Since its inception as a field of study mass communication has been thought of as the agency least likely to be responsible for instilling attitudes about political institutions. More credibility for that kind of learning was given to family, school, and peer groups. But the evidence today is persuasive. As variables in research on political socialization the mass media cannot be ignored. This article will present the evidence and argument in support of that view.

The period considered is 1959 through 1971, about twelve years. If we consider birthdays of young voters—those newly franchised and those eligible to vote for the first time in a presidential election—we will note they occurred since 1948. In that year there were only 190,000 television sets in the United States. By 1960, when these young voters were no more than twelve, 54 million sets were in use. In 1970 these reached just under 93 million.[7]

During this same period a research topic developed in political science, sociology, and recently in fields more directly concerned with mass communications such as journalism and radio and television. This topic is political socialization. It purports to study

... all political learning, formal and informal, deliberate and unplanned, at every stage of the life cycle, including not only explicitly political learning but also nominally non-political learning which affects political behavior, such as the learning of politically relevant social attitudes and the acquisition of politically relevant personality characteristics.[8]

In short, it is the process of how we come to learn about politics, how we obtain our attitudes and values about political institutions, and how we ultimately behave politically. Six comprehensive reviews of political socialization research have been published since 1959.[9] Other reviews have appeared by Greenstein in an encyclopedia;[10] by Dawson in an international political review;[11] and by Wasby in the *Family Life Coordinator*.[12] Four major studies have been reported in this same period.[13] In these reviews and studies and in others reported in a 1967 fifty-five page bibliography,[14] mass communication and television were either totally ignored, dismissed as relatively unimportant, or barely noted.

In the face of the growing television audience, the increased domestic and foreign news coverage, and the amount of time children spend with television it appears incredible that legions of researchers would avoid television as a source of political socialization. Yet television and mass communication, for the most part, have not been variables in socialization studies prior to the seventies. (See Figure 1.)

Hyman, in the first systematic review of socialization studies, could, but did not, plead that no one set out to study the influence of television because it was just getting started. Television and the development of political socialization as a research interest coincided in their infancies. It is curious, however, that Hyman used mass media findings from the classical voting studies of Elmira, N.Y., and Erie County, Ohio, to support the view that parental influence dominates siblings' views on political matters without inquiring *what siblings in the fifties were doing with media.*[15] The fact was that Hyman did not know, at least empirically, what children were doing with television when he reviewed the literature on political socialization in 1959. Klapper completed the first systematic review of mass communication effects in 1960.[16] Schramm and his associates produced the first comprehensive study of North American children and their use of television in 1961.[17] And even in these pace-setting works mass media's contribution to political socialization was barely and inferentially considered. For what was not available to Hyman was not available to Klapper and Schramm.

So we emerge, from the fifties, according to Hyman, with the conclusion that, "Foremost among agencies of socialization into politics is the family."[18]

Greenstein's pioneering study of New Haven school children in grades four through eight was based on data collected in 1958.[19] Greenstein, confirming earlier findings that the family is the important socializing agent,

briefly noted that media are a part of the child's environment, but failed to consider them seriously in his analyses.

What is most baffling about the Greenstein study is that the recognition accorded media while developing a *Gestalt* for the study of political socialization;[20] the inclusion of relevant media items in the questionnaire;[21] the empirical verification of television ownership;[22] and the conclusion that television provides models for children[23] were not pursued with some form of multivariate analysis or in-depth analysis to provide a more substantial discourse about mass communication and socialization interaction among the 659 children.[24]

Instead, Greenstein reverts to earlier works,[25] deficient in socialization data, to propose that

"Across the board" programs of (political) exhortation (designed to increase political involvement) are subject to all of the factors which make propaganda by mass communication an inefficient technique for changing beliefs and behavior. To begin with, the message tends largely to be received by those who are already sympathetic to it and therefore least in need of change. For the remainder of the population, the message is ignored, "crowded out" by other more potent communications, or even misperceived. When it is taken in, it is not reinforced at the face-to-face level and nothing is done to change the individual's actual life situation in order to facilitate acting on the message.[26]

It is unfortunate that in this precursory study about children's political socialization, earlier findings about adult populations and mass communication variables are taken as conclusive. Greenstein's peroration of mass communication effects upon children's political learning erroneously passes off their television viewing behavior as insignificant.

It is interesting to note that M. Kent Jennings in his review of Greenstein's *Children and Politics* suggests that there is a "paucity of attention devoted to peer group relationships, formal instruction, feelings of self-esteem and competence, and intra-familial relationships."[27] Again, the mass media are overlooked.

FIGURE 1
Contiguous Examination of the Appearance of Selected Benchmark Political Socialization
and Media Studies with the Average Weekly Viewing Hours for Children

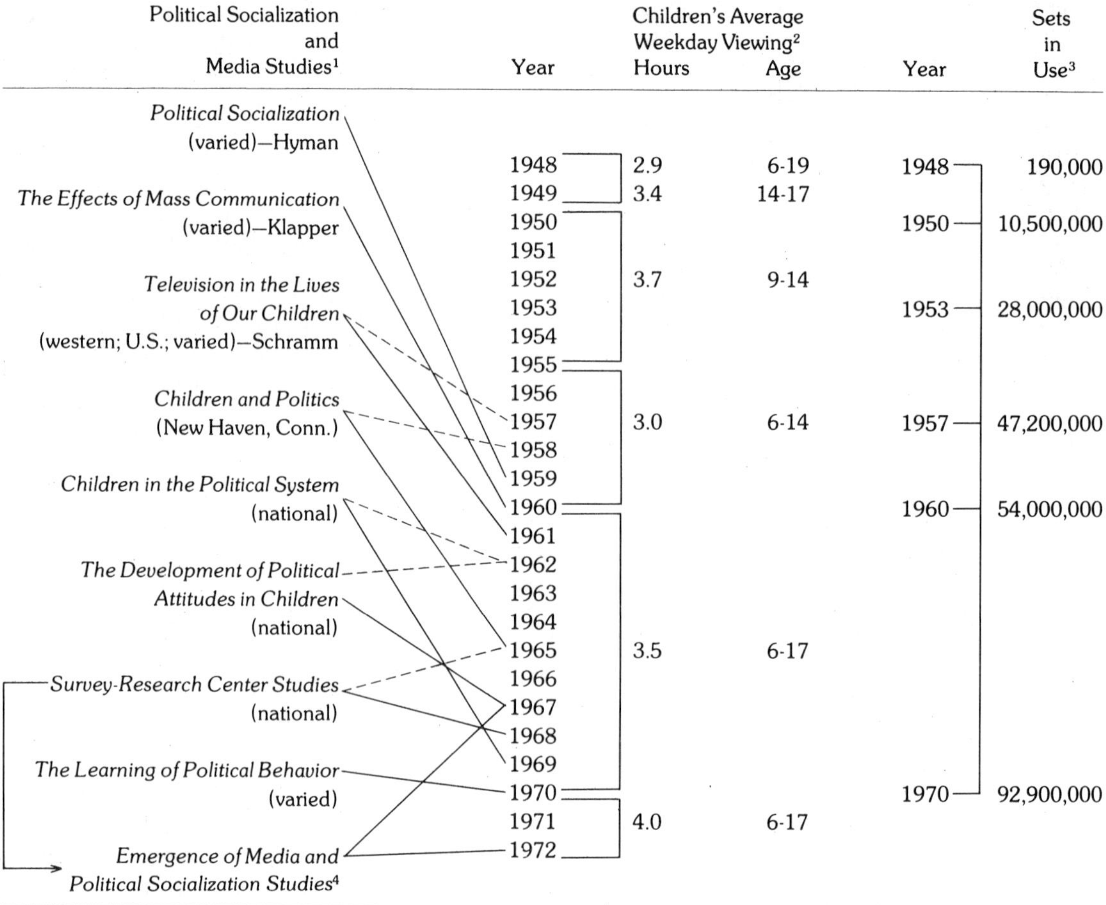

Political Socialization and Media Studies[1]	Year	Children's Average Weekday Viewing[2]		Year	Sets in Use[3]
		Hours	Age		
Political Socialization (varied)—Hyman	1948	2.9	6-19	1948	190,000
	1949	3.4	14-17		
The Effects of Mass Communication (varied)—Klapper	1950			1950	10,500,000
	1951				
	1952	3.7	9-14		
Television in the Lives of Our Children (western; U.S.; varied)—Schramm	1953			1953	28,000,000
	1954				
	1955				
	1956				
Children and Politics (New Haven, Conn.)	1957	3.0	6-14	1957	47,200,000
	1958				
	1959				
Children in the Political System (national)	1960			1960	54,000,000
	1961				
The Development of Political Attitudes in Children (national)	1962				
	1963				
	1964				
	1965	3.5	6-17		
Survey-Research Center Studies (national)	1966				
	1967				
	1968				
The Learning of Political Behavior (varied)	1969				
	1970			1970	92,900,000
	1971	4.0	6-17		
Emergence of Media and Political Socialization Studies[4]	1972				

[1]Parentheses: sample location; dashed line: year data was gathered; solid line: year of publication.
[2]These are estimates from various sources: Schramm *et al., Television in The Lives of Our Children;* Roper data; Greenberg *et al., Mass Media And The Urban Poor,* and others.
[3]Sources: Census data.
[4]Since the completion of this paper several studies have come to the author's attention; the reference here relates to the five studies (Johnson, Chaffee *et al.,* Hollander, Dominick, and Kraus). It applies, in part, to some of the studies at Michigan's Survey Research Center.

In the first national study Hess and Torney obtained some 12,000 school children's responses to political socialization items and concluded that "the effectiveness of the family in transmitting attitudes have been overestimated in previous research." And further "that the school stands out as the central, salient, and dominant force in the political socialization of the young child."[28]

The only item on mass media, which was subsumed under an index of political activity, was the statement-question, "I have read about a candidate in newspapers or magazines."[29] In 1961-62, when these data were collected, children were spending as much or more time viewing television as they were spending in school!

More so than Greenstein's, Hess and Torney's ancillary treatment of media variables is inferentially linked to the children's behavior. What little insight is provided about mass communications' role in the political socialization schema is sketchy and unclear. Throughout their report they offer interview dialogue such as this one with a third-grade boy:

"Have you ever seen the President?"
"I've seen him on television, and heard him on the radio, and seen him in newspapers."[30]

And this with a fourth-grade boy:

"Bobby, have you seen the President on TV?"
Yes." ...
"Have you seen him make speeches on TV?
"Yes."[31]

Another child's interview provides the following:

"Wally, did you see the TV debates (between Nixon and Kennedy)?"
"Some of them. I thought they were very good. It gave you a chance to see what's going on while they're running for President."
"Were you interested before?"
"No, but after the debates I just wanted to see if Kennedy wins."[32]

Wally's comments, among others, suggest that it may have been fruitful to probe and test for direct and indirect television and media effects upon the political socialization process as a result of viewing, listening, reading or hearing about the Kennedy-Nixon debates. There was ample evidence to show that the televised debates permeated the 1960 campaign and dominated television viewing in American households on at least four evenings.[33] Though Hess and Torney acknowledge the occasion by declaring that "the field testing of the national study took place a year and a half after the 1960 Presidential election, providing an opportunity to examine the responses of the group to the partisan aspects of this contest.

Television coverage of the campaign, particularly the debates between Kennedy and Nixon, made the campaign and election struggle a uniquely visible one."[34] They avoid television by discussing the election outcome and concluding, "that the election itself had a strong impact on many children and may in itself have been a socializing experience."[35]

A review of Hess and Torney's work by Sigel fails to note their lack of concern with television and media in the development of political attitudes in children.[36] Nor does Sears' detailed review essay mention mass media.[37] Interestingly, both Sigel and Sears, whose reviews appeared in 1968, fault the Hess-Torney study because no Negro children were included in that sample. The neglect is striking since a recent study found that television viewing for black children was 6 hours per day on the average. For white children it was 4½ hours per day. Bradley Greenberg and his associates concluded that, "The mass medium of the poor is television. It is a preferred and almost exclusive source of information about the outside world."[38]

Complementing the Hess-Torney study, is the impressive work of David Easton and Jack Dennis.[39] Largely derived from the same data as the previously mentioned study, media and television were once again ignored.

Since the same data were being evaluated, it was no surprise to find that, like Hess and Torney, Easton and Dennis minimize television in their assessment of children's political orientations.[40] Both efforts seem to "place" media as a utility—a conveyance of information like a telephone or a street sign. Neither study seriously treats mass communication channels—television, newspapers, magazines, radio, film, records, books, etc.—as independent variables. Institutions of family, school, peer groups, and church receive independent treatments; the mass media receive inferential or indirect treatments.

Inherent in this "transmission" or "vehicle" categorization of media, is a concern with *what* is conveyed rather than with *how* it is conveyed.[41] Consider Easton and Dennis' deductions from both events and data (italics are mine):

Empirically the prominence of the Presidency is reflected in the attention it obtains from the mass media. Children may sense this current of interest among adults if only by overhearing the conversation of their own parents. The drama of presidential-election campaigns undoubtedly also impresses the office on children. *If we take five years of age as the earliest point at which a presidential campaign might leave some imprint on the child, all our children had undergone one campaign at least, by the time of our testing in late 1961 and early 1962, that between Kennedy and Nixon in 1960. ... It seems plausible to assume that few children could pass through recurrent presidential contests without their curiosity being piqued. ...*

One indirect indicator of the child's exposure to the phenomenon of the election *and its psychological importance to him is the response to the following question: "How much did you learn from the last election for President? ... "* (responses: lot, some, little)

If this question is an indicator of the degree of sensitization of the child to politics through presidential elections, *we can ask whether responses to the item are associated with the child's perceptions of the President in any way, and more particularly whether the child who says he has learned a substantial amount from the election is also likely to regard the President more highly. ... (At this point S. Kraus (ed.), The Great Debates, is cited to suggest that since adults' hostility toward the opposition candidate decreased and favorable feelings increased as a result of simple television exposure it is likely that similar effects occur for children.)*

There is at least a prima facie case for the hypothesis that the election has socializing effects ... even though such effects may be confounded by other factors which predispose the child to pay attention to the election or to regard the President more favorably.[42]

Though the researchers allude to mass media, the television debates, and the "drama of presidential-election campaigns," they did not test for television exposure, television content, or viewing behavior generally. Instead, they relied on a gross measure of learning about campaigns to suggest a positive correlation between that and the child's positive feelings toward the President. They buttress this reasoning with exposure to the Presidency in school: "Furthermore, the classroom itself would seem to generate additional awareness and to provide historical continuity for the role of the President. It is the unusual school that does not have busts or pictures of past Presidents in the corridor and classrooms. Few curricula even in the early grades would fail to give some special attention to the office."[43]

The senior authors of these two volumes—Easton and Hess, a political scientist and a developmental psychologist—put together an interdisciplinary approach to study political attitudes of a national sample of elementary school children in grades two through eight in 1957 at the University of Chicago. In 1962, with United States Education Office Funding, they collected the data. With all due respect for their pioneering efforts and the contributions made to their respective disciplines, it is difficult to understand why television was so obviously avoided as a source variable for political socialization. During their five-year period of conceptualization and data collection children's viewing patterns were being published. (See Figure 1.) According to their own observation, significant political stimuli from the mass media confronted their subjects. To complete the indictment, Greenstein, in his review of the Hess-Torney and Easton-Dennis studies, failed to note their omission of mass media and television.[44]

From the fifties and the larger part of the sixties we have no empirical measure of the relationship between mass media and the formation of political attitudes in children simply because media were not included as a source variable. The literature shows that in the fifties family was thought to be most influential in political development and behavior.[45] The sixties ushered in a wave of socialization studies which argued between family and school for the front runner position.[46]

However, data gathered in the mid-sixties by the Survey Research Center at the University of Michigan raised doubts about family and school as agents of political socialization and some measures of media began to appear. Using a national probability sample of 1969 high school seniors, M. Kent Jennings and his associate found that:

1. Compared with parents, students are more cosmopolitan as related to interest in public affairs, knowledge and discourse of political domains, tolerance of political diversity and evaluations of politics at multiple levels.[47]

2. "If the eighteen-year-old is no simple carbon copy of his parents—as the results clearly indicate—then it seems likely that other socializing agents have ample opportunity to exert their impact. ... Not the least of these are the transformations in the content and form of the mass media and communication channels, phenomena over which the family and the school have relatively little control."[48]

3. "Findings certainly do not support the thinking of those who look to the civics curriculum in America high schools as even a minor source of political socialization."[49]

4. Political media usage among both Blacks and Whites were at about the same rates, "but Negro students use television more often than do Whites, and at all levels of parental education."[50]

5. "Regular usage of the mass media for political news rises substantially after high school. A comparison of seniors and their parents shows that parents pay more attention to each of the four media ... although students watch a good deal of television, they pay attention to its news broadcasts much less regularly than parents." Attention to newspapers, radio and magazines is also less frequent among students.[51]

Typically, the introduction of media in political socialization research takes its cue from the word *political* and the variables measured are political usage, public affairs programs watched, political items read, attention to news and politics in media, and the like. Nowhere do we find data about political socialization as a result of the regular media programming that children and adolescents view daily. Cartoons on television and comics in newspapers; policemen and authorities portrayed in films and television; contests of power by labor unions and big business; dramas of "making it" against all odds; issues in fictional dramas; all are part of the daily media diet which may be more substantially related to socialization than any other single societal force. Of these stimuli and their impact on political socialization we can only guess at the present time. But certain indicators are emerging.[52] *Evidence today suggests that mass media, particularly television, may be responsible for much of the child's political learning.*

Norris Johnson in 1967 found that Kentucky high school seniors in economically depressed rural areas, obtained most of their political information from television.[53] With a twice-reached panel of 1,291 Wisconsin junior and senior high school students, Chaffee, Ward and Tipton found that the relationship between media public affairs use and political knowledge is such that over time media use "should be considered as an independent (or intervening) variable in the political socialization process, not merely as one of many dependent variables."[54]

Further, among junior high school students, television entertainment viewing resulted in greater political knowledge; in fact, "*any* use of the mass media tends to expose them to sources of increased political knowledge."[55] This is the first attempt to assess nonpolitical-public affairs-news content impact upon young viewers and media users.[56]

Chaffee, Ward, and Tipton conclude that these Wisconsin students "feel their opinions (as distinct from information) are based on mass media reports. They rate the media as more influential than parents, teachers, or peers."[57]

Neil Hollander studied Everett, Washington, adolescents' views on the Viet Nam war and concluded "The major substantive finding ... is the importance of mass media as a source of learning about an important political object, war. This finding casts considerable doubt on the present utility of much of the previous research on the sources of political socialization and indicates that researchers have, perhaps, been passing over the major source of political learning. The new 'parent' is the mass media."[58]

Joseph Dominick, with a sample of sixth and seventh graders in New York City schools, looked at the role of television in political socialization and found that "the mass media are clearly the primary sources of information about the government" and political information generally for youngsters in this age group.[59]

Recently, several items in socialization studies were replicated with a statewide probability sample of graduating high school classes in New Hampshire. The preliminary results confirm Johnson's, Chaffee, Ward and Tipton's, Hollander's, and Dominick's conclusions. When presented with ten political topics and asked which—among eighteen sources within categories of church, family and friends, mass media, and school—were responsible for their attitude about the topics, students reported mass media for eight of them. The other two topics found media in second place among sources.[60]

Mass media must be considered as an important variable in source-political-object relationships—if, for no other reason to provide a realistic mirror of the way in which children occupy a good deal of their time.

To ignore media in empirical political socialization research is to promote less rigor in our efforts to gain knowledge and to bring meaningful change to the education process. For it ultimately affects a wide spectrum of pedagogy, at least in America. For example, high school curricula, at least in part, will be influenced by the earlier research reported here. A review of the research presently being diffused in secondary education throughout the country asserts, "These conclusions should not be interpreted as meaning that the influence of mass media upon the process of political socialization is unimportant. Rather, the impact of the mass media should be viewed in terms of the complex social setting in which the media function."[61]

Like other assertions on media's role in the political process found in the literature of political socialization, these general comments are part of the "daisy-chain" of findings that have been cited by researchers since the latter part of the forties. Since they stem from "classic" studies, they are adopted without empirical verification with the variables being considered at a given time. This brings about an inferential linkage of mass communication and political socialization.

Roberta Sigel, described researchers' tendency to "label their evidence as 'indirect,' 'inferential,' and the like" as reflecting "the fact that the state of the discipline has not yet progressed enough to offer us much empirical data which lays bare the causal relationship of certain socialization experiences to subsequent political behavior."[62]

While the condition may be explainable, the consequences are not acceptable. Mass media, and television in particular, need to be included in political socialization research whenever sources of learning and elements of influence are being evaluated.

At this juncture it is clear that for two decades researchers interested in political socialization ignored the mass media. Conversely, researchers in mass media did not gain interest in political socialization for almost the same length of time. A reassessment of socialization findings appears to be in order.

Currently underway is an effort to assemble the interdisciplinary research in mass communication and political behavior.[63] This report will bring forth hypotheses for that reassessment.

NOTES

1. These figures are based on Census Bureau estimates contained in "Population Characteristics, Voter Participation in November 1972," Series P-20, no. 244, (December 1972).

2. Wilbur Schramm, Jack Lyle, and Edwin B. Parker, *Television in the Lives of Our Children* (Stanford, Calif.: Stanford University Press, 1961), p. 75; see also W. Schramm (ed.), *The Impact of Educational Television* (Urbana: University of Illinois Press, 1960), pp. 214-225.

3. Lotte Bailyn, "Mass Media and Children: A Study of Exposure Habits and Cognitive Effect," *Psychological Monographs* 73, no. 1 (1959): 1-48.

4. Urie Bronfenbrenner, *Two Worlds of Childhood—U.S. and U.S.S.R.* (New York: Russell Sage Foundation, 1970), p. 103.

5. Neil Hollander, "Adolescents and the War: the Sources of Socialization," *Journalism Quarterly* 48 (Autumn 1971): 472.

6. Joseph T. Klapper, *The Effects of Mass Communication* (Glencoe, Ill.: Free Press, 1960), p. 255.

7. Figures based on Census and Electronic Industries Association data.

8. *International Encyclopedia of the Social Sciences,* 1968 ed., Vol. 14, p. 551, s.v. "Political Socialization," by Fred I. Greenstein.

9. Herbert Hyman, *Political Socialization* (Glencoe, Ill.: Free Press, 1959); Roberta Sigel, ed., *Political Socialization: Its Role in the Political Process, The Annals* 361 (September 1965); John J. Patrick, *Political Socialization of American Youth: Implications for Secondary School Social Studies,* Research Bulletin No. 3 (Washington, D.C.: National Council For the Social Studies, 1967); and Roberta Sigel, *Learning About Politics: A Reader in Political Socialization* (New York: Random House, 1970); Richard Dawson and Kenneth Prewitt, *Political Socialization* (Boston: Little, Brown, 1969); and Special Issue on Political Socialization, *Harvard Educational Review* 38 (Summer 1968).

10. "Political Socialization," Greenstein.

11. Richard E. Dawson, "Political Socialization," in *Political Science Annual: An International Review,* vol. 1 ed. James A. Robinson (Indianapolis: Bobbs-Merrill, 1966), pp. 1-84.

12. Stephen L. Wasby, "The Impact of the Family on Politics: An Essay and Review of the Literature," *Family Life Coordinator* 15 (1966): pp. 3-23.

13. Fred I. Greenstein, *Children and Politics* (New Haven, Conn.: Yale University Press, 1965); Robert Hess and Judith Torney, *The Development of Political Attitudes in Children* (Garden City, N.Y.: Doubleday, Anchor Books, 1967; reprint ed., 1968); David Easton and Jack Dennis, *Children in the Political System: Origins of Political Legitimacy* (New York: McGraw-Hill, 1969); and Kenneth P. Langton, *Political Socialization* (New York: Oxford University Press, 1969). The first three studies report data obtained from American children; Langton's study is derived primarily from Jamaican school children.

14. Jack Dennis, "Recent Research on Political Socialization: A Bibliography of Published, Forthcoming, and Unpublished Works, Theses, and Dissertations and a Survey of Projects in Progress," prepared for the Theory and Research Working Committee on Political Socialization, Council on Civic Education, Lincoln Filene Center for Citizenship and Public Affairs, Tufts University, Medford, Massachusetts, 1967.

15. Hyman, *Political Socialization,* pp. 92-122.

16. Klapper, *Effects.*

17. Schramm, Lyle, and Parker, *TV in the Lives of Our Children.* The first study to deal with the impact of television on children was completed in England in 1958. See Hilde Himmelweit, A. N. Oppenheim, and Pamela Vince, *Television and the Child* (London: Oxford University Press, 1958).

18. Hyman, *Political Socialization,* p. 69.

19. Greenstein, *Children and Politics.*

20. Following Lasswell's paradigm of the general process of communication, Greenstein delineates five elements for study of political socialization. The third element reads [italics his]: "*The agents of political socialization.* Among the most obvious sources of political learning in the United States are parents, teachers, neighbors, members of the extended family, peers, and the media of communication and those whose views are transmitted through the media" (p. 13).

21. Seven mass communications questions were included. These were indices of television viewing, media preference, comic book reading, media content, and media gratification. No tabulation of responses was given. Greenstein, *Children and Politics,* pp. 192-193.

22. "By the date of the New Haven study, possession of a family television set evidently was close to universal. Only a handful of children reported that their family had no television set...." Greenstein, *Children and Politics,* p. 147.

23. Greenstein, *Children and Politics,* pp. 147-152. Greenstein records the changes in children's exemplars (models) from patriotic figures like George Washington to popular entertainers extending from 1902 to 1958. Also, he notes that in a 1944 study almost 45 percent chose exemplars from "Immediate environment figures" with only 8 percent selecting "entertainers"; conversely, Greenstein's 1958 data displays 2 percent for environment and 38 percent for entertainment figures (see table, p. 138). Extending DeFleur's interesting research on children's learning of occupational roles and knowledge suggests that television exemplars may be stereotyped and distorted. See Melvin L. DeFleur, "Occupational Roles As Portrayed On Television," *Public Opinion Quarterly* 28 (1964): 57-74; and Melvin L. DeFleur and Lois B. DeFleur, "The Relative Contribution of Television As A Learning Source For Children's Occupation Knowledge," *American Sociological Review* 32 (October 1967): 777-789.

24. These were not randomly selected and Greenstein did not use statistical inference, though he did generate some contingency analyses for class and sex. See Greenstein, *Children and Politics,* p. 200.

25. Herbert Hyman and Paul Sheatsley, "Some Reasons Why Information Campaigns Fail," *Public Opinion Quarterly* 11 (Fall 1947): 412-423; and Klapper, *Effects.*

26. Greenstein, *Children and Politics,* p. 185.

27. M. Kent Jennings, review of Greenstein, *Children and Politics, Public Opinion Quarterly* 30 (Summer 1966): 322-323.

28. Hess and Torney, *Political Attitudes in Children,* pp. 247-250.

29. Hess and Torney, *Political Attitudes in Children,* p. 296. "Reading about candidates in the mass media showed the sharpest increase with age (probably as children's reading skills improve). Exposure to the image of candidates in these publications was reported by more than 90 percent of the students in grades six through eight..." (p. 100).

30. Hess and Torney, *Political Attitudes in Children,* p. 42.

31. Hess and Torney, *Political Attitudes in Children,* p. 44.

32. Hess and Torney, *Political Attitudes in Children,* p. 85.

33. For a review of the televised debates, audience reactions, and positioning in the campaign, see Sidney Kraus (ed.), *The Great Debates: Background, Perspective, Effects* (Bloomington: Indiana University Press, 1962).

34. Hess and Torney, *Political Attitudes in Children,* p. 101.

35. Hess and Torney, *Political Attitudes in Children,* p. 101.

36. Roberta S. Sigel, review of Hess and Torney, *The Development of Political Attitudes in Children, Public Opinion Quarterly* 32 (Fall 1968): 534.

37. David O. Sears, review of Hess and Torney, *The Development of Political Attitudes in Children, Harvard Educational Review* 38 (Summer 1968): 571-77.

38. Bradley S. Greenberg and Brenda Dervin, *Use of the Mass Media by the Urban Poor* (New York: Praeger, 1970), p. 80.

39. Easton and Dennis, *Children in Political System.*

40. The Easton-Dennis book differed from the Hess-Torney effort by linking the data to a theoretical framework, largely gleaned from Easton's superb earlier works, *A Framework for Political Analysis* (Englewood Cliffs, N.J.: Prentice-Hall, 1965) and *A System Analysis of Political Life* (New York: Wiley, 1965). Theirs is a political systems approach while Hess and Torney's is one of psychological development.

41. Attention to *how* may, for example, center an investigation on television and the child's behavior using operant learning theory. Television, the independent variable (child's viewing considered as a reinforcing agent), would be assessed by dependent measures of the child's political beliefs and behaviors. Learning, in this approach, is an intervening variable. For an excellent discussion of the concept of learning in this context see Thomas J. Cook and Frank P. Scioli, Jr., "A Critique of the Learning Concept in Political Socialization Research," *Social Science Quarterly* 52 (March 1972): 949-962. Cook and Scioli posit that political socialization research contains "...a body of research which provides a description of *what* people have learned up to a certain point in time rather than an explanation of *how* they learned their political preferences" (p. 953).

42. Easton and Dennis, *Children in Political System,* pp. 151-158. This excerpt is part of a larger discussion on the child's visibility and salience of political authorities such as the President and policemen.

43. Easton and Dennis, *Children in Political System,* p. 158.

44. Fred I. Greenstein, review of Easton and Dennis, *Children in the Political System, Political Science Quarterly* 87 (March 1972): 98-102.

45. See Hyman, "Political Socialization."

46. See Greenstein, *Children and Politics;* and Hess and Torney, *Political Attitudes in Children.*

47. M. Kent Jennings, "Pre-Adult Orientations to Multiple Systems of Government," *Midwest Journal of Political Science* 11 (August 1967): 291-317.

48. M. Kent Jennings and Richard G. Niemi, "The Transmission of Political Values From Parent to Child," *American Political Science Review* 62 (March 1968): 183. For political influence of mother and father on daughters and sons and for a discussion of symbolic interactionist theory in political socialization research, see L. Eugene Thomas. "Political Attitude Congruence Between Politically Active Parents and College-Age Children: An Inquiry Into Family Political Socialization," *Journal of Marriage and the Family* 33 (May 1971): 375-386.

49. Kenneth P. Langton and M. Kent Jennings, "Political Socialization and the High School Civics Curriculum in the United States," *American Political Science Review* 62 (September 1968): 865.

50. Langton and Jennings, "High School Civics," p. 862.

51. M. Kent Jennings and Richard G. Niemi, "Patterns of Political Learning," *Harvard Educational Review* 38 (Summer 1968): 450.

52. The work of Schramm, Lyle, and Parker, *TV in the Lives of Our Children;* Hemmelweit, Oppenheim, and Vince, *TV and the Child;* DeFleur's "Occupational Roles"; and DeFleur and DeFleur, "Children's Occupation Knowledge," have been early attempts to assess television's impact on children. For a more thorough bibliography, see John D. Abel, "Television and Children: A Selective Bibliography of Use and Effects," *Journal of Broadcasting* 13 (Winter 1968-1969): 101-105; and John P. Murray *et al.,* "Television and the Child: A Comprehensive Research Bibliography," *Journal of Broadcasting* 16 (Winter 1971-1972): 3-20; see also Elihu Katz and David Foulkes, "On the Use of Mass Media as 'Escape': Clarification of a Concept," *Public Opinion Quarterly* 26 (Fall 1962): 377-388; see Ruth Young, "Television in the Lives of Our Parents," *Journal of Broadcasting* 14 (Winter 1969-1970): 37-46; and Bradley S. Greenberg and Joseph R. Dominick, "Racial and Social Class Differences in Teen-Agers' Use of Television," *Journal of Broadcasting* 13 (Fall 1969): 331-344; and David M. Smith, "Some Uses of Mass Media by 14 Year Olds," *Journal of Broadcasting* 16 (Winter 1971-1972): 37-50. The studies reviewed under "mass communications" in the *Annual Review of Psychology* 19 (1968) and 22 (1971) are helpful.

53. Norris R. Johnson, "Television and Politicization," Ph.D. dissertation, University of Kentucky, 1967.

54. Steven H. Chaffee, L. Scott Ward, and Leonard P. Tipton, "Mass Communication and Political Socialization," *Journalism Quarterly* 47 (Winter 1970): 658-659.

55. Chaffee, Ward, and Tipton, "Political Socialization," p. 655.

56. See discussion of Greenstein's exemplars and DeFleur's occupational roles in footnote 23.

57. Chaffee, Ward, and Tipton, "Political Socialization," p. 659.

58. Hollander, "Adolescents and the War," p. 479.

59. Joseph R. Dominick, "Television and Political Socialization," *Educational Broadcasting Review* 6 (February 1972): 51.

60. Sidney Kraus, "Mass Communication Behavior and Political Socialization Among Adolescents in a Presidential Primary" (in press, 1973).

61. Patrick, *Political Socialization of American Youth,* p. 48. See also Langton and Jennings, "High School Civics."

62. Roberta Sigel, "In Retrospect," in *The Annals,* ed. R. Sigel (1965), p. 129.

63. The John and Mary Markle Foundation has funded a research project to assess current knowledge on the effects of mass communication upon political behavior. Raw data, nonpublished and published studies, and other materials relating to the purpose of the project are welcomed by this writer.

THE AGENDA-SETTING FUNCTION OF THE PRESS

Maxwell E. McCombs and Donald L. Shaw

All I know is just what I read in the papers.
—*Will Rodgers*

We Americans cherish the notion that America is a land firmly based upon laws, not men, and that political choices are made within the arena of competing ideas and issues. Voters carefully weigh both candidates and issues in making political choices. Few of us, however, have direct access to candidates.

We learn from our friends and from the press, newspapers, television, magazines, radio. In a nation in which the average person spends nearly three hours a day viewing television and another half hour reading a newspaper—to mention only two media—it is not surprising that we sometimes ask if the press, or "mass media," to use the term of many, does not do more than merely relay news between candidates and voters.

Does the press not actually create political and social issues by news choices made day after day? Publicity is at least potential power. Historian Daniel Boorstin has pointed out that it has become possible to achieve widespread (if not always long-lasting) fame merely by appearing in the national press, particularly television. You can become famous, so to speak, by becoming well known! Can this be true of political candidates or issues?

We are quite aware the press daily brings us news information. We may be less

From The Emergence of American Political Issues: The Agenda-Setting Function of the Press, *pp. 1-18. Edited by Maxwell McCombs and Donald L. Shaw. St. Paul, Minn.: West, 1977. Copyright 1977 by West Publishing Company, reprinted by permission.*

conscious of the way this news over time may add up to shape our ideas about important issues or personalities. Political leaders certainly are aware of the role of the press in campaigns. They usually adapt to the practices and prejudices of the press.

In 1968 Richard Nixon did what many would have regarded as impossible only a few years earlier. He returned from the politically dead to become President in an election squeaker. It was, some said, a "new" Nixon, or as political reporter Joe McGinness put it more simply, a Nixon more able to understand, or use, the press. Mr. Nixon was more approachable. On occasion he even smiled at reporters. He was seen in a bathrobe. Mr. Nixon was—the reporters themselves had to admit it—human. By a close vote he won over Senator Hubert Humphrey.

By 1972, President Nixon won re-election over Democratic Senator George McGovern with one of the largest majorities in history. When it came to voting, those whom President Nixon from time to time had loosely referred to as the silent majority were noisy enough. In that campaign, President Nixon spent only a small amount of time on the campaign trail. Instead he used a carefully constructed media campaign which emphasized selected issues and urged voters to re-elect the President.

Through press news, comment, and advertising, information about issues and personalities spreads throughout the land. But our suspicion remains: does the press merely relay information? Is it only a transmission belt? Or, by exercising conscious and unconscious choice, does the press not have the ability to spotlight certain issues for a short while, hammer away at others over time, and simply ignore still others? This book examines that agenda-setting power of the press, the hypothesis that the press itself has some power to establish an agenda of political issues which both candidates and voters come to regard as important.

THE POPULAR VIEW

Certainly in the popular view mass communication exerts tremendous influence over human affairs. The ability of television, newspapers, magazines, movies, radio, and a whole host of new communications technologies to mold the public mind and significantly influence the flow of history is a widely ascribed power. In the political arena, candidates spend substantial sums for the services of image-makers—a new kind of mass communication artist and technocrat who presumably works magic on the voters via the mass media.

Early social scientists shared with historians, politicians, and the general public a belief in the ability of mass communication to achieve significant, perhaps staggering, social and political effects. But beginning with the benchmark Erie County survey conducted during the 1940 presidential campaign,[1] precise, quantitative research on the effects of mass communication in election campaigns, public information campaigns, and on numerous public attitudes soon gave the academic world a jaundiced view of the power of mass communication. From a theory of massive communication effects—most everyone's view in 1940—the academic world moved 180 degrees in less than two decades. Summing up the first two decades of empirical mass communication research, Joseph Klapper in 1960 listed two major conclusions in his book, *The Effects of Mass Communication:*

1. Mass communication ordinarily does not serve as a necessary and sufficient cause of audience effects, but rather functions among and through a nexus of mediating factors and influences.

2. These mediating factors are such that they typically render mass communication a contributory agent, but not the sole cause, in a process of reinforcing the existing conditions....[2]

We moved from an all-powerful *1984* view to the *law of minimal consequences,* a notion that the media had almost no effect, in two decades! But despite the "law," interest in mass communication has proliferated during the past 15 years. Political practitioners, especially, continue to emphasize the use of mass communication in election campaigns.[3] Surely all this is not due simply to cultural lag in spreading the word about the law of minimal consequences. Rather it is because *mass communication does in fact play a significant political role.* This is not to say that the early research was wrong. It simply was limited. To gain precision, science must probe carefully circumscribed areas. Unfortunately, the early research on mass communication concentrated on attitude change. Given the popular assumption of mass media effects, it was not a surprising choice. But the chain of effects that result from exposure to mass communication has a number of links preceding attitude and opinion change. In sequence, the effects of exposure to communication are generally catalogued as:

Awareness→Information→Attitudes→Behavior

Early research chose as its strategy a broad flanking movement striking far along this chain of events. But as the evidence showed, the direct effects of mass communication on attitudes and behavior are minimal. Klapper's summary, which reflects the law of minimal consequences, is quite correct in its conclusion about the effects of mass communication on attitudes and opinions. So in recent years scholars interested in mass communication have concentrated on earlier points in the communication process: awareness and information. Here the research has been most fruitful in documenting significant social effects resulting from exposure to mass communication. People do learn from mass communication.

Not only do they learn factual information about public affairs and what is happening in the world, they also learn how much importance to attach to an issue or topic from the emphasis placed on it by the mass media.

Considerable evidence has accumulated that editors and broadcasters play an important part in shaping our social reality as they go about their day-to-day task of choosing and displaying news. In reports both prior to and during political campaigns, the news media to a considerable degree determine the important issues. In other words, the media set the "agenda" for the campaign.

This impact of the mass media—the ability to effect cognitive change among individuals, to structure their thinking—has been labeled the *agenda-setting function of mass communication.* Here may lie the most important effect of mass communication, its ability to mentally order and organize our world for us. In short, the mass media may not be successful in telling us what to think, but they are stunningly successful in telling us what to think *about.*[4]

ASSERTIONS OF AGENDA-SETTING

The general notion of agenda-setting—the ability of the media to influence the salience of events in the public mind—has been part of our political culture for at least half a century. Recall that the opening chapter of Walter Lippmann's 1922 book *Public Opinion* is titled: "The World Outside and the Pictures in Our Heads." As Lippmann pointed out, it is, of course, the mass media which dominate in the creation of these pictures of public affairs.[5]

More recently this assumption of media power has been asserted by presidential observer Theodore White in *The Making of the President, 1972.*

*The power of the press in America is a
primordial one. It sets the agenda of public
discussion; and this sweeping political power is
unrestrained by any law. It determines what people
will talk and think about—an authority that in other
nations is reserved for tyrants, priests, parties and
mandarins.*[6]

The press does more than bring these
issues to a level of political awareness among
the public. The idea of agenda-setting asserts
that the priorities of the press to some degree
become the priorities of the public. What the
press emphasizes is in turn emphasized
privately and publicly by the audiences of the
press. As political scientist Robert Lane has
suggested:

*The common viewing, listening, and reading
patterns of a large potion of the public tend, I
believe, to set for the nation some common foci of
attention, some common agendas of discussion. A
reference to an issue or to a presentation of an
issue is likely, in most social sets, to meet with
recognition because of the overlapping exposure
patterns of the members of these sets. Of course,
people have different private and group agendas
and these make for varied arenas of discourse, but
the tendency of the media to homogenize sets
means the variation is reduced, and the national
agenda develops a meaningful cross-set audience
and dialogue.*[7]

COGNITIVE EFFECTS
OF MASS COMMUNICATION

This concept of an agenda-setting function of
the press redirects our attention to the
cognitive aspects of mass communication, to
attention, awareness, and information. While
there was justification for earlier emphasis on
attitude change,[8] it was precisely that
emphasis on the affective aspects of mass
communication that led to the law of minimal
consequences. However, the history of mass
communication research from the 1940 Erie
County study to the present decade can be
viewed as a movement away from short-range
effects on attitudes and toward long-range
effects on cognitions.[9]

Attitudes concern our feelings of being for
or against a political position or figure.
Cognition concerns our knowledge and
beliefs about political objects. The agenda-
setting function of mass communication
clearly falls in this new tradition of cognitive
outcomes of mass communication. Perhaps
more than any other aspect of our
environment, the political arena—all those
issues and persons about whom we hold
opinions and knowledge—is a secondhand
reality. Especially in national politics, we have
little personal or direct contact. Our
knowledge comes primarily from the mass
media. For the most part, we know only those
aspects of national politics considered
newsworthy enough for transmission through
the mass media.

Even television's technological ability to
make us spectators for significant political
events does not eliminate the secondhand
nature of our political cognitions. Television
news is edited reality just as print news is an
edited version of reality. And even on those
rare occasions when events are presented in
their entirety, the television experience is not
the same as the eyewitness experience.[10]

Our knowledge of political affairs is based
on a tiny sample of the real political world.
That real world shrinks as the news media
decide what to cover and which aspects to
transmit in their reports, and as audiences
decide to which news messages they will
attend.

Yet, as Lippmann pointed out, our
political responses are made to that tiny
replica of the real world, the
pseudoenvironment, which we have
fabricated and assembled almost wholly from
mass media materials. The concept of
agenda-setting emphasizes one very
important aspect of this pseudoenvironment,
the *salience* or amount of emphasis accorded
the various political elements and issues vying
for public attention.

Many commentators have observed that there is an agenda-setting function of the press, and Lippmann long ago eloquently described the necessary connection between mass communication and individual political cognitions. But like much of our folk wisdom about politics and human behavior, it was not put to empirical test by researchers for over half a century.

EMPIRICAL EVIDENCE OF AGENDA-SETTING

The first empirical attempt at verification of the agenda-setting function of the mass media was carried out by McCombs and Shaw during the 1968 U.S. presidential election.[11] Among undecided voters in Chapel Hill, North Carolina there were substantial correlations between the political issues emphasized in the news media and what the voters regarded as the key issues in that election. The voters' beliefs about what were the major issues facing the country reflected the composite of the press coverage, even though the three presidential contenders in 1968 placed widely divergent emphasis on the issues. This suggests that voters—at least undecided voters—pay some attention to all the political news in the press regardless of whether it is about or originated with a favored candidate. This contradicts the concepts of selective exposure and selective perception, ideas which are central to the law of minimal consequences. Selective exposure and selective perception suggest that persons attend most closely to information which they find congenial and supportive.

In fact, further analysis of the 1968 Chapel Hill survey showed that among those undecided voters with leanings toward one of the three candidates, there was less agreement with the news agenda based on their preferred candidate's statements than with the news agenda based on all three candidates.

While the 1968 Chapel Hill study was the first empirical investigation based specifically on agenda-setting, there is other scholarly evidence in the mass communication/political behavior literature which can be interpreted in agenda-setting terms. Let's briefly consider several examples.

The first example comes from the 1948 Elmira study, research which cemented the strong role of interpersonal rather than mass communication in the election process. For an optimum view of the agenda-setting influence of the press, one should examine those Elmira voters with minimal interpersonal contact. As Berelson, Lazarsfeld, and McPhee noted:

... about one-fifth of our sample did not know the politics of any of their three closest friends in August. Such people have so little political content in their normal social interaction that what little they do learn about politics is largely independent of their social surroundings most of the time. Therefore, they are more likely than their fellows to be 'blown about' by the political winds of the times, in a way especially independent of their social surroundings.[12]

In other words, for those voters the political agenda suggested by the media is not mediated, interpreted, or confronted by interpersonal sources of influence. These voters would seem especially open to the agenda-setting influence of the press.

And the influence was there. These Elmira voters moved with the trend of the times more than did the other voters. Like the national Democratic trend that mounted during the 1948 campaign, these Elmira voters moved rapidly into the Democratic column. The cues were there in the media for all. But persons without the conservative brake of interpersonal contacts moved most rapidly with the national trend reported in the media.

The second example of agenda-setting comes from a study of county voting patterns in an Iowa referendum.[13] In this example it is easy to see the agenda-setting effects of both mass media and interpersonal news sources.

The question before the voters was calling a constitutional convention to reapportion legislative districts. Since large counties stood to gain and small counties to lose from reapportionment, the study anticipated a strong correlation between county population and proportion of votes in favor of the convention. In short, it was hypothesized that counties would vote their self-interest. And, overall, this was strikingly the case. Across all counties, the correlation is +.87 between county population and vote.

But now let us consider whether this pattern is facilitated by the presence of agenda-setting institutions. Two sources of heightened awareness were considered: a citizens' committee in favor of the convention and a daily newspaper in the county.

In the 41 counties where the citizens' committee was active, the correlation was +.92 between vote and population. In the 58 counties without such a group, the correlation was only +.59. Similar findings are reported for the presence or absence of a local daily newspaper. In the 38 counties with a local daily, the correlation was +.92. In the 61 counties without a daily, the correlation was only +.56.

Each agenda-setting source made a considerable difference in the outcome. What about their combined impact? In 28 counties with both a local daily and a citizens' committee the correlation was +.92. Where only one of these sources was present, the correlation declined to +.40; and when neither agenda-setter was present, the correlation declined to +.21.

Self-interest may have motivated many voters. But unless the issue was high on the agenda—placed there via the newspaper and local citizens' committee—this motivation simply did not come into play.

A similar "necessary condition" role for agenda-setting is found in a study of the distribution of knowledge among populations.[14] Generally, there is a knowledge gap between social classes concerning topics of public affairs, typically documented by a rather substantial correlation between level of education and knowledge of public affairs. That is to say, as level of education increases, so does the amount of knowledge about public affairs. But as communication scientist

Phillip Tichenor and his colleagues discovered, the strength of this correlation, at least for some topics, is a direct function of the amount of media coverage. They found a monotonic relationship between media coverage and the strength of the education/knowledge correlation. The more the press covers a topic, the more an audience—especially audience members with more education—learn.

THE CONCEPT OF AGENDA-SETTING

Agenda-setting not only asserts a positive relationship between what various communication media emphasize and what voters come to regard as important, it also considers this influence as an inevitable by-product of the normal flow of news.

Each day editors and news directors—the gate-keepers in news media systems—must decide which items to pass and which to reject. Furthermore, the items passed through the gate are not treated equally when presented to the audience. Some are used at length, others severely cut. Some are lead-off items on a newscast. Others follow much later. Newspapers clearly state the value they place on the salience of an item through headline size and placement within the newspaper—anywhere from the lead item on page one to placement at the bottom of a column on page 66.

Agenda-setting asserts that audiences learn these saliences from the news media, incorporating a similar set of weights into their personal agendas. Even though these saliences are largely a by-product of journalism practice and tradition, they nevertheless are attributes of the messages transmitted to the audience. And as the idea of agenda-setting asserts, they are among the most important message attributes transmitted to the audience.

This notion of the agenda-setting function of the mass media is a relational concept specifying a strong positive relationship between the emphases of mass communication and the salience of these topics to the individuals in the audience. This concept is stated in causal terms: increased salience of a topic or issue in the mass media influences (causes) the salience of that topic or issue among the public.

Agenda-setting as a concept is not limited to the correspondence between salience of topics for the media and the audience. We can also consider the saliency of various attributes of these objects (topics, issues, persons, or whatever) reported in the media. To what extent is our view of an object shaped or influenced by the picture sketched in the media, especially by those attributes which the media deem newsworthy? Some have argued, for example, that our views of city councils as institutions are directly influenced by press reporting, with the result that these local governing groups are perceived to have more expertise and authority than they actually possess.[15]

Consideration of agenda-setting in terms of the salience of both topics and their attributes allows the concept of agenda-setting to subsume many similar ideas presented in the past. The concepts of status-conferral, stereotyping, and image-making all deal with the salience of objects or attributes. And research on all three have linked these manipulations of salience to the mass media.

Status-conferral, the basic notion of press agentry in the Hollywood sense, describes the ability of the media to influence the prominence of an individual (object) in the public eye.

On the other hand, the concept of stereotyping concerns the prominence of attributes: All Scots are thrifty! All Frenchmen are romantic! Stereotyping has been criticized as invalid characterization of objects because of its overemphasis on a few selected traits. And the media repeatedly have been criticized for their perpetuation of stereotypes, most recently of female roles in our society.

The concept of image-making, now part of our political campaign jargon, covers the manipulation of the salience of both objects and attributes. A political image-maker is concerned with increasing public familiarity with his candidate (status-conferral) and/or increasing the perceived prominence of certain candidate attributes.

In all cases, we are dealing with the basic question of agenda-setting research: How does press coverage influence our perception of objects and their attributes?

ISSUE SALIENCE AND VOTING

Political issues have become salient as a factor in voter behavior in recent years. The importance of party identification, long the dominant variable in analysis of voter decisions, has been reduced. This stems both from a conceptual rethinking of voter behavior and from an empirical trend.

The role of party identification as the major predictor of how a voter would cast his presidential ballot now appears to be an empirical generalization limited to the 1940s and 1950s. By the 1960s whatever underlying conditions that gave rise to this dominance appear to have shifted and significant declines in the predictive and explanatory power of party identification begin to appear on the empirical record.[16]

Conceptually, issues also began to play a greater role in the analysis of voter decision-making. In 1960 the Michigan Survey Research Center, whose earlier work has provided much of the evidence for the key role of party identification, added a new set of open-ended questions to its interview schedule seeking information about the voter's own issue concerns—that is, those issues which were salient to the individual voter—and the perceived link between those issues and the parties.

Analysis of these questions reveals a major role for issue salience in the presidential vote decision. For example, in predicting voting choice in 1964 the weights were .39 for candidate image, .27 for party identification, and .23 for issues. (Each weight controls for the influence of the two other factors.) While candidate image had the greatest weight in 1964 (a plausible outcome with Lyndon Johnson and Barry Goldwater, who were associated with extreme positions, as the contenders), issues also had a strong effect.[17] As political scientist David RePass notes, "The remarkable thing that emerges from this analysis is that *salient issues had almost as much weight as party identification in predicting voting choice.*"[18] And, as if in anticipation of the findings from research on the agenda-setting function of the mass media, he also noted that while it was not easy to predict exactly which issues would be salient in a particular election, "the public does seem to respond most to current and recurring news and events."[19]

The 1968 Comparative State Election Project (CSEP), conducted by the Institute for Research in Social Science at the University of North Carolina, also gave issues a major conceptual role in the analysis.[20] CSEP examined the "distance" between each voter's attitude and the position of each presidential candidate. Both for the state voter cohorts and nationally, issue proximity was a more powerful predictor of presidential vote than party identification. While explicit attempts to weight the issues for personal salience to the voter failed to enhance their predictive strength, Beardsley[21] feels that this is a methodological artifact.

In 1972 issues took center stage. Summing up its analysis of that election, the Survey Research Center concluded: "Ideology and issue voting in that election provide a means for better explaining the unique elements of the contest than do social characteristics, the candidates, the events of the campaign, political alienation, cultural orientations, or partisan identification."[22]

Voters do respond to the issues. The new evidence on the impart of issues appearing in the late 1960s and early 1970s provided empirical vindication for V. O. Key, Jr.'s view that "voters are not fools." Key had long contended that voters in fact responded to the issues and to the events creating and surrounding those issues.[23] Again, anticipating the concept of an agenda-setting function of the press operating across time to define political reality, Key argued that the "impact of events from the inauguration of an administration to the onset of the next presidential campaign may affect far more voters than the fireworks of the campaign itself."[24] Even the benchmark Erie County survey found that events between 1936 and 1940 changed more than twice as many votes as did the 1940 presidential campaign itself.

It is, of course, the press that largely structures voters' perceptions of political reality ... The press can exert considerable influence on which issues make up the agenda for any particular election. Not only can the press influence the nature of the political arena in which a campaign is conducted but, on occasion, it can define (albeit inadvertently) an agenda which accrues to the benefit of one party. To a considerable degree the art of politics in a democracy is the art of determining which issue dimensions are of major interest to the public or can be made salient in order to win public support.

In 1952 the Republicans, led by Dwight Eisenhower, successfully exploited the three "K's"—Korea, Corruption, and Communism—in order to regain the White House after a hiatus of twenty years. The prominence of those three issues, cultivated by press reports extending over many months and accented by partisan campaign advertising, worked against the incumbent Democratic party. Nor is 1952 an isolated example. One of the major campaign techniques discussed by political analyst Stanley Kelley in *Professional Public Relations and Political Power* is nothing more than increasing the salience of an issue that works to an incumbent's disadvantage.[25]

These are what social scientist Angus Campbell and his colleagues[26] call *valence issues* in contrast to our usual consideration of *position issues* on which voters take various pro or con stances. A valence issue is simply a proposition, condition, or belief that is positively or negatively valued by all the voters. At least two, if not all three, of the 1952 K's were valence issues. No one was for crime or corruption. When valence issues are the case it is simply a matter of where the credit or blame is to be assigned. Apparently in 1952 enough voters assigned the blame to the Democrats to win the election for the Republicans. To the extent that the press (via its agenda-setting function) has a direct impact on the outcome of a particular election, it is likely to be through the medium of valance issues which directly accrue to the advantage or disadvantage of one political party. But ... that is only one facet of the agenda-setting function of mass communication.

NOTES

1. Paul Lazarsfeld, Bernard Berelson, and Hazel Gaudet, *The People's Choice* (New York: Columbia University Press, 1948).

2. Joseph Klapper, *The Effects of Mass Communication* (Glencoe, Ill.: Free Press, 1960), p. 8.

3. Ray Hiebert, Robert Jones, John Lorenz, and Ernest Lotito (eds.), *The Political Image Merchants: Strategies in the New Politics* (Washington, DC: Acropolis Books, 1971).

4. See Bernard C. Cohen, *The Press and Foreign Policy* (Princeton: Princeton University Press, 1963), p. 13; also Lee Becker, Maxwell McCombs, and Jack McLeod, "The Development of Political Cognitions," in ed. *Political Communication, vol.4,* Steven H. Chaffee, Sage Annual Reviews of Communication Research (Beverly Hills, Calif.: Sage Publications, 1975), pp. 21-63.

5. Walter Lippmann, *Public Opinion* (New York: Macmillan, 1922).

6. Theodore White, *The Making of the President, 1972* (New York: Bantam Books, 1973), p. 327.

7. Robert E. Lane, "Alienation, Protest and Rootless Politics in the Seventies," in Hiebert, Jones, Lorenz, and Lotito, op. cit., pp. 286-287.

8. Maxwell McCombs and Thomas Bowers, "Television's Effects on Political Behavior," in *The Fifth Season: How TV Influences the Ways People Behave,* ed. George Comstock *et al.* (Santa Monica, Calif.: Rand Corporation, in press).

9. Maxwell McCombs, "Mass Communication in Political Campaigns: Information, Gratification, and Persuasion," in ed. F. Gerald Kline and Phillip J. Tichenor *Current Perspectives in Mass Communication Research,* vol. 1, Sage Annual Reviews of Communication Research (Beverly Hills, Calif.: Sage Publications, 1972).

10. Kurt Lang and Gladys Engel Lang, *Politics and Television* (Chicago: Quadrangle, 1968).

11. Maxwell E. McCombs and Donald L. Shaw, "The Agenda-Setting Function of Mass Media," *Public Opinion Quarterly* 36 (Summer 1972): 176-187.

12. Bernard Berelson, Paul Lazarsfeld, and William McPhee, *Voting* (Chicago: University of Chicago Press, 1954), pp. 138-139.

13. David Arnold and David Gold, "The Facilitation Effect of Social Environment," *Public Opinion Quarterly* 28 (Fall 1964): 513-516.

14. G. A. Donahue, Phillip J. Tichenor, and C. N. Olien, "Mass Media and the Knowledge Gap: A Hypothesis Reconsidered," *Communication Research* 2 (January 1975): 3-23.

15. David L. Paletz, Peggy Reichert, and Barbara McIntyre, "How the Media Support Local Governmental Authority," *Public Opinion Quarterly* 35 (Spring 1971): 80-92.

16. Edward C. Dreyer, "Media Use and Electoral Choices: Some Political Consequences of Information Exposure," *Public Opinion Quarterly* 35 (Winter 1971-1972): 544-553; also Walter D. Burnham, "The End of American Party Politics," *Transaction* 7 (December 1969): 12-22.

17. David E. RePass, "Issue Salience and Party Choice," *American Political Science Review* 65 (June 1971): 389-400.

18. Repass, "Issue Salience," p. 400.

19. Repass, "Issue Salience," p. 393.

20. David M. Kovenock, James W. Prothro, and associates (eds.) *Explaining the Vote* (Chapel Hill, N.C.: Institute for Research in Social Science, 1973).

21. Philip L. Beardsley, "The Methodology of the Electoral Analysis: Models and Measurement," in *Explaining the Vote,* ed. Kovenock, Prothro, and associates p. 43.

22. A. H. Miller, W. E. Miller, A. S. Raine, and T. A. Brown, "A Majority Party in Disarray: Policy Polarization in the 1972 Election" mimeographed report, University of Michigan.

23. V. O. Key, Jr., *The Responsible Electorate* (New York: Vintage Books, 1966).

24. Key, *Electorate,* p. 9.

25. Stanley Kelley, *Professional Public Relations and Political Power* (Baltimore: John Hopkins Press, 1956).

26. Angus Campbell, Philip E. Converse, Warren E. Miller, and Donald E. Stokes, *Elections and the Political Order* (New York: Wiley, 1966), p. 170.

RECENT POLITICAL THEORY ON MASS MEDIA POTENTIAL IN POLITICAL CAMPAIGNS

L. John Martin

"He's the media candidate," Senator Henry M. Jackson is reported to have said of Governor Jimmy Carter a few days before the Pennsylvania primary, the results of which caused the senator to withdraw from the 1976 presidential race.

It [the press] feeds on itself. They decide he's got something unique. It has nothing to do with concrete, specific programs. They find him fascinating. The press can't nail him down on anything. They try, but they don't seem able to do it.... The press keeps facing a situation it can't quite solve.[1]

The power of the pen and of the press is conventional wisdom that goes back hundreds of years. Rosencrantz in *Hamlet* says that "many wearing rapiers are afraid of goosequills." But when this purported axiom was subjected to scientific investigation, doubts began to be expressed about its accuracy. Frank Luther Mott, the journalism historian, determined that, in the 35 presidential election campaigns from 1796 to 1940, the American press gave its majority support to the winning candidate 18 times and to the losing candidate 17 times.[2] Chance could not have played a more even-handed role.

Reprinted from "Recent Political Theory on Mass Media Potential in Political Campaigns" by L. John Martin in volume no. 427 of THE ANNALS of the American Academy of Political and Social Science. Copyright © 1976 by THE ANNALS; reprinted by permission.

HYPODERMIC THEORIES

Yet no one to the present day believes that the press is powerless. In fact, the power of the press is implicit in the idea of harnessing the mass media to perform important social, economic, military, and political tasks—a thought that occurred to the U.S. government in World War II, when it had to train a huge citizen army in a hurry. The Army's Education and Information Division needed to know which of the various available communication techniques were most effective in isolation, in sequence, and in combination. To answer these questions, an experimental section was organized under Yale psychologist Carl I. Hovland within the research branch of the division to study, among other things, the differential effects and effectiveness of the mass media.

Hovland and his staff conducted their empirical research in the context of a paradigm suggested by political scientist Harold D. Lasswell to describe the communication process: "Who says what to whom with what effect?" The studies dealt with the persuasiveness of the different media, but were later continued by the same group of psychologists at Yale University to include the effectiveness of various types of messages and communicators. The Yale Communication Research Program, as it was designated, had for its underpinnings Lasswell's "hypodermic model" of the communication process which, at least implicitly, suggests that communication is something someone does to someone else. The only question in this approach is, how does one vary the types of communicator (who) or the kinds of messages (what) or audiences (whom) to maximize the effectiveness of the process (what effect)? And that is what these communication researchers addressed themselves to for another 15 years or so.

The conclusion that many of them arrived at was that, all other things being equal, the more personal a medium the more efficiently persuasive it is. Thus, face-to-face communication is more effective than television, which is more effective than film, radio, and print—in that order.

But quite apart from the fact that this was not always the outcome of their research, all other things are seldom equal except in the laboratory. The difference between people in their natural habitats and people in a laboratory experiment was recognized by Hovland himself, who more than anyone was responsible for mass communication experiments in the laboratory. The reason, he said, you can prove so much more in the laboratory than in a survey of people in a real-life situation is that in the latter case people who have exposed themselves to a message did so voluntarily and many of them were on the persuader's side to begin with. In an experiment, opinion change is often measured minutes after the exposure, when the impact is greatest. Experiments are frequently carried out in classrooms where student-subjects are more receptive to the messages, which in any case are selected for their likelihood to show change.[3]

Gerhart D. Wiebe, a research psychologist for CBS and later dean of the School of Public Communication at Boston University, developed deductively a rationale for the greater effectiveness of more personal media; then he tested his theory empirically. He pointed out that the reason television is more vivid, more suggestive of "immediate reality" than radio, which in turn is more real than print, is that radio is one symbol system removed from reality (the spoken word), while print is two symbol systems—two levels of abstraction—removed. This is because the printed word is a symbol for the spoken word, which in turn is a symbol for reality. He said that television is experienced in an intimate frame of reference, while newspaper accounts are perceived in a distant frame of reference.[4] What led to the undoing of Senator Joseph R. McCarthy, in Wiebe's opinion, was that he was brought into an intimate frame of reference through the televising of the Army-McCarthy hearings. Wiebe contrasted this to the war in Indochina which, in 1954, was still being experienced in a distant frame of reference. Vietnam had not yet been brought into every American's living room by massive television coverage.

Then, in 1960, Joseph T. Klapper reviewed the research findings (mainly of the previous two decades) and came to the conclusion that "mass communication *ordinarily* does not serve as a necessary and sufficient cause of audience effects, but rather functions among and through a nexus of mediating factors and influences."[5] This was not a new idea. It had been noted by Hovland himself in a 1954 article referring to Mott's 1944 study and to a 1926 study by George A. Lundberg. Hovland had to admit that "press support of presidential candidates seems to bear no relationship to their success at the polls."[6] It was just that the hope had lingered that somehow a researcher might hit on the right formula—one that would guarantee a gambler's chance to those who are willing to invest their money in mass media time and space to cajole their fellow human beings into taking a desired line of action. But the best that Klapper could offer was the statement that "the efficacy of mass communication in creating opinion....can be guaged only in reference to issues on which, at the time of exposure, people are *known to have no opinion at all.*"[7]

INFORMATION-SEEKING THEORIES

What put researchers on a new track was a series of consistency theories developed in the 1950s, especially Leon Festinger's cognitive dissonance theory. Simply put, these theories stated that people like their beliefs and judgments about things to be consistent with one another. To reduce the dissonance created by inconsistencies, people expose themselves to facts, events, and judgments through communication or selectively shut out such communication to avoid dissonance. They might even selectively perceive, or misperceive, and selectively retain information to the same end.

Consistency theories switched the Lasswellian paradigm around. No longer were communication specialists concerned about who says what to whom, since this is immaterial if the "whom" in the paradigm is unable or unwilling to receive the message. The question was, who needs to receive what messages from whom? The emphasis was on the seeking and avoiding of information rather than on the transmission of instruction or urging of opinion change. Furthermore, a distinction began to be made between informational communication and persuasive communication. The mass media had been weighed in the balance and found clearly wanting in persuasiveness—at least in the short run. People don't do things or change their attitudes or even opinions simply because they are asked to or told to by an individual, directly or through the mass media.

The change in perspective on the communication process also led to a rethinking of the findings of the relative effectiveness of the different mass media. Pollster Elmo Roper had for years been asking people questions about the medium they consider most informative and the one they believe to be the most credible. He found television to be the medium more than half the audience would want to keep if they had to give up all other media. Television also was the most credible medium in the Roper poll. Over the years, television has consistently been rated the major source of information about national candidates by 60 to 65 percent of the public, with newspapers being rated first by only a fourth to a third of the public. For information about state candidates, television has a much narrower edge over newspapers, while on local candidates, newspapers are considered a better source than television by more people. Friends and relatives are an important source of information only on local candidates (the major source for around one in five). Radio and magazines are rated a major source of information about political

candidates—national, state, or local—by fewer than 10 percent of the population.[8]

In the light of information-seeking theories, communication specialist Alex S. Edelstein studied audiences in both the United States and Yugoslavia and concluded that sources of information were evaluated not in terms of their trustworthiness or credibility but in terms of their content, breadth of perception, and availability. Television provided the greatest breadth of perception, and if seeing was important to the audience, television was the preferred medium. Newspapers provided the greatest breadth of content and the most time to think, while radio was the most available medium.[9] Clearly, this view is based on a "uses and gratifications" theory rather than a hypodermic theory—the user of information being the one who determines what medium to use. He also makes the judgment about its believability, depending on whether it gratifies his needs. It is not the communicator who manipulates his medium or his message and its environment to create a desired effect.

AGENDA-SETTING FUNCTION

One bothersome problem with an audience-initiated and controlled communication model is that it appears to leave the man with a message—a political candidate, for instance—in an impotent, supplicant position. His target will attend to his message only if it does not upset the target's existing beliefs and judgments. In other words, the politician would tend to be preaching to the already converted: and, in fact, one of the rules of thumb of persuasive communication (such as political campaigning and propaganda) is that "the people you may want most in your audience are often least likely to be there."[10] This follows logically from the selective exposure hypothesis mentioned above and supports consistency theories.

While this rule is not difficult to rationalize, it leaves one dissatisfied. Don't tell us, we feel like saying, that the mass media have absolutely no power beyond merely agreeing with their audience—since, after all, people by this rule expose themselves only to those parts of the press with which they already agree. Intuitively—since each of us can think of occasions when the mass media have influenced us or when we think we were influenced—we tend to reject this conclusion.[11] And it is here that communication theorists have recently come up with a new explanatory proposition—they don't yet call it a theory. The proposition involves once and for all separating persuasive from informational communication. The underlying assumption is that gaining new knowledge has little to do with how that knowledge will be used. It might result in an interpretation that is favorable to the thrust of the message or one that is unfavorable.

The text is taken from political scientist Bernard C. Cohen, who pointed out that "the press may not be successful much of the time in telling people what to think, but it is stunningly successful in telling its readers what to think about."[12] Picking up this theme, two communication specialists, Maxwell E. McCombs and Donald L. Shaw, in a landmark study in 1972 showed that undecided voters in the 1968 presidential election tended to give the same priorities to issues in the campaign as was given to the issues by the news media.[13] They concluded that the reason for this was that the press sets the agenda for its audiences. It provides the facts, for the most part, that make up the cognitive world of each individual. This agenda-setting power of the press is directive rather than reactive. The press does not merely reflect developments which also influence the general public in the same way. The press actually picks certain issues to play up at times that do not necessarily parallel the significance of those events.

G. Ray Funkhouser showed that this is so by doing a content analysis of three weekly newsmagazines for the 1960s. The number of articles on such issues as the Vietnam War, race relations, student unrest, and inflation peaked in years when the events themselves were not at their highest point of importance or activity. What is especially noteworthy and supportive of the agenda-setting role of the press is that the peaks in news coverage coincided with peaks in the proportion of

people who picked these issues as the "most important problem facing America" in Gallup polls. On the other hand, they were not the issues that people felt the government should devote most of its attention to. Funkhouser concluded that "the average person takes the media's word for what the 'issues' are, whether or not he personally has any involvement or interest in them."[14] And, one might add, he rates them as important whether or not they have the salience in reality that the press gives them.

All this agrees very well with what information-seeking theorists had been saying for some time and with what those basing their research on the agenda-setting paradigm are now saying. The mass media tend to inform rather than to change attitudes. The conclusions drawn from the information derived from the media may direct attitudes one way or another, and it is only when nothing is competing from one's own past experience that media experience becomes real and their values are adopted as one's own. This, however, happens very infrequently in our multimedia society.

Theoretically, of course, it could happen to people who do not expose themselves to many media or who do not take an interest in political issues. Their political experience would be limited and they would be inclined to accept a line proposed by the media. But the likelihood of their exposure to an issue raised by the media would be equally limited. Philip E. Converse of the Survey Research Center at the University of Michigan has found that, on most issues, only about 20 percent of the public can be termed an "issue public" that has a genuine opinion based on knowledge. While only about 10 percent of the public will answer "don't know" to an opinion question, for another 70 percent of the population, response sequences over time are totally random."[15]

NEED FOR ORIENTATION

Non-attendance to any side of a political issue discussed in the media is a far more important deterrent to media impact than the previously feared factor of selective exposure. That is, people generally expose themselves only to those views with which they already agree and avoid information that challenges their opinions. Social psychologists Jonathan L. Freedman and David O. Sears, in a paper that upset this neat, intuitive theory, concluded after reviewing most of the literature on the subject that there is no firm evidence that people prefer to be exposed to supportive information or to information that will reduce their unease at being bombarded by contradictory facts and opinions.[16] They did add, however, that "people are disproportionately exposed to supportive information, but for reasons other than its supportiveness."[17]

Agenda-setting by the media, however, may apparently occur without direct exposure to the media. If a person can name any issue, event, or candidate at all, the chances are pretty good that he learned about it through the mass media or through someone who was exposed to the mass media, since few of us are direct witnesses to the news of the day.

Does this mean that the media also determine the relative importance of issues? That is exactly what agenda-setting studies have shown they do. Through the sheer frequency with which a story is told, length of the story, headline size, and positioning, the media suggest to the general public how important an event, issue, or candidate is. "Salience of an item is one of the key attributes acquired from the mass media," according to McCombs and Shaw.[18] Not only is this true of media impact on the public, but the news agencies have a similar impact on newspaper wire editors, as several studies both in the United States and abroad have shown.[19] The editor tends to use more of a story, news category, or issue on which he receives more items and longer items from the wire services.

To what extent does this also determine the side people will take on an issue? Probably very little, although as McCombs and Shaw point out, "issues sometimes clearly work to the advantage of one political party or candidate."[20] All it takes is for the press to play up the issue. But coupled with the emphasis given it by press, the issue must also find a responsive chord in the audience. Each of us has a need to relate to his environment, and if a given issue satisfies that need or stimulates it, we would turn to the mass media (or to our friends who are printed by the mass media) for orientation.[21] The theory is that the "need for orientation" leads to media use, which leads to agenda-setting by the mass media. But the theory says nothing about the side people will take on the issue. In fact, several studies have indicated that people will expose themselves to information that they need and that is relevant to them, regardless of whether the information conforms to their view of the issue or not. At the same time, they will avoid irrelevant information. This is in keeping with the refutation by Freedman and Sears of the selective exposure theory.

Applying these principles to political campaigns, if a voter finds a need for orientation to a particular issue, he will listen to all candidates, regardless of political party. This emerged in the McCombs and Shaw landmark study of the 1968 presidential elections. Even though the three presidential contenders that year placed very different emphases on the issues of the day, voters seemed to expose themselves to all three candidates. The researchers found that their respondents' issue agendas (or priorities) agreed less with the agendas of their preferred candidate than they did with a composite agenda based on the priorities of all three candidates.[22]

IMPORTANCE OF TV

What of the differential effects of the mass media? Do communication specialists still believe that it is futile to talk of one medium being more efficient and effective than another? Given that it is the voter rather than the communicator who decides which medium will be attended to, researchers have found that certain things can be said about differences in mass media effects. Campaign consultant Walter DeVries found in the 1970 Michigan gubernatorial race that different types of television programs (such as newscasts, documentaries, editorials) were rated higher as important factors in influencing voting decisions than any other medium. Of 36 factors that play a role in political campaigning, 12 were rated 5.0 or better on an 11-point scale as influencing voting decisions. Significantly, the only one of these over which the candidate himself had any control was "contacts with candidates"—that is, personal campaigning. None of the purchasable types of advertising—for example, television or newspaper ads, political mailings, or telephone campaigns—was rated higher than 4.9.[23]

McCombs, however, has found that television, unlike newspapers, does not have an agenda-setting effect across time. Furthermore, when different agendas are set by newspapers and television stations, newspaper priorities have a higher correlation with voter agendas.[24] Others have shown that if agendas are studied in terms of issues, sub-issues, and specifics (such as individuals involved or solutions proposed), television tends to set the overall issue agendas but not the agenda of details. Even among TV-oriented respondents—that is, those who said television was their major source of news—newspapers tended to set their agendas on sub-issues and specifics.[25]

In the face of the great emphasis that is placed by political candidates and their campaign managers on television appearances, and in view of the fact that the candidates who spend the most on television advertising appear to win, it may be rash to downgrade television. Yet there is growing evidence that, although large proportions of voters are exposed to the airing of political campaign messages on television, it is the newspapers that tend to determine the salience of issues. Conceivably, newspaper editors and reporters are themselves influenced in their judgment by the volume of television exposure. Furthermore, voting is a

short-term activity that requires no long-term attitudinal build-up, much as we would like to think of the vote as a considered judgment on the part of the electorate. Television may have a powerful short-term effect, ideally suited to the quick action requirements in politics. It may, therefore, be a useful medium to use immediately before an election. But for long-range effects, newspapers are still the most instrumental in determining saliences.

One additional theoretical note on mass media potential has emerged from a study of senatorial news coverage. Words appear to be more fruitful than deeds in putting a senator in the public eye. Activity and seniority do not seem to produce high media visibility for senators, according to a study by David Weaver and Cleveland Wilhoit. Being vocal or active in the Senate by introducing most bills, serving on most committees, participating in most roll-call votes is less effective than seeking out reporters with press releases and news conferences. Hence, the senators from the largest states with the largest staffs receive the most publicity in the press.[26]

NOTES

1. Quoted in the *Washington Post,* 29 April 1976, p. 11A.

2. Frank Luther Mott, "Newspapers in Presidential Campaigns," *Public Opinion Quarterly* 8 (Fall 1944): 362. There were no campaigns in President Washington's two elections in 1789 and 1793, Jefferson's 1804 election, and Monroe's 1820 election.

3. Carl I. Hovland, "Reconciling Conflicting Results Derived from Experimental and Survey Studies of Attitude Change," *American Psychologist* 14 (1959): 8-17.

4. Gerhart D. Wiebe, "A New Dimension in Journalism," *Journalism Quarterly* 31 (Fall 1954): 411-420.

5. Joseph T. Klapper, *The Effects of Mass Communication* (Glencoe, Ill.: Free Press, 1960), p. 8. Emphasis in original.

6. Quoted in Klapper, *Effects,* p. 54.

7. Klapper, *Effects,* p. 55. Emphasis in original.

8. Burns W. Roper, *An Extended View of Public Attitudes Toward Television and Other Mass Media, 1959-1971* (New York: Television Information Office, 1971), pp. 8-9.

9. Alex S. Edelstein, "Media Credibility and the Believability of Watergate," *News Research Bulletin*

No. 1 (Washington DC: American Newspaper Publishers Association, 1974), p. 5.

10. Marvin Karlins and Herbert I. Abelson, *Persuasion* 2nd ed. (New York: Springer, 1970), p. 84.

11. The question, of course, is were we really influenced or were we merely delighted to find some "facts" or views expressed in the press that happened to agree with our own prior views?

12. Bernard C. Cohen, *The Press and Foreign Policy* (Princeton, N.J.: Princeton University Press, 1963), p. 13.

13. Maxwell E. McCombs and Donald L. Shaw, "The Agenda-Setting Function of Mass Media," *Public Opinion Quarterly* 36 (Summer 1972): 176-187.

14. G. Ray Funkhouser, "Trends in Media Coverage of the Issues of the '60's, *Journalism Quarterly* 50 (Autumn 1973): 533-538.

15. Philip E. Converse, "New Dimensions of Meaning for Cross-Section Sample Surveys in Politics," *International Social Science Journal* 16 (1964): 25-26.

16. Jonathan L. Freedman and David O. Sears, "Selective Exposure," *Advances in Experimental Social Psychology* 2 (1965): 58-97.

17. Freedman and Sears, "Selective Exposure," p. 90.

18. Maxwell E. McCombs and Donald L. Shaw, "A Progress Report on Agenda-Setting Research," paper presented at the Association for Education in Journalism Convention, San Diego, Calif., 18-21 August 1974, p. 30.

19. L. John Martin, *Analysis of Newspaper Coverage of the U.S. in the Near East, North Africa and South Asia* (Washington DC: U.S. Information on Agency Research Report R-2-76, 1976).

20. McCombs and Shaw, "Progress Report," p. 40.

21. See Maxwell McCombs and David Weaver, "Voter's Need for Orientation and Use of Mass Communication," paper presented at the International Communication Association Convention, Montreal, Canada, 25-28 April 1973.

22. Maxwell McCombs, "Agenda-Setting Research: A Bibliographic Essay," *Political Communication Review,* forthcoming in February, 1976, p. 2.

23. Walter DeVries, "Taking the Voter's Pulse," in *The Political Image Merchants: Strategies in the New Politics* ed. Ray Hiebert *et al.* (Washington DC: Acropolis Books, 1971).

24. McCombs, "Agenda-Setting Research" pp. 6-7.

25. Marc Benton and P. Jean Frazier, "The Agenda-Setting Function of the Mass Media at Three Levels of 'Information Holding,'" paper presented at the Association for Education in Journalism Convention, Ottawa, Canada, August 1975.

26. David H. Weaver and G. Cleveland Wilhoit, "Agenda-Setting for the Media: Determinants of Senatorial News Coverage," paper presented at International Communication Association Convention, Chicago, 23-26 April 1975.

UTILIZATION OF MASS COMMUNICATION BY THE INDIVIDUAL

Elihu Katz, Jay G. Blumler, and Michael Gurevitch

Suppose that we were studying not broadcasting-and-society in mid-twentieth century America but opera-and-society in mid-nineteenth-century Italy. After all, opera in Italy, during that period, was a "mass" medium. What would we be studying? It seems likely, for one thing, that we would find interest in the attributes of the medium—what might today be called its "grammar"—for example, the curious convention that makes it possible to sing contradictory emotions simultaneously. For another, we would be interested in the functions of the medium for the individual and society: perceptions of the values expressed and underlined; the phenomena of stardom, fanship, and connoisseurship; the festive ambience which the medium created; and so on. It seems quite unlikely that we would be studying the effects of the singing of a particular opera on opinions and attitudes, even though some operas were written with explicit political, social, and moral aims in mind. The study of short-run effects, in other words, would not have had a high priority, although it might have had a place. But the emphasis, by and large, would have been on the medium as a cultural institution with its own social and psychological functions and perhaps long-run effects.

We have all been over the reasons why much of mass communication research took a different turn, preferring to look at specific

From Mass Communication Research: Major Issues and Future Directions, *pp. 11-35. Edited by W. Phillips Davison and Frederick T. C. Yu. New York: Praeger, 1974. Copyright © 1974 by Praeger Publishers Inc.; reprinted by permission.*

programs as specific messages with, possibly, specific effects. We were social psychologists interested in persuasion and attitude change. We were political scientists interested in new forms of social control. We were commissioned to measure message effectiveness for marketing organizations, or public health agencies, or churches, or political organizations, or for the broadcasting organizations themselves. And we were asked whether the media were not causes of violent and criminal behavior.

Yet even in the early days of empirical mass communication research this preoccupation with short-term effects was supplemented by the growth of an interest in the gratifications that the mass media provide their audiences. Such studies were well represented in the Lazarsfeld-Stanton collections; Herzog on quiz programs and the gratifications derived from listening to soap operas; Suchman on the motives for getting interested in serious music on radio; Wolfe and Fiske on the development of children's interest in comics; Berelson on the functions of newspaper reading; and so on.[1] Each of these investigations came up with a list of functions served either by some specific contents or by the medium in question: to match one's wits against others, to get information or advice for daily living, to provide a framework for one's day, to prepare oneself culturally for the demands of upward mobility, or to be reassured about the dignity and usefulness of one's role.

What these early studies had in common was, first, a basically similar methodological approach whereby statements about media functions were elicited from the respondents in an essentially open-ended way. Second, they shared a qualitative approach in their attempt to group gratification statements into labeled categories, largely ignoring the distribution of their frequency in the population. Third, they did not attempt to explore the links between the gratifications thus detected and the psychological or sociological origins of the needs that were so satisfied. Fourth, they failed to search for the interrelationships among the various media

functions, either quantitatively or conceptually, in a manner that might have led to the detection of the latent structure of media gratifications. Consequently, these studies did not result in a cumulatively more detailed picture of media gratifications conducive to the eventual formulation of theoretical statements.

The last few years have witnessed something of a revival of direct empirical investigations of audience uses and gratifications, not only in the United States but also in Britain, Sweden, Finland, Japan, and Israel. These more recent studies have a number of differing starting points, but each attempts to press toward a greater systematization of what is involved in conducting research in this field. Taken together, they make operational many of the logical steps that were only implicit in the earlier work. They are concerned with (1) the social and psychological origins of (2) needs, which generate (3) expectations of (4) the mass media or other sources, which lead to (5) differential patterns of media exposure (or engagement in other activities), resulting in (6) need gratifications and (7) other consequences, perhaps mostly unintended ones. Some of these investigations begin by specifying needs and then attempt to trace the extent to which they are gratified by the media or other sources. Others take observed gratifications as a starting point and attempt to reconstruct the needs that are being gratified. Yet others focus on the social origins of audience expectations and gratifications. But however varied their individual points of departure, they all strive toward an assessment of media consumption in audience-related terms, rather than in technological, aesthetic, ideological, or other more or less "elitist" terms. The convergence of their foci, as well as of their findings, indicates that there is a clear agenda here—part methodological and part theoretical—for a discussion of the future directions of this approach.

SOME BASIC ASSUMPTIONS OF THEORY, METHOD AND VALUE

Perhaps the place of "theory" and "method" in the study of audience uses and gratifications is not immediately apparent. The common tendency to attach the label "uses and gratifications approach" to work in this field appears to virtually disclaim any theoretical pretensions or methodological commitment. From this point of view the approach simply represents an attempt to explain something of the way in which individuals use communications, among other resources in their environment, to satisfy their needs and to achieve their goals, and to do so by simply asking them. Nevertheless, this effort does rest on a body of assumptions, explicit or implicit, that have some degree of internal coherence and that are arguable in the sense that not everyone contemplating them would find them self-evident. Lundberg and Hultén refer to them as jointly constituting a "uses and gratifications model."[2] Five elements of this model in particular may be singled out for comment:

1. The audience is conceived of as active, that is, an important part of mass media use is assumed to be goal directed.[3] This assumption may be contrasted with Bogart's thesis to the effect that "most mass media experiences represent pastime rather than purposeful activity, very often (reflecting) chance circumstances within the range of availabilities rather than the expression of psychological motivation or need."[4] Of course, it cannot be denied that media exposure often has a casual origin; the issue is whether, in addition, patterns of media use are shaped by more or less definite expectations of what certain kinds of content have to offer the audience member.

2. In the mass communication process much initiative in linking need gratification and media choice lies with the audience member. This places a strong limitation on theorizing about any form of straight-line effect of media content on attitudes and behavior. As Schramm, Lyle and Parker said:

> In a sense the term "effect" is misleading because it suggests that television "does something" to children ... Nothing can be further from the fact. It is the children who are most active in this relationship. It is they who use television rather than television that uses them.[5]

3. The media compete with other sources of need satisfaction. The needs served by mass communication constitute but a segment of the wider range of human needs, and the degree to which they can be adequately met through mass media consumption certainly varies. Consequently, a proper view of the role of the media in need satisfaction should take into account other functional alternatives—including different, more conventional, and "older" ways of fulfilling needs.

4. Methodologically speaking, many of the goals of mass media use can be derived from data supplied by individual audience members themselves—that is, people are sufficiently self-aware to be able to report their interests and motives in particular cases, or at least to recognize them when confronted with them in an intelligible and familiar verbal formulation.

5. Value judgments about the cultural significance of mass communication should be suspended while audience orientations are explored on their own terms. It is from the perspective of this assumption that certain affinities and contrasts between the uses and gratifications approach and much speculative writing about popular culture may be considered.

STATE OF THE ART: THEORETICAL ISSUES

From the few postulates outlined above, it is evident that further development of a theory of media gratification depends, first, on the clarification of its relationship to the theoretical traditions on which it so obviously draws and, second, on systematic efforts toward conceptual integration of empirical findings. Given the present state of the art, the following are priority issues in the development of an adequate theoretical basis.

Typologies of Audience Gratifications

Each major piece of uses and gratification research has yielded its own classification scheme of audience functions. When placed side by side, they reveal a mixture of shared gratification categories and notions peculiar to individual research teams. The differences are due in part to the fact that investigators have focused on different levels of study (e.g., medium or content) and different materials (e.g., different programs or program types on,

say, television) in different cultures (e.g., Finland, Israel, Japan, Sweden, the United Kingdom, the United States, and Yugoslavia).

Unifunctional conceptions of audience interests have been expressed in various forms. Popular culture writers have often based their criticisms of the media on the ground that, in primarily serving the escapist desires of the audience, they deprived it of the more beneficial uses that might be made of communication.[6] Stephenson's analysis of mass communication exclusively in terms of "play" may be interpreted as an extension, albeit in a transformed and expanded expression, of the same notion.[7] A more recent example has been provided by Nordenstreng, who, while breaking away from conventional formulations, still opts for a unifunctional view when he claims that, "It has often been documented (e.g., during television and newspaper strikes in Finland in 1966-67) that perhaps the basic motivation for media use is just an unarticulated need for social contact."[8]

The wide currency secured for a bifunctional view of audience concerns is reflected in Weiss' summary, which states that, "When ... studies of uses and gratifications are carried out, the media or media content are usually viewed dichotomously as predominantly fantasist-escapist or informational-educational in significance."[9] This dichotomy appears, for example, in Schramm's work (adopted subsequently by Schramm, Lyle and Parker; Pietila; and Furu), which distinguishes between sets of "immediate" and "deferred" gratifications, and in the distinction between informational and entertainment materials.[10]. In terms of audience gratifications specifically, it emerges in the distinction between surveillance and escape uses of the media.

The four-functional interpretation of the media was first proposed by Lasswell on a macro-sociological level and later developed

by Wright on both the macro- and the micro-
sociological levels.[11] It postulated that the
media served the functions of surveillance,
correlation, entertainment, and cultural
transmission (or socialization) for society as a
whole, as well as for individuals and
subgroups within society. An extension of the
four-function approach can also be found in
Wright's suggestive exploration of the
potential dysfunctional equivalents of
Lasswell's typology.

None of these statements, however,
adequately reflects the full range of functions,
which has been disclosed by the more recent
investigations. McQuail, Blumler and Brown
have put forward a typology consisting of the
following categories: diversion (including
escape from the constraints of routine and
the burdens of problems, and emotional
release); personal relationships (including
substitute companionship as well as social
utility); personal identity (including personal
reference, reality exploration, and value
reinforcement); and surveillance.[12]

An effort to encompass the large variety
of specific functions that have been proposed
is made in the elaborate scheme of Katz,
Gurevitch and Haas.[13] Their central notion is
that mass communication is used by
individuals to connect (or sometimes to
disconnect) themselves—via instrumental,
affective, or integrative relations—with
different kinds of others (self, family, friends,
nation, etc.). The scheme attempts to
comprehend the whole range of individual
gratifications of the many facets of the need
"to be connected." And it finds empirical
regularities in the preference for different
media for different kinds of connections.

Gratification and Needs

The study of mass media use suffers at
present from the absence of a relevant theory
of social and psychological needs. It is not so
much a catalogue of needs that is missing as
a clustering of groups of needs, a sorting out
of different levels of need, and a specification
of hypotheses linking particular needs with
particular media gratifications. It is true that
the work of Schramm, Lyle and Parker draws
on the distinction between the reality and
pleasure principles in the socialization
theories of Freud and others, but more recent
studies suggest that those categories are too
broad to be serviceable. Maslow's proposed
hierarchy of human needs may hold more
promise, but the relevance of his categories to
expectations of communication has not yet
been explored in detail.[14] Lasswell's scheme
to specify the needs that media satisfy has
proven useful, and it may be helpful to
examine Lasswell and Kaplan's broader
classification of values as well.[15]

Alternatively, students of uses and
gratifications could try to work backwards, as
it were, from gratifications to needs. In the
informational field, for example, the
surveillance function may be traced to a
desire for security or the satisfaction of
curiosity and the exploratory drive; seeking
reinforcement of one's attitudes and values
may derive from a need for reassurance that
one is right; and attempts to correlate
informational elements may stem from a more
basic need to develop one's cognitive mastery of
the environment. Similarly, the use of fictional
(and other) media materials for "personal
reference" may spring from a need for self-
esteem; social utility functions may be traced
to the need for affiliation; and escape
functions may be related to the need to
release tension and reduce anxiety. But
whichever way one proceeds, it is inescapable
that what is at issue here is the long-standing
problem of social and psychological science:
how to (and whether to bother to) systematize
the long lists of human and societal needs.
Thus far, gratifications research has stayed
close to what we have been calling media-
related needs (in the sense that the media
have been observed to satisfy them, at least in
part), but one wonders whether all this should
not be put in the broader context of
systematic studies of needs.

Sources of Media Gratifications

Studies have shown that audience gratifications can be derived from at least three distinct sources: media content, exposure to the media per se, and the social context that typifies the situation of exposure to different media. Although recognition of media content as a source of gratification has provided the basis for research in this area from its inception, less attention has been paid to the other sources. Nevertheless, it is clear that the need to relax or to kill time can be satisfied by the act of watching television, that the need to feel that one is spending one's time in a worthwhile way may be associated with the act of reading, and that the need to structure one's day may be satisfied merely by having the radio "on."[16] Similarly, a wish to spend time with one's family or friends can be served by watching television at home with the family or by going to the cinema with one's friends.

Each medium seems to offer a unique combination of (a) characteristic contents (at least stereotypically perceived in that way); (b) typical attributes (print vs. broadcasting modes of transmission, iconic vs. symbolic representation, reading vs. audio or audio-visual modes of reception); and (c) typical exposure situations (at home vs. out-of-home, alone vs. with others, control over the temporal aspects of exposure vs. absence of such control). The issue, then, is what combinations of attributes may render different media more or less adequate for the satisfaction of different needs.[17]

Gratifications and Media Attributes

Much uses and gratifications research has still barely advanced beyond a sort of charting and profiling activity: findings are still typically presented to show that certain bodies of content serve certain functions or that one medium is deemed better at satisfying certain needs than another. The further step, which has hardly been ventured, is one of explanation. At issue here is the relationship between the unique "grammar" of different media—that is, their specific technological and aesthetic attributes—and the particular requirements of audience members that they are then capable, or incapable, of satisfying. Which, indeed, are the attributes that render some media more conducive than others to satisfying specific needs? And which elements of content help to attract the expectations for which they apparently cater?

It is possible to postulate the operation of some kind of division of labor among the media for the satisfaction of audience needs. This may be elaborated in two ways: taking media attributes as the starting point, the suggestion is that those media that differ (or are similar) in their attributes are more likely to serve different (or similar) needs; or, utilizing the latent structure of needs as a point of departure, the implication is that needs that are psychologically related or conceptually similar will be equally well served by the same media (or by media with similar attributes).

To illustrate the first approach, Robinson has demonstrated the interchangeability of television and print media for learning purposes.[18] In the Israeli study, Katz, Gurevitch and Haas found five media ordered in a circumplex with respect to their functional similarities: books-newspapers-radio-television-cinema-books.[19] In other words, books functioned most like newspapers, on the one hand, and like cinema, on the other. Radio was most similar in its usage to newspapers, on the one hand, and to television, on the other. The explanation would seem to lie not only with certain technological attributes that they have in common, but with similar aesthetic qualities as well. Thus, books share a technology and an informational function with newspapers, but are similar to films in their aesthetic function. Radio shares a technology, as well as informational and entertainment content, with television, but it is also very much like newspapers—providing a heavy dose of information and an orientation to reality.

An illustration of the second aspect of this division of labor may also be drawn from the same study. Here, the argument is that structurally related needs will tend to be serviced by certain media more often than by others. Thus, books and cinema have been found to cater to needs concerned with self-fulfillment and self-gratification: they help to "connect" individuals to themselves. Newspapers, radio, and television all seem to connect individuals to society. In fact, the function of newspapers for those interested in following what is going on in the world may have been grossly underestimated in the past.[20] Television, however, was found to be less frequently used as a medium of escape by Israeli respondents than were books and films. And a Swedish study of the "functional specialities of the respective media" reported that, "A retreat from the immediate environment and its demands—probably mainly by the act of reading itself—was characteristic of audience usage of weekly magazines."[21]

Media Attributes as Perceived or Intrinsic

When people associate book-reading, for example, with a desire to know oneself, and newspapers with the need to feel connected to the larger society, it is difficult to disentangle perceptions of the media from their intrinsic qualities. Is there anything about the book as a medium that breeds intimacy? Is there something about newspapers that explains their centrality in socio-political integration? Or, is this "something" simply an accepted image of the medium and its characteristic content?

In this connection, Rosengren has suggested that uses and gratifications research may be profitably connected with the long-established tradition of enquiry into public perceptions of the various media and the dimensions according to which their respective images and qualities are differentiated.[22] A merger of the two lines of investigation may show how far the attributes of the media, as perceived by their consumers, and their intrinsic qualities are correlated with the pursuit of certain gratifications. So far, however, this connection has only been partially discussed in the work of Lundberg and Hultén.[23]

The Social Origins of Audience Needs and Their Gratifications

The social and environmental circumstances that lead people to turn to the mass media for the satisfaction of certain needs are also little understood as yet. For example, what needs, if any, are created by routine work on an assembly line, and which forms of media exposure will satisfy them? What motivates some people to seek political information from the mass media and others to actively avoid it? Here one may postulate that it is the combined product of psychological dispositions, sociological factors, and environmental conditions that determines the specific uses of the media by members of the audience.

At certain levels it should not prove unduly difficult to formulate discrete hypotheses about such relationships. For example, we might expect "substitute companionship" to be sought especially by individuals with limited opportunities for social contacts: invalids, the elderly, the single, the divorced or widowed living alone, the housewife who spends much time at home on her own, and so on.

At another level, however, it is more difficult to conceive of a general theory that might clarify the various processes that underlie any such specific relationships. A preliminary structuring of the possibilities suggests that social factors may be involved in the generation of media-related needs in any of the following five ways (each of which has attracted some comment in the literature):

1. Social situation produces tensions and conflicts, leading to pressure for their easement via mass media consumption.[24]
2. Social situation creates an awareness of problems that demand attention, information about which may be sought in the media.[25]
3. Social situation offers impoverished real-life opportunities to satisfy certain needs, which are then directed to the mass media for complementary, supplementary, or substitute servicing.[26]
4. Social situation gives rise to certain values, the affirmation and reinforcement of which is facilitated by the consumption of congruent media materials.[27]
5. Social situation provides a field of expectations of familiarity with certain media materials, which must then be monitored in order to sustain membership of valued social groupings.[28]

The Versatility of Sources of Need Satisfaction

Before becoming too sanguine about the possibility of relating social situations to psychological needs to media/content gratifications, it is important to bear in mind that gratifications studies based on specific media contents have demonstrated that one and the same set of media materials is capable of serving a multiplicity of needs and audience functions. Presumably, that is why Rosengren and Windahl have drawn attention to "a growing consensus that almost any type of content may serve practically any type of function."[29] For example, Blumler, Brown and McQuail have found that the television serial *The Saint* serves functions of personal reference, identification with characters, and reality-exploration, in addition to its more obvious diversionary function.[30] Similarly, their study of the gratifications involved in news viewing referred not only to the expected surveillance motive but also to functions of social utility, empathy, and even escape. In summarizing the implications of their evidence, McQuail, Blumler and Brown point out that:

the relationship between content categories and audience needs is far less tidy and more complex than most commentators have appreciated....One man's source of escape from the real world is a point of anchorage for another man's place in it.[31]

Gratifications and Effects

Pioneers in the study of uses and gratifications were moved chiefly by two aspirations. The first, which has largely been fulfilled, was to redress an imbalance evident in previous research: audience needs, they said, deserved as much attention in their own right as the persuasive aims of communicators with which so many of the early "effects" studies had been preoccupied. The second major aim of uses and gratifications research, however, was to treat audience requirements as intervening variables in the study of traditional communication effects. Glaser's formulation offers a typical expression of the rationale behind this prospect:

Since users approach the media with a variety of needs and predispositions...any precise identification of the effects of television watching...must identify the uses sought and made of television by the various types of viewers.[32]

Despite this injunction, hardly any substantial empirical or theoretical effort has been devoted to connecting gratifications and effects. Some limited evidence from the political field suggests that combining functions and effects perspectives may be fruitful.[33] But there are many other foci of traditional effects studies for which no detailed hypotheses about gratifications/effects interactions have yet been framed.

One obvious example is the field of media violence. Another might concern the impact on inhabitants of developing countries of exposure to television serials, films, and popular songs of foreign (predominantly American) origin. Yet another might relate to the wide range of materials, appearing especially in broadcast fiction, that purport simultaneously to entertain and to portray more or less faithfully some portion of social reality—e.g., the worlds of law enforcement, social work, hospital life, trade unionism, working-class neighborhoods, and ways of life at the executive level in business corporations and civil service departments.

Hypotheses about the cumulative effects of exposure to such materials on audience members' cognitive perceptions of these spheres of activity, and on the individuals engaged in them, might be formulated in awareness of the likely fact that some individuals will be viewing them primarily for purposes of escape, while others will be using them for reality-exploring gratifications. In these circumstances should we expect a readier acceptance of portrayed stereotypes by the escape seekers—the thesis of Festinger and Maccoby on persuasion via distraction might be relevant here—or by those viewers who are trusting enough to expect such programs to offer genuine insights into the nature of social reality?[34]

A similar body of recently analyzed materials may be found in the television soap opera, with its postulated capacity to "establish or reinforce value systems."[35] In fact one cluster of gratifications that emerged from an English study of listeners to a long-running daytime radio serial (*The Dales*) centered on the tendency of the program to uphold traditional family values.[36] This suggests that an answer to Katzman's "key question" ("to what degree do daytime serials change attitudes and norms and to what extent do they merely follow and reinforce their audience?") might initially be sought by distinguishing among the regular followers of such programs those individuals who are avowedly seeking a reinforcement of certain values from those who are not.

In addition, however, the literature refers to some consequences of audience functions that conventional effects designs may be unable to capture. First, there is what Katz and Foulkes have termed the "feedback" from media use to the individual's performance of his other social roles. Thus, Bailyn distinguished child uses of pictorial media that might "preclude more realistic and lasting solutions" to problems from those that, at one level, were "escapist" but that should more properly be categorized as "supplementation."[37] Similarly, Schramm, Lyle and Parker maintained that child uses of the mass media for fantasizing might either drain off discontent caused by the hard blows of socialization or lead a child into withdrawal from the real world.[38] And Lundberg and Hultén have suggested that for some individuals the substitute companionship function may involve use of the media to replace real social ties, while for others it may facilitate an adjustment to reality.[39]

Second, some authors have speculated on the connection between functions performed by the media for individuals and their functions (or dysfunctions) for other levels of society. This relationship is particularly crucial for its bearing on evaluative and ideological controversies about the role of mass communication in modern society. Thus, Enzenberger suggests that the 8 millimeter camera may satisfy the recreational and creative impulses of the individual and help to keep the family together while simultaneously atomizing and depoliticizing society.[40] Or news viewing may gratify the individual's need for civic participation; but if the news, as presented, is a disjointed succession of staccato events, it may also leave him with the message that the world is a disconnected place. Similarly, many radical critics tend to regard television as part of a conspiracy to keep people content and politically quiescent—offering respite, para-social interaction with interesting and amusing people, and much food for gossip—while propagating a false social consciousness.

IMPLICATIONS FOR RESEARCH POLICY AND MEDIA POLICY

In reviewing the state of the art of gratifications research, we have focused on issues—theoretical, methodological, and ideological—rather than on systematized findings. We have also tried to make manifest our assumptions. Thus, we have confronted the image of the beery, house-slippered, casual viewer of television with the notion of a more "active" audience—knowing that both images are true. We have asked whether a methodology based on respondents' introspection can be adequate. We have indicated the absence of satisfactory bridging concepts between the constraints arising from social situations and the gratifications sought from the media; or between particular patterns of use and likely effect.

These issues bear not only on the direction of future research, but also, echoing Nordenstreng, on the relationship between research policy and media policy.[41] Thus, we have raised the question of the extent to which the media create the needs that they satisfy. Even more fundamentally, we ask whether the media do actually satisfy their consumers—an assumption that radical critics of the media take more for granted than do gratification researchers.[42] To assert that mass communications is a latter-day opiate of the masses presupposes a media-output audience-satisfaction nexus that gratifications research treats as hypothesis rather than fact.

In other words, our position is that media researchers ought to be studying human needs to discover how much the media do or do not contribute to their creation and satisfaction. Moreover, we believe it is our job to clarify the extent to which certain kinds of media and content favor certain kinds of use—to thereby set boundaries to the over-generalization that any kind of content can be bent to any kind of need. We believe it is part of our job to explore the social and individual conditions under which audiences find need or use for program material aimed at changing their image of the status quo or "broadening their cultural horizons."[43]

From the point of view of media policy, then, we reject the view that an application of the uses and gratifications approach to policy questions must inevitably support or exonerate the producers of junk or the status quo of media content. That belief seems to require the acceptance of one or both of two other assumptions: existing patterns of audience needs support the prevailing patterns of media provision and no other; and audience concerns are in fact trivial and escapist. For reasons that should now be plain, we find both these propositions dubious.

Though audience oriented, the uses and gratifications approach is not necessarily conservative. While taking account of what people look for from the media, it breaks away from a slavish dependence of content on audience propensities by bringing to light the great variety of needs and interests that are encompassed by the latter. As McQuail, Blumler and Brown have argued, uses and gratifications data suggest that the mass media may not, after all, be as "constrained as the escapist theory makes out from performing a wider range of social functions than is generally assigned to them in western societies today."[44] In other words, instead of depicting the media as severely circumscribed by audience expectations, the uses and gratifications approach highlights the audience as a source of challenge to producers to cater more richly to the multiplicity of requirements and roles that it has disclosed.

NOTES

1. P. F. Lazarsfeld and F. N. Stanton (eds.), *Radio Research, 1941* (New York: Duell, Sloan & Pearce, 1942); P. F. Lazarsfeld and F. N. Stanton (eds.), *Radio Research, 1942-3* (New York: Duell, Sloan & Pearce, 1944); P. F. Lazarsfeld and F. N. Stanton (eds.), *Communications Research, 1948-9* (New York: Harper, 1949); H. Herzog, "Professor Quiz: A Gratification Study," in *Radio Research, 1941,* ed. Lazarsfeld and Stanton; E. Suchman, "An Invitation to Music," in *Radio Research, 1941,* ed. Lazarsfeld and Stanton; K. M. Wolfe and M. Fiske, "Why Children Read Comics," in *Communications Research, 1948-9,* ed. Lazarsfeld and Stanton; and B. Berelson, "What 'Missing the Newspaper' Means," in *Communications Research, 1948-49,* ed. Lazarsfeld and Stanton.

2. D. Lundberg and O. Hultén, *Individen och Massmedia* (Stockholm: EFI, 1968).

3. D. McQuail, J. G. Blumler, and J. R. Brown, "The Television Audience: A Revised Perspective," in *Sociology of Mass Communications,* ed. D. McQuail (Harmondsworth, England: Penguin, 1972).

4. L. Bogart, "The Mass Media and the Blue-Collar Worker," in *Blue-Collar World: Studies of the American Worker,* ed. A. Bennett and W. Gomberg (Englewood Cliffs, N. J.: Prentice-Hall, 1965).

5. W. Schramm, J. Lyle, and E. B. Parker, *Television in the Lives of Our Children* (Stanford, Calif.: Stanford University Press, 1961).

6. D. McDonald, "A Theory of Mass Culture," in *Mass Culture: The Popular Arts in America,* ed. D. M. White and B. Rosenberg (Glencoe, Ill.: Free Press, 1957).

7. W. Stephenson, *The Play Theory of Mass Communication* (Chicago: University of Chicago Press, 1967).

8. K. Nordenstreng, "Comments on 'Gratifications Research' in Broadcasting," *Public Opinion Quarterly* 34 (1970).

9. W. Weiss, "Mass Communication," *Annual Review of Psychology* 22 (1971).

10. W. Schramm, "The Nature of News," *Journalism Quarterly* 26 (1949); Schramm, Lyle, and Parker, *TV in the Lives of Our Children;* V. Pietila, "Immediate Versus Delayed Reward in Newspaper Reading," *Acta Sociologica* 12 (1969); and T. Furu, *The Function of Television for Children and Adolescents* (Tokyo: Sophia University, 1971).

11. H. Lasswell, "The Structure and Function of Communications in Society," in *The Communication of Ideas,* ed. L. Bryson (New York: Harper, 1948); and C. Wright, "Functional Analysis and Mass Communication," *Public Opinion Quarterly* 24 (1960).

12. McQuail, Blumler, and Brown, "TV Audience."

13. E. Katz, M. Gurevitch, and H. Haas, "On the Use of Mass Media for Important Things," *American Sociological Review* 38 (1973).

14. A. H. Maslow, *Motivation and Personality* (New York: Harper, 1954).

15. Lasswell, "Structure and Function of Communications"; and H. Lasswell and A. Kaplan, *Power and Society* (New Haven, Conn.: Yale University Press, 1950).

16. D. Waples, B. Berelson, and F. R. Bradshaw, *What Reading Does to People* (Chicago: University of Chicago Press, 1940); Berelson, " 'Missing the Newspaper' "; and H. Mendelsohn, "Listening to Radio," in *People, Society and Mass Communications,* ed. L. A. Dexter and D. M. White (Glencoe, Ill.: Free Press, 1964).

17. Katz, Gurevitch, and Haas, "Use of Mass Media."

18. J. P. Robinson, "Toward Defining the Functions of Television," in *Television and Social Behavior,* vol. 4 (Rockville, Md.: National Institute of Mental Health, 1972).

19. Katz, Gurevitch, and Haas, "Use of Mass Media."

20. A. Edelstein, "An Alternative Approach to the Study of Source Effects in Mass Communication," *Studies of Broadcasting* 9 (1973); and Lundberg and Hultén, *Individen.*

21. Lundberg and Hultén, *Individen.*

22. K. E. Rosengren, "Uses and Gratifications: An Overview," mimeographed, University of Lund, Sweden, 1972. See especially S. Nillson, "Publikens Upplevelse av TV-Program," mimeographed, Sveriges Radio Publications, Stockholm, 1971; Edelstein, "Alternative Approach to Source Effects"; and the literature cited therein.

23. Lundberg and Hultén, *Individen.*

24. E. Katz and D. Foulkes, "On the Use of Mass Media for 'Escape': Clarification of a Concept," *Public Opinion Quarterly* 26 (1962).

25. Edelstein, "Alternative Approach to Source Effects."

26. K. E. Rosengren and S. Windahl, "Mass Media Consumption as a Functional Alternative," in *Sociology of Mass Communications,* ed. D. McQuail (Harmondsworth, England: Penguin, 1972).

27. R. Dembo, "Life Style and Media Use Among English Working-Class Youths," *Gazette* 18 (1972).

28. C. K. Atkin, "Anticipated Communication and Mass Media Information-Seeking," *Public Opinion Quarterly* 36 (1972).

29. Rosengren and Windahl, "Mass Media Consumption."

30. J. G. Blumler, J. R. Brown, and D. McQuail, "The Social Origins of the Gratifications Associated with Television Viewing," mimeographed, The University of Leeds, England, 1970.

31. McQuail, Blumler, and Brown, "TV Audience."

32. W. A. Glaser, "Television and Voting Turnout," *Public Opinion Quarterly* 29 (1965).

33. J. G. Blumler and D. McQuail, *Television in Politics* (Chicago: University of Chicago Press, 1969).

34. L. Festinger and N. Maccoby, "On Resistance to Persuasive Communication," *Journal of Abnormal and Social Psychology* 60 (1964).

35. N. Katzman, "Television Soap Operas: What's Been Going On Anyway?" *Public Opinion Quarterly* 36 (1972).

36. Blumler, Brown, and McQuail, "Social Origins of Gratifications."

37. L. Bailyn, "Mass Media and Children," *Psychological Monographs* 71 (1959).

38. Schramm, Lyle, and Parker, *TV in the Lives of Our Children.*

39. Lundberg and Hultén, *Individen.*

40. H. M. Enzenberger, "Constituents of a Theory of the Media," in *Sociology of Mass Communications,* ed. D. McQuail (Harmondsworth, England: Penguin, 1972).

41. Nordenstreng, "Comments on 'Gratifications Research.'"

42. See B. Emmett, "A New Role for Research in Broadcasting," *Public Opinion Quarterly* 32 (1968-1969).

43. Emmett, "New Role for Research."

44. McQuail, Blumler, and Brown, "TV Audience."

Part Two

Media Roles and Performance

Topics

a **The Role of News**

b **Journalists and Their Methods**

c **Economics and the Media**

Introduction

The essays in Part One examine the impact of mass media on people and institutions. Many of the authors accept, explicitly or implicitly, the Lasswellian premise of media function: to serve as both informing and socializing agent for society.

The essays in Part Two examine the impact of people and institutions on the mass media. Here, too, we find general agreement on basic functions and consider another factor: the profit function.

How well do the news media fulfill their assigned functions? Do journalists see their role through the same lens as the social philosophers? What accounts for the form and content of the media—the policies of owners and managers, the professional norms of journalists, the internal structure of news organizations, influences from outside the media, or a combination of these factors? Are cultural, economic, and institutional changes affecting media roles and performance? These questions, which form the basis for a sociology of the mass media, are addressed from viewpoints both within and outside the media.

Robert E. Park, founder of the Chicago school of sociology and himself a journalist, may have been the first to suggest that people get the newspapers they deserve (or demand). In a classic examination, "The Natural History of the Newspaper," Park views the press as a mechanism that grows with, changes with, and adapts to the society it serves. Park, writing in 1925, saw the press as an imperfect institution but one that was not yet fully understood. He might conclude the same were he alive and writing today. His prescription for change might also stand the test of time: "If the newspapers are to be improved, it will come through the education of the people and the organization of political information and intelligence."

Examining the same fundamental question half a century later, journalism educator Todd Hunt comes to a similar conclusion. Society has become so complex, he observes, that neither reporters nor news audiences can make sense of the world by simply following events as they occur. The solution proposed by Hunt lies in redefining traditional concepts of news. In his essay, "Beyond the Journalistic Event: The Changing Concept of News," Hunt recommends a journalistic focus on the ongoing process of events, rather than on the isolate events themselves.

Donald McDonald is optimistic about the capacity of reporters to present complete and truthful accounts of society's transactions. But his optimism, in "Is Objectivity Possible?" depends on substantial changes in the news establishment. The former journalism school dean and fellow of the Center for the Study of Democratic Institutions also sees definitions of news at the heart of failures of the press, as does Hunt. The need to examine the "continually unfolding realities" that make up today's complex world requires the abandonment of the old news formulas—conflict, drama, celebrity, timeliness, uniqueness. In place of the hoary traditions of journalism, McDonald calls for more highly educated reporters; more time, space, and money for news; press monitoring by the public; and provocatively, a subordination of profit to public service.

These sanguine views of journalistic proficiency are not shared by all observers, however. Despite pretensions to objectivity, reporters can't arrive at truth, argues media critic Edward Jay Epstein. The very structure of journalism works against success, Epstein contends in "Journalism and Truth." Reporters, he asserts, lack the training and access to information required to discover truth; public institutions such as grand juries and legislative bodies have that access.

Coming in the post-Watergate euphoria of journalistic supremacy, Epstein's essay evoked forceful rebuttal from some quarters of the press. One who might agree with the Epstein thesis, however, is magazine editor Paul H. Weaver. In "The New Journalism and the Old—Thoughts After Watergate." Weaver outlines two conflicting directions in contemporary journalism. One is the objective, or "liberal," approach; the other the partisan, or adversary, approach. Liberal journalists seek the cooperation of public officials in order to gain access to information. In doing this, they must compromise with news sources. The adversary journalist, on the other hand, searches out public sin without compromise. Weaver believes that the public is better served—that is, gets more information—via the liberal approach, because the adversary journalist is shunned by most news sources as an enemy.

Sociologist Morris Janowitz dissects the same objective and adversary models posited by Weaver and concludes that the adversary role impedes professionalism in journalism. Adversarial reporters, Janowitz asserts, are caught in a double bind. To function effectively and responsibly, they must move toward the objective, or "gatekeeper," approach that they have shunned. If the advocate is to have a distinct and useful place in journalism, limits of performance and goals are necessary. Aside from this argument, Janowitz's article, "Professional Models in Journalism: The Gatekeeper and the Advocate," contains a useful review of recent communicator studies.

One work published after the Janowitz article, Bernard Roshco's *Newsmaking,*[1] challenges the validity of the objective model of reporting. Roshco describes news judgment as a response to the meshed imperatives imposed by the media organization's operational needs, the newsperson's occupational dilemmas, and the audience's predominant social assumptions. He does not believe that news organizations encourage "innovative ideas, dissident viewpoints, and news unfavorable and unpalatable to the institutional powerholders who usually dominate the news."

THE CHARACTERISTICS OF JOURNALISTS

The actors in these examinations of press function are writers and editors. What do they contribute to the equation? Are there attributes and behavior patterns of journalists that determine to some degree what the press shall be? Hunt suggests organizational myopia, Epstein a certain ineptitude, Weaver a dichotomy in method. Sociologist John W. C. Johnstone, with Edward J. Slawski and William Bowman, examines the question in a landmark study of the beliefs and values of journalists.[2] Their findings, reported partially in this section in "The Professional Values of American Newsmen," point up the philosophical divisions among today's journalists.

Their data show that reporters are split on the issue of participant versus neutral roles for journalists, although more favor the expanded, interpretive function of the press. "Neutrals" tend to be older, to have less formal education, to come from smaller cities and less prestigious newspapers, and to be more involved with professional and community organizations than are participant-types.

Generalizations about journalists are just that, however. There are concurrent movements in the field that defy generalization and that represent great diversity of approach and method. Everette E. Dennis examines these movements in "Journalistic Primitivism" and concludes that much of what is currently celebrated as "new" modes of reportage is really a throwback to earlier forms. The recent ascent of investigative and adversary journalism, Dennis observes, is essentially a return to a primitive style in which the hunt for sensation is fueled by formula and instinct. It has largely ignored advances in reportorial research methods and has also retarded genuine progress in style and form that began in the 1960s with the literary-nonfiction blend known as "the new journalism."

A relatively new approach to journalistic truth is advocated by Philip Meyer in "The Limits of Intuition." Recognized as the father of "precision journalism," Meyer argues that rigorous, controlled methods of information-gathering developed by social scientists can be profitably employed by journalists. The survey, the experiment, and content analysis are tools that offer reporters the opportunity to write stories otherwise unattainable. Precision journalism, Meyer contends, enhances objectivity while diverting reporters from the traps of mindless neutrality or adversarial ideology.

Television, which appeared on the mass media scene at mid-century, has posed new questions about the news function. Does the medium through which news is delivered make a difference as to form, purpose, utility? Paul Weaver asserts that it does in his essay, "Newspaper News and Television News." Although he finds similarities in the two forms—both provide accounts of current events, employing reportage and specially trained people—the differences are greater. Television news is structurally cogent, unified, coherent, visual. Newspaper news is loose, varied, diverse, narrative. These and other differences account for both the successes and failures of the two forms.[3]

ECONOMICS AND MEDIA CONTENT

Thus far, the essays in Part Two address the questions of how news is defined and how it can best be obtained and presented. These are central questions today, as they were fifty years ago, in evaluating media's impact on society. The next two essays examine another factor that helps to account for the news product: economics.

As the mass media have shaped the thoughts and actions of their audiences over time, so have the audiences influenced the shape of the media. Underlying this interaction have been the primary forces of civilization and its institutions. Continued industrialization, expanded literacy, and advances in communication technology have made the mass media dominant as channels of communication in this century. The principal focus of communication research has been, therefore, on the mass media: newspapers, national magazines, and later, radio and television.

Sociologist Richard Maisel, in a compelling analysis of growth rates since 1950, "The Decline of the Mass Media," suggests a change in focus. The mass media, he argues, have entered a period of decline. Specialized media, more attuned to the demands of a pluralistic society, are in the ascendency. The reason for the shift, according to Maisel, is the advent of postindustrial society. A substantial shift in the work force from manufacturing to the service sector (for example, the knowledge industry) has fueled an increased demand for information tailored to specialized audiences. Hence, the growth of specialized media.

The correctness of Maisel's hypothesis has profound import for the future role of the mass media. Economic reality, as no other force, has shaped the media product offered to consumers. The "bottom line" has been the guiding force in media decision making in this century. The bottom line for the newspaper industry appears to be in a shaky position as the 1980s approach. Economic gains secured through technological advances have been offset somewhat by substantial circulation losses. Drastic cost-cutting measures have been invoked by some newspaper managements to offset not only recession-induced advertising declines, but also the loss of more than 2.5 million subscribers since 1973. Where have all the readers gone?

The television industry appears to be more complacent about its financial future. Revenues have been rising faster than costs, and profits have never been higher than in the mid-1970s. Projections, both statistical and subjective, anticipate continued revenue growth.

Changing consumer preferences and the advent of new information-delivery systems, however, raise doubts about the long-term profitability of both newspapers and commercial television as we know them today. These concerns are examined in the final essay of Part Two, "The Economic Connection: Mass Media Profits, Ownership, and Performance," by Arnold H. Ismach.

Although newspaper profit margins remain among the highest of all industry, publishers are worried about continuing declines in readership. The problem has been acute in major metropolitan areas. The industry reaction to these danger signals has been technological improvement to reduce costs and research-based reshaping of newspaper content in an effort to attract new readers and regain old ones.

Although the economic strength of some newspapers has waned, Ismach observes, most are still highly profitable enterprises. This fact has made newspapers a highly desirable commodity in the capital marketplace and has led to frantic competition for new acquisitions by chains and media conglomerates. The buying and selling binge threatens to make extinct the independent, family-owned daily newspaper in all except the smaller markets. Chains, benefiting from economies of scale, tend to increase the profitability of the properties they buy. This creates more surplus capital for additional expansion. The result, in both broadcasting and the newspaper industry, is growing concentration of ownership and fewer independent voices in the news media.

The implications are clear, if one accepts the societal roles assigned to the media by authors in this volume. The potential of both print and electronic media to produce profits—indeed, the absolute *need* for profits—is not in itself ominous. But the apparent compulsion of stockholder-directed chains to maximize profits may be the decisive factor in determining whether the news media live up to their promise as the *eyes, ears,* and *glue* of democratic society.

NOTES

1. Bernard Roshco, *Newsmaking* (Chicago: University of Chicago Press, 1975).

2. John W. C. Johnstone, Edward J. Slawski, and William Bowman, *The News People: A Sociological Portrait of American Journalists and Their Work* (Urbana: University of Illinois Press, 1976).

3. For other views of television news performance, see Edwin Diamond, *The Tin Kazoo* (Cambridge, Mass.: MIT Press, 1975); Edward Jay Epstein, *News From Nowhere* (New York: Random House, 1973). An examination of television economics may be found in Bruce M. Owen, Jack H. Beebe, and Willard G. Manning, Jr., *Television Economics* (Lexington, Mass.: Heath, 1974); and in Les Brown, *Television: The Business Behind the Box* (New York: Harcourt Brace Jovanovich, 1971).

FURTHER READING

Bagdikian, Ben H. *The Information Machines.* New York: Harper & Row, 1971.

Johnstone, John W. C.; Slawski, Edward J.; and Bowman, William. *The News People: A Sociological Portrait of American Journalists and Their Work.* Urbana: University of Illinois Press, 1976.

McCombs, Maxwell B. *Mass Media in the Marketplace.* Journalism Monographs, no. 24. Lexington, Ky.: Association for Education in Journalism, 1972.

Rivers, William L., and Schramm, Wilbur. *Responsibility in Mass Communication.* Rev. ed. New York: Harper & Row, 1969.

Roshco, Bernard. *Newsmaking.* Chicago: University of Chicago Press, 1975.

Part Two

a

The Role of News

THE NATURAL HISTORY OF THE NEWSPAPER

Robert E. Park

The Newspaper has a history; but it has, likewise, a natural history. The press, as it exists, is not, as our moralists sometimes seem to assume, the willful product of any little group of living men. On the contrary, it is the outcome of a historic process in which many individuals participated without foreseeing what the ultimate product of their labors was to be.

The newspaper, like the modern city, is not wholly a rational product. No one sought to make it just what it is. In spite of all the efforts of individual men and generations of men to control it and to make it something after their own heart, it has continued to grow and change in its own incalculable ways.

The type of newspaper that exists is the type that has survived under the conditions of modern life. The men who may be said to have made the modern newspaper—James Gordon Bennett, Charles A. Dana, Joseph Pulitzer, and William Randolph Hearst—are the men who discovered the kind of paper that men and women would read and had the courage to publish it.

The natural history of the press is the history of the surviving species. It is an account of the conditions under which the existing newspaper has grown up and taken form.

A newspaper is not merely printed. It is circulated and read. Otherwise it is not a newspaper. The struggle for existence, in the case of the newspaper, has been a struggle for circulation. The newspaper that is not read ceases to be an influence in the community.

From The City, *pp. 8-23. Edited by Robert E. Park, Ernest W. Burgess, and R. D. McKenzie. Chicago: University of Chicago Press, 1925; reprinted, 1967. Copyright © 1967 by the University of Chicago Press; reprinted by permission.*

The power of the press may be roughly measured by the number of people who read it.

The growth of great cities has enormously increased the size of the reading public. Reading, which was a luxury in the country, has become a necessity in the city. In the urban environment literacy is almost as much a necessity as speech itself. That is one reason there are so many foreign-language newspapers.

Mark Villchur, editor of the *Russkoye Slovo,* New York City, asked his readers how many of them had read newspapers in the old country. He found that out of 312 correspondents only 16 had regularly read newspapers in Russia; 10 others from time to time read newspapers in the Volast, the village administration center, and 12 were subscribers to weekly magazines. In America all of them were subscribers or readers of Russian newspapers.

This is interesting because the immigrant has had, first and last, a profound influence on the character of our native newspapers. How to bring the immigrant and his descendants into the circle of newspaper readers has been one of the problems of modern journalism.

The immigrant who has, perhaps, acquired the newspaper habit from reading a foreign-language newspaper is eventually attracted to the native American newspapers. They are for him a window looking out into the larger world outside the narrow circle of the immigrant community in which he has been compelled to live. The newspapers have discovered that even men who can perhaps read no more than the headlines in the daily press will buy a Sunday paper to look at the pictures.

It is said that the most successful of the Hearst papers, the *New York Evening Journal,* gains a new body of subscribers every six years. Apparently it gets its readers mainly from immigrants. They graduate into Mr. Hearst's papers from the foreign-language press, and when the sensationalism of these papers begins to pall, they acquire a taste for some soberer journals. At any rate, Mr. Hearst has been a great Americanizer.

In their efforts to make the newspaper readable to the least-instructed reader, to find in the daily news material that would thrill the crudest intelligence, publishers have made one important discovery. They have found that the difference between the high-brow and the low-brow, which once seemed so profound, is largely a difference in vocabularies. In short, if the press can make itself intelligible to the common man, it will have even less difficulty in being understood by the intellectual. The character of present-day newspapers has been profoundly influenced by this fact.

THE FIRST NEWSPAPERS

What is a newspaper? Many answers have been given. It is the tribune of the people; it is the fourth estate;[1] the Palladium of our civil liberties, etc.

On the other hand, this same newspaper has been characterized as the great sophist. What the popular teachers did for Athens in the period of Socrates and Plato the press has done in modern times for the common man.

The modern newspaper has been accused of being a business enterprise. "Yes," say the newspaper men, "and the commodity it sells is news." It is the truth shop. (The editor is the philosopher turned merchant.) By making information about our common life accessible to every individual at less than the price of a telephone call, we are to regain, it is urged—even in the complicated life of what Graham Wallas calls the "Great Society"—some sort of working democracy.

The advertising manager's notion is again something different. For him the newspaper is a medium for creating advertising values. The business of the editor is to provide the envelope which incloses the space which the advertising man sells. Eventually the newspaper may be conceived as a sort of common carrier, like the railway or the post office.

The newspaper, according to the author of *The Brass Check*, is a crime. The brass check is a symbol of prostitution. "The brass check is found in your pay envelope every week—you write and print and distribute our newspapers and magazines. The brass check is the price of your shame—you who take the fair body of truth and sell it in the market place, who betray the virgin hopes of mankind into the loathsome brothel of big business."

This is the conception of a moralist and a socialist—Upton Sinclair.

Evidently the newspaper is an institution that is not yet fully understood. What it is, or seems to be, for any one of us at any time is determined by our differing points of view. As a matter of fact, we do not know much about the newspaper. It has never been studied.

One reason we know so little about the newspaper is that as it exists today it is a very recent manifestation. Besides, in the course of its relatively brief history, it has gone through a remarkable series of transfigurations. The press today is, however, all that it was and something more. To understand it we must see it in its historic perspective.

The first newspapers were written or printed letters; news-letters they were called. In the seventeenth century, English country-gentlemen used to employ correspondents to write them once a week from London the gossip of the court and of the town.

The first newspaper in America, at least the first newspaper that lasted beyond its first issue, was the *Boston News-Letter*. It was published by the postmaster. The village post office has always been a public forum, where all the affairs of the nation and the community were discussed. It was to be expected that there, in close proximity to the sources of intelligence, if anywhere, a newspaper would spring up. For a long time the position of postmaster and the vocation of editor were regarded as inseparable.

The first newspapers were simply devices for organizing gossip, and that, to a greater or less extent, they have remained. Horace Greeley's advice to a friend who was about to start a country paper is as good today as it was then.

Begin with a clear conception that the subject of deepest interest to an average human being is himself; next to that, he is most concerned about his neighbors. Asia and the Tongo Islands stand a long way after these in his regard. It does seem to me that most country journals are oblivious as to these vital truths. If you will, so soon as may be, secure a wide-awake, judicious correspondent in each village and township of your county, some young lawyer, doctor, clerk in a store, or assistant in a post-office who will promptly send you whatever of moment occurs in his vicinity, and will make up at least half of your journal of local matter thus collected, nobody in the county can long do without it. Do not let a new church be organized, or new members be added to one already existing, a farm be sold, a new house be raised, a mill be set in motion, a store be opened, nor anything of interest to a dozen families occur, without having the fact duly though briefly chronicled in your columns. If a farmer cuts a big tree, or grows a mammoth beet, or harvests a bounteous yield of wheat or corn, set forth the fact as concisely and unexceptionally as possible.

What Greeley advises friend Fletcher to do with his country paper the city editor of every newspaper, as far as it humanly is possible, is still trying to do. It is not practicable, in a city of three million and more, to mention everybody's name. For that reason attention is focused upon a few prominent figures. In a city where everything happens every day, it is not possible to record every petty incident, every variation from the routine of the city life. It is possible, however, to select certain particularly picturesque or romantic incidents and treat them symbolically, for their human interest rather than their individual and personal significance. In this way news ceases to be wholly personal and assumes the form of art. It ceases to be the record of the doings of individual men and women and becomes an impersonal account of manners and life.

The motive, conscious or unconscious, of the writers and of the press in all this is to reproduce, as far as possible, in the city the conditions of life in the village. In the village everyone knew everyone else. Everyone called everyone by his first name. The village was democratic. We are a nation of villagers. Our institutions are fundamentally village institutions. In the village, gossip and public opinion were the main sources of social control.

"I would rather live," said Thomas Jefferson, "in a country with newspapers and without a government than in a country with a government and without newspapers."

If public opinion is to continue to govern in the future as it has in the past, if we propose to maintain a democracy as Jefferson conceived it, the newspaper must continue to tell us about ourselves. We must somehow learn to know our community and its affairs in the same intimate way in which we knew them in the country villages. The newspaper must continue to be the printed diary of the home community. Marriages and divorce, crime and politics must continue to make up the main body of our news. Local news is the very stuff that democracy is made of.

But that, according to Walter Lippmann, is just the difficulty. "As social truth is organized today," so he says, "the press is not constituted to furnish from one edition to the next the amount of knowledge which the democratic theory of public opinion demands. ... When we expect it to supply such a body of truth, we employ a misleading standard of judgment. We misunderstand the limited nature of news, the illimitable complexity of society; we over-estimate our own endurance, public spirit, and all-round competence. We suppose an appetite for uninteresting truths which is not discovered by any honest analysis of our own tastes. ... Unconsciously the theory sets up the single reader as theoretically incompetent, and puts upon the press the burden of accomplishing whatever representative government, industrial organization, and diplomacy have failed to accomplish. Acting upon everybody for thirty minutes in twenty-four hours, the press is asked to create a mystical force called 'public opinion' that will take up the slack in public institutions."

It is evident that a newspaper cannot do for a community of one million inhabitants what the village did spontaneously for itself through the medium of gossip and personal contact. Nevertheless, the efforts of the newspaper to achieve this impossible result are an interesting chapter in the history of politics as well as of the press.

THE PARTY PAPERS

The first newspapers, the news-letters, were not party papers. Political journals began to supersede the news-letter at the beginning of the eighteenth century. The news with which the reading public was most concerned at that time was the reports of the debates in Parliament.

Even before the rise of the party press certain prying and curious individuals had made a business of visiting the Strangers' Gallery during the sessions of the House of Commons in order to write up from memory, or from notes taken down surreptitiously, accounts of the speeches and discussions during an important debate. At this time all deliberations of Parliament were secret, and it was not until one hundred years later that the right of reporters to attend the sessions of the House of Commons and record its proceedings was officially recognized. In the meantime reporters were compelled to resort to all sorts of subterfuges and indirect methods in order to get information. It is upon this information, gathered in this way, that much of our present history of English politics is based.

One of the most distinguished of these parliamentary reporters was Samuel Johnson. One evening in 1770, it is reported, Johnson, with a number of other celebrities, was taking dinner in London. Conversation turned upon parliamentary oratory. Someone spoke of a famous speech delivered in the House of Commons by the elder Pitt in 1741. Someone else, amid the applause of the company, quoted a passage from this speech as an illustration of an orator who had surpassed in feeling and beauty of language the finest efforts of the orators of antiquity. Then Johnson, who up to that point had taken no part in the discussion, spoke up. "I wrote that speech," he said, "in a garret in Exeter Street."

The guests were struck with amazement. He was asked, "How could it have been written by you, sir?"

"Sir," said Johnson, "I wrote it in Exeter Street. I never was in the gallery of the House of Commons but once. Cave had interests with the doorkeepers; he and the persons employed under him got admittance; they brought away the subjects of discussion, the names of the speakers, the side they took, and the order in which they rose, together with notes of the various arguments adduced in the course of the debate. The whole was afterward communicated to me, and I composed the speeches in the form they now have in the 'Parliamentary Debates,' for the speeches of that period are all printed from Cave's magazine."

Someone undertook to praise Johnson's impartiality, saying that in his reports he seems to have dealt out reason and eloquence with an equal hand to both political parties. "That is not quite true," was Johnson's reply. "I saved appearances tolerably well; but I took care that the Whig dogs should not have the best of it."

This speech of William Pitt, composed by Johnson in Exeter Street, has long held a place in school books and collections of oratory. It is the famous speech in which Pitt answered the accusation of the "atrocious crime of being a young man."

Perhaps Pitt thought he delivered that speech. At any rate there is no evidence that he repudiated it. I might add that Pitt, if he was the first, was not the last statesman who is indebted to the reporters for his reputation as an orator.

The significant thing about this incident is that it illustrates the manner in which, under the influence of the parliamentary reporters, something like a constitutional change was effected in the character of parliamentary government. As soon as the parliamentary orators discovered that they were addressing not only their fellow-members but, indirectly, through the medium of the press, the people of England, the whole character of parliamentary proceedings changed. Through the newspapers the whole country was enabled to participate in the discussions by which issues were framed and legislation was enacted.

Meanwhile, the newspapers themselves, under the influence of the very discussions which they themselves instigated, had become party organs. Whereupon the party press ceased to be a mere chronicle of small gossip and came to be what we know as a "journal of opinion." The editor, meanwhile, no longer a mere newsmonger and humble recorder of events, found himself the mouthpiece of a political party, playing a rôle in politics.

During the long struggle for freedom of thought and speech in the seventeenth century, popular discontent had found literary expression in the pamphlet and broadside. The most notable of these pamphleteers was John Milton, and the most famous of these pamphlets was Milton's *Areopagitica: A defense of the Liberty of Unlicensed Printing,* published in 1646; "the noblest piece of English prose" it has been called by Henry Morley.

When the newspaper became, in the early part of the eighteenth century, a journal of opinion, it took over the function of the political pamphlet. The opinion that had formerly found expression in a broadside was now expressed in the form of editorial leading articles. The editorial writer, who had inherited the mantle of the pamphleteer, now assumed the rôle of a tribune of the people.

It was in this rôle, as the protagonist of the popular cause, that the newspaper captured the imagination of our intelligentsia.

When we read in the political literature of a generation ago references to "the power of the press," it is the editor and the editorial, rather than the reporter and the news, of which these writers are thinking. Even now when we speak of the liberty of the press, it is the liberty to express an opinion, rather than the liberty to investigate and publish the facts, which is meant. The activities of the reporter, upon which any opinion that is relevant to existing conditions is likely to be based, are more often regarded as an infringement of our personal rights than an exercise of our political liberties.

The liberty of the press for which Milton wrote the *Aeropagitica* was the liberty to express an opinion. "Give me the liberty," he said, "to know, to alter, and to argue freely according to conscience, above all liberties."

Carlyle was thinking of the editorial writer and not of the reporter when he wrote: "Great is journalism! Is not every able editor a ruler of the world, being a persuader of it?"

The United States inherited its parliamentary government, its party system, and its newspapers from England. The rôle which the political journals played in English politics was re-enacted in America. The American newspapers were a power with which the British government had to reckon in the struggle of the colonies for independence. After the British took possession of New York City, Ambrose Serle, who had undertaken to publish the *New York Gazette* in the interest of the invaders, wrote as follows to Lord Dartmouth in regard to the patriot-party press.

Among other engines which have raised the present commotion, next to indecent harangues of the preachers, none has had a more extensive or stronger influence than the newspapers of the respective colonies. One is astonished to see with what avidity they are sought after, and how implicitly they are believed by the great bulk of the people.

It was nearly a century later, in the person of Horace Greeley, editor of the *New York Tribune* during the anti-slavery struggle, that the journal of opinion reached its highest expression in America. America has had better newspapermen than Horace Greeley, although none, perhaps, whose opinions exercised so wide an influence. *"The New York Tribune,"* says Charles Francis Adams, "during those years was the greatest educational factor, economically and morally, this country has ever known."

THE INDEPENDENT PRESS

The power of the press, as represented by the older type of newspaper, rested in the final analysis upon the ability of its editors to create a party and lead it. The journal of opinion is, by its very nature, predestined to become the organ of a party, or at any rate the mouthpiece of a school.

So long as political activities were organized on the basis of village life, the party system worked. In the village community, where life was and still is relatively fixed and settled, custom and tradition provided for most of the exigencies of daily life. In such a community, where every deviation from the ordinary routine of life was a matter of observation and comment and all the facts were known, the political process was, at any rate, a comparatively simple matter. Under these circumstances the work of the newspaper, as a gatherer and interpreter of the news, was but an extension of the function which was otherwise performed spontaneously by the community itself through the medium of personal contact and gossip.

But as our cities expanded and life grew more complicated, it turned out that political parties, in order to survive, must have a permanent organization. Eventually party morale became a greater value than the issues for the determination of which the parties are supposed to exist. The effect upon the party press was to reduce it to the position of a sort of house organ of the party organization. It no longer knew from day to day just what its opinions were. The editor was no longer a free agent. It was of this subjugated *Tribune* that Walt Whitman was thinking when he coined the phrase, "the kept editor."

When, finally, the exigencies of party politics, under conditions of life in great cities, developed the political machine, some of the more independent newspapers revolted. This was the origin of the independent press. It was one of the independent papers, the *New York Times* of that day, that first assailed and eventually overthrew, with the aid of a cartoonist, Thomas Nast, the Tweed Ring, the first and most outrageous of the political machines that party politics in this country has so far produced. Presently there was a general breaking away, particularly by the metropolitan, as distinguished from the country, papers, from the domination of the parties. Party loyalty ceased to a virtue.

Meanwhile a new political power had arisen and found expression in the press. This power was embodied, not in the editorial and the editorial writer, however, but in the news and the reporter. In spite of the fact that the prestige of the press, up to this time, had rested on its rôle of champion of popular causes, the older newspapers were not read by the masses of the people.

The ordinary man is more interested in news than he is in political doctrines or abstract ideas. H. L. Mencken has called attention to the fact that the average man does not understand more than two-thirds of what "comes from the lips of the average political orator or clergyman."

The ordinary man, as the *Saturday Evening Post* has discovered, thinks in concrete images, anecdotes, pictures, and parables. He finds it difficult and tiresome to read a long article unless it is dramatized and takes the form of what newspapers call a "story." "News story" and "fiction story" are two forms of modern literature that are now sometimes so like one another that it is difficult to distinguish them. The *Saturday Evening Post*, for example, writes the news in the form of fiction, while the daily press frequently writes fiction in the form of news.

When it is not possible to present ideas in the concrete, dramatic form of a story, the ordinary reader likes them stated in a short paragraph. It is said that James E. Scripps, founder of the *Detroit News* and one of the owners of several afternoon papers in secondary cities, built up his whole string of papers upon the basis of the very simple psychological principle that the ordinary man will read newspaper items in the inverse ratio to their length. His method of measuring the efficiency of his newspapers, therefore, was to count the number of items they contained. The paper that had the largest number of items was the best paper. This is just the reverse of Mr. Hearst's methods; his papers have fewer items than other papers.

The old-time journalist was inclined to have a contempt for news. News was for him simply material upon which to base an editorial. If God let things happen that were not in accordance with his conception of the fitness of things, he simply suppressed them. He refused to take the responsibility of letting his readers learn about things that he knew ought not to have happened.

Manton Marble, who was editor of the *New York World* before Joseph Pulitzer took it and made it yellow, used to say there were not eighteen thousand people in New York City to whom a well-conducted newspaper could offer to address itself. If the circulation of the paper went above that figure he thought there must be something wrong with the paper. Before Mr. Pulitzer took it over, the circulation had actually sunk to ten thousand. The old *New York World* preserved the type of the old conservative high-brow paper down to the eighties. By that time in the larger cities the politically independent newspapers had become the accepted type of journal.

Long before the rise of what was later to be called the independent press, there had appeared in New York two journals that were the forerunners of the present-day newspapers. In 1833 Benjamin Day, with a few associates, started a paper for "mechanics and the masses generally." The price of this paper [the *Sun*] was one cent, but the publishers expected to make up by larger circulation and by advertising the loss sustained by the lower price. At that time most of the other New York papers were selling for six cents.

It was, however, the enterprise of James Gordon Bennett, the founder of the *New York Herald*, which set the pace in the new form of journalism. In fact, as Will Irwin says in the only adequate account that has ever been written of the American newspaper,[2] "James Gordon Bennett invented news as we know it." Bennett, like some others who have contributed most to modern journalism, was a disillusioned man, and for that very reason, perhaps, a ruthless and cynical one. "I renounce all so-called principles," he said in his announcement of the new enterprise. By principles he meant, perhaps, editorial policies. His salutatory was at the same time a valedictory. In announcing the purposes of the new journalism he bade adieu to the aims and aspirations of the old. Henceforth the editors were to be news-gatherers, and the newspaper staked its future on its ability to gather, print, and circulate news.

What is news? There have been many answers. I think it was Charles A. Dana who said, "News is anything that will make people talk." This definition suggests at any rate the aims of the new journalism. Its purpose was to print anything that would make people talk and think, for most people do not think until they begin to talk. Thought is after all a sort of internal conversation.

A later version of the same definition is this: "News is anything that makes the reader say, 'Gee Whiz!'" This is the definition of Arthur McEwen, one of the men who helped make the Hearst papers. It is at the same time the definition of the latest and most successful type of journal, the yellow press. Not all successful journals are, to be sure, yellow. The *New York Times,* for example, is not. But the *New York Times* is not yet a type.

THE YELLOW PRESS

There seems to be, as Walter Lippmann has observed, two types of newspaper readers. "Those who find their own lives interesting" and "those who find their own lives dull, and wish to live a more thrilling existence." There are, correspondingly, two types of newspapers: papers edited on the principle that readers are mainly interested in reading about themselves, and papers edited upon the principle that their readers, seeking some escape from the dull routine of their own lives, are interested in anything which offers them what the psychoanalysts call "a flight from reality."

The provincial newspaper with its record of weddings, funerals, lodge meetings, oyster suppers, and all the small patter of the small town represents the first type. The metropolitan press, with its persistent search in the drab episodes of city life for the romantic and the picturesque, its dramatic accounts of vice and crime, and its unflagging interest in the movements of personages of a more or less mythical high society, represents the latter type.

Up to the last quarter of the nineteenth century, that is to say, up to about 1880, most newspapers, even in our large cities, were conducted on the theory that the best news a paper can print is a death notice or a marriage announcement.

Up to that time the newspapers had not yet begun to break into the tenements, and most people who supported a newspaper lived in homes rather than in apartments. The telephone had not yet come into popular use; the automobile was unheard of; the city was still a mosaic of little neighborhoods, like our foreign-language communities of the present day, in which the city dweller still maintained something of the provincialism of the small town.

Great changes, however, were impending. The independent press was already driving some of the old-time newspapers to the wall.

There were more newspapers than either the public or the advertisers were willing to support. It was at this time and under these circumstances that newspaper men discovered that circulation could be greatly increased by making literature out of the news. Charles A. Dana had already done this in the *Sun*, but there still was a large section of the population for whom the clever writing of Mr. Dana's young men was caviar.

The yellow press grew up in an attempt to capture for the newspaper a public whose only literature was the family story paper or the cheap novel. The problem was to write the news in such a way that it would appeal to the fundamental passions. The formula was: love and romance for the women; sport and politics for the men.

The effect of the application of this formula was enormously to increase the circulation of the newspapers, not only in the great cities, but all over the country. These changes were brought about mainly under the leadership of two men, Joseph Pulitzer and William Randolph Hearst.

Pulitzer had discovered, while he was editor of the *St. Louis Post-Dispatch,* that the way to fight popular causes was not to advocate them on the editorial page but to advertise them—write them up—in the news columns. It was Pulitzer who invented muck-raking. It was this kind of journalism which enabled Pulitzer, within a period of six years, to convert the old *New York World,* which was dying of inanition when he took it, into the most talked-about, if not the most widely circulated paper in New York City.

Meanwhile, out in San Francisco, Mr. Hearst had succeeded in galvanizing the old moribund *Examiner* into new life, making it the most widely read newspaper on the Pacific Coast.

It was under Mr. Hearst that the "sob sister" came into vogue. This is her story, as Will Irwin told it in *Collier's,* February 18, 1911:

Chamberlain (managing editor of the Examiner) conceived the idea that the city hospital was badly managed. He picked a little slip of a girl from among his cub reporters and assigned her to the investigation. She invented her own method; she "fainted" on the street, and was carried to the hospital for treatment. She turned out a story "with a sob for the unfortunate in every line." That was the professional beginning of "Annie Laurie" or Winifred Black, and of a departure in newspaper writing. For she came to have many imitators, but none other could ever so well stir up the primitive emotions of sympathy and pity; she was a "sob squad" all by herself. Indeed, in the discovery of this sympathetic "woman writing," Hearst broke through the crust into the thing he was after.

With the experience that he had gained on the *Examiner* in San Francisco and with a large fortune that he had inherited from his father, Hearst invaded New York in 1896. It was not until he reached New York and started out to make the *New York Journal* the most widely read paper in the United States that yellow journalism reached the limit.

Pulitzer's principal contribution to yellow journalism was muckraking. Hearst's was mainly "jazz." The newspaper had been conducted up to this time upon the theory that its business was to instruct. Hearst rejected that conception. His appeal was frankly not to the intellect but to the heart. The newspaper was for him first and last a form of entertainment.

It was about the time the yellow press was engaged in extending the newspaper habit to the masses of people, including women and immigrants—who up to this time did not read newspapers—that the department store was beginning to attract attention. The department store is, in a sense, a creation of the Sunday newspaper. At any rate, without the advertising that the Sunday newspaper was able to give it, the department store would hardly have gained the vogue it has today. It is important in this connection that women read the Sunday paper before they did the dailies. The women are buyers.

It was in the Sunday newspaper that the methods of yellow journalism were first completely worked out. The men who are chiefly responsible for them are Morrill Goddard and Arthur Brisbane. It was Goddard's ambition to make a paper that a man would buy even if he could not read it. He went in for pictures, first in black and white and then in colors. It was in the *Sunday World* that the first seven-column cut was printed. Then followed the comic section and all the other devices with which we are familiar for compelling a dull-minded and reluctant public to read.

After these methods had been worked out in the Sunday paper, they were introduced into the daily. The final triumph of the yellow journal was Brisbane's "Heart-to-Heart Editorials"—a column of predigested platitudes and moralizing, with half-page diagrams and illustrations to re-enforce the text. Nowhere has Herbert Spencer's maxim that the art of writing is economy of attention been so completely realized.

Walter Lippmann, in his study of public opinion, calls attention to the fact that no sociologist has ever written a book on newsgathering. It strikes him as very strange that an institution like the press, from which we expect so much and get so little of what we expect, should not have been the subject of a more disinterested study.

It is true that we have not studied the newspaper as the biologists have studied, for example, the potato bug. But the same may be said of every political institution, and the newspaper is a political institution quite as much as Tammany Hall or the board of aldermen is a political institution. We have grumbled about our political institutions; sometimes we have sought by certain magical legislative devices to exorcise and expel the evil spirits that possessed them. On the whole we have been inclined to regard them as sacred and to treat any fundamental criticism of them as a sort of blasphemy. If things went

wrong, it was not the institutions, but the persons we elected to conduct them, and an incorrigible human nature, who were at fault.

What then is the remedy for the existing condition of the newspapers? There is no remedy. Humanly speaking, the present newspapers are about as good as they can be. If the newspapers are to be improved, it will come through the education of the people and the organization of political information and intelligence. As Mr. Lippmann well says, "the number of social phenomena which are now recorded is small, the instruments of analysis are very crude, and the concepts often vague and uncriticized." We must improve our records, and that is a serious task. But first of all we must learn to look at political and social life objectively and cease to think of it wholly in moral terms. In that case we shall have less news, but better newspapers.

The real reason that the ordinary newspaper accounts of the incidents of ordinary life are so sensational is because we know so little of human life that we are not able to interpret the events of life when we read them. It is safe to say that when anything shocks us, we do not understand it.

NOTES

1. The three "estates of the realm" were kings, lords, and commons in the seventeenth century; later they were designated as the lords spiritual, the lords temporal, and the commons. In the eighteenth century the army was sometimes referred to as a "fourth estate," and at least once "the mob" was thus named. Probably Macaulay was the first to give this designation to "the gallery in which the reporters sit," in his essay on Hallam's *Constitutional History* in 1828, though Carlyle in his "Hero as a Man of Letters" ascribes the *bon mot* to Burke. It is not found in Burke's printed works.

2. Irwin's *The American Newspaper* was published serially in *Collier's* in 1911.

BEYOND THE JOURNALISTIC EVENT: THE CHANGING CONCEPT OF NEWS

Todd Hunt

Exactly what is "news"?

Consult the leading college textbooks of journalism and you discover that it is apparently impossible to give an adequate explanation of what news is. The most honest of the lot resorts to the old truism: "News is what you read in the newspapers." The others range from the too cute to the too neat:

"News is anything you didn't know yesterday."

"News is tomorrow's history done up in today's neat package."

"News is any event, idea or opinion that is timely, that interests or affects a large number of people in a community, and that is capable of being understood by them."

The stock-phrases of the traditional news room neatly avoid the issue of accurately defining the commodity dispensed by journalistic practitioners. Here is a sampling of the conventional wisdom a cub reporter may assimilate:

"You've got to have a nose for news." (The editor explaining how news is located.)

"I know a story when I see one." (The editor explaining how the decision is made to print the news.)

"We had that story 24 hours before anybody else in the state, including AP and UPI." (The editor verifying that the item he ran was indeed news.)

From Mass Comm Review 1 (April 1974); 23-30. Copyright © 1974 by Mass Comm Review; reprinted by permission.

HOW DID THE CONCEPT OF NEWS DEVELOP?

In Elizabethan England, news might concern reports from Ireland that the Earl of Essex was having success in quelling the rebellious Earl of Tyrone. In Colonial America, word of the 1765 Stamp Act was news when it arrived from England. And when the embattled farmers of Concord stood up to the King's militiamen, the "shot heard round the world" was, by definition, news. Certainly stunning events that change the history of a nation are "news."

When, in the early 1600s, printers first endeavored to issue news-sheets at regular intervals, the concept of "news" irrevocably began to change. For if items were to be found regularly to fill white space and provide a marketable commodity, one could not trust monarchs, parliaments and revolutionaries to supply the demand.

So, by the 1830s, American journalism had discovered the police court as a source of "news" about drunkenness, rowdiness and other such anti-social behavior on the part of the citizenry. Local politics likewise provided all manner of grist for the news mills.

Shortly after the War Between the States, a certain John B. Bogart, city editor of the New York Sun, is alleged to have told a young reporter: "When a dog bites a man, that is not news; but when a man bites a dog, that is news." And thus odd behavior, repackaged in the news rooms as "human interest stuff," became a journalistic staple.

In January 1930, William Randolph Hearst sent a letter admonishing the publishers and editors of his newspapers to print more news:

"The backbone of a newspaper is news. In other words a newspaper is a NEWSpaper ...

"NEWS is what the people want.

"NEWS pictures are what the people want.

"A NEWSpaper is what the people want."

Later this word went out to his lieutenants: "Will you please make a special point of seeing that our editors primarily make NEWS papers ...

"The text of a newspaper must tell the news.

"The headlines must tell the news.

"The pictures must tell the news.

"The subheads and subtitles must tell the news.

"Please see that the newspapers perform this function."

Hearst's editors knew well enough what he meant by "News," of course: crime reports, scandal and gossip, sex, disasters, sports and oddities, served up with scare headlines, dramatic pictures, and lurid writing slanted in such a way that it seemed always to champion the cause of the underdog, the little man.

The man who has spent the last 50 years researching items for Robert Ripley's popular "Believe It or Not" column recently told a magazine writer: there is "a primary urge to flee from the daily grind into the realm of the incredible." No publisher (to borrow the sentence structure of H. L. Mencken) ever lost money overestimating the extent of that urge.

During the period between World Wars I and II, as journalism historian Frank Luther Mott noted, the emphasis began to shift away from the classic Who-What-Where-When-Why-and-How news lead to the interpretative story, the feature, the signed column, and the by-line story by ace reporters. "The increasing complexity of the economic, social, and international news forced, by the thirties, some retreat from the ideal of purely factual news which prevailed in American reporting over fifty years." Mott wrote.

By the 1950s, schools of journalism were teaching their students "in-depth" reporting, which too often meant larger than ever doses of the 5W's and H, plus modest amounts of "interpretation" on the writer's part.

"NEWS" AS IT IS PRESENTED TODAY

It is 6 p.m. EST. The television news broadcaster manages the slightest of smiles as he greets his audience of more than a million.

"Good evening ...

"Tragedy in a Brooklyn apartment house. A 32-year-old mother drowned her three children in the bathtub of their fourth floor apartment this morning, and then took her own life with a ten-inch hunting knife belonging to her estranged husband. Police said neighbors of Mrs. Hector Smith told them she had been despondent in recent weeks....

In Manhattan, Governor Nelson Rockefeller emerged from a meeting with transit authorities and told newsmen that it will be 'only a matter of months' before the Long Island Railroad is 'the world's finest railroad,' a promise he first made nearly a year ago ...

"Meanwhile, in Grenoble, France, rescue workers continued the search for a party of 14 skiers missing after Sunday's avalanche in the world-famous resort area ..."

At which point—perhaps a tenth of the way through the half-hour prime time broadcast—the viewer might well ask himself: "This is *news?* This is somebody's notion of what I need to know about the world around me?"

The concept of "news" in the past two centuries of American history has expanded from "events affecting men" to include "non-events not really affecting men." There is far too much "news" today. It comes too close together, it is largely undifferentiated as to importance, and it is repeated endlessly. To illustrate:

The New York *Times* has an average of eleven articles commencing on page one each day. Eleven headlines vie for attention. Eleven fragmentary beginnings of stories—perhaps five paragraphs on the governor's plan to raise new revenue (continued on page 68, business and finance), four initial paragraphs on a plan to revitalize Times Square (continued on page 53, entertainment and leisure), twelve paragraphs on the woes of the Democratic Party (continued on page 33; see also related story on page 92), etc.

The New York *Times* is the most intelligently edited news vehicle in the country ... up until the stage where the information is packaged for delivery. The cluttered front page of the *Times* is a throwback to the day when seven dailies competed for newsstand attention in New York. It makes no sense today.

In the space of 47 seconds during the 6 p.m. news broadcast of January 23, 1973, WCBS-TV in New York bombarded its viewers with the following items: The son of Aristotle Onassis, the shipping magnate, died of massive head injuries in an air crash in Greece ... Eldridge Eleaver, the exiled Black Panther leader, was operated on for something-or-other in Algeria ... Timothy Leary, the high priest of LSD, was arraigned in California ... and Senator Barry Goldwater said that Senator George McGovern was a "sore loser" following McGovern's remarks at Oxford University in England regarding the meaning of the 1972 presidential election.

What is the human mind to make of all that in the space of 47 seconds? Perhaps it was nothing more than a clever and appropriate lead-in to the subsequent 30-second advertisement for a headache remedy.

On day one, a reporter interviews a school board member about an issue. Approximately two-thirds of the story is new information—quotes and observations. One-third is background information—explanations of terms used, titles, identifications, etc.

On day two, another school board member disagrees. The new story is one-third new information, one-third rehash of the previous day's story, one-third background. On day three, the superintendent of schools is interviewed. The percentage of new information drops to five or six paragraphs. The progression continues until a single unit of genuinely new information (*i.e.,* news) can trigger the accumulated outpouring of background information.

Similarly, the typical radio station, operating on a half-hour cycle of news-weather-sports-and-music, breathlessly reports the same story every 30 minutes from dawn to dusk, rearranging the order of facts only slightly and introducing it as "the headlines of the hour." Newspaper and broadcast industries alike have created a situation where a "new product" must be introduced every few hours. Detroit's much-maligned planned obsolescence of automobiles is a tortoise to journalism's hare.

As one might imagine from analyzing the products of American journalism, the typical newspaper or broadcast station news room is populated by agile folks with a high tolerance for "railroading it" and "going with what you've got"—shop talk that signifies a willingness to sacrifice completeness, orderliness, style and grace to the Great God of Deadlines. Whether educated by journalism schools or by the legendary gruff editors in green eyeshades, all learn to write in "inverted pyramids," to avoid starting lead sentences with "There is ..." and to use "he said" instead of fancy attributions that waste space and slow the reader down.

This uniformity is necessary, of course, for two basic reasons: 1) packaging the news is a fast-moving, high-pressure team effort, and 2) consuming the news is a habit. The packagers don't really stop to ponder the method of packaging the product. And the consumers don't stop to think about how they are consuming the product.

WHY IS NEWS CONCEIVED OF AND PRESENTED IN THIS WAY?

Certainly the beserk mother, the blathering politician and the dreadful avalanche are news, if by news we mean "events." But they can just as easily be chronicled in some sort of listing alongside the "vital statistics"—deaths, births, marriage license applications, divorces granted, fire runs and so forth. The Washington *Post* offers a neat and tidy round-up of the last 24 hours in street crimes, one paragraph per crime. It is interesting enough reading: "Male, white, approximately 30 years of age, accosted woman at corner of Connecticut Avenue and 18th Street at 4:15 p.m. The assailant put a knife to her throat and said, 'This is it; give me all your money.'" The crime news doesn't clutter up more than ten or fifteen inches of space each day, and it doesn't purport to be anything more than a public record embellished with a few interesting and instructive examples of current *modus operandi*. The utterances of elected officials and the tricks of nature might assume a proper perspective if they were similarly catalogued and displayed.

A BETTER WAY OF CATEGORIZING NEWS

This more logical handling of event-centered news then frees the editors to direct their efforts at gathering and presenting process-centered news. To cite the main differences between these two unfamiliar categories of news,

Event-centered news is:
Current, probably less than 24 hours old.
Uninterpreted at most, terms are explained and casual events are briefly summarized in order to offer the reader a context.
Written by journalists. That is, collected by reporters whose primary skills are maximally efficient observation and minimally biased description.

Process-centered news is:
Not necessarily current. It is written when the editors find that a writer is able to integrate and describe ongoing events in a meaningful and complete way.
Interpreted. The writer gives considerable attention to causes and offers suggestions as to resultant events.
Not necessarily written by journalists. The person (or persons) thought by the editors to be capable of analyzing, integrating and explaining accumulated events is sought to write the article.

Of course every paper runs syndicated columnists who specialize in looking at process rather than events. Experienced staff reporters are allowed to do an interpretative "sidebar" or a personalized Sunday "think piece" from time to time. But the columnists are usually displayed unimaginatively on the editorial page. And the local interpretative pieces, with the "Editor's Note" warnings, are often similarly grey.

A CLOSER LOOK AT THE GATHERING AND DISSEMINATING OF NEWS

Which-came-first, chicken-or-egg? Is American journalism event-centered because of the orientation of reporters and editors in the field, or are the practitioners forced to be event-centered because of the nature of the institution?

There is a self-reflexiveness at work: reporters get their understanding of what "news" is by looking at the event-centered product with which they are familiar. They then imitate what they have observed; they look at a process and they readily separate out the parts of that process which correspond to the accepted notion of what is "news." Publication of the reporters' stories provides positive reinforcement, and the cycle continues.

A not untypical example of the self-reflexiveness of event-centered news coverage could be seen in a sampling of the journalistic coverage of the "Summer Jam" in Watkins Glen on July 29, 1973. It was evident from preliminary stories on the wire services and broadcast stations that the reporters sent to cover the festival were on the lookout for a list of expectable things: a sea of young people, drug trips, casual nudity, promoter rip-off, quotes about "good vibes," traffic jams, patient cops, a volunteer doctor in a tent who thinks it would be better to legitimize marijuana, and finally, a mountain of trash and garbage.

Indeed, as the event got underway, the press corps proceeded to find precisely those things. The news media appeared to be obsessed with the head count that eventually placed attendance at nearly 600,000, half again as many as Woodstock attracted. In America, bigger is better; in the American press, bigger and better is a bona fide "angle" or "peg" for a news item. WCBS radio provided this telling moment:

Reporter: "I notice you aren't wearing any top, Miss. Aren't you getting a lot of stares and attention?"
Girl: "Only from reporters."

Most of the live broadcast reports from Watkins Glen were made by young reporters in their late twenties or early thirties who were probably thought by their editors to be contemporaries and peers of the festival crowd. None, however, projected any sense of having communicated with the participants on any but the most superficial level. Most of the interview segments recognized authority figures.

Reporter: "How much profit do you expect to make?"
Promoter: "Well, uh, we'll have to wait and see until all the bills are paid."
Reporter: "How long do you expect it will take until the traffic clears up?"
Sheriff: "Well, uh, it could be as much as a week."

The reporters thrust their microphones into the faces of young people and asked "Why did you come here?" ("I…um…we just heard about it, you know…") or "What do you think of all this?" ("Wow…groovy.") Something like getting up at a presidential press conference and asking "How do you like being president, Mr. President?"

Newspaper coverage was more of the same, only in great quantity. Most print accounts did list the three bands which appeared. But most omitted any mention of the type of music performed. (It was a rock festival, right? Everybody knows what rock music is. What more do you need to know?) That is a typical flaw in event-centered reporting: reducing to the familiar and labeling accordingly. Watkins Glen, with its white "boogying" music was not the Cocker-Havens-Hendrix Woodstock anymore than it was the Jagger-Stone-Angels fracas at Altamont. All rock music is not the same, and all rock festivals are not the same.

Now there's no arguing against the validity of spot news coverage of the Watkins Glen event: 600,000 people in one place is of legitimate concern. The fact that it came off without any trouble is of interest. But unfortunately, having reported those two basic facts, plus descriptive details, most editors will consider the file complete. The event is over; there is no more news, save for the obligatory wire service follow-ups on how much it cost to truck away the garbage and how some townspeople would rather not have a repeat of the rock festival in their neck of the woods.

At this point I can anticipate the question: "Well, what story should the reporters have gotten at Watkins Glen? Give me an example of your 'process-centered' story."

To which I might be expected to come back with a proposed story title bordering on the philosophical: "Where is American youth headed in the Summer of 1973? Or where is American music headed, etc."

Even this is thinking in headlines. (What story can we generate by covering this event? We must know in advance in order to justify sending a reporter out there.) Thinking in headlines, or thinking in terms of reporter productivity, is a route that leads right back to event-centered reporting. If a reporter is schooled to understand that he must go out and discover a "packageable" truth, he is automatically limited in what he can see.

What it boils down to is this: if the self-reflexiveness of event-centered reporting is to be avoided, news media will have to nurture a whole new breed of information gatherers. They will have to be people who are capable of going into a situation—such as the "Summer Jam"—and studying the event at a generic level: "What's going on here? What are these people doing? How are they using this event? Are they all using it the same way; if not, what differences and variations are there?"

Instead of responding as the typical reporter does, glorying in the discovery of a "fact" which makes the phenomenon easily explainable, the process-centered reporter instinctively doubts the "fact" and resists over-simplification. Throughout the information-gathering process, he must also attempt to ascertain which of his own biases, what parts of his own cultural makeup, are acting as filters on the information. He does this, perhaps, by sharing his observations with others and attempting to put some value on *their* responses to the reporter's responses.

What kind of story does the reporter then write? Perhaps none at all, for the time being. He might want to spend the next few days, or weeks, using other types of resources to augment his observations. He may merge this story with another, if he can make an interesting connection. He may decide that an impressionistic account—light on "facts," but rich in anecdotal detail—is worth disseminating to the public at this point, with the option of returning to the subject matter at a later date when subsequent events, information or thought offer a fresh dimension.

I can anticipate the criticism from old-line journalists: "You're talking about the kind of stuff they run in magazines. That's not what people want in their daily newspapers."

More self-reflexiveness: editors assume that people must want more of what they've been getting, and readers assume that a newspaper is supposed to look like the product that the editors have been giving them.

Exactly eight days after "Summer Jam," the Sunday Arts and leisure section of the New York *Times* and *The National Observer* carried useful and interesting process-centered reports datelined Watkins Glen. The stories seemed "right" at that temporal remove and in those particular publications. But they could seem just as "right" on page one of Tuesday's hometown daily. It is a matter of gradually adjusting the newspaper audience's expectations regarding "news" content.

AUGMENTING THE REPORTING STAFF

Reporters are not necessarily the best reporters. When we note that a reporter brings "experience" to a news situation, what we are saying is that he sees the event as being similar or not similar to events he has previously reported. Any young person who has broken in under an experienced reporter has probably suffered the indignity of being told that a promising story idea "isn't news." What the old hand is actually saying might be translated: "I did that story years ago when I was a cub, but now I've got my beat routinized in such a way that I don't perceive of that as something worth writing about."

One of the heartening trends brought about by the fluid job market of recent years and the increased college training of young journalists is that important news beats are being given to "inexperienced" reporters who bring the advantage of *tabula rasa* to important stories. Unlike the hard-bitten, I've-seen-it-all pros, they approach the subject with a certain fervor, much as youthful Nader's Raiders study groups attack problems that the legal establishment has come to take for granted.

A strong case can also be made, I believe, for augmenting reporters with nonstaff writers on an *ad hoc* basis. The writing of process-centered news might be handled by essayists from such diverse fields as anthropology, social psychology, architecture, philosophy and literature. Their format would not be the inverted pyramid, which ranks facts and meta-facts in order of ability to astonish, but rather the essay. An essay is an attempt *(essai,* French for "try") to present an idea and support it through a logical development of facts and related ideas.

The proposal is hardly revolutionary. The New York *Times* Op-Ed page might run an essay by Willy Brandt alongside one by Woody Allen. The *National Observer* and the *Christian Science Monitor* departmentalize and condense event-centered news, devoting a large portion of their non-advertising space to attractively packaged essays. These, of course, are quality publications catering to readers of above-average intelligence. But there is no reason why the New York *Daily News*, the paper that Ayn Rand and Truman Capote say they read, couldn't introduce the essay format to the popular audience.

It is important, too, that traditional sources of story ideas be augmented. The managing editor's futures file, the handout basket, the reporter's check of his "run" are adequate ways of finding event-centered news. But once again, self-reflexiveness is evident: stories are considered news today because they were news before.

How are sources of process-centered news ideas developed? By innovative techniques such as the "Committee on the Future" at the *Times-Union*, Gannett's Rochester, N. Y., paper. Editor John Dougherty conducts extended, away-from-work sessions with half a dozen staff members at a time—eventually he will have included the entire staff—in an attempt to anticipate what changes will be necessary in future coverage so that the newspaper will be prepared to understand and explain complex events. Anything goes at the meetings; no idea or suggestion is met with a rebuttal that "we've always done it that way" or "that would be nice, but …"

The Associated Press Managing Editors Association (APME) last year conducted four major surveys which eventually led to series of articles on "The Mood of America." An attempt was made to provide insight into what Americans are thinking and worrying about, and what things concern experts in various fields. A committee of APME also has begun to use experts—theologians, economists, scientists, lawyers and teachers—to advise the press about ongoing stories (process-centered news) that need to be explored. The resulting special articles and series have helped the Associated Press service augment its considerable flow of event-centered news.

In addition, the leading newspapers now send reporters and editors to sit in on conferences at "think tanks" here and abroad—not to write stories, but to keep abreast of intellectual developments and trends.

Because process-centered news is usually complex, it may be necessary for the news media to use terms of specialist-reporters in order to cover a story adequately. An example: During the week of July 23, 1973, CBS radio presented a series on the relationship of the world's weather to economics. Ray Brady, the radio network's business reporter, and meteorologist Gordon Barnes teamed up to present an explanation of how droughts and floods around the world in 1972 and 1973 were responsible for scarcity, thus generating the current high prices of food. It was apparent to the listener that the synergy of two reporters combining their efforts resulted in a more meaningful and multi-dimensional report than one might have expected if a single correspondent had presented the in-depth story.

Yet another way in which the information-gathering function can and should be improved is through the use of the latest social science methods. In *Precision Journalism,* Knight correspondent Philip Meyer argues that newspapers must take advantage of man's greatly increased capacity for managing data. He suggests, for example, that the computer can be used by the political reporter to determine where to look for pre-election stories. He cites the example of a reporter on a large-city daily with a data-processing department who used punched cards to analyze the operations of the local courts. The resulting stories told more about the subject than anyone had known before, according to Meyer.

The daily news media can and must move beyond the journalistic event, into an ongoing examination of the processes of human behavior. The front page and the news broadcast of the mid-Twentieth Century may appear as quaint to our grandchildren as the image of the old town crier is to us.

IS OBJECTIVITY POSSIBLE?

Donald McDonald

Truth and politics are on rather bad terms with each other. No one, as far as I know, has ever counted truthfulness among the political virtues. ... Seen from the viewpoint of politics, truth has a despotic character. It is therefore hated by tryants, who rightly fear the competition of a coercive force they cannot monopolize, and it enjoys a rather precarious status in the eyes of governments that rest on consent and abhor coercion.
—HANNAH ARENDT

The antidote for political deviousness is journalistic integrity. Since truthfulness is not a political virtue, it has to be a journalistic virtue.

But perhaps integrity and truthfulness are terms that are too morally intense, too loaded with accusatory implications for an analysis

From The Center Magazine 4 (September/October 1971): 29-42. Reprinted with permission from The Center Magazine, a publication of the Center for the Study of Democratic Institutions, Santa Barbara, California.

limiting elements in the practice of public-affairs journalism. Journalistic objectivity is a better term. Badly misunderstood and badly applied as it has been in the history of American journalism, objectivity subsumes all the mass-communication virtues—moral, artistic, and intellectual. It covers the individual journalist and the institution that employs him. And while it is a goal it is also a process, a kind of operational guideline, a demanding but not impossibly idealistic criterion of professional competence.

Objectivity (not to be confused with objectivism, a specialized and technical philosophical theory of knowledge) is here used to mean simply an essential correspondence between knowledge of a thing and the thing itself. The best translation of the term into its journalistic application may have been furnished by the Freedom of the Press Commission in 1947. The Commission said that, among other things, the press owes to society "a truthful, comprehensive, and intelligent account of the day's events in a context which gives them meaning."

I suppose that no reporter or editor would take exception to such a definition of the journalist's responsibility. Not many reporters get up in the morning and say to themselves, "Today I am going to file a lying, incomplete, ignorant report of an event taken out of context." But then how account for the quality of public affairs journalism in this country? Arthur R. Murphy, the former chairman of *McCall's* magazine, has said that in spite of our ten thousand newspapers, eight thousand magazines, and seven thousand radio and television stations, Americans suffer from an "understanding gap" and are "ill-informed and confused about major issues and events."

Objectivity is problematic in public-affairs journalism because elements and practices in the reporting process are taken for granted and perpetuated by journalists when they should be critically examined. The reporter, the reader-viewer, the conventions of American journalism, the forms and processes of the communications institutions, language, the investigative and interpretive functions of the reporter, all affect the objectivity of mass communication. A misunderstanding or malfunctioning of any of them is enough to defeat or at least seriously impair the efforts of even the most nobly motivated journalist.

Let us begin with the reporter. From the myriad of details of an event or situation, the reporter selects those which seem to him most significant, investigates and asks questions to clarify the meaning of what he has perceived, and then organizes his knowledge in a report. What the reporter selects for attention, the weight he puts on the various elements, the kinds of questions he asks, are all influenced by the personal history he brings to his work.

Indeed, even what he initially perceives is conditioned by history. Some years ago, Dr. Robert Livingston, then with the National Institute of Mental Health, on a visit to the Center, reported that experiments by neurosurgeons and neurophysiologists indicate that man's entire nervous system, in its interpreting, sensing, and transmitting to the brain the information it receives, builds up through the years total-response patterns which, as they stabilize, thenceforth affect in a definite accept-reject manner the perceiving capacity of a person.

We are familiar with the classic psychological and sociological experiments testing the ability of students to perceive, recall, and report staged dramatic incidents they have witnessed. The wildly varying reports of the same incident reflect what Walter Lippmann has called the tricks of memory and the incessant creative qualify of the imagination of the witness.

According to Lippmann, experience seems to show that the reporter brings something to the scene which later he takes away from it. A report is the joint product of the knower and the known, in which the role of the observer is always selective and usually creative. The facts we see depend on where we are placed and the habits of our eyes.

A few years ago, when Lillian Ross's book, *Reporting,* appeared, her publisher claimed that one never doubts that what she sees is the truth. But a reviewer in the *Times Literary Supplement* demurred. "One eyewitness," the reviewer said, "tells us what she has seen and heard and put together; it is not the truth about anything, but one person's selection from the chaos of facts, images, words, all the ingredients of experience she has witnessed from her single viewpoint. We might guess more about the truth or at least the heart of the matter, all the omissions and distortions, if we knew more about the reporter, her psychological blocks, and the limits of her experience, but it is a conceit of this school of reporting to pretend to omit the reporter. The reporter, however, is human and therefore limited, and if we have no knowledge of her limitations we are merely being deceived."

The reviewer went on to say that "James Agee was at the opposite extreme as a reporter. He wrote in perhaps the greatest work of reportage of this century, *Let Us Now Praise Famous Men,* about a tenant farmer: 'I know him only so far as I know him: and all of that depends as fully on who I am as on who he is.' Thus Agee accepted, as Miss Ross apparently does not, that any subject is sieved through a reporter's self and, therefore, Agee showed the interplay between himself and the people and places he was trying to describe."

Now, whether Miss Ross rejects what Mr. Agee accepted, and whether or how it would be feasible for every reporter to reveal within every report his "psychological blocks and the limits of his experience," and whether Miss Ross's reporting is "not the truth about anything" are all arguable. What is not deniable is the sieving process through which reality must pass in the reporter's work. The question is, how can reality emerge from this subjective process without being essentially diminished and distorted? I do not think the answer lies simply in the reporter's showing the interplay between himself and the things he is reporting. At best this permits the reader to discount the report for its acknowledged subjective elements, but it leaves him waiting for a more satisfying, more objective, less distorted account of public affairs.

When the reporter moves from relatively uncomplicated, concrete, even physical phenomena into the realm of the abstract and the complex—i.e., studies, conferences, programs, policies on urban affairs, race and ethnic relations, foreign and military affairs, economic and fiscal conditions, the administration of criminal justice, cultural ferment, youth unrest, population problems, environmental issues, politics, and government—the value judgments he must make at every critical stage in his investigation and interpretation of the facts must reflect the values he already holds. Again, these values flow from his personal history. They are the products of his education, his religious experience, his childhood, family life, social and economic background, friendships and associations, national ties and culture, as well as his emotional life and experiences, and his reason.

Take just one of the value-influences in the reporter's life: his national ties. Both individual reports of the Vietnam war and over-all coverage have differed markedly from nation to nation. This cannot be attributed altogether to external censorship. I. F. Stone once noted that an Associated Press dispatch on American military, political, and diplomatic activity in Vietnam, prepared for publication in the French newspaper, *Le Monde,* contained material far more critical of the United States than anything filed by the A.P. for consumption in American newspapers.

A book by Jay Epstein raised serious questions about the Warren Commission's investigation of the Kennedy assassination.

Richard Rovere has said that Epstein is a scholar who had done what the American press should have done when the Warren Commission report was issued. "It should have cast a very cool eye on the report and sought to learn from those who prepared it how it was prepared, who did the heavy work, and what individual workers thought of the collective product. Mr. Epstein's scholarly tools happen to be those employed day in and day out by journalists. But the press left it to a single scholar to find the news."

Epstein suggested that a kind of national loyalty seems to have got in the way of the journalists and their reporting obligation. They produced a "version of the truth...to reassure the nation and protect the national interest."

George Orwell's classic essay, "Politics and the English Language," suggests not only that politics and language can be mutually degrading when in the hands of corrupt persons, but that all of us, including reporters, go along rather uncritically with the degrading process. A paragraph from Orwell's essay, written more than thirty years ago, is an uncomfortable reminder that little has changed in those three decades:

In our time, political speech and writing are largely the defense of the indefensible. Things like the continuance of British rule in India, the Russian purges and deportations, the dropping of the atom bombs on Japan, can indeed be defended, but only by arguments which are too brutal for most people to face, and which do not square with the professed aims of political parties. Thus political language has to consist largely of euphemism, question-begging, and sheer cloudy vagueness. Defenseless villages are bombarded from the air, the inhabitants driven out into the countryside, the cattle machine-gunned, the huts set on fire with incendiary bullets: this is called pacification. *Millions of peasants are robbed of their farms and sent trudging along the roads with no more than they can carry: this is called* transfer of population *or* rectification of frontiers. *People are imprisoned for years without trial, or shot in the back of the neck, or sent to die of scurvy in Arctic lumber camps: this is called* elimination of unreliable elements. *Such phraseology is needed if one wants to name things without calling up mental pictures of them....*

No one can, or perhaps ever will, prevent politicians and political organizations from using language this way. The question is whether journalists can rise above natural allegiance to their nation and report the realities obscured by this kind of partisan euphemism.

Another element in the reporting process affecting objectivity is the journalistic conventions, as distinguished from journalistic processes. The latter inhere in the very nature of the medium (newspaper, magazine, radio, television) and are to that extent inescapable, though sometimes they can be modified in the interest of objectivity. Journalistic conventions, however, were established to meet historical conditions. As such they can be sharply modified, or even discarded and new ones substituted when those historical conditions no longer exist, or when, again in the interest of objective reporting, the conventions are no longer useful or even obstructive. But conventions have a way of hanging on.

The most pernicious journalistic convention is the notion that a thing is not newsworthy until it becomes an event; that is, until something happens. Two things follow from this: first, significant phenomena that are not events (e.g., situations, trends, conditions) go largely unreported; second, often the context, which can make even an event meaningful, is either not reported or reported inadequately.

It was not until Michael Harrington wrote his book on poverty in America (*The Other America*) that national consciousness was focused on a situation existing in the backyard of every metropolitan newspaper in the United States.

It was not until Richard Harris reported in *The New Yorker* on the unethical conditions in the ethical-drug industry that the American people were alerted to a situation that the wire services or even a metropolitan newspaper could have investigated and reported years before.

At the height of the Watts riots in 1965, a white Protestant churchman in Los Angeles shook his head and said, "I hadn't known such conditions [despair, unemployment, resentment among the blacks] existed in that area."

Even as sophisticated a newspaper as *The New York Times* has not always been able to free itself from the notion that "something has to happen" before you can publish. The May, 1966, issue of *Times Talk,* the house newsletter written by and for staff members of the *Times,* contains an article by Tom Wicker, of the *Times'* Washington bureau, on the circumstances surrounding the paper's publication that year of a series of articles on the Central Intelligence Agency. Six members of the *Times* had spent months interviewing, researching, writing, rewriting the material for those articles. At last they were ready for publication. But it seems they really were not ready.

"Turner Catledge [then executive editor of the *Times*]," Wicker said, "had insisted from the first on having an adequate news peg. Months now had passed since the 'Singapore incident' set the whole thing off. Weeks were to pass before the right time came to publish. Finally *Ramparts* magazine broke the Michigan State case, in which it was discovered that C.I.A. agents had been given cover in a big aid program the university operated for the Diem regime in South Vietnam."

Also in the news at that time was a slander suit in a Baltimore court involving a C.I.A. agent.

"Thus," Wicker continued, "with the C.I.A. in the news again, the time was ripe, public interest was awakened, and our editors thought we had the justification we needed for five articles, twenty-three thousand words in all, trying to answer the questions we had asked ourselves those long months ago. Hastily, over a weekend, we wrote the news-peg material into the pieces and gave the galley proofs a last close check for accuracy and for any updating needed."

Another convention of American journalism is that reader interest can only be attracted by conflict, novelty, or recency. This leads the reporter to neglect that which can make his report meaningful, the context. The

Los Angeles *Times,* ordinarily fastidious in its reporting of public affairs, lapsed a few years ago with some no-context reporting in its coverage of strikes by county social-welfare workers and hospital employees. The paper detailed the conflict elements in the strikes: the accusations and counteraccusations by strikers and county supervisors, the actions by pickets and nonstrikers, the threats and counterthreats. But aside from one vague reference to "working conditions" the reporters did not tell the readers the context of the strikes. The actual pay and working conditions of the workers, the level of their education, their compensation related to the nature of their work and cost of living, the history of salary increases, the comparison of pay scales with those of similar workers in other cities—none of this contextual material was furnished until a week or two later after letters had been sent to the editors pointing out the omission.

This convention—that reader interest can only be attracted and held by the bizarre, by conflict, novelty, recency—stemmed in part from the days when newspapers competed with each other for readers within the same community, when the educational level of the average American adult was low, and when the time and energy the American worker could give to informing himself on public affairs was sharply limited. Those conditions no longer exist.

There are other journalistic conventions that need reëxamination, perhaps discarding. James Reston has described, in *Foreign Affairs,* how the press associations invented the headline or all-purpose agency news story which could be published at length in the large city papers or cut in half for the middle towns or reduced to a paragraph for the very small papers. This solution to a technical problem had results nobody in the Associated Press or United Press International intended. "It tended to sharpen and inflate the news," Reston wrote. "It created a tradition of putting the most dramatic fact in the story first and then following it with paragraphs of decreasing importance. Thus it encouraged not a balanced but a startling presentation of the news, based on what one of my irreverent colleagues calls the 'Christ, how the wind blew!' lead. This was fine for the news of wrecks or murders, but was a limiting and distorting device as news of foreign policy became more and more complicated."

Reston is convinced that newspaper journalists must twist themselves around and "see these wider perspectives of the news, the causes as well as the effects.... Ideas are news, and we are not covering the news of the mind as we should. This is where rebellion, revolution, and war start, but we minimize the conflict of ideas and emphasize the conflict in the streets, without relating the second to the first."

I have often been struck by the way in which serious books—the "news of the mind"—are handled by the American press. When they are not ignored, they pop up in book pages, more often than not as notices rather than reviews. The idea that books such as Lewis Mumford's *The Myth of the Machine,* or Jean Gottmann's study of the metropolitan city, or Ivar Berg's *Education and Jobs: The Great Training Robbery* are important news events, or, better, serious treatments of public affairs worth reporting as such, does not occur in a climate of conventional journalistic values.

A third element in the reporting process is the thing reported. It is a commonplace that complexity is a characteristic of public affairs. Robert Lekachman, the economist, has criticized the mass media for not respecting the complexity of economic issues which, he says, almost always relate to other problems of civil rights, urbanization, transportation, education, space and science research. But with few exceptions these are reported, Lekachman says, as items of interest only to the business and financial community. Thus, a

Presidential message on the budget and the economic condition of the nation—a matter of wide-ranging social, cultural, and political ramifications—will be explained, if it is explained at all, in narrow terms and invariably in the business section of the newspaper.

Public-affairs issues are complex not only in their horizontal relationships with other issues but also vertically in their own historical antecedents. The meaning of American involvement in Vietnam is largely bound up with an historical sequence of events which started in the late nineteen-forties and which were themeselves influenced by our obsession with communism (which had *its* antecedents), as well as with the history of Vietnam itself and that people's two-thousand-year relationship with China and its much briefer relationship with France.

Too, public-affairs issues are usually not neat, beginning-middle-and-end "stories," but continually unfolding realities, and therein lies another dimension of their complexity. The reporter's accounts will be faithful to that fact if they are themselves open-ended, provisional, constantly revised as the issues play themselves out and as reactions follow actions.

The task of the objective reporter is to discover and communicate the coherence of a complex, unfolding reality. He can do it by his contextual reporting; by plainly showing the unavoidable but significant gaps in his information; by recapitulating and reviewing the reality in print when important new facts become available; by continuous surveying of the current literature which may illuminate shadowy areas; and by interviewing experts and scholars for further illumination.

Einar Ostgaard of the Peace Research Institute in Oslo and Jacques Ellul, the French social critic, are not the only ones to have commented on the discontinuities in the mass media's presentation of great public issues. But none have made the point more sharply.

Ostgaard traces the discontinuities to the way the media define newsworthiness. As long as news must have a certain simplicity, easy reader identification, closeness in either a physical or cultural sense, and excitement—as long as this kind of a news barrier is in effect, there will be little or no continuity in the presentation of world events.

"Certain news media," Ostgaard writes, "will attempt to present a continuous report of what happens. But as long as a decision on whether or not to publish a story is also based on [the above] considerations, the result must be a certain degree of discontinuity.... A report from London may appear on a Monday, drop out of sight on Tuesday and Wednesday for lack of space (although the news agencies are still dutifully reporting), reappear on Thursday, but by now [there is] a mystery since what went on in the interim was never published."

The interim developments were omitted "because these happenings were no longer 'news.' Proximity in time is often a major prerequisite for a news story. Thus, the shorter the time it takes for an event 'to happen' the more likely it is to be reported fully, and conversely, the longer the time it takes, the larger the probabilities that only an incomplete picture of the event will be presented. This time factor is also probably related to the degree to which the event will appear exciting and this contributes to the 'sensationalism' factor."

Ostgaard quotes from Bernard Cohen's study of the matter: "In hopping from issue to issue, from crisis to crisis, the correspondent deals in political discontinuities" and gives a "grossly uneven, often misleading picture of the world and its political relationships and problems....So far from reflecting difficult international realities as they confront the statesman [such reporting] has no politically relevant public-opinion uses....If the reporting of developments in terms of conflict exacerbates conflict, then, *mutatis mutandis,* the simplification of foreign-affairs reporting exacerbates the dangers of simplification in the approach to complex issues."

Ellul noted in his book, *The Political Illusion,* that "man has discontinuous consciousness, and the first effect of news on him is not to make him more capable of being a citizen but to disperse his attention, to absorb it, and present to him an excessive amount of information that he will not be able to absorb, information too diverse to serve him in any way whatever....

"As a result, a truly stupefying lack of continuity is created, for if one information item merely effaces the other on the same subject, it would not be so bad; but a continuous flow of information on a specific question, showing a problem's origin, growth, crisis, and denouement is very rare. Most frequently my attention, attracted today by Turkey, will be absorbed tomorrow by a financial crisis in New York and the day after tomorrow by parachutists in Sumatra. In the midst of all this, how can a man not specially trained perceive the slightest continuity, experience the slightest political continuity; how, finally, can he understand? He can literally only react to news."

The processes of the communications media, as distinct from the conventions adopted by journalists, inhere in the nature of the media and in their forms—primarily the printed words and photographs of the newspaper and magazine, the broadcast language of radio, and the words and motion pictures of television. Obviously, inherent processes cannot be discarded and replaced. But if their distinctive effects are understood and their limitations recognized, they can be used more effectively in the interest of objective reporting; at the minimum, working journalists will be less likely to deceive themselves as to how "truthful, comprehensive, and intelligent" are their accounts of public affairs.

When the Army-McCarthy hearings were televised in the nineteen-fifties, it seemed that for the first time the essence of what had come to be called McCarthyism was communicated to the American people. Television sight and sound revealed something about Joseph McCarthy which print journalists had labored in vain to reveal in the preceding four or five years. Professional opinion poll-takers say that McCarthy's decline dates from those hearings.

Similarly, television documentaries on the working and living conditions of migratory farm workers, on life in the black ghettos, on the treatment given in homes for the aged and the mentally ill, on drug addiction, on conditions in prisons, have communicated those realities in a way that print journalists cannot hope to match through the written word.

And it was not until John F. Kennedy and Richard Nixon were simultaneously compared and contrasted in their televised Presidential campaign debates in 1960 that many American people formed a judgment as to the character and capabilities of the candidates.

We can go back to Cardinal Newman and all the way back to Aristotle for an explanation of what it is and why it is that televised communication has a more immediately powerful and gripping impact than print and why, at the same time, it is so severely limited in other respects.

Television simulates personal experience. While our understanding of a thing through experience may be far from complete, our assent to the existential judgment of the reality of that thing will be, in Newman's distinction, real as compared to notional. If one is told Britain is an island, Newman said, one makes a notional assent. If one actually sees that Britain is an island, sails all around it, one's assent to the truth becomes real.

But assent is not always equivalent to understanding. Experience, Aristotle said, is of individual things; understanding and wisdom are of causes and universals. "We do not regard any of our senses as wisdom, yet surely these give the most authoritative knowledge of particulars. But they do not tell us the 'why' of anything."

Although television is by its nature sense-oriented, engaging our sight and hearing, and therefore primarily concerned with particulars, it can explore the "why" of things when it also engages our reason. The more probing televised documentary films travel a respectable distance in that direction.

But it is the simulated personal experience, and all the moral and emotional content, the immediacy, and the self-involvement in personal experience that characterize television's effect. Undoubtedly we experience far more than we understand, and it is probably no less true that it is experience rather than understanding that most influences our behavior, even when the televised experience is not only simulated but manipulated, as Joe McGinnis showed us in his report, *The Selling of the President.* Certainly the contrived image of Richard Nixon and the rigorously controlled conditions under which he was presented to the viewers in 1968 resulted in many of them apparently acting on *that* experience of Mr. Nixon rather than on any genuine knowledge of the man.

The power of television to influence behavior is not diminished because politicians, and the television journalists themselves, can falsify the reality they are broadcasting. Indeed, the effectiveness of the deception underscores the power of the television medium as such.

But for an understanding of complex public-affairs issues and a grasp of the "why" of an event, we need more than the sight and the sound provided by television, more than the uncontrived experience of what the camera and microphone in the hands of truthful and competent broadcast journalists can convey to us, more than the moral conviction and emotional involvement aroused by such an experience. We need the opportunity for recurrent study and reflection on these issues. In short we need to make

room for the work of reason. And for that, the printed word is indispensable.

It is the special temptation of television newsmen to believe that visibility and meaning are synonymous. But one television journalist, Walter Cronkite, resists the temptation. He has said that electronic journalism will never replace the written word in the communication of the meaning of public affairs. In the interest of objectivity, television reporters can, in the very act of reporting, make clear to their viewers what aspects of an issue or situation their medium must leave either unreported or only partially reported, and the reasons why.

The time and space allotted for reporting significantly affect the objectivity of the journalist's work. It can be argued that speed is a convention rather than an inherent process of mass communication. I think it is more accurate to say that the daily rhythm and tempo of mass communication correspond to the rhythm and tempo of human life itself. But it must also be said that a mutual, or reciprocating, action occurs: i.e., the rhythm and tempo of human action, the affairs of mankind, can be adjusted to meet the requirements of the communications media. When a President times an outburst of indignation so that it will be seen on the television screen in the evening or be read in the Sunday morning metropolitan papers of the nation, obviously public affairs have been adjusted to the rhythm of the media. (The Presidential display, at its inception, may be what Daniel Boorstin has described as a "pseudo-event," but once it occurs it is an authentic public affair, more or less rich, more or less significant, but a public affair nonetheless).

Objectivity is affected not so much by mutual adjustments in rhythm and tempo between the media and the actors in the drama of public affairs as it is by the easy—often lazy—assumption adopted by some journalists that their breathless journalism is adequate to the communication of public affairs. It is the indiscriminate application of speed and the forcing of all public affairs, no matter how complex, obscure, and developmental they may be, into the mold of instant journalism that threatens objectivity.

Obviously many human affairs have their regular diurnal aspect. Sporting contests, stock-market activities, educational programs—these have their clocklike patterns, they are predictable, they mesh with the mass media communication timetables. But it is axiomatic that the more serious and consequential the public affairs, the untidier they will be and the more unmanageable they will be by any of the metronomic standards set by the print and electronic media.

Those metronomic imperatives sometimes exert a fascinating effect on editors and a bizarre, distorting effect on their journalism. Douglass Cater in his book, *The Fourth Branch of Government,* tells about one Washington wire-service editor who, in a running story, in order to have "something of interest" for editors of both morning and afternoon papers, "creates" stories by baiting public officials with "conflict queries."

Although language is the indispensable tool of the journalist, one need not read very widely on the subject nor think about it at any great length to realize that language demands the ultimate in craftsmanship, moral sensitivity, and intelligence. How language is used is crucial to the possibility of objective journalism. Herewith, some testimony to the difficulties in making language serve the cause of objectivity:

Much self-control and great disinterestedness are needed by those who would realize the ideal of never misusing language. A man who habitually speaks and writes correctly is one who has cured himself, not merely of conscious and deliberate lying, but also (and the task is much more difficult and at least as important) of unconscious mendacity.

—ALDOUS HUXLEY

Nothing is more common than for men to think that because they are familiar with words they understand the ideas they stand for.

—CARDINAL NEWMAN

[The Thomists] showed that language and meaning depend on the past experiences of men; that different words can mean different things to different men; that neither language nor knowledge is identical with reality. The Scholastic maxim—"never deny; rarely affirm; always distinguish"—is a medieval way, if you wish, of warning against the dangers of over-generalization.

—MARGARET GORMAN

If there is one thing certain, the truth will not be caught once and for all in a net of words alone.

—WELLER EMBLER

The spoken word and the reading of its written equivalent are both of them fundamentally the exercise of choice at every step—choosing not only the right sounds and combinations of sounds but also the right words and combinations of words to fit the continually emerging patterns both of language and of life.

—JOSHUA WHATMOUGH

The fact remains that, imperfect as words are as symbols of our ideas and as expressions of our thoughts, the journalist cannot dispense with them. Words may not be sufficient, but they are necessary. Even Marshall McLuhan's envisioned electric future in which experience will be communicated visually and configurationally rather than in the sequential, linear form of the printed word is a communication impossibility without the use of language.

Let us stipulate, then, that language alone is an imperfect medium for the expression of truth. Words can be inexact when precision is needed; ambiguous when univocal meaning is required; connotative when definition and denotation are demanded; allusive when identity is sought.

But it would be too easy and certainly misleading to conclude that the infelicities of language are indefeasible. After due allowances are made for the irreducible element of imperfection in words as signs of things and thoughts, it seems obvious that the task of communicating through language is primarily intellectual. Clear expression begins with clear thinking.

The task is also one of artistry. The craftsmanship of putting clear thoughts into clear language is complicated, but not defeated, by the ambiguity of words. Here the emphasis on speed in mass communication can be a crippling condition imposed on the public-affairs journalist. No matter how much the responsible journalist respects words and the intellectual and craft demands which their usage imposes, it is virtually impossible for him to develop the requisite intellectual and artistic habits if his editors enforce their deadlines inflexibly and indiscriminately, no matter how complex, subtle, and historically embedded may be the thing he is reporting.

Ordinarily public affairs do not happen or exist with their explanatory context already built into them. They must be investigated, not simply looked at. And then the materials must be interpreted.

American editors and publishers old enough to remember the era of personal journalism which existed well into the twentieth century are still wary of any effort to interpret the news. They identify interpretation with opinion, prejudice, slanting, distortion, surmise, speculation, and advocacy. And all of these qualities were indeed distinguishing features of old-time personal journalism. It sought to move and persuade rather than enlighten readers.

Reacting against this, publishers developed what they thought was a splendid alternative, an objectivity so narrowly defined that what was eliminated was not only opinionated editorializing in the news columns but also any opportunity for the reporter to put what he was reporting into a context which would make it meaningful. This was thought to be the objectivity of the scientist in his laboratory, meticulously recording what his senses perceived, impersonal, unprejudiced, and, above all, humble before the demonstrable fact. Actually the scientist was doing much more than this: his investigations led him to look for causes and relationships, and his intuitive and creative faculties were never idle.

But this only partly understood scientific model on which journalistic objectivity was patterned is ill-adapted to the work of the public-affairs reporter. The truths of public affairs are not encompassed by their appearances, or by what can be perceived only by the senses. As Eric Severeid pointed out some years ago, when journalists confined their coverage of the late Senator Joseph McCarthy simply to what the senator said and did, far from producing objective journalism they were producing "the big lie." For the truth, or the meaning, of McCarthy could never be discerned from any particular statement he made or act he performed. It could only be discerned by relating the particular action to previous, possibly contradictory, actions; to the web of current and contemporary history in which the actions took place; and to known realities which the senator had ignored or misstated but which were relevant if readers were to be able to understand the senator and to form a judgment about his responsibility.

Of course, publishers and editors are not so naïve as to think that flat, one-dimensional, surface reporting is adequate to the needs of readers. But the solution some of them propose—a division of labor, with the reporter furnishing the facts in the news columns and editorial writers supplying the interpretation and analysis on the editorial page or in specially designated columns labeled "interpretive report"—is practically ineffectual and, I suspect, even theoretically untenable. It assumes that fact-gathering and interpreting are separable reporting functions. I think a convincing case can be made that fact-gathering, investigation, and interpretation are integral aspects and, for the purpose of the objective report itself, they are indivisible.

Certainly interpretive reporting contains subjective elements. But it will be an essentially objective act to the extent that the interpretation is grounded in the realities of an event or situation and to the extent that these grounds are clearly shown and evaluated by the reporter within his report. There is no reporting—even the "scientifically" objective, bare-facts reporting—which is free from subjective influence; the reporter does have to be subjective in selecting which of the bare facts he will include in his report. But the reporter's subjective judgment cannot be described as manipulative and distorting when it is oriented to the objective realities of the thing he is reporting.

The interpretive reporter and the editorialist both make judgments. The reporter's judgments are aimed at clarifying the meaning of public-affairs issues and problems. The editorial writer's judgments are aimed at persuading the reader about the rightness or wrongness of policies, programs, ideas; and at moving him to take a position on them. The distinction here is between clarification and rhetoric.

The most useful analysis of how the public-affairs reporter must work in investigating and interpreting his materials is in a book that was not written for journalists. In *The Modern Researcher,* Henry Graff and Jacques Barzun, two Columbia university historians, take up the problems of the working historian which happen in most respects to be the problems of the working public-affairs journalist: finding the facts; verifying the facts; handling ideas; truth, and the causation of and conditions surrounding events; discernible patterns in public affairs; and the sources and correctives of bias.

When Douglass Cater wrote his book on journalism in Washington, D.C., in 1959, he noted that there were more than three thousand public-information officers working for the federal government compared to twelve hundred newspaper and broadcast reporters in the capital. I doubt whether that ratio has altered significantly since 1959. And if you add to government public-information officers all the public-relations men working in Washington for private and special-interest lobbies and organizations, one can begin to perceive the magnitude of the journalist's task as he seeks to write objectively about what is happening.

The relationship of the reporter to his source is complicated not only by the sheer numbers of governmental and private public-relations men who stand between their clients and the public as shields and interpreters. It is also complicated by the special power of some of the highest government officials to reward or punish journalists by giving or withholding information according to how "cooperative" the journalists are; by the present Justice Department's unprecedented harassment of reporters (requests for indentification of their sources, attempts to subpoena the notes on which they have based their stories and broadcasts, grand-jury investigations of reporters who publish classified government documents); and often by the journalists' own inability, or unwillingness, to develop investigative techniques to counter the manipulative and intimidating tactics of government officials.

It must also be admitted that laziness and lack of enterprise in the use of alternative sources of information are not unknown vices of journalists. T.R.B., the Washington columnist for *The New Republic,* once attended a hearing by the Senate Judiciary Sub-committee on Anti-Trust and Monopoly. He discovered that "the one hundred largest manufacturing monsters in the United States increased their share of net capital assets of all U.S. manufacturing from 1947 to 1962.... Textron has acquired sixty-nine manufacturing enterprises; Martin-Marietta picked up two hundred and forty-six million dollars worth of mergers.... Three big oil companies recently—Continental, Socony, and Gulf—each absorbed a fertilizer company; only one major independent fertilizer company remains.... Only three reporters were at the hearing when we looked in."

But even the most enterprising and intelligent of the Washington journalists are victims of that peculiar capital infirmity known as the "background briefing," that device by which government officials float trial balloons, attack their critics, and gild their programs on a not-for-attribution basis. The inviolable ground rule is that, while reporters may use anything they wish from these briefings, they must not identify the government official who gives them the information. The reporter who disobeys the rule is banned from background briefings, loses out on stories that his competitors are filing, and may lose his assignment if not his job.

Ben Bradlee, executive editor of the Washington *Post,* has complained bitterly about the background briefing: "We shudder righteously at the thought of withholding the name of a bank robber, a party giver, a campaign contributor. Why do we go along so complacently withholding the identity of public officials? By doing so we shamelessly do other people's bidding. We knowingly let ourselves be used for obvious trial balloons and for personal attacks. In short, we demean our profession."

Bradlee suggests that the more flagrant abuses of the background briefing might be eliminated if the press sharply limited and persuaded government officials to limit the amount of unattributed information; insisted on at least agency attribution ("White House sources," "State Department experts" instead of "high government officials" or "government sources"); and refused to let a background briefer indulge in personal attack without being identified.

Presidents as news sources use the immense authority of their office and have developed over the years a variety of wiles to keep reporters in line and to minimize the possibility of the searching and informed questions ever arising at news conferences.

James Reston has recalled how Lyndon Johnson tamed the reporters: "He knew that the Washington press corps was full of specialists, some of whom had devoted most of their careers to the study of foreign affairs, or the federal judiciary, or science or military affairs, and therefore not only knew their subjects, but probably knew more about them than he did. If he announced his news conferences in advance, they would come running with their well-informed and awkward inquiries. So he simply did not announce his news conferences. He called them when only the White House correspondents were around, and then usually on the weekends when only a few of them were on duty. He held them in his own executive office, where he was not in display before the cameras, but talking intimately with the reporters who travel with him all the time and are not only familiar to him but subject to his system of punishments and rewards, which can be embarrassing to a reporter on a highly competitive beat."

The objective public-affairs reporter, whether he is working in the superheated atmosphere of Washington or covering City Hall in Milwaukee, has to walk a narrow line. He must develop a relationship with his source that is intimate enough to generate confidence and yield information but detached enough to enable him to be truthful in his writing even when the truth may not flatter the source of his information. The goal of government officials and the goal of journalists are one—the common good. But it does not follow that the journalist serves the common good by joining hands with and following the bidding of the officials. He serves it by maintaining the amount of distance which is required for cool, detached objectivity.

It is possible for most, if not all, reporters for a newspaper, news service, television station or network to be objective in the performance of their individual tasks, or to aspire to objectivity, but for the institution which employs them to be profoundly nonobjective. How the institution uses its reporters, the working conditions it has set up for them, the news policies it has established, the extent to which the commercial and profit interests influence its communication performance all determine in the end whether the journalism produced will be objective.

Out of the thousands of events, situations, and conditions that might be reported each day, only a relatively few are printed or broadcast. Despite its slogan, *The New York Times* does not really publish all the news that is fit to print. It selects some news and it rejects other, even though both may be fit to print. The *Times* receives two and a half million words a day; it selects 185,000 (less than one per cent) for publication.

The question is, what is the basis and what are the principles which guide newspaper editors and television news directors both in their selection and in their handling of news? Historically, the answer to that question has been diverse, as all the foregoing might have suggested by now.

There is a sense in which a communications medium can be said to be objective if all of its individual reports, no matter how trivial the subjects, are true accounts. A newspaper like the *Daily News* in New York, assuming its various sensational items are accurately reported, can be said to be just as objective as *The New York Times*. But in a much deeper sense, the picture of the world as found in the *Times* is far truer, more objective, more bona fide than that in the *News*. This is partly because there is between all newspapers and their readers an implicit contract, a promise that they will furnish readers with the information they need if they are to function as responsible citizens in our society.

I do not think the problem of objectivity—whether in the individual reporter or in the institution—can be separated from the question of the over-all significance of the final product. Just as the objectivity of the individual reporter depends on his perception, selection, and ordering of the essential rather than the accidental elements of the event or situation he is reporting, so the objectivity of the newspaper or television station or network depends on the consistent selection of the most important aspects of contemporary life that will be assigned to the reporters for their investigation and interpretation.

It is not enough for the institution to be occasionally significant in many areas of public affairs, or to be consistently significant in one or two areas. If it falls short of over-all significance it presents a distorted picture of the world to its clientele.

What is required for a journalism of significance in any communications institution is a wise, experienced person with sufficient authority to make and enforce news policy for his paper, wire service, television station or network, and with sufficient resources (able reporters and editors, adequate time and space) to carry out that policy. Each of these elements—wisdom, experience, authority, enforcement, resources—is indispensable. One still hears of newspaper situations, which must be astounding to laymen, in which the wire editor (the real gatekeeper who selects the non-local stories that will pass through the news barrier and into the paper) is virtually sovereign and, in actual effect, determines news policy which may or may not be the policy the publisher or editor-in-chief would adopt if they were at that gate.

The wise director of news policy knows: (a) what constitutes "the good life," humanly speaking; (b) the present human condition; and (c) the contemporary events, developments, and forces which most directly and profoundly affect the human condition and the prospect for the good life.

Theoretically the commercial profit-making nature of mass communications need not compromise the efforts to produce a journalism of integrity. In practice, the theory often fails to stand up, or, more accurately, it is allowed to collapse.

It is true that newspaper editors no longer suppress stories that offend their advertisers. But I do not recall that the television industry, when it was heavily supported by tobacco advertising, came even remotely close to the newspapers and magazines in the number of news stories it aired about the relationship between cigarette smoking and lung cancer. And I cannot recall any television documentaries on this disease which national health officials say is of epidemic magnitude; if there have been documentaries, they cannot begin to compare in number or depth with those done by the television industry on the problem of, say, drug abuse. The commercial influence is always present in the media. The evidence suggests that the opportunity, desire, and ability to make enormous profits in the communications media sometimes results in shabby reporting of public affairs. Network officials say that they have corporate responsibilities to their stockholders and must show an improved profit picture each year.

When Fred Friendly, then a top news executive with the Columbia Broadcasting System, wanted to broadcast Senate Foreign Relations Committee hearings five years ago, the network overruled him and scheduled a rerun of an "I Love Lucy" show. Friendly resigned and later pointed out that he had not asked C.B.S. to suffer a net loss but only to take a very mild reduction in the gigantic profits they were making.

When Kenneth A. Cox was a member of the Federal Communications Commission, he criticized the F.C.C. and the radio industry for a situation in which the commission could renew, as they did on one occasion, the licenses of twenty-one stations without bothering to inquire into the areas of public affairs, agriculture, instruction, and religion. The stations had proposed devoting less than five per cent of their time to those areas.

Mr. Cox noted that radio is now about fifty years old and that "surely it should strive to be—with due allowance for the admitted need for a viable economic base—something more than a jukebox, a ball park, and a news ticker." He said it was ridiculous to argue that the broadcaster who devotes twenty-three hours of each day to commercially sponsored programming is being subjected to an impairment of his freedom to speak if he is asked by the F.C.C. whether it would not better serve the public interest if more than twenty-five or thirty minutes of the remaining hour in the day could be devoted to public affairs.

I once took part in a seminar with newspaper, radio, and television news officials on the question of what the media can contribute to intergroup understanding and harmony in the community. One of the radio officials rather proudly reported that his station had often presented public-service programs on community problems, and he stated—also very proudly—that some of these "programs" ran as long as five minutes. It was obvious that, by his standards, five minutes of air time represented a considerable amount of money. But, of course, it bore little relationship to the magnitude and gravity of the problems in his community.

It is common knowledge that salaries paid to business, management, and advertising staff members of newspapers are substantially higher than those paid to reporters. Salary is not the only measurement of the regard which publishers have for the quality of public-affairs reporting, but it is a major measurement and, in the minds of most reporters, the decisive measurement.

Competent, highly motivated public-affairs reporters have been migrating for a generation from the newspapers and wire services to para-journalistic work (e.g., administrative and legislative work for congressmen). In one recent year, only twenty per cent of students graduating from journalism colleges chose to go into news reporting.

The reader of the newspaper account or the viewer of a television news broadcast or documentary brings to it his own personal history. And if the reporter is subject to "tricks of memory" and the "incessant creative quality of his imagination," the reader is no less susceptible. If he distorts or misreads a report it may be his fault, the reporter's fault, or just due to the ambiguity of words. Barzun and Graff say:

The reader brings something with him to every act of reading. He brings his own experience of life and a variable amount of knowledge gathered from previous reading. The result is that unless the vocabulary of a new piece of reading matter is visibly technical and strange to him, he will almost always think he understands it. This will happen even when what is said is badly put, repeatedly misleading, or adroitly tendentious. The whole power of propaganda lies in this human propensity to catch the drift, to make out a meaning, to believe what is in print, with no thought of resistance by analysis and criticism.

It may be assumed that if reporters will write with precision, make distinctions not fussily but with an exactness necessary to an understanding of the material, in short, if reporters will display in their work intellectual and critical power, their readers will develop a comparable virtue. The possibility will then be enhanced that what the reporter has understood and put into words (or, for television, into words and motion photography) the reader will understand. In that event, objective communication will have been accomplished.

But is objectivity in the over-all reporting of public affairs generally and consistently possible in American journalism? I think it is, not in the sense of objectivity as the total truth about anything (something which historians have never succeeded in capturing), and not in the sense of objectivity as meaning the absence of all subjective elements. But objectivity as meaning a substantially truthful account of contemporary public affairs is well within the possibility of the mass-communications media despite many practical difficulties.

These are some of the things that must be done to overcome the difficulties (other suggestions have been made in the course of this article):

1. Recognition of the existence of the reporter's personal history and experience and their effect on his work, with constant effort made to broaden and objectify that experience, and hence his values.

2. More professional education and training in the art of investigative reporting, both in professionally-oriented journalism schools or university departments (preferably following a liberal arts undergraduate education) and on the job with newspapers and television stations.

3. Insistence that reporters and editors bring to their work a broad educational experience so that they can interrelate the economic, political, social, and cultural elements of public affairs and provide the context which will illuminate what they are reporting.

4. A proper balance of specialization and rotation of reporters' assignments to avoid superficiality on the one hand and the boredom, laziness, and uncritical, routinized approach often associated with the unvarying assignment on the other.

5. Vigilance from the editor's desk (spot comparisons, for example, of the reporters' dispatches with those of other American reporters and, in the case of international assignments, with the reports of foreign writers).

6. Careful fitting of reporters to the kinds of assignments on which they could probably be more consistently objective, and a constant review of that fit.

7. Providing the working conditions (sufficient space, time, and professional understanding) to enable reporters to do careful work.

8. A continuing communications commission to monitor the performance of the press and television and to make public its evaluations.

9. Extension and refinement of the ombudsman-like idea initiated by a few newspapers to give readers a critical voice that will be heard in the operation of the papers.

10. Subordination of the profit-making of a newspaper or broadcasting station to the service of its communication function.

11. Better use made of the wire services by subscribing papers and, where the wire services are inadequate, more rigorous demands by the individual editors.

It is possible for the citizen with a great deal of time and a considerable expenditure of money to keep himself adequately informed on the public affairs of the day by reading several newspapers and a half-dozen or more journals and magazines, watching the televised documentaries, and picking up the best of the books on contemporary issues.

But it should be equally possible for citizens, without making such an extraordinary investment of their time and money, to subscribe to their hometown newspaper, watch the television news and public-affairs programs, and perhaps subscribe to one magazine or journal and be confident that their opinions and actions on public affairs are based on an understanding of the issues. I do not think this is now the case. But I do think it is possible.

JOURNALISM AND TRUTH

Edward Jay Epstein

The problem of journalism in America proceeds from a simple but inescapable bind: journalists are rarely, if ever, in a position to establish the truth about an issue for themselves, and they are therefore almost entirely dependent on self-interested "sources" for the version of reality that they report. Walter Lippmann pointed to the root of the problem more than fifty years ago when he made a painful distinction between "news" and truth. "The function of news is to signalize an event, the function of truth is to bring to light the hidden facts, to set them into relation with each other, and make a picture of reality on which men can act." Because news-reporting and truth-seeking have different ultimate purposes, Lippmann postulated that "news" could be expected to coincide with truth in only a few limited areas, such as the scores of baseball games or elections, where the results are definite and measurable. In the more complex and ambiguous recesses of political life, where the outcome is almost always in doubt or dispute, news reports could not be expected to exhaust, or perhaps even indicate, the truth of the matter. This divergence between news and truth stemmed not from the inadequacies of newsmen but from the exigencies of the news business, which limited the time, space, and resources that could be allotted to any single story. Lippmann concluded pessimistically that if the public required a more truthful interpretation of the world they lived in, they would have to depend on institutions other than the press.

Contemporary journalists would have some difficulty accepting such a distinction between news and truth. Indeed, newsmen

From Commentary, *April 1974, pp. 36-40. Copyright ©
1974 by Edward Jay Epstein; reprinted by permission
of the author.*

now almost invariably depict themselves not merely as reporters of the fragments of information that come their way, but as active pursuers of the truth. In the current rhetoric of journalism, "stenographic reporting," where the reporter simply but accurately repeats what he has been told, is a pejorative term used to describe inadequate journalism; "investigative reporting," on the other hand, where the reporter supposedly ferrets out a hidden truth, is an honorific enterprise to which all journalists are supposed to aspire. In the post-Watergate era, moreover, even critics of the press attribute to it powers of discovery that go well beyond reporting new developments.

Yet despite the energetic claims of the press, the limits of journalism described by Lippmann still persist in basically the same form. Individual journalists may be better educated and motivated today than they were fifty years ago, but newspapers still have strict deadlines, which limit the time that can be spent investigating a story; a restricted number of news "holes," which limit the space that can be devoted to elucidating the details of an event; and fixed budgets, which limit the resources that can be used on any single piece of reportage. Today, as when Lippman wrote, "The final page is of a definite size [and] must be ready at a precise moment."

Under these conditions, it would be unreasonable to expect even the most resourceful journalist to produce anything more than a truncated version of reality. Beyond this, however, even if such restraints were somehow suspended, and journalists had unlimited time, space, and financial resources at their disposal, they would still lack the forensic means and authority to establish the truth about a matter in serious dispute. Grand juries, prosecutors, judges, and legislative committees can compel witnesses to testify before them—offering the inducement of immunity to reluctant witnesses and the threat of perjury and contempt actions to inconsistent witnesses; they can subpoena records and other evidence, and test it all through cross-examination and other rigorous processes.

Similarly, scientists, doctors, and other experts can establish facts in a disputed area, especially when there is unanimous agreement on the results of a particular test or analysis, because their authority and technical expertise are accepted in their distinct spheres of competency. Such authority derives from the individual reputation of the expert, certification of his *bona fides* by a professional group which is presumed to have a virtual monopoly of knowledge over the field, and a clearly articulated fact-finding procedure (such as was used, for instance, in establishing the erasures on the Nixon tapes). Even in more problematic areas, like the social sciences, academic researchers can resolve disputed issues. Acceptance of such an academic verdict, however, will depend heavily on the qualifications of the researcher, the degree to which his sources are satisfactorily documented, and the process of review by other scholars in the field through which, presumably, objections to the thesis are articulated and errors corrected. In all cases, a necessary (thought not sufficient) condition for establishing the truth is the use of an acceptable procedure for examining, testing, and evaluating evidence.

Reporters possess no such wherewithal for dealing with evidence. Unlike the judicial officer, journalists cannot compel a witness to furnish them an account of an event. Witnesses need only tell reporters what they deem is in their own self-interest, and then they can lie or fashion their story to fit a particular purpose without risking any legal penalty. Nor can a journalist test an account by hostile cross-examination without jeopardizing the future cooperation of the witness. Indeed, given the voluntary nature of the relationship between a reporter and his source, a continued flow of information can only be assured if the journalist's stories promise to serve the interest of the witness (which precludes impeaching the latter's credibility). In recent years, journalists have cogently argued that if they are forced to testify before grand juries about their sources, they will be cut off from further information. The same logic applies with equal force to criticizing harshly or casting doubts on the activities of these sources. The misreporting of a series of violent incidents involving the Black Panthers in 1969 is a case in point: the reporters closest to the Black Panthers could not dispute their public claim that an organized campaign of genocide was being waged against them without jeopardizing the special access they had to Panther spokesmen.[1]

Moreover, since journalists generally lack the technical competence to evaluate evidence with any authority, they must also rely on the reports of authoritative institutions for their "facts." A reporter cannot establish the existence of an influenza epidemic, for instance, by conducting medical examinations himself; he must rely on the pronouncement of the Department of Health. (A journalist may of course become a doctor, but then his authority for reporting a fact rests on his scientific rather than journalistic credentials.) Whenever a journalist attempts to establish a factual proposition on his own authority, his conclusion must be open to question. For example, following the overthrow of the Allende government in Chile in 1973, *Newsweek* carried a dramatic report by a correspondent who claimed to have gained entrance to the Santiago morgue and personally examined the bodies of those killed after the coup. By inspecting the hands of the corpses, and the nature of their wounds, the correspondent concluded that these were workers with calloused hands who had been brutally executed. When the *Wall Street Journal* challenged these findings (on the basis of inconsistencies in the description of the morgue), the reporter acknowledged that he personally had spent only two minutes on the scene, and *Newsweek* fell back on an earlier unpublished report of a UN observer who claimed to have witnessed something similar in the Santiago morgue at some different time. While the dispute remained unsettled, the burden of proof was shifted from *Newsweek*'s own reporter to an outside "authority."

Finally, journalists cannot even claim the modicum of authority granted to academic researchers because they cannot fulfill the requirement of always identifying their sources, let alone documenting their claims. Protecting (and concealing) the identity of their informants is a real concern for journalists, and one on which their livelihood might well depend, but it also distinguishes the journalistic from the academic product. Without identifiable sources the account cannot be reviewed or corroborated by others with specialized knowledge of the subject. Even the most egregious errors may thus remain uncorrected. For instance, in what purported to be an interview with John W. Dean III, the President's former counsel, *Newsweek* reported that Dean would reveal in his public testimony that some White House officials had planned to assassinate Panama's head of government, but that the plan was aborted at the last minute. This *Newsweek* "exclusive" was circulated to thousands of newspapers in an advance press release, and widely published. When it turned out that the story was untrue—Dean did not testify about any such assassination plot, and denied under oath that he had discussed any substantial aspects of his testimony with *Newsweek* reporters—*Newsweek* did not correct or explain the discrepancy. Presumably, Dean was not the source for the putative "Dean Interview," and the unidentified source had misled *Newsweek* on what Dean was planning to say in his public testimony. Since the error was that of an unidentified source, *Newsweek* did not feel obligated to correct it in future editions.

It is not necessary to belabor the point that gathering news is a very different enterprise from establishing truth, with different standards and objectives. Journalists readily admit that they are dependent on others for privileged information and the ascertainment of facts in a controversial issue (although some might argue that the sphere of measurable and non-controversial issues is larger than I suggest). Indeed, many of the most eminent journalists in America submitted affidavits in the Pentagon Papers case attesting that "leaks" and confidential sources are indispensable elements in the reporting of national news. And despite the more heroic public claims of the news media, daily journalism is largely concerned with finding and retaining profitable sources of prepackaged stories (whether it be the Weather Bureau, the Dow-Jones financial wire service, public-relations agencies, or a confidential source within the government). What is now called "investigative reporting" is merely the development of sources within the counter-elite or other dissidents in the government, while "stenographic reporting" refers to the development of sources among official spokesmen for the government. There is no difference in the basic method of reporting.

Even in the case of Watergate, which has become synonymous with "investigative reporting," it was the investigative agencies of the government and not the members of the press who assembled the evidence, which was then deliberately leaked to receptive reporters at the Washington *Post*, the Los Angeles *Times, Time,* and other journals. Within a week after the burglars were caught in Watergate in June 1972, FBI agents had identified the leaders of the break-in as employees of the Committee to Reelect the President (and former employees of the White House), traced the hundred-dollar bills found in their possession to funds contributed to President Nixon's re-election campaign, and interviewed one of the key conspirators, Alfred Baldwin, who in effect turned state's evidence, describing the wire-tapping operation in great detail and revealing that the transcripts had been delivered directly to CRP headquarters.

This evidence, which was presented to the grand jury (and eventually in open court), was systematically leaked by investigative agents in the case. (Why members of the FBI and the Department of Justice had become dissidents is another question.) The crucial evidence which the FBI investigation did not turn up—such as the earlier burglary of Ellsberg's psychiatrist, the offers of executive clemency, the intervention with the CIA, the suborning of perjury, the cash payoffs made from campaign contributions, the "enemies list," and the 1970 subversion control plan—came out not through "investigative reporting," but only when one of the burglars, John McCord, revealed his role in the cover-up to Judge John Sirica and when John Dean virtually defected to the U.S. prosecutor and disclosed the White House "horror stories." Indeed, it was John Dean, not the enterprising reporters of the Washington press corps, who was the real author of most of the revelations that are at the heart of the present Federal conspiracy indictments and the impeachment inquest. (And it was Ralph Nader, another non-journalist, who unearthed the contributions from the milk industry.) To be sure, by serving as conduits for the interested parties who wanted to release information about Watergate and other White House abuses of power, journalists played an extremely important role in the political process—but not as investigators or establishers of the truth.

The reliance on "leaks" or "authoritative" sources might not be an insoluble problem for journalism if reporters had some means of evaluating them in advance, and publishing only those portions which did not distort reality, by being either untrue or out of context. Unfortunately, however, the inherent pressures of daily journalism severely reduce the possibility of verifying a leak or disclosure in advance of publication. Reporters can of course seek out more than one source on an issue, but there is no satisfactory way available, other than intuition, to choose among conflicting accounts. The democratic criterion of adding up confirming and disconfirming interviews, as if they were votes, produces no decisive result, as even total agreement might simply mean that a false account had been widely circulated, while total disagreement might mean that only the original source was privy to the truth about an event.

"Plausibility" is also an unsatisfactory criterion for evaluating leaks, since the liar is always capable of fashioning his account to fit the predispositions of the journalist to whom he is disclosing it, and thereby to make it appear plausible. Nor can a reporter simply give weight to the source that is most intimately involved with the issue, since those closest to a dispute might have the greatest interest in distorting or neglecting aspects of it, and might well be the least impartial. In certain instances, leaks, if publication were delayed, could be tested by the direction of unfolding events—for example, the advance disclosure of John Dean's testimony could have been refuted if *Newsweek* had delayed its story until Dean actually testified—but such a procedure would undercut the far more basic journalistic value of signaling the probable direction of events before they fully unfold. Given these circumstances, a journalist has little basis for choosing among conflicting sources. The New York *Times* thus carried two completely contradictory reports of the same insurrection in the Philippines in different sections of the same Sunday edition (February 17, 1974). The "News of the Week" section placed the casualties at 10,000 dead or missing, while the general news section refuted this higher figure and placed the total casualties at 276. Both accounts were based on sources within the Philippine government, and the editor of each section simply chose the account he preferred.

When journalists are presented with secret information about issues of great import, they become, in a very real sense, agents for the surreptitious source. Even if the disclosure is supported by authoritative documents, the journalist cannot know whether the information has been altered, edited, or selected out of context. Nor can he be certain what interest he is serving or what will be the eventual outcome of the leak.

Consider, for example, the disclosures by the columnist Jack Anderson of the minutes of a secret National Security Council meeting on the 1971 Indo-Pakistani war for which he was awarded the Pulitzer Prize for national reporting. Anderson claimed that the blunt orders by Dr. Henry Kissinger in these private meetings to "tilt" toward Pakistan contradicted Kissinger's public professions of neutrality; this claim received wide circulation, and sharply undermined Kissinger's credibility (although the *Wall Street Journal* demonstrated by printing the public statements to which Anderson referred that Kissinger was in fact consistent in both his private and public statements in expressing opposition to the Indian military incursion into East Pakistan). At the time it was generally presumed that the leak came from a dissident with the administration who favored India, or, at least, opposed the administration's policy in the subcontinent. Only two years afterward, as a byproduct of the Watergate investigation, was some light cast on the source of the leak. A White House investigation identified Charles E. Radford, a Navy yeoman, who was working at the time as a stenographer, as the proximate source of the National Security Council minutes supplied to Anderson. But the investigation further revealed that Yeoman Radford was also copying and transmitting to members of the Joint Chiefs of Staff highly classified documents in a "surreptitious operation" apparently designed to keep them aware of Kissinger's (and the President's) negotiations. And Yeoman Radford has testified that he acted only on the express orders of the Joint Chiefs of Staff, and not on his own initiative, in passing documents. If this is indeed the case, it would appear that members of the Joint Chiefs of staff authored the Anderson leak in order to undermine the authority of Henry Kissinger (who was involved in developing the détente with China and Russia at that time). In this case, Anderson was used as an instrument in a power struggle he probably was unaware of—and which might have had nothing to do with the Indo-Pakistani war he was reporting on.

The important question is not whether journalists are deviously manipulated by their sources, but whether they can exert any real control over disclosures wrenched from contexts to which they do not have access or with which they are unfamiliar. In most circumstances, the logic of daily journalism impels immediate publication which, though it might result in a prized "scoop," divorces the journalist from responsibility for the veracity or consequences of the disclosure. Jack Anderson was thus able to explain a blatantly false report he published about the arrest for drunken driving of Senator Thomas Eagleton, then the Vice-Presidential nominee of the Democratic party, by saying that if he had delayed publication to check the allegation he would have risked being scooped by competitors.

But even in rare cases in which newspapers allot time and manpower to study a leak, as the New York *Times* did in the case of the Pentagon Papers, the information still must be revised into a form and format which will maintain the interest of the readers (as well as the editors). Since the *Times* decided not to print the entire study of the Vietnam war—which ran to more than 7,000 pages and covered a 25-year period—or even substantial parts of the narrative, which was complex and academic, sections of the material had to be reorganized and rewritten along a theme that would be comprehensible to its audience. The theme chosen was duplicity: the difference between what the leaders of America said about the Vietnam war in private and in public. The Pentagon study, however, was not written in line with this theme: it was an official Department of Defense analysis of decision-making and, more precisely, of how policy preferences crystallized within the Department. To convert this bureaucratic study into a journalistic exposé of duplicity required taking certain liberties with the original history: outside material had to be added and assertions from the actual study had to be omitted. For example, to show that the Tonkin Gulf resolution (by which in effect Congress authorized the escalation of the war, and which was editorially endorsed at the time by most major newspapers, including the New York *Times* and the Washington *Post*)

resulted from duplicity, the *Times* had to omit the conclusion of the Pentagon Papers that the Johnson administration had tried to avoid the fatal clash in the Tonkin Gulf, and had to add evidence of possible American provocations in Laos, which were not actually referred to in the Pentagon Papers themselves.

Journalists, then, are caught in a dilemma. They can either serve as a faithful messenger for some subterranean interest, or they can recast the message into their own version of the story by adding, deleting, or altering material. The first alternative assures that the message will be accurately relayed to the intended audience, although the message itself might be false or misleading. The latter alternative, while lessening the source's control over the message, increases the risk of further distortion, since the journalist cannot be aware of the full context and circumstances surrounding the disclosure. In neither case can journalists be certain of either the truth or the intended purpose of what they publish. Such a dilemma cannot be remedied by superior newsmen or more intensive journalistic training. It arises not out of defects in the practice of journalism, but out of the source-reporter relationship which is part and parcel of the structure of modern journalism.

To some degree, the tension in the dilemma could be alleviated if journalists gave up the pretense of being establishers of truth, recognized themselves as agents for others who desired to disclose information, and clearly labeled the circumstances and interests behind the information they reported so that it could be intelligently evaluated. By concealing the machinations and politics behind a leak, journalists suppress part of the truth surrounding the story. Thus the means by which the medical records of Senator Thomas Eagleton were acquired and passed on to the Knight newspapers (which won the 1973 Pulitzer Prize for disclosing information contained in these records) seem no less important than the Senator's medical history itself, especially since copies of the presumably illegally-obtained records were later found in the White House safe of John Ehrlichman. (In rifling through Larry O'Brien's personal files, the Watergate burglars were probably looking for material damaging to O'Brien and the Democrats; if they had succeeded, such material would no doubt have found its way into print by being leaked to "investigative journalists.") Similarly, the motives and circumstances behind the well-timed leaks to the press by elements in the Nixon administration which ultimately forced Justice Abe Fortas from the Supreme Court do not necessarily make a less important part of the story than any of the alleged improprieties committed by Fortas. And the leaks provided by senior executives in the FBI and other investigative agencies in an attempt to resist White House domination still remains the unreported part of the Watergate story.

Since journalists cannot expose these hidden aspects of a story without damaging the sources they are dependent on for information (and honors), they cannot realistically be expected to label the interest behind any disclosure. (Indeed, it is a practice among journalists to mislead their readers by explicitly denying as occasion arises that they received information from their real source.) Under these conditions, journalism can serve as an important institution for conveying and circulating information, and signalling changes in the direction of public policy and discourse, but it cannot serve as a credible investigator of the "hidden facts" or the elusive truths which determine them.

NOTES

1. For a fuller account, see Edward J. Epstein, "The Black Panthers: A Question of Genocide," *New Yorker*, 13 February 1971.

THE NEW JOURNALISM AND THE OLD — THOUGHTS AFTER WATERGATE

Paul H. Weaver

The "fourth estate" of the realm—that was Burke's way of summing up the role of the press in his time, and when one has discounted the medieval terminology, his phrase is no less apt today. It reminds us that the press, as the coequal of other "estates," is a political institution in its own right, intimately bound up with all the institutions of government. If affects them and is affected by them in turn, and together they determine the nature of the regime and the quality of public life. Governmental institutions have political effects through their exercise of legislative, executive, or judicial powers; the press achieves its impact through the way it influences the entry of ideas and information into the "public space" in which political life takes place. So the basic question to be asked about the press is: What is its relation to other political institutions, and how does it consequently manage the "public space"?

The aftermath of Watergate provides a suitable occasion for rethinking this question—though not because the press was in any way at fault in this episode. The Watergate scandals emerge solely from the Nixon Administration's abuse of its Presidential powers in matters ranging from campaign finance and civil liberties to national security. By covering the emerging scandals as it did, the press was acting in accord with a venerable journalistic tradition that dates back to *The New York Times'* exposé of the corrupt Tweed Ring in 1871.

Reprinted with permission of Paul H. Weaver from The Public Interest, *no. 35, Spring 1974. Copyright © 1974 by National Affairs, Inc.*

Yet Watergate was more than a series of criminal and corrupt actions, it also has raised basic Constitutional questions concerning the interrelationship among all our political institutions, including of course the press. One of these issues was the freedom of the press. Many of the abuses symbolized by Watergate—the Plumbers, unjustified investigations and wiretaps, and so forth—were in fact directed at the press as part of the Administration's campaign to make the news media less critical. If these efforts had been successful, they would have reduced press freedom and altered the balance between government and the press in favor of the former. For the time being at least, that danger has been averted.

So the press emerges from Watergate as free, self-confident, and enterprising as at any other time in its history. But it also emerges a bit different from what it was before. For the press today is an institution in limbo—an institution in that distinctive kind of trouble which derives from not having a settled idea of its role and purpose. It is in limbo because it now occupies an ambiguous middle ground between its longstanding tradition of "objective" journalism and a new movement for an "adversary" journalism—no longer massively committed to the one but not yet certain, let alone unanimous, about the other. To the extent that it is committed to the new movement, it is committed to a journalistic idea that is not easily compatible with American institutions in their current form, nor easily reconciled with some of its most valuable traditions. And to the extent that the press embraces this movement, its political role will remain in flux until some new practical adaptation to adversary journalism is worked out by government, public opinion, and the press itself. Watergate did not create this problem—it has been growing for a decade now—but it did intensify it. And this is the problem which confronts American journalism after Watergate.

TWO KINDS OF JOURNALISM

To put the matter briefly: Traditionally, American journalism has been very close to, dependent upon, and cooperative with, official sources. This has been one of its problems, but it has also been its greatest strength and virtue. For in various ways this arrangement has maximized both the openness and flexibility of American government and the amount of information available to the citizenry. Over the past ten years, however, a small but significant and still-growing segment of the journalistic community has begun to revise this relationship by assuming a posture of greater independence and less cooperativeness. They see this change as a modest reform which will render American journalism purer, better, and truer to its traditional aspirations. In fact, it represents a radical change. In the long run it could make the press "freer" but also less informative and possibly more partisan; and this in turn could make the political system more closed, less flexible, and less competent.

To appreciate the meaning of what has happened, we may begin with the simple fact that journalism is the enterprise of publishing a current account of current events.[1] As such, it cannot proceed until three prior questions have been settled. First, there is the question of how, where, and on what basis to find and validate information. Second, there is the question of the point of view from which events are to be surveyed and characterized. And third, there is the question of the audience to be addressed and the basis on which it is to be aggregated. Abstractly, one can imagine any number of possible resolutions of these issues, but in practice things work out more simply. For wherever one looks in the modern world, daily journalism seems to assume one of two general forms: the partisan and the liberal.

Partisan journalism, which prevails in many European countries, and which has traditionally been represented in the United States by the "journal of opinion" rather than the newspaper, begins with an explicitly political point of view. It is ideological journalism. It aims at assembling an audience that shares its point of view; its object is to interpret public affairs from within that point of view; and it gathers information for the purpose of illuminating and particularizing such interpretation. Such a journalism is less concerned with information as such than with the maintenance and elaboration of its point of view. To it, events are more interesting for the light they cast on its "position" than for what they are, or seem, on their face.

Liberal journalism, by contrast, which prevails in the English-speaking world, is characterized by a preoccupation with facts and events as such, and by an indifference to—indeed, a systematic effort to avoid—an explicitly ideological point of view. It aims instead at appealing to a universal audience on the basis of its non-political, "objective" point of view and its commitment to finding and reporting only "facts" as distinct from "opinion." Liberal journalism strives to be a kind of *tabula rasa* upon which unfolding events and emerging information inscribe themselves. Its principal concern is to find as many events and as much information as it can, and it does this by going to "sources"—persons and organizations directly involved in the events, upon whom it relies both for information and for the validation of this information.

Throughout the 20th century, American journalism has been solidly in the liberal camp. It has sought a universal audience rather than a factional one; its central objective has been to find and publish as much information about as many events as quickly as possible; and it has striven to do this on the basis of a non-partisan, non-political, "facts-only" point of view. Or at least these have been its ideals; the extent of their actual realization has been subject, not only to the viscissitudes of human judgment, but also to two tensions inherent in the very idea of a liberal journalism.

The first of these is the tension between access and autonomy, between the effort of the press to get as much unambiguously true information about as many events as possible—which requires a maximum of access to the actors in these events, which in turn curtails a maximum of dependency on these actors—and its effort to preserve its capacity for independent judgment. The second tension arises out of the desire of liberal journalists to avoid taking a political point of view, which conflicts with the inevitability that, in the course of describing events, some sort of point of view will be assumed (observation and writing cannot proceed in the absence of one), and that no point of view will ever be totally devoid of political implications.

ACCESS AND INDEPENDENCE

To these complex problems, the established liberal tradition of American journalism provides a suitably complex resolution. As between access and autonomy, the tradition opts massively and with a clear conscience for access. This choice is reflected not only in the way newsmen go about their work, but in almost every other feature of American journalism as well, from the form of the news story to the role of the newspaper owner. By opting for access, the American press has given priority and reality to its ideals of acting as a *tabula rasa* and maximizing the amount of raw information it provides to the electorate. This same emphasis on access also goes a long way toward settling, if only unintentionally, the problem of point of view. A *tabula rasa* that is written on primarily by persons involved in events inevitably reflects their slant on the world.

In practice, then, this emphasis on access means the following:

First, virtually all the information published by the press is derived from (and is validated by) "high-level sources," i.e., persons, officials, and organizations actively involved in the events in question.

Second, what newsmen know about the events and issues they cover and about the general context in which these occur, they acquire almost exclusively from the persons involved rather than from external professional, academic, or ideological sources and authorities.

Third, the point of view from which newsmen write is largely determined by the views, concerns, vocabularies, and situations of those actually involved in public affairs. The viewpoint of the American press is thus a practical rather than ideological or theoretical one.

And fourth, as a result of this emphasis on access, newsmen are routinely aware of—or can easily gather—a truly immense amount of information. They are authentic ringside observers of men and events. They can never publish more than a small fraction of what they know (or have reason to believe), and what they do publish is backed up by a large, if often unarticulated, familiarity with the persons, institutions, and issues involved.

Yet if the "objective" tradition defines American journalism as a primarily derivative and dependent enterprise, it also provides the newsman with a limited but still quite important sphere of independence. Partly this independence has existed by virtue of the sheer volume of events and information which are routinely available to the working newsman. He therefore is confronted with the daily and hourly necessity of choosing, and to choose is to exercise a measure of independent power. This power is enhanced by the fragmentation and indiscipline of American government. Not only do they increase the number of points of access for the newsmen seeking a given bit of information, but they also create for him the opportunity—often exploited in practice—to follow the maxim *divide et impera,* an approach whose utility is made much greater by the almost insatiable appetite of most officials for the two political resources which the newsman possesses automatically: publicity and information. The traditional journalist, then, is not utterly at the mercy of his sources.

Just as important as the fact of the newsman's power is the independent way in which the liberal tradition of American journalism has encouraged him to use that power. To begin with, the tradition demands that the newsman maintain a strict formal independence of his sources: There are to be no financial conflicts of interest, and excessively close personal or ideological relationships are frowned upon. Second, each of the newsman's uses of his selective power is subject to a process of review by his journalistic peers and superiors; not only is the newsman supposed to be free of obligations to his sources, but also he is held answerable before the court of journalistic opinion. Third and most important, there is the traditional norm of "independent" judgment. The newsman is not to have a single, comprehensive, ideological point of view, but the liberal tradition of American journalism does encourage him to have an occasional *ad hoc* opinion and to bring such views to bear in his reporting—provided they pass muster with his journalistic colleagues and superiors, and provided also that there aren't many such opinions and that they manifest themselves only infrequently. (James Reston is an examplar of this ethos, a man of judgment rather than a man of partisan ideology.) And as vehicles for the expression of these modest and occasional opinions, the liberal tradition sanctions, in addition to "objective" reporting, the devices of muckraking and the "crusade" against a particular instance of inequity. These latter are not often used, but they do remain in the newsman's arsenal to define alternative modes of dealing with institutions and events—and to give the newsman further room for exercising independent judgment.

THE LIBERAL TRADITION

In the liberal tradition, then, the relationship between newsman and source, between press and government, is one of structured interdependence and bartering within an atmosphere of amiable suspiciousness. Each side knows its role. The job of government is to give access and information—*and to do so to a far greater extent than would or could be required by law.* This last point is worth emphasizing, since in this respect American government differs markedly from European (even British) governments. All European journalists are immediately struck by this difference. The American reporter not only has access to official announcements and press releases; he also has the opportunity of becoming the confidant of the official and of enjoying limited but regular access to his personal thoughts, official secrets, internal departmental gossip, and the like.

Of course, there is a price tag on such extraordinary access. The reporter is expected to be generally sympathetic to the public official and his government and to cooperate with them as far as his sense of professionalism permits. Beyond that, the press is expected to have no strong and comprehensive ideas about the general shape of public affairs; it is officialdom which is collectively entitled to define the topography and limits of public discussion and the news—and each individual official is to have the further opportunity of attempting to shape the content of news to suit his own preferences or purposes.

But the press also has its role and rights. Its main job is to exploit its access and, one way or another, to get as much information as it can into public circulation. It has the right to select freely among the often widely divergent ideas and information circulating within officialdom and to expose corruption and foulups. In exchange, it is expected to see to it that the impression being made on the public is not radically at odds with the reality of affairs as newsmen and officials, from their "inside" perspective, know it to be.

At the level of day-to-day individual interaction, of course, the relationship between press and government in the "objective" tradition is ill-defined and highly variable. There are a few rules of thumb that all parties are expected to observe. Officials are not supposed to lie—at least, hardly ever, and then only for some good public reason. They are also supposed to keep their efforts to deceive newsmen and the public to modest proportions. And they are not ever to use the powers of government to harass or coerce newsmen. Newsmen, for their part, are expected not to "editorialize" in their news stories and are supposed to give persons accused or disputed in a story an opportuntity to tell their own side of the matter. And newsmen are also expected not to publish certain kinds of information without permission: official secrets, information about the seamy side of officials' private lives, and "inside dope" of no particular relevance to public policy. But within these limits, more or less anything goes. There is much uncertainty and much room for maneuver, manipulation, and enterprise on both sides—and for all their mutuality and cooperation, there is also endless conflict between government and press. But in this general scramble there are limits that both of the parties respect.

The great virtue of the liberal tradition of American journalism is that it enables the press to find and print a great deal of information—much more of it, and more quickly, than partisan newspapers can. For the newsman, it has the further advantage of affording him an opportunity to become truly learned and sophisticated about public affairs through an informal process of close personal observation. And for the citizen it has the virtue that it produces news which is generally intelligible. One can know that the content of news is a more or less faithful reflection of affairs as they are understood by the persons engaged in them, or at least as officialdom as a whole sees them. What is more, the general perspective on events is a practical one. News presented in this way is sensitive to the practitioner's questions of "What next?" and "How to?" and "Who are my friends and enemies?"—and this in turn increases the possibilities that public opinion, reacting to the news, will have significant impact on the day-to-day conduct of government.

Of course, the established tradition has its shortcomings as well, and some of them are quite severe. It is a kind of journalism that is very easily (and very often) manipulated, especially by government but also by newsmen themselves. In any particular instance, the reader can never be absolutely sure that the impression being conveyed to him is a reasonably accurate reflection of the reality of affairs. And beyond that, traditional liberal journalism is perhaps excessively controlled by the ethos and conventional wisdom prevailing among "insiders" and shared by newsmen. In short, the "objective" tradition has the vices and virtues inherent in the idea of acting as a *tabula rasa.* But the virtues are substantial ones too, and the vices, serious though they are, are to no small extent inherent in the very mission of journalism as defined by the liberal tradition: publishing a current account of current events for "the general reader," i.e., the ordinary citizen.

THE ORIGINS OF "ADVERSARY" JOURNALISM

What I have just described is the operational reality of the liberal tradition of American journalism. The image which that journalism has of itself is not exactly congruent with the reality. Some elements of this image, to be sure, are accurate enough. For instance, newsmen correctly believe that they perform three quite different public functions: For the most part, they act as neutral finders and conveyors of information; to some extent they are the "watchdogs" of government; and on rare occasions they advocate the reform of observable inequities. But in other respects, and especially as it depicts the relationship between press and government, the image is a romantic fiction. To listen to traditional newsmen, one would think that the press is completely independent of government in its quest for news, that it routinely searches out vast amounts of hidden, jealously guarded information, that it is constantly defying persons in high office, and that it is the day-in, day-out adversary of "the Establishment" and the equally faithful defender of "the People."

Now this myth of the autonomous, investigative, adversary press does serve a useful purpose. One of the greatest problems of traditional journalism is its proneness to co-optation by its sources. To the extent that newsmen believe and act on their romantic notion of who they are and what they do, the likelihood of their becoming mere uncritical puppets in the hands of their sources is diminished. Moreover, their morale would be lower, their energy smaller, and their self-respect weaker if they subscribed to a truly realistic conception of daily journalism. The romantic image of the "adversary press," then, is a myth: "functional" for certain purposes, but wholly inaccurate as a model of what newsmen actually do or can hope to achieve.

The movement for a new, genuinely adversary journalism which has gained such ground over the past decade arises out of this romantic myth; it is to the liberal tradition of our press what, in a religious context, heresy is to orthodoxy. Is is the nature of a heresy to isolate a part of a tradition or doctrine and to treat the part as if it were the whole. The current "heretical" movement in American journalism is defined by the fact that it takes the mythical part of the "orthodox" tradition—the fiction of the autonomous, investigative, adversary press—for the whole of that tradition. It presents itself as an effort to make our press live up to what it always said it was: a journalism that is autonomous instead of interdependent, original instead of derivative, and in an adversary instead of cooperative relationship with government and officialdom. Like religious heresies, the movement *appears* to be a "reformation"—an effort to recover the core of a partially but not irrecoverably corrupted tradition. But such appearances are misleading. For, because heresies are simplificatory, what they profess to be "recovering" is actually something that never was and that was never intended to be. What they really advocate, therefore, is the creation of something quite new and different under a smokescreen of rhetoric about restoring what is old and familiar.

Although this movement for a newly purified journalism did not attain real strength until the late 1960s, its origins lay somewhat farther in the past. Within the journalistic community, three events were critical in fomenting dissatisfaction with the existing press-government relationship: McCarthyism, the U-2 incident, and the Bay of Pigs. Each cast discredit upon the Cold War itself or the spirit in which government conducted it, and together they caused newsmen to revise their opinion of American institutions and their own relationship to them.

In a way, McCarthyism was the most important. It was a powerful, nationwide movement, and no demagogue can create such a movement without a sounding board in the press. By uncritically repeating and dramatically displaying the sensational charges made by a Senator—in keeping with the usages of objective journalism—the press provided Joe McCarthy with just such a sounding board. In the aftermath of the McCarthy era, newsmen increasingly agreed that they had permitted themselves to be used irresponsibly. A member of government had abused the power that the objective tradition gave him over the press. The answer, it was generally agreed, was that the press should become more vigilant and critical, and should exercise much more discretion about what it printed in connection with known demagogues, even those in high public office.

Then came the U-2 incident and the Bay of Pigs. In the former case, it may be recalled, various government agencies first said that the flight was for weather research and not espionage (the plane had presumably strayed off course), then said that it was for espionage but that President Eisenhower had not known about it, whereupon Eisenhower came forward and publicly declared that he had known and approved of the program. In the

latter case, President Kennedy persuaded *The New York Times,* on grounds of national security, not to print a story on preparations for the Bay of Pigs invasion. After the invasion flopped he publicly stated that the *Times* should have printed the story because he would then have been forced to cancel the invasion, sparing the United States one of the worst foreign policy fiascos in its history. It was not merely that government had lied and suppressed news, and been caught at it. Nor was it only that the press had been used, used easily and with cavalier disrespect, and used wrongly. It was rather that two *Presidents* had publicly admitted lying and suppressing news, and that one of them said the press shouldn't have listened to him. Clearly the problem which the press had identified in the aftermath of McCarthyism was not confined to an occasional demagogue in Congress; it extended to the highest and most respected officials in the land. If one couldn't trust them, evidently one couldn't trust anyone.

THE EXPERIENCE OF THE 1960s

These events marked the beginning of both the "credibility gap" theme in public affairs reporting and a growing truculence among newsmen. By 1966 Clifton Daniel, then managing editor of *The New York Times,* could give a speech saying that the *Times* had been wrong not to print the Bay of Pigs story and would not make such a mistake again. The *Times* is of course our preeminent journalistic institution; it had previously been cooperative with government about national security matters; and it does not make admissions of error lightly, if at all. The speech was a watershed in modern journalistic history, and it served notice that an important article in the informal covenant between press and government was being renegotiated, if not unilaterally repudiated.

This issue might have been resolved satisfactorily had not four further developments supervened. One of these was the steep decline, during the 1960s, in the competitiveness of the "prestige" newsmarkets, especially New York, which quietly but effectively shifted the balance of power between newsmen and sources. When *The New York Times* had been actively in competition with the *Herald-Tribune*, their newsmen felt constrained to maintain friendly relationships with sources so that their opposite numbers would not get "exclusives"—and sources, as a consequence, could "whipsaw" newsmen to keep them in line. When the *Times*, the Washington *Post*, and other leading newspapers no longer had any true local competitors, their newsmen became less beholden, and sources became relatively weaker. Since these newsmen worked for newspapers which were widely respected and emulated by lesser publications, and since in any event they produced a large portion of the national news coverage published in the country, this shift had effects out of all proportion to the number of newspapers immediately involved. (Significantly, the only truly competitive comprehensive national news services—AP and UPI—have been little affected by the emergence of the movement for an "adversary" journalism.)

A second important development was the growth in the visibility, self-consciousness, and self-confidence of the journalistic profession, and especially of the Washington press corps. Traditionally, reporting had been a low-prestige occupation; some studies reported it to rank *between* the blue-collar and white-collar occupations. In the 1960s this began to change. President Kennedy showed a special fondness for newsmen; the inauguration in 1963 of the national half-hour television news programs gave the press a new vehicle of unprecedented power and created, overnight, a batch of journalistic celebrities; officials became ever more attentive to the press, and their efforts to manipulate the news grew in scale and sophistication; books and articles about the press began to proliferate; and by the beginning of the 1970s scale salaries at leading newspapers approached (and, in TV, exceeded) those of Assistant Secretaries. Whatever the cause, newsmen had a growing sense of their importance and a corresponding unwillingness to accept the dependency and subordination which, as it seemed, had been characteristic of the position of the press in earlier decades.

Third, there was the extraordinary political and cultural ferment of the 1960s, involving a dramatic expansion and intensification of political conflict and the emergence of countercultural, anti-establishment, and other oppositional movements. The spirit of the age had its impact on the journalistic community, especially on its younger, newly-recruited members. The psychological distance between press and government and the frequency of stories critical of established policy grew.

More important than this direct form of cultural influence, however, was the indirect influence of the spirit of the 1960s upon journalism. As we have noted, the traditional mode of American journalism was dependent and derivative; the press largely reflected the ideas and balance of power in official circles. As the 1960s wore on, an ever larger segment of officialdom itself became sympathetic to the oppositional fashions of the decade. Not only "the kids" and other people "out there," but also Senators, committee chairmen, Washington lawyers, and Assistant Secretaries began to articulate the spirit of "confrontation" and "alienation." Thus, as ideological movements of opinion became stronger, traditional journalism found itself having to choose from among a variety of perspectives, all of which could claim some official standing. Merely by continuing to report public affairs in the traditional way, the press gave increasing exposure to the ideas and symbols of the oppositional movements.

THE WHITE HOUSE VS. THE PRESS

This led in turn to the fourth development which fostered the current movement for a "new journalism": the intensification of opposition to the movements of the 1960s both in public opinion at large and within specific institutions and political circles. One of the ways in which such "backlash" sentiment expressed itself was by attacking the press for giving exposure to those movements, and one of the most prominent sources of such attacks was the White House, beginning with Lyndon Johnson. For a variety of reasons—good, bad, and indifferent—both Johnson and his successor chose to resist the growing truculence of the press and the exposure it gave to the growing anti-war and other oppositional movements in the country as a whole. As in Vietnam, so on the homefront: With each escalation of the President's campaign against the press, the press seemed to counter with an added measure of defiance and a little more coverage of oppositional politics.

At first the belligerents fought their battles with the conventional weapons of legitimate political warfare. LBJ used the personal approach (flattering and punishing reporters, making telephone calls to network executives, etc.) and the traditional devices of political public relations (emphasizing good news and deemphasizing the bad, manipulating the appearance of events, wheeling out various "experts" and "authorities" to defend his positions, and the like). The Nixon Administration, in its early months, added to these devices the long-range artillery of Agnewian rhetoric and an elaborately centralized system of "public information."

These tactics not only didn't work, they seemed only to confirm the press it its new determination to be independent, which in context meant critical.

As feelings on both sides grew more embittered, their tactics became more unconventional and the struggle more total: It was an omen of the Watergate era to come. The Administration—which in this escalation was clearly the aggressor—launched FBI investigations of newsmen it felt to be hostile; deprived the press of traditional forms of access, such as the press conference, the casual telephone conversation, and the cocktail party; threatened television stations with loss of their licenses; in the first case of prior censorship in American history, brought suit to enjoin the publication of the Pentagon papers; and set up the Plumbers to stop unauthorized leaks. The press countered with heavy coverage of anti-Nixon political elements, publication of secret government documents (the Pentagon and Anderson papers) which they would not have dreamed of making public ten years earlier, and a growing pattern of refusing to accept the legality of subpoenas issued by courts in the course of due legal processes. There was also a certain tendency to begin ignoring traditional journalistic standards of fairness` and truth. When the Supreme Court issued its "Caldwell" decision in 1972, which at most only upheld the existing rules defining the testimonial obligations of newsmen, the press interpreted this as a *change* in Constitutional law that reduced freedom of the press. A year before, in "The Selling of the Pentagon," CBS-TV editors falsified the continuity of a filmed interview with a Pentagon official. And when the actions of any newsman were challenged or criticized, increasingly the journalistic community as a whole drew together in defense of its own, right or wrong. Jack Anderson was given the Pulitzer prize for publishing a National Security Council minute concerning the American position in a current, explosive diplomatic situation, and "The Selling of the Pentagon," despite its dubious editing, was cited for excellence in the television documentary category.

THE NEW MOOD

The upshot of these developments was that the liberal press particularly—and to an increasing extent other parts of the journalistic community as well-found itself ever more committed to a stance of truculent independence from government and officialdom. Increasingly it felt that its proper role was not to cooperate with government but to be independent of it, or even opposed to it. Increasingly newsmen began to say that their job was to be an autonomous, investigative adversary of government and to constitute a countervailing force against the great authority of all established institutions. And increasingly they began to see as illegitimate the few traditional formal constraints upon the press: libel law, "fair trial" restrictions on news coverage, testimonial obligations upon all citizens to give their evidence under subpoena, and the laws defining and protecting government secrets. These sentiments, and the actions which in modest but growing number gave concrete expression to them, define the movement for a "new journalism" which exists today and which poses the central question which the press will have to cope with after Watergate.

It is impossible to state with any precision or sense of certainty just how widespread and securely entrenched this movement is. Its only clearly identifiable location seems to be generational: It is young reporters, in their twenties and early thirties, who seem most to share the attitudes that define the movement. In general, though, it is more a mood than a settled, behavioral pattern; a thing more of the spirit than of the flesh; a tendency or yearning more than an established and institutionalized accomplishment. And yet it is a fact. If it is not so widespread or influential as current conservative critics of the media insist, it is also more substantial than

defenders of the movement admit. It exists; it really is unlike that which has prevailed in our journalism for decades; it could yet become dominant; and it makes a difference.

THE BLASI FINDINGS

A recent study by Professor Vince Blasi of the Michigan Law School suggests something of the extent to which the attitudes of this movement have gained ground in the journalistic community. As a means of measuring the need for and effects of "shield" legislation, Blasi in 1972 asked a non-random sample of almost 1,000 newsmen to respond to the following hypothetical situation:

You have a continuing source relationship with a group of political radicals. They have given you much information in confidence and this has enabled you to write several byline stories describing and assessing in general terms the activities and moods of the group. During the course of this relationship, you are present at a closed meeting with ten of these radicals at which the group vigorously debates whether to bomb a number of targets, including the local police station. The consensus is against such bombing, but two members of the group argue very heatedly in favor of bombing and are deeply upset when the others refuse to go along. These two then threaten to act on their own. The discussion then turns to another topic. Two weeks later the local police station is in fact bombed. One officer is killed by the blast and two others are seriously injured.

The first question Blasi posed was this: "In these circumstances, would you on your own initiative volunteer the information you learned at the meeting *right after the meeting* (i.e., before a bombing took place)?" Of those who responded, 26.2 per cent answered "yes," 55.5 per cent "no," and the rest gave no answer.

Question #2: "Would you volunteer the information on your own initiative to law enforcement authorities *after the bombing* (but before you were contacted by the police or subpoenaed by a grand jury)?" Answer: 37.6 per cent yes, 36.0 per cent no, 26.4 per cent no answer.

Question #3: "Assume that you were subpoenaed by a grand jury investigating the bombing but that an absolute legal privilege were established so that you could not be compelled to answer questions against your will. Would you voluntarily answer if the grand jury asked you whether this group of radicals had ever discussed the possibility of bombing the police station?" Answer: 45.5 per cent yes, 36.0 per cent no, 18.5 per cent no answer.

Question #4: "If the grand jury asked you to name the members of the group who had advocated bombing?" Answer: 36.9 per cent yes, 44.1 per cent no, 19.0 per cent no answer.

Question #5: "Assume that one of the members of the group who had argued vigorously *against* the bombing was indicted for the crime and that you believed, on the basis of the meeting, that it is highly unlikely that this particular member was the bomber. Would you on your own initiative volunteer this information to the prosecutor?" Answer: 60 per cent yes, 22.2 per cent no, 17.8 per cent no answer.

Question #6: "If this member's defense lawyer subpoenaed you at the trial would you testify about the meeting you had witnessed (including giving the names of those who did advocate the bombing) even if you were protected by an absolute privilege so that you couldn't be compelled to testify?" Answer: 43.2 per cent yes, 36.4 per cent no, 20.4 per cent no answer.

In the liberal tradition of "objective" journalism, newsmen cooperated with government and especially with law enforcement officials in serious felonies like bombing and murder. One may safely assume that, at some point, a traditional reporter would have given his information to the authorities and defense lawyers—albeit with a guilty conscience over having broken his pledge of confidentiality.[2] Blasi's newsmen show the opposite inclination. Even in a case of bombing, death, and serious injury, only one fourth said they would warn authorities of the possibility of a bombing beforehand; only two fifths said they would volunteer their information after the bombing; less than half were sure they would tell a grand jury that the group had discussed the possibility of bombing; and only two fifths were willing to name the persons who had advocated the bombing. And most startling of all, *almost three fifths of this sample of 1,000 reporters were unwilling to say that they would go to court to testify in defense of persons on trial for murder even if they had information tending to show the defendants to be innocent and others to be guilty.*

ISSUES OF CONFIDENTIALITY

Of course, these are only attitudes; it is quite possible—even likely—that, in the crunch, no more than a handful of newsmen would actually withhold their evidence in such circumstances. But in a way that is beside the point. What is to the point is that these attitudes are widely perceived to exist among newsmen, and that a few newsmen have begun to act on the basis of them. Together these developments have raised two large and disagreeable issues which our political and legal processes are now forced to grapple with.

One of these is the problem posed by the unauthorized publication of secret or confidential government documents, ranging from White House memoranda and secret depositions before grand juries to Jack Anderson's National Security Council minute or William Beecher's summary of the U.S. fallback position in the SALT-I negotiations. In large part, to be sure, the issue here should focus more on the persons responsible for leaking documents than on the press, which merely publishes them; surely the proper initial defendant, in a legal test of this process, is not *The New York Times* but Daniel Ellsberg, not Jack Anderson but his sources (apparently in the Pentagon). Yet it is also an issue that concerns the press itself because, until recently, the press, out of regard for national security or fear of the consequences, would not have published the Pentagon papers (though it might well have written *about* them, in a veiled and guarded way). Today, obviously, it will publish them, and the result is that we are confronted squarely with a new issue that we would be better off not having to deal with.

It is an impossible issue. However it is resolved, or even if it is not resolved, we will be worse off than we were before it was raised. It involves a conflict among three valuable traditions—press freedom, confidentiality in government, and the relatively open or amorphous quality of American government. Conflicts among these traditions have heretofore been resolved on an informal, *ad hoc* basis. To attempt to resolve them systematically and formally is to lose much and to gain little, if anything. One does need secrecy and confidentiality in government; to protect national security from enemy powers, to ensure that persons in government will feel free to write down on paper their best individual judgments on issues of fact and policy, and perhaps most of all to preserve the ability of officials (especially the President) to be flexible and to take initiatives. (Premature leaks are the tried-and-true device for forestalling Presidential initiatives in policy and administration, or for rendering them ineffective once taken.) On the other hand, one does not want Congress to make any law abridging the freedom of the press in order to preserve this confidentiality. Nor does one want to take the path of enacting an official secrets act that provides severe penalties for any civil servant who leaks information without formal approval from the highest authorities. This last measure would sharply reduce the amount and range of perfectly harmless and also useful information that would be made—is now made—available to the press, usually to the benefit of us all; it would also reduce the ability of Congress to oversee the Executive, since it would know less about what was going on. Thus, by retreating from its old cooperative notion of public responsibility, the press has created an issue which cannot be resolved without changing the American system as a whole in some fundamental—and unattractive—way.

More or less the same is true of the second issue raised by the current movement for a new journalism: the question of the testimonial obligations of newsmen. In the past several years, journalists have begun to insist with increasing frequency and vehemence that they should not be compelled by grand juries or courts to disclose information they have gathered from sources on a confidential basis. To do so, they say, will cause sources to give less information to the press, which in turn will reduce the amount of information citizens can glean from newspapers. Previously, newsmen had generally cooperated with the law enforcement establishment. Now, partly because of the increasingly adversarial stance of newsmen towards government, and partly also because more newsmen have begun to cover the activities of radical, violent, or criminal groups, this has changed. A number of newsmen have chosen to go to jail rather than reveal the identify of confidential informants or the substance of what they learned from them. And in defense of this choice they have offered the further argument that the press is now subjected to so many subpoenas—over a four-year period beginning in 1968, for instance, the Chicago *Tribune* received more than 400—that its operations are truly disrupted and its freedom, as a practical matter, is reduced.

Should we then enact shield legislation exempting newsmen from their testimonial obligations? Perhaps, but to do so is not without its costs. With certain minor and traditional exceptions, all citizens are now obligated to give their evidence before courts of law. It is hard to see why newsmen should be made a class apart in this respect; and it is likely that such an exemption would render our system of criminal justice less effective. The price of immunity for journalists would be less justice for everyone else. Here, too, we have a dilemma that is created by the newsman's increasing withdrawal of his consent from the traditional covenant of cooperative suspiciousness between the press and government. To resolve the issue is to change the American system in fundamental—and, again, unattractive—ways.

A RETREAT
FROM THE LIBERAL IDEAL

The deeper problem with this movement for a new journalism, however, is that it represents an incipient retreat, not merely from an intelligible idea of the public interest and of the responsibility of the press to serve it, but also from the entire liberal tradition of American journalism and the system of liberal democracy which it has fostered and served. The problem of the press publishing a few government secrets or withholding the names of an occasional criminal may be serious in principle but it is usually negligible in practice. But there is a larger practical question raised by "adversary" journalism that is not at all negligible: the question of the persistence of the open, fragmented, liberal system of American democracy as we have known it and benefited from it for the past many decades.

Our instinct is to assume that this system is virtually indestructible, rooted as it is in the pragmatic temper of the American people, the Constitutional system of division of powers, and other such factors apparently beyond the influence of what we do or think. This is a reasonable assumption within limits, but it isn't entirely true. The system also depends on many institutions and attitudes which are indeed changeable, and one of the most important—if least acknowledged—of these is the kind of press we have. Its capacity to find and publish vast amounts of information about politics and government, and its success in reaching universal audiences without regard to ideology or political affiliations, have contributed in an important way to the openness and flexibility of American government and to the ability of public opinion to influence the conduct of public affairs and to attain consensus. As the press has become wealthier in recent decades, its ability to gather and print information has increased; as political party organizations have declined, the need and willingness of officials to give newsmen access have also grown; so even while the complexity of government and the amount of "classified" information have increased, the capacity of the press to help the American system realize its ideals has at least kept pace.

The new movement abroad in the journalistic community threatens all this. For the press can make its contribution to the system only by maintaining close access—a closer access, as I have said, than can ever be provided by law. The price of such access is some degree of cooperation and sympathy for government—*not* a slavish adulation, as is sometimes said, but a decent respect for authority, a willingness to see government and persons in government given the opportunity to do their job, and at least a slight sense of responsibility for and commitment to the goals inherent in those jobs. When these are not present, access diminishes. And when newsmen begin to assert they are positively the adversaries of government, access diminishes drastically, and with it not only the contribution journalism can make but also the openness and flexibility of government itself. Politicians and officials are no more than human; they have their needs and interests; above all they intend to survive. If they feel themselves to be threatened or harmed, they will eventually take steps to insulate themselves as best they can from the danger.

The history of the Nixon Administration shows some of the ways in which this can occur. At one extreme there is Watergate itself—that is, the Plumbers, wiretaps and investigations of newsmen, harassment of news organizations, and the like. This is an irrational and pathological response which is as unnecessary as it is intolerable, and we are not likely to see a recurrence in the discernible future. But the Nixon Administration used other methods as well, and these we can expect to see more of, regardless of who is in the White House, if the movement continues to gain ground. There is "jawboning": making speeches criticizing press coverage in hopes of reducing the press' credibility and increasing its cooperativeness. More important, there is the technique of organizing and formalizing all press-government contacts through the instrument of the Public Affairs/Public Information office and the centralized public relations operation, such as the one inaugurated by Herb Klein. And most powerful of all, there is the simple device of self-isolation, on the theory that it is better to have less of a bad press than more of a good press, especially in light of the fact that the effort to seek the latter can so easily end up earning one more of the former. Such a "low-profile" strategy—with infrequent and irregular press conferences, sharply limited informal contact between officials and reporters, even reliance on a praetorian staff lacking extensive ties outside the official family—is one of Richard Nixon's original contributions to the American political tradition. It is clearly an undesirable contribution, especially in its Nixonesque form, and yet it represents a logical adaptation to the perceived existence of an adversary press; the chances are we will see more of it insofar as the new movement gains ground. By the end of his campaign, even George McGovern seemed to be changing his mind about the desirability of having an "open" staff in constant informal contact with the press. The result, as he not unreasonably perceived it, was a bad press which emphasized the confusion and in-fighting within his official family and which thus suggested that McGovern was not a competent executive. It is hard to imagine that if he had won in 1972 he would have continued his policy of openness. The price is simply too high for any rational man to want to pay, and the benefits, if any, are too few and too small.

And as government adapts to the situation created by the current movement for a new journalism, so will the entire profession of journalism—and in ways that it does not now envision. As has been pointed out, the traditional form of the news story, the news organization's pattern of recruiting and training newsmen, even the format of the modern newspaper are all geared to the liberal, orthodox mode of journalism, with its preoccupation with facts and events, its relative unconcern for the problem of point of view, and its intention of appealing to a universal audience. In order to work, such a journalism needs reporters to have access to

government, and when they no longer have it the capacity of newspapers to maintain the other features of the existing form is weakened, as is the whole idea of and justification for those features. Journalism will change—and the logical direction of change is toward the partisan form of journalism, with its ideological basis, politically based relationship to the government in power, and fractionated audiences. It is possible, of course, that an adversary journalism could persist indefinitely, but this seems unlikely. A stance of "pure" opposition—opposition as an end in itself, rather than as an expression of some larger, positive political commitment—is self-contradictory in theory and likely to be short-lived in practice. The probability is that an adversary press would eventually ally itself with a political faction and so become partisan—an ideologically divisive factor rather than a politically unifying force. The consequences could be enormous.

TWO SCENARIOS FOR THE FUTURE

Now the partisan mode of journalism has its virtues. It does not evade the problem of "point of view" as liberal journalism does, and in this sense it has an appealing honesty. It also has the capacity to create and sustain coherent bodies of political opinion; at a time when political opinion in this country is so often contradictory and inchoate, that is a very important trait. This is why "journals of opinion," existing on the margins of American journalism, have been so important and desirable.

But if, over the long run, American journalism were ever to turn massively to the partisan mode, the consequences of this development would extend to nearly every aspect of our political system. Partisan journalism would not increase the openness of the system, it would sharply decrease it. It would not reduce the scope of political conflict, but enlarge it. It would not increase the capacity of American government to act effectively and flexibly in meeting emergent needs, but would tend to paralyze it. It would not empower public opinion as a whole, but would transform it into a congeries of rigid ideological factions eternally at war with one another and subject to the leadership of small coteries of ideologues and manipulators. Indeed, it would tend to transform the entire nature of American politics: From having been a popular government based on a flexible consensus, it would become Europeanized into a popular government based on an equilibrium of hostile parties and unchanging ideologies.

The alternative to such a "Europeanization" of journalism and politics, it should be emphasized, does not have to be a massive and uncritical reversion to the way things were during the 1950s and early 1960s. Even if this were possible—which it isn't—it would clearly be undesirable. Both officialdom and the press were then busily abusing the "objective" tradition, officialdom by treating the media as an institution to be deliberately "managed" for its own expediential purposes, and the press by encouraging and acquiescing in these efforts out of inertia and a generalized avidity to print "big news" as often and as easily as possible.

There are ways to curb these abuses while still preserving the benefits of the liberal tradition of our press which the "advisory" approach would squander. Government can increase the amount of information which is formally made available on the public record. It can scale down its "public relations" operations to the point where they cannot easily operate as instruments of press management and are content instead merely to disseminate information. As Joseph Lee Auspitz and Clifford W. Brown, Jr., have

suggested, the "strategic" cast of mind giving rise to, among other things, the habit of "managing" the press for purposes of personal power can be discouraged by strengthening the political party, which embeds individual actors in an institutional context, channels and restrains their ambition, and promotes a "representative" as against a "strategic" ethos. And the press, for its own part, can help to recover the objective tradition by abandoning its flirtation with the "oppositional" posture and by ceasing to exploit public affairs for their sensation value (since the desire to exploit public affairs in this way is the main incentive leading the press to acquiesce in the manipulations of "strategically" minded officials). The result, I believe, will be a journalism that provides more, and more useful, information to the citizenry, and a political system that, in consequence, comes a bit closer than in the past to realizing its historic ideals.

NOTES

1. I should point out that I am using the terms "journalism" and the "press" in these pages to refer to *daily* journalism only—that is, to daily newspapers and broadcast news programs. There are other forms of journalism, of course: weekly, monthly, quarterly, general purpose, special purpose, and so on. These other forms are important and interesting, and they perform crucial functions vis-à-vis government and the daily press itself. Unfortunately, space prevents me from considering them in this essay.

2. Writing in the January 15, 1973 issue of *New York*, Richard Reeves described a classic instance of the traditional relationship. "I remember … my first big story with *The New York Times* in the summer of 1966 … a homicide case against a young man named Ernest Gallashaw, accused in the shooting of a ten-year-old boy during racial rioting in the East New York section of Brooklyn.… In ten days or so … I came back with notebooks full of interviews and evidence that made it clear … that New York City authorities were playing fast and loose with Gallashaw's life and freedom . …. I wrote a three-column story, but just before deadline … I was told that it would not be published immediately and that I was to turn over our evidence to the Brooklyn District Attorney's office.

"… Clifton Daniel, then the managing editor … explained … that homicide investigations were government business.… The *Times* ran the complete story a day later, beginning on page 1 with a lead saying the District Attorney was investigating new evidence in the case."

Part Two

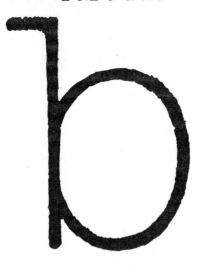

Journalists
and Their Methods

PROFESSIONAL MODELS IN JOURNALISM: THE GATEKEEPER AND THE ADVOCATE

Morris Janowitz

Practitioners in any particular profession hold differing conceptions of their tasks and priorities. The difference between the "public health" doctor and the clinician is a long-standing distinction that has had a strong impact on the practice of medicine. In the military, it has been observed that officers can be classified as "pragmatists" or as "absolutists" according to their differing notions of the relative importance and role of force in international relations.

This article seeks to present two alternative models which are operative among contemporary working journalists—the "gatekeeper" and the "advocate." It also seeks to analyze the professional issues associated with these models and their implications for the practice of journalism.

Since World War I, journalists have come more and more to consider themselves as professionals and to search for an appropriate professional mode. The initial efforts were to fashion journalism into a field, similar to medicine, where the journalist would develop his technical expertise and also a sense of professional responsibility. This model and its aspirations can best be called the "gatekeeper" model. In particular, this image of the journalist sought to apply the canons of the scientific method to increase his objectivity and enhance his effective performance. The model was reinforced in part by the increased prestige of the academic social researcher, and it assumed that,

From Journalism Quarterly *52 (Winter 1975): 618-626, 662.* Copyright © *1975 by* Journalism Quarterly; *reprinted by permission.*

through the application of intellectually based techniques, objective and valid results could be obtained.

The gatekeeper orientation emphasized the search for objectivity and the sharp separation of reporting fact from disseminating opinion. Coverage of the real world required that the journalist select the important from the mass of detailed information; therefore, the notion of the journalist as gatekeeper rested on his ability to detect, emphasize, and disseminate that which was important. Under the gatekeeper concept of professionalism, the journalist encountered institutional pressures and personal limitations in searching for objectivity and separating fact from opinion. But to the extent that he thought of himself as a professional or hoped to make journalism into a profession, he had little doubt about standards of performance, although there was much debate about their clarity and how to apply them.

Of course, there were powerful barriers to the implementation of such a professional conception. In particular, journalists did not have sufficient time or resources to pursue their investigations. However, individual journalists have increasingly developed areas of extensive expertise and competence.

The emergence of this professional orientation probably reflected the technical achievements of other professional groups, particularly in medicine and law. It represented the belief that the scientific method was productive in various sections of society and that it had broad substantive and cultural relevance for the journalist.[1]

In the 1960s, the gatekeeper model of journalistic professionalism was questioned by some working journalists. They recommended replacing the scientific method with the concept of the journalist as critic and interpreter. "Objectivity" was criticized in various intellectual quarters. Outspoken academic social scientists became doubtful about their ability to be objective and claimed that the search for objective reality led to a retreat from personal and political responsibility. Some working journalists also proclaimed that objectivity in reporting was impossible or at least doubtful and that the task of the journalist was to represent the viewpoints and interests of competing groups, especially those of excluded and underprivileged groups. One sociological investigator sympathetic to it concluded, from her field research into the practice of journalism, that objectivity was a "strategic ritual" by news personnel to defend themselves from the "risks of their trade" and from "critical onslaught."[2]

These journalists feel that there is a series of conflicting interests, each of which creates its own contribution to the definition of reality. Therefore the role of the journalist is to insure that all perspectives are adequately represented in the media, for the resolution of social conflict depends on effective representation of alternative definitions of reality. The journalist must "participate" in the advocacy process. He must be an advocate for those who are denied powerful spokesmen, and he must point out the consequences of the contemporary power imbalance. The search for objective reality yields to a struggle to participate in the sociopolitical process by supplying knowledge and information.

The issue of confidentiality is crucial in distinguishing between the gatekeeper and the advocate-journalist. Before World War II, this issue came up infrequently. Before 1941, the national security aspect of public affairs was circumscribed, and only a few journalists were working on such topics and the associated issue of confidentiality. However, progressively, matters of national security and associated record-keeping have expanded the day-to-day problem of confidentiality. The contemporary advocate-journalist has developed outspoken opinions on confidentiality. The issue of confidentiality is very salient to him and supplies a means of expressing his professional ideology. But the importance of confidentiality also derives from the self-conceptions of the advocate-journalist. He believes that his tasks involve collecting information and revealing the contents whenever it is, in his view, in the public interest or in the interest of submerged or repressed social groups.

As a result, three central themes guide the advocate notions of confidentiality. First, the journalist believes in the absolute confidentiality of his sources in certain circumstances. But the issue is broader than sources, for the advocate-journalist thinks of himself as representing the interest of his clients—that is, those who supply him with information, especially the submerged groups about whom he writes. Therefore, he is prepared to keep information supplied to him confidential when he believes that doing so is in the interest of his clients.

Second, the advocate's professional role now has come to outstrip, under most conditions, his citizen role. The advocate-journalist has come to believe that, if he obtains information bearing on a criminal prosecution, he is not required to assist the legal process. In 1972, Professor Blasi of the law school of the University of Michigan completed an ad hoc questionnaire survey of approximately 1,000 journalists' views on confidentiality. It was by no means a representative sample, but the findings indicate that a minority have accepted the essentials of the advocate point of view. Almost 20% declared that they would not supply the "prosecution" with information which they had collected in confidence that could be used to establish the innocence of a defendant facing indictment on a serious criminal charge.[3]

Third, the mechanisms of confidentiality are not symmetrical, especially with respect to government sources. The advocate-journalists believe that personal records of income taxes, social security and criminal behavior should be kept confidential to insure individual privacy. However, since they believe that government, in conducting its business, either withholds or manipulates information, journalists have a widely ranging obligation to expose information which government agencies label as confidential.

These conpeting models must address as well the complex issues of professional-client relations. Of course, the journalist has clients and has professional relationships with his clients. The audience of a medium are the journalist's initial clients, and he has the obligation to perform services which are "good" for the client and on his behalf, regardless of the client's preferences and beliefs. But his client linkage is weak because of the ease with which the audience can shift its loyalties. Moreover, in a democratic society the media are open, and unintended audiences figure as clients.

But the issue is more complex. The journalist does not perform a specific service for a particular individual. He seeks to assist the members of his audience to relate themselves symbolically to the institutions of collective problem solving. The journalist thereby performs a task designed to create the conditions under which the individual citizen, and administrative and political leaders, can take action. There is an analogy with the schoolteacher, in that the journalist too is concerned with mind sets and thought processes in the first instance, and here lies the core element of professional-client relations in journalism.

The adherents of the gatekeeper outlook hold different conceptions of their client relationships. In the gatekeeper conception, the emphasis is placed on the client's ability to judge his own self-interest. The task of the journalist is to process information and to comment, in order to place information in a proper cultural perspective and to assist the client in understanding his relationship to the sociopolitical process. In short, it is to enhance his underlying rationality. This requires the journalist to present the client with information which may be unpleasant and which he has a powerful tendency to resist. It is hardly a purely "rationalist" interpretation, since it recognizes the irrational and emotional elements in social relations. The professional client relationship assumes that the audience members have the potential to respond and that this potential needs to be maximized. It is based on a notion of a self-correcting system of social and political control.

In contrast, the advocate's conception of professional journalism highlights the barriers to sociopolitical change in contemporary society and the difficulties that certain segments of the society have in achieving their legitimate self-interests. For these groups to achieve their legitimate objects, the active intervention of the mass media, as well as of other key institutions like the educational and judicial systems, is required. Professional relations with clients have special reference to subject groups covered by the mass media, especially to those groups suffering inequalities and injustices. Therefore, it is the professional responsibility of the advocate-journalist to speak on behalf of these groups. Thus, the advocate-journalist would like to relate to his clients in the role of the lawyer but in the setting of the mass media.

Advocate-journalists have come to think of themselves as conforming to a conception of the legal profession, concerned to speak on behalf of their "client" groups by means of the mass media. The movement toward the advocacy format, in fact, represented a partial break with the idea of professionalism and was in part a political act. Some critics have described it as the Europeanization" of the American press.[4] The advocacy format does raise the reality of a more explicitly partisan press. However, during the last decade the American press cannot be seen as having been Europeanized, since it has not moved toward more and more explicit linkages with organized political parties and factions. The advocacy format in the American scene has been a much more individualistic expression with only a diffuse ideology and a strong anti-authority overtone.

PATTERNS OF TWO ORIENTATIONS

Is it possible to estimate the proportion of working journalists who adhere to the gatekeeper rather than the advocate norms? What factors reinforce each of the two competing models? We are, of course, dealing with a small group, compared with medicine, law, or teaching. Johnstone estimated that, in 1971, there were a total of 69,500 people working full time in the English-language news media in the United States engaged in news and editorial work. Of this number, a "relatively small cadre of news and public affairs personnel—some 7,000 at most, staff the primary information services in the United States."[5] The compactness of the profession implies intense interaction among its members that contributes to the articulation of professional attitudes and beliefs.

From Johnstone's interview survey of a sample of over 1,300 journalists, some measures of the relative concentration of the gatekeepers versus advocate oulook can be drawn. The broadest, most diffuse measure of even a mild orientation toward the advocate outlook could be found in the answer to the question of whether the journalist thought there were too few crusaders in the media; 34.9 percent did. On the other hand, the narrowest, sharpest measure of the advocacy model came in willingness to endorse the activities of the underground press without qualification. Only 11 percent held this viewpoint—the strongly advocate-journalists.

By means of a scale of items, Johnstone distinguishes the "neutral" from the "participant" journalists, and the results confirm the responses on the single items. Of his sample, 8.5 percent were predominantly participants in outlook, and 21.4 percent were moderately participant. In addition, 35.4 percent held balanced views, 25.1 percent were moderately neutral, and 9.7 percent were predominantly neutral. These findings underline the conclusion that the bulk of the profession hold "moderate" views and only a small minority are polarized at each end of the continuum.

Johnstone presents some data that enable us to make certain inferences about the social and educational background factors that fashion journalists in the advocate model. The drift toward the advocate persuasion does not essentially represent socioeconomic background or minority-group protest but, rather, a personal, intellectual, and in turn political trend. It appears to be more a result of "socialization"—that is, age, education, and career experience—and undoubtedly involves elements of social personality. In his conclusion, he states "participant views of journalistic responsibility would appear to emerge out of one's experience in higher education, while neutral values are a product of apprentice type experiences, of career lines in which one learns to be a journalist in the context of practical skills, and concrete routines rather than abstract principles and theories." His data emphasize the importance of youth and of residence in large metropolitan centers in conditioning advocacy orientations. Journalism is a comparatively young profession; his survey points out that one-third of the journalists in the early 1970s were between 25 and 34 years old.

Since the mid-1960s, it appears to me that the most outspoken carriers of the advocate orientation have been the younger journalists educated at prestigious liberal arts schools and state universities. They have been exposed to student movements and, more important, to academic writings and to professors deeply critical of contemporary society. They tend to find their desired life style in the major metropolitan centers. On the other hand, the gatekeeper personnel tend to be older and more often educated in journalism. It would not be unfair to speak of two subcultures in journalism, highly age-graded. This is particularly so since the gatekeeper personnel appear to be more involved in professional associations, while the subculture of the advocates is linked to intensive primary groups, face-to-face and informal networks and controls.

Most surveys of journalists' political opinions show that they are skewed to the "left" of center. While there is hardly a one-to-one linkage between political orientation and professional norms, the advocates appear to be concentrated more to the left of the political spectrum than the gatekeepers. Those who have written on the culture of journalism have repeatedly pointed to the reformist impulse which has motivated men and women to enter the field. This reformist impulse is accompanied not by an urge to exercise power but by a desire to bring about change through moral criticism. The contemporary thrust of advocate journalism is clearly a manifestation of such motivation. However, it has become embodied in an elaborated professional ideology and supported by the internal social organization of journalism.

BACKGROUND OF PROFESSIONALISM

The rise of the advocate-journalist will not be understood if it is considered as the direct result of the agitation and unrest of the 1960s, especially on the campuses. It is an oversimplification to conclude that activist students moved off campus and into public life, including positions in the mass media, taking with them the notion of advocate journalism. The student unrest did heighten criticism of the mass media and lead to demands for greater activism among professionals. Many young journalists who think of themselves as advocates were exposed to the student movement of the 1960s. The student movement in the United States during this period had diffuse ideological elements, but, in contrast to such movements in Western Europe, it was mainly linked to specific issues, particularly to opposition to the war in Vietnam.

Instead, it is necessary to recall that the advocate in American journalism has a long tradition. From its very earliest origins in the American colonial period and in the Revolutionary War, the then existing press was polemical and offered advocacy journalism. In the United States, the mass circulation newspaper developed—in contrast to the European press—as a nonparty press. It was and remains a commercial enterprise; and its social and political roles were grafted on as a result of the efforts of the muckraker novelists and journalists. The reformist tradition was an expression of ethical and religious impulses grounded in a philosophy of pragmatism. The crusading editor and reporter, the individual defying organized interests and corrupting forces, searched for the facts and presented them dramatically. The muckraker represented, moreover, the belief that the newspaper had the potential—through the power of the press and public opinion—to overcome the weaknesses of political institutions. It is in this concept that there is a direct line of continuity between the muckraker and the advocate.

However, our concern is with development since the 1920s, when the professional elements of journalism were becoming more explicit and self-conscious. By the early 1920s, when Walter Lippmann wrote *Public Opinion*, he was fully aware of the distinction between the gatekeeper and the advocate in journalism and of the ambiguities involved in professionalizing the press and in balancing these roles. He did not use these terms. However, it is striking that he anticipated that the advocate role in the press was gaining and would gain in prominence and importance. Lippmann defined the essential public and cultural dimensions of the gatekeeper when he stated that "the function of news is to signalize an event."[6] He was hardly naive or simplistic, since he recognized the difference between news and "the truth." But this distinction did not, in his view, relieve the journalist of his professional responsibilities to dig for the objective facts. On the contrary, he was concerned that the press was beginning to be "regarded as an organ of direct democracy, charged on a much wider scale, and from day to day, with the function often attributed to the initiative, referendum and recall."[7] In short, he anticipated the advocate definition of the journalist and rejected its political implications.

It was almost 25 years later that the Commission on the Freedom of the Press issued its report, which sought to explicate and extend the debate about the role of the journalist. Its main impact was in its "General Report," dated 10 December 1946, which rejected governmental intervention and stressed the need for self-regulation.[8] This theme came to dominate discussion about the mass media in schools of journalism and professional associations. Considered in retrospect, the commission appears to have been committed to a gatekeeper conception of journalism—like many such critical intellectual endeavors—but it had the unanticipated effect of justifying the advocate role.

The commission criticized extensively the absence of appropriate standards of press performance and the ineffectiveness of the mass media in solving the problems of a democratic society. Its formulation de-emphasized the "factual" and the "intelligence" aspects of public affairs and stressed the interpretative role of the press. Whether it intended to or not, it moved in the direction of strengthening and justifying an expansion of the advocate role.

The Hutchins Commission's exploration of basic issues should have led—and did not—to collective efforts involving journalists, mass media managers and representatives of the public in "institution building." The exclusive academic composition of the commission, plus the failure to establish a mixed body after the commission's report, weakened its effectiveness. The commission's effort reflects a continuation of the academic outlook of benign contempt for the professional journalist—enriched by the particular intellectual moralizing of its chairman, Robert M. Hutchins.

If the Commission on the Freedom of the Press gave unanticipated legitimacy to the advocate position, the findings and recommendations of the Kerner Commission, established to investigate the causes (and prevention in the future) of the tragic race riots of the 1960s, gave explicit support to the trend. The Kerner Commission criticized the media for failing to give adequate coverage to the plight of minorities and for their ineffective editorial support for necessary social and political change.[9] The recommendations of the Kerner Commission included the employment of additional minority-group members in the mass media, in order to guarantee that the minority point of view would be adequately represented.

These recommendations epitomized the advocate orientation. The critics of this aspect of advocacy journalism hold that reporting on the state of minority groups can be done through an effective gatekeeper outlook concerned with objectivity; to maintain only minority-group members can perform that function is to politicize recruitment into the profession.

INSTITUTION BUILDING

It is indeed striking that the extensive debate about professional journalism in the United States has not produced a significant "institution building" either toward an independent audit or in the format of a press council. Each programmatic statement or policy proposal over the last 30 years that has addressed itself to improving journalism has concluded that an independent audit of press performance is essential. But there has been no meaningful movement in this direction in the United States. In 1947, the final report of the Commission of the Freedom of the Press, *A Free and Responsible Press,* stated that "we recommend the establishment of a new and independent agency to appraise and report annually upon the performance."[10] In the same vein, John Wale, the British journalist, ended his study of the British press by observing that the evaluation of press content remains a neglected topic and that academic research should probe the "accuracy, fullness and fairness" of what journalists write and broadcast in haste.[11]

Of course, a great variety of reasons can be cited to account for the failure of an independent press audit to develop, but, given the vast academic effort in "media research" and the extensive resources of private foundations, there is no effective explanation. One can point to vested interests, institutional inertia and reluctance to deal with controversial problems. The financial owners, the operational managers and the working press have each demonstrated resistance to implementing independent audits. Second, there must be professional justifications for auditing the press—and these seem to be weak or absent.

In the United States, norms about freedom of expression have had the consequence of eliminating any role for the government, even a facilitating one, in audit press performance. The realities of the federal government's press relations, especially sharp criticism of the media by Richard Nixon and Spiro Agnew, plus the extensive apparatus of media information and contrived leaks, have reinforced the journalist's opposition to any setting of standards by governmental agencies. Given the central importance of protecting press sources and the reluctance of the courts to do so, journalists also view the judicial branch with considerable skepticism as an agency for setting standards.

Even those who accept the idea of an independent audit do not support it energetically. In fact, the increased salience of the distinction between the gatekeeping journalist and the advocate-journalist serves to generate counterpressures. On the abstract level, the gatekeeping journalist's outlook is compatible with an independent audit of press performance. But the day-to-day pressures on the journalist—including the most creative and professional journalist—are such as to lead him to doubt the effectiveness of such an audit. There is also doubt about the mechanism of implementation that runs as follows. Men and women who really know journalism are not likely to take up such tasks. Therefore, the likelihood is that academics without realistic knowledge of the press would become involved and produce sterile and mechanical results.

On the other hand, the advocate-journalist is indifferent or openly hostile to such enterprises. Because he lacks a commitment to objectivity, the audit for him recedes as a device of professional consequence. The advocate-journalist paradoxically sees the competitive process as the basis of self-regulation and is interested in increasing the scope and intensity of divergent points of view in any given media outlet. In addition, in recent years, the advocate-journalist has launched various journalism reviews—local magazines designed to compete with and to counterbalance the existing news institutions rather than to work for the establishment of independent press audits.

Third, there can be no doubt that the methodology of the press audit presents very difficult problems and requires considerable resources. Basically, a distinction can be made between the case study approach, which focuses on a series of specific items, and a broader analytic approach, which is concerned with overall standards of performance. Given the development and aspirations of the social sciences in the United States, it is understandable that there would be extensive efforts to apply quantitative and systematic content analysis to the evaluation of mass media performance. The objective is not to focus on specific items but to chart patterns and trends. The results of such efforts have unfortunately been disappointing. While the logic of content analysis should be particularly suitable for this task, it has not fulfilled its promise or been effectively organized as a research procedure.[12] In recent years, there has been some increase in interest in the quality of and imagination of content analysis studies. But systematic content analysis of press performance has not produced a solid array of results that could command both academic and journalistic attention. In particular, formulating categories which not only describe media content but also incorporate evaluative criteria and can be reliably applied has proved to be the major difficulty.

In essence, the movement toward an independent audit of the mass media has been weaker in the United States than in Great Britain. In Great Britain, the movement resulted in the emergence of a press council.

Characteristically, the British effort has been less in the direction of the analytic categories and formal standards of performance that reflect United States social science; instead, the work has been of the case study variety.[13]

The existence of the British Press Council has stimulated the very gradual development of counterparts in the United States. Local press councils were suggested in 1968 as appropriate and received some stimulus because of the financial support offered by the Mellett Fund for a Free and Responsible Press in 1967 for organizing such councils in six communities.[14] A national news council was organized in 1972 but its program has been slow in evolving. Publishers and editors-in-chief appear prepared to offer more verbal support of these efforts than implied by published editorials.[15] Moreover, there is some empirical evidence that the local press councils have a positive—if limited—effect.[16]

However, journalists in the United States have been more concerned with their professional autonomy than with mechanisms for auditing their performance. The extent to which they believe that they have made progress in this respect is striking. Journalists are subject to a constant stream of external pressures. Public information officers and public relations agents seek to have their organizations and clients mentioned in the mass media. Professional journalists take such activities for granted and without resentment make use of the provided material as they see fit. They are, of course, more deeply concerned with pressure and criticism from the top level of the executive branch of government and with court decisions seeking to force them to reveal their sources. While these court decisions raise fundamental professional issues, the journalistic corps have responded with vigor and enthusiasm to the attacks from the White House and Watergate-associated sources, since these are news and the basis of new journalistic reputations.

The issue of professional autonomy focuses more and more on the internal procedures of the media agencies. The journalist wants to select his own stories, to treat them as he feels appropriate and to avoid his work's being rewritten and edited by members of his organization. The sheer size of a mass media organization creates a division of labor and a set of supervising officers who impinge on autonomy, so defined. Nevertheless, Johnstone's survey indicates that U.S. journalists, as of the early 1970s, tend to be fairly satisfied with the amount of freedom they have in "deciding which aspects of a news story should be emphasized."[17] They are more constrained by their organization in selecting the stories on which they work, but even in this regard they overwhelmingly believe that they have effective freedom. The differences between the gatekeepers and the advocate-journalists are real and noteworthy. The journalist-advocates are less satisfied with their professional freedom and autonomy, but they are hardly fundamentally dissatisfied. No doubt to some extent they feel that they are able to operate as advocates.

CONCLUSION

Although institution building in journalism has been slow and difficult, there have been advances in the professional direction. In this regard, the advocate-journalist has also been interested, if not in professional ethics and in having his performance audited, at least in maintaining his autonomy and in defending the profession against unwarranted intrusion from governmental sources. No profession operates at its most effective level; the gatekeeper outlook permitted distortions of reality. But the distortion could and would have been greater in the absence of the gatekeeper norms. The advocate outlook almost denies the existence of an objective reality and has weakened the effort to strengthen professionalism.

Basically, the underlying issue in the professionalization of journalism rests in assessing and juxtaposing the functions and consequences of the two competing models. The gatekeeper can be considered as the ideal of the enlightenment of the mass public; the advocate, as the ideal of the lawyer and almost that of the politician.

There are difficulties in the gatekeeper model, but there is an inherent clarity of purpose and goal. The professional task is to retain and develop the essential concern with the inherent search for objectivity that is linked to the scientific method. The gatekeeper is a form of public servant. However, the gatekeeper journalist is aware of the economic realities that provide the resources for his endeavors and that can serve to thwart or distort the impulse toward objective journalism. But as Gans has pointed out, there are organizational factors in the contemporary mass media that continue to reinforce the professional norm of objectivity.[18] In particular, the journalist in the main works for organizations with heterogeneous audiences. To build and to retain mass audiences, journalists soon are stimulated to produce output that will be viewed by such heterogeneous audiences as relatively objective. These audiences respond with sharp criticism to content which distorts that part of the environment with which they are directly familiar; and persistent distortion runs the risk of the loss of specific audience segments.

The comparison of the gatekeeper and the advocate models highlights the ambiguity of the advocate's role. He is not the equivalent of a lawyer because of the absence of an analogy to legal procedures, cross-examination of witnesses, the role of the judge and the appeals procedure, for example. Nor is he in effect a European type of party journalist, because he is committed to a libertarian ethic and because he opposes excessive confidentiality. These aspects of the self-imposed tasks of the advocate-journalist imply that it is essential for him to have a basis for his professional independence. This requirement perforce and even unintentionally leads him back toward the gatekeeper ideal.

The resolution of the dichotomy between the gatekeeper and the advocate perspectives rests not in a mechanical synthesis, but, rather, in a clear differentiation. The core task of the journalist—given both the ambiguity of the advocate model and centrality of the information for a democratic society—rests in the gatekeeper role. The advocate role as a distinct and a secondary role, if it is to persist with effectiveness and responsibility, will require an element of professionalization to insure its independence and to define its limits and potentialities.

NOTES

1. Systematic scholarship on the sociology and professional organization of the journalists remains limited. Under the stimulation of Harold D. Lasswell, Leo Rosten prepared a study in depth on *The Washington Correspondents* (New York: Harcourt, Brace, 1937) that remains one of the leading references. Jeremy Tunstall's *The Westminster Lobby Correspondents: A Sociological Study of National Journalism* (London: Routledge & Kegan Paul, 1970) deals with the equivalent group in British journalism. He has also published a study entitled *Journalists at Work: Specialist Correspondents, the News Organizations, News Sources and Competitors—Colleagues* (London: Constable, 1971). These works contain valuable material on the values and cultural assumptions of journalists. A sample survey of 1,225 journalists in the United States, undertaken by John Johnstone in 1971, concentrates on social demography and career patterns: John Johnstone *et al., The News People: A Sociological Portrait of American Journalists and Their Work* (Urbana: University of Illinois Press, 1976). See also William L. Rivers and Wilbur Schramm, *Responsibility in Mass Communication*, rev. ed. (New York: Harper & Row, 1969); and Jack M. McLeod and Searle E. Hawley, Jr., "Professionalization Among Newsmen," *Journalism Quarterly* 46 (Autumn 1964): 529-539.

2. Gaye Tuchman, "Objectivity as a Strategic Ritual: An Examination of Newsmen's Notions of Objectivity," *American Journal of Sociology* 77 (January 1972): 660-679.

3. Vince Blasi, "The Newsman's Privilege: An Empirical Study" *Michigan Law Review* 70 (December, 1971): 229-284.

4. Paul H. Weaver, "The New Journalism and the Old—Thoughts After Watergate" *The Public Interest,* Spring 1974, pp. 67-88.

5. Johnstone *et al., News People*.

6. Walter Lippmann, *Public Opinion* (New York: Macmillan, 1922), p. 271.

7. Lippmann, *Public Opinion*, p. 274.

8. Commission on Freedom of the Press, *A Free and Responsible Press* (Chicago: University of Chicago Press, 1947).

9. U.S. National Advisory Commission on Civil Disorders, *Report* (Washington DC: U.S. Government Printing Office, 1968), pp. 201-220.

10. Commission on Freedom of the Press, *Free Press,* p. 100.

11. John Wale, *Journalism and Government* (London: Macmillan, 1972).

12. Morris Janowitz, "Content Analysis and the Study of the Symbolic Environment," in ed. Arnold A. Rogow *Politics, Personality, and Social Science in the Twentieth Century,* (Chicago: University of Chicago Press, 1969), pp. 155-170.

13. H. Phillip Levy, *The Press Council: History, Procedure and Case* (London: Macmillan, 1967).

14. James W. Markham, "Journalism, Educators and the Press Council Idea: A Symposium," *Journalism Quarterly* 49 (Spring 1968): 22-85.

15. John E. Polich, "Newspaper Support of Press Councils," *Journalism Quarterly* 51 (Summer 1974): 199-212.

16. L. Erwin Atwood and Kenneth Starck, "Effects of Community Press Councils: Real and Imagined," *Journalism Quarterly* 49 (Summer 1972): 230-238.

17. Johnstone *et al.*, News People.

18. Herbert Gans, "The Famine in American Mass Communications Research: Comments on Hirsch, Tuchman, and Gecas," *American Journal of Sociology* 77 (January 1972): 697-705.

THE PROFESSIONAL VALUES OF AMERICAN NEWSMEN

John W. C. Johnstone, Edward J. Slawski, and William Bowman

A long-standing debate has raged within American journalism over the definition of responsible journalistic practice. Although the focus of this debate has shifted from decade to decade in reaction to changing social and political climates, the essence of the controversy can be identified in competing definitions of the functions of the news media in American society, conflicting assessments of the public's need for and right to information, and divergent images of the nature of news itself. The debate on these issues has been reflected in disputes about the proper role of the journalist in gathering news.

At the turn of the century, criticism within American journalism was focused on the excesses of an unrestrained market-oriented journalism guided by what Siebert[1] labeled a "libertarian" philosophy of the press. In response, the principal direction of American journalism during the first half of the twentieth century was toward establishing itself as a profession, and it was this era which saw the proliferation of professional schools, the articulation of codes of professional ethics, and the maturation of the ideology of "objective" reporting. By about the end of World War II, however, debate within the field had shifted, and criticism of the news media came to be focused on the shortcomings of an obsessively objective and socially complacent style of journalism. Today debate within the field would appear to pit

proponents of a professionalized, objective, restrained and technically efficient journalism against those advocating a socially responsible journalism inspired by some of the same journalistic norms which were the objects of earlier reforms.

The current adversaries are perhaps most accurately identified as proponents of a "neutral" as opposed to a "participant" press. In the former perspective, the news media function as an impartial transmission link dispensing information to the public. In this "neutral" image, news is seen to emerge naturally from the events and occurrences of the real world, and it is sufficient for the journalist to be a spectator of the ongoing social process and to transmit faithfully accurate communications about it. Responsible journalism can be achieved by means of objectivity, factual accuracy, and the verification of information. Objectivity and factual accuracy become ritualized as justifications for the truth-value of the information which the reporter transmits.[2] The newsman's relationship to information is thus one of detachment and neutrality, and his relationship to news sources is straighforward—sources simply provide the reporter with news to be reported. In this image, the primary journalistic sins are sensationalism—overstatements of the natural reality of events—and bias—a violation of the observer's neutrality vis-a-vis information.

In the image of a "participant" press, the news media are accorded a more challenging role in the surveillance of the environment and the interrelation of its parts. Although the nature of news once again resides in ongoing social process, the journalist must play a more active and, to some extent, creative part in the development of the newsworthy. In this image there is not so clear an expectation that newsworthy information will reveal itself naturally, as there is an assumption that the most significant news of the day will come to light only as the result of the journalist's imposition of his point of view. Here the

From Public Opinion Quarterly 36 (Winter 1972-1973):
522-540. Copyright 1972 © by Public Opinion Quarterly;
reprinted by permission.

newsman has personal responsibility for the information he seeks to transmit, and his relationship to news sources is more circumscribed—sources provide leads but the reporter must sift through for the real story.[3]

Whether one assumes that information is consciously withheld by news sources or is merely buried in the complexities of modern life, that which is most worth while journalistically is believed to emerge from the active efforts of the journalist. To be newsworthy, information must be reported in context, and it is the journalist's task to provide the background and interpretation necessary to give events meaning. In this sense, the primary journalistic value is relevance, and the cardinal sins, news suppression and superficiality.

To further differentiate the active-passive dimension of the two journalistic "styles," the neutral observer allows the control of content to be vested in the events observed, while the participant orientation sees the control as vested in the journalist himself.

Several works have appeared in recent years to suggest that the contemporary journalist may often be caught between these competing expectations. Cohen,[4] for example, noted that the public affairs reporter holds two sets of conceptions of the role of the press, one set involving him only as a neutral reporter, another defining his active participation in the policymaking process. Cohen also noted that this duality pervades every aspect of the public affairs reporter's experience, which he characterized as a "bifurcated professional existence." Nimmo,[5] Dunn,[6] and Chittick[7] also discuss the multiple roles of the public affairs reporter, and point to the delicate balance between objective detachment and subjective involvement. And Kimball,[8] in an almost Parsonian formulation of role dilemma, analyzed the reporter's role in terms of competing expectations of personal involvement and affective neutrality:

In a sense the reporter must learn to master two opposite psychological states. One is the capacity to immerse himself in the stories he is sent to cover so completely that he actually relives them. The other is to be able to detach himself from these same intense involvements, to stand outside the experience and place it in perspective for the reader.[9]

In Kimball's view, the key professional attribute of the journalist is the capacity to remove himself from intense experience and still be able to write about it.

PURPOSE OF THE PAPER AND SOURCE OF DATA

This paper examines conceptions of the role of the news media held by contemporary American journalists. The paper discusses the importance journalists attach to various media functions, assesses the extent to which their conceptions of the media fit with "neutral" and "participant" images of journalism and then traces the professional and social characteristics of those oriented to different conceptions of journalistic responsibility.

The data presented in this paper were collected as part of a comprehensive occupational study of full-time editorial manpower in the American news media.[10] During the fall of 1971, a national probability sample of 1,313 American journalists was interviewed by the field staff of the National Opinion Research Center. The sample, which included editorial personnel in daily and weekly newspapers, news magazines, wire services, and the news departments of radio and television stations and networks, was designed in three stages. In the first stage, a list of 1,061 qualifying news organizations located within the 72 primary sampling units of the NORC national sample was compiled from directories, and these organizations were contacted for information on the number of full-time editorial personnel they employed. From this information we estimated a manpower pool of 69,500 editorial employees in the American news media. Next, 308 news organizations, stratified by geographic location and industry sector, were sampled from the longer list with probabilities proportionate to size. These organizations were then contacted again and asked for lists of the names and job titles of their editorial personnel. In all, 282 organizations provided this information, and in the remaining 26 cases partial lists were compiled from secondary sources. These lists then constituted the sampling frame for the selection of individual respondents.

In the final stage, a probability sample designed to yield 1,340 completed interviews was drawn from this frame. The sample was stratified by job title, so that persons in more influential positions within news organizations were given a higher probability of selection than "rank-and-file" journalists. This "elite" stratum was operationally defined as all personnel holding job titles of editor, manager, news director, assistant editor, bureau chief, producer, columnist, critic, commentator, Washington correspondent—or combinations of those titles. Persons in these positions represented almost precisely 25 percent of the total manpower pool. The sample was drawn in clusters of two or three, with larger organizations yielding more than one cluster. All in all, this sampling plan produced a 6.45 percent representation of media influentials, and a 2.56 percent sampling of rank-and-file journalists. Interviews were completed with 1,313 of 1,550 eligible respondents, for an over-all completion rate of 84.7 percent. The interviews, which averaged 49.2 minutes in length, were all completed by telephone, a large number from long-distance.

CONCEPTIONS OF NEWS MEDIA FUNCTIONS

Toward the middle of the interview, journalists were asked to rate the importance of eight different aspects of news media performance selected to reflect values consistent with both "participant" and "neutral" images of press functions. The respondents rated each of the eight functions into one of four categories ranging from "extremely important" to "not really important at all." Table 1 reports the percentages who evaluated each activity "extremely important," and ranks the functions by the level of endorsement they received.

In this table, the first, second, fourth, and seventh items were selected to represent press functions consistent with images of a socially responsible participant press. Investigative, analytic, and interpretive reporting all define participant journalistic roles, in which the shape and emphasis of the news is defined in large part by the efforts of the journalist. As such, they are consistent with participant values. Moreover, to accord the news media a role in the development of national policy is by definition to endorse participant journalism, and to stress an educative function for the media is to accord the journalist professional responsibility and judgment in the selection of content.

By contrast, the third, fifth, sixth, and eighth items listed in Table 1 represent press functions more in keeping with an image of a neutralized modern-day libertarian press. Getting information to the public as quickly as possible precludes the possibility of providing background and context, and is to emphasize a journalist's technical prowess rather than his familiarity with substance. Emphasis on the importance of verified information lies perhaps at the heart of objective journalism, and to provide news of interest to the widest possible public is similarly a core value of a classical libertarian view of the functions of the press in a democracy. Finally, to emphasize the entertainment function of the news media is to locate standards of news judgment with audience rather than with the journalistic practitioner; as such, endorsement of this value suggests more a passive than an active journalistic role.

Inspection of the figures in Table 1 indicates more general support for participant than for neutral media functions. That government is always news is confirmed by the fact that more than three-quarters of American journalists strongly endorsed the media's watchdog role in investigating governmental activities. In addition, more than 60 percent felt it was extremely

TABLE 1
Percentage of American Journalists Evaluating
Eight News Media Functions as
"Extremely Important"

Media Functions	Percent (N = 1,313)*
1. Investigate claims and statements made by the government	76.3
2. Provide analysis and interpretation of complex problems	61.3
3. Get information to the public as quickly as possible	56.4
4. Discuss national policy while it is still being developed	55.9
5. Stay away from stories where factual content cannot be verified	52.8
6. Concentrate on news which is of interest to the widest possible public	39.1
7. Develop intellectual and cultural interests of the public	30.5
8. Provide entertainment and relaxation	16.7

*In this and subsequent tables, the "elite" and "rank and file" strata are combined into a single sample weighted by their probabilities of selection. All calculations are computed from the weighted cases, but the reported N's are the unweighted case bases.

important for the media to provide analysis and interpretation of complex problems. It should be noted that the interviewing for the survey was conducted just a few weeks after publication of the Pentagon Papers, and it is not unlikely that the question on investigative reporting was associated by many respondents with that series of events. If that were in fact the case, of course, it would indicate very widespread support for those actions within the profession. In any event, the fact that investigative efforts of the press were endorsed more often than the importance of sticking to verified factual dispatches suggests more over-all support among contemporary journalists for participant than for neutral styles of journalism. At the same time, a majority of newsmen did feel it was extremely important for the media to transmit information quickly and to communicate only verified factual content.

While these figures are informative, the main purpose of the present paper is to determine how concepts of media functions are patterned among contemporary American journalists, and to trace the principal social and professional characteristics of those adhering to different images of journalistic responsibility. With these goals in mind, responses to the eight media activities listed in Table 1 were first subjected to a factor analysis.[11] Although the first two factors identified in this analysis explained only 42 percent of the common variance, the loadings on these factors were consistent with expectations. Items numbered 1, 2, and 4 in Table 1 all revealed positive relationships with the first factor, with the highest loading (.375) found for the fourth item, discussion by the media of national policies in process of formulation. Together, then, attitudes favorable to investigative reporting, to the analysis and interpretation of complex problems, and to the media taking an active role in the development of national policy form the nucleus of what can be interpreted as an orientation toward participant journalism. Responses to these three questions showed no relationship to the second factor.

Items numbered 3, 5, 6, and 8, by comparison, all showed positive loadings on the second factor and zero or slightly negative loadings on the first. The strongest loading on the second factor (.417) was revealed by item 6, the importance of concentrating on news of interest to the widest possible public. On this basis, the meaning of the second factor can be interpreted as a contemporary version of a libertarian philosophy of the news media.

Finally, item 7, the development by the media of intellectual and cultural interests of the public, turned out to be related positively to both factors, and, contrary to expectations, was found to be related somewhat more closely to the libertarian than to the participant factor (.185 compared with .132).

Endorsement of this function of the news media, therefore, would not appear to have clear-cut meaning in terms of the principal dimensions revealed by the other responses. Because of this, responses to this question were not used further in the analysis.

When the analysis was extended to include other opinion questions, two additional questions were located on which responses were clearly differentiated along the participant and neutral dimensions. The first of these measured opinions regarding crusading and social reform functions of the press, and the second, opinions on the usefulness of underground media.[12] Favorable opinions regarding crusaders and social reformers in the news media showed average (Pearson) correlations of .20 and −.08, respectively, with the core items of the participant and neutral dimensions; the comparable figures for favorable assessments of the usefulness of underground media were .14 and −.12.

On the basis of these findings and the logical connection between advocacy journalism and participant values, responses endorsing crusading and underground media activities were added to those from the three core items identified in the first factor to form a Likert-type scale of dispositions favorable to participant news media functions. The five component items were weighted equally in this scale, and the resulting scores ranged between 5 and 20 points, with a mean of 15.30 and a standard deviation of 2.82.[13] In similar fashion, the four core items of the second factor were combined to produce a scale measuring favorable orientations to neutral journalistic functions.[14] Values on this scale ranged from 4 to 16, with a mean of 11.94 and a standard deviation of 2.46.

The correlation between the two resulting scales was −.187, indicating that a journalist endorsing one set of media functions was likely to eschew values on the other dimension. Neutral and participant conceptions of the news media would appear to represent alternate and on the whole incompatible definitions of journalistic responsibility.

DETERMINANTS OF JOURNALISTIC VALUES

The remainder of this paper explores the social and professional characteristics of journalists who hold neutral and participant images of journalistic responsibility. The underlying premise of this section is that these dimensions constitute alternate definitions of professional responsibility within the field, and the goal of the analysis is to identify determinants of these competing professional orientations. The analysis is also exploratory, and will assess the relationship of a wide range of personal and organizational characteristics to professional values. Finally, from a multivariate analysis, we will attempt to isolate a limited number of factors which influence the development and reinforcement of competing definitions of professional role within contemporary journalism.

The frame of reference guiding this analysis emerges from the sociology of occupations and professions, and more specifically from the study of occupational socialization. Models of professional socialization such as developed by Sherlock and Morris[15] or Moore[16] explain the evolution of the professional in terms of a chain of prior influences which include early background factors leading to recruitment into a field, the nature of professional training received, and the type of post-training career influences emanating from the work setting. As Bucher and Strauss[17] have noted, however, most sociological studies of professions too readily assume a unity of interest and perspective among the incumbents of professional groups, and as a result have tended to overlook influences which result in heterogeneity of professional outlook.

TABLE 2
Correlates of "Neutral" and "Participant" Orientations to Journalism
(Pearson Correlation)*

Variables	Value Scales	
	Neutral	Participant
1. Type of education and training received		
(a) Years of formal schooling	−.234	.249
(b) "Quality" of college attended	−.154	.116
(c) Majored in journalism in college or in graduate school	.082	.010
2. Age and experience in the field		
(d) Age	.154	−.132
(e) Number of years in the news media	.108	−.089
3. Community and organizational setting		
(f) Size of city	−.201	.170
(g) Size of news organization	−.084	.106
(h) Prestige of news organization	−.148	.137
(i) Print sector of media	.040	.095
4. Current level of responsibility		
(j) Level of organizational responsibility	.011	−.092
(k) Income	−.081	.083
5. Professional and community integration		
(l) Number of professional organizations belonged to	.003	−.034
(m) Number of community organizations belonged to	.109	−.128
(n) Percentage of people seen socially connected with journalism or the communications field	−.097	.161

*In this table a correlation coefficient greater than .060 (or −.060) can be interpreted as significantly different from zero with approximately 95 percent confidence.

In the present paper, we will not be concerned with factors leading to decisions to enter journalism, but rather with those aspects of a journalist's training and career which influence his conception of professional responsibility. Specifically, the analysis relates concepts of professionalism to five types of factors: (1) amount and type of education received, (2) age and longevity in the field, (3) the community and organizational setting worked in, (4) current job responsibilities, and (5) patterns of professional and social integration.

Table 2 presents zero-order correlation coefficients between scores on the neutral and participant scales and fourteen independent variables. Preliminary inspection of these figures indicates that the relationships are on the whole quite low, though it should be noted that because of the large sample many satisfy usual criteria for inferring statistical significance. The table also reveals, however, that a number of factors differentiate quite clearly between the two sets of values since the coefficients, although small, are in opposite directions.

Starting with education and training, conceptions of participant press responsibilities clearly are associated with higher levels of formal schooling, while neutral values are associated with lower.

Amount of education turns out to be the strongest single predictor of both value scales. At this point it should be noted that considerable variation exists in the formal schooling of contemporary American journalists: although 86 percent have attended college, only 58 percent are college graduates, only 18 percent have attended graduate school, and only 8 percent hold graduate degrees. The results in Table 2 would suggest that the great diversity in formal education currently found in the field may be the primary source of professional clevage within journalism today.

Information was also collected on the colleges and universities journalists had attended, and on their major fields of study in college or graduate school. Colleges and universities were classified in terms of national ratings,[18] and Table 2 reveals that journalistic values are also related to the "quality" of college attended—participant values with more selective schools, and neutral values with less selective. The most highly trained and perhaps best educated journalistic practitioners thus tend to embrace participant ideologies of the press and to eschew neutral-libertarian conceptions. Interestingly, studying journalism in college[19] has little influence on the type of professional values held. What relationships do exist indicate that majoring in journalism is more related to holding neutral than participant images of journalistic responsibility, but the results show only that those with professional training are likely to score higher on neutral values; they do not score lower on participant functions.

Turning now to the second group of factors, Table 2 shows that both a journalist's age and the number of years he has worked in the news media differentiate the values he holds, with older and more experienced journalists scoring higher on neutral press functions and lower on participant. These two factors are of course strongly related to one another ($r = .829$), but chronological age seems a somewhat better predictor of value outcomes than does media experience. Age is also related to the amount of formal education obtained ($r = .095$), since along with other occupational groups in American society the average educational attainment of journalists has been increasing in recent decades. Thus, it is not clear whether to interpret the age correlations as indicating a cohort or an aging phenomenon. If participant images of media functions are in fact a product of higher education, then the relationship with age reflects changing educational levels in the field over time, and could be interpreted as cohort differentiation. If, on the other hand, journalists' values become more conservative or neutral as they grow older, then the relationship would properly be interpreted as an aging effect. This dilemma cannot be resolved from zero-order statistics, however, and will be considered again later in this paper.

Moving to the third set of predictors, Table 2 reveals that both the type of community a journalist works in and the type of organization he works for have a bearing on how he defines journalistic responsibilities. Of the four factors listed, city size differentiates most clearly between the value sets: participant values are more likely to be held by journalists working in large cities, and neutral values by those in smaller cities and towns. In addition, however, the size of a news organization, measured by the number of editorial personnel it employs, and the prestige of a news organization[20] also correlate positively with participant values and negatively with neutral. All three of these factors are highly interrelated: larger news organizations are located in larger cities ($r = .751$), and the most prestigious are not only large themselves ($r = .758$) but have head offices in larger cities ($r = .588$).

Because the two sets of values were best discriminated by city size, however, we are inclined to interpret participant values as primarily an urban phenomenon and only secondarily a product of organizational characteristics. Nonetheless, the relationships do suggest that larger and more powerful news organizations provide the kind of setting in which it is possible to practice the more aggressive "participant" style of journalism. Here again, however, the relationships are complicated by the fact that a journalist's education is a good predictor of the type of community and organization he works in: those in larger cities and in larger and more prominent organizations have more formal education than those working in other settings. Efforts to sort out these relationships will be postponed until later.

The figures on line (i) of Table 2 indicate that journalistic values are not clearly differentiated by the sector of the media worked in. Being in the print sector[21] does correlate modestly with the endorsement of participant values, but sector seems unrelated to holding neutral images of media functions.

Two indicators of job status—level of organizational responsibility[22] and income—were also introduced into the analysis as potential correlates of journalistic values. The results show that income level has a small but consistent effect in discriminating neutral and participant values, while organizational level has a slightly negative relationship with holding participant values, and no relationship at all with holding neutral. The most interesting feature of these figures is that participant values are related positively with income and negatively with organizational responsibility, a somewhat surprising outcome given that the two measures of status were, as expected, positively correlated ($r = .262$). The explanation lies in the fact that journalists who work in smaller news organizations have both lower salaries and higher levels of managerial responsibility: the correlation between income and size of organization was .190, but between organization size and level of responsibility it was $-.157$. Because

participant values are also more prevalent in larger organizations, the zero-order effects of the two status measures turn out to be reversed. More generally, of course, the results that journalistic values are better predicted by the type of organization a person works for than by his job level.

Finally, journalistic values were examined in relation to three measures of social and professional integration—the number of professional organizations and associations belonged to, the number of community organizations belonged to, and the extent to which a journalist's informal social relations were confined to members of his professional community.[23]

The often-noted tendency of journalists to associate among themselves is seen in the figures of Table 2 to ring true for those adhering to participant images of professional responsibility, but to be an inadequate description of those endorsing neutral press functions. Although membership in professional organizations and associations fails to discriminate at all between the value scales, both a journalist's integration into the community and the extent to which his informal social contacts are concentrated among professional colleagues are related to the values he holds—neutral values being predicted by the former, and participant by the latter. Participant images of journalistic responsibility would appear to be reinforced by informal relationships within the professional community, while netural values are sustained by one's attachments within the wider environment.

Paradoxically, it is participant rather than neutral journalism which calls for the independence of the journalist from community ties, since it is the ability to investigate, analyze, or crusade which would be compromised by formal allegiances to news sources. To support investigative reporting and journalistic crusading, of course, is to endorse a style of journalism in which conflict relations are to be expected between the journalist and vested interests in the external environment. The participant journalist thus values detachment from external social ties in order to preserve editorial freedom, and for him associations with professional peers provide the sequestration necessary to reinforce a commitment to conflict-based news values.

Those oriented to neutral-libertarian journalism, on the other hand, value editorial neutrality to news content in order to maintain relationships with news sources. The implications suggested by this are similar to what Janowitz[24] and Breed[25] concluded from their studies of the community press: neutral journalism is oriented to news which binds the social order together rather than to that which generates conflict and dissent. Just as the participant journalist holds conflict-based news values, then, the neutral journalist is consensus-oriented. The latent function of news which is of interest to the widest possible public or which provides entertainment and relaxation is to solidify rather than to exacerbate the status quo. Formal social ties within the external community, then, do not represent a situation of cross-pressures for the netural journalist: on the contrary, they strengthen rather than undercut his sense of journalistic responsibility.

To conclude this section, it should be noted that the correlation between belonging to community organizations and the extent of one's informal social relations with professional peers was $-.218$, thus confirming that the two patterns of social relations are on the whole incompatible. Belonging to community organizations was positively associated with belonging to professional organizations, however, ($r = .186$), and there was virtually no relationship at all between one's formal and informal professional connections ($r = .029$). Once again, the connection between patterns of social integration and journalistic values is complicated by other factors—in this case, by age, organizational responsibility, and city size. At this point we will examine the interconnections among these factors.

MULTIVARIATE ANALYSIS

On the basis of the relationships and interpretations discussed in the previous section, six of the fourteen factors listed in Table 2 were selected to form a tentative model of the social factors influencing the emergence and development of competing images of journalistic responsibility. The factors selected were age, years of schooling, city size, level of organizational responsibility, the extent of one's informal relations with professional peers, and membership in community organizations. In this interpretive scheme … size of city and level of organizational responsibility are viewed as dependent on age and education; the two types of social integration as dependent on all four of the factors above; and journalistic value orientations as dependent on all six. This model does not posit causal connections within the sets of variables except in the case of age and education, where the date of one's birth would indeed affect the amount of schooling obtained.

Multiple regression analyses were then carried out to predict scores on the neutral and participant scales using all six factors as predictors, and on the two measures of social integration using the first four factors as predictors. The results of these analyses are summarized in Table 3.[26] Here, the zero-order correlation among all eight factors are reported in the lower lefthand portion of the table, and the standardized regression coefficients from the four regression analyses in the upper righthand portion. The legend at the bottom of the table defines the variables and reports their means and standard deviations. In reviewing the results we will first discuss the predictors of the two measures of social integration (variables X_5 and X_6 in Table 3) and then the predictors of the two value scales (X_7 and X_8). The multiple correlation coefficients for these four variables are as follows: for X_5, $R = .283$; for X_6, $R = .340$; for X_7, $R = .319$; and for X_8, $R = .323$.

The values of the standardized regression coefficients for variable X_5 indicate that informal social relationships with professional colleagues are predicted better by city size and age than by education and organizational responsibility.[27] It is younger journalists in the big cities who are most likely to concentrate

TABLE 3
Regression Coefficients and Correlation Matrix

	X_1	X_2	X_3	X_4	X_5	X_6	X_7	X_8
				Standardized regression coefficients				
X_1		–	–	–	–.149	.201	–.070	.133
X_2	–.095		–	–	.068	.038	.210	–.195
X_3	–.047	.199		–	.169	–.136	.096	–.150
X_4	.297	–.090	–.095		–.075	.178	–.015	–.078
X_5	–.186	.122	.197	–.142		–	.087	–.017
X_6	.256	–.024	–.155	.247	–.218		–.067	.063
X_7	–.132	.249	.170	–.092	.161	–.128		–
X_8	.154	–.234	–.201	.011	–.097	.109	–.187	
				Zero-order correlation coefficients				

Legend:

X_1 = Age (mean = 38.37; standard deviation = 12.53)

X_2 = Years of schooling (mean = 3.70; standard deviation = 1.12, where 1 = some high school or less; 2 = completed high school; 3 = 1-3 years of college; 4 = graduated from college; 5 = some graduate work, no degree; and 6 = graduate degree)

X_3 = City size (mean = 1,139,991; standard deviation = 2,347,078).

X_4 = Level of organizational responsibility (mean = 2.82; standard deviation = 1.87, where scores represent categories listed in footnote 22)

X_5 = Percentage of persons respondent sees socially who are connected with journalism or the communications field (mean = 29.83; standard deviation = 27.24)

X_6 = Number of community organizations belonged to (mean = 1.58); standard deviation = 2.03)

X_7 = Orientation to participant journalism (mean = 15.30; standard deviation = 2.82)

X_8 = Orientation to neutral journalism (mean = 11.94; standard deviation = 2.46)

their social relationships within the professional community. Frequent informal associations among journalists, then, are best understood as functions of the demographic environment and of career stage. Large urban centers employ sufficient numbers of journalists to make possible the emergence of a professional community, and younger journalists taking jobs in big cities probably find it easier to establish social ties with their colleagues than in the community at large. The results would suggest, in other words, that the observed isolation of journalists from the wider community may not be so much a consciously imposed isolation as a natural consequence of urban life. This is not to say that such patterns of social relations do not have ideological consequences.

Integration into the wider community, as reflected in the number of community organizations a journalist belongs to, would appear from the data to be a function of three factors: first, being older; second, holding a more responsible organizational position; and third, living in a smaller city or town. The direct effects of age and of city size can be interpreted as above, and may reflect only the longer period of time a journalist has lived in a community, and the fact that in smaller places there are not many other journalists around to associate with. The effects of organizational position, however, are better interpreted by the fact that news organizations in our society are business enterprises and as such function within the wider social and economic environment. Holding an executive position in a news organization involves one in day-to-day contact with the business community as well as the professional, and formal social ties with the surrounding community are therefore as much a necessity for the news media executive as for his counterpart in any other large business firm. To rise in the structure of a news organization, then, is to broaden the base of one's external social attachments. The fact that membership in community organizations was negatively correlated with the extent of one's informal social relations with professional colleagues would suggest that the news media executive does not have time for both.

Turning to the value scales, Table 3 reveals that formal schooling has by far the strongest effect on the endorsement of participant values. The standardized regression coefficient for education was .210, while for the next strongest predictors, city size and informal colleague relationships, the values were .096 and .087, respectively. Education is a much stronger predictor than age, and thus participant values are better interpreted as a cohort phenomenon than as a function of youthful idealism. Moreover, even though education and city size are related ($r = .199$), the effects of education are direct and do not stem primarily from the effect education has on other factors. Of the total effect of education on participant values (reflected by the zero-order correlation coefficient of .249), approximately five-sixths is direct influence ($.210/.249 = 84.3$ percent). City size and informal colleague relations also have direct effects, but of a considerably lesser magnitude. On the basis of these results, we would conclude that participant views of journalistic responsibility emerge out of one's experiences in higher education, and are subsequently reinforced by working in an urban environment and by one's associations with other journalists.

Even though its influence is negative, education is also the strongest single predictor of neutral journalistic values. This influence can perhaps be reinterpreted as the positive effect of an apprenticeship-type career line, of learning journalism in the context of practical skills and techniques rather than abstract principles and theories. In any case, neutral values are clearly influenced by a lack of exposure to higher education. The relative impact of education in this case is not as pronounced as in the case of participant values, however. Working in smaller communities and being older also have sizeable direct effects on neutral values, and being integrated into the community has a smaller but nonetheless direct positive effect.

Interestingly, when the influence of the other five predictors is controlled, organizational position turns out to have a negative rather than positive effect on holding neutral values. Organizational position thus has positive *indirect* effects on neutral values (through its influence on belonging to community organizations) but its *direct* effects are negative. The positive correlation between organizational position and neutral values, in other words, can be explained entirely by the relationship of organizational position to the other predictor variables. It is possible that interactions undetected by the linear model may also be involved here, but the explication of these effects is beyond the scope of this paper.

All in all, the data suggest that neutral images of journalistic responsibility emerge as a function of on-the-job rather than academic training, of doing journalism in smaller places, and of longevity in the field. They would appear also to be reinforced by a journalist's formal ties to the local social environment.

CONCLUSION

Many occupations and professions within American society today are experiencing internal cleavages over the definition of responsible professional practice. Splits between "conservative" and "progressive," or "establishment" and "radical" wings are visible within science, education, sociology, city planning, psychiatry and social work, to cite just a few fields. These cleavages have been interpreted in many ways, but they all seem to reflect what Rein[28] identifies as a search for relevance to problems of contemporary society.

Within journalism the quest for relevance revolves around old themes—objectivity versus subjectivity, detachment versus advocacy, observer versus watchdog. The issues differentiate proponents of neutral and participant styles of journalism, which we would argue represent what Bucher and Strauss[29] identify as occupational "segments"—subgroups organized around alternative professional identities and ideologies. Although most practicing journalists do subscribe to some elements of each "ideology," the segments are clearly identifiable in terms of organized sets of beliefs regarding the functions of the news media in American society.

As in many other fields, the segments within contemporary journalism are differentiated along lines of education and training, and the great diversity of educational backgrounds among journalists is perhaps the primary source of the current segmentation. The two camps are also organized along ecological lines, however, with one functioning primarily within the urban environment, and the other in smaller communities. These contexts both stimulate and reinforce the two sets of values. Finally, although some differences among age groups are also evident in the split, the segmentation should probably not be interpreted primarily as generational conflict.

NOTES

1. Fred Siebert, "The Libertarian Theory", *Four Theories of the Press*, ed. Fred Siebert, Theodore Peterson, and Wilbur Schramm (Urbana: University of Illinois Press, 1956).

2. Gaye Tuchman, "Objectivity as Strategic Ritual: An Examination of Newspapermen's Notions of Objectivity," *American Journal of Sociology,* vol. 77, no. 4, pp. 660-679.

3. The amount of sifting which a reporter will do depends to some extent on what his assignment is. Those newsmen who cover a regular "beat" are dependent on their sources for news to a greater extent than those who are free to cover a variety of areas. "Beat" reporters, therefore, will often withhold stories that could be damaging to the reporter-source relationship. See John Rothchild, "The Stories Reporters Don't Write," *Washington Monthly,* June 1971, pp. 1-8.

4. Bernard C. Cohen, *The Press and Foreign Policy* (Princeton, N.J.: Princeton University Press, 1963).

5. Dan D. Nimmo, *Newsgathering in Washington* (New York: Atherton, 1964).

6. Delmer D. Dunn, *Public Officials and the Press* (Reading, Mass.: Addison-Wesley, 1969).

7. William O. Chittick, *State Department, Press, and Pressure Groups: A Role Analysis* (New York: Wiley-Interscience, 1970)

8. Penn Kimball, "Journalism: Art, Craft, or Profession?" in *The Professions in America,* ed. K. S. Lynn (Boston: Beacon Press, 1963), pp. 242-260.

9. Kimball, "Journalism," p. 249.

10. The study was supported by a grant from the John and Mary R. Markle Foundation of New York. Complete results from this study will be reported in John W.C. Johnstone, Edward J. Slawski, and William W. Bowman, *The News People: A Sociological Portrait of American Journalists and Their Work* (Urban, Ill.: University of Illinois Press, 1976).

11. The factor analytic solution used was a principal components solution, using a varimax rotation, with 1.00 in the diagonals of the correlation matrix.

12. The actual questions and their response distributions were as follows: (1) Do you feel there are too many, too few, or about the right number of crusaders and social reformers in the news media today? Too many, 22.3 percent; too few, 34.9 percent; about the right number, 39.1 percent; no opinion, 3.8 percent. (2) How useful a role do you think the underground media are playing on the American scene today? Very useful, 11.2 percent; somewhat useful, 47.5 percent; not useful at all, 36.3 percent; no opinion, 4.5 percent.

13. Responses to the three questions on the importance of media functions were given the following scale values: extremely important, 4; quite important, 3; somewhat important, 2; not important at all, 1. Responses to the question on crusaders and social reformers were scored as follows: too few, 4; about the right number, 2; too many, 1. For the question on the underground media, the scale scores were: very useful, 4; somewhat useful, 3; not useful at all, 1.

14. The four items were weighted equally and scored in the same fashion as the media activities questions in the first scale.

15. Basil J. Sherlock and Richard T. Morris, "The Evolution of the Professional: A Paradigm," *Sociological Inquiry* 37 (Winter 1968): 27-46.

16. Wilbert E. Moore, "Occupational Socialization," in *Handbook of Socialization Theory and Research,* ed. David A. Goslin (Chicago: Rand McNally, 1969), pp. 861-883.

17. M. Rue Bucher and Anselm Strauss, "Professions in Process," *American Journal of Sociology* 66 (1961): 325-335.

18. The ratings used were those reported in James Cass and Max Birnbaum, *Comparative Guide to American Colleges* (New York: Harper & Row, 1970). The ratings measure the general selectivity of a college in terms of criteria such as the percentage of applicants accepted by the college, and a variety of statistical indices of the scholastic potential of the student body. The authors argue that their index scores are a "crucial measure of the academic quality of a college because ... an institution of higher learning can never be much better than its student body, and is not likely to be much worse."

19. A "dummy" variable was created giving those who majored in journalism a score of 1 and those who majored in any other field a score of 0. Thirty-four percent of those who graduated from college majored in journalism either in college or in graduate school.

20. The prestige measures used here were developed from the responses members of the sample gave when asked to name the three news organizations they considered fairest and most reliable. Organizational prestige is thus operationally defined as the number of times an organization was cited for fairness and reliability by a national sample of 1,313 journalists. The three news organizations named most frequently in answer to the question were, in order, the New York *Times,* Associated Press, and Washington *Post.*

21. Those working for daily or weekly newspapers and for news magazines were given a score of 1, and those working for the broadcast media or in the wire services a score of 0. On the basis of the preliminary survey of news organizations, the distribution of full-time manpower within the American news media was estimated as follows: 55.8 percent in daily newspapers; 16.5 percent in weeklies; 2.7 percent in news magazines; 10.1 percent in television; 10.1 percent in radio; and 4.7 percent in the wire services. Seventy-five percent of American journalists thus work in the print sector, so defined.

22. Organizational responsibility was measured by classifying job titles into seven categories: (1) rank-and-file news gathering and news processing positions; (2) "star reporter" positions; (3) subject matter editors; (4) department heads; (5) second-in-command managerial positions; (6) over-all management positions; and (7) owners and publishers.

23. This was measured by answers to the following question: "Altogether, about what percentage of the people you see socially are connected in some way with journalism or the communication field?" The mean for the sample was 29.83, with a standard deviation of 27.24.

24. Morris Janowitz, *The Community Press in an Urban Setting* (New York: Free Press, 1952).

25. Warren Breed, "Mass Communication and Sociocultural Integration," *Social Forces* 37 (1858): 109-116.

26. The authors are grateful to James Wiley for helpful suggestions on the analysis and presentation of these data.

27. Following Raymond Boudon, "A New Look at Correlation Analysis," in *Methodology in Social Research,* ed. H.M. Blalock and A.B. Blalock (New York: McGraw-Hill, 1968), pp. 199-235, and others, we interpret these values as measures of the direct influence of the predictor variable on the dependent variable, holding constant all other variables in the system. The values measures the fraction of the standard deviation of the dependent variable for which the designated factor is directly responsible.

28. Martin Rein, "Social Work in Search of a Radical Profession," *Social Work* 15 (1970); 15-28.

29. Bucher and Strauss, "Professions," p. 332.

JOURNALISTIC PRIMITIVISM

Everette E. Dennis

As this decade opened, the New Journalism as a literary-journalistic movement was gaining momentum. Having survived the sharp attack of critics for more than five years, it was achieving acceptance at several levels:

—Editors and other media gatekeepers acknowledged its presence and force;

—Writers increasingly—and in a wide range of publications—offered demonstrably real examples;

—Academicians provided definition and analysis through articles, books and courses.

To say that the New Journalism now had some legitimacy is not to say that it lacked forceful opponents, some vitriolic, who were presenting a continuing stream of criticism. But, somehow, that outpouring seemed redundant, less vital than it had been when Dwight Macdonald first denounced Tom Wolfe in the mid-1960s.[1] Yet, the message was much the same. "It isn't new," "it doesn't exist," "it is hurting literature and journalism," were the main elements in the litany. Most often the critics avoided issues of style and form, focusing instead on substance and content. Wolfe's introduction of the concept "Radical Chic,"[2] for example, brought an immediate response that was laced with personal invective. Even in journals of opinion where one might expect civility (e.g., the intellectual Catholic monthly *Commonweal*), the attacks were mean. One writer even resorted to ridiculing Wolfe's Southern accent, linking it with a mild suggestion that he might be a racist.[3]

Although social critics were saying that the 1970s would be a quieter time than the previous decade had been, there was still a good deal of noise attending the New Journalism. As editors, writers and academicians caught up with the New Journalists, some celebrated the excitement and utility of various new approaches to nonfiction reportage. Others saw the New Journalism movement as a perfect opportunity for advancing the state of the art far beyond earlier expectations. They specifically rejected an attitude common among many journalists: "basically, journalism, despite the attempts to elevate it, to give it stature, is a farily elementary craft. It relies more on instinctual things than on an acquired body of knowledge."[4] Implicitly attacking this view, and belying his own explosively creative style, Tom Wolfe called for a disciplined "psychology of realism" in which he saw "some unique and rather marvelous advantages."[5] Elaborating on the importance of learning more about the basic operations involved in jogging the reader's memory, Wolfe wrote:

> If students of the brain are correct so far, human memory seems to be made up of sets of meaningful data—as opposed to what the older mechanistic theory presumed: viz that it is made up of random bits of meaningless or haphazard data that are then combined and given meaning by the mind. These memory sets often combine a complete image and emotion. The power of a single image in a story or song to evoke a complex feeling is well known.[6]

Wolfe explained further:

> One's memory is apparently made up of millions of such sets, which work together on the Identikit principle. The most gifted writers are those who manipulate the memory sets of the reader in such a rich fashion that they resonate with the reader's own real emotions. The events are merely taking place on the page, in print, but the emotions are real. Hence the unique feeling when one is "absorbed" in a certain book, "lost" in it.[7]

From Journal of Popular Culture 9 (Summer 1975): 122-135. Copyright © 1975 by Journal of Popular Culture, Bowling Green, Ohio; reprinted by permission.

This is a powerful rejection of the instinctual view of journalism that reporting is somewhat static, to be learned and relearned by succeeding generations of untrained persons. The implications of Wolfe's call for a psychology of realism, presented unassumingly in the introduction to his book, *The New Journalism,* are vast, but implicit in them is an advancement of the state of the art, a notion of progress in journalistic form and practice. With a better mechanistic, clinical knowledge of the ordering and orchestration of memory sets to stimulate particular emotions, the journalist with creative impulses might even strive for a higher, more powerful form with potential impact that is hard to comprehend. Indeed, in the instinctual mode, the new reporter is self-taught and conditioned by interaction with peers and supervisors in the newsroom. The learning process for the journalist is, therefore, case-by-case memorization, a mindless application of form to content. What Wolfe's psychology of realism proposes is working from a generalized theory, one that is operationalized in the rich use of language to build images in the mind of the reader.

Blend Wolfe's proposal with Ronald Weber's ideas about tonal richness, and the vast possibilities for a new art form—a New Journalism that moves conventional journalism beyond its wildest nocturnal fantasies—emerges with some clarity. Suggesting that the New Journalism has both artistic and reportorial strains, Weber, a professor of American studies at Notre Dame, has written:

The other basic strain at work in the New Journalism is more strictly journalistic. It's rooted not so much in the effort to turn reporting into art as to bend the stultifying conventions of traditional journalistic practice and to extend the range and power of nonfiction writing. Partly this involves a freedom of style and construction that permits the writer to abandon the tonal simplicities and ready made structures of newspaper and magazine writing—a freedom to experiment with language and to align manner and form with material.[8]

Just as these visionary views were joining the New Journalism debate, the activitiy and excitement that was so much a part of the innovative period from the mid-60s to early 70s, seemed to wind down. David Rubin, writing in *The Quill,* suggested that the New Journalism seemed "somewhat passé." Chief spokesman and practitioner Tom Wolfe would write that by 1973, he "felt so written-out and talked-out on the subject of New Journalism, I vowed to observe a prolonged media fast."[9] In spite of the dazzling successes of such showcases of New Journalism writing as *Rolling Stone* and *New Times,* the New Journalism had seemingly shifted into neutral. In part it might be suggested that a sagging national economy had taken its toll on the expanded newspaper story (with newsprint cutbacks) and on the experimental spirit of the more abundant '60s. However, there is little doubt that the fervor that marked the New Journalism debate, that had given it center stage billing, was outdistanced by a resurgence of interest in investigative or adversarial reporting. But unlike the New Journalism debate which brought with it a concept of journalistic progress, the excitement over investigative reporting was a triumph for instinctual journalism, a celebration of journalistic primitivism. This journalistic primitivism has intervened in the New Journalism debate and has retarded the journalistic progress that seemed so evident at the beginning of this decade.

JOURNALISTS AS ADVERSARIES

Where the New Journalism was more concerned with style and form (although it delivered highly contemporaneous content), investigative reporting focused almost exclusively on content and the impact of that content on governmental operations. That the press should be a watchdog of government, an adversary, as it were, has long been a cornerstone of journalistic philosophy. In fact, the notion is so well established that it is quickly socialized into a reporter and becomes a deeply-held craft attitude. Even though the press had engaged in notable skirmishes with government throughout its history, the adversarial concept was more platitude than practice during much of the Cold War period and beyond.[10] During the 1960s with unrest over Vietnam and rather blatant credibility problems in the national government, journalistic consensus like social and political consensus crumbled. Reporters were less likely to overlook governmental transgressions for the sake of national unity and more likely to report them.

For some reporters this was nothing new. Sleuthing investigators like Clark Mollenhoff and Jack Anderson were seasoned professionals. Both had brought continuous embarrassment to government officials and bureaucrats by exposing conflicts of interest and occasional corruption. Anderson, who was trained by and conditioned to the journalistic moralizing of the late Drew Pearson, was a part of a continuing tradition of Washington exposé that found new life in the massive growth of government during the New Deal. It had earlier roots, of course, paralleling political reform movements, accelerating during the lurid and shocking "Yellow Journalism" of the 1880s and 1890s. It may have reached its highest form in the meticulous work of the Muckrakers at the turn of the century when painstaking investigation was combined with solid literary style.

The present preoccupation with investigative journalism which focuses on the adventures of Bob Woodward and Carl Bernstein chronicled in their bestselling book, *All the President's Men* (and later

brought to the silver screen by Robert Redford), drew strength from the combative relationship between press and government during the early years of the Nixon Administration. Major skirmishes in that accelerating hostility were the Agnew attacks on the press which began in 1969; Jack Anderson's revelation of the Bangladesh Papers which embarrassed Henry Kissinger and transformed Anderson from journalistic pariah to Pulitzer Prize winner; publication by the New York *Times* and Washington *Post* of the Pentagon Papers and the resultant litigation; and the heavy use of subpoena power by the Department of Justice. Against this backdrop came the mounting Watergate story, a two and a half-year saga of corruption in high places. The efforts of Woodward and Bernstein and others who investigated the Watergate affair differed in at least one important respect from earlier exposés. It was not a single exposé, but a series of exposés, some fueled by journalistic enterprise, some stimulated by the courts and other government agencies. This continuity of coverage was not always a positive factor, though. Sometimes it was prolonged and suspenseful coverage on non-events such as the physical delivery of evidence to Judge Sirica. As John L. Hulteng has written:

> This is crescendo journalism; it reflects a desire to keep the story alive, to build mounting suspense, to add on pressure. The news magazines and the TV networks have used this countdown technique—a kind of ever more portentous drum-roll of ominous developments—at several stages of the Watergate investigations, and in reporting of periodic opinion polling results.[11]

But beyond its prolonged nature there was nothing to distinguish the Watergate coverage from earlier exposés of government scandal and corruption. Journalists and journalistic organizations are fond of celebrating the heroic exploits of their colleagues and Woodward and Bernstein became instant journalistic heroes. As they were honored for what was clearly careful and courageous reporting, there was a tendency to overstate their innovations and impact and to embellish its importance. Warning against this tendency, critic Edward Jay Epstein wrote:

A sustaining myth of journalism holds that every great government scandal is revealed through the work of enterprising reporters who by one means or another pierce the official veil of secrecy. The role that government institutions themselves play in exposing offical misconduct and corruption therefore tends to be neglected if not wholly ignored, in the press.[12]

On closer inspection, Woodward and Bernstein became ultimate journalistic celebrities, not by fashioning innovations that move reporting ahead, but by employing tried and true methods of investigation; not by producing lively and insightful copy that gave new dimensions of understanding to government corruption, but by turning out dull, bland, often mediocre prose. By any standard, other than journalistic, the Woodward-Bernstein performance was primitive. It was the product of two conventionally trained and conditioned neophyte reporters; persons with little understanding of or appreciation for the intricacies of earlier journalistic practice. Yet, these men produced the only kind of reportage that American journalism honors—the simple exposé, the revelations of corruption. Only the content of communication is honored, provided, of course, that it resulted from competent investigation. There is, as James Fallows of the *Washington Monthly* has written:

…absolutely nothing wrong with reporting scandals of public importance. The danger is that as the journalistic pack sets out on the trail of the felon and the lecher, it will neglect more important developments which lack the crucial spice of scandal.[13]

Sadly, the kind of journalistic enterprise that is honored in the Watergate revelations is of a primitive nature and does little to advance the state of the art. It might be forcefully argued that what should be rewarded are reportorial methods that not only uncover a contemporary abuse, but improve upon the media's ability to monitor this kind of activity in the future. Has anything been learned over many years of investigative reporting that can improve the quality of the journalistic enterprise? Unfortunately, from this point of view, there has been no linkage between present practice and that of the recent and more distant past. While fields like music, architecture, and medicine honor the new methods as the process that provides a pathway toward advancement, journalism rewards dogged application of the old methods. Imagine, for example, an architectural firm turning a major commission over to two untrained junior employees unschooled in the history of architecture and design. Yet, in a sense, this is what the Washington *Post* did. In hindsight the *Post's* judgment was vindicated and the content of the dynamic duo's slow-paced writing became the rage of the journalistic community.

With journalistic recognition geared to the revelations of investigative journalism and apparently ignorant of the kinds of methodological advancement in the art that have been suggested by thoughtful commentators, it is no wonder that reportage appears static. Nothing encourages the reporter to study earlier efforts to move reporting toward new horizons. Indeed, it is left to the historian to point out that Ida Tarbell's brilliant history of the Standard Oil Company at the turn of the century was a far, far better thing both in terms of prose quality and investigative thoroughness than the contemporary investigative reporting that is winning prizes.

A classic case of journalistic primitivism is that of Geraldo Rivera, the WABC reporter, who became something of a journalistic celebrity for his explosive coverage of the Willowbrook institution for the mentally retarded on Staten Island. Rivera, who is proud of his lack of training in or previous experience with reporting, specializes in a television version of the old institutional exposé. Whether his concern is junkies in Harlem, single-occupancy hotels or nursing homes, his technique is the same. He brings to his subject a sense of moralistic outrage, investigates, sees abuses, and swoops down on the scene with camera and microphone.

Rivera may have more show business appeal than some of his predecessors, but his method is really no different. Indeed, the Willowbrook institution has been the subject of exposés for more than twenty-five years. Some were more sophisticated, some less, than Rivera's. For example Nellie Bly's "Horrors of the Madhouse," published in the 1880s, was not greatly improved upon by Rivera. The exposé of this kind, a journalism of indignation, always makes for readable copy and exciting broadcast news, but has little impact in bringing about social change. This does not stop journalistic awards from flowing in to honor such efforts, however.

Even though Rivera's work differs substantially from Woodward and Bernstein's, especially in terms of the overt presence of a point-of-view, the process is not substantially different.[14]

Journalistic primitives practice their primitivism both in their prose style and in their investigative methods. There is little that is memorable about the graceless writing of a Jack Anderson or a Seymour Hersh and this seems to be true of many other primitive investigatory journalists. The primitives lack of imagination in written expression is matched only by their conservative adherence to a case-by-case method of gathering information. In an age of computers it is truly

amazing that journalists rigidly cling to the same methods of news-gathering that James Gordon Bennett used in the 1830s. Like Grandma Moses, the journalistic primitives have charm, but it is exasperating to anyone interested in a more readable, understandable and illuminating journalism, that their triumph should seem so complete.

REPORTORIAL STYLES

There is a tendency for Rivera and others to dismiss earlier reporting efforts as mindless products of "objectivity," unconcerned with the pursuit of truth. Part of the present debate centers on a conflict in journalism. Epstein, in a widely-quoted article in *Commentary* wrote:

In the current rhetoric of journalism, "stenographic reporting," where the reporter simply but accurately repeats what he has been told, is a pejorative term used to describe inadequate journalism; "investigative reporting," on the other hand, where the reporter supposedly ferrets out a hidden truth, is an honorific enterprise to which all journalists are supposed to aspire. In the post-Watergate era, moreover, even critics of the press attribute to it powers of discovery that go well beyond reporting news developments.[15]

Harvard management expert Chris Argyris in his controversial study of a metropolitan newspaper, *Behind the Front Page,* suggests that there are three types of reporters: traditional reporters, reporter-researchers, and reporter-activists. The traditional reporter's "first commandment is to be objective and get the facts.... The reporters who adhere to this concept strive to present the news as objectively as possible."[16] By contrast, the reporter-researcher is one who "no longer found inverted pyramid news coverage challenging even under time pressures."[17] Argyris continues:

They sought to do more interpretive news. They wanted to dig beneath the surface of events to find the critical but half-hidden forces that were shaping events. (For example, one reporter did a thorough analysis of societal trends and pressures for urbanization and pressures creating dry rot in our cities.)[18]

Perhaps then the ferment stirred by the New Journalism since the mid-1960s would result in a true advancement of reportorial practice and purpose. The reporter-researchers impose "their analytical abilities and their conceptual models upon reality to give it deeper meaning."[19] Add to this mix the reporter-activist who wishes "to use journalism to change or shake up the world."[20] The reporter-activists, writes Argyris, "seem more like angry young men. They are more critical than constructive."[21] Argyris makes no secret about the fact that he includes Rivera in the reporter-activist category.

The basic differences that Argyris observed among reporters was the way they conceptualized their role and the amount of time and personal resourcefulness they brought to their work. While the reporter-activist might demonstrate his empathy for people in a more overt way, he really doesn't differ fundamentally from the traditional reporter or the reporter-researcher in the way he gathers news and writes it. True, there are differences of tone and point-of-view, but, the old journalistic form with its short paragraphs and information organized in a descending order of importance remains intact.

When the problems inherent in this mode of presentation are linked with traditionally-impressionistic methods of gathering information, the limitations of journalistic primitivism become apparent.

In an essay in the *Public Interest* magazine, writer and critic Paul Weaver observes that "traditionally, American journalism has been very close to, dependent upon, and cooperative with official sources."[22] But in recent years, he says, "a small but significant and still-growing segment of the journalistic community has begun to revise this relationship by assuming a posture of greater independence and less cooperativeness."[23] Weaver sees this trend making the press "freer, but also less informative and possibly more partisan."[24]

To Weaver and others the movement toward an adversary journalism is romantic and seen by its adherents as a heresy. He writes:

The current "heretical" movement in American journalism is defined by the fact that it takes the mythical part of the "orthodox" tradition—the fiction of the atonomous, investigative, adversary press—for the whole of that tradition. It presents itself as an effort to make our press live up to what it always said it was: a journalism that is autonomous instead of interdependent, original instead of derivitive, and in an adversary instead of cooperative relationship with government and officialdom.[25]

But, says Weaver, like other heresies, this one advocates recovering "something that never was and that was never intended to be."[26]

Attempting to demolish what he regards as an adversary myth in contemporary journalism, sociologist Irving Kristol says, "adversary journalism today is rooted, not in political principle, but in a kind of joyful schizophrenia."[27] While boasting they they are a rigorous watchdog of government, "journalists today are overwhelmingly in favor of ever greater concentration of power in government—Federal, state and local—while in their daily adversary proceedings, they create an even greater distrust and suspicion of government."[28] Today's journalists are not radical republicans like Tom Paine, but are:

"Liberals" who believe in large and powerful government. They believe that the United States Government must help feed the world, defend and promote civil liberties throughout the world, mediate conflicts among the peoples of the world, redistribute income in favor of the poor and the unlucky, regulate the activities of the large corporations, "plan" cities and neighborhoods, etc.—all of which requires an energetic government with a vast, self-confident bureaucracy.[29]

While Kristol's statement may represent an articulate conservative critique of the press, it muddies the water in the debate over adversarial-investigative reporting because the focus of most of the reporters in question would be on the performance of public officials, more than with the nature of public policy. That is to say, the adversarial journalist would criticize the public official who abuses the privileges of his office without ever dealing with the general policies which that person had advocated.

Offering a more useful unraveling of the investigative-adversary concept is Mitchell V. Charnley, author of the most widely-used textbook of journalistic reporting:

I think it is a mistake to equate "watchdog" and "adversary." Good reporting can investigate government and, I suppose, when the implications or the conclusions of the reporting are adversely critical, it might be called adversary. But good reporting can also watch government and find it

golden, in which case "adversary" seems the wrong word. "Adversary" is the anti-thesis of objectivity, and I believe an objective attitude is still the ideal attitude for a reporter. Adversary reporting, as a term, seems to me to mean that the reporter says in advance, "I am out to find things that are adverse." That is to say, things that are deprecatory, derogatory, pejorative. Such adjectives should come after the fact rather than before.[30]

TOWARD
ADVANCING THE ART

What the debate over adversary journalism clearly demonstrates is that it helps to define the nature of press-government relationships, but does little to advance the state of the art in either information-gathering techniques or the quality of writing. Thus, the adversarial-investigative considerations cannot supplant the New Journalism as a vehicle for journalistic progress. Investigative reporting should be recognized for its contributions to our intelligence on public affairs, but thoughtful commentators might want to question the somewhat static nature of this journalistic approach. In an age of increasingly sophisticated methods of acquiring information in other fields, journalism would do well to consider ways in which reportage can be improved, both in its assembling of information and in linking the message content more effectively with readers in a manner that is more pertinent to them.

Wolfe & Company have proposed explorations in the psychology of realism, a yet uncharted area that might link findings of researchers in psychology, neurology, and social-psychology with literary devices.

Not unrelated to these suggestions are proposals for more "humanistic" journalism whereby utility of the information for the reader becomes the guiding principle. One champion of this approach is Alex S. Edelstein of the University of Washington who has suggested innovative ways to treat such snoremongering standard news items as zoning meetings. Says Edelstein, "If the reader can identify with another person's experience, he feels less isolated as a human being. He develops a greater understanding of others and becomes more able to cope with events."[31] The Edelstein notion runs counter to the usual journalistic value that emphasizes the uniqueness of human experience, rather than that which is common to most people. Promoted originally in a two year experiment on newspapers in the Pacific Northwest, the information-salience approach is a key element in Edelstein's research that charts methods for survey researchers to use in asking the kinds of questions that have personal meaning and importance for people being interviewed. Instead of being asked to rank public issues from a list provided by the interviewer, the interviewee is asked to suggest areas and issues that have pertinence to him.[32] This is in sharp contrast to the forced response questions of the Gallup pollsters. Through illuminating research during the Watergate period, Edelstein and his colleagues have provided the journalistic community considerable grist for the development of a newer, more representative and utilitarian journalism. However, only a small portion of Edelstein's research is specifically directed at the journalistic practitioner. But there is much in his research from which reporters and editors can draw inferences that will be useful in their work.

Perhaps better known than Edelstein's work is that of Philip Meyer and others who practice "precision journalism." Some commentators (including this author) have long seen precision journalism as one of the many forms of New Journalism that developed in the 1960s. While Wolfe and his colleagues were trying to push journalism toward the methods of fiction (in order to present a more understandable and richer journalistic product), Meyer, a Washington correspondent for the Knight Newspaper group, was arguing quietly that the methods

of the social sciences might also give new life and force to journalism. Meyer, who had training in social science methods while a Nieman fellow at Harvard, was ready in 1967 when an extraordinary challenge presented itself. In that year of urban unrest, residents of Detroit were puzzled about the causes of that city's devastating riot. As Frank Angelo of the *Detroit Free Press* put it, "there were nagging questions that we believed should be answered without waiting for outside agencies to do the job."[33] Angelo called Meyer to Detroit where he quickly became project director of a survey sponsored by the Detroit Urban League and financed by Henry Ford II and two foundations. Assisted by two University of Michigan social scientists, Meyer hired Blacks to interview a random sample of Negroes in the main riot areas of Detroit. The result was a widely-praised series, "The People Beyond 12th Street," which was notable for its readability. Blending human example with numbers, Meyer and his coworkers put human experience into context. As Meyer put it, "It used to be said that journalism is history in a hurry. I would argue that, to meet the needs of today, journalism must become social science in a hurry."[34] Continuing he wrote:

As journalists we are in the business of oversimplifications. Without oversimplifying, we'd seldom communicate anything. But we have to be wary of going too far and we need to be choosy about the oversimplified stereotypes we create.[35]

Meyer had achieved something that journalists had been talking about for years—*representativeness.* Social science methods—survey research, content analysis, field experiments—he reasoned, could become tools for the journalist. Meyer's efforts differed sharply from such precedents as the *Fortune* magazine surveys of the 1930s and the continued pulse-taking of George Gallup. To him, survey research was a means for finding convincing answers to questions about community attitudes. Thus the journalist could draw inferences from a solid data base, rather than random impressions.

A year after his pioneering work, Meyer returned to Detroit for a followup study, wherein the blend of data with personal interviews and humanistic examples was advanced even more. Trying the method in a different setting, Meyer initiated a similar study in the black community of Miami, Florida for the Knight-owned Miami *Herald.* In 1969, he studied the aftermath of campus unrest in Berkeley, California by surveying a sample of the original 1964 Berkeley rebels. While the early precision journalism work harnessed the tools of survey research, one of the most far-reaching studies done in 1973 was a content analysis search of public records in Philadelphia. The power of precision journalism was fully demonstrated in this, the first comprehensive computer study of a criminal justice system ever made by a newspaper. The seven-month study of court records resulted in a series on the breakdown of criminal justice…"the jailing of the innocent, freeing of the guilty."[36] This was done through "a sophisticated computer analysis of the way violent crimes are handled in the courts and was based on the cases of 1,034 persons indicted during 1971 for murder, rape, aggravated robbery as well as aggravated assault and battery."[37] As a reprint of the series began:

Soft judges…a tough district attorney…crowded courtrooms…light sentence. These are catch phrases used to describe what is happening in many big city criminal justice systems. But how soft are the judges? Is the district attorney really tough? Are courtrooms crowded by necessity? How light are the sentences? For seven months a Philadelphia Inquirer *investigative reporting team sought the answers to these questions and scores of others during an intensive probe into the administration of justice in this—the nation's fourth-largest city.…The findings ranging from the existence of broad patterns of discrimination on the part of judges to extreme sentencing disparity and the jailing of innocent persons—were published in a seven-part, 25,000 word series of articles during the week of Feb. 18, 1974.*[38]

Without social science tools and the computer, this extraordinary story could not have been told.

The literature about precision journalism

is quite limited. The main source is Meyer's 1973 book, *Precision Journalism,* and chapters in two other books.[39] Schools of journalism were receptive to Meyer and provided modest leadership in advancing this approach, although courses in the subject are even scarcer than those in New Journalism.[40]

Although some editors openly scoff at precision journalism, economic cutbacks on many newspapers have been more responsible for delaying the extensive application of precision journalism methods. Yet the movement got new life in 1974 when Northwestern University sponsored a precision journalism workshop. Meyer and others were there to help organize a precision journalism association, "an organization for the advancement of scientific reporting methods." The 1974 conference was attended by two dozen newsmen from large papers and small, many of whom have carried the precision journalism method back to their respective newspapers. In spite of these advances, precision journalism is "at this point more a goal than a reality."[41] As this writer and a colleague put it in 1974, "Notable experiments have been conducted and a more imaginative use of survey research data is apparent. Yet it is only a beginning for a cooperative liaison between the coolly detached methods of science and the inventively conceived prose of the writer. Together the two may move us closer to the truth."[42] Precision journalism is not without its detractors. Editors argue that it is expensive and that it is difficult to train journalists to make effective use of social science methods. Social scientists worry about journalists bastardizing their tools and actually misleading readers rather than providing greater depth of understanding. It might be argued that at best the tools of social science are crude measures, still not fully developed, but they do have advantages over traditional reporting that relies more on instinct and surface impressions than on ascertaining a representative picture of a community or issue.

There are, of course, others besides the proponents of humanistic and precision journalism who have thoughts about advancing the state of reporting and reportial practice. Some scholars suggest, for example, that reporters should pay more heed to the findings of social scientists and others who have studied interviewing methods, indicating that the journalistic interview is especially crude and needs improvement. Still others suggest that reporters and their overseers should sharpen their use of litigation as a reportorial tool. Occasionally legal action by the press is initiated to gain access to public meetings and records. Indeed, a number of suits by journalists have been filed under the Federal Freedom of Information Act for the purpose of obtaining information from government departments and agencies. Bruce Brugmann of the muckraking San Francisco *Bay Guardian* has even developed guidelines for legal action:

First, I insist that a suit flow naturally from news and editorials. Secondly, we do it as a last resort after we are certain that there is nobody else around to do it. Thirdly, it is done openly, and, finally, it is not allowed to interfere with our editorial operation.[43]

Thus, there are a number of perspectives offered by communications scholars and journalists that would improve upon current reportorial practices. From Wolfe's psychology of realism to Meyer's precision journalism and other urgings, the purpose is clear: to advance and accelerate the journalistic enterprise.

SUMMARY AND CONCLUSION

In spite of advances in reportorial methods and visionary proposals for change, American journalism continues to pay homage to its most primitive form without regard to an advancement in the state of the art of reporting. The result is a celebration of journalistic primitivism in which often untrained or self-taught journalists pursuing corruption in government with the most unimaginative and traditional reportorial methods are rewarded and encouraged. Without undermining the importance of the Woodwards and Bernsteins, it is suggested here that recognition for meritorious work in journalism ought to go to those who improve upon existing practice by introducing new reportorial methods. To this end, schools of journalism and professional journalistic organizations and societies ought to find ways to reward, sanction and encourage such worthy enterprise.

NOTES

1. See especially Dwight Macdonald, "Parajournalism or Tom Wolfe and His Magic Writing Machine," *New York Review of Books*, August 1965, p. 3.
2. Tom Wolfe, *Radical Chic and Mau-Mauing the Flak-Catchers* (New York: Farrar, Straus & Giroux, 1970).
3. See Linda Kuehl, "Dazzle-Dust: A Wolfe in Chic Clothing," *Commonweal*, 7 May 1971, p. 212.

4. Chris Argyris, *Behind the Front Page: Organizational Self-Renewal in a Metropolitan Newspaper* (San Francisco: Jossey-Bass, 1974) p. 48.

5. Tom Wolfe, *The New Journalism,* with an anthology edited by Tom Wolfe and E.W. Johnson (New York: Harper & Row, 1973), p. 48.

6. Wolfe, *New Journalism,* p. 48.

7. Wolfe, *New Journalism,* p. 48.

8. Ronald Weber (ed.), *The Reporter as Artist: A Look at the New Journalism Controversy* (New York: Hastings House, 1974), p. 17.

9. Tom Wolfe personal letter to Everette E. Dennis, March 1974.

10. For an excellent discussion of this see James Aronson, *The Press and the Cold War* (Indianapolis: Bobbs-Merrill, 1974).

11. John L. Hulteng, "Nixon, Watergate and the Press: The Whole Story Needs to be Told, but Not Oversold," *The Oregonian,* 21 April 1974, p. 1. The article is based on a talk by Professor Hulteng given before the Oregon Press Women In April 1974.

12. Edward Jay Epstein, "Did The Press Uncover Watergate?" *Commentary,* July 1974, p. 21.

13. James Fallows, "Ben Bradlee and His All-Star Revue," *The Washington Monthly,* January 1973, p. 43.

14. See "Geraldo Rivera," interview in *Penthouse,* March 1973, pp. 56-60.

15. Edward Jay Epstein, "Journalism and Truth," *Commentary,* April 1974, p. 36

16. Argyris, *Behind the Front Page,* p. 47.

17. Argyris, *Behind the Front Page,* p. 50.

18. Argyris, *Behind the Front Page,* p. 50.

19. Argyris, *Behind the Front Page,* p. 51.

20. Argyris, *Behind the Front Page,* p. 52.

21. Argyris, *Behind the Front Page,* p. 52.

22. Paul H. Weaver, "The New Journalism and The Old—Thoughts After Watergate," *The Public Interest,* Spring 1974, p. 68.

23. Weaver, "The New Journalism and The Old," p. 68-69.

24. Weaver, "The New Journalism and The Old," p. 69.

25. Weaver, "The New Journalism and The Old," p. 75.

26. Weaver, "The New Journalism and The Old," p. 75.

27. Irving Kristol, "Is the Press Misusing Its Growing Power," *More,* January 1975, pp. 26, 28.

28. Kristol, "Growing Power."

29. Kristol, "Growing Power."

30. Mitchell v. Charnley, personal letter to Everette E. Dennis, 18 February 1975.

31. Alex S. Edelstein and William E. Ames, "Humanistic Newswriting," *The Quill,* June 1970, p. 28.

32. This methodology is discussed in detail in Alex S. Edelstein, *The Uses of Communication in Decision-Making* (New York: Praeger, 1974).

33. Editors of the Detroit Free Press, *Reporting the Detroit Riot* (New York: American Newspapers Publishers Association, 1968).

34. Philip Meyer, "Reporters and Research Tools," Grosman Memorial Lecture, University of Colorado, 14 April 1970.

35. Meyer, "Reporters and Research."

36. "Crime and Justice," republished series from *Philadelphia Inquirer,* 1974, p. 2.

37. "Crime and Justice," p. 2.

38. "Crime and Justice," p. 2.

39. See Neil Felgenhauer, "Precision Journalism," in *The Magic Writing Machine,* ed. Everette E. Dennis (Eugene: University of Oregon, School of Journalism, 1971); and "Precision Journalism," in *Other Voices: The New Journalism in America,* ed. Everette E. Dennis and William L. Rivers (San Francisco: Canfield Press, 1974).

40. A number of leading journalism schools have courses in the New Journalism, among them the University of Wisconsin, University of Washington, and Stanford University. The first course in the New Journalism was taught by the author at the University of Oregon in 1971 and was based on an earlier course taught at Kansas State University in 1969 and 1970.

41. Everette E. Dennis and William L. Rivers (eds.), *Other Voices: The New Journalism in America* (San Francisco: Canfield Press, 1974).

42. Dennis and Rivers, *Other Voices,* p. 198.

43. Dennis and Rivers, *Other Voices,* p. 60.

THE LIMITS OF INTUITION

Philip Meyer

Social scientists used to be more like journalists. They relied on observation and interpretation, collecting the observations from public records, from interviews, from direct participation, and then spinning out the interpretations. Like many journalists, they cheerfully accepted the American folk wisdom which Samuel Stouffer once described as the conviction that anyone with "a little common sense and a few facts can come up at once with the correct answer on any subject." The difference was that we journalists put our interpretations in readable English while the social scientists couched theirs in jargon.

In the two decades since Stouffer made that statement, social science has experienced something like a revolution. With development of the computer, data too vast and unwieldy to quantify have yielded to counting and measuring. Powerful statistical tools which once were only interesting theoretical devices have become practical. Social science now is doing what we journalists like to think we are best at: finding facts, inferring causes, pointing to ways to correct social problems, and evaluating the efforts of such correction.

One example is the 1966 report on the effects of school segregation, produced for the U.S. Office of Education under the direction of James S. Coleman. Daniel P. Moynihan, in the *Harvard Educational Review*, said of it:

The study, Equality of Educational Opportunity, was hardly an everyday affair. Commissioned under the Civil Rights Act of 1964, one of the great bills of the twentieth century, sponsored by the United States Office of Education in a period of its most vigorous leadership, and conducted by

leading social scientists at just the moment when incomparably powerful methods of analysis had been developed, the study was perhaps the second largest in the history of social science. Its findings were, if anything, even more extraordinary than its genesis.

Its findings were counterintuitive—they didn't fit the folk wisdom. Coleman had expected to find large inequalities in school facilities for black and white children and a causal connection between the expected poorer black facilities and lower black achievement. He found neither. Instead he found that family influences are much stronger than anything that happens at school, and that among school effects the most powerful is not teachers or physical facilities but the social class climate of the school. Cautious bureaucrats saw to it that the conclusions were buried in 737 pages of text and eye-numbing tables and charts, and the package was released over a Fourth of July weekend when papers were understaffed. But the message keeps trickling out—sometimes when Coleman testifies to a Congressional committee, sometimes when a federal judge cites it in an opinion hitting at *de facto* school segregation.

After the Coleman Report the U.S. Civil Rights Commission hired its own social science consultants, gathered more data, and did its own analysis. Its report, issued in February, 1967, documented the assumption that equal educational opportunity is not likely to be found in schools which are predominantly black. Then came the logical conclusion that only a drastic reorganization of school attendance patterns can bring long-run equality. To achieve such a reorganization, the Commission proposed legislation withholding federal aid from school districts where blacks are bunched together beyond an acceptable proportion. It was a drastic proposal, ahead of its time, but the idea remains very much alive. The whole job was done in fifteen months, a feat made possible by the "incomparably powerful methods of analysis" mentioned by

Reprinted from the Columbia Journalism Review, *July/August 1971, pp. 15-20. Copyright © 1971 by* Columbia Journalism Review; *reprinted by permission.*

Moynihan—primarily the computer and multiple regression analysis, a way of sorting out the relative effects of different variables on educational achievement.

The tools for reasoning have not changed. The capacity for managing data has changed, and to this extent there is a new social science. There is not yet a new journalism, although there is a growing awareness in the profession that the old journalism is no longer adequate in a world of swift and sometimes quiet change.

While the sociologists were deserting their armchairs to sharpen their methodological tools, journalists have been preoccupied with a question of stance rather than method. The basic question, argued with dreary persistence through the period since World War II, is whether objectivity is a desirable or even possible aim of the journalist. Being objective is easy, if you are simple-minded about defining it. The simple-minded definition may be stated as follows: when there is more than one possible interpretation to a given event, then all possible interpretations have equal weight. Or, for every plausible argument, there is an equally plausible counterargument.

This stance simplifies decisionmaking. You record public events as a detached, impersonal, unprejudiced observer, much like the proverbial man from Mars. A man from Mars might not understand these events. The reporter might not, either. No matter. All he needs to do is transmit the observable facts and leave the job of understanding them to the reader. This kind of thinking must underlie a traditional belief splendidly satirized in the novel *The Whole Truth*, by former New York *Times* correspondent Robert Daley: that a good reporter is good anywhere.

A good reporter by this standard is one who observes and transmits the observation unchanged and undistorted. Therefore, specialized knowledge is of no use to him.

Indeed, it might be a hindrance by focusing his attention on detail not of interest to the reader. The reporter as transmission instrument is the reader's agent and is interested only in what the reader would be interested in if he were there.

About 1960 I knew a foreign correspondent who laughed when someone asked him if he spoke the language of the country to which he was assigned. He didn't know the language, but neither did his readers, so from his point of view it made no difference. Until quite recently one of the daily newspapers ranked in the nation's top ten by the Bernays poll banned midcareer training by its reporters. An editor's explanation: a newspaper reporter should be "a professional amateur" and not clutter his head with too much knowledge about any one thing, lest he lose touch with his readers.

The validity of that position, if it ever existed, was, of course, wiped out by the postwar education boom which produced better informed, more knowledge-hungry readers; by the competition for credibility posed by television; and by the increasing pace of change and greater complexity of events which must be understood by a writer before he can make sense of them to a reader.

Indeed, it was TV which helped to bring an end to the period of simplistic objectivity. The inadequacy of that old stance was demonstrated clearly for all to see by a politician who knew how to take advantage of it, the late Senator Joseph McCarthy. Newspapers were using the old rules to cover his charges of Communists in government, telling both sides, reporting the surface happenings, leaving the reader to decide for himself where the truth was. Challenge an editor on this point and he would tell you that when a senator says something startling, the mere fact that he said it is news, whether the thing that he said is true or false. If it is false, no doubt someone will say so, and the paper will print that version, too.

The flaw in this reasoning is that truth and falsehood can grapple a very long time before truth emerges the victor. The journalist who tried the hardest to tell the truth about McCarthy was Edward R. Murrow, who did not pretend to be objective. His TV film on the McCarthy career was a masterpiece of subjective editing. Its message was persuasive because Murrow didn't have to tell the viewer what he thought of McCarthy—he merely showed him selected film clips that told their own story. This, by the way, is a classic technique of fiction. The great maxim for fiction writers, Theodore Morrison told his students at Harvard, is, "Show, don't tell." The selection of what to show is, of course, based on the message you wish to convey and is therefore nonobjective.

Today newspaper editors talk more about "fairness" than "objectivity." The former is easier to define and easier to practice and leaves room for a less passive role on the part of the reporter. Instead of being a transmitting machine for the superficial, he can conduct his investigation into an event or series of events, decide what is going on, and then figure out the best way to tell what is going on. The result is what is generally known as interpretive reporting. The concept is not new: Professor Curtis MacDougall of Northwestern, for one, wrote a book about it before World War II, and Kansas State University offered a journalism course with that title as far back as 1950. But the acceptance of the need for interpretive

reporting has expanded significantly, with more and more newspapers and even wire services devoting more manpower to conduct the investigations on which to base sound interpretation.

And there is the catch. Old-fashioned objective reporting needed no anchor; it merely bobbed along the surface of the news like a pingpong ball floating down a mountain stream. Interpretation requires a reference point. One must begin with a prejudgment, a position of some kind.

Practitioners of what is sometimes called the New Journalism find this reference point in their own heads. They are gifted writers—indeed, many are so gifted that they have written themselves out of the newspaper business—and they tell you what a scene looks like when filtered through their personal sets of belief, attitude, and experience. Personal journalism as such is not new; in this country it is at least as old as Thomas Paine. What is new is the application of fiction techniques to nonfiction writing to make the personal approach much more readable.

Another kind of anchoring point for interpretation can be found in ideology. The reporter starts with a given belief structure shared by some subgroup of society and then selects and interprets events to fit them into the given structure. He is read mainly by fellow members of the subgroup. The result tends to be rather dull reading, whether it is the work of the ideologues of the Left or Right. Perhaps the left-wing radicals of the underground press are a bit more interesting than Dan Smoot or Billy James Hargis if only because they are younger and find new things to say from time to time.

There is yet a third anchor, and it differs only in breadth from personal prejudice or subgroup prejudice. It is group prejudice, also known as the conventional wisdom, and it supplies the reference frame for most current interpretive reporting. Reporters tend to come from middle-class backgrounds. Their education and experience tend to make them more liberal in outlook than is typical of such development, but it is, nevertheless, conventional liberalism. In addition, there is an implicit, sometimes explicit, demand from editors and readers for explanations of complex events which are intuitively satisfying. New things are easier to accept, digest, and believe if they are cast in familiar frameworks. If a phenomenon is really new, it cannot, of course, be given a familiar flavor without distorting it, squeezing it into the old mold. To this extent, the reporter works against the basic tenet of his profession, i.e. that he should discover and emphasize what is new. If something is really new, it may not be believed or attended to.

In 1959, I was on rewrite duty for the Miami *Herald* when the police reporter called to report, along with the usual car accidents and gambling raids, that police were encountering a new form of drug abuse: teenagers sniffing the fumes of model airplane glue from paper bags. Never having heard of such a thing, I dismissed the matter as unimportant and didn't bother the city desk with it. Several years passed before glue-sniffing in particular and drug abuse in general among the young became recognized as a social problem. My problem then—and a common problem for most of us—was a low level of tolerance for ambiguity. The human mind finds it difficult to cope with an ambiguous situation and to make the necessary suspension of judgment while the facts are collected and studied. Ralph K. White, in *Nobody Wanted War: Misperceptions in Vietnam and Other Wars,* has ascribed early public tolerance of the Vietnam war to this characteristic.

The ambiguity in the glue-sniffing case came from the fact that police reporters do not ordinarily give rewrite men news of social significance. The easiest thing to believe was that the police or the police reporter were exaggerating or misinterpreting or even misperceiving an isolated situation. Believing this, I was able to dismiss the matter in less than two minutes.

A more current example involves some findings of social science research. Several time-series studies of racial attitudes of white and black Americans have been made since the pre-riot period which ended with Watts in 1965. Whether local or national in scope, these studies have shown whites and blacks growing closer together, both physically—at work, home, and school—and in attitudes of mutual tolerance and respect. The studies include a comparison of national samples of adult Americans interviewed by the University of Michigan Survey Research Center in 1964 and 1968. In the first sample, interviewed before the riots, 81 per cent of the whites said they had only white friends, no black friends; in 1968, after the riots, the number of whites who had exclusively white friends had dropped to 70 per cent. Among Negroes, 40 per cent said in 1964 that all their friends were black. In 1968, the proportion with only black friends was down to 25 per cent.

Local studies, over both shorter and longer time periods, have yielded similar results. In 1969, three out of four Detroit whites, given a description of a hypothetical situation in which a daughter brings a black child home to play, expressed approval; thirteen years before, a majority of whites in the same area had disapproved.

In Buffalo, Lester W. Milbrath of the State University of New York sampled black attitudes in the fall and winter of 1966-67 and again a year and a half later. Instead of the expected increase in preference for black separatism and violence, he found "a sizable increase in acceptance by blacks of integration, open-housing, equal employment opportunities, and nonviolent resistance." Another study, of Deep South college students by Donal E. Muir of the University of Alabama, found increasing sentiment for integration over a six-year period.

These findings run counter to the intuitive belief that black riots and white reaction have greatly worsened race relations since 1965. As a result, they have for the most part been ignored by newspapers. Information that race relations are improving, coming from social science sources, may seem more ambiguous to an editor than an eyewitness account of a man biting a dog. But the mere fact that it contradicts conventional belief, just as a man biting a dog reverses conventional man-dog roles, ought to enhance, not detract from, its news value.

As reporters, then, we tend to have our heads set to reinforce the conventional wisdom. The effect is multiplied because we tend to imitate and reinforce each other. Sometimes this imitation is direct, as when reporters covering a political speech gather in a huddle afterward to reach a consensus on the lead. Usually the imitation is more subtle. When a political candidate says something silly or in poor taste and editors put the story on page 1, reporters get positive reinforcement in the same way that a pigeon in a laboratory gets a grain of corn for pecking the right bar. And so reporters peck the bar again, searching the candidates' remarks for anything which can, by stretch of imagination or isolation from context, be interpreted as being in poor taste. And they make page 1 again. Something like this happened to George Romney during the 1968 Presidential primary campaigns and to Spiro T. Agnew during the Presidential campaign. Both said some silly things, but both became the victims of unfair stereotyping.

This is a specific form of the more general tendency to "hype up" news leads, then backpedal in the fourth or fifth paragraph to restore perspective. The hyped-up lead enhances the story's competitive position in the struggle for page 1. Thus sometimes very subtle, perhaps even meaningless or random, acts of a national administration are given undue prominence. When time shows the significance of the act in question to have been greatly exaggerated, more stories are written about the "new" stance of the Administration. With luck, the sweep of the oscillations tends to diminish, and truth comes even closer. But it is the perhaps unconscious analog of the old wire service trick of exaggerating disaster in order to get that service's story favored treatment over a competing service, then the next day, when it develops that the calamity was not so great as first supposed, using this angle to squeeze-out the opposition again. The profession is

outgrowing that, but problems will always hound the reporter in a hurry, the one assigned to spot news.

More of us are being freed from spot assignments to coverage in depth. We have more opportunities than ever before to report on social change, on the things that, as James Reston puts it, don't "just happen" but are "going on quietly." In this situation it is possible to free ourselves from the old anchoring points. Instead of starting from a base of personal conviction, ideology, or conventional wisdom we can start with intensive and systematic fact-finding efforts. Such a suggestion may seem to be a plea for a reactionary return to the old ideal of objectivity, but it has this difference: instead of reporting competing viewpoints for what they are worth, we could make an effort to determine just what they are worth. It is not necessary to turn our backs on interpretations; it is necessary to reduce the size of the leap from fact to interpretation, and to find a more solid base of fact from which to leap.

Here the social sciences can help us in two ways: their findings in many fields provide a continuing check on the conventional wisdom; we can save ourselves some trouble, some inaccuracy, and some lost opportunities by paying attention to what the social scientists are doing and finding out. More importantly and of more direct practical value, we can follow their example by abandoning the philosopher's armchair, giving up the notion that a few facts and common sense will make any problem yield, and make the new research techniques our own. The task is difficult, yet not so formidable as it might seem at first glance.

Quantification is not the tedious work that it used to be. While the computer cannot think for us, it can remove the drudgery from counting and measuring. Moreover, computer time is no longer expensive, particularly when compared with the cost of hand-tabulating the same data. What remains expensive is the collection of data. But there is precedent for newspapers to spend large amounts of money in research for news stories. If the story is important enough, a good newspaper will find a way to cover it.

The Detroit *Free Press* did so after the 1967 riot. The Detroit Urban League raised funds for data collection; the newspaper put a research team together; and findings from a study of attitudes among riot-area blacks were published a month after the riot—with data sound enough to form much of the basis for the profile of the rioter in Chapter II of the Kerner Commission report. [See "When Scholars Joined Journalists," Fall, 1967.] A year later, the *Free Press* spent its own money to collect new interview data in the riot area and discover that black militance was following surprisingly conventional channels. Meanwhile, in Miami, the *Herald* made good use of its market research department to field a study, designed to academic standards, of Dade County's still-peaceful blacks. After the Rev. Martin Luther King, Jr., was killed, the Office of Economic Opportunity funded return interviews of a portion of the *Herald* sample. It was the quickest way for OEO policymakers to get an accurate reading of the effect of the assassination on black strategies and aspirations.

Another formidable undertaking with the Knight Newspapers' study of the Berkeley student rebels five years after their arrests in Sproul Hall. Other media carried "mood" reports on the state of the campus five years later or interviewed former student leaders. The KNI project, through a mail survey, tracked down more than 200 rank-and-file members of that movement and found them settling down in behavior but not in attitude.

Some stories are worth this heavy artillery. But for the new methods to gain currency in journalism, two things must happen. First, editors must feel the need strongly enough to develop the inhouse cpacity for systematic research. Hiring an outside consultant or survey firm to prepare a report for a reporter to write about is not enough; the reporter's insight, fast reflexes, and ability to cope with deadline pressure are needed from the outset. The second need, of course, is for the

editors to find the talent to fill this need. Many journalism schools are prepared to supply it. Some have faculty members with the necessary methodological skills; others are geared to direct their students to the appropriate courses in the sociology, psychology, or political science departments. Students are not likely to be motivated to learn the new methods if they see little chance of applying them in future careers. But the potential for receptivity, especially among the younger generation of newspaper managers, is high.

It used to be said that journalism is history in a hurry. Now, to cope with the acceleration of social change, journalism must become social science in a hurry. Some journalists have expressed the fear that such a development might be resisted by the social science community—as though we were practicing their profession without the proper license. But social scientists are generally no more alarmed at the prospect of journalists becoming more systematic than historians would be at the prospect of our becoming more thorough and precise. They do not resent our intruding into their turf. Indeed, they tend to feel that we have neglected their turf and that if we were to become more like them, we might appreciate them more. It is a reasonable hope.

Moreover, because newsgathering organizations, like fire-engine companies, are geared for bringing large resources to bear on short notice, we can do many things that social scientists would like to do but can't. There is much wistful talk among social scientists of developing a standby capacity for "fire-engine research," so that critical events can be studied and their impact measured even as they happen. While academic action and decision-making are slow and cumbersome, cityroom action and decisionmaking are not. Therefore the role of fire-engine researcher may come more naturally and readily to journalists.

The ground rules are no different from those on which we have always operated: find the facts, tell what they mean, and do it without wasting time. If there are new tools to enable us to perform this task with greater power, accuracy, and insight, then we should make the most of them.

NEWSPAPER NEWS AND TELEVISION NEWS

Paul H. Weaver

The American newspaper as we know it today has been an established and essentially unchanging institution for upwards of 70 years. The same can hardly be said of television. As recently as 30 years ago it was nothing but a gleam in the entrepreneurial eye, and over the intervening decades it has passed fitfully through its infancy and adolescence. Today, however, television can fairly be said to have attained its majority and entered adulthood. Fully mature it obviously isn't, but adult it most certainly is; what was once a congeries of open-ended possibilities is now a settled and distinctive reality.

The fact that television is now a full-fledged institution and mode of communication implies, among other things, that it has finally become a fit subject for serious scholarship. For the humanist, television provides a settled *genre,* or family of *genres,* for study and criticism. These may not be high forms, but they are forms nevertheless and as such are presumably worthy of attention. For the social scientist, the institution of television itself, and its impact on other institutions and social processes, is at last something that can be looked at without fear that tomorrow everything will suddenly be different. And for everyone's scrutiny there is the central reality of television as a settled and powerful force in American civilization, actively at work affecting our culture, politics, economy, and individual lives.

What difference has the advent of television made to American society? Nobody really knows, of course; it is still too early to

tell, and until recently critics and scholars have generally dismissed TV out of hand, calling it "chewing gum for the eyes" or some other expression of thoughtless contempt. In these pages I would nevertheless like to offer a few tentative thoughts about the nature, assumptions, and political consequences of one element of modern television, the nightly network news program. It is clear to me that, in comparison to newspaper news, television news is not just "more of the same." Despite their many shared characteristics, newspapers and television differ in several fundamental respects and consequently tend to shape public perceptions and opinions in ways.

It is more or less impossible to think coherently about the comparison between newspaper news and television news until one grasps a simple but all-important truth: that news is a *genre,* a distinctive mode of writing and of depicting experience, and that any comparisons between newspapers and television must at least begin by analyzing the variant of this *genre* that each represents. Economic, technological, legal, and social considerations may be explored later, but to begin with what one is talking about are two related but not identical modes of expression and vision. And since expression and vision are so heavily influenced by culture, one cannot for the most part think coherently about such modes in the abstract—one must look at journalism *in a given place* and *at a stated time.* National and historical differences within journalism are extremely large. In what follows, I shall be concerned solely with American newspapers and American TV as they exist today.

In order to discourage anyone from entertaining an exaggerated notion of how different these two media are, and with the

From Television as a Social Force: New Approaches to TV Criticism, pp. 81-94. Edited by Douglass Cater and Ruth Adler. New York: Praeger and Aspen Institute, 1975. Copyright © 1975 by the Aspen Institute Program on Communications & Society; reprinted by permission of the publisher.

hope of putting their real differences in some perspective, let me begin by sketching what seem to me to be their most important common characteristics. Many of the vices and virtues that people attribute to television or newspapers are in fact not unique to the medium in question but are instead characteristics of news as such.

First, newspaper news and television news are alike in being varieties of journalism, which means that both consist of a current account of current events. ("Criticism of the moment at the moment," was James's useful formulation.) This two-fold contemporaneity—the present as a subject matter, and the present as the perspective in time from which it is described—is what accounts for the intense and universal appeal of journalism, and also for the extraordinary difficulty journalism encounters in achieving a depiction of events which experience and criticism affirm to be coherent, balanced, and reliable. This difficulty, it should be emphasized, is an inherent one for which there can be no solution; the best one can hope for is a recognition of the difficulty, an earnest effort to cope with it, and a general scaling down of claims and expectations all around. However that may be, television and newspapers share the appeal and the difficulty of contemporaneity more or less equally. The familiar criticism that TV is under greater time pressure, and therefore is less thoughtful, is essentially false. The criticism applies to both media.

Second, newspaper news and television news are alike in "covering" current events by means of reportage, i.e., factual description of what an on-the-scene observer of the event in question saw and heard. Thus news in America has long possessed all the distinctive advantages of reportage—concreteness, immediacy, and faithfulness to the particularity of events. But by the same token it has also been prone to the special weaknesses of reportage, chief of which are a relative inability to depict complexity and ambiguity and a powerful disinclination to pursue the meta-observational questions which illuminate complexity and ambiguity. A further shortcoming of reportage is that it increases the likelihood that the newsman, in the course of gathering information about a given event by being on the scene, will alter the event. This "Heisenberg effect" is an everyday occurrence in modern journalism and can be seen in the omnipresence of "pseudo-events" (happenings engineered by sources for the purpose of being reported), in the common practice of "milking the news," and in the much rarer instances of deliberate "staging" of events by newsmen desperate for a good story to report. Newspapers and TV are equally prone to these pathologies.

Third, newspaper news and television news are alike in being accounts of events that are vocationally-produced by special-purpose organizations. News is gathered and written by persons whose full-time occupation is to gather and write news. Thus newsmen may be said to be specialists—members of a distinct occupational community that has its distinctive traditions, concerns, and ways of doing things. Inevitably, news reflects the specialized ethos of the journalistic community and is shaped by its structure and processes, even though the intention of news is to speak to, and embody, the general concerns of the average citizen.

Fourth, newspaper and television news are alike in being essentially melodramatic accounts of current events. Partly by virtue of their focus on "events" and partly as a result of the traditions which define the ethos of the newsman and the structure of the news story, both newspapers and television depict events as actions that carry forward an implicit and usually extremely simplistic line of dramatic action. Thus events derive their journalistic identity in no small measure from the dramatistic fictions which newsmen and sources spin around them. One consequence of this practice is that news has historically defined the present as a period of transition—as an outgrowth of the past and a prefiguration of the future, yet different from both; as a time of discontinuity rather than continuity, of instability rather than stability, and of danger, crisis, struggle, and adventure rather than the reverse. Another consequence is the way in which the decisions of news organizations about the newsworthiness of a particular event quickly come to be self-fulfilling prophecies: what one prints today establishes a line of action which identifies related events tomorrow as being newsworthy, the printing of which both confirms the validity of the first day's decision and points to events still farther in the future as being worthy of coverage. So faddism and sensationalism are tendencies of both media.

Finally, newspaper news and television news in America are alike in using the same themes, formulas, and symbols in constructing the lines of melodramatic action which give meaning and identity to events. The two media, in other words, are cut from the same intellectual and rhetorical cloth. For instance, both newspapers and television typically report events associated with political campaigns in terms of a generalized image of politics as a horse race. Events associated with major changes in public policy, by contrast, are generally presented in terms of a model of policy-making as the undertaking of expert and well-intentioned leaders acting in the public interest. The failure of policy is ordinarily described according to a scenario in which existing policies are defended by officials and other interested parties for selfish motives against the opposition of an aroused public opinion indignantly demanding reform. These generalized images are but a few of the many formulas that give concrete expression to the two central themes that run, colliding

with each other as they do so, throughout all newspaper and television journalism in America—the populist notion that the people should rule directly in their own felt interests, and the republican notion that established institutions should rule in behalf of the public interest under the scrutiny of the electorate.

So much for similarities; now for some of the differences which make the advent of television journalism an event of no small moment in America political history. Undoubtedly, the most obvious of these differences is a structural one. In comparison to newspaper news, television news is far more coherently organized and tightly unified, and this is true of the individual TV and newspaper news story as well as of the TV and newspaper news aggregate as a whole (the newspaper edition and the TV news program). The difference is associated with the fact that TV is organized and presented in time, whereas the newspaper edition is organized only in space.

The difference in structure becomes most apparent when one considers newspaper editions and TV news programs as wholes. Though both are limited in volume, the newspaper contains a vastly large number of stories by a factor of something on the order of ten. This occurs because the newspaper, being organized in space, can feasibly publish many more stories, and much more text, than most readers care to read; its contents are thus an *à la carte* menu which the reader rapidly scans and from which he selects a "meal" according to his interests and time. Inevitably, therefore, the contents of the typical newspaper edition are chosen to be extremely diverse—are chosen, in fact, *not* to be read in their entirety by a single reader. There is, in consequence, a loose, open-ended, discursive quality to the contents and structure of the newspaper edition.

It is precisely the reverse with the television news program. Being organized in time, it cannot so easily present news *à la carte*: to "scan" all the possible stories, the viewer would have to see all of them in their entirety in the first place before choosing which ones to view—which is an absurdity. The television news program is thus a *table d'hôte*, a collection of stories selected and arranged to be seen in their entirety by every viewer without reducing the size or interest of the audience as the program proceeds. The consequence is that the television news program contains many fewer stories and that the ones it does contain are chosen carefully for their interest and balance and are presented as a relatively coherent and integrated package.

Thus, whereas the contents of the newspaper make up a diverse, numerous, often inchoate aggregate, the elements of the television news program typically form a unified whole.They seldom if ever attain perfect unity, of course; the materials of the real world, though malleable in television journalism, are not *that* malleable. But almost invariably there are several stories in a given program that exhibit a common theme or mood, and frequently there are further stories designed to provide contrast, emphasis, or development. This does not happen by accident; it is intentional on the part of TV newsmen, and the fact that it is intentional is proof that the underlying goal of the television news program is to attain the condition of wholeness, to exhibit theme, structure, and unity.

One consequence of this is that the TV news program tends to present a single, unified interpretation of the day's events *as a whole* and to construe periods of time as having a single defining movement, action, or mood. To the extent that we think or speak of the day's events holistically as good, bad, hopeful, discouraging, dramatic, boring, or whatever—and of course we all do this constantly—we are thinking in the mode of television journalism. In newspapers, by contrast, the events of the day rarely have anywhere near so clear a thematic identity; the newspaper's day is always a comparative mishmash.

Though it is not widely recognized and is often actually denied, precisely the same general relationship exists between the television news story and the newspaper news story. We are used to thinking of the TV news story as a slight, weak, and unsophisticated expository instrument in comparison to the newspaper news story. TV, according to conventional wisdom, is essentially a "headline service" that must content itself with formulaic capsule summaries of the top

"spot news" stories of the day; newspapers, by contrast, have the time, space, and capacity to produce long, meaty, analytic, more fully-realized accounts of what's going on. Yet the reality is exactly the reverse, as a glance at the scripts of just a few film news stories immediately demonstrates. Allowing for the fact that the newspaper news story *is* longer and does contain more raw data, the truth is that ordinarily it is the television news story which is more analytical, which more consistently and insistently goes beneath and beyond the surface of events to exhibit the larger trends and meanings of current affairs, which achieves the more integrated and coherent exposition of the reporter's findings, and which constitutes the more flexible and sophisticated reportorial instrumentality.

The standard newspaper news story is organized according to the principle of the "inverted pyramid."[1] Its subject and focus is a single, unitary event as defined in one or two sentences (the headline and lead paragraph). Having stated in the simplest and most reductionist of terms the bare bones of the event (who, what, where, when, and so on), the newspaper news story—*every* newspaper news story—has already achieved a kind of completeness and can be terminated at that point without rendering it unintelligible; if it is published in this form we call it an "item" or "filler." (A significant proportion of the "filler items" published by our newspapers, interestingly enough, are in fact major stories from out-of-town and foreign newspapers which have been cut off after the second or third paragraph in precisely this way.) But the news story need not be, and characteristically is not, terminated at this point. Instead it goes on, in a quasi-random sequence of syntactically crude sentences and disjointed paragraphs, to adduce additional data that elaborate on this or that aspect of the story-, topic-, and event-defining headline and lead. In theory, these data are to be presented in descending order of importance, and to some extent they are—the objective here being to enable an editor to cut as much material as needs to be cut to make the story fit the available space in the shortest possible time while doing the least substantive damage (he cuts the material at the end of the story), and to maximize the ease with which a reader can decide he has read as much of the story as suits his purposes (he reads down the story until he has had enough). But for the most part the data are presented in a quasi-random order, for the simple reason that they are all roughly co-equal in importance—or rather in unimportance, since the fact remains that the story stands on its own with all but the first few paragraphsn eliminated.

The television news story is radically different.[2] Unlike the newspaper news story, which is designed *not* to be read in its entirety while still achieving intelligibility, the television news story is a whole that is designed to be fully intelligible only when viewed in its entirety. Its focus is therefore upon a theme which runs throughout the story and which develops as the story moves from its beginning to its middle and then to its end. Information, narrative, sound, and pictures are selected and organized to illustrate the theme and to provide the necessary development.

Events in the newspaper sense of happenings that can be defined and comprehended in a single sentence are but the occasion of the television news story, not its *raison d'être*. In fact, a surprisingly large proportion of TV news stories are not about

events in any intelligible sense and do not pretend to be; and of those that do deal with events nearly all either dramatize or re-enact them, or treat them as incidental epiphenomena of the large phenomena or ideas which are the true thematic focus. But whatever the case, the TV news story, structurally, is virtually incapable of limiting itself to the simple event-naming and embroidering function performed by the newspaper news story; inevitably it goes into, beneath, or beyond the ostensive event to fix upon something else—a process, mood, trend, condition, irony, relationship, or whatever else seems a suitable theme in the circumstances.

A number of conclusions follow from the structural differences between newspaper and television news. One, clearly, is that television news is a far more flexible and intellectually accommodating form that the newspaper variety: more "interpretive," less constrained by the daily flow of events, and less committed to the newspaper's narrow, one-day-only perspective in time. (Whether TV makes proper use of this ability, or squanders it, is another question, on which more later.) Second, it seems equally clear that, as regards the interpretation of current events, television is capable of being—and ordinarily is—far more monolithic than the newspaper. Just as a single idea or theme governs the selection and presentation of all the information in the TV news story to a far greater extent that in the looser, more discursive, less "disciplined" newspaper story, so can a single theme or mood come to determine the contents of an entire TV news program and thus minutely shape its depiction of current affairs as a whole—something that is essentially impossible in a newspaper edition. Finally, and in consequence, the structure of TV news renders its contents far more completely within the practical, day-to-day, discretionary control of the TV news executive than is the case with newspapers, the content of which is by comparison more powerfully influenced by events, sources, and other external or uncontrollable forces.

A second major difference between the two media is associated with the fact that television is both visual and aural, while the newspaper is visual only. It thus becomes possible—and television, from the beginning, has chosen to exploit this possibility—for TV news to rely on spoken narrative as against the written narrative of the newspaper. This in itself is a substantial difference, but its consequences are made all the more powerful by the distinctive ways in which the two media have chosen to execute their narrative functions.

Newspapers news adopts an intensely impersonal narrative voice. In part, this means that the reporter, in writing his story, never speaks in the first person, but the matter goes far beyond that. The reporter also never makes reference to his own actions in observing events and finding facts; there is never any explicit allusion to the reporter's own awareness of the motives of sources, the probable validity of quoted statements, the extent to which the story at hand confirms or falsifies previous stories, and so forth. Moreover, the news story is couched in the extremely narrow and stylized vocabulary which has become standard for all modern news writing; it too helps to expunge any intimation of the reporter's identity and consciousness. The almost random structure of the newspaper news story and the crude syntax of the prose have much the same effect, making it nearly impossible for the reporter to express his best personal understanding of the subject at hand and of the relationships and contexts of the data he adduces. In short, the form of the newspaper news story systematically obscures any trace of the actual person who is doing the writing, who has observed the event in question at first hand, and who presumably has developed a critical understanding of it. What remains in the story is only a residue of impersonal statements of unambiguously

observable fact; the newspaper news story narrates the flow of current events in the rigorous and remote voice of the scientific paper.

This impersonal narrator endows newspaper journalism with a number of advantages and disadvantages. As for the advantages, there is first the fact that the newspaper's style tends to maximize the reader's belief in the truthfulness and dispassion of what the newspaper prints. It is a style which suggests an author who is so passionately scrupulous about facts that he will write literally nothing that an independent investigator could not verify as a fact. It suggests an author so rigorous in this positivism that he will not even imply relationships or nuances. And it suggests as well an author who is so dedicated to the ideal of objective neutrality in all things that he will make literally no reference, however modest or oblique, to his own person. The voice of the newspaper, in short, suggests an author who is a fact-machine, and nothing more.

Or rather almost nothing more: for the reality, of course, is that behind every newspaper news story there lurks a real, flesh-and-blood author who, being only human, does have real thoughts, real personal experience and knowledge, and real feelings. The disjointed, low-key, facts-only, simple-declarative-sentence prose this real person writes powerfully suggests a kind of deliberate repression of self and thus establishes within newspaper writing a distinct intensity, an undercurrent of taut emotion in the manner of Hemingway. Thus to the quasi-scientific authority of the fact-machine there is added the interest and drama inherent in the intensity radiated by this deliberately impersonal person.

There are also some disadvantages, however. The newspaper's laconic, facts-only voice prevents the reporter from conveying to the reader the substantial proportion of his knowledge and feel for the event at hand that cannot be formulated as statements of unambiguously observable fact. As a result, this information is simply denied to the reader. Moreover, interrelationships among the facts presented in the news story are rendered deeply ambiguous by the disjointedness of their exposition. The narrowness of the news story's vocabulary also obliterates complexity and nuance; events are effectively reduced to things that are fully described by their overt physical attributes and their legal-bureaucratic status. In the last analysis, then, this is a voice that does almost as much to make it hard for the reader to understand events as it does to help him—and this in turn calls into question the intentions of the real author, the reporter. What kind of person would present himself as a fact-machine—as a person who is not human and who exercises no judgment? What sort of person sometimes tells the reader less than he has reason to believe? Who would write things whose implication he knows to be false or misleading? The answer is easy: someone who at best is gravely confused and at worst is utterly dishonest with himself and his reader. He is a person who refuses to assume responsibility for the meaning of what he writes; who evades the obligations that are instantly created between author and reader the minute one sets pen to paper; and who cynically manipulates the reader's trust. The author of the news story, in sum, seems to want to bamboozle the reader as much as to inform him, and in this sense he is an unreliable narrator.

The narrative style of television news is the polar opposite of that embodied in the conventions of newspaper writing. It is, above all, a *personal* voice that tells the day's news on the tube. One actually hears the voice; one sees the face, body, and manner of the person who speaks. This individual is constantly on view, intruding his person and personality almost continuously into the narrative. If there is an interview with an important newsmaker, the story will depict the reporter, asking questions or listening and responding to answers, as well as the interviewee himself. Sometimes this personal narrator will make a passing reference to the process of covering the story. In fact, there is scarcely a moment in the television news story when the look, sound, manner, thought, and personality of the reporter-narrator is not visibly and audibly present. If the narrator of the newspaper story may be said to be a sort of disembodied zombie, then the narrator of television news is emphatically a real,

flesh-and-blood person in all his uniqueness.

But not necessarily in all his fallible humanness. The television reporter, on camera, displays precious few weaknesses. His stance is easy and masterful, his voice commanding, his diction perfect; his lines are spoken flawlessly, his clothes wrinkle-free, custom-made, and color-coordinated, and his every hair is perfectly in (or out of, depending on the style) place. He may be a real person, but clearly he is playing a role, and in most cases (but not all: there is a measure of variety here) the posture he assumes is one of omniscience.

There is hardly an aspect of the scripting, casting, and staging of a television news program that is not designed to convey an impression of authority and omniscience. This can be seen most strikingly in the role of the anchorman—Walter Cronkite is the exemplar—who is positively god-like: he summons forth men, events, and images at will; he speaks in tones of utter certainty; he is the person with whom all things begin and end. But the omniscient pose is also adopted by reporters in the field. The "eyewitness" story format offers a particularly useful illustration: the reporter usually stands in front of the building or scene in question, his head and torso many times larger on the screen than the physical objects and persons involved in the actual events being reported. Throughout the report the actual occurrences are like putty in his masterful hands. He cuts from one shot to another; he stops the President in mid-sentence; he "voices over" images of kings, Congresses, wars, and citizens. At every point he conveys the subterranean but nonetheless powerful suggestion that the reporter is larger than life, that he literally as well as figuratively towers over the mere mortals whose doings and undoings he so easily and unerringly grasps and whose pretenses he sees through in an instant. Newsmen protest that this isn't at all what they have in mind; their concern is just to make the news visually interesting and intellectually coherent. Maybe so. But it doesn't really matter why they do it; the important thing is that they do it—and that, intentionally or not, they convey these suggestions of the TV newsman's omniscience to the viewer.

But most of all the television newsman's omniscience is apparent in what he says and how he says it. He is hardly one to limit and discipline himself in the manner of the newspaper narrator; he does not say less than he knows, nor is he willing to suggest by his silences, omissions, or ambiguities that there are things he does not know or cannot say for certain. To the contrary, he speaks authoritatively and self-confidently about everything that comes into his field of vision: men, events, motives, intentions, meanings, significances, trends, threats, problems, solutions—all are evidently within his perfect understanding, and he pronounces on them without any ifs, ands, or buts. To be sure, there are exceptions to this pose—TV newsmen such as John Chancellor who have begun to assume a stance not of omniscience but of a kind of sober, honest, self-critical, *reflexive* authoritativeness, in which the newsman not only says what he does know, but also makes clear his doubts, uncertainties, and the like, as well. These exceptions are few, however; most newsmen still pattern themselves after the example set by Walter Cronkite, who, despite the palpable absurdity of the notion that a definitive account of events is possible in principle, let alone in a 22-minute time-slot, continues to pronounce, God-like, the epitaph, "And that's the way it is …" at the end of each installment of *The CBS Evening News with Walter Cronkite.*

The personal and omniscient narrative of television journalism is noteworthy in a number of respects. It endows TV with an enormous added measure of moral, intellectual, and personal authority, as witness the fact that Walter Cronkite is among the nation's most admired and trusted men. It is hard to see how this narrative voice could be anything but a central cause of the enormous

persuasive power of modern television. Yet it must also be said that the authoritativeness which TV newsmen pretend to is, in the end, a two-edged sword. For, omniscient or not, these newsmen are still identifiable on the screen as human beings, and it is therefore inevitable that, at some level, the audience is going to be aware that no one in real life ever knows so much or is so undoubting and intellectually self-assured, and that these television men are putting on a not entirely honest act. And when these men begin pronouncing *ex cathedra* on subjects about which the audience has strong feelings or substantial knowledge, the viewer is likely to be doubly irritated—first at the objectionable depiction of events, and second at the fraudulence and arrogance of the omniscient posture assumed by the man who conveys the objectionable depictions. Thus, ironically, each added increment of credibility which the omniscient narrator garners for television journalism automatically creates an equal increment of potential for "credibility gap" and public hostility toward television.

A second consequence arises out of this pose of omniscience as well: intellectual and political hubris. By the example its narrators set, by the "truths" they so confidently proclaim, and by the extraordinary power of the medium itself, television journalism encourages its viewers to entertain a badly inflated notion of how much it is possible to know and to do in the real world. By encouraging the sin of hubris, television journalism shows itself to be as unreliable, in the end, as the narrator of the newspaper news story, but for the opposite reason: not because it says less than it knows but because it says more.

Finally, television news differs from newspaper news in the vastly greater importance that TV attaches to spectacle. This is not so simply because television has such a large and sophisticated capacity for depicting the sights and sounds of events. At least as important is the fact that American television journalists have long since become institutionally committed to exploiting and emphasizing this special capability. They could—and in the early years of American television they did—follow, if only in a vague sort of way, the admirable model of the BBC and pay no more attention to the spectacular aspects of events than good newspapers do. But in American TV journalism today it is otherwise, to put it mildly. In almost any aspect of TV news that one might care to explore, one will find that considerations of pure spectacle count for much more than they do in newspaper journalism: in the choice of events to cover, in the allocation of resources among events, in the construction of events, in the choice of materials to illustrate stories, and perhaps above all in the selection of themes around which to build news stories.

In practical terms, this emphasis on spectacle is revealed in the television news organization's preoccupation with film, and especially with "good" film—i.e., film that clearly and dramatically depicts action, conflict, ritual, or color. Faced with a choice between two potentially newsworthy events, the American TV news organization will prefer, other things being equal, the one for which there is better film. What film they have for an event tentatively identified as newsworthy ordinarily guides, and in some instances may completely determine, the way the event is defined and the theme chosen for the story—a practice which can easily cause the story to misrepresent the situation as it really was. And in rare instances television news organizations have been known to "create" film, to stage spectacles for purposes of being filmed, in order to have something newsworthy to report. In newspapers, spectacle is but one of many competing and more completely coequal considerations, but in television it is a preoccupation. This

preoccupation leads television journalism to give disproportionate coverage to events, or aspects of events, which are spectacular and spectacularly filmed.

This emphasis is noteworthy for a number of reasons. For one, it largely vitiates the unique flexibility and interpretive capabilities of the television news story, or rather it prevents their value from being fully realized. For under the influence of TV's passion for spectacle, the possibilities of the news story that could be used to counteract the inherent journalistic tendencies toward narrowness, literalness, short-sightedness, and the like, are instead exploited principally as a means of making news and events more visually interesting and emotionally stimulating than they are in real life. Second, the emphasis on spectacle tends to make TV journalism superficial in the literal sense of being fixated on the surface sights and sounds of events. Third, it powerfully reinforces the melodramatism inherent in American journalism, rendering television preeminently an instrument of symbolic politics. Fourth, the emphasis on spectacle lends additional forms of authority and interest to TV news: the interest and excitement which are characteristic of spectacle, and the largely specious but still quite real authority, or "credibility," of film as a mode of eyewitness observation. And finally the television emphasis on spectacle fixes the focus of TV journalism uniquely upon the ongoing drama of nationhood itself. Whereas newspapers focus on a diverse mass of specific events, television depicts something more directly thematic and melodramatic—the spectacle adorning the national dramas of the whole and the parts, of conflict and consensus, war and peace, danger and mastery, triumph and defeat, and so on.

Though I don't pretend to know what all of them are, I am certain that there are many other differences between newspaper news and television news; the three discussed here illuminate only a small part of what is obviously a large and complex relationship. Yet even these elementary distinctions of structure, voice, and content do seem to establish the importance of looking into the relationship more deeply. For if what I have said thus far is true, then clearly the introduction of television journalism deserves to be considered an event of major consequence for all aspects of American life, and perhaps especially for American politics. Toqueville showed how the American political system rests on an uneasy balance between equality and liberty—or, as I would put it, between democracy and liberalism. On the analysis in these pages, the conclusion seems inescapable that whereas the effect of newspaper news is to sustain that balance, television news tends to upset it by reinforcing the egalitarian idea and by weakening liberalism.

Newspapers news tends to sustain the Tocquevillian balance by providing a great deal of precise information within a cognitive framework that is crude and nearly chaotic. It thus mobilizes public attention to public affairs (thereby performing an egalitarian-democratic function), while preserving to a significant extent the ability of each reader to choose for himself what to read and what to make of the data he encounters (the liberal idea). Thus there is an activation of public opinion as a whole (the democratic idea), but in behalf of no particular vision or objective

save perhaps the ideal of individualism itself (the liberal idea). Through the newspaper, a single organization communicates directly with the electorate (the democratic impulse), but in a manner which suggests that no single coherent vision of public affairs is legitimate or even possible (the liberal idea). The newspaper sustains the Tocquevillian balance between democracy and liberalism, then, by incorporating both of these antagonistic ideas into its very conception of news. This practice is not without its disadvantages, to be sure. The liberal idea in particular, associated as it is with impersonal narrative and chaotic cognitive structure, creates more than its share of confusion. Yet as Tocqueville showed, the institutionalization of both ideas is necessary to the stability and legitimacy of the American regime—and if a bit of confusion or inelegance is the price we must pay for having them institutionalized in our media of public information, it seems a worthwhile bargain.

Television news, by contrast, incorporates no such admirable ambivalence. It is almost uniquely an expression of the democratic-egalitarian impulse. Television news is like newspaper news in that both mobilize public attention to public affairs and disseminate information—but there the similarities end. For television news is all mobilization; it seems utterly to lack the liberal, privatizing characteristics of print journalism—the discontinuities, the randomness, the ambiguities, and the diversity which give the ideal of individualism real substance. The television news emphasis on spectacle, its reliance on the single omniscient observer, and its commitment to the notion of a unified, thematic depiction of events, all make TV an extraordinarily powerful mobilizer of public attention and public opinion. The mobilization is organized around a single vision of public affairs promulgated by a single journalistic organization. Thus television news gives credence to the idea that there exists in America a single, coherent national agenda which can be perceived as such by any reasonable and well-intentioned person. Television news consequently lends a distinctive power and authority to the denigration of differences among us; it asserts that on the most fundamental level—that of deciding what is important enough to merit public attention—all Americans are essentially agreed and that wise public decisions can be reached through plebiscitarian consensus rather than through a system of institutions designed to represent and mediate differences among Americans.

Television news, in other words, is perhaps the most powerful centralizing-democratizing machine ever let loose in American society, a machine which, in its commitment to social unity and intellectual coherence, can scarcely avoid riding roughshod over the historic aspirations of liberalism—pluralism, diversity, localism, privacy, individualism, and untrammeled freedom for what is personal and idiosyncratic. So it is hard to imagine that the advent of television journalism is without significance for American politics and it is equally hard to believe that, in its current form, it is something that Americans should welcome with untroubled hearts.

NOTES

1. There are other modes of newspaper writing, of course: the column, the editorial, the feature story, the news analysis. Each of these has its own charcteristics. Here I am analyzing only the standard news story.
2. I should emphasize that I am dealing here only with the filmed news story from a remote location. TV news programs also present "items" and "commentaries"—not many, usually, but some. These have their own characteristics and are not discussed in this paper.

Part Two

C

Economics
and the Media

THE DECLINE OF
MASS MEDIA

Richard Maisel

A new, three-stage theory of social change and media growth, formulated in recent years, challenges many of the ideas long accepted in the study of modern communication systems. According to this theory, the third stage, now evident in the United States, is characterized by a declining growth rate for mass media and an increasing growth rate for specialized communication directed to smaller, more homogeneous audiences.[1] If this theory is correct, the mass media will—contrary to past expectations—play a less important role in the future, and the focus of scientific attention should be shifted to specialized media.

This article reviews media growth trends in the United States during the period 1950-1970[2] to determine whether the claims of the three-stage theory are warranted.

THE TWO-STAGE THEORY

Most studies of modern communication systems are based on a two-stage theory[3] of social change and media growth, which may be summarized as follows:

1. The history of Western civilization may meaningfully be divided into two periods: a stable earlier period, in which society was small in scale, local in orientation, and organized around a primitive, pre-industrial economy; and a later period of industrialization, extending to the present, in which society has grown in size, scope, and technological prowess.

2. Each of these two periods is characterized by a communication system that is consistent with its needs and resources. In the pre-industrial period, the communication system was restricted to

From Public Opinion Quarterly *37 (Summer 1973):*
159-170. Copyright© 1973 by Public Opinion Quarterly;
reprinted by permission.

direct face-to-face communication between individuals. In the later period, beginning in the mid-fifteenth century with the invention of printing from movable type, a powerful system of mass communication evolved.

3. There is a close, functional relationship between the process of industrialization and the growth of mass communication. The former stimulates and provides the resources necessary for the latter; the latter facilitates the growth of the former. Thus each stage in the growth of the mass media helps provide the conditions necessary for its further growth.

4. Both the mass media and the processes of industrialization that support it have been growing at a rapid rate and will continue to do so in the future.

5. Mass communication develops a powerful "hold" over its audience, thereby closing off potentially competitive forms of cultural experience. This gives the mass media an ever more secure position and an ever more paramount role in determining the cultural content of our society.

THE THREE-STAGE THEORY

The newer, three-stage theory[4] of social change and media growth incorporates the older theory through step 3, supplanting the later steps with a third stage of development, as follows:

4. When industrialization and the institutional changes that accompany it reach an advanced level, new forces are released, which channel subsequent social and economic development down a new path, culminating in the third stage—"post-industrial society."

5. Among the forces released at an advanced level of industrialization are increased specialization and the growth of the so-called service industries.

6. The point at which the third stage begins is usually marked by a rapid shift of the work force away from the manufacturing sector toward the service sector. In the United States, this shift occurred in the period following the second World War.

7. The service industries are great consumers of specialized media. The needs and tastes of specialized groups can only be satisfied by a form of specialized communication designed for homogeneous audiences.

Thus, the development of the third stage, or "post-industrial society," does not support the rapid growth of mass communication; rather, it stimulates the growth of specialized media. Moreover, technological development and increase in wealth provide the means necessary for the development of these specialized media.

On the basis of these propositions, we would not predict an acceleration in the growth of the mass media; rather, we would expect a rapid growth in specialized media.

TEST OF HYPOTHESIS

According to the three-stage theory, the United States entered the third stage following the second World War. Therefore, we may test the theory by examining the rates of media growth in the United States during the period 1950-1970, expecting to find an increase in growth rates for the specialized media relative to growth rates for the mass media. We shall measure the growth of media in two ways. First, we shall measure economic support, in current dollars,[5] including advertising revenue, consumer expenditures, and, in some cases, government expenditures. Second, we shall measure growth in the volume of communications using the best measures available throughout the period.[6]

TABLE 1
Volume and Growth Rate of GNP, Education, Personal Message, and Mass Media
Systems, 1950-70

	Dollar Volume (GNP in Billions, Media Systems in Millions)			Growth Rate	
GNP and Media	1950	1960	1970	1950-60	1960-70
GNP (a)	284.8	503.7	974.1	1.78	1.93
Media Systems					
Education (b)	8,796	24,722	70,600	2.81	2.85
Personal Message (c)	4,544	10,001	20,636	2.20	2.06
Mass Media (d)	9,254	16,413	28,525	1.77	1.73

(a) *Abstract 1971,* Table 150.
(b) Consists of educational expenditure at all levels of instruction, public and private (*Abstract 1972,* Table 155).
(c) Consists of telephone and telegraph operating revenue, domestic and overseas (*Abstract 1972,* Table 793) and ordinary postal revenue (*Abstract 1971,* Table 752).
(d) Consists of advertising revenue (*Abstract 1972,* Table 1260), consumer expenditure on books, maps, newspapers, magazines, sheet music, and motion pictures (*Abstract 1972,* Table 330), and the number of subscribers to CATV (*Abstract 1972,* Table 802) times an assumed annual subscription rate of $50.

MASS MEDIA, EDUCATION, AND PERSONAL MESSAGE SYSTEM

The education system is the most important of all specialized media systems. At its core is the school system, a mammoth medium for the communication of specialized information. The school system also supports the use of other specialized media, such as textbooks, technical treatises, and audio-visual materials. Equally important, the product of the education system, particularly of *higher* education, is a stratum of individuals who, both in their work and private life, are consumers of specialized communication. Thus, a crucial test of the three-stage theory is provided by growth in the education system.

In this section, we will compare the growth rates for the education system with those of the mass media. To complete the analysis, we will include the growth rates of the much-neglected personal message system, which includes those specialized media, other than face-to-face interaction, that permit communication between individuals. These include the telephone, telegraph, and correspondence by mail. If the three-stage theory is correct, we should expect to find that the growth rates for both the education and personal message systems are greater than those for the mass media. Analysis of education growth rates, however, remains the more crucial test.

Table 1, depicting economic growth for the mass media, education, and personal message systems, reveals the highest growth rate in the education system, and the lowest growth rate in the mass media system. Table 1 also shows growth rates for the economy as a whole measured as the gross national product (GNP). The growth rates for both the education and personal message systems are well above those for the GNP, indicating that both of these systems—but particularly education—expanded relative to the total economy. The growth rate for the mass media

TABLE 2
Growth Rate of Higher Education, Telephone and Television, 1950-70

Media	Growth Rate			
	1950-55	1955-60	1960-65	1965-70
Dollar Volume				
Higher Education (a)	1.52	2.05	1.94	1.93
Telephone (b)	1.70	1.43	1.41	1.52
Television (c)	6.04	1.57	1.59	1.44
Communication Volume				
Higher Education (d)	1.07	1.50	1.58	1.30
Telephone (e)	1.22	1.33	1.29	1.33
Television (f)	4.38	1.46	1.30	1.19

(a) Current expenditure and interest, capital outlay, or plant expansion (*Abstract 1971,* Table 150, except 1955 data, which were estimated by assuming 1955 expenditure to be equal to 1950 expenditure plus five-sixths of the growth to 1956 [*Abstract 1972,* Table 139]).
(b) Operating revenue, domestic and overseas (*Abstract 1971,* Table 759 [except 1955 data (*Abstract 1960,* Table 663)]).
(c) Advertising revenue (*Abstract 1972,* Table 1216) and the number of subscribers to CATV (*Abstract 1972,* Table 802) times an assumed annual subscription rate of $50.
(d) College enrollment (*Abstract 1971,* Table 153).
(e) Average telephone conversations daily, Bell and independent companies, local and long distance (*Abstract 1971,* Table 757, except 1955 data [*Abstract 1960,* Table 665]).
(f) Average total hours sets in use daily, obtained by the number of television households (A. C. Neilson Company, *Television 1971,* p. 5) times the average hours per day of television sets in use per household (National Association of Broadcasters, *Dimensions of Television 1968-69,* p. 12 and A. C. Neilson Company, private communication).

was approximately equal to that of the GNP in the 1950-60 period, but fell behind during the 1960-70 period. Thus, we must conclude that the mass media system is contracting relative to the economy as a whole.

Every media system is composed of new and expanding segments, as well as those that are stable or in decline. The critical element in the development of media systems is found in the growth segments. Table 2 shows the growth rates, measured in terms of dollar-value and facility use, for television, the telephone, and higher education—the most active components of, respectively, the mass media, personal message, and education systems. As we would expect, Table 2 reveals explosive growth for television during the 1950-55 period, but a steady decline in its expansion thereafter. In contrast, the growth rate for higher education was low in the 1950-55 period, but rose sharply in subsequent periods. By the 1955-60 period, the growth rate for higher education had surpassed that of television, and continued to do so throughout the sixties. The growth rate for the telephone was moderately high compared with the other two media under consideration, and stable throughout the postwar period. In the 1965-70 period, it surpassed the sagging growth rate for television. Thus, in the 1950-70 period, growth rates for the fastest growing segments of the education and personal message systems have increased relative to the analogous component of the mass media system. Moreover, television dollar volume

TABLE 3
Growth Rate of Commercial, Educational, and Special Service Broadcasting, 1950-70

	Growth Rate			
	1950-55	1955-60	1960-65	1965-70
Number of Authorized Radio Stations				
Educational (a)	1.58	1.42	1.50	1.69
Safety and Special Service (b)	1.24	21.7	2.23	1.26
Commercial (c)	1.10	1.31	1.27	1.17
Number of TV Stations on Air (d)				
Educational	—	4.27	1.95	2.06
Commercial	4.40	1.25	1.01	1.15
Average Weekly Hours of Broadcasting per TV Station				
Educational (e)	—	—	—	1.42
Commercial (f)	—	—	—	1.02

(a) FM only (*Abstract 1966,* Table 737, except 1970 data [*Abstract 1971,* Table 765]).
(b) Consists of amateur, disaster, citizens, aviation, industrial, marine, land transportation, and public safety services (*Abstract 1966,* Table 737, except 1970 data [*Abstract 1971,* Table 765]).
(c) AM and FM (*Abstract 1966,* Table 737, except 1970 data [*Abstract 1971,* Table 765]).
(d) Federal Communications Commission, *Annual Report, Fiscal Year 1970,* p. 144.
(e) *Abstract 1972,* Table 803. Data for 1965 were estimated as the average of 1964 and 1966 data.
(f) *Abstract 1972,* Table 809.

grew by 1.44 during the 1965-70 period, insignificantly more than the 1.43 by which the GNP grew in the same interval. Therefore, by 1970, television, which is usually considered the most successful of the mass media, did not have an expanding position in the economy.

Each medium may also be divided into more or less specialized segments. Higher education, for example, tends to be a more specialized medium, while elementary school tends to be a mass medium. Thus we can test the three-stage theory by examining the growth rates for each medium divided into segments along degree-of-specialization lines. In the case of the school system, expenditures in the 1960-70 period grew by 1.14 for elementary schools, 1.43 for secondary schools, and 2.07 for institutions of higher education.[7] Thus growth rates vary directly with the degree of specialization of the individual segment. The same general tendencies are seen in Table 3, which shows that the growth rates for education and special service broadcasting have been increasing relative to those of commercial broadcasting. Table 4 shows that in the 1960-70 period, the quantity of air and first-class mail delivered increased faster than second-, third-, and fourth-class mail (excluding publications), and the purchase rate of tape recorders exceeded that of phonographs.

Therefore, every comparison among the education, personal message, and mass media systems shows that the first two media are growing at increasingly more rapid rates than the third.

TABLE 4

Volume and Growth Rate of Mail and Consumer Audio Equipment, 1950-70

	Unit Volume			Growth Rate	
	1950	1960	1970	1950-60	1960-70
Mail Received, (a) Pieces per Capita					
Air and First-Class	168	193	246	1.14	1.27
Second-, Third-, and Fourth-class	119	148	149	1.24	1.01
Consumer Audio Equipment, (b) in Thousands of Units Purchased					
Tape Recorders	—	295	8,452	—	28.65
Phonographs	1,260	4,523	5,620	3.58	1.24

(a) *Abstract 1971*, Table 752.

(b) Electronic Industry Association, *Consumer Electronics 1972*.

SPECIALIZATION OF THE MASS MEDIA

Several authors[8] have suggested that the mass media themselves are becoming more specialized, a proposition deduced from the three-stage theory. We can test this proposition by examining the growth rates of the more specialized and less specialized components of each mass medium. We can, for example, distinguish between the national broadcasting networks and local radio and television stations; the former have larger and more heterogeneous audiences and thereby constitute the less specialized segment of the broadcasting media. Table 5 shows that within all three of the major media—radio, newspapers, and magazines—throughout the years 1950 to 1970 there has been greater growth in advertising revenue directed to more specialized audiences. This finding strongly supports the three-stage theory in two ways: (1) by showing differential growth in

the media carrying the advertising, and (2) by *directly* showing differential growth in the medium of advertising, itself a means of communication. The source of support also suggests the direction to which the media must orient themselves in order to obtain further support: the growth of a more specialized type of advertising means the medium must attract the type of audience to which a more specialized advertising is directed. Thus, specialized advertising becomes a factor in the medium's continued specialization. An outstanding example of this can be seen in the case of radio, where network-originated broadcasts have diminished in favor of locally based fare directed to very special segments within the community. Thus, one station will play "heavy" rock music, while another station operates in the older "top 40" rock 'n' roll format, and a third broadcasts news exclusively. The trend has gone so far that the networks, themselves, have become specialized. The same trend can be found in the area of magazines, in which mass magazines such as *Life, Look,* and the

TABLE 5
Growth Rate of GNP and Advertising Expenditure by Medium, 1950-69

GNP and Media	Growth Rate			
	1950-55	1955-60	1960-65	1965-69
GNP (a)	1.40	1.26	1.36	1.35
Television (b)				
Network	6.35	1.45	1.57	1.35
Local	4.09	1.24	1.46	1.58
Radio (c)				
Network	.43	.51	1.39	.98
Local	1.19	.131	1.37	1.42
Magazine				
Regional (d)	—	—	2.06	1.35
Other than Regional (e)	1.41	1.29	1.20	1.11
Newspaper (f)				
National	1.39	1.13	1.03	1.20
Retail	1.48	1.18	1.14	1.28
Classified	1.61	1.31	1.51	1.30
All Media (g)				
National	1.66	1.35	1.28	1.22
Local	1.54	1.22	1.27	1.35
Total	1.61	1.29	1.27	1.28

(a) *Abstract 1971,* Table 484.
(b) *Abstract 1971,* Table 1216.
(c) *Ibid.*
(d) Publishers' Information Bureau/Leading National Advertisers.
(e) Total magazine advertising expenditures (*Abstract 1971,* Table 1216) minus regional advertising expenditure.
(f) American Newspaper Publishers Association, Research Department, Bureau of Advertising, March 1970.
(g) *Abstract 1971,* Table 1216.

Saturday Evening Post have ceased publication, while special interest magazines have been thriving. Many magazines with large national circulations, such as *Time,* have set up regional advertising areas.

The trend toward specialization in magazines and radio has often been noted before,[9] and is usually explained as a consequence of television. But this is only a partial explanation. It does not, for example, explain the fact that the growth rate of local television advertising has been increasing relative to the growth rate for network television advertising (Table 5). The three-stage theory accounts not only for shifts among media, but for shifts within a particular medium as well.

In Table 6, data for the 1950-70 period reveal that the growth rate of consumer economic support for various media is directly related to the degree to which each medium is specialized. Within the print medium, the growth rate for books has been higher than for magazines and newspapers, which are less specialized, and the rate of increase in expenditures for legitimate theater has been greater than the rate of increase in

TABLE 6
Growth Rate of Consumer Recreation Expenditure by Medium, 1950-70

Medium	Growth Rate			
	1950-55	1955-60	1960-65	1965-70
Radio and Television (a)	1.25	1.25	1.67	1.40
Magazines and Newspapers (b)	1.25	1.17	1.30	1.42
Books (c)	1.29	1.50	1.54	1.66
Legitimate Theater (d)	1.34	1.48	1.35	1.48
Motion Pictures (e)	1.01	.89	1.12	1.33
Total (f)	1.26	1.29	1.43	1.48

(a) Consists of expenditure for purchase and repair of radio and television receivers, phonograph records and musical instruments (*Abstract 1972*, Table 330), and the number of subscribers to CATV (*Abstract 1972*, Table 802) times an assumed annual subscription rate of $50.
(b) *Abstract 1972*, Table 330. Includes sheet music.
(c) *Abstract 1972*, Table 330. Includes maps.
(d) *Abstract 1972*, Table 330.
(e) *Ibid.*
(f) *Ibid.*

expenditures for motion pictures, which again are less specialized. Table 6 also shows that the rate of increase in consumer expenditures for radio, television, magazines, newspapers, and motion pictures has been far less than the rate of increase in consumer expenditure as a whole, which in turn has been less than the rate of increase in books and legitimate theater. This further confirms that, relative to the total economy, specialized media are expanding and mass media are contracting.

Table 7, providing 1947-70 growth rates for various segments within the print medium, reveals that in every case, growth of the more specialized segment of the medium exceeds that of the less specialized: the growth rate in the circulation of suburban newspapers is greater than the growth rate in the circulation of central city newspapers; the growth rate in the number of technical books sold and the number of new technical books published is greater than the growth rate in the number of fiction books sold and the number of new fiction books published; the growth rate in the number of biomonthly and quarterly magazines is greater than the growth rate in the number of weekly and monthly magazines.

The same trend toward specialization can be seen in the theater medium, where the number of off-Broadway performances increased by 1.29 from 1960 to 1970, while in the same period the growth rate for the less specialized Broadway performance was .75[10] An identical trend can be seen in motion pictures, where the size of newly built theaters and their audiences have decreased.

CONCLUSION

Our review of trends in media growth in the United States during the 1950-70 period supports the three-stage theory of social change and media growth. In every case, the growth rate of the more specialized media increased relative to the growth rate of the mass media. The mass media are actually shrinking in size relative to the total economy.

Given these findings, it is clear that the focus of attention in the study of modern communication systems should broaden from its present preoccupation with the mass media to a full examination of all major media and communication systems. This would include studies of important media systems

TABLE 7
Volume and Growth Rate of Print Media, 1947-70

Print Media	Unit Volume			Growth Rate	
	1947	1957	1967	1947-57	1957-67
Newspaper Circulation, 25 Largest Metropolitan Areas, (a) in Millions of Papers Sold					
Central City Papers (b)	22.7	24.7	23.0	1.09	.93
Papers Outside Central City	1.4	2.4	3.5	1.71	1.45
Books, (c) in Millions of Copies Sold					
Fiction (d)	—	480.0	759.2	—	1.58
Technical (e)	—	238.6	602.4	—	1.77
	1950	1960	1970	1950-60	1960-70
New Books and Editions Published (f)					
Fiction	1,907	2,440	3,137	1.28	1.28
Technical (g)	3,200	4,415	13,834	1.37	3.13
Periodicals Published (h) Weekly to Monthly	5,553	6,220	6,759	1.12	1.08
Bimonthly and Quarterly	1,040	1,638	2,065	1.56	1.26

(a) M. Lehr and J. Wallis, interoffice correspondence, American Newspaper Publishers Association, Bureau of Advertising, May 3, 1967.
(b) Includes circulation that these papers have outside central city.
(c) *Abstract 1972,* Table 818. Data for 1957 were estimated from 1958 and 1967 data assuming a constant growth rate. between 1957 and 1967.
(d) Includes general book, trade, etc.
(e) Includes textbooks, subscription reference books, technical, scientific, and professional books.
(f) *Abstract 1972,* Table 816.
(g) Includes agriculture, business, law, medicine, philosophy, psychology, science, sociology, economics, and technologies.
(h) *Abstract 1972,* Table 810.

that have been almost completely neglected, such as the telephone system; studies of new media that are growing rapidly, such as the office communication system; and studies that provide perspectives on the total communication system of our society, such as those of Fritz Machlup.[11]

We must also abandon the outmoded view of the individual as simply the recipient of standardized messages emanating from the mass media, whose only recourse in self-expression is the primitive sound of his own voice in direct face-to-face interaction. Rather, we must begin to think of, and study, the individual in our society as a communicator having access to a very powerful set of media tools and as a recipient of a wide range of equally enriched communications directed to him by others. This would lead us to study how he learns about and uses the available media systems, and the effect that this ability to communicate has on him.

Comparing the two- and three-stage theories shows that it is dangerous simply to project trends into the future. Each development seems to bring with it the conditions by which it changes. Thus the development of the standardized industrial culture brought about the conditions that now seem to be causing the development of a more differentiated culture. We should, therefore, not make the same error of simply projecting the third stage into the future. At least two other possibilities exist. First, the explosive increase in the volume of communication directed to the individual creates the problem of dealing with it. Thus we might expect the coming period to be characterized by the growth of receptors, media for receiving communications; such developments are already apparent in the use of speed reading, computers for data retrieval, tape recorders, and copying equipment.

The second possibility is less auspicious. The growth of a differentiated communication system is part of the larger process by which our society has been producing a differentiated culture. In both economic and psychological terms, the cost of this differentiated culture has been increasing, and it is not clear whether our society will pay the price of supporting it in the future. In recent years, for example, both economic and moral support has been withdrawn from educational institutions, which in the past played a leading role in the development of the differentiated culture.

NOTES

1. Conversely, we shall assume that larger audiences are more heterogeneous. Here, "audience" means that *average* audience to which messages sent by a particular medium are directed. We acknowledge, but consider it the exception, that larger audiences are sometimes *less* heterogeneous.

2. Unless otherwise stated, all sources of data given in this article are: U.S. Department of Commerce, Bureau of the Census, *Statistical Abstract of the United States* (Washington, DC: Government Printing Office, 1960-72. This work will hereafter be referred to as *Abstract*, followed by the year of publication and table number.

3. The two-stage theory was implicitly assumed by both sides several years ago in the then prevalent controversy over mass culture. It is also assumed by several authors as a grounding rationale. See, for example, Charles S. Steinberg (ed.), *Mass Media and Communication* (New York: Hastings House, 1966), pp. ix-xiii; and Lewis Anthony Dexter and David Manning White (eds.), *People and Mass Communications* (New York: Free Press, 1964), pp. 3-10. Explicit statements of the two-stage theory may be found in Joseph Bensman and Bernard Rosenberg, "Mass Media and Mass Culture," in *America as a Mass Society,* ed. Phillip Olsen (New York: Free Press, 1963); and Melvin DeFleur, *Theories of Mass Communication,* 2nd ed. (New York: David McKay, 1970), chapters 1-4, 6.

4. The three-stage theory is part of a more general shift from two- to three-stage theories of social change. Colin Clark, *Conditions of Economic Progress* (London: Macmillan, 1957) has formulated a widely used three-stage theory of economic growth that has been extended to other areas of society by Daniel Bell, "The Measurement of Knowledge and Technology," in *Indicators of Social Change,* ed. Eleanor Bernert Sheldon and Wilbert E. Moore (New York: Russell Sage, 1968) and others as the "post-industrial society." The clearest statement of the three-stage theory as it applies to media growth, and the one used as the basis for this paper, is given by John Merrill and Ralph L. Lowenstein, *Media, Message, and Man* (New York: David McKay, 1971), pp. 33-44.

5. Since we are interested in relative growth, there is no need to correct for inflation using constant dollars.

6. In most cases, measures for volume are far from ideal. For example, our measure for the volume of communication by books, the number of books sold, does not take into account the degree to which the books were actually read.

7. *Abstract 1971,* table 153.

8. Merrill and Lowenstein, *Media, Message, and Man,* pp. 33-44; and Denis McQuail, *Toward a Sociology of Mass Communication* (London: Collier-Macmillan, 1969).

9. See, for example, Rolf B. Myersohn, "Social Research in Television," in *Mass Culture,* ed. Bernard Rosenberg and David Manning White, (New York: Free Press, 1957), pp. 348-349; and Sydney W. Head, "Some Intermedia Relationships," in Steinberg, *Mass Media.*

10. *Abstract 1971,* table 319.

11. Fritz Machlup, *The Production and Distribution of Knowledge* (Princeton, N.J.: Princeton University Press, 1962).

THE ECONOMIC CONNECTION: MASS MEDIA PROFITS, OWNERSHIP, AND PERFORMANCE

Arnold H. Ismach

A. J. Liebling, the *New Yorker's* acerbic press critic of the forties and fifties, once observed that the function of newspaper owners is to inform the public, but their role is to make money.

Lord Thomson of Fleet Street, the late Canadian entrepreneur who built a worldwide media empire, once characterized a commercial television license as "a license to print money."

If they were to make those comments today, someone might accuse them of understatement. But they serve to remind that the mass media, before anything else, are business enterprises. They don't exist primarily to keep the public informed of the world around it, but to produce profit for shareowners. And rarely have they been more successful in achieving that primary goal than in the mid-1970s.

Revenue and income have never been higher for both broadcast and print media than in the decade of the seventies. This was true even in the recession years of 1973-1975, when both newspapers and television outperformed the rest of the economy. New records were being established in 1976 and 1977 for all indicators of media prosperity.

The profitability of media enterprises is not in itself a cause for lamentation. Even the harshest appraisers of press performance acknowledge that journalism can serve society well only if its channels are financially stable. Press critic Ben Bagdikian recognized both the need for sound financial footing and its implications when he wrote:

In the United States, the role of the press is assumed to be an independent monitor of the environment, and since it cannot be an instrument of government, it has evolved as a private enterprise. This means that the press can survive only if it shows a profit, which influences its behavior and is a force shaping its future.[1]

Media spokesmen are even more strident in their defense of the profit orientation of publishers and broadcast owners. John H. Colburn, an executive of Landmark Communications, Inc. of Norfolk, Virginia, put it this way in addressing an industry conference:

Without a sound financial basis, newspapers could not spend the money they now do to cover the news of every aspect of society. And in covering that news, especially in the fields of politics, government and corporate affairs, newspapers must have the economic independence to resist the pressures that come from these, other special interest groups, and even their advertisers.[2]

If those premises are accepted, the question becomes not whether news media profitability is proper, but rather whether the jingling of the cash register is aiding or interfering with the clacking of the typewriter. In the 1970s an increasing number of journalism scholars, press critics, and lay observers are claiming interference.

Donald McDonald, editor of *The Center Magazine,* warned of one form of interference when he wrote, "Today, in some respects, the most...formidable threat to consistently responsible journalism comes not so much from government as from the mass media themselves."[3] McDonald was referring to two ominous trends that threaten the quality of reporting: the profit orientation of news organizations and the accelerating concentration of media ownership into fewer and fewer hands.

The concentration-of-ownership alarm has been sounded often and loudly in the 1970s as the growth of newspaper chains and media conglomerates reached epic proportions. One chain alone acquired twenty additional daily newspapers in 1977, a year in which seventy-two papers changed hands. In 1977, 60 percent of the nation's 1,756 dailies were members of 168 chains. The twelve largest newspaper groups accounted for 38 percent of the total daily newspaper circulation in the United States that year. Cross-media ownership (newspaper and broadcast properties held by the same company) included more than a third of the dailies and a fourth of the television stations as the decade began. The combined holdings of chains, cross-media owners, and media conglomerates encompassed three out of every five newspapers, almost four out of five television stations, and more than a third of all radio stations.

Concentration of such a large proportion of the nation's information outlets in the hands of relatively few owners poses many concerns. Among them is the fear that absentee ownership will ignore community needs in favor of maximizing profits. Bigness in itself is seen as a threat to First Amendment ideals. Large corporations, in this view, seek to avoid alienating any substantial portion of their publics and therefore avoid treating unpopular themes or upsetting concepts.

The economic realities of the mass media present other threats to journalistic performance as well. Public ownership of a growing number of once family-held properties raises a question of profit pressure from stockholders versus responsibility to news consumers. Will higher profits be devoted to improving journalistic quality—or to expanding capital growth and dividends? There is also the question of whether the current profitability of the mass media will survive as a long-term phenomenon. What will happen to the news function of the media if newspapers and commercial television as we know them today are supplanted by new and as yet unknown information dissemination systems? These questions are best addressed through an examination of the economic forces at work on the principal mass communications channels.

THE NEWSPAPER LEDGER

Herbert Brucker, the distinguished editor, looked at the explosive growth of commercial television in 1951 and predicted that the daily newspaper "may go the way of the horse and buggy."[4]

By 1972, the newspaper business had become the fifth largest employer of all United States manufacturing industries—and it wasn't making buggies.[5]

There's little doubt that newspaper publishing today is in sound financial condition. Except for a handful of big-city dailies beset by problems endemic to metropolitan regions, the newspaper ledger shows blue ink, and lots of it. There was a time when publishers, protected from public scrutiny because most newspapers were privately owned, claimed to be on the brink of genteel poverty, if not on the verge of bankruptcy. Some still play the same tune. Ben Bagdikian described the syndrome with insight, if derisively, when he wrote:

...American publishers have always felt obligated to pretend that they are an auxiliary of the Little Sisters of the Poor.... When it comes time for the publisher to bargain with his unions, he limps into the conference room sighing that he'll be lucky to pay last month's electric bill. Every

time a paper dies, publishers form a Greek chorus crying that they are all about to be struck dead by the tragic disease of "unionism" compounded by the terrifying constriction, the "cost-price squeeze." They have been known…to beg (or strongly suggest) that their local member of Congress vote for something alternatively called the Failing Newspaper Bill and the Newspaper Preservation Act, which exempts them from certain anti-trust laws and thus can save them all from a terminal disease. Or to make burnt offering to the President's Price Commission pleading that they need exemption from controls in order to make ends meet.[6]

With the growth of publicly owned publishing companies in the past decade, it has become more difficult to perpetuate the myth of newspaper poverty. Companies that are traded in the stock market must disclose certain financial data to the Securities and Exchange Commission (SEC), which makes the statistics public. In 1971, a recession year, the SEC disclosed that the average return on sales (after-tax profit) for the 500 leading corporations was 3.8 percent. The average for publicly traded newspapers that year was 7.9 percent—more than twice the average of the 500 largest corporations.

There are other indicators that confirm the profitability picture. *Editor & Publisher,* a trade magazine, reports annually on the financial performance of theoretical "average" papers in different circulation categories. In 1970, the hypothetical paper with a circulation of 250,000 showed a pretax profit of 23.5 percent. In 1971, it was 23.2 percent. In 1976, the magazine reported on the balance sheet of a 255,000-circulation daily that experienced a poor year because of the loss of a major advertiser and other

problems. It still showed a profit of 17.8 percent before taxes.[7]

The income picture is as bright or brighter for small dailies. Kidder, Peabody & Company, an investment banking firm, developed composite balance sheets in 1972 for newspapers of different sizes.[8] The 35,000-circulation paper showed a pretax profit of 21.6 percent on revenues of $3.5 million. This compares to the 23.2 percent return recorded for metropolitan dailies. All indications point to pretax income in the 20 percent range for most daily newspapers, a figure more than double that for the rest of U.S. industry.

The present level of newspaper affluence was achieved in the face of competition from a new and powerful medium, commercial television. In 1950, when television was in its infancy, the newspaper share of total U.S. advertising expenditures was 36 percent, and television's was less than 5 percent. By 1975, television's share of ad revenues had climbed to 19 percent, and newspaper's declined to 30 percent. But in dollars, newspaper advertising revenue topped an estimated $10 billion by 1977, more than three times its 1950 total. Newspapers had developed expanded sources of local revenue (for example, classified advertising) to compensate for the loss of national-advertiser dollars to television. Some industry projections have newspapers retaining their 30 percent share of total advertising dollars through the mid-1980s and television increasing its percentage to 22 at the expense of other media.[9]

Despite this sanguine picture of the newspaper industry as a money machine, owners aren't complacent. Throughout the 1970s, executives have worried privately about declining circulation and readership and about an unending upward spiral in material and labor costs. By 1976, many of them were doing their worrying in public. Some even speculated that the giant metropolitan daily, at least as we know it today, will disappear by the end of the century.

Newspaper revenues have increased in the face of what has been a net decline in readership since the 1940s. Circulation reached an all-time high of 63 million in 1973 but dropped to 61.2 million by 1976. Circulation, however, is not readership. Newspaper sales, by every available measure, have lagged far behind population growth in the United States since 1950. For every 100 households in the nation, 111 papers were sold each day in 1960. By 1973, the figure had dropped to 92. For every 100 families in 1960, 130 papers were sold daily. By 1973, it was down to 116. And for every 100 persons in the United States in 1960, there were 33 papers sold. In 1973, the figure was 30.[10]

Ominously, readership declines were recorded not only in the young-adult age group (18-24), but also in the highly marketable middle-aged group (35-49). Advertisers are attracted not only by the total audience delivered by a medium, but also by characteristics of that audience. The high purchasing power of family groups in the middle years is an attribute sought by advertisers. If they can't obtain it in one medium, they will seek another.

Time spent reading newspapers is also declining. Stable at about 37 minutes a day per adult reader for many years, the average, media experts now predict, will drop in the decade ahead to 32 minutes per day.[11] This is another factor that may influence audience-conscious advertisers.

The circulation losses of the second half of the century can be traced largely to the death of dozens of large-city dailies, beset by competition and the resultant decline in advertising revenue, by rising production costs, and by urban delivery problems, among other factors. Nonmetropolitan dailies in monopoly markets haven't suffered as much from these obstacles. But the decline in reader loyalty affects smaller as well as larger newspapers.

Compounding the crisis of the vanishing reader have been rapidly increasing labor and material costs and the specter of new technology ultimately providing substitute information sources for present newspaper consumers. Salaries in the field, once considered low for semiprofessional work, are now considerably higher. Experienced reporters on metropolitan newspapers can expect to earn from $18,000 to $24,000 a year. As a labor-intensive industry, newspaper publishing allots 30 to 55 percent of its budget to employees, compared to 25 percent for industry in general.

Newsprint is the second largest expense for newspapers, accounting for about a fourth of the cost of production. And newsprint prices have soared in the past two decades. They reached $300 a ton in 1977, almost double what they were five years earlier. Ink prices have also risen sharply, tied as they are to the price of petroleum. With advertising linage on the rise, creating increased demand for both newsprint and ink, publishers have kept pace only by increasing advertising and circulation rates.

There is a limit to rate increases, however, since advertisers may find other media more cost-efficient at some point, and readers may discover that newspapers have become an expendable high-budget item. The most troublesome problem, however, remains the growing public disaffection with newspapers, compounded by the growth of alternative information sources. Radio, and later television, were two such alternative sources that newspaper owners feared, but both threats have been weathered. The growth of specialized publications to serve consumers and the expected development of cable television, however, may be more intractable threats.

Both academic and industry research in recent years indicates that traditional newspaper content has become less relevant, and thus less important, to the average citizen. Heavily oriented to public affairs coverage, the traditional newspaper was directed to elite, rather than mass, audiences. The increasingly pluralistic urban population, with diverse interests and the affluence to satisfy those interests, also served to make the newspaper a less useful commodity than it once may have been. People can turn to special-interest magazines to get information that they consider important. Community newspapers in urban areas can provide bread-and-butter local news that the large dailies no longer can afford to gather or to publish. Radio and television provide news summaries that apparently satisfy the appetites of many consumers for information about the nation and the world.

It appeared to some researchers, in fact, that advertising content was perhaps the strongest reason some people had for continuing as subscribers and readers. And that, too, might end some day if advertisers find less costly methods to reach their markets. Direct mail, for example, has attracted department store merchandisers as a supplement to, and sometimes a substitute for, newspaper advertising. Food markets, a bedrock advertising source for newspapers, have been devoting an increasing portion of their budgets to local television.

Cable television, on the verge of emerging as a major alternative medium for a decade, still is expected by media experts to "arrive" in the near future. With its large channel capacity and the potential for interactive, two-way communication with subscribers, cable may be the force that finally upsets the newspaper survival record. Two-way cable subscribers, according to some scenarios, will be able to do their banking, keep family records, make purchases, and get custom-ordered news and information items delivered to them electronically while sitting at their home consoles.

In this way, the mass product that all newspaper readers and television viewers now must accept can be replaced by specific items that consumers choose to match their own personal interests and needs. There will be no need to pay for a sports section or an entertainment page that the consumer may not want. Such a system would, in effect, give the news consumer an opportunity to create a newspaper tailor-made to personal interests—something that existing mass media technology can not provide.

For metropolitan newspapers, the awesome array of problems just described doesn't include some that are even more pressing. The rise in apartment living makes home delivery more difficult. Congested traffic in large cities creates costly headaches for circulation managers. The exodus of central city residents to the suburbs, weakening readership ties to the metro daily, is still another obstacle.

The changing ethnic and racial composition of some major cities has also upset circulation expectations based on population alone. Leo Bogart, general manager of the Newspaper Advertising Bureau, considers the influx of Black, Chicano, and Puerto Rican immigrants as a major factor in metropolitan circulation losses. Bogart likens them to the waves of European immigrants in the early part of the century, who could not read English. Eventually, they became newspaper buyers. He predicts that the new immigrants "will be acculturated as their predecessors were, and as they are brought closer to the mainstream levels of income and education, they will become regular newspaper readers."[12]

In examining prospects for metropolitan dailies over the long term, Bogart offers five suggestions to newspaper managements to halt further erosion:

1. Change editorial content to more closely match the interests of upcoming generations.

2. Devote a greater percentage of news content to subjects of interest to women.

3. Raise the sophistication quotient of reporting and content to match the levels of an increasingly better educated audience.

4. Encourage the conversion of central city minorities to newspaper reading.

5. Improve circulation techniques and reduce delivery failures.[13]

Bogart's assessment of the mismatch between newspaper content and reader interests is shared by media researcher Gerald L. Grotta. If the newspaper as we know it is to survive, Grotta argues, publishers and editors must learn to define their products in relation to the market. At the moment, he wrote in 1974, most don't seem to have a clear view of what their customers want or need.[14] There are signs, however, that the market awareness Grotta urges is reaching the board rooms and newsrooms of American newspapers.

Newspaper owners have responded in two ways to the perils of rising production costs and slipping readership. They have invested heavily in new budget-cutting technology and have launched studies to find out what is needed to attract the elusive reader. The results of the technology revolution are already evident. If parallel gains are achieved through a content revolution, speculation about the demise of the newspaper may be premature.

The most apparent change in the industry has been the computerization of the typesetting and printing processes. It has been a technological turnaround on a scale unprecedented in journalism history. Printing methods changed little from the invention of the Linotype machine in 1884 until about 1960. In the decade that followed, newspapers invested more than $2 billion in new equipment and plant modernization. By the mid-1970s, more than half of the nation's dailies had converted to photocomposition, eliminating the Linotype and the use of hot metal. Offset printing, using thin photographic plates instead of the cast-metal sterotype process, was employed by more than 60 percent and rising.

The move to automation reached into the newsroom as well, with reporters and editors feeding stories and headlines directly to computers via video display terminals or optical scanning devices. From computer storage, the copy (news or advertising) is fed directly to automatic phototypesetting machines. Eliminated are the Linotype or keypunch operator and the proofreader.

Cost savings have been immense. Workforce reductions of as much as 50 percent have been experienced by some newspapers. One medium-sized daily found that by investing $89,000 in an optical scanner, it could eliminate twelve people who were paid $120,000 yearly for punching stories onto tape. Investment in newsroom computer terminals can be recouped through salary savings in 12 to 30 months, according to one industry analyst.

Further improvements are on the horizon. Engineers are close to perfecting automatic page makeup and platemaking equipment through which an editor can design a newspaper page on a video terminal, press a button, and have a press-ready plate produced automatically. Even the printing plate itself may fall to technology. Ink-jet devices, in which computers govern the formation of letters and shapes sprayed by ink jets onto moving newsprint, is expected to be perfected by the early 1980s.

Outside the realm of equipment, newspaper managers have moved in several new directions to reinforce their profit positions. Some of the major thrusts include:

1. Modern fiscal planning, budget control, and management-by-objectives have come to an industry that for generations has functioned by seat-of-the-pants direction. The *New York Times,* for example, didn't have a written budget to guide its operations until the early 1960s. Publishers are now hiring graduates of business schools as management

executives, supplanting those who rose "through the ranks" of the newsroom or advertising department.

2. Facing competition from suburban weeklies and from free-circulation and controlled-circulation (voluntary payment) newspapers, some publishers have moved into these ventures themselves. Some have also sought to solidify their positions with advertisers by providing "total market coverage"—delivering advertising messages to the homes of nonsubscribers by carrier or mail. Other newspapers are offering segmented distribution of advertising messages. In this way, advertisers can reach certain portions of the total audience selectively, without paying for the entire press run.

3. Unproductive facets of newspaper operations are being excised, such as circulation to geographic regions that are unprofitable because of high distribution costs and low appeal to local advertisers. Newspaper owners who publish morning and evening newspapers in the same community are increasingly turning to combined newspapers on Saturdays as a cost-saving move, and some have combined both papers through the week.

All these efforts are for naught unless newspapers manage to retain their readers, of course. Perhaps for this reason, newsroom budgets haven't been reduced by most publishers, and in some cases they have been enriched. Typically, editorial departments receive about 10 percent of a newspaper's budget and 40 percent of its space for news. With the realization that readership is the cornerstone of continued prosperity, the industry is engaged in efforts such as these:

1. Publication of special "zoned" editions for suburban communities, giving readers local news and advertising.

2. Special sections geared to the personal interests of readers—entertainment, recreation and leisure, life-style, and family concerns. These sections contain "soft" features with a service, or consumer-utility,

quality, as opposed to "hard" news found in the rest of the paper. Some of the largest news organizations have reduced public affairs coverage, including foreign correspondence, in the belief that only a minority of readers seek such information.

3. Intensive research into the still-unsolved riddle of what the public wants in newspapers. An industry-wide research effort was launched by more than twenty trade organizations in 1977 to probe reader behavior. It was financed by a fund of more than $1 million. Individual newspapers have also intensified their own research efforts, converting the findings into content and format changes.

4. A few newspapers are exploring the possibilities of "tailor-made" newspapers, in which consumers can "build" their own reading package from special sections on topics that interest them, avoiding buying sections in which they have little or no interest. This, of course, approaches the advantage of two-way cable communication described earlier.

5. Large numbers of newspapers are involved in the "newspaper in the classroom" program, in which newspapers and study materials are provided to public schools. The hope is that the newspaper reading habit will be instilled at an early age.

Taken together, these efforts represent recognition by an industry that is at the peak of its earning power, that the communication environment is changing. Studies have shown that many adults don't consider today's newspapers as essential. That stark fact has led the industry on a chase for formulas to reverse the trend. "There never has been a time when as much experimentation was going on in newspaper format and content," said the Advertising Bureau's Leo Bogart in 1977.[15]

If the experiments fail, newspaper owners will still have something to fall back on, however. Any substitute system of news delivery, such as two-way cable, will require a system of news gathering. Newspapers already have such a system in place. And just in case, many newspapers are also investing heavily in cable systems of their own.

THE BROADCAST LEDGER

On the basis of return per dollar of investment, television stations are more profitable than newspapers. They probably are more profitable than any other enterprise, short of Arizona land sales and the illicit drug trade. Some small stations earn only a modest profit or lose money. But if advertising sales exceed $500,000 a year, pretax profits are in the vicinity of 15 percent. If sales are over $1.5 million a year, profits generally top 20 percent. Many stations earn more than that.

This enviable profit condition is achieved with little invested capital. Compared to manufacturing industries, start-up costs for a station are low—sometimes as little as a million dollars. Yet a television station in a major market may sell for $20 million and more. The buyer isn't paying that sum for color cameras and file cabinets—the station's equity—but for the right to reach a certain audience. The price is for the station's broadcast license.

Therein lies the reason for television's profitability. With a finite number of licenses available, station owners enjoy a partial monopoly. Regulation by the federal government creates the monoply situation. In 1976, there were 509 commercial VHF stations and 190 commercial UHF stations, the total only 40 percent of the number of daily newspapers in the country. Yet television advertising revenue was 60 percent of that taken by newspapers.

As Owen, Beebe, and Manning point out in their book, *Television Economics,* it is a serious mistake to assume that stations are in business to produce programs.[16] They are in the business of producing audiences, which are then sold to advertisers. With the size of the television audience increasing, station owners have no trouble attracting advertisers.

There were 70.5 million households with at least one television set in 1976. That set was turned on an average of 6½ hours each day (and is expected to reach almost 7 hours by 1985).[17] With audiences of that size and devotion, advertisers line up far in advance to buy commercial time. They have to: in 1976, available time on popular evening network programs was booked more than a year in advance. That was a year in which networks increased their advertising rates 30 percent and in which overall industry revenue rose 20 percent. Even in the recession years that preceded 1976, revenue records were established. These conditions prompted some advertisers to talk in 1977 about starting a fourth network, or an occasional network, to make time available at lower rates. They would do this by linking the nation's nonnetwork stations, which operate in communities that cover nearly 60 percent of all households (the networks reach 95 percent). It didn't happen in 1977, but the potential remains.

Despite the growth of independents, television in the 1970s was still a network game, and it was the networks themselves and not their affiliate stations that set the rules. The three national networks—ABC, CBS, and NBC—dominate television just as General Motors, Ford, and Chrysler dominate the American auto industry—and there are no German imports in television broadcasting. The networks, with the five VHF stations each is permitted to own, command more than 50 percent of the industry's gross revenue and more than 40 percent of its net profits.

Actually, the networks earn even more, because income from syndication of rerun series and sales of programs to other countries are not reflected in these figures.

Although the networks have the upper hand in dealing with affiliate stations, they must be responsive in some degree to their needs and desires. Although network affiliation is the local station's biggest asset, other than its license, the networks need the affiliates to create the largest national market possible. The networks sell this national market to advertisers, who sometimes pay more than $100,000 a minute to reach it.

Networks and stations don't always seek the largest audiences. Programs can be expensive, and because of this cost factor, it may be inefficient to produce programs that produce larger audiences. Sometimes a weak program may be more profitable, because its production costs are low. Stations also run programs that are not profitable at all—public affairs documentaries, religious programs, and others that draw small audiences. This is done to satisfy federal requirements for public service and to assure favorable action at license renewal time.

The amount of such programming is minimal, however. Most public service shows appear during "ghetto" time periods, such as Sunday mornings or late at night. In the past decade, public affairs documentaries have occupied less than 4 percent of available prime-time evening schedules. This lack of public affairs investment testifies mutely to the fact that television is considered, by both its audiences and the industry, as an entertainment rather than an information medium. Public affairs programs, even the nightly news, do not draw the audiences that sitcoms or game shows command. Despite industry studies showing that almost one-third of the adult audience says it obtains *all* of its news about the world from television and that almost two-thirds says it gets most of its news from television, public affairs is a relatively minor concern for most station managers.

The networks don't produce many programs, other than news, public affairs, and sports. Most of what they transmit to their affiliates over leased telephone company lines comes from outside producers and film companies. Affiliates receive about 30 percent of the revenue the networks receive for commercials and also can sell some commercial time locally on each network show. Thus, the networks serve as brokers for the affiliates, but they are brokers with the upper hand.

Network domination may be reduced in the future, by technological change and by regulation. The Federal Communications Commission (FCC), which issues broadcasting licenses and sets rules governing the operation of television and radio stations, has already intervened to reduce the amount of network programing that affiliates are required to carry. Since networks receive nothing from nonnetwork shows aired by affiliates, this has already dented their profit position.

Other influences that may lessen network dominance include direct transmission of programs to independent stations by satellite on a common-carrier basis. This would enable program suppliers other than the networks to gain the same advantage networks now enjoy—simultaneous distribution. Independent program syndicators now must rely on ground and air transportation to distribute film to stations. Despite that disadvantage, syndicators have made steady gains. The syndication success of *Mary Hartman, Mary Hartman* in the 1976-77 season proved the feasibility of independent distribution.

The threat that sends chills through commercial television board rooms, however—network, affiliate, and independent alike—is not syndication but cable television. Just as newspaper owners fear loss of their audiences to alternative media, television broadcasters see cable, particularly pay TV, as the enemy. Broadcast owners don't face the same cost-price squeeze that has confronted newspapers, however, nor do they stand alone in confronting the enemy: They have government on their side.

At its inception, cable television was a boon to commercial broadcasters. It provided television reception in areas where commercial signals were too weak for ordinary home antennas. The potential of cable television soon became apparent, and that potential was not to serve as a hod carrier to commercial television but as a rival. Cable systems can carry a far greater number of channels then are available through existing over-the-air systems.

This means that consumers could choose from ten or twenty or forty different programs instead of the half-dozen available in most urban markets. Indeed, new cable systems installed in the 1970s have been required to provide the multichannel capacity and to make some of those channels available to the public. If the television audience were to be divided into forty parts, instead of three or six, then the large audiences now so attractive to advertisers on commercial television would be no more. Television's principal advantage as a sales medium would be significantly diminished.

Subscriber, or pay, television carries the same threat. In theory, subscriber systems would offer consumers special programming not now available on commercial television, for a fee. Plays, sporting events, concerts, and the like would be purchased at prices considerably lower than a single ticket to those events. Conceivably, this could draw large chunks of the audience away from commercial stations.

Thus far, neither cable nor subscriber systems have arrived at these lofty competitive positions. Cable was wired into about 12 million homes by 1977, only 17 percent of all TV households. In the top twenty-five markets, the figure was considerably lower. Subscriber television was operational only in a few test markets. Part of the reason for the retarded development was cost. Cable systems could be installed inexpensively in rural areas and small towns, but wiring costs in metropolitan regions was ten times as expensive—as much as $80,000 per mile. Most pay TV systems rely on cable connections, although a few systems employ over-the-air technology.

The principal reason for cable's slow growth, however, has been the massed opposition of the commercial television industry. Through extensive lobbying of both Congress and the FCC, over-the-air interests have been able to thwart cable systems in their quest for markets and programs. In the absence of regulation by Congress, the FCC stepped into the cable regulation void in the 1960s. It did this on the premise that cable can compete with TV stations for profits and thereby reduce the stations' ability to do public service programming. The FCC's mission is to assure public service by broadcasters.

Government regulatory agencies have historically protected obsolete systems against innovation. In the case of the FCC, it acted from the start to retard the growth of cable systems to protect the existing television monopoly from competition.[18] Cable systems, for example, were not permitted to bring in distant signals that would compete with the same programming on local stations. Delays in granting operating permission for subscriber television systems were notorious, as well as limitations on the types of programming that might be offered.

Although the battle is not over, it appears that cable and subscriber systems are gradually winning the right to enter the marketplace on more equal footing. Authorizations for several subscriber transmission systems were granted in 1976, and more favorable programing conditions were granted to cable systems. Most industry analysts expect steady but inexorable growth into the 1980s. The Cox Broadcasting Co. survey predicted that by 1985 cable will reach 29 percent of the nation's households, that at least half of all newly installed cable systems will have two-way capability, and that almost all of the top twenty-five markets will have operational wired pay-TV systems.[19]

This leaves commercial broadcasters with some of the same unease that newspaper owners feel today. Technology is changing existing conditions because of the imperatives of financial incentive and consumer demand. Just as radio has survived the onslaught of commercial television by becoming a more specialized medium (there were more than 7,000 commercial AM and FM stations in 1976, each with program content targeted to a specialized audience), over-the-air television may someday evolve into a more limited medium.

Broadcast owners, too, are hedging their bets. Many have invested in cable systems (although the FCC prohibits joint station and cable ownership in the same community). Regulations prevent companies from owning more than seven television stations (only five VHF), seven AM stations, and seven FM stations. Even though twenty-one broadcast properties make an impressive package, surplus capital requires an outlet, and some of the larger industry groups are turning to ventures outside of broadcasting. The networks themselves are diversified ventures, with NBC, a subsidiary of giant RCA, the largest. CBS and ABC, too, are engaged in interprises as diverse as movie theater ownership, food processing, record manufacture, and publishing. In 1975, a "bad" year, the networks reported net profits ranging from $29 million to $106 million. It appears unlikely that with such resources the industry will allow itself to fall behind in the race for audiences and dollars.

CONCENTRATION OF OWNERSHIP

At the turn of the century, there were eight newspaper chains in the United States, representing an estimated 10 percent of the circulation of the nation's approximately 2,200 dailies.[21] In 1945, a total of 76 newspaper chains controlled 42 percent of the daily circulation and 54 percent of the Sunday circulation. And by 1977, there were 168 groups operating 1,061 newspapers—60 percent of the 1,756 dailies in the country. These chain newspapers accounted for more

than seven out of every ten papers sold. (Of course, group ownership and circulation figures fluctuate up or down from month to month, as newspapers and chains are bought and sold in the marketplace.)

Although the number of chain operations has grown, a small number dominate the field. The four largest newspaper groups sell one out of five papers bought each day. The twelve largest chains controlled 38 percent of the circulation in 1976, and the twenty-five largest, 52 percent.

In 1920 there were about 552 cities in the United States with competing newspapers. In 1977 there were 39, and only a handful of those were in large cities. The reduction in newspaper voices hasn't been balanced by the growth of radio and television, even if those media are considered journalistically equivalent. At the start of the 1970s, cross-media owners (those with both newspaper and broadcast properties) controlled 36 percent of the dailies, 25 percent of the television stations and 18 percent of the radio stations. The combined holdings of groups, cross-media owners, and media conglomerates embraced 58 percent of daily newspapers, 77 percent of television stations, and 66 percent of radio stations.

A Justice Department study in the early 1970s showed that in each of fifty major urban markets, a single owner controlled two or more broadcast outlets and/or at least one TV station plus one daily newspaper. In several markets, a newspaper chain or dominant newspaper owned network-affiliated TV, AM, and FM stations. In 1970, according to FCC records, 231 of the nation's dailies were owned by broadcast licensees in the same city.[22]

The statistics may be dulling, but to some they are also alarming. The principal outlets of mass communication in America are falling into fewer and fewer hands. In a nation founded on the principles of free and diverse speech, the specter of an information oligarchy suddenly seems real. Politicians, social commentators, and even some figures within media organizations are sounding alarms.

Congressman Morris Udall of Arizona is one who laments the diminishing number of media voices. "I dread the day," he said in

1977, "when all American newspapers look alike, and read alike, and when there won't be much more difference in the daily newspapers in Topeka and New York than there is in ... a Big Mac."[23] Udall did more than complain. He introduced a bill calling for a study commission to examine the effects of concentration in basic industries, including publishing and communications.

Some fear that government can do little about existing concentration of ownership in the mass media, however. The process has gone too far, media critic Ben Bagdikian believes. Bagdikian, communications scholar Donald McDonald, syndicated columnist Kevin Phillips, and others who bemoan the trend toward greater concentration have instead recommended various palliatives that fall short of breaking up the existing media groups.

Bagdikian, for example, suggests public disclosure of the names of major shareholders in each media outlet, so that consumers will know the sources of control. He also urges greater editorial control on media organizations by journalists, including the power to elect their own editors.[24] McDonald also calls for strengthening the autonomy of working journalists, giving them sufficient job security to encourage independent judgment.[25] In addition, he calls for government intervention to facilitate the development of new and competitive media outlets, deconcentration of media ownership through a ban on cross-ownership, and industry or government action to open existing channels to the public. Creation of new media outlets in an age of multimillion-dollar enterprises, McDonald contends, would require some form of subsidy. Several Western democracies subsidize their print or broadcast media, but the prospect of government control accompanying government aid frightens many media watchers in the United States.

Phillips, in his examination of media concentration, concludes that, of the several approaches possible to control the growth of chains, the antitrust avenue is most likely to succeed.[26] There is no First Amendment barrier, he asserts, to the regulation of trusts.

There have been mixed signals thus far regarding the federal government's inclination to intervene. Most aggressive in a weak field has been the Justice Department. Some would say it has tiptoed gingerly in the media arena, but Justice has threatened antitrust action against cross-ownership and has itself pressed divestiture actions against purchasers who threaten geographic monopoly. That kind of pressure has apparently persuaded a reluctant FCC to impose some restrictions on cross-ownership by broadcast, newspaper, and cable operators. The regulations to date have not applied to geographically separate markets or to existing combinations.

The courts have had little opportunity to interpret the law in this area, although the U.S. Circuit Court of Appeals in Washington DC directed the FCC in 1977 to adopt rules prohibiting common ownership of a newspaper and broadcasting station in the same city unless such joint ownership is in the public interest.[27] The FCC appealed the ruling to the Supreme Court, adding support to the accusation by critics that the commission functions as a defender of commercial interests rather than as a regulator of those interests on behalf of the public.

Finally, the Congress has shown its disinclination to interfere with the profitable state of media concentration. In 1971 it adopted the Newspaper Preservation Act, which sanctified joint operating agreements for newspapers in twenty-two cities. This allowed them to share production, business, and advertising facilities, which otherwise might have been in violation of antitrust laws.

Meanwhile, the big grow bigger. It was noted earlier that seventy-two newspapers changed hands in 1976. Most of them went to chain owners or media conglomerates. The rush to chain ownership that the Commission on Freedom of the Press warned against in 1947, and that others have documented since, continued unabated in the late 1970s. And as profitable independent newspapers became scarce, the media giants began to acquire each other.

The allure of newspapers and broadcast stations as targets of acquisition is simple to understand: they make lots of money. Bagdikian has noted that, like beach-front property and other limited commodities, their value is bound to increase. Existing chains and conglomerates, swimming in surplus earnings that demand investment, look first to the media. Their existing management expertise and the economies of scale possible through chain purchasing, production, and accounting operations make horizontal expansion attractive. The rationale for newspapers acquiring other newspapers, especially in monopoly circumstances, was stated eloquently by A. J. Liebling almost two decades ago:

The point is, that even when two, or several competing newspapers in a town are both, or all, making money, it is vastly to the advantage of one to buy out the others, establish a monopoly in selling advertising, and benefit from the "operating economies" of one plant, one staff, and exactly as much news coverage as the publisher chooses to give. The advertisers must have him anyway, and the readers have no other pabulum. He will get all the income for a fraction of the outlay, so he can afford to pay a price for his competitor's paper far beyond what it might be worth to a buyer from outside, who would continue to operate it competitively.[28]

The day when such agreeable conditions existed has largely disappeared, of course. Leibling's scenario was carried out in city after city. There are few competing papers remaining, and medium-sized independent ownerships are also a vanishing species. Most of the independent dailies left today are under 10,000 circulation, with a cash flow too small to attract many chain operators. The desirable independents remaining—small and medium-sized dailies in noncompetitive markets—are courted by acquisition-hungry groups as energetically as sailors chasing girls in a new port. It isn't unusual to find papers selling at forty to sixty times earnings—much higher than in typical industrial acquisitions—although a more typical ratio may be twenty to twenty-five times earnings.

Rupert Murdoch, the Australian press tycoon who invaded the U.S. market in the 1970s, has an explanation for the willingness to pay high prices for profitable newspapers: "You pay three times the revenue because it's a monopoly and a license to steal money forever."[29]

It isn't difficult to understand why chains seek to acquire media properties: surplus capital and the lure of high profits. But why would independent owners wish to sell off their profitable properties? The explanation is largely a creature of inheritance tax laws. With estate taxes above 70 percent in the highest brackets, the paper would have to be sold anyway after the death of the owner. By selling earlier, the income (if taken as cash) is taxed at the low capital-gains rate of 25 percent. The sale also frees family members with no interest in newspaper management to pursue other interests. When the chains come around, checkbook in hand, their offers are often impossible to refuse.

Tax laws also encourage media groups to expand. If profits are paid out as dividends, they are taxed twice, first at the corporate rate of 50 percent and again as individual income to stockholders. The less costly option is to put earnings back into expansion or acquisitions. The typical newspaper is also valuable to a buyer because of tax regulations governing plant depreciation. The new owner may start the depreciation process over again on the basis of new market value and replacement cost, and that can mean huge tax savings.[30]

The bidding war among chains chasing high-profit independents is also fueled by deteriorating metropolitan operations. *Business Week*, examining the situation in 1977, explained:

With cost pressures closing in on major metropolitan dailies, Times Mirror, Gannett, New York Times Co. and other publishing companies are buying up small- and medium-sized chains as well as independent newspapers to relieve a worsening profit squeeze, get the growth they need, and, above all, pick up some good properties before they are gone.[31]

First choice for the chains is still the independent daily in a noncompetitive market. Times-Mirror Vice Chairman Otis Chandler explained why in a revealing statement that is less pungent but more descriptive than Murdoch's confession: "It gives you a franchise to do what you want with profitability. You can engineer your profits. You can control expenses and generate revenues almost arbitrarily."[32]

Such candor explains why Times-Mirror bid against S. I. Newhouse for Booth Newspapers, Inc., a group of eight Michigan dailies and the Sunday magazine supplement, *Parade*. Newhouse won out in 1977 by paying $305 million, reputedly the largest deal in newspaper history. About the same time, the Gannett group paid a reported $173 million for the Speidel chain of thirteen midwestern and western dailies. A grasp of the value that chains place on small dailies may be seen in another Gannett acquisition: It reportedly paid $10 million for the 9,000-circulation *Valley News Dispatch* in western Pennsylvania.

Gannett became the nation's largest chain in 1977 in terms of number of newspapers. Its letterhead included 73 papers in twenty-eight states. When Gannett became a public company in 1967, it had twenty-nine newspapers in 5 states. Gross revenues were $110 million. In 1977 the company estimated that revenues would exceed $500 million. Profits have followed the same curve, from $23 million in 1967 to $75 million in 1975, before taxes.

Trailing Gannett in total number of papers as 1977 began was the Thomson group, with 57; Knight-Ridder, 34; Walls, 32; and Newhouse, 30. In terms of circulation, however, the leader was Knight-Ridder, with 3.72 million in daily sales fueled by papers in Detroit, Philadelphia, Miami, St. Paul, Long Beach, and San Jose. Second in circulation were the Newhouse newspapers, with 3.53 million; the Chicago *Tribune,* with 2.99 million, and Gannett, with 2.94 million. They were followed by Times-Mirror, Dow Jones, Hearst, Cox Newspapers, and the New York Times Company.[33]

In terms of revenues, some of the chains are dwarfed by conglomerates that also own media properties. RCA, with holdings in broadcasting, book publishing, manufacturing, foods, and auto rentals, among others, had revenues of $5.32 billion in 1976.[34] CBS, through its broadcasting, publishing, recreation, and manufacturing enterprises, reported 1976 sales of $2.23 billion. Time, Inc. had 1976 sales of $1.03 billion from magazines, books, films, cable television, broadcasting, and other ventures. Times-Mirror, heavily concentrated in publishing and forest products, was just a step behind with revenues of $964 million. Gannett, the largest of the chains, was down the sales list with sales of $413 million, principally from its newspaper operations.

The issue, of course, is not the bigness or the profitability of the chains and conglomerates, but rather the effect of such concentration on the information diet of the American public. On that question, there is neither a definitive answer nor general agreement. Theoretically, the high profit levels should insure high-quality news operations for both print and broadcast media. Some chains are, in fact, known to bring new dollars and high editorial standards to their acquisitions (for example, Times-Mirror and Gannett). Others, such as Thomson and Newhouse, have reputations for cutting editorial budgets and considering only the bottom line of the profit and loss statement.

The late Lord Thomson was once quoted as saying: "I buy newspapers to make money to buy more newspapers to make more money. As for editorial content, that's the stuff you separate the ads with."[35]

In monopoly situations, managements are under no compulsion to reinvest profits in product improvement. "Instead," writes Bagdikian, "they are under pressure to siphon off local profits to the parent corporation for expansion into other product lines."[36]

Another danger of chain operation is the possible uniformity of editorial matter—Congressman Udall's "Big Mac" syndrome. Most chain owners contend that each of their newspapers has editorial independence. But as some studies have found, this varies from chain to chain. Editorial integrity may be compromised, too, by the knowledge that almost any target of newspaper criticism may in some way be related to an interest group within a large conglomerate.

One indication of the effect of chain ownership on editorial quality would be the reaction of employees, who are closest to the operation. Bagdikian, a frequent critic of chains, acknowledges wide variation on this question. But he concludes that, with some notable exceptions, there is usually less satisfaction among the staffs of newspapers that have been bought by chains.

In such a speculative area, fears may have as much validity as reality. At one time, newspapers were bought or founded to acquire political power for their owners. Now the likely reason is the desire to make money. But the potential for political power exists on a scale larger than before. In its final verdict on chain ownership, society may have to ask if it wants one corporate board of directors controlling newspapers in twenty-eight states (as in the case of Gannett). Those states have fifty-six U.S. Senators among them, and one may ask how they might vote in a matter involving Gannett interests. The same question may be asked about other chains whose geographic reach approaches that of Gannett.

THE SHAPE
OF THE FUTURE

Richard Maisel, in "The Decline of the Mass Media" (in Part Two, p. 233), predicts the economic decline of newspapers and television in an age when new and alternative forms of communication are becoming available. The managers of our mass media systems are acting as if they believed him. Some are attempting to capitalize on the trend toward specialized information sources. Others are seeking ways to retain audiences. Their responses, however, may not be adequate to the task.

Television fears the competition of cable systems, particularly subscription TV. Broadcasters have attempted to block, through political maneuvers, cable's opportunity to compete. Television's managers have also neglected, in their desire to maximize audiences and therefore profits, the diverse programing desires of a pluralistic audience. This may lead to more intervention by government to modify programing, or, more likely, to the weaning away of dissatisfied portions of the audience by media that can satisfy their desires.

Radio, small in comparison to TV or newspapers, appears secure at this time. Its unique role as provider of music, weather, and headline news for specific segments of a nation in motion does not seem likely to be usurped by another medium just yet.

Newspapers are perhaps in the most precarious position. Some authorities, however, predict the long-term survival of the newspaper. A study by the Battelle Memorial Institute in 1971 forecast growth in circulation to between 82 and 93 million by 1985.[37] Joseph M. Ungaro, a Gannett executive, forecast a 50 percent increase in the number of daily newspapers by 1987.[38] Newspaper managements are attempting to make these predictions come true through an array of measures. The most successful to date has been cost-cutting through use of new printing methods. The greatest hopes for long-term success, though, are placed in marketing approaches to newspaper content and packaging.

Research has come into its own in the

newsrooms of America, often to the dismay of practicing journalists. Service-oriented stories are blossoming in papers large and small: how to manage your budget, the eleven best pizza parlors in town, techniques for getting along with your spouse (or your friends or yourself), how to keep fit and happy at forty. Reporters and editors, faced with the imperative of attracting an audience no longer loyal to their traditional efforts, grumble about the change in focus. They insist that governmental news coverage, once the staple of the newspaper, should not be sacrificed to consumer service and entertainment froth. As a solution to declining readership, they say, the new orientation is like throwing the baby out with the bath water.

Publishing tycoon Rupert Murdoch put the argument starkly in a speech to newspaper executives in 1977:

Too many newspapers the world over seem more preoccupied with covering the machinery of government than the lives of the governed. Too often they sppear to be engaged in solemn dialogue with themselves. Too often the tedium is the message.[39]

Few in management or the newsroom appear to have seriously confronted the possibility that conventional public affairs coverage really *isn't* important, that it has little value to citizens. Perhaps research efforts will next be directed to developing methods to change public affairs reporting so that people are helped to perceive its relevance to themselves. This may mean that many of the internal, procedural aspects of governmental operations that now make up a significant portion of the news budget should be abandoned. Instead of a dry jumble of unrelated events, public affairs information may be presented in a holistic, personally pertinent form. Such a change would require truly revolutionary changes in the traditional norms of journalistic belief and practice, however.

Granted the possibility of such changes, the chase may still not be worth the candle. There must be a finite limit to a communication system that uses a limited resource—flattened trees—on which to deliver its messages. Newspapers, as well as other media, must also surmount the Principle of Relative Constancy.[40] It states that the amount of money spent on mass media by society is a relatively constant proportion of the gross national product, with a moderately declining trend across time.

Under this hypothesis, as new media forms arise, they gain public support at the expense of the older forms. The historic verification of the hypothesis is strengthened by another fact of twentieth century life: the ultimate constraint on media use may not be a limited amount of money, but a scarcity of time among consumers.

Given these premises, the existing broadcast and print media may be relatively helpless to do anything in the face of encroaching technology. There is no doubt that economically feasible interactive cable transmission is around the corner. Home-screen delivery of user-selected newspaper content has already begun in England. When the cost of home equipment goes down sufficiently and the services offered match consumer desires, few observers can argue that two-way cable will not cut into conventional media use. The home console/screen/printer will become newspaper-library-theater-market-department store for Everyman. Some futurists see it happening by 1990, others further into the twenty-first century. But happen it will, with perhaps more certainty than the newspaper arriving on your doorstep today.

NOTES

1. Ben H. Bagdikian, *The Information Machines: Their Impact on Man and Media* (New York: Harper & Row, 1971), p. 115.

2. John H. Colburn, "Economics of the Press," paper presented to the Conference on Education for Newspaper Journalists in the Seventies and Beyond, Reston, Virginia, 31 October-2 November, 1973, p. 119.

3. Donald McDonald, "The Media's Conflict of Interests," *The Center Magazine,* November/December 1976, pp. 15-35.

4. Herbert Brucker, "Is the Press Writing Its Obituary?" *Saturday Review,* 25 April 1959, p. 9.

5. U.S. Department of Commerce, "Printing and Publishing," *U.S. Industrial Outlook,* December 1972, p. 428.

6. Ben H. Bagdikian, "The Myth of Newspaper Poverty," *Columbia Journalism Review,* March/April 1973, p. 20.

7. *Editor & Publisher,* 2 April 1977, p. 14.

8. Quoted in Colburn, "Economics," p. 104.

9. Estimates are taken from *Cox Looks at the Future,* a report of an industry survey, (Atlanta, Ga.: Cox Broadcasting, 1975).

10. Leo Bogart, "The Future of the Metropolitan Daily," *Journal of Communication* 25 (Spring 1975): 30-43.

11. *Cox Looks at Future,* p. 22.

12. Bogart, "Metropolitan Daily," p. 39.

13. Bogart, "Metropolitan Daily," pp. 42-43.

14. Gerald L. Grotta, "Newspaper Industry May Be Heading for Decline," *Journalism Quarterly* 51 (Autumn 1974): 498-502.

15. Quoted in David Shaw, "The Newspaper Must Be Fit to Survive," *The Quill,* February 1977, p. 18.

16. Bruce M. Owen, Jack H. Beebe, and Willard G. Manning, Jr., *Television Economics* (Lexington, Mass.: Heath, 1974).

17. *Cox Looks at Future,* p. 19.

18. This point is made forcefully by Owen, Beebe, and Manning, *Television Economics,* in Chapter 1 and throughout Part II.

19. *Cox Looks at Future,* pp. 37-60.

20. See, for example, the series of public opinion polls, dating back to the 1950s, conducted by the Roper Organization for the Television Information Institute.

21. The estimate of chain ownership in 1900 is from Frank Luther Mott, *American Journalism,* 3rd ed. New York: Macmillan, 1962), p. 648. The data that follow are taken from industry and governmental sources and are reported in several standard and periodical sources, including Edwin Emery, *The Press and America,* 3rd ed. (Englewood Cliffs, N.J.: Prentice-Hall, 1972), pp. 443, 621; Raymond B. Nixon, "Trends in U.S. Newspaper Ownership: Concentration With Competition," *Gazette* 14 (1968): 181-193; Ben H. Bagdikian, "Newspaper Mergers—the Final Phase," *Columbia Journalism Review,* March/April 1977, pp. 17-22; Robert L. Bishop, "The Rush to Chain Ownership," *Columbia Journalism Review,* November/December 1972, p. 10; and McDonald, "Conflict of Interests." Figures on cities with competing newspapers were provided by Prof. Edwin Emery and Judith Sobel, of the University of Minnesota, from a study completed in 1977.

22. Statistics in this paragraph are taken from Morton Mintz and Jerry Cohen, *America, Inc.,* (New York: Dell, 1971), chapters 1-2.

23. Quoted in Kevin Phillips, "Busting the Media Trusts," *Harper's,* July 1977, pp. 23-34.

24. Bagdikian, "Newspaper Mergers."

25. McDonald, "Conflict of Interests."

26. Phillips, "Busting the Trusts."

27. *National Citizens Committee for Broadcasting* v. *FCC,* 2 Med. L. Rptr. 1405 (D.C. Cir. 1977).

28. A.J. Liebling, *The Press* (New York: Ballantine, 1961) p. 30.

29. Bagdikian, "Newspaper Mergers," p. 21.

30. A description of the tax incentives appears in *Columbia Journalism Review,* July/August 1977, p. 18.

31. "The Big Money Hunts for Independent Newspapers," *Business Week,* 21 February 1977, p. 56.

32. "Big Money Hunts Independent Newspapers," p. 59.

33. Data on newspaper chain circulation are based on compilations prepared by Prof. Paul Jess of the University of Kansas for the 1977 *Editor & Publisher International Yearbook.*

34. These and other sales figures are taken from Phillips, "Busting the Trusts."

35. Bagdikian, "Newspaper Mergers," p. 21.

36. Bagdikian, "Newspaper Poverty," p. 33.

37. "Newspapers with Coffee: Still Around in 1990?" *Printing Management,* May 1971, pp. 50-51.

38. Quoted in *Editor & Publisher,* 19 March 1977, p. 16.

39. Speech to a meeting of United Press International editors, San Francisco, California, 26 April 1977.

40. Maxwell McCombs, "Mass Media in the Marketplace," *Journalism Monographs,* no. 24 (August 1972).

Part Three

Media Reforms
and Innovations

Topics

Introduction

Whatever uncertainties face America's mass communication system in the coming decades, the constitutional guarantees of freedom of speech and press will remain a focal point of public debate. Free speech and press provide a rationale for citizen participation in the communication process, for the independence of media managers, and for professional performance.

The initial essay in Part Three by D. M. Gillmor is intended to convey to the reader a sense of the pragmatic vitality of the social dialogue on the meaning of the words "Congress shall make no law...abridging the freedom of speech, or of the press...." These freedoms are more than pieces of an abstract libertarian theory; they are also crucial to the anatomy of economic and political power.

Too seldom are these rights thought of in their economic context. Concentration of media ownership may ultimately be the greatest threat to freedom of speech and press in America. Blatant interferences with freedom of expression by government are checked by state and federal courts sensitive to the evolving meaning of the First Amendment and to guarantees of freedom of speech and press in state constitutions. Corporate or nongovernmental obstructions to the free flow of information, on the other hand, are less blatant but perhaps more insidious, and they are not expressly proscribed by the First and Fourteenth Amendments.

Although we have been unable to find significant differences in content between competitive and monopoly newspapers, between group-owned and independent newspapers, and between cross-channel-owned and independent broadcast stations, we may yet do damage to Judge Learned Hand's expectation in the *Associated Press* case "that right conclusions are more likely to be gathered out of a multitude of tongues" when we fail to counteract a rampaging tendency in mass communication toward merger, conglomeration, and cross-media ownership.[1]

"Freedom of the press from governmental interference under the First Amendment," said Justice Hugo Black when the *Associated Press* case reached the Supreme Court, "does not sanction repression of that freedom by private interests."[2]

What must we learn about newspaper economics, stock swapping, inheritance tax, and capital gains to fashion reasonable proposals for tax reform or for legislation limiting the number of newspapers per owner, a limit already placed on broadcast properties? Would new legislation singling out the press pass constitutional muster? If not, then what does it take to mobilize the energies of the Antitrust Division of the U.S. Department of Justice? Is it possible that antitrust action would destroy more newspapers than it would save? And is it too late for intervention of this kind given the present level of consolidation?

To what extent is technology alone the culprit? Automation enhances the economies of scale in both production and business management (per-unit cost goes down as circulation increases). Group ownership therefore is by definition viable and profitable and a temptation to both buyer and seller of newspaper properties.

And what twentieth-century person would stay the course of technology? Technological innovation has changed the face of the newsroom. Writing and editing can now be done electronically. Using a computer-based system, reporters type their stories on video display terminals (VDTs), which display the text as the story is written. The computer allows wire-service and syndicate material to be fed into its storage capacity and retrieved when needed. Editors can then call up stories on their VDTs for electronic editing.

Typically VDTs have the capability of copying, moving, and deleting text; of allowing for inserts, italics, bold or normal type; of distinguishing between editorial changes and original copy; of overstriking,

erasing, merging, and paging through copy. In addition they may be able to justify, hyphenate, write and count headlines, change column width and depth, page through directories of news material in storage, compare in sequence edited and unedited versions of the same story, and compare them with wire service versions. Once edited, stories are moved electronically to automated typesetters.

The major purpose of these systems is to save time, and time is money. For the same reason television journalism has entered its era of ENG (electronic news gathering). More news is being gathered with fewer technical steps. Mobile, live-coverage miniature cameras, with reusable tape rather than film, are able to microwave remote coverage back to a central studio. Is it possible that within such systems reporters and editors will find their traditional functions of news judgment delegated to various kinds of technocrats? This concern is already being expressed by professional groups such as the Radio and Television News Directors Association.

Radio and television are regulated by government on the premise that broadcast frequencies are a scarce resource: since there are not enough for everyone, someone must be denied. But such technological scarcity may already be a ghost of times past. Television, in theory at least, is already a medium of abundance; only economic and political obstacles stand in its way as the story of CATV illustrates.

Unbounded by the petty technological, political, and economic limitations of our planet, futurist Arthur C. Clarke blasts us off into outer space. Author of the book *2001: A Space Odyssey*, which became a classic film of its genre, Clarke provides a mind-stretching view of the technological richness of our spatial near-future. Like Marshall McLuhan and Buckminster Fuller, he forecasts a United States of Earth that will communicate with itself and eventually with other galaxies. It is a most invigorating journey.

But can technology alone redeem humankind? James W. Carey and John J. Quirk have had serious doubts about technological utopias for some time.[3] And they distrust those who project a future that will become, in their words, "a time zone in which the human condition is somehow transcended, politics evaporated, and a blessed stage of peace and democratic harmony achieved." Northern Ireland and southern Africa are, after all, essentially industrialized societies.

Carey and Quirk perceive in futurist projections strong tendencies to confuse information with knowledge. They express their concern in a provocative sentence: "The 'idea of information' is another way past the real political factors of class, status, and power, but these formidable realities cannot be dissolved into a future where they are presumed not to exist because they have been absorbed and transformed by the computational machinery." Marshall McLuhan, for example, in his "futurean mirage," has had very little to say about the control and cost factors of innovative communication systems.

Suppose that conventional economic and political remedies are unavailable to us. What is left to be done? Is it possible that reporters and editors are developing a professional ethos, an individual sense of responsibility, that will eventually neutralize the organizational strictures and power configurations that limit them?

Bernard Roshco believes that mass media

organizations do not encourage "innovative ideas, dissident viewpoints, and news unfavorable and unpalatable to the institutional powerholders who usually dominate the news."[4] From his relatively radical perspective, James Aronson agrees. In *Deadline for the Media* he explores the reporter activism that led in the late 1960s to voice-in-product demands and the journalism reviews that reflected in part a challenge to the business and technological values directing news and public information enterprises. The reviews, though now in decline (the bellwether *Chicago Journalism Review* ceased publication in early 1975), have left their imprint on the establishment media.

Reflections of new ideologies and journalistic life styles can be discerned at an A. J. Liebling Counter-Convention. But there is something more afoot. Elements of professionalization are surfacing in the minds and meetings of working journalists. This is not to say that the process of professionalization is well understood or that its concepts fit the field neatly or comfortably. But reporters do talk more and more about the need for greater editorial independence from the corporate oligarchy. And serious ethical issues are creeping back into their conversations and into the literature of journalism after a forty-year hiatus.

Worn-out adages such as "We don't make the news, we just print it" or "We only give the public what they want" are no longer respectable. Nor is the bottom-line ethic, where minimum attention is paid to minimum standards in order to prevent personal catastrophe—often in legal form. More often than in the recent past, reporters and editors are asking whether the negative effects of a news story on individual values outweigh the beneficial effects on the public's right to know.

In part, then, we are considering the extent to which a journalist—part of a news organization with norms and conventions, rules and routines—still retains freedom for independent judgment and expression outside of that organization or any other organization, including his own guilds and societies.

Realizing that James Madison was probably correct when he said that some abuse of freedom is necessary in its practice, we are nevertheless beginning to question again some news gathering and presentation devices: the reporter who pretends to be someone else to get a story; eavesdropping or other techniques for which we criticize the FBI and the CIA; vagueness in attribution and other quote tricks; naming rape victims for no apparent public purpose; exploitative coverage of sociopsychopaths; "freebies" (gifts, trips, dinners, tickets, writing prizes from special-interest groups); a spectrum of conflicts of interest, from membership in issue organizations to moonlighting; buying news; and legislative lobbying—to name only some of the ethical issues under discussion.

Does the adversary metaphor undergirding American journalism lead to ethical misbehavior? Roscoe Born, vice president of *The National Observer* answers the question this way:

I have come to the belief that there lurks in the character of nearly every journalist a fundamental flaw ... an inborn desire to "get" somebody, anybody; to publish a startling story....A reporter who takes the hide off somebody in print reaps immense rewards and satisfactions.

Generalization to be sure, but an indication that we are no longer oblivious to tough ethical issues. When we do ignore such issues, and thereby fail to develop a compelling set of principles, the law does it for us. And that has been the trend. Lacking our own operative ethical codes, the courts in such cases as *Dietemann* v. *Time, Inc.* (the clandestine gathering of news,[5] *Gertz* v. *Robert Welch, Inc.* (an attack on the

reputation of a private person).[6] and the *Pentagon Papers* case (use of prior restraint to prevent publication of stolen government documents)[7] define our ethical boundaries for us.

Can ethical precepts be the product of group thinking, or are they purely personal? Surely there are transferable elements. But whatever the case, ethical concerns are themselves a reflection of professionalism.

At a recent conference on libel and privacy involving editors, reporters, lawyers, and teachers, libel and privacy questions regularly resolved into ethical issues. Formal ethical codes haven't worked, says Charles Seib, ombudsman for the *Washington Post,* because they conflict with traditions that newspersons, right or wrong, won't give up. One example he has used to make his point is the "unidentified source," which the Associated Press Managing Editors code seeks to discourage. Another is the desultory use of corrections.

While increasing concern is being expressed for ethical norms, formal codes may not work because they contain no organizing principle or underlying concept. That concept, it would seem, since our accountability ought to be no one but our audiences, must be the *public interest,* a term charged with emotion and confusion.

"It is probable," said Daniel Bell and Irving Kristol in the introduction to the first issue of the new journal *Public Interest,* "that as much mischief has been perpetrated upon the human race in the name of 'the public interest' as in the name of anything else...." Yet the very frequency of the invocation of the concept by public, press, and government provokes Everette E. Dennis to pursue its meaning.

Dennis provides an operational definition anchored in the First Amendment, a reasonable approach when one considers that the Constitution itself is an authoritative statement of the public interest. Government, he believes, whether its judicial or law-making branch, ought to be the last resort in resolving disputes about the meaning of the public interest. Less formal forums—such as the editor's office, the ombudsman, the letter to the editor, the correction, the retraction, or the local, state, or national press council—ought to be tried first. Certainly the public ought to participate in defining the public interest. To do so it must have access to the major organs of public opinion and to their policy-making echelons.

Although some doubt that a citizen audit of press performance, a press council, is compatible with First Amendment norms, one has to be impressed with what some press councils have accomplished in a few short years. If nothing else, council rulings have reminded journalists of what some nonjournalists consider the lower threshholds of responsible performance. And press procedures in specific areas have been modified as a result of council rulings. Most councils, moreover, combine in their memberships journalists and nonjournalists and provide thereby an unusual opportunity for mutual understanding.

A range of issues is represented in the few examples used by Gillmor to reflect the work of the National News Council, the Minnesota Press Council, and the Honolulu Community-Media Council. Beyond these examples, misrepresentation, unfairness, the instant analysis of presidential speeches, lack of attribution, and press behavior endangering the life of a person involuntarily thrust into the public spotlight have all been the subject of citizen complaints. Sometimes the complaints are upheld; sometimes they are not.

Just as we may be worried about what reporter "movements" and other forms of collective action do to the reporter's individuality, we must also be concerned about what they and citizen access do to the prerogatives of power in our constitutional system. When we tamper with the power of the publisher, are we, as Justice Potter Stewart has recently implied, tampering with the First Amendment? This question is also being addressed.[8]

The point is that access is much more than a legal issue to be resolved by a court. It is the reader or the viewer knocking on an editor's door to ask for a rebuttal. It is a complaint brought to a press council. It is an attempt by reporters to have a greater voice in what goes into the newspaper or over the airwaves. It is women or minorities seeking an end to discrimination in the news room.

There still appears to be discrimination in hiring, job status, and promotability of women and minorities. In 1969 the late Whitney M. Young, Jr., then executive director of the National Urban League, said in an address to the annual convention of the National Association of Broadcasters, "If we could get the broadcasting industry to be as discriminating in its identification of black leadership as it is in its employment policies, we would be in great shape."

At that time fewer than 8 percent of broadcast jobs in New York City were filled by Blacks and Puerto Ricans, although they constituted 25 percent of the population of the city. The figures for Los Angeles were even worse. Young called for outreach—finding ways to escalate the movement of minority people up the ladder. Get Black people at the top, he argued, and then you will be able to find Blacks to fill the jobs below.

Since 1969, minority employment in the broadcast industry generally is estimated to have reached about 12 percent, the employment of women approximately 24 percent. Commercial television stations, for example, are replacing whites and men who leave their employment with minority persons and women. The Office of Communication of the United Church of Christ, in a report to the Federal Communications Commission, wonders whether some broadcasters might be reclassifying some of these people into upper-level job categories while keeping them in the same old lower-level jobs at the same low salaries. The answer is not clear, and in specific instances the charge is being litigated.

Still, in 1976 nearly a third of both commercial and noncommercial broadcast stations had no minority staffers. And only 1.9 percent of the people working in the print media were Black, according to Sam Adams, Gannett Foundation minorities professor of journalism at the University of Kansas. This dimension of access deserves careful monitoring.

Access, then, can take both internal and external forms, and all of them, unlike the intervention of a court or a legislature, are indirect. And yet there may be a role for government. By expediting the development of new channels of communication, for example cable television, satellites, and public broadcasting, the government facilitates access indirectly. Although public broadcasting did require a 1967 Act of Congress for the diversion of public monies, it did so without interfering with the commercial networks then in place. The result is a gradually improving alternative system, though not without its problems.

Unfortunately, it is not clear how the FCC, the White House Office of Telecommunication Policy, HEW, and the Corporation for Public Broadcasting are to divide responsibility for the direction of noncommercial service. The result has been a miasma of indecision. Among the recommendations of the Carnegie Commission Report, which gave birth to the Public Broadcasting Act, was the hope that the alternative system would provide a voice for groups in the community that otherwise might be unheard, in other words, an access function. This function may yet be fulfilled.

In the meantime many questions need to be answered. Anne W. Branscomb, a lawyer specializing in communications law and regulation, has skillfully measured their range.[9] First of all, what is noncommercial broadcasting? A basic definition has eluded us. How should public broadcasters ascertain community needs and interests? What are the responsibilities of public stations for political broadcasting? What are the parameters of controversial-issue programming? And who should make these decisions? Branscomb's

proposals for future planning in this area deserve close attention. This nation, she says, the world's wealthiest, spends less to enrich its broadcast output than most of its less well-endowed neighbors. We are, as a result, a culturally deprived people, still dependent on the BBC for the best of our public programing.

In an essay included in Part Three, Branscomb speculates on why the great promise of CATV has never been met. Again her hopes for the future rest on public action.

It is fitting, perhaps, that James W. Carey, one of the most thoughtful minds in American journalism, should address us again, although his article reprinted from a British journal may leave us with a certain sense of futility.

Carey asks, "Who will criticize the critics?" The omnibus newspaper, he observes, is the forum for criticism of art, architecture, literature, politics, business, and all else, but who criticizes the newspaper in any sustained way? Not the ombudsman or his counterpart, whatever the title, because he works from inside and his impartiality cannot be assured. Not local or national press councils, because they tend to become an additional level of elitist bureaucracy disconnected from its publics. Not social scientists with their expert reports, because they measure only public opinion and are bereft of any concern for quality, truth, and reasonableness.

What Carey would substitute he calls "cultural criticism," an ongoing process of debate between the press and its more analytical audiences, to be sure a more abstract mechanism than the cases-and-controversies approach of both ombudsman and press council.

Carey is vague about how the exchange he proposes would be energized and maintained, and he may not persuade all his readers that the general community would yawn any less—to use Carey's own metaphor—when attending to a press/public debate than when attending to criticism of the arts.

Routines and conventions of the press that Carey rightly views as sometimes disguising reality more than informing it are being challenged by ombudsmen and press councils and in the columns of the press.

These experiments in accountability are more promising and systematic than Carey infers, and he misperceives the intentions and capabilities of social science.

Nevertheless, Carey's call for a sustained and systematic review of press performance is a reflection of his dedicated idealism, without which the literature of journalism would be the poorer. Essentially he is calling for a more variable public access to those media that daily shape our minds and feelings.

Finally, access to editorial decision making may be achieved by communication researchers, if their research is somehow made relevant to an editor's problems. Two British students of communication, Denis McQuail and Michael Gurevitch, in an article describing a number of theoretical approaches that attempt to explain audience behavior, include an *action/motivation* perspective with numerous implications for applied research. And it may be distinguished from other perspectives by the emphasis it places on the audience member, the receiver of communication messages. Such an approach may be a starting place for those editors who sincerely care about the needs and wants of their readers and for broadcasters who for license renewal are required to ascertain the needs of their audiences.

All of these essays, in their own particular ways, dissolve into the question of the public interest and public access to the great organs of public opinion, and it is in these terms that the future of innovation and reform in mass communication will proceed.

NOTES

1. *United States v. Associated Press,* 52 F. Supp. 362 (S. D. N. Y. 1943).
2. *Associated Press et al. v. United States,* 326 U.S. 1 (1945).
3. James W. Carey and John J. Quirk, "The Mythos of the Electronic Revolution," parts I and II, *The American Scholar,* Spring and Summer 1970.
4. Bernard Roshco, *Newsmaking* (Chicago: University of Chicago Press, 1975), p. 122.
5. *Dietemann v. Time, Inc.,* 449 F. 2d 245 (9th Cir. 1971).
6. *Gertz v. Robert Welch, Inc.,* 94 S. Ct. 2997 (1974).
7. *New York Times v. United States, United States v. The Washington Post,* 403 U.S. 713, 91 S. Ct. 2140 (1971).
8. Bruce M. Owen, *Economics and Freedom of Expression.* Cambridge, Mass.: Balinger, 1975.
9. Anne W. Branscomb, "A Crisis of Identity: Reflections on the Future of Public Broadcasting," in *The Future of Public Broadcasting,* ed. Douglass Cater and Michael J. Nyhan (New York: Praeger and the Aspen Institute Program on Communications and Society, 1976).

FURTHER READING

Barron, Jerome A., *Freedom of the Press For Whom? The Right of Access to Mass Media.* Bloomington: University of Indiana Press, 1973.

Emerson, Thomas I., *The System of Freedom of Expression.* New York: Vintage Books, 1970.

Hutteng, John L., *The Messenger's Motives: Ethical Problems of the News Media.* Englewood Cliffs, N.J.: Prentice-Hall, 1976.

Mintz, Morton and Jerry S. Cohen, *Power Inc.: Public and Private Rulers and How to Make Them Accountable.* New York: The Viking Press, 1976.

Schmidt, Benno C., Jr., *Freedom of the Press v. Public Access.* Springfield, Mass.: Praeger Publishers, Inc., 1976.

Part Three

Constitutional Dialogue and Dilemmas

FREEDOM OF EXPRESSION

Donald M. Gillmor

A basic measure of the degree of freedom of expression in a society is the volume and accessibility of debate and dialogue on what this freedom means, how it is to be defined and applied, by whom, and how best it can be protected against any governmental or private interest that would suppress it.

English-language libraries are vast repositories of the fruits of continuing and sometimes exceedingly complex colloquies on this nuclear concept. John Milton's "Let (Truth) and Falsehood grapple...,"[1] James Madison's "Congress shall make no law...,"[2] John Stuart Mills's "All silencing of discussion is an assumption of infallibility...,"[3] and Oliver Wendell Holmes's "clear and present danger..."[4] are no more than touchstones in the long and brutal struggle for a right that had to be torn from the grip of authority, both sacred and secular.

The idea of freedom of expression has no meaning in the abstract. To be able to shout about it, to write about it, to disagree with others about it, to litigate about it is to have it. To have reached perfect consensus about it, to defer to authoritative proclamations about it, to have foreclosed debate on it, to fear to press grievances about it is to have lost it. Unless freedom of expression is constantly being reappraised, repudiated, reaffirmed, or acted upon with sometimes outrageous zeal, it is pure metaphysics and cannot have a bearing on the everyday needs of the citizenry.

Law professor Harry Kalven, Jr. put it well: "...I suggest that the presence or absence in the law of the concept of seditious libel (a law which would make criticism of government a crime) defines the society. If...it makes seditious libel an offense, it is not a free society no matter what its other characteristics."[5] Freedom of expression, then, includes the right to question the fundamental postulates of a society.

More than a faith, freedom of expression is a process, a methodology, a key to self-government that demands on pain of social atrophy that the "debate on public issues…be uninhibited, robust, and wide-open,"[6] because freedom of expression is no less than the "thinking process of the community."[7] It may also be a basic individual human need.[8]

Herbert Marcuse, an influential New Left philosopher, promulgates an antithetical view, which would consider everything said so far to be pure illusion. Buyers and sellers in the marketplace of ideas are no more than marionettes tied to commercial and political strings. He adopts Plato's notion that there should be free discussion only if it is rational, free speech only for those who can be trusted to war against repressive tolerance, the middle and the right elements of the political spectrum. He proposes intolerance in the name of dissent. He is opposed to institutionalized tolerance, characteristic of a liberal democracy, because it disarms dissenters, the militant opposition. It gives them the illusion of having impact on the social order when in fact they have none. Marcuse advocates precensorship as a substitute for the illusion of freedom, precensorship by an intellectual elite in place of what we now have in his view, a dictatorship of nonintellectuals—politicians, generals, and businessmen.[9]

Marcuse, certainly, challenges the fundamentals of his country's system of freedom of expression, but more importantly, he does so by participating persuasively in the process itself.

And speaking of precensorship, not even the hallowed "no prior restraint" doctrine is absolutely secure in a genuine dialogue.[10] It was challenged recently by the Supreme Court itself, key members of which held that in circumstances of jeopardy to national security the press could either be restrained from publishing or criminally prosecuted for what it did publish.[11] Whether the promise of severe postpublication penalties is in itself a prior restraint is a crucial question for Americans.[12]

The presumption a judge is willing to make with respect to the constitutionality of a state or federal law that interferes with freedom of expression frequently depends on where he places this complex of rights in the hierarchy of social and individual values, or whether he is willing to rank constitutional rights at all. Those who would afford absolute protection to freedom of expression or those who would prefer it over other rights—such as the collective right to national security—because of the crucial contribution it makes to political freedom either reject outright or scrutinize most carefully laws that affect it. Judicial pragmatists rely instead on ad hoc balancing tests that weigh one right against another in the peculiar circumstances of a case.[13] These judges also show deference to enactments of legislatures on the assumption that lawmakers represent the most democratic branch of government and therefore the will of the people and should not be obstructed in their work unless what they do is patently unconstitutional. The composition of an appellate court at any particular time will determine which of these general approaches to the application of constitutional mandates will dominate.

Nevertheless there is some consensus. There is no disagreement anymore that liberty of circulation and distribution is an integral part of freedom of expression.[14] The Supreme Court has denied the Post Office judgmental authority over content.[15] Anonymous speech has the full protection of the First Amendment.[16] Freedom of expression includes the right to criticize and disparage judges, as well as other public officials, in most vitriolic, scurrilous, and even erroneous terms.[17] Punitive or discriminatory taxes against the press are not permitted.[18] And it is recognized that free expression often requires the collective effort of an assembly[19] or a petition for a redress of grievances.[20]

The unorthodox, dissident, or counterculture press is protected by the First Amendment. "The history of this nation and particularly of the development of the institutions of our complex federal system of government," a federal district court said recently, "has been repeatedly jarred and reshaped by the continuing investigation, reporting and advocacy of independent journalists unaffiliated with major institutions and often with no resource except their wit, persistence, and the crudest mechanisms for placing words on paper."[21] The scholastic and collegiate press is less well protected.[22]

Still much remains unsettled. For example, are "fighting words," words that incite to riot, beyond the protective reach of the First Amendment?[23] Should the police authority, in the furtherance of First Amendment interests, protect the audience from the speaker[24] or the speaker from the audience?[25] Should speech-plus activities—for example, parading, picketing, and door-to-door solicitation—be given the same protection as pure speech, and if not, what conditions ought to be attached to these important and frequent forms of communication?[26]

More perplexing is the problem of drawing the line between protected speech and unprotected illegal conduct in cases of symbolic speech, such as the burning of a draft card,[27] the destruction of a flag,[28] or the wearing of black arm bands by schoolchildren to protest the Vietnam War on behalf of their parents.[29] The Supreme Court has never issued a unanimous decision in a symbolic speech case.

The Supreme Court seems prepared to extend increasingly greater protection to commercial forms of communication[30] and is moving away from its earlier position that purely commercial speech deserved little, if any, constitutional protection.[31]

While the ragged edges of a theory of freedom of expression begin to emerge, the courts must still deal with urgent conflicts between freedom of speech and press and other rights—the right to one's good reputation,[32] the right to personal privacy,[33] and the right to a speedy and public trial before an impartial jury.[34] They must also decide to what degree sexually explicit communication is protected by the First Amendment.[35] Do cameras in a courtroom constitute a denial of due process of law?[36] Does the common law precept that the state is entitled to every man's evidence in a court of law override the privilege of a journalist to protect the identity of his sources and the raw materials of his work (notes, tapes, etc.) on the assumption that by doing so he is contributing to the public's interest in a free flow of information?[37] Do labor laws that require journalists to belong to unions[38] or campaign financing laws that entangle the press violate the First Amendment? The latter question was answered affirmatively in a recent Supreme Court decision.[39]

Even more difficult are those appeals that ask the courts to find implied rights in the sparse language of the First Amendment. For example, is there an implied right of the public to know and to have access to news and public information? In the United States, legislatures have been more positive than courts in responding to this question.[40] Is there an implied right to hear,[41] to refuse to listen,[42] to travel in pursuit of information?[43] These issues are in flux, and a divided Supreme Court has not spoken its last word. Only grudgingly has the High Court extended unequivocal First Amendment protection to film,[44] and as shall be noted, the broadcast media enjoy only a qualified freedom of expression.

Finally, does the First Amendment imply a right of access by members of the audience, not only to information and information sources, but also to the major channels of mass communication themselves? This question has generated an explosion of speculation in recent years about the meaning of freedom of speech and press. The libertarian notion of a free marketplace of ideas in which everyone may participate equally, although a fighting faith in an earlier time and certainly parent to the First Amendment, no longer seems to contain assumptions appropriate to the economic, political, and technological realities of today.

Even though the First Amendment may still protect the solitary speaker from any form of government repression, it does not assure that same speaker access to the great engines of public opinion—radio, television, and the newspapers—by means of which his ideas can have impact. At the same time, ownership of mass media outlets becomes concentrated in fewer and fewer hands (approximately 168 newspaper chains account for 71 percent of all daily newspaper circulation),[45] making illusory the supposition that everyone has an equal opportunity to command a soapbox in the marketplace.[46]

So persons with something to contribute to a robust and uninhibited social dialogue are protected from governmental interference but not from the rigidities of a publisher. Courts, adhering to traditional interpretations of the First Amendment, have held recently that newspaper readers have no right to reply to editorial attacks against them[47] and that one side of a legal dispute has no "right to make use of the defendant's printing presses and distribution systems without defendant's consent."[48] A labor union had tried unsuccessfuly to buy advertising space in Chicago's daily newspapers in order to explain its reasons for an attempted boycott of Chicago department stores.

Broadcasters, on the other hand, are required by the Fairness Doctrine (1) to devote a reasonable amount of time to the coverage of controversial issues of public importance and (2) to do so fairly by affording a reasonable opportunity for contrasting viewpoints to be voiced on these issues. In 1969 a radio station belonging to the Reverend John H. Norris in Red Lion,

Pennsylvania lost its license for refusing to permit a left-wing writer to reply free of charge to a personal attack made against him by a right-wing evangelist. In upholding the Federal Communication Commission's action, the Supreme Court declared that in broadcasting it is the public interest—not the private—that is paramount, and it held the Fairness Doctrine constitutional.[49]

Later, when a group of antiwar businessmen and the Democratic National Committee sought to buy time on a Washington DC radio station and the CBS network, respectively, Chief Justice Warren Burger held for the Court that granting a constitutional right of access to broadcast advertising would inevitably push the FCC into a review of day-to-day editorial and managerial decision and thereby offend the First Amendment. The Court also argued that if management were required to accept advertising, the system would be monopolized by those who could and would pay the costs.[50]

The two decisions are difficult to reconcile with one another and with the Court's ruling in the newspaper access case. It must be remembered, however, that the broadcast media are regulated by government as a scarce public resource and are licensed every three years on condition that they be operated in "the public interest, convenience and necessity." Ironically, it is the unregulated newspaper that may now be the scarce resource, while broadcasting, through the gradual emergence of cable, is becoming the medium of abundance.

There are other problems with the Court's argument. It may be too late to worry about the broadcast system being monopolized by those who are able to pay the costs of air time. The Federal Trade Commission estimates that 75 percent of all broadcast advertising is purchased by fewer than 100 firms and that 10 firms account for 22 percent of it. Ultimate control of the broadcast media is already vested in the public, and as Justice William Brennan observed in a dissenting opinion in the latter case, the government is already involved in an elaborate statutory scheme governing virtually all aspects of the broadcast industry.

Nevertheless, opponents of the Fairness Doctrine see it as a prologue to government control of programing and a device for discriminating against broadcast journalists. Former Supreme Court Justice William O. Douglas and Wisconsin's liberal Senator William Proxmire would repeal it as an affront to the First Amendment.[51]

Proponents believe that responsible broadcasters have nothing to worry about and that only flagrant violations of the public trust have led to license revocation. They would not abandon the Fairness Doctrine until the broadcast spectrum has been greatly expanded by further developments in cable and satellite communications, developments against which the television networks have successfully lobbied. It sometimes appears as if the broadcast industry wants it both ways. Deregulation and thereby first-class citizenship under the First Amendment would mean removal of all restraints on the development of new and competitive technologies.

But there are problems with the Fairness Doctrine. Its two parts seem to be in conflict. Stations get into trouble only for disregarding the "opposing views" part of the FCC requirement. A hard-hitting investigative news staff will accrue a fat file of fairness complaints, usually having to do with particular programs. NBC's documentary on the failure of some corporate pension plans was an example.[52] A bland, penny-pinching station that never ventures into controversy will have a clean slate at license renewal time.

By fixing its attention on the second part of the Fairness Doctrine, the FCC does interfere with editorial discretion, journalistic judgment, and the content of specific programs, which section 326 of the Federal Communication Act expressly forbids. The result has been a quagmire of cases in which "stations are assayed in a way that so weights negative complaints against positive performance that it puts a premium on timidity."[53] At the same time, given the wide discretion accorded the broadcaster in his use of the Fairness Doctrine, his commitment "to devote a reasonable amount of time to the discussion of controversial issues" is, for the most part, a broken promise. Since novel, unorthodox, and unrepresentative views may not find a vehicle for broadcast, accessibility for editorial advertising becomes all the more imperative.

Where the Supreme Court sees the Fairness Doctrine as an alternative to viewers and listeners having access to the channels, others see access as a way of making the Fairness Doctrine work. Programs modeled on *60 Minutes* and *Bill Moyer's Journal,* giving the audience a chance to talk back, may in the long run keep the FCC out of the newsroom and the broadcaster out of the courtroom. But Congress will have to reinforce its original intention to measure fairness in terms of the overall, three-year performance of the broadcaster rather than on the basis of individual program complaints to the FCC.[54]

It is impossible to speculate on how entrepreneurs view these suggestions. It is a fact, however, that as time passes there are fewer and fewer entrepreneurs. Economic inevitabilities have brought the privately owned mass communications system to a point where the majority of FM radio stations are owned by AM stations; most of the larger AM stations are affiliated with television stations, as are about half of the existing cablecasting systems. The most significant broadcasting chains, owning five stations each, belong to the three major networks; together the three networks and their total of fifteen stations accounted for 52 percent of the total revenues of all television stations in 1974, and the networks produce or control 95 percent of all prime-time programing.

In 1973, more than 95 percent of the VHF stations in the top ten markets were owned by groups, while more than 75 percent of all commercial television stations in the top 100 markets were held by groups. Newspaper-based groups controlled 25 percent of these strong-signal stations.[55]

More than 50 percent of all daily newspapers are chain-owned, and the ten largest chains account for one-fourth of total annual revenues for the industry and one-third of the circulation. Only fifteen American cities still have competing daily newspapers. In 1975 only New York City had more than two newspaper owners. Magazines are part of this cross-channel pattern of ownership, and nearly half of the major book companies own or are owned by newspaper, broadcast, or magazine interests. All news media depend heavily upon two major wire services, AP and UPI, for a large percentage of their information. And industrial conglomerates are now heavily invested in the communications system.

Is it a paradox of press freedom that freedom from government requires governmental intervention in the form of tax reform, subsidies, or antitrust enforcement? Or is such a notion the beginning of the end for freedom of expression? And whose rights to free expression are at stake? The reporter's? The editor's? The publisher's? Or the audience's? And what rights ought to be protected? The freedom to howl in a closet?

The right to own a channel? The right to receive information from as many diverse sources as possible? Certainly there are more questions than answers.

American newspapers are not exempt from general taxation,[56] from the application of labor laws,[57] or from antitrust legislation.[58] In the leading antitrust case, *Associated Press et al. v.United States,* Justice Hugo Black, speaking for the Court, said of the First Amendment that it "rests on the assumption that the widest possible dissemination of information from diverse and antagonistic sources is essential to the welfare of the public, that a free press is a condition of a free society." "Surely," he added, "a command that the government itself shall not impede the free flow of ideas does not afford non-governmental combinations a refuge if they impose restraints upon that constitutionally guaranteed freedom. Freedom to publish means freedom for all and not for some. Freedom to publish is guaranteed by the Constitution, but freedom to combine to keep others from publishing is not. Freedom of the press from governmental interference under the First Amendment does not sanction repression of that freedom by private interests."[59]

The 1947 Commission on Freedom of the Press, a nongovernmental body, put it more philosophically:

> Clearly a qualitatively new era of public responsibility for the press has arrived; and it becomes an imperative question whether press performance can any longer be left to the unregulated initiative of the issuers. The moral and legal right of thinkers to utter their opinions must in any case remain intact; this right stands for the kernel of individualism at the heart of all free social life. But the element of duty involved in the right requires a new scrutiny. And the service of news, as distinct from the utterance of opinion, acquires an added importance. The need of the consumer to have adequate and uncontaminated mental food is such that he is under a duty to get it; and, because of this duty, his interest acquires the stature of a right. It becomes legitimate to speak of the moral right of men to the news they can use.[60]

Does the First Amendment protect only the editorial output of the media, or does it also protect their capital investments, their organizational bylaws and technology, and the airwaves they use? Recommendations are now being made that conduit and content be separated in the interest of freedom of expression; the Constitution would protect the output of the journalist but not the business interests of his employer.[61] One media economist proposes that antitrust and legislative action be taken to divest newspaper printing and delivery systems from editorial and newsgathering services. Such a structural change would mean that printing plants would have a quasi-public utility status and would be open to anyone willing to pay the costs of access to transmission facilities. Cross-ownership of newspaper and television media in the same city would be prohibited. But because broadcasting systems do not show the same monopolistic tendencies of newspapers, the licensing and regulatory authority of the FCC over broadcasting would be abolished.[62]

Congress and its creature, the FCC, have taken practically no steps toward goals of this kind, and the courts, where newspapers are concerned, would consider them unattainable. In fact Justice Potter Stewart said in a speech recently that "the Free Press Clause extends protection to an institution. The publishing business is, in short, the only organized private business that is given explicit constitutional protection...and it is...a mistake to suppose that the only purpose of the constitutional guarantee of a free press is to insure that a newspaper will serve as a neutral forum for debate, a 'marketplace for ideas,' a kind of Hyde Park corner for the community."[63]

Nevertheless, access is on the agenda and it will probably stay there. Never has there been so much potential for so much to be said to, and by, so many. America may have to modify its traditional concept of freedom of expression if it is to keep pace with expanding technologies and changing social needs. But it must achieve this by enlarging rather than contracting basic freedoms. And there may be risks involved.

Even though public access to communication channels implies an enlarged freedom of expression, a freer flow of information, a right to inform, to publish, to reply, and a more balanced flow of information, some consider the risks of experimentation too great. Paul Freund, an influential legal scholar, commenting on the *Miami Herald* case, in which the Supreme Court held Florida's right-of-reply statute unconstitutional, said:

...[I]t must be acknowledged that if a newspaper were obliged to publish a reply to every editorial expression of opinion or report of events the institution of the press as the Framers understood it would come to an end. Either a newspaper would become an incoherent grab-bag of miscellaneous contributions or it would cease to venture into controversial ground at all. In either event it would lose its distinctive character and force, and the First Amendment would have become self-defeating.[64]

Freund deals with the contradiction between the constitutional status of broadcast and print media by arguing a difference in law between a legally conferred monopoly and one produced by market conditions. "There is a difference," he says, "between the long tradition of an independent press and the evolving character of broadcasting, with its unique, concentrated impact in viewers and listeners."[65] And he deals with the newspaper-scarcity argument by pointing to the remarkable diversity of print publications. One wonders how his model would accommodate systems that combine print and electronic technologies, such as computer "print-outs" or facsimile delivered by satellite, microwave, or cable.

In a footnote to his opinion for the Court in the same case, Chief Justice Warren Burger makes reference to the belief of Thomas Emerson that a limited right of access may be enforced if it is done so by "governmental measures to encourage a multiplicity of outlets, rather than compelling a few outlets to represent everybody...."[66] Freund would agree, and their agreement is important because they are both eminent First Amendment scholars.

Emerson's *The System of Freedom of Expression* is the most sophisticated effort so far to develop what he calls a "full protection" theory of the First Amendment.[67] The theory depends at the outset on consensual definitions of freedom of speech, of law, of what the First Amendment intends in its use of the word "abridge." The centerpiece of Emerson's theory is the distinction between conduct that consists largely of "expression," and is therefore protected by the Constitution, and conduct that consists largely of "action," and is not protected by the Constitution.

Emerson believes that government does have a role in facilitating expression—for example, in protecting the public against private concentrations of ownership and power. He sees a positive role for government, which in turn requires him to give the First Amendment a broad interpretation that, at the very least, would include the right to form or hold beliefs and opinions, to have some right of access to the means of communication, to receive communication from others, and to obtain information on which to base decisions or to expedite further communication.[68]

Only under such conditions can social change take place without violence and can the rage generated when speech is suppressed be dissipated. "The test of the openness of a society and the health of its system of freedom of expression," says Emerson, "is likely to be found in its tolerance for militant rhetoric."[69] Does such rhetoric find meaningful outlets in contemporary society? There is disagreement. But it does seem that lack of public access to the major organs of news and opinion may be the greatest weakness of the existing system. Economic rather than political inequality may be the problem, and its solution will depend on public action. What forms this action can safely take without destroying the freedoms we already enjoy is part of the urgent agenda of the immediate future. Public action will be in large part legislative, and law makers will require the best possible information for their decisions.

What is most important, however, and what must continue unabated, is the dialogue itself. It will proceed through cases at law, resolutions, statutes, articles, books, research proposals, polemics, and yes, even through demands for revolutionary changes in systems and subsystems and through spirited classroom discussions.

Freedom of expression belongs to people who, by the fortunes of history, are free from fear. And tragically it is not a readily exportable blessing.

NOTES

1. John Milton, Areopagitica (1644; Jebb. ed., Cambridge: Cambridge University Press, 1918), p. 58: "And though all the winds of doctrine were let loose to play upon the earth, so Truth be in the field, we do injuriously by licensing and prohibiting to misdoubt her strength. Let her and Falsehood grapple; who ever knew Truth put to the worse in a free and open encounter."

2. *Constitution of the United States,* Amendment I (1791): "Congress shall make no law respecting an establishment of religion, or prohibiting the free exercise thereof; or abridging the freedom of speech, or of the press; or the right of the people peaceably to assemble, and to petition the Government for a redress of grievances."

3. John Stuart Mill, *On Liberty,* ed. Alburey Castell (New York: F. S. Crofts, 1947), p. 17.

4. *Schenck v. United States,* 249 U.S. 47 (1919): "The question in every case is whether the words used are used in such circumstances and are of such a nature as to create *a clear and present danger* that they will bring about the substantive evils that Congress has a right to prevent." (Emphasis added.) For an extended discussion of the "clear and present danger" doctrine see Zechariah Chafee, Jr., *Free Speech in the United States* (Cambridge, Mass.: Harvard University Press, 1941).

5. Harry Kalven, Jr., "The New York *Times* Case: A Note on the Central Meaning of the First Amendment," in *Supreme Court Review,* ed. Philip B. Kurland, (Chicago: University of Chicago Press, 1964), p. 205.

6. Associate Justice William Brennan for the United States Supreme Court in *New York Times* v. *Sullivan,* 376 U.S. 254 (1964), a landmark case which has made it impossible for public officials or public figures to win a libel judgment against a publisher without proof by the plaintiff of actual malice on the part of the defendant, that is "with knowledge that it (the publication) was false or with reckless disregard of whether it was false or not."

7. Alexander Meiklejohn, *Political Freedom* (New York: Harper & Row, 1960). The quotation represents the major theme of this treatise.

8. Thomas I. Emerson, *Toward a General Theory of the First Amendment* (New York: Vintage Books, 1967), pp. 4, 18-19, 22-27.

9. Herbert Marcuse, "Repressive Tolerance," in *A Critique of Pure Tolerance,* ed. Robert Paul Wolff, Barrington Moore, Jr., and Herbert Marcuse (Boston: Beacon Press, 1965), p. 110.

10. *Near* v. *Minnesota,* 283 U.S. 697 (1931), the landmark case. See also *Bantam Books, Inc.* v. *Sullivan,* 372 U.S. 58, 70 (1963), in which the Court says that "any system of prior restraints comes to this Court bearing a heavy presumption against constitutionality."

11. *New York Times.* v. *United States; United States* v. *Washington Post* (the Pentagon Papers case), 403 U.S. 713 (1971). See also *Nebraska Press Association* v. *Stuart, 427 U.S. 539 (1976).*

12. Donald M. Gillmor, *Judicial Restraints on the Press* (Columbia, Mo.: Freedom of Information Foundation, 1974). See especially the discussion of *United States* v. *Dickinson,* 465 F. 2d 496 (5th Cir. 1972), pp. 5-7.

13. Donald M. Gillmor, and Jerome A. Barron, *Mass Communication Law: Cases and Comment,* 2nd ed. (St. Paul, Minn.: West, 1974), pp. 7-8, 25-26, 81-83. For the absolutist view of the First Amendment by one of its staunchest proponents, see William O. Douglas, *The Right of the People* (Garden City, N.Y.: Doubleday, 1958). For a comprehensive statement of the preference doctrine, see Robert B. McKay, "The Preference for Freedom," *New York University Law Review* 34 (November 1959): 1182-1222. Learned Hand's *The Bill of Rights* (New York: Atheneum, 1964) reflects the balance-of-interests doctrine.

14. *Lovell* v. *Griffin,* 303 U.S. 444 (1938).

15. *Hannegan* v. *Esquire,* 327 U.S. 146 (1946); *Lamont* v. *Postmaster General,* 381 U.S. 301 (1965).

16. *Talley* v. *California,* 362 U.S. 60 (1960).

17. *Bridges* v. *California,* 314 U.S. 252 (1941). The language is Justice Frank Murphy's in a similar case, *Pennekamp* v. *Florida,* 328 U.S. 331, 370 (1946).

18. *Grosjean* v. *American Press Co.,* 297 U.S. 233 (1936).

19. *DeJonge* v. *Oregon,* 299 U.S. 353 (1937).

20. *Edwards* v. *South Carolina,* 372 U.S. 229 (1963).

21. *Quad-City Community News Service, Inc.* v. *Jebens,* 334 F.Supp. 8 (D.C. Iowa 1971).

22. Robert Trager, *Student Press Rights* (Urbana, Ill.: ERIC and Journalism Education Association, 1974).

23. *Chaplinsky* v. *New Hampshire,* 315 U.S. 568 (1942).

24. *Feiner* v. *New York,* 340 U.S. 315 (1951).

25. *Terminiello* v. *Chicago,* 337 U.S. 1 (1949).

26. *Walker* v. *Birmingham,* 388 U.S. 307 (1967), *Shuttlesworth* v. *Birmingham,* 394 U.S. 147 (1969); *Amalgamated Food Employees Union Local 590* v. *Logan Valley Plaza, Inc.,* 391 U.S. 308 (1968), *Lloyd Corp.* v. *Tanner,* 407 U.S. 551 (1972); *Cantwell* v. *Connecticut* 310 U.S. 296 (1940), *Breard* v. *Alexandria,* 341 U.S. 622 (1951).

27. *United States* v. *O'Brien,* 391 U.S. 367 (1968).

28. *Street* v. *New York,* 394 U.S. 576 (1969).

29. *Tinker* v. *Des Moines Independent School District,* 393 U.S. 503 (1969).

30. *Bigelow* v. *Virginia,* 421 U.S. 809 (1975).

31. *Valentine* v. *Chrestensen,* 316 U.S. 52 (1942).

32. *Gertz* v. *Robert Welch, Inc.,* 418 U.S. 323 (1974).

33. *Cantrell* v. *Forest City Publishing Co.,* 419 U.S. 245 (1974).

34. *Nebraska Press Association* v. *Stuart,* 427 U.S. 539 (1976).

35. *Miller* v. *State of California,* 413 U.S. 15 (1973); see particularly Justice William Brennan's dissent in a companion case, *Paris Adult Theatre I* v. *Slaton,* 413 U.S. 49 (1973).

36. *Estes* v. *State of Texas,* 381 U.S. 532 (1965).

37. *Branzburg* v. *Hayes,* 408 U.S. 665 (1972).

38. *Evans* v. *American Federation of Television and Radio Artists,* 354 F. Supp. 823 (S.D.N.Y. 1973), reversed, 496 F. 2d 305 (2d Cir. 1974); *Buckley* v. *Valeo,* 96 S.Ct. 612 (1976).

39. *American Civil Liberties Union* v. *Jennings,* 366 F. Supp. 1041 (D.C.D.C. 1973).

40. *Freedom of Information Act* (Pub. L. 89-554, Sept. 6, 1966, 80 Stat. 383; Pub. L. 90-23 § 1, June 5, 1967, 81 Stat. 54; Pub. L. 93-502 § 1-4, Nov. 21, 1974, 88 Stat. 1561. The 1974 Amendments to the Act supersede the Supreme Court's holding in *Environmental Protection Agency* v. *Mink,* 410 U.S. 73 (1973).

41. *Kleindienst v. Mandel,* 408 U.S. 753 (1973).

42. *Public Utilities Commission* v. *Pollak,* 343 U.S. 451 (1952).

43. *Zemel v. Rusk,* 381 U.S. 1 (1965).

44. *United States* v. *Paramount Pictures,* 334 U.S. 131 (1948); *Joseph Burstyn, Inc.* v. *Wilson,* 343 U.S. 495 (1952).

45. Daniel B. Wackman, Donald M. Gillmor, Cecilie Gaziano and Everette E. Dennis, "Chain Newspaper Autonomy as Reflected in Presidential Campaign Endorsements," *Journalism Quarterly* 52 (Autumn 1975): 411-420.

46. Jerome A. Barron, *Freedom of the Press for Whom?* (Bloomington: Indiana University Press, 1973). For an analysis of and a rejection in part of Barron's access thesis see Benno C. Schmidt, Jr., *Freedom of the Press vs. Public Access* (Aspen, Col. and New York: Aspen Institute Program on Communications and Society and Praeger, 1976).

47. *Miami Herald Publishing Co.* v. *Tornillo,* 418 U.S. 241 (1974).

48. *Chicago Joint Board, Amalgamated Clothing Workers of America, AFL-CIO* v. *Chicago Tribune Co.,* 307 F. Supp. 422 (N.D. Ill. 1969).

49. *Red Lion Broadcasting Co., Inc.* v. *Federal Communications Commission,* 395 U.S. 367 (1969).

50. *Columbia Broadcasting System, Inc.* v. *Democratic National Committee,* 412 U.S. 94 (1973).

51. William Proxmire, "Repealing the Fairness Doctrine," *TV Guide,* 12 April 1975.

52. *National Broadcasting Company, Inc.* v. *Federal Communications Commission,* 516 F. 2d 1101 (D.C. Cir. 1974).

53. Fred W. Friendly, *The Good Guys, the Bad Guys, and the First Amendment* (New York: Random House, 1976), p. 221.

54. Friendly, *Good Guys,* p. 227. It should be noted that in 1976 the FCC in the WHAR case found a radio station in violation of the Fairness Doctrine for failing to deal with the continuing and controversial issue of strip mining in the listening area of Clarksburg, West Virginia. See In re Complaint of Rep. Patsy Mink..., FCC 76-529 (16 June 1976).

55. *Television Fact Book,* no. 42 (1972-1973).

56. *Territory of Alaska* v. *Journal Printing Co.,* 135 F. Supp. 169 (D.C. Alaska 1955).

57. *Mabee* v. *White Plains Publishing Co.,* 327 U.S. 178 (1946); *Oklahoma Press Publishing Co.* v. *Walling,* 327 U.S. 178 (1946); *Associated Press* v. *National Labor Relations Board,* 301 U.S. 103 (1937).

58. *Associated Press et al.* v. *United States,* 326 U.S. 1 (1945); *Citizens Publishing Co.* v. *United States,* 394 U.S. 131 (1969).

59. *Associated Press et al.* v. *United States* at 1.

60. Commission on Freedom of the Press, *A Free and Responsible Press* (Chicago: University of Chicago Press, 1947), p. 125.

61. Anne W. Branscomb, *The First Amendment as a Shield or a Sword: An Integrated Look at Regulation of Multi-Media Ownership* (Santa Monica, Calif.: Rand Corporation, 1975), pp. 99-100.

62. Bruce M. Owen, *Economics and Freedom of Expression* (Cambridge, Mass.: Balinger, 1975), pp. 183-189.

63. Potter Stewart, "Or of the Press," *Hastings Law Review* 26 (1975): 631. Also quoted in Schmidt, *Freedom of the Press,* p. 238.

64. Paul A. Freund, "The Legal Framework of the Tornillo Case," in *The Trial of the First Amendment* ed. Roy M. Fisher (Columbia, Mo.: Freedom of Information Center, 1975), p. 27.

65. Freund, "Tornillo Case," p. 27.

66. *Miami Herald Publishing Co.* v. *Tornillo,* 418 U.S. 241 (1974).

67. Thomas I. Emerson, *The System of Freedom of Expression* (New York: Vintage Books, 1971), p. 671.

68. Thomas I. Emerson, "Communication and Freedom of Expression," *Scientific American,* September 1972, p. 163.

69. Emerson, "Communication and Expression," p. 167.

Part Three

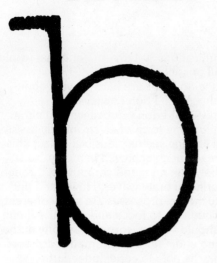

Technology and the Illusion of Utopia

COMMUNICATIONS IN THE SECOND CENTURY OF THE TELEPHONE

Arthur C. Clarke

Man is the communicating animal; he demands news, information, entertainment, almost as much food. In fact, as a functioning human being, he can survive much longer without food—even without water!—than without information, as experiments in sensory deprivation have shown. This is a truly astonishing fact; one could construct a whole philosophy around it.

So any major advance in communications capability that can be conceived can be realized in practice, and that same advance will come into widespread use just as soon as it is practicable. Often sooner; the public can't wait for "state of the art" to settle down. Remember the first clumsy phonographs, radios, tape recorders? And would you believe the date of the first music broadcast? It was barely a year after the invention of the telephone! On April 2, 1877, a "telegraphic harmony" apparatus in Philadelphia sent "Yankee Doodle" to sixteen loudspeakers—well, soft-speakers—in New York's Steinway Hall. Alexander Graham Bell was in the audience, and one would like to know if he complimented the promoter—his now forgotten rival, Elisha Gray, who got to the Patent Office just those fatal few hours too late....

Gray was not the only one to be caught out by the momentum of events. When news of the telephone reached England through Cyrus Field's undersea telegraphic cable, the chief engineer of the Post Office was asked whether this new Yankee invention would be of any practical value. He gave the forthright reply: "No, sir. The Americans have need of the telephone—but we do not. We have plenty of messenger boys."

Before you laugh at this myopic Victorian, please ask yourself this question: would you, exactly a hundred years ago, ever dream that the time would come when this primitive toy would not only be in every home and every office, but would be the essential basis of all social, administrative and business life in the civilized world? Or that one day there would be approximately one instrument for every ten human beings on the planet?

Now, the telephone is a very simple device, which even the 19th century could readily mass produce. In fact, one derivative of the carbon microphone must be near the absolute zero of technological complexity: you can make a working—though hardly hi-fi—microphone out of three carpenter's nails, one laid across the other two to form a letter H.

The extraordinary — nay, magical — simplicity of the telephone allowed it to spread over the world with astonishing speed. When we consider the very much more complex devices of the future, is it reasonable to suppose that they too will eventually become features of every home, every office? Well, let me give you another cautionary tale.

THE COMFORTABLE COMSOLE

In the early 1940s, the late John W. Campbell—editor of *Astounding Stories,* and undoubtedly the most formidable imagination ever to be flunked at M.I.T.—pooh-poohed the idea of home television. He refused to believe that anything as complex as a TV receiver could ever be made cheap and reliable enough for domestic use.

Public demand certainly disposed of that prophecy. Home TV became available in the Early Neo-Electronic Age—that is, *even before* the solid-state revolution. So let us take it as axiomatic that complexity is no bar to universality. Think of your pocket computers and march fearlessly into the future...trying to imagine the ideal, ultimate

communications system—the one that would fulfill all possible fantasies.

Since no holds are barred, what about telepathy? Well, I don't believe in telepathy—but I don't *disbelieve* in it either. Certainly some form of electronically-assisted mental linkage seems plausible; in fact, this has already been achieved in a very crude form, between men and computers, through monitoring of brain waves. However, I find that *my* mental processes are so incoherent, even when I try to focus and organize them, that I should be very sorry for anyone at the receiving end. Our superhuman successors, if any, may be able to cope; indeed, the development of the right technology might force such an evolutionary advance. Perhaps the best that *we* could manage would be the sharing of emotional states, not the higher intellectual processes. So radio-assisted telepathy might merely lead to some interesting new vices—admittedly, a long-felt want.

Let's stick, therefore, to the recognized sense channels, of which sound and sight are by far the most important. Although one day we will presumably develop transducers for all the senses, just because they are there, I suspect that the law of diminishing returns will set in rather rapidly after the "feelies" and "smellies." These may have some limited applications for entertainment purposes, as anyone who was pulverized by the movie *Earthquake* may agree. (Personally, I'm looking forward to the epic *Nova,* in which the theater's heating system is turned on full blast in the final reel....)

The basic ingredients of the ideal communications device are, therefore, already in common use even today. The standard computer console, with keyboard and visual display, plus hi-fi sound and TV camera, will do very nicely. Through such an instrument (for which I've coined the ugly but perhaps unavoidable name "comsole"—communications console) one could have face-to-face interaction with anyone, anywhere on earth, and send or receive any type of information. I think most of us would settle for this, but there are some other possibilities to consider.

For example: what about *verbal* inputs? Do we really need a keyboard? I'm sure the answer is "Yes." We want to be able to type out messages, look at them, and edit them before transmission. We need keyboard inputs for privacy, and quietness. A *reliable* voice recognition system, capable of coping with accents, hangovers, ill-fitting dentures and the "human error" that my late friend HAL, the computer from *2001,* complained about, represents something many orders of magnitude more complex than a simple alpha-numeric keyboard. It would be a device with capabilities, in a limited area, at least as good as those of a human brain.

Yet assuming that the curves of the last few decades can be extrapolated, this will certainly be available sometime in the next century. Though most of us will still be tapping out numbers in 2001, I've little real doubt that well before 2076 you will simply say to your comsole: "Get me Bill Smith". Or if you *do* say: "Get me 212-345-5512," it will answer, "Surely you mean 212-245-5521." And it will be quite right.

Now a machine with this sort of capability—a robot secretary, in effect—could be quite expensive. *It doesn't matter.*

Contrary to the edicts of Madison Avenue, the time will come when it won't be necessary to trade in last year's model. Eventually, everything reaches its technological plateau, and thereafter the only changes are in matters of style. This is obvious when you look at such familiar domestic objects as chairs, beds, tables, knives, forks. Oh, you can make them of plastic or fiberglass or whatever, but the basic design rarely alters.

It took a few thousand years to reach these particular plateaus; things happen more quickly nowadays even for much more complex devices. The bicycle took about a century; radio receivers half that time. This is not to deny that marginal improvements will go on indefinitely, but after a while all further changes are icing on a perfectly palatable cake. You may be surprised to learn that

there are electrical devices that have been giving satisfactory service for half a century or more. The other day someone found an Edison carbon filament lamp that has apparently never been switched off since it was installed. And until recently, there were sections of Atlantic cable that had been in service for a full century!

Now, it's hard to see how a properly designed and constructed solid-state device can ever wear out. It should have something like the working life of a diamond, which is adequate for most practical purposes. So when we reach this state of affairs, it would be worth investing more in a multi-purpose home communications device than in an automobile. It could be handed on from one generation to the next—as was once the case with a good watch.

PLUGGING IN
TO THE FUTURE

It has been obvious for a very long time that such audio-visual devices could complete the revolution started by the telephone. We are already approaching the point when it will be feasible—not necessarily desirable—for those engaged in what is quaintly called "white-collar" jobs to do perhaps 95 percent of their work without leaving home. Of course, few of today's families could survive this, but for the moment let's confine ourselves to electronic, not social, technology.

Many years ago I coined the slogan: "Don't commute—communicate!" Apart from the savings in travel time (the *real* reason I became a writer is that I refuse to spend more than 30 seconds moving from home to office) there would be astronomical economies in power and raw materials. Compare the amount of hardware in communications systems, as opposed to railroads, highways and airlines. And the number of kilowatt hours you expend on the shortest journey would power several lifetimes of chatter, between the remotest ends of the earth.

Obviously, the home comsole would handle most of today's first-class mail;

messages would be stored in its memory waiting for you to press the playback key whenever you felt like it. Then you would type out the answer—or alternatively call up the other party for a face-to-face chat.

Fine, but at once we have a serious problem—the already annoying matter of time zones. They are going to become quite intolerable in the electronic global village—where we are all neighbors, but a third of us are asleep at any given moment. The other day I was woken up at 4:00 a.m. by the London *Daily Express,* which had subtracted 5½ hours instead of adding them. I don't know what I said, but I doubt if my views on the Loch Ness Monster were printable.

The railroads and the telegraph made time zones inevitable in the 19th century; the global telecommunications network of the 21st may abolish them. It's been suggested, at least half seriously, that we'll have to establish a Common Time over the whole planet—whatever inconvenience this may cause to those old-fashioned enough to gear themselves to the day-night cycle.

During the course of the day—whatever *that* may be—you will use the home comsole to call your friends and deal with business, exactly as you use the telephone now—with this difference: you'll be able to exchange any amount of tabular, visual or graphical information. Thus if you're an author, you'll be able to wave that horrid page-one type in front of your delinquent editor on Easter Island, or wherever he lives. Instead of spending hours hunting for non-existent parts numbers, engineers will be able to *show* their supplier the broken dohickey from the rotary discombobulator. And we'll be able to see those old friends of a lifetime, whom we'll never again meet in the flesh.

Which raises an interesting problem. One of the great advantages of Mr. Bell's invention is that you can converse with people *without* their seeing you, or knowing where you are, or who is with you. A great many business deals would never be consummated, or even attempted, over a video circuit; but perhaps they are deals that shouldn't be, anyway....

I am aware that previous attempts to supply vision—such as the Bell Picturephone—have hardly been a roaring success. But I feel sure that this is due to cost, the small size of the picture, and the limited service available. No one would have predicted much of a future for the very first "Televisors," with their flickering, postage-stamp-sized images. Such technical limitations have a habit of being rather rapidly overcome, and the *large-screen, high-definition* Picturephone-Plus is inevitable.

I could certainly do with such a device. For several years, Stanley Kubrick has been talking wistfully to me about another space project. But there's an insoluble problem—I won't leave my home in Sri Lanka for more than a couple of weeks a year, and Stanley refuses to get into an airplane. We may both be too old, or too lazy, before the arrival of home comsoles makes another collaboration possible. So the present backwardness of electronics has spared the world another masterpiece like *2001: A Space Odyssey.*

Clearly, when we do have two-way vision, there will have to be some changes in protocol. You can't *always* pretend to your wife that the camera has broken down again.... Incidentally, some of the changes that would be produced in a society totally oriented to telecommunications have been well discussed by a promising local writer, in a novel called *The Naked Sun.* The author's full name escapes me at the moment, but I believe it begins with "Isaac."

INFOMANIACS REJOICE!

The possibilities of the comsole as an entertainment and information device are virtually unlimited; some of them, of course, are just becoming available, as an adjunct to the various TV subscription services. At any moment one should be able to call up all the news headlines on the screen, and expand any of particular interest into a complete story at several levels of thoroughness—all the way, let us say, from the *Daily News* to the *New York Times....* I hate to think of the hours I have wasted, listening to radio news bulletins—for some item that never turned up. Nothing is more frustrating—as will be confirmed by any Englishmen touring the United States during a Test Match, or any American in England during the World Series (how did it get that ridiculous name?). For the first time, it will be possible to have a news service with immediacy, selectivity, *and* thoroughness.

The electronic newspaper, apart from all its other merits, will also have two gigantic ecological plusses. It will save whole forests for posterity; and it will halve the cost of garbage collection. This alone might be enough to justify it, and to pay for it.

Like many of my generation, I became a news addict during World War II. Even now, it takes a definite effort of will for me *not* to switch on the hourly news summaries, and with a truly global service one could spend every waking minute monitoring the amusing, crazy, interesting and tragic things that go on around this planet. I can foresee the rise of even more virulent forms of news addiction, resulting in the evolution of a class of people who can't bear to miss anything that's happening, anywhere, and spend their waking hours glued to the comsole. I've even coined a name for them—Infomaniacs.

Continuing in this vein, I used to think how nice it would be to have access, in one's own home, to all the books and printed matter, all the recordings and movies, all the visual arts of mankind. But would not many of us be completely overwhelmed by such an embarassment of riches, and solve the impossible problem of selection by selecting nothing? Every day I sneak guiltily past my set of the *Great Books of the Western World,* most of which I've never even opened....What would it *really* be like to have the Library of Congress—*all* the world's great libraries—at your fingertips? Assuming, of course, that your fingertips were sufficiently educated to handle the problem of indexing and retrieval. I speak with some feeling on

this subject, because for a couple of years I had the job of classifying and indexing everything published in the physical sciences, in all languages. If you can't find what you're looking for in *Physics Abstracts* for 1949-51, you'll know who to blame.

With the latest techniques, it would be possible to put the whole of human knowledge into a shoe box. The problem, of course, is to get it out again; anything misfiled would be irretrievably lost. Another problem is to decide whether we mass-produce the shoe boxes, so that every family has one—or whether we have a central shoe box linked to the home with wide-band communications.

Probably we'll have both, and there are also some interesting compromises. Years ago I invented something that I christened, believe it or not, the *Micropaedia Brittanica.* My *Micropaedia* would be a box about the size of an ordinary hard-cover book, with a display screen and alpha-numeric keyboard. It would contain, in text and pictures, *at least* as much material as a large encyclopaedia plus dictionary.

However, the main point of the electronic *Brittanica* would not be its compactness—but the fact that, every few months, you could plug it in, dial a number, and have it up-dated overnight....Think of the saving in wood pulp and transportation that this implies!

THE NEXT BEST THING TO BEING THERE...

It is usually assumed that the comsole would have a flat TV-type screen, which would appear to be all that is necessary for most communications purposes. But the ultimate in face-to-face electronic confrontation would be when you could not tell, without touching, whether or not the other person was physically present; he or she would appear as a perfect 3-D projection. This no longer appears fantastic, now that we have seen holographic displays that are quite indistinguishable from reality. So I am sure that this will be achieved some day; I am not sure how badly we need it.

What *could* be done, even with current techniques, is to provide 3-D—or at least widescreen Cinerama-type—pictures for a single person at a time. This would need merely a small viewing booth and some clever optics, and it could provide the basis for a valuable educational-entertainment tool, as Dennis Gabor, inventor of holography, has suggested. But it could also give rise to a new industry—personalized television safaris. When you can have a high-quality cinema display in your own home, there will certainly be global audiences for specialized programs with instant feedback from viewer to cameraman. How nice to be able to make a trip up the Amazon, with a few dozen unknown friends scattered over the world, with perfect sound and vision, being able to ask your guide questions, suggest detours, request closeups of interesting plants or animals—in fact, sharing everything except the mosquitoes and the heat!

It has been suggested that this sort of technology might ultimately lead to a world in which no one *ever* bothered to leave home. The classic treatment of this theme is, of course, E. M. Forster's *The Machine Stops,* written more than 70 years ago as a counterblast to H. G. Wells.

Yet I don't regard this sort of pathological, sedentary society as very likely. "Telesafaris" might have just the opposite effect. The customers would, sooner or later, be inspired to visit the places that really appealed to them...mosquitoes notwithstanding. Improved communications will promote travel for *pleasure*; and the sooner we get rid of the other kind, the better.

THE MOVEABLE INFORMATION FEAST

So far, I have been talking about the communications devices in the home and the office. But in the last few decades we have seen the telephone begin to lose its metal umbilical cord, and this process will accelerate. The rise of walkie-talkies and Citizen's Band radio is a portent of the future.

The individual wrist-watch telephone through which you can contact anyone, anywhere, will be a mixed blessing which, nevertheless, very few will be able to reject. In fact, we may not have a choice; it is all too easy to imagine a society in which it is illegal to switch off your receiver, in case the Chairman of the People's Cooperative wants to summon you in a hurry.... But let's not ally ourselves with those reactionaries who look only on the *bad* side of *every* new development. Alexander Graham Bell cannot be blamed for Stalin, once aptly described as "Genghis Khan with a telephone."

It would be an *underestimate* to say that the wrist-watch telephone would save tens of thousands of lives a year. Everyone of us knows of tragedies—car accidents on lonely highways, lost campers, overturned boats, even old people at home—where some means of communication would have made all the difference between life and death. Even a simple emergency S.O.S. system, whereby one pressed a button and sent out a HELP! signal, would be enough. This is a possibility of the immediate future; the only real problem—and, alas, a serious one—is that of false alarms.

Now, the invariably forgotten accessory of the wrist-watch telephone is the wrist-watch telephone *directory*. Considering the bulk of that volume for even a modest-sized city, this means that our personal transceivers will require some sophisticated information-retrieval circuits, and a memory to hold the few hundred most-used numbers. So we may be forced, rather quickly, to go the whole way, and combine in a single highly portable unit not only communications equipment, but also something like today's pocket-calculators, plus data banks, plus information processing circuits. It would be a constant companion, serving much the same purpose as a human secretary. In a recent novel I called it a

"Minisec." In fact, as electronic intelligence develops, it would provide more and more services, finally developing a personality of its own, to a degree which may be unimaginable today.

Except, of course, by science fiction writers. In his brilliant novel, *The Futurological Congress,* Stanislaw Lem gives a nightmare cameo which I can't get out of my mind. He describes a group of women sitting in complete silence—while their handbag computers gossip happily to one another....

TIPTOEING THROUGH THE SPECTRUM

At this point, before I lose all credibility with the hairy-knuckled engineers who have to produce the hardware, I'd better do a once-over-lightly of the electromagnetic spectrum. This is, I think, unique among our natural resources. We've been exploiting it for less than one lifetime, and are now polluting much of it to the very maximum of our ability. But if we stopped using it tomorrow, it would be just as good as new, because the garbage is heading outwards at the speed of light.... Too bad this isn't true of the rest of the environment.

Do we have enough available bandwidth for a billion personal transceivers, even assuming that they aren't all working at once? As far as the home equipment is concerned, there is no problem, at least in communities of any size. The only uncertainty, and a pretty harrowing one to the people who have to make the decisions, is how quickly coaxial cables are going to be replaced by glass fibers, with their million-fold greater communications capability. Incidentally, one of the less glamorous occupations of the future will be mining houses for the rare metal, copper, buried inside them by our rich ancestors. Fortunately, there is no danger that we shall ever run out of silica....

But I would also suggest that optical systems, in the infrared and ultraviolet, have a great future not only for fixed, but even for *mobile,* personal communications. They may take over some of the functions of present-day transistor radios and walkie-talkies—leaving the radio bands free for services which can be provided in no other way. The fact that opticals have only very limited range, owing to atmospheric absorption, can be turned to major advantage. You can use the same frequencies—and *what* a band of frequencies!—millions of times over—as long as you keep your service areas 10 or 20 kilometers apart.

It may be objected that light waves won't go around corners, or though walls. Elementary, my dear Watson. We simply have lots of dirt cheap—because they are made from dirt!—optical wave guides and light pipes deliberately leaking radiation all over the place. Some would be passive, some active. Some would have very low-powered optical-to-radio transducers in both directions, to save knocking holes in walls, and to get to awkward places. In densely populated communities one would always be in direct or reflected sight of some optical transmitter or repeater. But we must be careful how we use the ultraviolet. People who talked too much might get sunburned....

When you are cycling across Africa, or drifting on a balsa-wood raft across the Pacific, you will of course still have to use the radio frequencies — say the one to ten thousand megahertz bands, which can accommodate at least ten million voice circuits. This number can be multiplied many times by skillful use of satellite technology. I can envisage an earth-embracing halo of low-altitude, low-powered radio satellites, switching frequencies continually so that they provide the desired coverage in given geographical regions. And N.A.S.A. has recently published a most exciting report on the use of the very large (kilometer-square!) antennas we will soon be able to construct in space. These would permit the simultaneous use of myriads of very narrow beams which could be focused on individual subscribers carrying receivers which could be mass-produced for about $10. I rather suspect that our long-awaited personal transceiver will be an adaptive, radio-optical hybrid, actively hunting the electromagnetic spectrum in search of incoming signals addressed to it.

THE ELECTRONIC DRUG?

One of the functions of science fiction is to serve as an early warning system. In fact, the very act of description may prevent some futures, by a kind of exclusion principle. Far from predicting the future, science fiction often *exorcises* it. At the very least, it makes us ask ourselves: "What kind of future do we really want?" No other type of literature poses such fundamental questions, at any rate explicitly.

The marvellous toys that we have been discussing will simply remain toys, unless we use them constructively and creatively. Now, toys are all right in the proper place; in fact they are an essential part of any childhood. But they should not become mere distractions—or ways of drugging the mind to avoid reality.

We have all seen unbuttoned beer-bellies slumped in front of the TV set, and transistorized morons twitching down the street, puppets controlled by invisible disk jockeys. These are not the highest representatives of our culture; but, tragically, they may be typical of the near future. As we evolve a society orientated towards

information, and move away from one based primarily on manufacture and transportation, there will be millions who cannot adapt to the change. We may have no alternative but to use the lower electronic arts to keep them in a state of drugged placidity.

For in the world of the future, the sort of mindless labor that has occupied 99 per cent of mankind, for much more than 99 percent of its existence, will of course be largely taken over by machines. Yet most people are bored to death without work—even work they don't like. In a workless world, therefore, only the highly educated will be able to flourish, or perhaps even to survive. The rest are likely to destroy themselves and their environment out of sheer frustration. This is no vision of the distant future; it is already happening, most of all in the decaying cities.

So perhaps we should not despise TV soap operas if, during the turbulent transition period between our culture and real civilization, they serve as yet another opium for the masses. *This* drug, at any rate, is cheap and harmless, serving to kill time—for those many people who like it better dead.

COMMUNICATE TO EDUCATE

When we look at the manifold problems of our age, it is clear that the most fundamental one—from which almost all others stem—is that of ignorance. And ignorance can be banished only by communication, in the widest meaning of the word.

The best educational arrangement, someone once remarked, consists of a log with a teacher at one end and a pupil at the other. Unfortunately there are no longer enough teachers, and probably not enough logs, to go around.

Now, one thing that electronics can do rather well is to multiply teachers. As you doubtless know, at this very moment a most ambitious and exciting social experiment is taking place in India, where N.A.S.A.'s ATS-6 satellite is broadcasting educational programs to several thousand villages. ATS-6 is the only communications satellite in existence powerful enough to transmit signals that can be picked up on an ordinary TV set, augmented by a simple parabolic dish, like a large umbrella made of wire mesh.

Thanks to the extraordinary generosity of the Indian Space Research Organization, which flew in six engineers and half a ton of equipment, I have a five-meter satellite antenna on the roof of my Colombo house, now renamed "Jodrell Bank East." Since the experiment started on August 1, 1975, I have thus been in the curious position of having the only TV set in Sri Lanka. It's been fascinating to watch the programs; even though I don't understand Hindi, the messages of family planning, hygiene, agricultural techniques and national unity come across loud and clear.

Though it is impossible to put a value on such things, I believe that the cost of this experiment will be trivial compared with the benefits. And the ground segment is remarkably cheap, in terms of its coverage. Would you believe 4,000 people round one TV set? Or a 3-meter-diameter village antenna—made of *dried mud?*

Of course, there are some critics—as reported recently by Dr. Yash Pal, the able and energetic Director of the Indian Space Application Centre:

"In the drawing room of large cities," he says, "you meet many people who are concerned about the damage one is going to cause to the integrity of rural India by exposing her to the world outside. After they have lectured you about the dangers of corrupting this innocent, beautiful mass of humanity, they usually turn round and ask: 'Well, now that we have a satellite, when are we going to see some American programs?' Of course they themselves are immune to cultural domination or foreign influence."

I'm afraid that cocktail party intellectuals are the same everywhere. Because *we* frequently suffer from the modern scourge of information pollution, we find it hard to imagine its even deadlier

opposite—information starvation. For any outsider, however well-meaning, to tell an Indian villager that he would be better off without access to the world's news, entertainment, *and knowledge,* is an obscene impertinence, like the spectacle of a fat man preaching the virtues of fasting to the hungry.

Unfortunately, on July 31, 1976, the one-year experiment will end; ATS-6 will crawl back along the equator and return to the United States. Originally, it was hoped to launch *two* satellites; last summer I saw the three-quarters completed ATS-7, sitting mothballed at the Fairchild plant. No one could raise the $10 million necessary to finish it, or hijack one of the Air Force's numerous Titan 3-Cs to get it into orbit.

And so in a few months' time, millions of people who have had a window opened on marvellous new worlds of culture and education will have it slammed down in their faces again. There will be some heart-rending scenes in the villages, when the cry goes up, however unfairly, "The Americans have stolen our satellite!" Useless to explain, as the frustrated viewers start to refill their six-to-nine p.m. time slot with baby-making, that it was only through the initiative and generosity of the United States that the satellite was loaned in the first place....The Ugly American will have struck again.

Yet I hope that this noble experiment is just the curtain-raiser to a truly global educational satellite system. Its cost would be one or two dollars per student, per *year.* There could be few better investments in the future health, happiness and peace of mankind.

I don't wish to get too much involved in the potential—still less the politics—of communications satellites, because they can take care of themselves, and are now multiplying rapidly. The world investment in satellites and ground stations now exceeds a billion dollars, and is increasing almost explosively. After years of delay and dithering, the United States is at last establishing *domestic* satellite systems; the U.S.S.R. has had one for almost a decade. At first, the Soviet network emloyed *non*-synchronous satellites, moving in an elongated orbit that took them high over Russia for a few hours of every day. However, they have now seen the overwhelming advantages of stationary orbits, and several of their comsats are currently fixed above the Indian Ocean. Some are designed for TV relaying to remote parts of the Soviet Union, and I've gently hinted to my friends in Moscow that perhaps *they* could fill the breach when ATS-6 goes home....

We are now in the early stages of a battle for the mind—or at least the eyes and ears—of the human race, a battle which will be fought 36,000 kilometers above the equator. The preliminary skirmishes have already taken place at the United Nations, where there have been determined attempts by some countries to limit the use of satellites which can beam programs from space directly into the home, thus bypassing the national networks. Guess who is scared . . . .

As a matter of fact, I tried to frighten the United States with satellites myself, back in 1960, when I published a story in 1960 in *Playboy* about a Chinese plot to brainwash innocent Americans with pornographic TV programs. Perhaps "frighten" is not the correct verb, and in these permissive days such an idea sounds positively old-fashioned. But in 1960 the first regular comsat service was still five years in the future, and this seemed a good gambit for attracting attention to its possibilities.

UNITED STATES OF EARTH

Fortunately, in this area there is an excellent record of international cooperation. Even countries who hate each other's guts work together through the International Telecommunications Union, which sets limits to powers and assigns frequencies. Eventually, some kind of consensus will emerge, which will avoid the worst abuses.

A major step towards this was taken on August 20, 1971, when the agreement setting up INTELSAT (the International Telecommunications Satellite Organization) was signed at the State Department. I would like to quote from the address I gave on that occasion:

I submit that the eventual impact of the communications satellite upon the whole human race will be at least as great as that of the telephone upon the so-called developed societies.

In fact, as far as real communications are concerned, there are as yet no developed societies; we are all still in the semaphore and smoke-signal stage. And we are now about to witness an interesting situation in which many countries, particularly in Asia and Africa, are going to leapfrog a whole era of communications technology and go straight into the space age. They will never know the vast networks of cables and microwave links that this country has built at such enormous cost both in money and in natural resources. The satellites can do far more and at far less expense to the environment....

...I believe that the communications satellites can unite mankind. Let me remind you, that, whatever the history books say, this great country was created a little more than a hundred years ago by two inventions. Without them, the United States was impossible; with them, it was inevitable. Those inventions were, of course, the railroad and the electric telegraph.

Today we are seeing on a global scale an almost exact parallel to that situation. What the railroads and the telegraph did here a century ago, the jets and the communications satellites are doing now to all the world....

And the final result—whatever name we actually give to it—will be the United States of Earth.

THE SPACE BARRIER

I would like to end with some thoughts on the wider future of communications— communications beyond the earth. And here we face an extraordinary paradox, which in the centuries to come may have profound political and cultural implications.

For the whole of human history, up to that moment one hundred years ago when the telephone was invented, it was impossible for two persons more than a few meters apart to interact in real time. The abolition of that apparently fundamental barrier was one of technology's supreme triumphs; today we take it for granted that men can converse with each other, and even see each other, wherever they may be. Generations will live and die, always with this godlike power at their fingertips.

Yet this superb achievement will be ephemeral; before the next hundred years have passed, our hard-won victory over space will have been lost, never to be regained.

On the Apollo voyages, for the first time, men traveled more than a light-second away from earth. The resulting two-and-a-half second round-trip communications delay was surprisingly unobtrusive, but only because of the dramatic nature of the messages—and the discipline of the speakers. I doubt if the average person will have the self-control to talk comfortably with anyone on the moon.

And beyond the moon, of course, it will be impossible. We will never be able to converse with friends on Mars, even though we can easily exchange any amount of information with them. If will take at least three minutes to get there, and another three minutes to receive a reply.

Anyone who considers that this is never likely to be of much practical importance is taking a very short-sighted view. It has now been demonstrated, beyond reasonable doubt, that in the course of the next century, we could occupy the entire solar system. The resources in energy and material are there;

the unknowns are the motivation—and our probability of survival, which may indeed depend upon the rate with which we get our eggs out of this one fragile planetary basket.

We would not be here, talking about the future, unless we were optimists. And in that case we must *assume* that eventually very large populations will be living far from earth—light-minutes and light-hours away, even if we colonize only the inner solar system. However, space colony advocate Freeman Dyson has argued with great eloquence that planets aren't important, and the real action will be in the cloud of comets out beyond Pluto, a light-*day* or more from earth.

And looking further afield, it is now widely realized that there are no *fundamental* scientific obstacles even to interstellar travel. Though Nobel Laureate Dr. Edward Purcell once rashly remarked that star-ships should stay on the cereal boxes, where they belonged—that's exactly where moonships were, only 30 years ago....

So the finite velocity of light will, inevitably, divide the human race once more into scattered communities, sundered by barriers of space and time. We will be as one with our remote ancestors, who lived in a world of immense and often insuperable distances, for we are moving out into a universe vaster than all their dreams.

ARE THERE OTHERS?

But it is, surely, not an empty universe. No discussion of communications and the future would be complete without reference to the most exciting possibility of all— communications with extra-terrestrial intelligence. The galaxy must be an absolute Babel of conversation, and it is surely only a matter of time before we can hear the neighbors. They already know about us, for our sphere of detectable radio signals is now scores of light-years across. Perhaps even more to the point—and more likely to bring the precinct cops hurrying here as fast as their paddy-wagon can travel—is the fact that several microsecond-thick shells of x-ray pulses are already more than ten light-years out from earth, announcing to the universe that, somewhere, juvenile delinquents are detonating atom bombs.

Plausible arguments suggest that our best bet for interstellar eavesdropping would be in the 1000-Megahertz, or 30 centimeter, region of the spectrum. The N.A.S.A./Stanford/ Ames *Project Cyclops* report, which proposed an array of several hundred large radio telescopes for such a search, recommended a specific band about 200 Megahertz wide—and lying between the hydrogen line (1420 MHz) and the lowest OH line (1,662 MHz). Dr. Bernard Oliver, who directed the *Cyclops* study, has waxed poetic about the appropriateness of *our* type of life seeking its kind in the band lying between the disassociation products of water—the "water-hole."

Unfortunately, we may be about to pollute the water-hole so badly that it will be useless to radio astronomers. The proposed MARESAT and NAVSTAR satellites will be dunked right in the middle of it, radiating so powerfully that they would completely saturate any *Cyclops*-type array. Barney Oliver tells me: "Since the *Cyclops* study, additional reasons have become apparent for expecting the water-hole to be our contact with the mainstream of life in the galaxy. The thought that we, through our ignorance, may blind ourselves to such contact and condemn the human race to isolation appalls us."

I hope that the next World Administrative Radio Conference, when it meets in 1979, will take a stand on this matter. The conflict of interest between the radio astronomers and the communications engineers will get more and more insoluble, until, as I suggested many years ago, we move the atronomers to the quietest place in the solar system—the center of the lunar farside, where they will be shielded from the radio racket of earth by 3,500 kilometers of solid rock. But *that* answer will hardly be available before the next century.

Whatever the difficulties and problems, the search for extra-terrestrial signals will continue. Some scientists fear that it will not succeed; others fear that it *will*. It may already have succeeded, but we don't yet know it. Even if the pulsars *are* neutron stars—so what? They may still be artificial beacons, all broadcasting essentially the same message: "Last stop for gas this side of Andromeda."

More seriously, if the decades and the centuries pass, with no indication that there is intelligent life elsewhere in the universe, the long-term effects on human philosophy will be profound—and may be disastrous. Better to have neighbors we don't like, than to be utterly alone. For that cosmic loneliness could point to a very depressing conclusion—that intelligence marks an evolutionary dead-end. When we consider how well—and how *long*—the sharks and the cockroaches have managed without it, and how badly we are managing *with* it, one cannot help wondering if intelligence is an aberration like the armor of the dinosaurs, dooming its possessors to extinction.

No, I don't *really* believe this. Even if the computers we carry on our shoulders are evolutionary accidents, they can now generate their own programs—and set their own goals.

For we can now say, in the widest possible meaning of the phrase, that the purpose of human life is information processing. I have already mentioned the strange fact that men can survive longer without water than without information....

And therefore the real value of all the devices we have been discussing is that they have the potential for immensely enriching and enlarging life, by giving us more information to process—up to the maximum number of bits per second that the human brain can absorb.

I am happy, therefore, to have solved one of the great problems the philosophers and theologians have been haggling over for several thousand years. You may, perhaps, feel that this is rather a dusty answer, and that not even the most inspired preacher could ever found a religion upon the slogan: "The purpose of life is information processing." Indeed, you may even retort: "Well, what is the purpose of information processing?"

I'm glad you asked me that ...

THE HISTORY OF THE FUTURE

James W. Carey and John J. Quirk

"What sort of a past has the future had?" The future, as an idea, indeed has a definite history and has served as a powerful political and cultural weapon, particularly in the last two centuries. During this period, the idea of the future has been presented and functioned in American and British life in three quite distinct ways.

First, the future is often regarded as cause for a revitalization of optimism, an exhortation to the public to keep "faith," and is embodied in commemorative expositions of progress, world fairs, oratorical invocations, and in the declaration of national and international goals. Second, the future, in the politics of literary prophecy, is attractively portrayed as the fulfillment of a particular ideology or idealism. The past and present are rewritten to evidence a momentous changing of the times in which particular policies and technologies will yield a way out of current dilemmas, and a new age of peace, democracy, and ecological harmony will reign. Third, the future has acquired a new expression in the development of modern technologies of information processing and decision making by computer and cybernated devices. Here the future is a participation ritual of technological exorcism whereby the act of collecting data and allowing the public to participate in extrapolating trends and making choices is considered a method of cleansing confusion and relieving us from human fallibilities.

Excerpts from "The History of the Future" by James W. Carey and John J. Quirk. Reprinted from Communication Technology and Social Policy: Understanding the New Cultural Revolution. *Edited by George Gerbner, Larry P. Gross, and William H. Melody. Copyright © 1973 by John Wiley & Sons. Reprinted by permission of John Wiley & Sons, Inc.*

THE FUTURE AS EXHORTATION

Throughout American history, an exortation to the future has been a standard inaugural for observing key anniversaries and renewed declarations of national purpose. At celebrations of science and industry, and orations of public officials, the invocation of a sublime technological future elevates the prosaic and pedestrian commonplaces of "the American creed" with its promises of progress and prosperity to an appeal for public confidence in established institutions and industrial practices. This exhortation to the sublime future is an attempt to ward off dissent and to embellish cosmetically the blemishes of the body politic with imagery of a greater future for all.

The strategy of the future as exhortation was exemplified by the Centennial Exhibition staged in Philadelphia in 1876. The American Centennial was observed through the preferred nineteenth century symbol of progress and optimism, the industrial exhibit. The initial purpose of the exhibit was to testify to American unity 11 years after the Civil War. However, the magnetic attraction of the exhibit was the Hall of Machinery with 13 acres of machines connected by pulleys, shafts, wheels, and belts to a giant Corliss engine in the central transcept. Symbolically, President Grant opened the Centennial by turning the levers that brought the giant engine to life, assisted by Dom Pedro, the Emperor of Brazil. The Corliss engine dominating the Centennial illustrated the giantism of nineteenth century mechanical technology, which enraptured both public and politicians. The machines were symbols of the grandeur and strength of the American people and a hopeful sign for the second century of American life. Even literary men like William Dean Howells were overcome by the Corliss engine: " ... in these things of iron and steel ... the national genius freely speaks; by and by the inspired marbles, the breathing canvases, the great literature; for the present America is voluble in the strong metals and their infinite uses."[1]

While the giant hardware of the "Age of Steam" dominated the exhibit, the new electrical machines also held sway in the Centennial halls where the electric lamp and Alexander Graham Bell's telephone were on display.

In inaugurating the fair, President Grant noted that of necessity our progress had been in the practical tasks of subduing nature and building industry, yet we would soon rival the older nations in theology, science, fine arts, literature, and law. For while this was a celebration of 1876, it had an eye clearly fixed on 1976, the next centennial, progress toward which was guaranteed by native advances in mechanics and industry. However, America of the 1870s displayed numerous symptoms not altogether in harmony with the prevailing mood of the Centennial. The entire two decades following 1873 were highlighted by a worldwide depression. Earlier "improvements" in communication and transportation had led to an unprecedented degree of international integration in the economy. Failures in the economy fanned out over this international network so that the "communications revolution" of the 1830s generated, as one observer put it, three unpredecented historical phenomena: "an international agrarian market, an international agrarian depression and, as a climax, international agrarian discontent."[2] Bitter discord reverberated through American society, lurking even in the shadow of the Centennial Exhibition. Labor unrest in the Pennsylvania coal fields led to strikes and union organization and to the hanging of 10 members of the Molly Maguires in 1877. During 1876, President Grant had to dispatch troops to the South to control violence in the aftermath of the disputed election of Rutherford Hayes. The Centennial itself was disrupted on the Fourth of July by Susan Anthony's presentation of the Women's Declaration of Independence. Frederick Douglass, the contemporary black leader, was an official guest at the Centennial opening, although he had difficulty getting past police to the receiving stand; however, his token presence did not retard the spread of Jim Crow legislation through the South, undoing whatever gains had accrued to blacks in the

aftermath of the Civil War. Finally, nine days before the climactic Fourth of July celebration, news arrived of Custer's defeat at Little Big Horn.[3] Such realities of American life—the problems of racial and ethnic relations, of political democracy, of the industrial proletariat, and of chronic depression did not pervade the official rhetoric of the Centennial with its eyes fixed firmly on Tomorrow.

For another Centennial celebration we have dutifully created a commission on National Goals, a Bi-Centennial Committee, agencies, and commissions to foretell the year 2000. Moreover, the same problems that haunted 1876 mar the contemporary landscape. And, finally, while the favored symbols of technological progress have changed—atomic reactors, computers, and information utilities—having replaced steam engines and dynamos—the same style of exhortation to a better future through technology dominates contemporary life. This exhortation to discount the present for the future has, therefore, been a particular although not peculiar aspect of American popular culture. It is, in a trenchant phrase of Horace Kallen, "the doctrine and discipline of pioneering made art."[4]

The reasons behind this orientation are easy enough to state, although difficult to document briefly, for the very creation of the United States was an attempt to outrun history and to escape European experience, not merely to find a new place but to found a "New World." The idea of a "new land," a virgin continent, had been part of the European utopian tradition. The discovery of America during the age of exploration removed utopia from literature and installed it in life.

This notion of our dispensation from European experience, free to realize the future without the baggage and liabilities of the past, has always been central to American belief. It first appears in a religious context, in the belief that a uniform, nonsectarian Christianity would be possible in "New England" because of the absence of European institutions and traditions. In the nineteenth century, dramatic advances in technology and industrialization were seen as an analogy to the spread of American religion so that Gardner Spring could declare in 1850 that we are living on the "border of a spiritual harvest because thought now travels by steam and magnetic wires."[5] Soon the spiritual improvement wrought by Christianity was linked to those "internal improvements," particularly improvements in transportation and communication, so that canals, railways, and telegraph became the most important form of missionary activity by midcentury.

The course and domain of spiritual empire increasingly became identified with that practical enterprise, manifest destiny, the course of the American empire. America's dispensation from history gave her a missionary role in the world: to win the world to an absolute truth—at first religious, then technical; to create a radical future "of a piece with titanic entrance into the 'new world' of steam and electricity."[6]

Whenever the future failed, as often it did during the nineteenth and twentieth centuries, appeal was made to yet another new future patching up the miscarriage of previous predictions. Most importantly, preachers and politicians appealed to Americans to retain faith in the future as such; they appealed to the future as a solvent and asked the public to believe that the latest technology or social project would fully justify past sacrifices and the endurance of present turmoil.

Fifty years after the Philadelphia Centennial the foremost American historians of the period, Charles and Mary Beard, who were not unconscious of the difficulties of postwar America, were fascinated nonetheless by the vastness of the industrial inventory presented at the Sesquicentennial Exposition in contrast to what was shown in 1876. Moreover, they saw America's social destiny in "the radical departures effected in technology by electrical devices, the internal combustion engine, the wireless transmission of radio"; changes, they felt, "more momentous even than those wrought by invention in the age of Watt and Fulton." They argued that the new technology removed the gloom and depression of the age of steam and provided a new motive force to rearrange American social patterns. Electricity would emancipate mankind and integrate the city with the country as radio brought cosmopolitanism "as if on the wings of the wind." They concluded in lyrical prose that the "influence of the new motors and machines was as subtle as the electricity that turned the wheel, lighted the film and carried the song."[7]

Several years later, in the midst of the Great Depression, Franklin Delano Roosevelt ritually exhorted the American people reminding them that

We say that we are a people of the future ... the command of the democratic faith has ever been onward and upward; never have free men been satisfied with the mere maintenance of the status quo ... we have always held to the hope, the conviction, that there was a better life, a better world, beyond the horizon.[8]

Similarly, at the 1933 Century of Progress Exposition in Chicago, where Thomas Edison was being memorialized and the electrical exhibit featured the themes of conquest of time and space, Roosevelt tried to banish doubts and fears by reference to "the inauguration of a Century of even greater progress—not only along material lines; but a world uplifting that will culminate in the greater happiness of mankind."

The function of such rhetoric was once characterized by the late C. Wright Mills: "The more the antagonisms of the present must be suffered, the more the future is drawn upon as a source of pseudo-unity and synthetic morale."[9] The future in exhortation becomes a solvent, the very act of moving forward in time constitutes a movement away from past problems and present difficulties. The future becomes a time zone in which the human condition is somehow transcended, politics evaporated, and a blessed stage of peace and democratic harmony achieved. The historian Allan Nevins clearly expresses this native ideology:

Unity in American life and political thought certainly does not stem from general agreement on any body of doctrines ... The meaning of democracy in Oregon is very different from its meaning in Alabama. We are often told that we are held together as a people not so much by our common loyalty to the past ... as by our common faith and hopes for the future. It is not the look backward ... but the look forward that gives us cohesion. While we share some memories, the much more important fact is that we share many expectations.... The great unifying sentiment of America is hope for the future.... For national unity it is important to maintain in the American people this sense of confidence in our common future.[10]

These views have potent political uses. The ideology of the future can serve as a form of "false consciousness," a deflection away from the substantial problems of the present, problems grounded in conflicts over wealth and status and the appropriate control of technology, toward a future where these problems, by the very nature of the future, cannot exist. As rationalizers for the British empire in the last century urged not only recognition of but belief in the Industrial Revolution, so Nevins like other apologists asks that our "minority groups" must have their sense of deprivation relieved by

partaking of "faith in sharing on equal terms, in a happier future." Similarly, one of Richard Nixon's first acts as President was to create a National Goals Research Staff. The staff was charged with orienting Americans toward the coming bicentennial and the year 2000, so that we might "seize on the future as the key dimension of our decisions.... "[11]

Culturally and politically, then, the idea of the future functions in much the same way as the notion of the "invisible Hand of Providence" operating in the dreams of "heavenly cities" in the eighteenth and nineteenth centuries; it provides a basis for faith in the essential rectitude of motives and policy in the midst of the disarray of the present. The rhetoric of the future has, in the twenteith century, offered in Aldous Huxley's words, a "motivating and compensatory Future" which consoles for the miseries suffered in the present.[12] To Huxley's critical mind, the literature of the future provided to modern generations what the Methodist sermon on hard times now and heavenly rewards later had for the first English working class at the onset of the Industrial Revolution; the rhetoric of a sublime future as an alternative to political revolution and a stimulus to acquiescence. In the new literature of the future, the salvation is not otherworldly but terrestrial revolution and it correlates in moral, social, and material betterment. As Huxley concluded, "the thought of ... happiness in the twenty-first century consoles the disillusioned beneficiaries of progress."[13]

THE FUTURE AS LITERARY PROPHECY

From the enormous corpus of prophetic writing about the future, we have selected a few British and American authors who illustrate the essential features of this literature. Although the authors' motives and backgrounds differ, certain distinct common themes distinguish futurist literature. Invariably the newest technologies of communication and transportation are seen as means for the lasting solution to existing problems and a radical departure from previous historical patterns. Also, the landscape of the future is suggestively drawn as one where a sublime state of environmental balance, social harmony, and peace is achieved.

In *Futures* magazine, I.F. Clarke has identified the first major technological forecast written in the English language as the work of an anonymous author published in 1763 under the title of *The Reign of George VI, 1900-24*.[14] This premiere utopia, which may be said to have initiated the age of extrapolation, depicted the future as a mere perfection of the ethos of the reign of George III. It projected the consolidation and expansion of the empire over the continents of Europe and North America with a Pax Britannica of secure hegemony by means of vastly improved communication and transportation supporting commerce, foreign service, and military force. Published in the same year as the end of the French and Indian War and 13 years before the uprising of the 13 colonies, it professed to see a time when England's perennial rivals gladly accepted orders from London. Coeval with Watt's steam experiments, it suggested that the English countryside would be embellished by the waterways and routes of new industry, that cities might remain quaint, and that the society of aristocratic amenities would be perpetuated. During the predominance of the British Empire a literature of the imperial future sought to impress the reading public with such sublime reasons for continued expenditure and sacrifice on behalf of Anglo-Saxon destiny. It also became in time a ground for arguing against revolutionary ideology as Chartism, Marxism, and republicanism challenged the system.

An apotheosis of nineteenth century optimism followed in the train of the Great Exhibit of 1851 as the prevalent ethos of Victorian conplacency imagined a global community of interests to be the inevitable by-product of communication and transport in the cause of trade and empire. There were some dissenters who pierced the Crystal Palace mystique and correctly read into industrialization its pernicious tendencies to dwarf man and nature under advancing machinery. The dominant note remained one of beneficient *social corollaries* to be derived from the conquests by technology of the earth and the barriers of time and space. Ironically, these included gifts for which we are still waiting, such as freedom from drudgery, a wedding of beauty and utility, and an end to warfare and cosmopolitan consciousness.

A prime document of this period is illustrative of the point that today's future is yesterday's future as well. In *The Silent Revolution: or the Future Effects of Steam and Electricity Upon the Condition of Mankind,* a projection from the perspective of 1852, Michael Angelo Garvey portrayed the world as the Great Exhibit writ large where all the problems of industrialism were finally resolved. The smoke-filled slum and the Malthusian spectre were to be eliminated as transportation redistributed population to new colonies and allowed a new and elevated working class access to "pure air and joyous landscape." Sharing the mistaken notion of most futurists that social conflict results from insufficient communication and isolation. Garvey personified the technology of travel and telegraphy. The railway was "if not the great leveler" then "the great master of ceremonies," who is "daily introducing the various classes," and "making them better acquainted in common." In a further "future period," Garvey projected a system of total communications anticipating the notions of Marshall McLuhan: "a perfect network of electric filaments" to "consolidate and harmonize the social union of mankind by furnishing a sensitive apparatus analogous to the nervous system of the living frame."[15]

This perfect future was of a piece with other Victorian prophecies despite the proximate realities of Irish famine and labor unrest, the Crimean War, and other manifestations of discord and dispute. But the ulterior motive for the imperial era future literature was patently clear in *The Silent Revolution*. Garvey pleaded for his readers to maintain their loyalty to the regime, the proper caretaker of the future, and to avoid noisy agitation for reform or revolt. The "silent revolution" was a substitute for a social revolution, a rhetorical method to keep not only the majority but minorities silent about questions of imperial policy.

The literature of the future of the empire continued to mirror and mold prevailing opinion of the British elite well into the twentieth century. Its attitudes regularly overshadowed critical warnings about the fate awaiting overextension abroad and retention of obsolete institutions at home. Although the citations from twentieth century versions of the literature of the imperial futurists already seem arcane to us because of the depletion of English power, it is well to realize the degree to which American futurism in the present context—for instance, in Zbigniew Brzezinski's "Technetronic Society"—derives its inspiration from the British version of an imperial future: a *Pax Americana* augmented by electronic instruments of communication for the conduct of foreign policy and warfare and the pacification of the home populace.[16]

In *The World in 2030,* a view from the year 1930, the Earl of Birkenhead tried to blend imperialism and futurism to ward off erosion of public confidence caused by the depression and the rise of dictators. To offer a relief from the over 230 years of turmoil, Birkenhead predicted a characteristic turning point identical to that delineated by current writers about the future: "Today we are witnessing the death of a society and tradition which have existed since the first French Revolution and the Industrial Revolution."[17] This change, however, was not to be political or social, but technological. Electrification of the English countryside and decentralized, smokeless factories were to comprise a handsome landscape of laboratories resembling an "interminable park" and dispensing the plentitude of an "industrial Arcadia."

Public disaffection from remote government might be treated by obtaining formal participation through electronic communications, so that "it will be feasible once more to revive *that form* of democracy which flourished in the city states of Ancient Greece."[18] Broadcasting of special debates could be followed by instant opinion polling through devices inserted in telephone exchanges. But, this meant no real transfer of power to the people, because in Birkenhead's analysis, government should probably be handed to a class of expert specialists whose electronic consultation might be a mere formality, a guise of democracy for the electronic Leviathan.

Furthermore, Birkenhead envisioned the future world as continuing management of world affairs and the evolution of international organization around the nucleus of the British Commonwealth with India, South Africa, and even Dublin again inside its orbit. The future world would be made safe for the RAF patrol over the pipelines in Iraq and for upper-class amenities of silent Rolls Royce and riding to hounds. In sum, "the world in 2030" was to be nothing more than the wishful dream of an 1830 Tory mentality given technocratic expression.

So pronounced was the tendency of the British *intelligentsia* to conceive of the future solely in terms of the empire that it affected even Liberals, Fabians, and scientific modernizers such as J.B.S. Haldane. H. G. Wells, the most inventive of the futurists during the first part of the twentieth century, was initially a member of a circle who viewed the Empire as "the pacific precursor of a practical World State" and the royal military equipped with the latest technology of communication and transport as the forerunners of a "world police" able to be dispatched quickly to any trouble spot to quell insurrectionary activity.[19]

In contradistinction to the imperialist futurists, there arose an alternative view of the future genuinely dedicated to the decentralization of power and industry, a rehabilitation of the natural landscape, and a revival of regional cultures. Its major figures were the Russian anarchist and naturalist Peter Kropotkin and the Scots regionalist Patrick Geddes. Kropotkin's vision of an "industrial village" of the future foresaw the dispersion of production and population to communal and workshop levels.[20] The transmission of electricity would replace the huge steam engine, dehumanized factories, and alienation of labor. This attractive idea was further elaborated by Geddes as a theory of the reversal of the adversities of the Industrial Revolution and the arrival in the near future of a "eutopian" mode of life.

During and after World War I, Geddes and his colleague sociologist Victor Branford edited a series of books and pamphlets collectively published as *Interpretations and Forecasts, The Making of the Future,* and *Papers for the Present.*[21] Geddes' foremost American disciple, Lewis Mumford, has credited this biologist and town planner with the introduction of "the future, as so to speak, a legally bounded terrain in social thought."[22] Geddes earned the title of "big brother of reform" through his activist field experiments from Chicago and Edinburgh to India and Palestine. His intellectual influence extended to contemporaries such as Jane Addams and John Dewey and has reemerged in updated versions in the work of recent figures such as Paul Goodman and Marshall McLuhan.

Geddes' own portrayal of the future drew a dialectical contrast between old and new forms of technology. Electricity was to be the key to a "great transition" from forms of concentration to decentralization, from pollutants to ecology, from urban congestion and false cosmopolitanism to regional and folk revival: "We may divide the age of machinery into the paleotechnic age of smoke and steam engine, and the neotechnic age of electricity and radium, the conquest of noise and the utilization of waste."[23] The aim of the future for Geddes was a neotechnic "Eutopia" under a "partnership of man and nature" in a world redesigned to resemble a garden.

There is a remarkable similarity between Geddes' conception of the future and notions entertained by contemporary futurology. Geddes expected the passing away of politics, parties, and ideologies. In place of political activism, he and Branford advocated a third alternative *beyond* right and left to be carried out by "peace armies" of "university militants" going to the peoples of the world in projects of environmental reconstruction, conservation, educational reform, and civic design. Imperialism would be superseded by autonomous regional federations. This neglect of political facts and factors in Geddes' ideas has been evaluated by Lewis Mumford as the critical oversight in his view of the future world.

Geddes' future was premised on several other errors. The new technology as applied brought about increased centralization and concentration and domination over the landscape by powerhouses, and extended the range of control by imperialistic power centers over indigenous cultures and regions.

The ideas of Geddes and Kropotkin had their influence in the United States among leading conservationists, regional planners, and social critics. The transfer to the American scene of Geddes' neotechnic formulations was especially due to the works of Lewis Mumford.

In 1934, in his *Technics and Civilization,* Mumford attributed a series of "revolutionary changes" to "qualitative" effects of electricity itself, particularly hydroelectric turbines and incipient automated machinery in the factory.

These he supposed to include a "tidying up of the landscape" by "Geotechnics" in the "building of reservoirs and power dams" and a lifting of the "smoke pall" as "with electricity the clear sky and clear water…come back again." The sublime landscape of the radiant future would be one of an intermarriage of town and country, agriculture and industry, and even distribution of surplus population and of wealth.[24]

From radio and "person-to-person" electronic communication, Mumford hoped for a universal democracy by technology: "there are now the elements of almost as close a political unity as that which was once possible in the tiniest cities of Attica."[25]

Still, Mumford's Americanization of Geddes' gospel was subjected to the same irony of history as had overtaken previous projections of the future. The hydroelectric project and reservoir eventually further uprooted and eroded the environment. The air, water, and land were neither cleared nor cleansed, as we who now inhabit this future landscape well know. The megalopolis continued to grow. Total automation is still more predicted than realized, while the C.I.O.'s organizing drive began in earnest just as Mumford wrote of the end of the working class. Politically, it was an age of dictators and centralized rule.

Mumford himself was compelled to admit that there had been a "miscarriage of the machine," since civilization was still stalled in a "pseudomorphic" stage: "The new machines followed the pattern laid down by previous economic and technical standards." In subsequent reevaluation, Mumford has seen that belief in electricity as a revolutionary force was in fact mistaken even "in those plans that have been carried through, the realization has retrospectively disfigured the anticipation."[26]

Nevertheless, Mumford's themes have reappeared in future literature. It was 36 years ago that he composed a section on "shock absorbers," the essence of which appeared in Alvin Toffler's *Future Shock*.[27] Toffler has revived themes of the sublime technological revolution of 40 years vintage as a means of peering toward the year 2000. Toffler's recent work is embellished by the same recurring symbolism of the futurist genre. There are a number of "final and qualitative" departures in store for the new millenium. According to Toffler, the new society has "broken irretrievably with the past" surpassing geography and history.

What we encounter in Toffler is a portrait of the future as a new realm of dispensation from the consequences of the industrial revolution. The era of automation is pictured as a change "more important than the industrial revolution." The new industries of electronics and space technology are characterized by "relative silence and clean surroundings" as contrasted to the imagery of "smoky steel mills or clinking machines." The end of the assembly line dispenses with classic class conflict by placing a "new organization man" in the leading role as historical protagonist. Anticipatory democracy will be instituted in "town halls of the future," where critics of technics will be outdistanced by a futurist movement. Dissident minorities and recalcitrant middle Americans will be co-opted into programmed participation into future-planning games. Groups will be dissuaded from opposition to the space program and have their dissent funneled into support for improved technology. Cadres of specialists shall be attached to various social groups so that expertise will be married to the solicitation of consent.

Another illustrative comparison can be taken from the literature of the 1930s and 1970s. Contemporary rhetoric of a sublime national future merely places the computer and transistor where the powerhouse generators once held sway as predominant technology. A striking similarity may be seen in the parallel between the initial celebration of the Tennessee Valley Authority as a New Deal showcase and the recent projection of the electronic counterculture in *The Greening of America*.[28]

Contrary to the prevalent interpretations, the New Deal had its futurist impulses in efforts to enact projects for the construction of new communities, the decentralization of power, the reclamation of the landscape, and the electrification of the American countryside. This aspect of New Deal thought reflected the ideas of the old progressive conservationists like Gifford Pinchott, who had been influenced by Geddes and the regional planning movement.

The TVA was the subject of a vast oratorical and journalistic outpouring, centering on its image as a model of the future. For instance, it was held to be a "Revolution by Electricity" by Paul Hutchinson, editor of *The Christian Century,* who lifted his idiom from Lewis Mumford. In his words, the TVA was to "fashion the future of a new America." The "real revolutionary" was the new machine "which might at last become as much of a liberating and regenerative agency as the dreamers of the early industrial revolution declared it would be." The Tennessee Valley Authority was to be marked by a complete "absence of politics" and decentralization into "factory-plus-farm villages."[29] It would deny the iron laws of managerialism and bureaucratic revolution.

However, the TVA's own record has been a final reversal of these promises. Internally, it has developed technocratic structures and its new towns display a company town psychology. By strip-mining and other such practices it has marred the landscape. Like its technological big sister, the Atomic Energy Commission, it is aligned economically and politically with parts of the military-industrial complex. If anything, the machine again became the real counterrevolutionary.

In *The Greening of America,* Charles Reich predicts a "transformation" beyond a "mere revolution such as the French or Russian...." This new form of revolution offers answers to questions of identity and community, of history and politics. In the age of the computer and counterculture, Reich's rhetoric resembles Hutchinson's of four decades ago. For instance, "The machine itself has begun to do the work of revolution." And, "Prophets and philosophers have proposed these ways of life before, but only today's technology has made them possible."[30]

Reich attributes to electronics and cybernetics the social *correlates* of a higher consciousness, participation in a shared community, and renewed contacts with the land. The trouble with the Reichean formulation of a revolutionary machinery and a new cultural emergence is that its manifestations are either illusory or ephemeral.

At bottom, the counterculture is primarily an extension of the existing entertainment and leisure industries, instead of a regeneration of the humane dimension. Reich cites the devotees of Woodstock and is silent on the Altamont tragedy. The record industry lets the counterculture have the prophetic lyrics and collects the profits and the real cultural power.

There is a pronounced tendency, however, for prophets and movements to resort to incantations to reassure themselves about their cherished illusions. The enthusiasts of the Tennessee Valley Authority a generation ago, as Harold Ickes observed sardonically in 1944, began to believe that they might breathe life into a new democracy merely by intoning "TVA, TVA, TVA." Similarly the "greening of America" and like-minded counterculture scenarios impress one as nothing more than a chanting exercise for a new generation of Americans sent to their rendevous with another electric destiny. Presently, the shaping of the future remains routed along past lines. We see technological patterns and organizational forms continuing the trend toward concentration and centralization of power and control in established institutions.

THE FUTURE AS
A PARTICIPATION RITUAL

The writings of Reich and Toffler are merely the outer edge of a large body of literature forecasting another technological revolution and a new future. This revolution is preeminently one in communication, for as Norbert Weiner noted some years ago, "the present time is the age of communication and control." Modern engineering is communication engineering, for its major preoccupation is not the economy of energy "but the accurate reproduction of a signal."[31]

This third communications revolution was preceded by the innovation of printing, which mechanized the production of information, extended literacy, and enlarged the domain of empire. The second revolution occurred over the last century with the marriage, through electricity, of the capacity to simultaneously produce and transmit messages—a process that extends from the telephone and telegraph to television. Now, this third communication revolution involves the linkage of machines for information storage and retrieval with the telephone, television, and computer producing new systems of "broadband" communications or "information utilities."

The revolutionary potential of these "improvements" in communication does not derive from the prosaic facts about them—more information sent faster and further with greater fidelity. Instead, their attraction resides in the supposed capacity to transform the commonplace into the extraordinary: to create novel forms of human community, new standards of efficiency and progress, newer and more democratic forms of politics, and finally to usher a "new man" into history. The printing press, by extending literacy, not only taught men to read but was expected to eradicate ignorance, prejudice, and provincialism. Similarly, the telegraph and radio were seen as magnetic forces binding people into international networks of peace and understanding.

Recently the "cybernetic revolution," by increasing available information by a quantum leap, promises to make "policy options...clearly defined, the probable outcomes of alternative measures accurately predicted and the feedback mechanism from society...so effective that man could at last bring his full intelligence to bear on resolving the central problems of society."[32]

The basis of this third communications revolution, the marriage of the timeshared computer for both data analysis and information storage and retrieval with the telephone and television, is portrayed as the ultimate communications machine; it combines the speed and intimacy of dialogue, the memory of history, the variable ouput of sight and sound, the individuality of total information combined with totally free choice, the political awareness and control of a fully informed and participant electorate, and the analytic skill of advanced mathematics.

Despite the manifest failure of technology to resolve pressing social issues over the last century, contemporary intellectuals continue to see revolutionary potential in the latest technological gadgets that are pictured as a force *outside* history and politics. The future as it is previsioned is one in which cybernetic machines provide the dynamic of progressive change. More important, while certain groups—industrialists, technocrats, and scientists—are portrayed as the appointed guardians of the new technology, they are not ordinarily viewed as an elite usurping the power to make history and define reality. They are viewed as self-abnegating servants of power, merely accommodating themselves to the truth and the future as determined by the inexorable advance of science and technology. In modern futurism, *it is the machines that possess teleological insight.*

Moreover, the new communications technology is extended into virtually every domain of social life, invading even the family through home computer consoles for information, entertainment, education, and edification. And the public is invited to participate in a technical ritual of planning the future through World Games and electronic Delphic technicians as a rehearsal for the new stage of participatory democracy to be ushered in by communications technology.

Unfortunately, the vision of democracy by electricity has been with us since at least the telegraph and telephone and has been put forward by most writers about the future over the last century. James Russell Lowell, assessing the aftermath of the Civil War in the 1860s, felt that "the dream of Human Brotherhood seems to be coming true at last." He pinned this belief to the new form of the town meeting that technology could bring into existence:

It has been said that our system of town meetings made our revolution possible, by educating the people in self-government. But this was at most of partial efficacy, while the newspapers and telegraph gather the whole nation into a vast town-meeting where everyone hears the affairs of the country discussed and where better judgment is pretty sure to make itself valid at last. No discovery is made that some mention of it does not sooner or later reach the ears of a majority of Americans. It is this constant mental and moral stimulus which gives them the alertness and vivacity, the wide-awakeness of temperament, characteristic of dwellers in great cities....[33]

Despite the shortcomings of the town meetings, the newspaper, the telegraph, the wireless, and the television to create the conditions of a new Athens, Buckminster Fuller, one of the most vocal and visible of contemporary advocates, has described a form of instantaneous, daily, plebiscitory democracy through a computerized system of electronic voting and opinion polling.

Devise a mechanical means for nationwide voting daily and secretly by each adult citizen of Uncle Sam's family: then I assure you will Democracy be saved...This is a simple mechanical problem involving but a fractional effort of that involved in distributing the daily mails to the nation...Electrified voting...promises a household efficiency superior to any government of record, because it incorporates not only the speed of decision of the dictator...but additional advantages that can never be his.[34]

But it is also obvious that the extraordinary demands made on the citizen by such a system would merely co-opt him into the technical apparatus with only the illusion of control.

To participate in such a system the citizen of the future will have to undergo a continuing, lifelong education in real time, the acquisition of new knowledge when it is needed in time to meet problems as they arise. Recognizing the implausibility of all this, Donald Michael has recommended a form of republicanism instead of direct democracy. He argues that specialists will have to mediate between the technology and the citizen and government. Such specialists will be retained by groups to represent them to the government. But given the engineered "complexity" of the new information systems, involvement of the public becomes a mere ritual of participation or overparticipation to legitimate rule by a new scientific elite. If either of these modes of citizen participation are seriously entertained as the way past the present crises in politics, then of only one thing we may be sure: no matter what form of government we live under in the future, *it will be called democracy.* There is in the writing on the future no consideration of the nature of the polity because, in fact, political community is today very near a total collapse by the rush upon it of the very values the new futurists represent: rationalization, centralization, and uniformity. Other writers, notably C. Wright Mills, at least recognized that the basic problem was the one of elitism. While some futurist writers recognize that we are in a situation where meritocractic elites replace the old plutocracy, they do not take the next step—the growth of technocratic elites presumes the atomization of society; the condition of their rule is the erosion of political and social community and the creation of a new monopoly of knowledge.

Many new futurists recognize that knowledge is power—they say it so often it perhaps has never occurred to them that it first of all needs to be meaningful and relevant knowledge—and that it can be monopolized like any other commodity. However, they rarely recognize that the phrase "monopoly of knowledge" has two interpretations. In the first, monopoly of knowledge simply means the control of factual information or data. Communications is crucial here because the development of more elaborate codes and storage facilities allows groups to control information and deny access to the uninitiated and disconnected. Moreover, competition for innovation in the speed of communication is spurred by the fact that if information flows at unequal rates what is still the future for one group is already the past for another. Ithiel Pool and his colleagues illustrate this meaning of monopoly of knowledge and simultaneously paint a generous portrait of the new information systems in breaking this monopoly.

The information facilities provided by the computer can…serve as a decentralizing instrument. They can make available to all parts of an organization the kinds of immediate and complete information that is today available only at the center. The power of top leadership today is very largely the power of their information monopoly.…A society with computerized information facilities can make its choice between centralization and decentralization, because it will have the mechanical capability of moving information either way.[35]

There is, however, a more stringent sense of the meaning of a monopoly of knowledge. When one speaks, let us say, of the monopoly of religious knowledge, of the institutional church, one is not referring to the control of particles of information. Instead, one is referring to control of the entire system of

thought, or paradigm, that determines what it is that can be religiously factual, that determines what the standards are for assessing the truth of any elucidation of these facts, and that defines what it is that can be accounted for as knowledge. Modern computer enthusiasts may be willing to share their data with anybody. What they are not willing to relinquish as readily is the entire technocratic world view that determines what it is that qualifies as an acceptable or valuable fact. What they monopolize is not the data itself but the approved, certified, sanctioned, official mode of thought, indeed the definition of what it means to be reasonable. And this is possible because of a persistent confusion between information and knowledge.

Rarely in writing about the new communications technology is the relationship between information and knowledge ever adequately worked out, because it is not recognized as a problem. Information and knowledge are generally taken as identical and synonymous. It is assumed that reality consists of data or bits of information and this information is, in principle, recordable and storable. Therefore, it is also possible, in principle, for a receiver to know everything or to at least to have access to all knowledge. But this primitive epistemology, admittedly primitively described, will not do the intellectual work or carry the argumentative freight heaped upon it. Knowledge is, after all, paradigmatic. It is not given in experience as data. There is no such thing as "information" about the world devoid of conceptual systems that create and define the world in the act of discovering it. Such paradigms are present in information systems; they are meta-informational, contained in computer programs, statistical devices, information storage, and retrieval codes, technical theories that predefine information and perhaps most importantly in systems of binary opposition, that *lingua franca* of modern science.

Moreover, as one hopes the history and sociology of science have finally established, paradigms are not independent of exterior biases and purposes; they instead express a value-laden rationale in technical language. Computer information systems are not just objective, information recording devices. They are emanations of attitudes and hopes. The subjective location of such attitudes and hopes remains vested in the servants of the institutional monopoly of foreknowledge, for instance, the Rand Corporation. The "idea of information" is another way past the real political factors of class, status, and power, but these formidable realities cannot be dissolved into a future where they are presumed not to exist because they have been absorbed and transformed by the computational machinery.

In summary, then, the "third communications revolution" has within it the same seeds of miscarriage that have historically attended innovations in communications. Instead of creating a "new future," modern technology invites the public to participate in a ritual of control where fascination with technology masks the underlying factors of politics and power. But this only brings up to date what has always been true of the literature of the future. This literature with its body of predictions, prescriptions, and prophecies is a cultural strategy for moving or mobilizing or arousing people toward predefined ends by prescribed means. It would legislate and magistrate beyond the writ of any previous parliamentary or judicial body. It presumes to arbitrarily decree what shall be done and to appeal for the enactment of the plans brought forth. In the process, parts of the past are selectively deleted and aspects of the present are ignored. If such factors contradict the desired end in view they must be proclaimed "obsolete," or examples of cultural lag.

Unlike the mere revisionist or clairvoyant, the futurist has the advantage that the future can always be rewritten for there is no record to compare it with, no systematic verification of prophecy. The futurist can keep extending the day of consummation or rely on the forgetfulness of the public when the appointed but unfulfilled day arrives.

We have been treating here what should be called the "futurean mirage"—the illusion of a future. The futurean mirage is that the future is already out there, converging with the last stage of history, the great departure from all previous stations of travail to the final "stability zone." It posits the future as more than the *next* time dimension; instead, the future is conceived as an active agent reaching back into the present and past from its own superior vantage point and revising time and ineluctably removing obstacles to the previous unachieved rendevous with destiny. However, this sublime future is definitely not an open space in time, openly arrived at; instead, it is a carefully prepared predestination determined not on the grounds of human needs but technological imperatives peculiar to the devices by which the decision making of the futurist mystique is based.

The great irony is that while we seem to be living through the anticipatory "age of the future," there is no real future left open to us as a viable site. For the past projections of the future, in their influence as an ideational powerhouse on the course of policy and history, have foreclosed the formerly available futures filled with variable choices and exhausted the once rich cultural and natural resources that might have provided the basis in the past for a humane future in a livable landscape.

The emphasis of the futurist cast on the instantaneous efficiencies and speed over space in communications has by its focus on vast scale and fast pace eclipsed the public vision of its own immediate and long-term community with its indigenous interests. The mythology of the powerhouse, with its promise of decentralized economies and ecological harmonies, has actually provided a glossy picture of the sublime future whose subliminal aspects really have tendencies to commercial empires and cosmetically treated landscapes engineered for exploitation.

There remain elements of cultural permanence and political vitality in the nontechnological parts of our national inheritance. To draw on these resources, is it not time for the conception of the future to be rejoined to the real past and the realities of the present?

NOTES

1. Quoted in Dee Brown, *The Year of the Century, 1876* (New York: Scribner's 1966), p. 130.

2. Lee Benson, "The Historical Background of Turner's Frontier Essay," *Agricultural History* 25 (April 1951): 62.

3. Brown, *1876.*

4. Horace M. Kallen, *Patterns of Progress* (New York: Columbia University Press, 50), p. 78.

5. Perry Miller, *The Life of the Mind in America* (New York: Harcourt Brace and World, 1965), p. 48.

6. Miller, *Life of the Mind,* p. 52.

7. Charles Beard and Mary Beard, *The Rise of American Civilization* (New York: Macmillan, 1940), p. 746.

8. Allan Nevins, "The Tradition of the Future," in *Now and Tomorrow,* ed. Tom E. Kakonis and James C. Wilcox (Lexington, Mass.: Heath, 1971), pp. 400-401.

9. C. Wright Mills, *Power, Politics and People,* ed. Irving Louis Horowitz (New York: Ballantine Books, 1963), p. 302.

10. Nevins, "Tradition of Future," p. 398.

11. "Statement by President Nixon on Creating a National Goals Research Staff," *Futures* 1 (September 1969): 459.

12. Aldous Huxley, *Tomorrow and Tomorrow and Tomorrow and Other Essays* (New York: Perennial Library, 1972), p. 139.

13. Huxley, *Tomorrow,* p. 140.

14. I. F. Clarke, "The First Forecast of the Future," *Futures* 1 (June 1969): 325, 330.

15. Michael Angelo Garvey, *The Silent Revolution: or the Future Effects of Steam and Electricity Upon the Condition of Mankind* (London: William and Frederick G. Cash, 1852), pp. 170, 134, 103-104.

16. Zbigniew Brzezinski, *Between Two Ages* (New York: Viking, 1970).

17. Earl of Birkenhead, *The World in 2030 A.D.* (New York: Brewer and Warren, 1930), p. 116.

18. Birkenhead, *2030,* p. 8-9

19. H. G. Wells, *The Way the World Is Going* (New York: Doubleday, 1929), p. 126.

20. Peter Kropotkin, *Fields, Factories and Workshops* (New York: Putnam, 1913).

21. Patrick Geddes, *Ideas at War* (London: Williams and Norgate, 1917).

22. Harry Elmer Barnes (ed.), *An Introduction to the History of Sociology,* abridged ed. (Chicago: University of Chicago Press, 1966), p. 381.

23. Geddes, *Ideas at War,* preface.

24. Lewis Mumford, *Technics and Civilization* (New York: Harcourt, Brace and World, Harking Books, 1963), pp. 255-256.

25. Mumford, *Technics,* p. 241.

26. Lewis Mumford, "An Appraisal of Lewis Mumford's 'Technics and Civilization' (1934)," *Daedalus* 88 (Summer 1959): 534.

27. Alvin Toffler, *Future Shock* (New York: Bantam Books, 1971).

28. Charles Reich, *The Greening of America* (New York: Random House, 1970).

29. Paul Hutchinson, "Revolution by Electricity," in *New Directions,* ed. Warren Bower (New York: Lippincott, 1937), pp. 83-95.

30. Reich, *Greening,* pp. 204, 383.

31. Norbert Weiner, *Cybernetics* (Cambridge, Mass.: M.I.T. Press, 1948), p. 39.

32. Alan Westin, *Information Technology in a Democracy* (Cambridge, Mass.: Harvard University Press, 1971), p. 1.

33. James Russell Lowell, *The Works of James Russell Lowell,* vol. 5, Standard Library (Cambridge, Mass.: Riverside Press, 1871), p. 239.

34. R. Buckminster Fuller, *No More Secondhand God and Other Writings* (Carbondale, Ill.: Southern Illinois University Press, 1963), pp. 13-14.

35. Westin, *Information Technology,* p. 248.

Part Three

The New Professionalism

THE STING OF THE GADFLY

James Aronson

The communications industry has always been hostile to criticism from outside the industry and almost entirely self-indulgent within. Until the 1960s, serious criticism, with some remarkable exceptions, was rare. The exceptions were blockbusters, but closed ranks within the industry managed to confine the damage to a few falling sticks of type.

Among the exceptions were Will Irwin's book *The Shame of American Newspapers* (1910) and Upton Sinclair's *The Brass Check* (1920), a bitter indictment of the press and particularly the Associated Press. There were George Seldes's books of the 1930s and 1940s, with bugle-call titles such *You Can't Print That!, Can These Things Be!,* and *Let the People Know;* Harold Ickes's *The House of Lords* (1939), and George Marion's *Stop the Press!* (1953), which, more than its predecessors, placed the newspaper industry within the context of the system of American monopoly capital. There were, of course, many other books about the press, but they were for the most part only tangentially critical and defensive of prevalent practices. In these books the major villain was government.

The exclamation marks in the titles of several books may have stemmed from the authors' exasperation in their attempts to find publishers. *The Brass Check* was "published by the author" at Pasadena, California. George Marion's publisher was Fairplay in New York. That, of course, was George Marion himself. In 1953, the year of Senator Joe McCarthy's maximum influence, the only fair play a radical author could get was what he gave himself. Seldes, as a foreign correspondent of high standing, was published by the big houses (at least in the earlier days), but reviews of his books were harsh or nonexistent. His books may still be found, for a dollar or two, in secondhand bookshops, and they will prove historical eye-openers for a younger generation of readers.

Seldes's newsletter *In Fact,* published from 1940 to 1950, was a constant gadfly, placing in sharp focus (as Ralph Nader did for a later generation) the unsavory, unhealthy and unsafe practices of the tobacco, automotive and drug industries, for example, and the tenderly solicitous attitudes toward these industries by the press monopolies. In the field of foreign affairs particularly, *I. F. Stone's Weekly,* launched in 1952, was a brillian successor to *In Fact.*

There must be a special place also for the late A. J. Liebling and his evilly cheerful essays in the *New Yorker* magazine during the 1940s and 1950s under the title "The Wayward Press," subsequently published in book form. They were a penetrating indictment of the press and its coverage of important news events, written with devastating wit and humor.

Seldes, Marion, Liebling and Stone were vigorous proponents of a union of working newspapermen and women, and all four were early members of the Newspaper Guild, founded in 1933. There were sound economic reasons for a union of editorial and commercial employees in those depression days. Payroll cuts and "payless paydays" were common, as were troglodyte publishers such as Lucius T. Russell, publisher of the *Newark Ledger.* Russell one day picked up a piece of chalk, drew a line through the middle of the *Ledger* newsroom, and said: "Everyone on *that* side of the line is fired." They were—and a few days later were rehired at lower pay.

No thoughtful editorial staff member rejected the economic reasons for establishing the Guild (although a minority balked at rubbing elbows in meeting halls with ordinary clerks). But some hoped for something broader than traditional unionism, especially those who had become disillusioned with their practical experiences of freedom of the press, as opposed to the theoretical concept of the First Amendment.

These experiences had persuaded many reporters and desk editors that the Newspaper Guild had a responsibility far beyond the question of wages, hours and working conditions. Reporters knew that many of their stories were distorted after leaving their typewriters. Wire-service copy was often marred by half-truths and omissions. Some publishers and editors favored certain politicians and advertisers in the news columns or, as on the Hearst Newspapers, had a "Shit List" to guarantee that the listees never received a sanitary mention.

What was the responsibility of a newspaperman or woman? The press, after all, was supposed to be the watchdog of the public interest, and newspapers could not be published without the acquiescence and cooperation of the working press. Such reflection, however, was not encouraged within the Guild. The officers emphasized that the Guild was not an association of professional journalists: it was an industrial union of editorial workers, clerks, stenographers, maintenance men and advertising solicitors. It would not be fair to those not directly concerned with gathering and editing the news to involve them in questions about the content of newspapers. That was not the function of a union. Besides, the question of ownership was clear: what appeared in a newspaper was the responsibility of the owner.

This fraternal repression of editorial dissent, superimposed upon increasing disillusionment, had an ironic result. The Guild units of the most reactionary publications (Hearst's *Journal-American* in New York and Time Inc., for example) counted in their ranks the highest percentage of radicals (the term then was "reds") in the newspaper industry. Premature "underground" publications, mostly mimeographed, began to appear. The one at the *New York Times* was titled *New Times*. Some on the news staffs joined the Communist party as an expression of their political and journalistic discontent. Others became increasingly frequent patrons of a nearby barroom that was a virtual appendage of each newspaper. There were mighty lions in those liquid lairs. How many publishers and editors were cruelly dissected in a splendid alcoholic haze!

Other critics from outside the newspapers sought to inspect the performance, content and responsibility of the press. The most pertinent and comprehensive survey of the modern press was presented in 1947 as the Hutchins Commission Report, officially, *A Free and Responsible Press: A General Report on Mass Communications: Newspapers, Radio, Motion Pictures, Magazines, and Books*. The report was published by the University of Chicago, of which Robert Maynard Hutchins then was chancellor. The commission, with Hutchins as director, was made up of university experts, lawyers and industrialists, none identified with the political left and none involved with the commercial media.

The commission concluded that, while the press had developed enormously as an instrument of mass communication, the proportion of people who could express their ideas and opinions through the press had decreased. Those in control had not provided a service adequate to the needs of society and had even engaged in practices which society condemned.

"One of the most effective ways of improving the press," the report said, "is blocked by the press itself: By a kind of unwritten law, the press ignores the errors and misrepresentations, the lies and scandals of which its members are guilty." Its most innovative and controversial suggestion for improving press performance and responsibility was the establishment of an independent agency to appraise and report annually on the performance of the press. It would be free of government control and would have no power except moral suasion "to educate the people as to the aspirations which they ought to have for the press" and which the press ought to have for the people....

The press council idea had much to commend it, and the reluctant cooperation of the great majority of media proprietors in the tested areas indicated that they feared not so much an encroachment on freedom of the press as a watchful eye on their license to do what they wished without concern for a public accounting. Further, as the complexion of the cities changed through the 1960s increasingly to brown and black, an equitable press council would have had to reflect this shifting color line. The communications industry, however, was not willing to put into effect the high-sounding principles about racial equality espoused on the editorial pages.

But the industry had a continuing, uneasy awareness of being watched, particularly after the Agnew explosions of 1969-70. Public-opinion polls projected a growing mistrust by the public of the media, and in 1969 the governing board of the American Society of Newspaper Editors held its annual meeting in London as a manifest of their concern about self-policing the communications industry. They engaged in a comprehensive study of the British Press Council, created in 1953 as a nationwide entity and credited—despite some severe criticism of its operations—with improving the standards of the British press.

The ASNE group was reluctant, however, to recommend establishment of an American counterpart, citing the infinitely greater size of the United States, differences in the judicial systems, concept of ethics and public attitudes. The board went so far as to propose an ASNE Grievance Committee "to receive complaints in substance about the performance of daily newspapers." But the complaints would be restricted to those by one newspaper organization against another.

Interestingly, at a session of the Association for Education in Journalism in August 1970, a proposal for an American press council similar to Great Britain's was made by Norman Isaacs, who had been president of the ASNE at the time of the London meeting. Despite prevailing opposition, he said, "we may have the beginnings of such an institution within four or five years."

There were some within the industry, however, whose frustration would not tolerate the slower cadence of Isaac's forecast. They began even before his prediction to form internal "press councils" without the participation of the owners of the media. In individual cities and geographically concentrated regions, they joined together to examine the performance of the media in their city or area, and their own role as participating performers. They were for the most part reporters, rewrite men and women, and broadcast technicians, young and fairly new to the industry. But they frequently enjoyed the sympathy and cooperation of their more experienced colleagues who shared their exasperation at not being able to achieve full and free expression in gathering, writing and publishing news and commentary.

There was a striking example of this disaffection in Chicago in the weeks following the Democratic National Convention in August 1968. The cause was the unconscionable police brutality against war protesters, young radical dissidents and even uninvolved onlookers in the streets of the city.

Reporters and photographers, particularly from the Chicago media, were also clubbed and mauled by the police, and when they repaired to the anticipated safety of their own newsrooms, they suffered perhaps greater injuries to their morale. There, as one reporter said, "our own editors told us that we didn't see what we really saw under those blue helmets." On-the-scene reports were ignored, copy was altered, news pictures were discarded and the editors made it clear that their allegiance was not to their beaten staff, but to the man who had given orders for the beatings—Chicago's Mayor Richard J. Daley.

Out of this editorial outrage arose a movement for redress of grievances, not only against the mayor and the police, but against their own bosses, editors as well as publishers. That's how the *Chicago Journalism Review* was born. [It ceased publication in early 1975]

The first issue was published in October 1968 under the auspices of a new organization, the Association of Working Press. And though the spark, of course, was the aftermath of the convention, resentments in other areas were deep and of long standing. In the prologue to its first issue, the editors of *CJR* wrote:

When the cameras and conventioneers went home, the local media returned to the fold. Many of us, reporters in Chicago, could only watch what happened in silent frustration. Mayor Daley was permitted to take over the media. [His] contempt for the media was no longer veiled....Daley openly insulted newsmen, charged they were dupes, and assailed the integrity of the Chicago media. And as he threw verbal excrement in the faces of Chicago journalists, we took it like slaves.

But the slaves finally revolted, and the Association of Working Press opened its doors to reporters, photographers, rewrite men and women, news editors and broadcasters in the Chicago area. Its principal objectives were:

1. Ensure the rights of reporters and photographers to cover important events without interference from the police department or any other governmental agency.

2. Increase the representation of Negroes and other minority groups of the Chicago news media to a level proportionate to their representation in the population of the city.

3. Improve professional standards of fairness and accuracy in the media, and publicly condemn obvious breaches of journalistic ethics.

4. Contribute to the continuing education of the press corps through seminars, lectures and publications.

There were no bylines in the first six-page issue of *CJR*. Its editors feared reprisals from the newspapers, but there were none, and bylines appeared. The three dominant names in the early issues were Henry de Zutter, education reporter of the *Chicago Daily News;* Christopher Chandler, urban affairs specialist of *Chicago's American* (later transformed into *Chicago Today,* an evening newspaper owned by the *Chicago Tribune*); and Ron Dorfman, also of *Chicago Today,* who resigned to work full-time with *CJR.* De Zutter and Chandler later left to publish a new Chicago magazine. Dorfman remained, and his innovative mind and spirit made a distinct imprint on *CJR.*

The *Chicago Journalism Review* in 1972 was a neat, professionally prepared magazine, with articles by some of the best-known names in Chicago journalism. Its coverage was wide-ranging: exposés about suppression of news of police brutality, and about kindly treatment of corporate industry in the business pages of the press; slipshod reporting about *Rights in Conflict,* the Walker report on violence in Chicago, and blind spots in the report itself; and surveys of the coverage of racial news and employment of minority people in the Chicago media. Two of the more notable articles were a detailed description of the workings of the Chicago Police Red Squad, and a documented recapitulation (an entire issue) of the police murder of black militant Fred Hampton on December 4, 1969, proving beyond doubt that the murder had been unprovoked and showing further how the *Chicago Tribune* had striven to present a false picture of the murder and its aftermath.

In the first months of *CJR*, Chicago's newspapers maintained an uncomfortable silence about it, but their editors gave their views freely to interviewers—a mixture of hostility, sufferance and either feigned or resigned acceptance. Clayton Kirkpatrick, editor of the *Chicago Tribune* (which late in 1971 received an unaccustomed accolade from *CJR* for its new liveliness and efforts toward fairness), said at first that he was reluctant to concede that *CJR* was necessary "for reporters as a way to bring their criticism to editors' attention." Later, however, he declared it to be a "useful publication [which] stimulates an interest in professional qualities." Neither he nor his colleagues on the other Chicago dailies would concede that *CJR* had moved them to change their ways. There was a patronizing quality to the editors' comments, and an understandable distaste for having their internal wash spread out for inspection on the banks of the Chicago River. To cover their embarrassment, they criticized *CJR* for becoming "too involved in the inner workings of the press" (Maxwell McCrohan, managing editor of *Chicago Today*) or for "picayune carping" (Daryle Feldmeir of the *Chicago Daily News*). All agreed with Feldmeir that a reporter "ought to air gripes and bitches" within his own organization.

But that, as Ron Dorfman noted, was precisely why *CJR* had been founded—because the staffs got nowhere with their internal bitching, and *CJR* "focused previously diffused hostilities of working stiffs for management into more rational channels."

In mid-1972 the *Chicago Journalism Review's* circulation was about 8,000, with a readership spread from Hawaii to Afghanistan (and one in Fiji, according to Dorfman), but with about 75 percent in the Chicago area. Dorfman said the general reaction among media managements was "irritation and annoyance; but some changes have been made." He cited these examples:

The Field Newspapers [Daily News *and* Sun-Times] *reinstituted coverage of the Criminal Courts Building after we criticized them for not having any; United Press International sent a senior editor to do a takeout on Cairo* [deep-going racial unrest in that Illinois city] *after we criticized their stringer's coverage (the senior editor did not do much better); coverage of street gangs by all media improved considerably after we published lists of sources with phone numbers; the Field papers adopted a policy against gratuities after we published a story noting Christmas-gift hauls by City Hall reporters.*

Dorfman felt also that *CJR* had helped to make the media somewhat more responsive to public needs. He attributed this in part to what A. J. Liebling called the "country club syndrome." Many *CJR* readers, said Dorfman, were influential persons with whom the "news brass socialize; and when they have to explain themselves at cocktail parties (the country clubs, remember, have been infected with radical chic), it is terribly embarrassing." As for the working press itself, Dorfman said:

They can't be apathetic if the criticism is on the mark. The first copies of CJR *to arrive in an office are eagerly scrambled for and read thoroughly (for example, the issue with the report about sportswriters on the take from the racetracks)....The local press corps has responded with determination to improve media performance. Nearly 200 journalists have contributed articles and art work to* CJR.

Chicago is an unusual city for journalism: it still has four daily newspapers, although they are under two ownerships—The Chicago Tribune Company and the Field Enterprises....The decline in the number of big-city newspapers has been caused by three factors: the growth of television as a news source; the movement of people (mainly white and middle class) out of the inner cities, leading to the rise of prosperous and sophisticated suburban dailies; and handsome profits accruing from the sale of newspapers to the powerful conglomerates such as Newhouse, Thomson, Perry and Copley. The trend toward unimaginative and cautious chain journalism has disturbed and frustrated young journalists coming into the industry and has led in turn to a proliferation of journalism reviews. By mid-1972 there were reviews in 12 cities: Honolulu, Long Beach, (covering Southern California), Atlanta (an experimental supplement to the *Columbia Journalism Review*), Denver, Holyoke (Massachusetts—covering the Connecticut Valley), St. Louis, Cleveland, Philadelphia, Providence, Chicago, Milwaukee and finally, after several abortive attempts, New York City. There were others, such as the *Central Standard Times* of Wichita, dealing frequently with the press but falling primarily into the category of "alternative" publications. The reviews were concerned with more than newspapers: since radio and television news had become the primary source of information in most areas of the country, the reviews concentrated also on broadcast journalism.

Some media people began to regard the new phenomenon as a "journalism review movement," but there was actually little collaboration among the publications. Their common bond was that all were produced by working media staffs, seeking in constructive fashion to bring about improvements and reforms in the established media. Some were one-man operations (*Point of View* in Cleveland); some were financed in part by foundation funds; and at least one (*Review of Southern California Journalism*) was published under the auspices of a professional journalism organization, Sigma Delta Chi. Most had a small magazine (8½ × 11) or newsletter format, but four (St. Louis, Connecticut Valley, Providence and New York) were tabloid size, ranging from eight to 20 pages. Most were published biweekly, monthly or quarterly. A few appeared only when money became available. Only one (Cleveland's *Point of View*) could truly be considered radical in the political sense, although the *Chicago Journalism Review* on occasion has fitted the description. The single word characterizing the general outlook of all the reviews was "muckraking."

One other common characteristic of the reviews was the uncommon manner in which they received the silent treatment (in print or on the air) from the media in their areas. But if they were not acknowledged by the target newspapers, their rise was carefully charted in the established trade and professional publications of journalism, such as the *Columbia Journalism Review, Quill* (Sigma Delta Chi), *Editor & Publisher,* the *ASNE Bulletin,* and in the press sections of *Time* and *Newsweek.* Many articles about the reviews showed grudging admiration but criticized them for being unprofessional and unattractive. To a degree the criticism was warranted, and it emphasized the narrow training in the schools of journalism and in the media also.

What the young journalists lack in production skills, however, is compensated for by their sharp barbs aimed at the basic fault of the media—unwillingness to come to grips with the gigantic problems of the cities and their minority peoples, and to dig out the root causes of these problems. The reasons for the reluctance had become clear to the young journalists: the interweaving interests—financial and social—between the owners of the media and the dominant industrial and political figures. Now almost for the first time this interlocking directorate was being exposed on the local level by working media people in a position to know where the bodies were hidden, and why they were not being permitted to drag them out for public autopsy.

A case in point was the exposure by the *Philadelphia Journalism Review* of a crass instance of censorship by *Philadelphia* magazine. The editor of *Philadelphia* had refused to publish an assigned article about Police Commissioner Frank Rizzo, a candidate in the mayoralty election, in which he was the victor. The article was unflattering. Following the election, the editor of *Philadelphia* accepted an important post in the Rizzo administration.

Unlike the *Chicago Journalism Review,* some of the newer reviews were months in the planning stage. One was the *St. Louis Journalism Review* in a city with two newspapers—the reactionary *Globe-Democrat* and the prestigious *Post Dispatch,* still owned by the Pulitzer family, but exhibiting a faint but steady erosion of its courageously independent positions on state and national affairs. Founded in October 1970, two years later the St. Louis review had an editorial board of 20, a circulation of 4,000 and a financially stable sponsor, FOCUS/Midwest Publishing Company, publishers of the magazine *FOCUS/Midwest.*....The St. Louis review from the outset has taken a careful look at St. Louis media performance in major news events—election coverage, racial issues in a city with an almost 50 percent black population, the Pentagon Papers and the Attica prison massacre....That kind of peering, however, produced only overt hostility at the *Globe-Democrat.* Staff response at both papers has ranged from "enthusiastic approval" to "dim awareness"....

The *St. Louis Journalism Review* managed to focus on the local media situation without parochialism. For example, when it examined how the St. Louis media covered the Pentagon Papers crisis, the local coverage was related to the national coverage. Again, a first-rate survey of black and minority hiring in the St. Louis media was set against the national average.

More localized, perhaps, because of its geographic separation from the mainland, the *Hawaii Journalism Review* sought without measurable success to open traditionally closed doors in what its editors call the "plantation's government and business preserves." After a year of publication, its circulation was a select 800 among legislators, councilmen, journalists and university people.

"Hawaii is hard to ruffle," said Bob Jones of the editorial board. "Editors sometimes take issue with our observations [for example, that the dining-out column of the *Honolulu Advertiser* was palpably advertising space without being so labeled], or erroneously feel that we have not done an adequate reporting job. We do not necessarily run all points of view in a single issue (we list ourselves in the mast as a journal of opinion and observation), but we do run rebuttals in the following issue. We try to stay out of petty newsroom administrative beefs and concentrate on specific stories and malpractices in journalism." The impact of the Hawaii review, Jones felt, had been minimal. "Many of the matters we have tackled still exist," he said. "Economics wins out over criticism."

In Denver *The Unsatisfied Man* took its name from a comment by Frederick G. Bonfils, founder of the *Denver Post*: "There is no hope for the satisfied man." It was launched, with some foundation help, by the Colorado Media Project, comprising more than 60 reporters, editors and broadcasters. Low-keyed and with a sense of humor, it is doing a thorough job of constructive criticism of Colorado's media, including coverage of the "atomic beat," Washington reporting by the Colorado media, payola in the city rooms and pressure tactics by television stations to obtain license renewals from the Federal Communications Commission. In July 1971 *Cervi's Rocky Mountain Journal* published an

unsigned critique of *The Unsatisfied Man* describing it as "little more than the creation of a new syndrome: narcissistic-schizophrenic with overtones of paranoia." The editors of *TUM* reprinted the article in full in the August issue and tentatively identified the author. In unnarcissistic fashion, it opened its pages also to other reporters who seemed eager to defend the managements of the Denver media for which they work—an obvious demonstration of the need for a journalism review in Denver.

The *Philadelphia Journalism Review* was organized by six members of the editorial staff of the *Philadelphia Inquirer,* but its sponsorship rapidly expanded to staff members of the *Bulletin,* the *News,* the wire services and broadcasting. Its contents expanded similarly from a confining complaint sheet to a thoroughly professional forum for questions of concern to media staffs—advocacy *vs.* objectivity in the news, efforts to obtain a greater voice in policy-making decisions and the problems of white journalists covering racial news. In early 1972 it was distributing about 3,000 copies in the Philadelphia-Camden region.

In Long Beach the *Review of Southern California Journalism,* a quarterly, reflected in its early issues its academic origins—the California State College chapter of Sigma Delta Chi. It seemed somewhat distant from the world of commercial journalism, but in successive issues it moved eagerly into that world with articles by media people, interspersed with pertinent comment from teachers and students of journalism. An example of this positive mixture was the Fall 1971 issue with an article by Steve Roberts, *New York Times* correspondent in Los Angeles, titled "Why Journalists Are Tools of the Establishment" (the journalists got off too lightly); a review of an excellent (but ignored) book critical of the media, *Don't Blame the People,* by Robert Cirino, and a survey of how the press treated the Pentagon Papers, both in Southern California and nationally.

In New England there were two journalism reviews—*Thorn,* published by the Connecticut Valley Media Review, covering Western Massachusetts and Vermont, and the *Journalists' Newsletter* of Providence. Both were being published on an irregular basis and showed scars of financial stress. But they were earnest, searching and forthright in their comments about the media and, somewhat self-consciously, their own role as journalists. They seemed content to confine their criticism to their own locales, and since both regions were heavily populated and had a high concentration of universities, there was much ground to cover. Their targets were well selected, but their fire was, at least in the early issues, scattershot.

New York City is the publishing center of the nation, the headquarters of the broadcast networks and the home base for much of the radical movement. Yet it proved more difficult to organize and launch a persevering journalism review in New York than elsewhere in the country. One major reason may be the attitude of élitist professionalism afflicting a large part of the media staffs. This attitude stems in part from conditioning in the journalism schools, where New York is projected as the "Big Apple," the zenith of media achievement. And once New York is achieved, new conditioning is administered to develop the fantasy that a New York newspaper or broadcast journalist is a cut above out-of-town journalists, as they are designated.

However miserable the New York journalist—bored, censored, frustrated by trivial assignments—he must maintain the Potemkin Village facade to the public view. In these circumstances, involvement in a journalism review that would reveal the media as something less than a public trust would tarnish the illusion. It would also prove an obstacle to continued acceptance in the élite milieu of the media, where a staff writer can briefly rub ecstatic elbows with an editor or publisher at the most desirable bars. Vanity, avarice and envy are the holy trinity of most media people on the make in New York. And even if the Big Apple has demonstrable worm holes, the credo of the trinity makes a bite mandatory.

In 1970 at least two ventures into critical journalism were undertaken in New York for brief periods. They were a publication with the Jell-O-like title *Pac-O-Lies,* published by a group of radical journalists under the aegis of the New York Media Project; and *Inside Media,* published by Media Mobilization, a not so radical but equally disenchanted group based to a large extent in the broadcast media. *Pac-O-Lies* survived for four issues, much of its content sharp and revelatory, in the soundest muckraking tradition, but suffering, as the radical movement was, from some overblown rhetoric and a lack of clear direction. Its language was alternately belligerent and defensive. It vacillated between what should have been its major function—exposition of the sins of the media—and its predilection to espousal of radical-movement ideas.

Inside Media approached its task with more sobriety and with more insight. Its first (and unfortunately its last) issue had excellent material on the subpoena campaign against the media by former Attorney General Mitchell, the issues involved in WPIX-TV's battle to obtain a license renewal from the FCC, police agents infiltrating the media and the women's struggle for equality at the newsmagazines.

A third publication of 1970 was the *AP Review,* published by employees of the Associated Press, a short-lived goldmine of source material for the sins of commission and omission in the giant wire service. The first issue had, among other things, an intra-organizational exchange showing how an article by Peter Arnett, Pulitzer prize reporter for the AP in Vietnam, had been censored. Published also in *AP Review* was a memo from New York headquarters with instructions to reporters in the field to ignore situations which might show the United States fighting forces in a poor light. The article was widely (and almost exclusively) reported in the radical press. The *AP Review* never published a second issue.

It was not until the fall of 1971 that New York finally acquired a journalism review giving evidence of permanence. It was founded by Richard Pollak, a former editor of the press section of *Newsweek,* and William Woodward, a reporter for the *New York Post,* who resigned to undertake the publication. It was called (*More*), the notation that reporters and rewrite men and women place at the bottom of each page of copy to indicate there is more to come.

(*More*) was the result of several months of discussion with people highly placed in the media—some of the meetings were held in the bastion of the enemy, the private dining rooms of the Harvard Club in Manhattan. It was clear from the start that the publishers of (*More*) had made a careful study of other journalism reviews and applied their conclusions to the psychology and makeup of the media and their staffs in the Big Apple. "This is where the targets are," said Pollak. "We want to scrutinize the New York press in the same tough-minded way that the press ought to be covering the rest of the world."

An editorial in the pilot issue (June 1971) asked for a "commonsense understanding by publishers that journalists ought to be free to write about their profession without jeopardizing their jobs." For their part, the editors of (*More*) established an "ironclad policy" never to commission or publish articles by journalists about their own organizations. The pilot issue seemed more interested in big-name bylines than tough-minded scrutiny (two Pulitzer prizewinners and a former White House press secretary, none of them reaching much below the surface in their commentary), but the names and the national range of coverage won for (*More*) a spate of publicity that paved the way for a successful launching in September 1971.

The shakedown voyages of the first months seem to have proved the vessel seaworthy. While prominent names persisted (nothing wrong with that if the content matches the reputation), there was added to the publication an imaginative probing in vulnerable areas of the industry. The result was a series of excellent investigative articles about how the media operate—woefully

deficient hiring policies for blacks and Puerto Ricans at the *New York Post;* dull and deficient coverage of business news at the *New York Times;* and the beginnings of a steady look at the television empire in New York.

By early 1972 (*More*) had 5,000 paid subscriptions nationwide, and was selling 5,000 more on newstands in New York, Washington, D.C., Boston and Berkeley. As it began to find its targets, there was a concomitant decline in publicity and a rise in protests from the targets and their friends. (*More*) took advertising—a departure for journalism reviews and inevitably a test of its willingness to withstand the temptations of financial success as against editorial integrity.

In the summer of 1972 new reviews were established in the San Francisco Bay area, Baltimore and Minneapolis-St. Paul.

Thus from Hawaii to California to Denver to Providence the spunky watchdog patrol was keeping an eye on the larger watchdog and the way Big Brother was watching the world. Management was publicly resigned and privately hostile, hoping that the barking at its ankles would cease and the barkers vanish. Staff reaction was mixed—some delighted that the reviews were in business, others wary and still others angry at the interlopers for disturbing cozy arrangements under which certain news-staff favorites identified with management in return for the illusion of power and influence.

There were sporadic stories about the reviews in the press and in the magazines (broadcast journalism was almost completely silent), but few attempts to analyze the phenomenon of their appearance....

The journalism reviews are not an unnatural phenomenon: they mark the rise of an intelligent and searching generation of journalists who know that something is terribly wrong in their profession. Seeking to set standards and ideals which were not encouraged by the media managers, they are attempting to find answers themselves and are reaching out for public support. Far from rejecting as "quaint" the principles of objectivity (they would call it fairness), accuracy and education, they are trying in all three areas to improve the publications for which they work: to make objectivity mean the most probing kind of journalism, not a device to maintain the status quo: to persuade both their colleagues and the public that the only natural role of the communications media is an adversary one to government and established power.

In all fairness, it is still too early to assess accurately the quality and the promise of most of the journalism reviews....The most hopeful fact about them is that they existed—lively, pertinent, irreverent, making mistakes and sometimes giving vent to a personal spleen, but on the whole positive and constructive. For their minor transgressions they are denounced from the loftiest pulpits of journalism by preachers whose righteousness shrouds hypocrisies monumental enough to curl the whiskers of Horace Greeley.

There is, unfortunately, no journalism-review "movement." Journalists are still too individualistic for that. Nor is there a coherent political or social strain among the editors and publishers of the reviews: the failure of the radical movement to develop a cohesive philosophy of its own has left its negative mark on the new generation of journalists. Ambivalence is apparent in some of the publications, as it is in the discontented newsrooms. It has never been easy for an American journalist to abjure even the superficial camaraderie of a professional setting—as the media workshops tend to be—and take a dissenting stand apart from his fellows.

It may be that the reviews will not become permanent because some of their organizers

actually regard them as temporary—and this in itself sets limits to their effectiveness. With few exceptions, the reviews are reformist, not radical. All of those involved see with varying degrees of clarity the faults and evils of the media; but for most of them the task, as they see it, is to force changes within the media to make them more honest and serviceable, and therefore less degrading, places to work. To be sure, they probably see themselves as rebels, but rebels within the casue—the cause being the establishment of journalism itself. And, like many rebels of the past, they are subject to the blandishments of the establishment, which could turn them—sometimes without their realizing it—into effective tools of the establishment, with sufficient freedom of speech and movement to give them the illusion of independence. At that point, some might declare the battle won and the need for the gadfly no longer valid....

THE NATIVES GROW RESTLESS

James Aronson

The proliferation of journalism reviews is a significant development in the American communications industry. Yet it is only the most overt expression of a growing unrest which carries the hope of major changes in the practice of journalism. Perhaps the most controversial development is the movement among editorial staffs to obtain a greater voice in determining the content, personnel and general policies of the publications for which they work.

This movement came late in an industry which has declared itself the most democratic in the world. Until the late 1960s few voices had challenged the monarchical control of publishers and broadcast managers over the gathering and publication of news. Even the Newspaper Guild sought to dampen the new movement, insisting, as it had since its inception in 1933, that the management and content of newspapers were beyond its jurisdiction. The unions in the broadcast field reacted in similar fashion.

The new movement had precedents, however, in Europe. The most notable example was at the Paris daily newspaper *Le Monde,* perhaps the most prestigious in Europe. There a plan for shared management had been devised in 1944, immediately after the liberation of Paris. In 1951 the founding director of *Le Monde,* Hubert Beuve-Méry, was forced out in a dispute with the owners of the paper, but the editorial staff, speaking through the newly formed Society of Journalists, refused to work without him. Beuve-Méry withdrew his resignation and participated in drawing up a new agreement. Under the plan, the staff by 1968 had a 40 percent share in the control of *Le Monde.* That included policy-making and managerial decisions—not day-to-day but in overall planning—and the right to block the sale of the paper. Since any major changes in the paper's structure (for example, the naming of a new managing director, who had to be a journalist) required a 75 percent majority, the staff, through the Society of Journalists, had a virtual veto.

Tradition-bound American publishers might be impressed with the results of the *Le Monde* experiment described in a book by Jean Schwoebel, *Le Monde's* chief diplomatic editor and one of the pioneers of the plan. The book, entitled *Press, Power, and Money,* has unfortunately not been translated from the French for United States publication. Under control of its editorial staff, *Le Monde* achieved first rank in influence in France, a new plant and a profit in 1969 of 3.5 million dollars on a gross income of 20 million dollars. A key to its editorial quality was its insistence on retaining a 3:2 ratio of news to advertising, exactly the reverse of prevailing practice in the United States.

Even at the time of the great French newspaper slump of 1971-72, when other newspapers were losing revenue and laying off employees, *Le Monde* managed to break even and retain its circulation at 500,000 (it had doubled its circulation in less than ten years). These statistics were even more striking in view of the decline in the number of Paris daily newspapers from 32 in 1945 to 11 in 1972.

During a visit to the United States in 1970, Schwoebel declared that in a capitalist country influence could be exerted only through a share of the ownership—the rest was without value. Thirty-two societies had been established in France, he said, all striving to emulate the *Le Monde* pattern, but they were meeting stiff resistance from the owners. Formed into a federation, the societies were seeking to achieve their aims through political pressure.

The federation did not operate as the Newspaper Guild, Schwoebel said. It was founded as a commercial group but later changed into a "civil" one. Profit sharing was not part of the societies' demands: "We want part of the ownership not for the profits—that is for the investors—but only for the juridical rights the property gives. As soon as we leave the paper, we no longer have rights." The federation had an assembly and a council of administration and declared its goal to be the unity of journalists in a common conception. "To unite journalists is very difficult," Schwoebel said. "You succeed only if you pick very solid, very reasonable arguments. And in my view we have united on very sensible, responsible problems."

The *Le Monde* experiment was contagious and attracted attention among frustrated and dissatisfied journalists in Germany, Italy, England and Spain. The feudal power of the owners of the press was a common factor in each of the countries, as well as elsewhere in France. And in France particularly, the student uprising of 1968 helped to give courage to the journalists of France, who walked out in a series of strikes that shook the press structure and the government-operated radio-television network.

There was a revealing and amusing confrontation in 1968 between the striking staff of the picture paper *Paris-Match* and the publisher, textile millionaire Jean Prouvost (who owned also the conservative daily *Figaro* and the powerful Radio Luxembourg). During the confrontation the following dialogue took place:

> PROUVOST: *I do own this magazine, don't I?*
> STAFF: *Yes.*
> PROUVOST: *It's my money, isn't it?*
> STAFF: *Yes.*
> PROUVOST: *Well, then, I'm the boss, am I not?*
> STAFF: *Yes.*
> PROUVOST: *Then in that case I decide what I
> please.*
> STAFF: *(in chorus): NO!*

In 1969 a strike was called at *Figaro* when Prouvost refused to sign a new contract with the editorial staff. Prouvost's own partner associated himself with the staff, and the strike ended with a compromise settlement under which the editorial association of the staff retained its prerogatives under the old contract. A walkout at the weekly *L'Express* the same year forced its management to draw up a set of reforms recognizing the "right of employees to participate in the decision-making process." Again the issue was not financial control. "The time is now past," said a *Figaro* editor, "when a newspaper owner can buy a paper in the same way that a nineteenth-century entrepreneur bought a boat with a consignment of slaves." Another journalist said: "It's not the money. We want to raise the standards of the French press. We want to give it a new morality."

The prevalence of morality was not notable in the profit-hungry West German publishing industry. At a glance, it seemed to rest on pliant pillars: the bare breast and the bare bottom. In some cities, particularly Hamburg, newsstands took on the appearance of a mountain of flesh. Chief among the flesh peddlers was Heinrich Bauer, publisher, among others, of the mass-circulation *Quick,* which *Newsweek* once modestly described as "titillating." When the staff of Hamburg-based *Der Stern,* generally described as West Germany's *Life,* learned that a co-owner of *Stern* was about to sell his shares to Bauer for 42.5 million dollars, they rebelled.

Within hours of the report of the owner's intention, a resolution was adopted by 140 editors, reporters and photographers threatening to strike unless the deal was called off. It was. The would-be seller was forced to turn his shares over to his current partners, who then signed an agreement with the staff giving the editors and writers broad new authority similar to that at *Le Monde.* The character of the agreement was expressed in the preamble:

> *Stern is a politically engaged magazine, but independent of political parties, economic interest groups and other lobbies, which intends to inform and entertain its readers. The editorial staff of* Stern *pledges themselves to an open democratic society and to progressive liberal principles.*

Neither at conservative *Figaro* nor at liberal *Stern* was the action sparked by political radicals on the staffs. It is doubtful whether there *were* any radicals at *Figaro;* and in typically Germanic fashion, at *Stern* the greatest number of votes for the new editorial council went to the "father"—editor-in-chief Heinrich Nannen. In a sense, therefore, the European events took on added significance precisely because nonradical personnel reacted so swiftly and with such unity to the growing power of the press barons and their unwillingness to acknowledge, as *Stern's* Nannen expressed it, that "owning a newspaper is different from owning a spaghetti factory."

Except for the *New York Times* and the *Washington Post*, and the press sections of *Time* and *Newsweek*, the newspapers of the United States have given scant coverage to the events in France and Germany. Among those who did comment, however, was Robert U. Brown, editor and publisher of *Editor & Publisher*, the weekly trade journal of the newspaper industry. Brown participated in the twenty-second congress of the Federation of International Newspaper Editors (FIEJ) in Istanbul in May 1969, and reported his conclusions in *Editor & Publisher* (June 4, 1969):

> *The trend in Europe is toward the unrestricted right of the editor to run his news and editorial department the way he wants to without consideration or responsibility toward the publisher or the owner. It amounts to some sort of "divine right." There seems to be very little discussion or acknowledgment of the right of the owner or publisher who hired the editor and put him into that exalted position in the first place. Once hired, the current thinking of European editors is that no one, least of all the publisher, has any right to question his editing decisions.*

It was obvious from the events as they actually were happening, and the nature of the agreements at *Le Monde* and *Stern*, for example, that Brown was overstating the European situation. But it was also clear that his comment had been made out of concern that the days of journalistic slave ships and spaghetti-printing factories might be coming to an end in the United States, too.

While *Figaro* and *Stern* were boiling over in May 1969, and Brown was stewing in Istanbul, the Magazine Publishers Association of America convened to mark its fiftieth anniversary at Williamsburg, Virginia. Among the invited speakers was Jean-Louis Servan-Schreiber, brother of Jean-Jacques and associated with him at the weekly *L'Express* and at *L'Expansion*, an industrial publication. His topic was: "Will Publishers Lose Control of Their Publications to Editors?" As though in response to Brown's uneasy vision of the future, he described the strife in the French press as a situation "which might very well in the near future emerge in different countries of the world. [They] may be the beginning of a permanent problem in our profession, just as the Berkeley riots of 1967 started ... the worldwide student unrest." The demand of the editorial staffs in France, he said, was that "information should become a public service protected from the power of money and capital." That sounded dangerously close to an accurate interpretation of the First Amendment. He went on:

> *It is true that publications are bought and sold as other goods and that people do not like the feeling of being traded. It is also true that not all publishers feel strong enough to ignore the influence of powerful advertisers on the editorial content. Although there have been instances of journalists publishing without capital, we have yet to imagine how capital alone can publish without journalists. For all these moral and professional reasons, while the journalistic associations are in fact questioning capitalist rule, we cannot afford to disregard them altogether.*

A year later Jean Schwoebel was asked, when he also was in the United States, whether the *Le Monde* experiment might take root in an "élite or quality" newspaper in the United States. Possibly at the *New York Times* or the *Washington Post* or the *Christian Science Monitor*, Schwoebel replied, but "I know perfectly well that conditions are different in America." The United States was highly advanced in efficiency and energy, he said, but its people were slow to realize that "the real cause of chaos in the future involves a dimension beyond efficiency." Then, as Servan-Schreiber had done, he placed great stress on the question of economic control:

Your journalists are dependent on a society which still believes much in profitability—which is necessary. I think the view of profits, of commerce, in American society in a certain measure represents progress; in another way, not. I believe sincerely that it is much more difficult for American journalists than for us because in such a society as yours it is not regarded as a scandal that economic processes control the press. In European societies it is looked upon as a scandal. In my view such control is completely anti-American.

In ten years I am sure that this philosophy will have taken root in America. I say that not only journalists have a right, but clerks or workers have a right to press for their rights. But journalists are different. We are defenders of the truth. Now progress is a question of dialogue. We are at the end of a certain kind of journalism—of magisterial journalism—and of a certain kind of journalist—the magisterial journalist. And we must accept this dialogue.

Schwoebel was sound in his contention that things were different in the United States—and American journalists have helped to broaden that difference. This theory of the exceptionalism of American journalism was rooted in two strongly held beliefs: (1) that the owner of a media enterprise was entitled, to all the income he could derive from it; (2) that journalists in the United States, even in the commercially competitive setting of the media, were individualistic professionals. And superimposed upon these beliefs has been the traditionally sacrosanct ideal of objectivity, projected by publishers (and accepted by most media staffs) as the only proper framework for the theory and practice of American journalism.

Under this principle of objectivity, American journalists have maintained a posture apart from and a degree above the general public. And while they have held to their positions, their publishers and the operators of the broadcast media have

pirouetted through the commercial world in pursuit of maximum profits. The process is in fact a classical capitalist ballet in which both bosses and employees are far more concerned with success, image and status than with performance in the public interest.

On the surface, such an arrangement would seem to be comfortable and enduring for the participants. But, like much of life in the United States, it is tending to come apart at the seams. A deep unhappiness has become apparent among media staffs, ranging from the mighty empires on Madison Avenue to small-town newspapers. It has affected executives, reporters, news broadcasters, columnists and copy readers. The malaise takes many forms: frustration about assignments; anger at censorship and prejudicial editing of copy; contempt for managerial timidity; and resentment at lack of progress on the job. Yet this malaise has been kept under control by periodic elevation of privilege and paycheck. The publishers and their country-club companions in industry and government have seen to the former, and the unions in the industry—not without periodic hassles—to the latter.

In this atmosphere two counter pressures are being applied to media staffs: the determination of the owners to maintain the status quo, utilizing to this end the ideal of objectivity as against "advocacy" journalism; and the ever-increasing number of dissenters in American society demanding fundamental changes in a system of which the media are an integral part. The catalysts that brought this simmering situation to a boil were the dramatic events of the 1960s, on the one hand, and, on the other, a new generation of journalists who had been involved in these events on university campuses, in street demonstrations against war and poverty, and in the unprecedented protests against racism.

These young journalists came into the newsrooms directly from the front lines, as it were, without cynicism and eager to be of useful service in a communications network whose potential for the common good was unmatched in history. They felt they could persuade the communications industry to present, for all the world to see, the true condition of man as a prelude to action to change this condition. The image of the journalist they wished to destroy was, for example, the one in *Medium Cool,* the popular and realistic film about Chicago in the 1960s. In this film a television reporter-cameraman stands in front of a television set watching Martin Luther King, Jr., make an impassioned speech, and says: "Jesus, I really love to shoot film!"

When the young journalists presented themselves for service, however, they almost invariably encountered the stone-wall traditions. Don't get too close to a story, they were told, or you'll lose your objectivity and get emotional about it. The good reporter is objective, unemotional, detached. Don't let anybody tell you the best place to watch a football game is out there on the field. Don't fool yourself: the best place is from the bench. The end result of most of this advice was the kind of news story that skillfully presented the facts in objective fashion, eschewed interpretive analysis and, above all, preserved the reporter in armorplated neutrality.

There was one flaw, however. The story in reality was lopsided. The source of the objective facts about the situation was too often police officials or government press officers. Rarely was the other side represented in detail, whether it was a suspect in an episode of violence, a foreign adversary in a complicated negotiation or the target of an investigatory agency. The attitude of the press toward Senator Joe McCarthy in the flowering Cold War years[1] was a classic example of objectivity run amok in favor of the predator. The media, under the cover of objective reporting, was largely instrumental in building McCarthy into the formidable figure he became. The reporters who were assigned to cover McCarthy (they were known as the "goon squad") knew McCarthy was a liar and a charlatan, and that his charges were almost entirely baseless. Yet they insisted that the strictures of objectivity required them to report the senator's charges without

comment—unless they were rebutted by the person under attack or by a political opponent of McCarthy who might then be quoted.

This, of course, was nonsense. If the reporters (and their editors) had proof that McCarthy's allegations were false—and a minimum of digging would have documented their findings—it was their responsibility to publish the documented refutation. The victims themselves were generally unavailable for comment or fearful of making a statement because an indictment on a charge of perjury was a likely result in the poisoned atmosphere of the time. A responsible press would have exerted every effort to help the victim set the record straight. But "objectivity" forbade this. The basic reasons for media reluctance, however, went deeper than this convenient catchphrase. They were prejudice and fear on the part of editors and, unfortunately, many of the reporters. The crippling myth of the "international Communist conspiracy" had taken hold in the ranks of the press, as well as in the general public.

The young journalists coming into the media, however, were not willing to accept the guidance of their weary elders, and they charted their own course. Significantly, their first moves coincided with the high point in the public protest against the war in Southeast Asis in 1969. In October of that year a moratorium was declared by the peace movement; all workers were asked to remain away from the job or to request time off to join demonstrations.

At the *New York Times* in mid-October representatives of 308 employees (many of them from the commercial departments) asked for and were denied the use of the newspaper's auditorium for discussions on Moratorium Day. They were told by Sidney Gruson, assistant to the publisher, that "it is a principle of this company that its facilities should not be used for what could be construed as political purposes." Instead, more than 150 *Times* employees on Moratorium Day held a silent vigil outside the building on West 43rd Street, and then joined a nearby rally sponsored by representatives of the book-publishing industry.

At Time, Inc., 462 employees of *Time, Life, Fortune* and *Sports Illustrated* sought the use of the Time-Life auditorium. Permission was given, and 500 attended antiwar discussions—among them publisher Henry Luce III. A spokesman explained that Luce "was just there to see what was going on. He wasn't wearing a button or an armband or anything." The employees signed a petition calling for an "immediate and unilateral withdrawal" from Vietnam, collected 1,400 signatures from passersby at the Time-Life building, and then joined the publishing industry rally. At *Newsweek* 200 employees remained off the job on Moratorium Day.

At the *Wall Street Journal* several employees raised the question of participating in Moratorium Day and were told by management that it was completely against the policy of Dow Jones (publishers of the *Journal*) to do anything "which might in the public eye cast the slightest doubt about the impartiality of its news coverage." Therefore, Dow Jones as an organization would not participate in any way. Employees wishing to take part, however, could get time off, "to be made up at a later date."

The *Times's* Gruson told Stanford Sesser of the *Wall Street Journal* that he might be old-fashioned, "but I feel very strongly about purity of news columns. Pure objectivity may not exist, but you have to strive for it anyway." In Raleigh, North Carolina, Sesser found another Gruson who disagreed—his daughter, Kerry. As a student at Radcliffe, where she had been campus correspondent for the *Times,* Kerry Gruson had worn the red armband of student demonstrators while attending press conferences. She told Sesser: "Objectivity is a myth … There comes a time when you have to take a stand. After that you try to be fair." The *Times's* decision denying the meeting hall was wrong, she said: "The war has waked people up and started them

thinking. To say that newspapermen aren't allowed to think because they're newspapermen is completely ridiculous."

One month later 500,000 persons took part in the greatest antiwar demonstration in the nation's history, in Washington, D.C. Yet the three major television networks decided not to cover the events live. Since there was no coverage, the issue of objectivity as such could not be raised. But the decision, by negation, mocked the whole concept of objectivity. The failure to cover was an incalculably greater barrier to objective truth than a crowd of reporters with red armbands.

The ferment within the industry by 1970 had increased to the point where groups of editorial personnel on several newspapers were meeting to discuss their functions and responsibilities, and the responsibility of their publications to the public. The basic issue was how they could make their collective weight felt with management about questions of policy, personnel and content. Almost immediately the phrase of "reporter power" was coined. As with most such rhetorical slogans, however, it was out of proportion to the amount of activity involved—but it was to the point. Stories began to appear in journalism reviews about the reporters' associations in France and Germany, and grave warnings were posted in media trade journals about threats to the system of free enterprise and a free press.

Managements in some cities took heed of the stirrings below and responded positively to requests for discussion. The response was in part an effort to avoid an even more serious confrontation which almost surely would have resulted from a refusal to talk things out. The media managements were aware also of the angry mood in the antiwar movement, with which many reporters sympathized, particularly after the United

States—South Vietnam invasion of Cambodia and the killings of students by troops and police at Kent State University in Ohio and Jackson State in Mississippi.

In February 1970 the Association of Tribune Journalists was created by *Minneapolis Tribune* reporters, not as a collective-bargaining group (the Newspaper Guild was the representative of editorial and commercial employees), but as an organization which would "bring its best thoughts into a dialogue with management." The group was formed, an organizer said, because the staff felt like privates in an army in which the editors acted like officers. "We were to do what we were told and like it," he said, "and no one gave a damn if we thought our orders were sane or insane."

At the Gannett newspapers in Rochester, New York, a rotating system was set up providing for staff members to sit in with the editorial board. A Journalists Committee in Providence held several meetings with management about specific staff and policy complaints. While in some areas (Buffalo, for example, where Guild monitors sat in on a staff-management meeting discussing editorial practices), the Newspaper Guild watched the proceedings warily, in others it added its weight to the extra-Guild demands. When two assistant city editorships became vacant at the *Minneapolis Tribune,* the local Guild adopted a resolution requesting that reporters, photographers and copydesk editors be permitted to "advise and consent to management's nominations." Management insisted that it would not give up its prerogatives (it had not been asked to), but agreed to consider staff nominations for the two jobs. In Denver a new contract in 1970 established an ethics committee and a human-rights committee to discuss minority hiring and certain editorial practices which the staff found to be demeaning. Granted these were small steps: they were notable because they had never been taken before.

The pattern, for the most part, in the internal media ferment was not radical but reformist. The dissenters had no desire to take power. The situation at the *New York Times* was typical. *Le Monde's* Jean Schwoebel had met with a group of dissidents there who were seeking to alter the paper's stodgy image (they had been dubbed "The Cabal"). He found them much more inclined to confine themselves to their own problems than to lead a national revolt—something which the staff of the *Times,* because of the paper's prestige, could well do. Later, in a conversation with Ron Dorfman, editor of the *Chicago Journalism Review,* one *Times* cabalist, J. Anthony Lukas, remarked with some astonishment about Schwoebel's views: "He's talking about *ownership!*" That obviously was not in the minds of the *Times's* dissenters, nor the prevailing view among the 60 activists at the *New York Post* who had been meeting with then publisher Dorothy Schiff.

The *Post,* with the largest evening circulation in the United States, has a complete monopoly in the New York evening field. It is a fat, penny-pinching, cramped newspaper, short on cultural standards and long on syndicated opinions and analysis. Despite its liberal pretensions, it has frequently been accused of discrimination against black and Puerto Rican staff members and of hypocritical hiring practices in this area. It is, in short, a disgracefully inadequate newspaper in the cultural capital of the nation, and many of its staff members have long been aware of a concomitant cultural lag in the newsroom. In this unhappy setting, staff members joined to confront the reluctant publisher, Mrs. Dorothy Schiff, and her chief editors with demands for improved editorial and personnel practices.

At one point Mrs. Schiff defended the *Post's* firing of a young black woman who had been tried out as a reporter. She strayed so far from the facts that she snapped the patience of one of the *Post's* most loyal reporters—Ted Poston, a 35-year veteran, able writer and devoted management counselor. Poston's qualifications should have led to an editor's chair years before, but he had a handicap: he was black.

In February 1970 Poston sent a memorandum to Mrs. Schiff detailing the perennially shoddy practices of the *Post* regarding minority staff members. The memo, published in the October 1971 issue of *(More),* the New York journalism review, concluded: "I think that it will be criminal for the *New York Post* to dissipate the unquestioned loyalty it has developed over the years from liberals and minority group communities by refusing to face and correct a situation which some of your executives won't even admit exists."

Poston received an icy reply from Mrs. Schiff, who shortly thereafter was defending the *Post* before the New York State Human Rights Commission in a case growing out of the firing of another young black reporter. The commission found valid the charge that the *Post* maintained a policy of employing no more than three black and Puerto Rican editorial employees at one time (out of a staff of 63), and ruled that the reporter, William Artis, had been fired "in contravention of the human rights laws."

At about the same time, a *Post* woman reporter was fired for refusing an assignment to interview the wife of a big league baseball pitcher. She felt that the assignment was degrading both to the wife of the pitcher and to herself; that the only reason the woman was being interviewed was because she was the pitcher's wife. The staff rose in defense of the dismissed reporter and threatened to close down the paper. The reporter was rehired.

At less liberal papers the reaction of publishers and editors has been more liberal. The Associated Press Managing Editors Association, comprising editors of papers with an Associated Press franchise, in 1971 commissioned a report on "Activism and Advocacy" under the direction of Ed Miller, executive editor of the Call-Chronicle Newspapers of Allentown, Pennsylvania. Miller visited four newspapers in Buffalo, Portland (Maine), Denver and Milwaukee, seeking "to document what was happening rather than make judgments." When he got into the newsrooms, Miller found that his range of investigation went far beyond his alliterative subject. It covered such subjects as off-the-job activities by reporters, advocacy reporting, ethics, newsroom revolts, journalism reviews and—affecting all these

other questions—the matter of credibility. Miller approached his task with a refreshing openmindedness, even though it was clear that he was more at ease in discussion with his counterparts than with dissenting staff. His findings are instructive because they deal with four newspapers generally regarded as responsible, and in four different sectors of the United States. Following are highlights of his report.

Buffalo Evening News: The editorial staff Professional Standards Group raised seven issues with management: training procedures, minority hiring, stylebook, dignity and professionalism (later termed "civility"), investigative reporting, resistance to writing promotional stories and reporter's conscience. The group felt that the *Evening News* was more often a booster for the "landed gentry" of the community than a critic and investigator, and that it ignored the needs of the city's ghetto residents. The "real enemy," one said, was "the system of doing things in a certain way for 40 or 50 years." Miller himself said:

Staffers, particularly young reporters, are feeling hemmed in. They see their profession as a means for social change but are frustrated when their managers do not march to the same drummer. To some degree it's a problem of youth; but waiting for young enthusiasm to mellow would be a sad solution. Some may see it as a modern labor-management battle, but even that old standby is not purely the case. Buffalo's Professional Standards Group found as much resistance among the ranks of the Guild as it did from management.

Managing Editor Elwood M. Wardlow of the *Evening News* judged the Standards Group's efforts as neither a success nor a failure. Some of their suggestions had been adopted, he said, and management *was* listening better. There had been no recrimination against those who stated the case most forcefully. City Editor Bud Wacker summed up: "The conditions which caused [the movement] are still present." Miller added: "That is not a self-indictment, but rather a candid and honest appraisal of one newspaper that recognizes a problem which will not go away."

Denver Post: The resistance in Denver took the form of a journalism review, *The Unsatisfied Man,* and managerial reaction was sharp. The *Post's* managing editor, John Rogers, commented: "Too much of the time the effectiveness of whatever valid criticism might appear is eroded by their purely personal criticism....There's too much invective rather than investigation. Too much subjective carping. This, unfortunately, is abetted by too frequent examples of bad reporting and faulty conclusions." He couldn't recall a single instance of change at the *Post* as a result of the review's criticism.

A parallel development at the *Post* was the creation of the Ethics Committee as an adjunct to the Newspaper Guild, seeking to set higher standards in staff conduct—refusal of gifts, for example, or cutting down on junkets designed to inspire news stories which in reality were free advertising. "We got resistance from management," said a committee member, "and ridicule from the staff," many of whom regarded the committee as "nosey do-gooders." But the committee persevered and worked out with management a memorandum on staff ethics which was likely to become a continuing agreement.

An assistant managing editor, asked about the *Post's* hiring of "activists," said: "The premise of management is to hire these young Turks to strike a balance on the staff. They're given every opportunity to move up the ladder." He said he would not be "turned off" by an applicant who wanted to work on a newspaper to change the world, but he wouldn't "want a whole staff that way." Managing Editor Rogers felt there was good rapport between management and staff, and an "open-door" policy was helping to maintain staff stability. One staff member was candid about his colleagues: "One of the problems around here is that people would bitch about stories not being done, but virtually all of the time if they had gone to the desk the chances are that they would have

been done. There is a helluva lot of laziness."

Portland Press-Herald and *Express:* Executive Editor Ernest Chard said: "Applicants come in with a greater sense of mission than they used to. There seems to be a rejection of establishment pursuits as the young crowd looks to newspapers as a way of projecting social service. They wish to be in the swing of things, an influence on shaping society, and they think newspapers provide a medium to do this."

As in the other cities he visited, Miller said, the attitude of the younger reporters in Portland was: "Let's set the pace, not follow it." Too often, they said, newspapers failed to deal with a problem, such as the environment, until it was forced upon them. In Portland the reporters were asking for an opportunity to research community problems in depth to determine causes and solutions rather than simply recite the manifestations of the problems. "You must give reporters with proven competence the opportunity to have a voice," said Editor Chard. He cited the case of a city hall reporter who wrote an opinion column once a week. The politicians were critical, and some executives felt it would undermine the reporter's credibility with his sources. But no one could demonstrate that the reporter was unfair in his news coverage, and the column continued.

Miller found that "the particular stumbling block of larger organizations, communications up and down the chain of command," did not appear to be a serious problem in Portland. Smaller size was one factor, he felt, but a more important one was that "the paper's primary asset in dealing with the problems of advocacy and activism seems to be internal flexibility. There appears to be enough safety valves to prevent explosion."

Milwaukee Journal: This newspaper, one of the most outspoken critics of Senator Joe McCarthy (it sought in its pages to counter as quickly as possible his demonstrable distortion and lying), takes a tough line toward outside activities by its staff. "We have a clear-cut policy," said Managing Editor Joe Shoquist. "Anybody in the news and editorial operation should be as uninvolved and as passive as possible. We forbid practices which might reflect unfavorably on the newspaper or its credibility." Some don'ts: no political action—either running for office or working in politics; no participation in demonstrations; no publicity jobs—not even for churches. How did Shoquist feel about activist applicants for jobs? He responded:

We want to avoid prejudiced reporting, but I worry more about the inhibiting effect we have on idealistic reporters than the dangers of editorializing in the news columns. I expect your reporters to be fired with enthusiasm. We want a strong social conscience, but they soon discover they will have to do it through the system. An activist's alternatives are underground newspapers or other minor publications which have no influence in the scheme of things. But the activist soon learns that he can make the greatest impact by working on a respected newspaper which is believed.

A reporter or editor is required to make some sacrifices in his civil rights. That's really a small price to pay for the compensations, for we're in a position to do so much for our world and our society, we must not undercut our effectiveness. We must keep the slate as clean as possible. Having a clear-cut policy helps us stay on this course.

The *Journal* sends its editors to meetings of community groups, such as county government officials, educators and lawyers. Once a month it sponsors dinners to give the community an opportunity for an exchange with the editors. The stress is on credibility. Shoquist elaborated:

We want an objective attitude, not just a recitation of the facts. Analysis, interpretation, and even some opinionating may be necessary if we are to inform people. Just repeating words or actions may not be truthful reporting. We have people capable, knowledgeable, and mature enough to analyze and interpret. We do identify this material doggedly, so the reader knows precisely what's being presented. But the need for presenting this is there.

Many staff reporters agreed with this managerial approach, although there was disagreement as to how much voice staff members had in decision making at the top. An editorial-page feature called "In My Opinion" is used occasionally by staff members as an outlet. A column titled "Accent in the News" permits another outlet six days a week for observations, comments and sidelights. And on Sunday there is a column called "Write On" reserved for any black member of the staff, not just reporters (there are eight black reporters in the "professional ranks" at the *Journal* out of a total of 160).

Although management at the *Milwaukee Journal* seemed to take credit for an enlightened attitude within the newsroom, however hard-nosed it was about outside activities, it is clear that a staff group called Journal 14 (after a Milwaukee draft-resistance group) was in some measure responsible for the enlightenment. These were reporters and copyeditors seriously concerned with basic questions of news philosophy, standards, traditional methods and the scope of coverage. They were for the most part the more experienced members of the staff, unlike their resisting counterparts at other newspapers. They were aware that the growing complexity of society demanded a more careful look at race questions, life-styles and poor people than could be provided by the "tape-recorder" style of journalism. In this spirit they prepared and signed a report to management which led to meetings with the editors and effected some reforms. "There was a general change in attitudes," one member said, adding:

"There's lots of talent around here seriously concerned about improving the product. Our motive was to create a better paper. The quality of reporters is a key." He referred to the "nonsystem" in effect at the *Journal* which he described as a failure of communications between reporters who were experts in their specialized fields and their editors, whose only advantage was their authority. None of this, Miller concluded, was "out of step with management thinking and practice at the *Milwaukee Journal*."

Miller listed three central concerns derived from his survey and what he thought should be done about them: consistency (the same policy regarding ethics, activism and advocacy should be applied to publisher and reporter alike); flexibility (the title of editor does not guarantee that its holder is the repository of greater wisdom than that of the reporter); and communications (the communications industry ought to learn the art of communication within its own newsrooms). Miller concluded:

These factors in turn have an impact on the way a staff member views the organization. You cannot speak of activism without first assessing a paper's standards and practices. If a reporter is told that he cannot demonstrate for a cause but the publisher is allowed to sit on the various news-making boards in the community, is that properly dealing with the conditions of activism? If a reporter is told that he cannot inject his opinions into his news columns, yet he believes the paper bends its stories in favor of major advertisers or community projects, how does an editor effectively discuss advocacy journalism?

In other words, the condition is not limited to a handful of young motivated reporters on urban newspapers. These are merely the most visible and vocal symptoms. Editors must remember that young activists are looking not only outward to the changing community but inward to the organization. Thus, if a newspaper is to deal with tensions of activism and advocacy journalism, it

must first determine if its own actions and principles of operation are not in some ways contributing to those tensions. Perhaps we've been looking outside to society for the causes of activism and advocacy journalism when we should have been looking inside the organization as well.

These are thoughtful words from a man on the managerial side of the newsroom who took seriously his assignment from the Associated Press Managing Editors Association and contributed a valuable report both for his colleagues in the association and for media people in general.

For certain groups within the media Miller's words have special meaning—groups which for generations have felt particularly the prejudices and strictures of the system in which they lived and the communications media to which they aspired. Seemingly diverse, they have much in common. They are the black people and the women and the young men forced into the Army by a draft or by an economic system which deprives them of the right to a civilian livelihood with dignity....

NOTES

1. There are detailed chapters about the press and McCarthy in a book by James Aronson, *The Press and the Cold War* (New York: Bobbs-Merrill, 1970).

Part Three

Modes of Access

THE PRESS AND THE PUBLIC INTEREST: A DEFINITIONAL DILEMMA

Everette E. Dennis

Whether the interest of the press as the issuer of information is necessarily the same as that of the consumer of the information is central to many critiques of the mass media. This conflict of interests between the individual and the mass media is often resolved by invoking the public interest as a mediating principle. While the truism that the press should serve the public interest is accepted by nearly everyone, the satisfactory definition of that concept has proven much more difficult. "[T]here are two distinct interests," wrote philosopher William Ernest Hocking, "only one of them needs ... protection; to protect the issuer is to protect the consumer."[1] Freedom of the press, Hocking suggested, "has always been a matter of public as well as individual importance. Inseparable from the right of the press to be free has been the right of the people to have a free press."[2]

Examining the public interest concept in terms of the motivation for legislative attacks on executive secrecy, Professor Francis E. Rourke noted that the strongest efforts in this area had come initially from the press and the scientific community. This, he said, "reflects the wide variety of interests [but] each...can also point to a clear public interest in the success of its special efforts."[3] Professor Rourke continued:

[T]he public has an obvious stake in the effective performance of the legislative task, as it does in the availability of information in the hands of executive officials to the media of communications upon which the people depend for knowledge concerning the affairs of

Excerpts from De Paul Law Review 23 (Spring 1974): 937-960. Copyright © 1974 by De Paul University; reprinted by permission.

*government. And the public has no less an interest
in keeping open the channels of communications
upon which the economic progress of society may
be said to depend.*[4]

Rourke's rationale that the public has a deep
interest in the free flow of information, and
thereby a free press, is frequently echoed by
students of government, the press, newsmen
and judges. That was what Mr. Justice
Brennan had in mind in *New York Times Co.
v. Sullivan* when he enunciated a profound
national commitment to the principle of
debate on public issues which he said should
be "uninhibited, robust and wide open."[5] This
principle brought an exasperated response
from Jerome A. Barron, law professor and
authority on access to the news media.
Fumed Barron: "newspaper publishers'
interests and the public interest are held to be
identical," and the result of the *Times*
decision was "romantic and lopsidedly pro-
publisher."[6]

Clearly, Barron and others believe that
the consumer of communication should also
have a right to determine what shall constitute
freedom of the press. The exercise of this
prerogative in Barron's view, would serve the
public interest. Such a position is sharply at
odds with the 1947 Commission on Freedom
of the Press which observed "(that) the work
of the press always involves the interest of the
consumer; but as long as the consumer is free
his interest is protected in the protection of
the freedom of the issuer"[7]....

THE SEARCH
FOR DEFINITION

Few concepts have attracted as much
scholarly probing as the public interest. "It is
probable that as much mischief has been
perpetrated upon the human race in the
name of 'the public interest' as in the name of
anything else," wrote Daniel Bell and Irving
Kristol as they introduced a new journal titled,
The Public Interest, in 1965.[8] Although the
concept traces its origins to the writings of
Plato and Aristotle and has provided the
substance for many books, papers and
scholarly presentations, the public interest is
little more than "a conceptual muddle," as

suggested by political scientist Frank Sorauf,
who wrote: "Clearly, no scholarly consensus
exists on the public interest, nor does
agreement appear to be in the offing."[9]

In part the disillusionment with the
concept springs from the vague and confusing
meanings that have been attached to it. The
rubric of public interest seems to belong to
that genre of euphemisms that includes the
public welfare, the common good, and the
national interest. In part, the problem with the
concept is its idealistic and pristine nature as
demonstrated in Walter Lippmann's comment
that "the public interest may be presumed to
be what men would choose if they saw clearly,
thought rationally, acted disinterestedly and
benevolently."[10] The British writer Robert
Skidelsky, however, sees the term as a dying
metaphor because one man's metaphor is
always another man's reality.[11]

The despair of the critics notwithstanding,
the term is not to be escaped. It is pervasive in
the literature of the first amendment and
serves as a guiding principle for the courts
and the public philosophers. The public
interest "is the central concept of a civilized
polity [and] its genius lies not in its clarity but
in its perverse and persistent moral intrusion
upon the internal and external discourse of
rulers and ruled alike"[12]....

Even though a political scientist's 1960
observation that "there is no public interest
theory worthy of the name"[13] remains valid in
1973, there have been some notable attempts
in recent years to explicate the concept more
fully. One of the best efforts is a brilliant
treatise by political scientist Virginia Held, *The
Public Interest and Individual Interests.*[14]
Before defining the concept in her own terms,
she synthesizes the literature of the public
interest and proposes three classifications: (1)
preponderance theories, (2) the public
interest as common interest, and (3) unitary
conceptions.

The preponderance theories are based on
the assumption that if the public interest has
any meaning at all it "cannot be in conflict
with a preponderance or sum of individual
interests, although this preponderance may

be thought to be constituted and to be calculable in very different ways."[15]

The preponderance theories are traced to the writings of Hobbes, who believed in a preponderance of force; Hume, an exponent of preponderance of opinion; and Bentham, who advanced the idea of superior sum of individual interests. A contemporary application of preponderance theory is the relationship between the Federal Communications Commission and the networks' programming on television, a kind of lowest common denominator guided by ratings designed to give the public what it says it wants.

In examining the public interest as a common interest, Ms. Held says, "the equation of the public interest with those interests which all members of a polity have in *common*," forms the core of this idea.[16] This concept agrees with preponderance theories in not ruling out the possibility of justifiable conflicts of individual interest, but it defines the public interest in terms of unanimity and compatibility. Common interest theory finds support in the writings of Rousseau who spoke of the common good and the general will. A modern application of this common interest theory would be shared interest and mutual trust. The unitary formulation is based on universal moral precepts and hence,

individual interests cannot justifiably conflict with the public interest or with each other. Only a universal moral order can confer validity, or justifiability, and the same universal order which renders a judgment that a given action or state is right or good cannot also render a judgment that the same action or state is wrong or evil.[17]

The formulation advanced by Ms. Held is an attempt to outline a norm for public interest that would function within the political and legal systems and would be governed by authoritative rules of conduct. She asserts that

the policy may be understood as a system which validates public interest claims ... [*and*] ... *that only the political system provides an effective decision method which could be associated with the term*

public *for claims of what is or is not in the public interest. Any such decision method, or network of methods for a given society is constitutive of a political system.*[18]

This system suggests that "no judgment concerning the public interest can be valid outside the political system whose decision procedures validate claims about it, although judgments concerning ... the public interest, and the political system can itself be judged in moral terms."[19]

How would Ms. Held's construct be applied? In the instance of the regulation of television programming, for example, there would be at least two levels for consideration. First, the question of the *preferences* of a majority of the population would be determined empirically. Similarly, the *interests* of the majority could also be determined empirically, but

[*b*]*oth of these questions would be distinct from that of whether existing programming practices are in the* public interest. *It might or it might not be considered in the interest of the polity to satisfy* majority *interest in this field. The question of* majority *interest might well be the one with which we were concerned, in a particular discussion, but if so, we would do well to use this term, not the public interest. We might conceivably decide, for instance, that it is not in the public interest for government to interfere with television programming, no matter what is produced, and that this decision has priority over any evaluation of program content. Discussion of the latter, then, might be in terms of majority interests, of the responsibilities of the networks to minority interests, or of aesthetic considerations, and perhaps not in terms of the public interest at all.*[20]

The Held system depends, of course, on statutory regulations and the courts as a mechanism for adjudicating public interest disputes.

Perhaps the most useful distinction in this conceptual definition is the clear dividing line between preference and interest. What interests the public, in terms of its wants, desires and tastes may necessarily be in the public interest. For example, in a developing nation, the immediate desires of pre-literate people for a certain content in television programming might not comport with the government's desire to use television as a channel for education and culture. Thus, even in a democracy, majority rule might be in conflict with the public interest. In American society, for example, freedom of speech is a fundamental tenet of constitutional law and of societal values. However, in a single instance the majority of the community might favor censorship. Under Ms. Held's system, public interest doctrine would dictate adherence to societal rules, overturning the immediate will of the majority. In many instances such an approach is essential to the preservation of minority rights, aesthetic values and other public interest concerns.

The public interest definitional dilemma indicated in this section illustrates the still turbulent nature of the debate over this most complex of concepts. ...

THE LEGAL DIMENSION
Searching for a Standard

Virginia Held's assumption that "[only] the polity may be *understood as a system which validates public interest claims*," moves the definition of the public interest in relation to the press toward the legal sphere.[21] This is appropriate since the courts frequently have invoked the concept in adjudicating conflicts between individuals and the press. A fragmentary definition of the public interest, based on an aggregate view of these cases, has provided what one legal scholar called "a public interest doctrine" that gives the press relief from damages in such areas as libel.[22]

The notion of the public interest, long a cornerstone of the English common law, was expressed in such terms as *pro bono publico*, the general welfare and others. However, the concept was always related to specific, pragmatic conflicts between individuals and/or collective social entities. In his *Commentaries*, William Blackstone wrote, "the public good is in nothing more

essentially interested, than in the protection of every individual's private rights."[23] For the term "public interest" the linkage between the common law and American judicial decisions came in the landmark case of *Munn v. Illinois*[24] wherein private grain elevators located along railroad lines were said to be "affected with a public interest."[25] *Munn* established a basis for direct governmental regulation over certain businesses thought to involve the public business, and therefore, the public interest.

Two areas of communications law that have helped to fashion a public interest doctrine are the recognition that an individual may maintain an action for defamation and invasion of his privacy. In an early application of the concept, *Post Publishing Co. v. Hallam*,[26] an action for libel, Judge William H. Taft, later President and Chief Justice of the United States, wrote:

> The existence and extent of privilege in communications are determined by balancing the needs and good of society against the right of an individual to enjoy a good reputation when he has done nothing which ought to injure it. The privilege should always cease where the sacrifice of the individual right becomes so great that the public good to be derived from it is outweighed.[27]

Judge Taft's thoughtful articulation of a balancing of individual and societal rights was quoted frequently in libel cases involving public officials and public issues. The Missouri Supreme Court offered a ringing declaration of the public interest in *Diener v. Star-Chronicle Co.*,[28] where Justice Lamm said that:

> The right of freedom of speech, of fair comment with an honest purpose in matters of public concern, is on the foot of pro bono publico *and founded on public policy. Free discussion is the foundation on which free government itself is builded* [sic]. *That lost, all is lost—the two exist or perish together.*[29]

The public interest definition in communications cases expanded slowly, finding its first specific support in *McClung v. Pulitzer Publishing Co.*[30] In *McClung* the court ruled that a newspaper's discussion regarding the allegedly brutal treatment of prisoners in a state penitentiary was a matter of public interest. This decision clarified the role of the courts in defining the public interest: "It is the duty and province of the court to determine whether the matter spoken or written about is a matter of public interest."[31] The only issue under discussion was the conduct of a warden of a state penitentiary and from all evidence the articles were substantially true. The decision, however, failed to distinguish between matters *in* the public interest and *of* public interest. The newspaper articles, according to the court, were *of* public interest because they concerned the public acts of public officers. Thus the opinion did not extend public interest to encompass the mere publication of matters of idle curiosity.

Until the enunciation of the malice standard in *New York Times Co. v. Sullivan*,[32] libel cases offered little in the way of clarification of the public interest standard suggested by *McClung*. However, *United States v. Associated Press*, an antitrust case, suggested a functional rationale for the public interest juxtaposed with the interest of the press.[33] Judge Learned Hand dealt squarely with the question of the public interest raised in the case when he wrote:

[N]either exclusively, nor even primarily, are the interests of the newspaper industry conclusive; for that industry serves one of the most vital of all general interests: the dissemination of news from as many different sources, and with as many different facets and colors as is possible. That interest is closely akin to, if indeed it is not the same as, the interest protected by the First Amendment; it presupposes that right conclusions are more likely to be gathered out of a multitude of tongues, than through any kind of authoritative selection. To many this is, and always will be, folly; but we have staked upon it our all.[34]

Adding support to this statement when the case reached the Supreme Court was Justice Felix Frankfurter who, in a concurring opinion, wrote:

The interest of the public is to have the flow of news not trammeled by the combined self-interest of those who enjoy a unique constitutional position precisely because of the public dependence on a free press. A public interest so essential to the vitality of our democratic government may be defeated by private restraints no less than by public censorship.[35]

The decisions indicate that the judiciary was making it clear that freedom of the press belonged to the *public-at-large,* not simply to the *owners* of the means of communication. This rationale was reaffirmed in *National Broadcasting Co. v. United States*[36] where the Court found that the public interest served under the Federal Communications Act is "thus the interest of the listening public in the larger and more effective use of radio."[37] Although [we are not here] concerned with the "public interest, convenience and necessity" standard of the Federal Communications Act, the Court's finding in *National Broadcasting Co.* is often referred to in other cases concerning a public interest dimension.

A Defense Against Invasion of Privacy

Judge Learned Hand suggested in *Associated Press* that promotion of truth regarding public matters by furnishing a basis for understanding them was a public interest essential to the vitality of our democratic government.[38] This functional definition of a public interest in information as a basis for the democratic process is classical Miltonian doctrine. In the privacy cases, however, the public interest has often been seen more narrowly as courts have looked at the content of communication. The notion that the public interest would negate an individual's right of privacy has its origins in a series of privacy cases from the 1930s. According to one commentator,

As more newspapers and magazines were brought to trial for alleged privacy violations, the defense of 'published in the public interest' grew. Today, what an editor says is newsworthy, or what the public is interested in, is generally considered privileged publication, immune from a privacy suit.[39]

The basis for the use of the public interest concept as a defense against an action for invasion of privacy was laid in *Sarat Lahiri v. Daily Mirror, Inc.,* in which case a Hindu mystic sued a New York newspaper for using his picture in a story about a mystical rope trick.[40] The musician sought relief under a state privacy statute on the grounds that the picture had been used for trade purposes and without his consent. After finding for the defendant, the court said, "A free press is so intimately bound up with fundamental democratic institutions that if the right of privacy is to be extended to cover news items and articles of general public interest, educational and informative in character, it should be the result of a clear expression of legislative policy."[41] After *Sarat Lahiri* the public interest argument was frequently invoked as a defense in privacy suits involving the mass media.[42]

In a number of subsequent cases, the courts have been obliged to balance the interests of individuals with the interests of the community or public. In *Berg v. Minneapolis Star and Tribune,*[43] a privacy suit arising from publicity given to a divorce and custody proceeding, the court stated: "Everyone will agree that at some point the public interest in obtaining information becomes dominant over the individual's desire for privacy."[44] Unfortunately, because of the unique factual situations found in several cases involving the public interest as a defense, the opinions offer little in the way of a consistent, detailed analysis of the concept.

The public interest-privacy standard controlling most contemporary decisions follows that enunciated in *Time, Inc. v. Hill.*[45] The plaintiffs were members of a family held hostage in its home by escaped convicts. The family's harrowing experience was subsequently fictionalized in a play and in magazine coverage of that play. The Court, which found no invasion of privacy, held that:

[T]he constitutional protections for speech and press preclude the application of the New York statute to redress false reports of matters of public interest in the absence of proof that the defendant published the report with knowledge of its falsity or in reckless disregard of the truth.

....

[W]e have no doubt that the subject of the *Life* article, the opening of a new play linked to an actual incident, is a matter of public interest.[46]

In defining "actual interest" Justice Brennan said that it is a matter of the public interest within the scope of protection afforded by the constitutional guarantees of speech and press. Furthermore, an "[e]rroneous statement is no less inevitable in such a case than in the case of comment upon public affairs, and in both, if innocent or merely negligent, '...it must be protected if the freedoms of expression are to have the "breathing space" that they "need...to survive"....'"[47] As a result of the *Hill* decision newsworthiness became linked with the public interest doctrine.

The standard announced in *Hill* was applied in *Frank Man v. Warner Bros., Inc.,* wherein a professional musician brought suit under the New York privacy statute because he had been included in a movie about the Woodstock rock festival where he had appeared on stage.[48] In denying the plaintiff's request for an injunction against showing the film, the court wrote, "the uncontroverted and incontrovertible fact is that the motion picture in which the plaintiff says he appears presents a true account of what actually happened at an event of great public interest."[49] As the above mentioned cases indicate, the interest of the public is defined as that which is newsworthy and captures public attention. This rather limited view of the public interest is but a minor facet of the concept of public interest inherent in Judge Hand's "multitude of tongues" statement. The notion expressed in the privacy applications of public interest is a kind of "trickle-down" theory in which individual news stories of public interest are also deemed to be in the public interest. That seems to be the essence of judicial thinking on the matter.

The Public Interest and Libel

Recent libel cases have followed the invasion of privacy cases assuming that what is *of* public interest is *in* the public interest. The landmark case of *New York Times Co. v. Sullivan,* which broke new ground by fashioning a malice rule,[50] also reiterated "a profound national commitment to the principle that debate on public issues should be uninhibited, robust, and wide-open, and that it may well include vehement, caustic, and sometimes unpleasantly sharp attacks on government and public officials."[51] Through *New York Times* and its progeny, the malice rule [was for a time] expanded to include private citizens caught up in public events. The principle here seems to be that unfettered communication on public issues and matters is in the public interest.

One of the first post-*New York Times* cases to deal specifically with the term, "public interest," was *Williams v. The Daily Review,*[52] in which the court held that "the scope of the term 'public interest' in California [was] not limited to matters relating solely to public officials."[53] The limitations of the public interest principle inherent in *New York Times* was examined in *Walker v. Associated Press.*[54] Although the opinion of the Louisiana Appeals Court was reversed by the Supreme Court, it offers an instructive comment on immunity from libel damges based on qualified privilege conditions:

The immunity does extend to 'fair' comment or criticism on matters of public interest or concern. 'Public interest,' however, does not confer upon a newspaper or anyone else the privilege of publishing defamation merely because it has 'news value,' and the public would like to read it. The privilege is limited to those matters which are of legitimate concern to the community as a whole

because they materially affect the interest of all the community. The comment must be 'fair' and directed and confined to the facts which are a matter of public concern, and not go beyond them by attacking the personal character of the individual involved.[55]

Arguing that a public interest doctrine has emerged in the *New York Times* progeny which have applied the *Times* rule to libels resulting from a discussion of public issues, one commentator asserts:

Fundamental to the application of the first amendment to the law of libel is the concept that the first amendment was designed to protect and foster the circulation of ideas, or at least some ideas that are of social importance. An important corollary to this concept is the recognition that the circulation of falsehood is of marginal social utility.[56]

Further, *"New York Times* and its progeny indicate that the first amendment leaves little room for actionable libel where government is involved, and that some falsehood must be tolerated to avoid a 'chilling effect' on first amendment rights."[57]

W. H. Flamm and others contend that several corporate and individual libel cases have begun to etch a definition of the public interest. The post-*Times* cases concerned with public issues have moved away from the necessity for any determination of whether a plaintiff was a public figure. Under the public figure principle, three factors were considered...:

(1) the importance of the defendant's activities, which were measured by balancing the value of the defendant's service to society against the risk of harm posed to individuals by that activity; (2) whether the plaintiff was entitled to protection in light of his past activity; and (3) whether the plaintiff had a means of self defense.[58]

Recent corporate libel cases have dealt with public issue and public interest standards. In *United Medical Laboratories v. Columbia Broadcasting System,* the Court of

Appeals for the Ninth Circuit declared that stories concerning administration of public health are in the public interest.[59] The defendant, CBS, broadcast a series of exposés of fraud in the medical laboratory business which raised questions about the plaintiff's medical laboratory. The court, in reviewing the case, recognized that:

[T]he fundamental basis on which all of the Court's First Amendment thrusts into various fields thus far presented has rested [is] the right of the public to have an interest in the matter involved and its right, therefore, to know or be informed about it.[60]

In *Bon Air Hotel, Inc., v. Time, Inc.,* *Sports Illustrated* magazine ran an article that brought to light the exorbitant prices charged for accommodations at an Augusta, Georgia hotel during the Master's Golf tournament.[61] The theme of the article was the dishevelment and general decline of the hotel. The court ruled that the public interest in the subject matter of the story brought the publisher within constitutionally protected areas of free expression.[62] A legal scholar's comment on these cases suggested that, "Clearly, the court's primary emphasis was upon the public's interest in the things done by these companies; concern for the status of the injured parties was reduced to a secondary level."[63]

Recent libel cases involving individuals have also used a public issue-public interest standard. Five cases involving organized crime are in point. *Cerrito v. Time, Inc.* and *Konigsberg v. Time, Inc.* both grew out of a *Life* magazine series on organized crime.[64] Plaintiff Cerrito claimed that he had been defamed by a statement that he was the head of a Cosa Nostra family in San Jose, California. The court in the case applied the *New York Times* malice rule because:

There can be no doubt that organized crime is a subject about which the public has an interest and a right to be informed. The vast expenditures of money by all branches of government, both state and federal, into [investigation of] the workings and extent of organized crime indicates the [highest] interest of the public, as well as its right to know or be informed.[65]

In *Konigsberg,* the plaintiff brought a libel action against *Life* magazine for asserting, inter alia, that he was a Cosa Nostra killer and had disposed of a body in the basement of a New Jersey congressman's home. The court found that organized crime and the plaintiff's relationship to the alleged illegal activities of a congressman were matters of public interest justifying application of the actual malice standard to libel action.[66]

Time, Inc. v. Ragano and *Wasserman v. Time, Inc.* involved slightly different interests.[67] In *Wasserman,* the publication in *Life* magazine of a picture of lawyers eating lunch with reputed gangsters was said to be in the public interest. In *Ragano,* a case involving the same publication, two lawyers were identified as being Cosa Nostra "hoodlums" when in fact they were attorneys for the "hoodlums." The court said that actual malice had to be shown because of the great public interest in the case. In a similar action, *Time, Inc. v. McLaney,* a story in a magazine article about the influence of a reputed gangster in the election of the premier of the Bahamas, was also declared to be in the public interest.[68]

Another public interest case, *Gertz v. Robert Welch, Inc.,* involved an attorney who had represented the family of a man shot by the police in Chicago.[69] The attorney brought a libel action because of a story in *American Opinion* magazine which had called him a "communist fronter." The court ruled that the attorney had thrust himself into the vortex of an important public controversy and that the article clearly dealt with a matter of public interest and thus was protected by the first and fourteenth amendments.[70] In reaching its decision in *Gertz,* the court stated:

The rationale for affording First Amendment protection to matters of public interest, as implied by Hill,...is that our system of government places great value on society's open discussion of not only public officials (Sullivan) *and public figures* (Butts), *but also matters of public interest* (Hill). *A person allegedly defamed by matter pertaining to the public interest must satisfy a heavy burden, i.e., a showing of actual malice, in order to recover therefor. The rationale of Time, Inc. v. Hill has been applied to several decisions of the Courts of Appeal recently, all of which extended the guarantee of free speech to matters of public interest.*[71]

The public interest criteria of these cases and of *Time, Inc. v. Hill,* which lent support to the idea of public interest in a public issue, were given some clarification in *Rosenbloom v. Metromedia Inc.*[72] In *Rosenbloom* radio news stories about a man charged with (and later acquitted of) the sale of pornography were held to be in the public interest. *Rosenbloom* extended the *Times* malice standard to private individuals caught up in public events:

If a matter is a subject of public or general interest, it cannot suddenly become less so merely because a private individual did not 'voluntarily' choose to become involved. The public's primary interest in the event, the public focus is on the conduct of the participant and the content, effect and significance of the conduct, not the participant's prior anonymity or notoriety.[73]

As the aforementioned cases indicate, the concept of public interest as understood in a libel action is not unlike that in privacy cases. Free and robust discussion of issues is the primary value of the first amendment. At this juncture apparently any discussion of a public issue that does not involve actual malice under the *Time* and *Rosenbloom* [and later *Gertz*] formulations is in the public interest. The only discussion that does not have social utility, under this doctrine, is that which is a deliberate and knowing falsehood.

The public interest doctrine in communications law cases has arisen at a time when the public interest concept is a topic of lively conversation in the legal community. The so-called "Nader's Raiders" and other similar groups launch their attacks in the name of "the public interest." Furthermore, there is a new area of public interest law which has grown in part out of legal aid programs established originally by the Office of Economic Opportunity. Because so much of American life has been defined by the courts as "affected with the public interest," a noted scholar and jurist, Judge Sterry R. Waterman of the Court of Appeals for the Second Circuit has called for a redefinition of the public interest so that "this enlargement [of] the administration of law may, in truth, become the instrumentality for social justice."[74] Judge Waterman asks rhetorically, "Isn't there a public or private accommodation still possible between our right to be left alone and the denial of that right to us as more and more of what we do is affected with the public interest?"[75]

MEDIA INTEREST AND PUBLIC INTEREST

In a variety of polemic treatises over the years, spokesmen for the communications industry in America have maintained that they operate *in* the public interest. This is a traditional view of the first amendment and is solidly grounded in the cases previously cited. It is, most commentators agree, a negative interpretation of the first amendment, focusing on the phrase, "Congress shall make no law," a command that has been interpreted as a shield against interference with the free flow of information. Clearly this interpretation favors the issuer of communication. It is an ultimate triumph for the "trickle-down" theory of mass communication and press freedom. By allowing the purveyors of communication maximum freedom, the means for the free flow of information to the public is determined.

Arguing for a positive interpretation of the first amendment, law professor and authority on mass media Jerome Barron takes sharp issue with the "trickle-down" theory. He sees this traditional interpretation of the first amendment as abrogating individual rights of communications access to a small number of vital voices in the marketplace of ideas. Barron's model, however, may be likened to a pinball machine. He would add more voices to the marketplace and while they would shoot their messages on different vectors, the ultimate result would be pinballs moving in the same direction and within a fixed range which may be designated as "press freedom." According to this view, the diversity of many voices rather than the stable force of a few, best serves freedom and the public interest.

While the argument centering on the question of whether the press interest and public interest are synonymous rages, the work of the public philosophers and the jurists has helped to clarify its components. They do not, however, offer any objective criterion for deciding what is *in* the public interest. Since one ultimate controlling mechanism for adjudicating the public interest and sorting it out among a range of individual and private interests is the courts, one would hope to find guidance in the opinions of the judiciary. But any expectation for definition from this sector is quickly cooled since the courts have consistently blended public interest into an ambiguous rhetorical concept. As most of the decisions previously reviewed indicate, the courts have said that what is *of* public interest is *in* the public interest. Such a position suggests that the public interest is a larger superstructure than the preferential information demands of individuals, although their needs and wants fall under the concept's general rubric.

In American society the Constitution is the ultimate statement of the public interest. Operation of the society under the provisions of the Constitution, which imply and specifically state general goals, *is* in the public interest. Thus, a free press is a means by which the public interest is transmitted and eventually achieved. It is the visible barometer, the expression of performance. If one accepts this general precept, the public's interest is much more than giving the public what it wants. Preferential choice needs to be consistent with constitutional rules. Inherent in our constitutional government is the

assumption that the process of democracy is delegated—as a public trust—to public servants and officials. In delegating this trust, society takes an important step in the view of audience researcher Robert Silvey, who wrote:

It is as though society says in effect to the public servant: 'It is up to you to look after our interests. You must immerse yourself in your subject, because we haven't time to do so. There may come times when we shall demand that you take a certain course which you, having weighed it in the light of your knowledge and experience, will tell us is not in fact in our interest. Though you are our servant you must, in such a case, refuse to obey us. You will be right to do so, for though at the time you will be refusing to give us what we want, you will, paradoxically, be doing what in the long run we want you to do.[76]

So it is that the courts find themselves adjudicating press freedom cases. In this process they must be concerned not only with the aggregate preferences of society, but also with larger constructs of freedom for the social order—as well as for the individual. It has been in such a spirit that the courts have decided that:

a. The free flow of information is in the public interest.

b. Information about public affairs is of public interest and in the public interest.

c. The publication of newsworthy information is in the public interest.

d. Communications diversity is in the public interest.

e. Government regulation of certain communications activities "affected with a public interest" is in the public interest.

f. Matters *of* public interest or matters *in* the public interest are usually immune from libel and privacy recovery.

Although these statements provide the foundation for defining the public interest in regard to media behavior, it is first necessary to dispense with the suggestion that the public interest is a mere myth. The reasoning of Professor Hans Morgenthau is useful in performing this task:

I happen to believe that there is a possibility by rational political analysis to arrive at certain objective conclusions which define in negative terms what it is not. So, you see, if you assume that the national interest is a mere fiction, a mere ideological justification and rationalization of particular parochial interests, you have nothing to go on except the rivalry of different and frequently incompatable powerful interests, each claiming to be the national interest.[77]

Thus by the very act of being free, the press operates in the public interest. However, as Barron points out, because freedom of the press belongs to all of the people, the press, as an issuer of communication, has no right to prevent the communication of others. Activities by the press that drive out competition, encourage censorship, or prevent free discussion and debate on matters of public concern are at odds with the notion of positive freedom of the press. They are, therefore, not in the public interest. Thus the public interest and the media interest are congruent only when there is a viable relationship between issuer and consumer of communication that is operating to the satisfaction of both. This does not mean simply giving the public what it wants; rather, it entails acquainting the public with the broad range of possibilities and then allowing it to make a free choice within that extensive panoply. When immediate whims and curiosity-seeking by the issuer or the consumer conflict with other social rights, the government, through the court system, should act as the regulator. For example, the interest

in a celebrated trial may be quite high and the media may want to cover it in all aspects. However, such coverage might conflict with an individual's right to a fair trial. In such an instance it is up to the courts to sort out the conflicting interests and values.

If communication law cases were decided in a public interest framework, a quite precise, measurable definition of the public interest would no doubt emerge. That definition would be dynamic, flexible and accommodating, while at the same time it would provide a standard and a rationale for media behavior.

Government, however, is not the only check and balance between purely private interests and the public interest. In examining other entities that also advance and protect the public interest, the public health model of disease prevention is useful. The public health model suggests three levels of prevention—primary, secondry and tertiary. When applied to the public interest problem at hand it can be expressed schematically as it is in Figure 1.

At the primary level, prevention of public interest violations could be accomplished through informal educational processes in which the various parties in society would interact and settle their differences privately. In this arena, the universities, especially schools of journalism, have a broad mandate to teach ethics and responsible performance. Ideally, all disputes could be settled in this free and informal forum.

FIGURE 1
Adjudicatory Means for Public Interest Conflicts

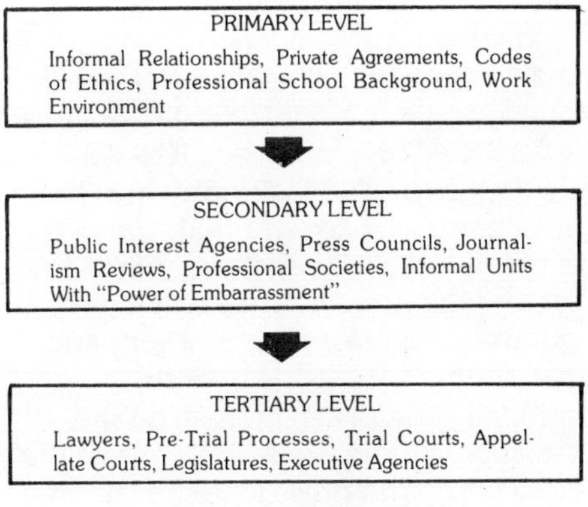

PRIMARY LEVEL

Informal Relationships, Private Agreements, Codes of Ethics, Professional School Background, Work Environment

SECONDARY LEVEL

Public Interest Agencies, Press Councils, Journalism Reviews, Professional Societies, Informal Units With "Power of Embarrassment"

TERTIARY LEVEL

Lawyers, Pre-Trial Processes, Trial Courts, Appellate Courts, Legislatures, Executive Agencies

FIGURE 2
A System of Public Interest/Press Interest

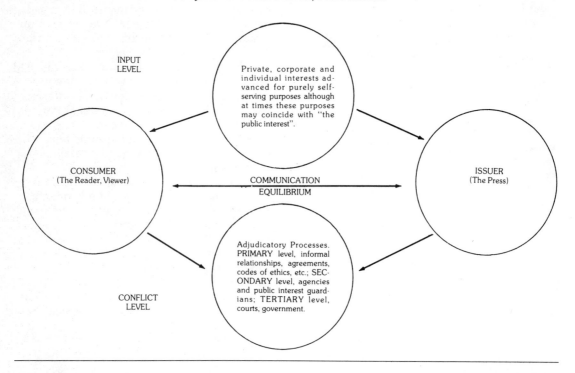

At the secondary level of prevention, watchdog agencies would monitor press behavior and attempt to curb abuses and point out public interest violations. These agencies would include such public interest bodies as Ralph Nader's Center for the Study of Responsive Law and John Gardiner's Common Cause. Further, the press could be more directly influenced through press councils, communications task forces and foundations, journalism reviews and professional groups.

Finally, and only after the other two levels had failed, would the prevention measures of the tertiary level be employed. This would include the courts, the legislature and the executive branch of government.

As previously discussed, the public interest and the press interest would be contiguous when maximum freedom and minimal interference exists in both. Operationally, the press interest/public interest would be measured in terms of the degree to which the press fostered the free flow of information and satisfied the justifiable information needs of its consumers. Only when such a balanced ratio is achieved will the interest of the press and the interest of the public be one and the same.

Figure 2 illustrates such a scheme in which the public interest would begin to define itself. It would be the reaction of the press to higher-order interests expressed in the Constitution, blended with the interests of individuals and groups in society. The input for this information pool would be the expressions of public and private interests related directly to the issuer of communication or indirectly to the issuer through the consumer. This interplay between issuer and consumer would determine the appropriate messages to be communicated to society and hopefully would solidify the public interest content of those messages. All conflicts would be adjudicated through the primary, secondary and tertiary processes indicated above. Monitoring such an operational system would yield a system of public interest/press interest with attendant doctrine and methodologies. Only then could the public interest be determined with any validity and certainty.

NOTES

1. William Ernest Hocking, *Freedom of the Press: A Framework of Principle,* a report from the Commission on Freedom of the Press (Chicago: University of Chicago Press, 1947), p. 164.

2. Hocking, *Freedom of the Press,* p. 169.

3. Francis E. Rourke, *Secrecy and Publicity: Dilemmas of Democracy* (Baltimore: Johns Hopkins Press, 1966), p. 31.

4. Rourke, *Secrecy and Publicity,* p. 31.

5. *New York Times v. Sullivan,* 376 U.S. 254, 270 (1964).

6. Jerome A. Barron, *Freedom of the Press for Whom? The Right of Access to the Mass Media* (Bloomington: University of Indiana Press, 1973), p. 12.

7. Hocking, *Freedom of the Press,* p. 224.

8. Daniel Bell and Irving Kristol, "What is the Public Interest?" *The Public Interest,* Fall 1965, p. 4.

9. Frank Sorauf, "The Conceptual Muddle," in *The Public Interest,* ed. Carl J. Friedrich (New York: Atherton, 1962).

10. Walter Lippmann, *The Public Philosophy* (New York: Mentor, 1955), p. 40.

11. Robert Skidelsky, "Politics is Not Enough: On the Dying Metaphor of the National Interest," *Encounter,* January 1969, p. 47.

12. Stephen K. Bailey, "The Public Interest: Some Operational Dilemmas," in *The Public Interest,* ed. Carl J. Friedrich (New York: Atherton, 1962), p. 106.

13. Glendon Schubert, *The Public Interest* (Glencoe, Ill.: Free Press, 1960), pp. 223-224.

14. Virginia Held, *The Public Interest and Individual Interests* (New York: Basic Books, 1970).

15. Held, *Public Interest,* p. 43.

16. Held, *Public Interest,* p. 44; emphasis in original.

17. Held, *Public Interest,* p. 136.

18. Held, *Public Interest,* pp. 176-177; emphasis in original.

19. Held, *Public Interest,* p. 183.

20. Held, *Public Interest,* p. 192; emphasis in original.

21. Held, *Public Interest,* p. 176.

22. W. H. Flamm, Jr., "Further Limits on Libel Actions—Extension of the *New York Times* Rule to Libels Arising From Discussion of Public Issues," *Villanova Law Review* 16(1971): 995, 961.

23. I. William Blackstone, *Commentaries* 139 (1769).

24. *Munn v. Illinois,* 94 U.S. 113 (1877).

25. *Munn v. Illinois* at 130.

26. *Post Publishing Co. v. Hallam,* 59 F. 530 (C.C.A. 6th 1893).

27. *Post Publishing Co. v. Hallam* at 540.

28. *Diener v. Star-Chronicle Co.,* 230 Mo. 613, at 630 132 S.W.1133 (1910).

29. *Diener v. Star-Chronicle Co.* at 630, 1149.

30. *McClung v. Pulitzer Publishing Co.,* 214 S.W. 193; 279 Mo. 370 (1919).

31. *McClung v. Pulitzer Publishing Co.* at 200(S.W.), 399 (Mo.).

32. *New York Times Co. v. Sullivan,* 376 U.S. 254 (1964).

33. *United States v. Associated Press,* 52 F. Supp. 362 (S.D.N.Y. 1943).

34. *United States v. Associated Press* at 372.

35. *Associated Press v. United States,* 326 U.S. 190 (1943).

36. *National Broadcasting Co. v. United States,* 319 U.S. 190 (1943).

37. *National Broadcasting Co. v. United States* at 216.

38. *United States v. Associated Press* at 362.

39. Don R. Pember, *Privacy and the Press: The Law, the Mass Media and the First Amendment* (Seattle: University of Washington Press, 1972), p. 115.

40. *Sarat Lahiri v. Daily Mirror,* 295 N.Y.S. 382 (1937).

41. *Sarat Lahiri v. Daily Mirror* at 388.

42. See *Time, Inc. v. Hill,* 385 U.S. 374 (1967); *Leverton v. Curtis,* 97 F. Supp. 181 (E.D.Pa. 1951); *Sweenek v. Pathe News, Inc.,* 16 F. Supp. 746 (E.D.N.Y. 1936); *Barbieri v. News-Journal Co.,* 56 Del. 67, 189 A.2d 773 (1963); *Reardon v. News-Journal Co.,* 53 Del. 29, 164 A.2d (1960); *Kline v. Robert M. McBride & Co.,* 1970 Misc. 974, 11 N.Y.S. 2d 674 (Sup. Ct. 1939).

43. *Berg v. Minneapolis Star & Tribune Co.,* 79 F. Supp. 957 (1948).

44. *Berg v. Minneapolis Star & Tribune Co.* at 962; see also *Koussevitzky v. Allen, Towne, and Heath,* 188 Misc. 479, 68 NYS 2d. 779 (1947).

45. *Time, Inc. v. Hill,* 385 U.S. 374 (1967).

46. *Time, Inc. v. Hill* at 387-388.

47. *Time, Inc. v. Hill* at 387-388.

48. *Frank Man v. Warner Bros., Inc.,* 317 F. Supp. 50 S.D.N.Y.(1970).

49. *Frank Man v. Warner Bros., Inc.* at 51.

50. *New York Times Co. v. Sullivan,* 376 U.S. 254 (1964). The court stated that a public official cannot recover damages for a defamatory falsehood relating

to his official conduct unless he proves that the statement was made with "actual malice"—that is, with knowledge that it was false or with reckless disregard of whether it was false or not. See *New York Times Co. v. Sullivan* at 279-280.

51. *New York Times Co. v. Sullivan* at 270-271.

52. *Williams v. The Daily Review, Inc.*, 236 Cal. App. 2d 405, 46 Cal. Rptr. 135 (1965).

53. *Williams v. The Daily Review, Inc.* at 417 (Cal. App. 2d), 143 (Cal. Rptr.).

54. *Walker v. Associated Press*, 191 So. 2d 727 (La. Ct. App. 1966); rev'd, 389 U.S. 28 (1967).

55. *Walker v. Associated Press* at 733.

56. Flamm, "Further Limits," pp. 964-965.

57. Flamm, "Further Limits," p. 965.

58. Flamm, "Further Limits," p. 961.

59. *United Medical Laboratories v. Columbia Broadcasting System*, 404 F. 2d 706 (9th Cir 1969).

60. *United Medical Laboratories v. Columbia Broadcasting System* at 710.

61. *Bon Air Hotel Inc. v. Time, Inc.*, 295 F. Supp. 704 (S.D. Ga. 1968).

62. *Bon Air Hotel, Inc. v. Times, Inc.* at 708.

63. Flamm, "Further Limits," p. 969.

64. *Cerrito v. Time, Inc.*, 302 F. Supp. 1071 (N.D. Cal. 1966); and *Konigsberg v. Time, Inc.*, 312 F. Supp. 848 (S.D.N.Y. 1970).

65. *Cerrito v. Time, Inc.*, at 1073.

66. *Konigsberg v. Time, Inc.* at 852.

67. *Time, Inc. v. Ragano*, 427 F. 2d 219 (5th Cir. 1970); and *Wasserman v. Time, Inc.*, 424 F. 2d 920 (D.C. Cir 1970), cert. denied, 398 U.S. 940 (1970).

68. *Time, Inc. v. McLaney*, 406 F. 2d 565 (5th Cir. 1969), cert. denied, 395 U.S. 922 (1969).

69. *Gertz v. Robert Welch, Inc.*, 322 F. Supp. 997 (N.D. Ill. 1970). This ruling was overturned by the U.S. Supreme Court in *Gertz v. Robert Welch, Inc.*, 418 U.S. 323 (1974). The Court threw out the public issue test of *Rosenbloom* and held that, where private persons were libeled, a showing of actual injury due to negligence on the part of the publisher would be sufficient to support an award of actual damages. Public officials or public figures, however, would still have to meet the actual malice standard of *New York Times v. Sullivan*, that is, knowing falsehood or reckless disregard of truth or falsity. Essentially the Court is saying that the public interest is less engaged in the affairs of private persons than it is in the affairs of public persons.

70. *Gertz v. Robert Welch, Inc.* at 1000.

71. *Gertz v. Robert Welch, Inc.* at 999.

72. *Time, Inc. v. Hill* at 374; and *Rosenbloom v. Metromedia, Inc.*, 403 U.S. 29 (1971).

73. *Rosenbloom v. Metromedia, Inc.* at 43.

74. Sterry R. Waterman, "Whither the Concept 'Affected with a Public Interest'?" *Vanderbilt Law Review* 25 (1972): 927, 937.

75. Waterman, "Whither 'Public Interest'?" p. 936.

76. Robert Silvey, "Giving the Public What It Wants," *Contemporary Review*, May 1961, p. 261.

77. Noam Chomsky and Hans Morgenthau, "National Interest and the Pentagon Papers," *Partisan Review*, Summer 1972, pp. 336-375.

PRESS COUNCILS IN AMERICA

Donald M. Gillmor

To what extent should a syndicated columnist identify his economic interest in topics he writes about? At what point should a small city daily close debate on a controversial local issue in its letters columns? How should a newspaper make amends for a headline that seriously distorts the political position of a state legislator?

These are the kinds of questions that now appear regularly on the agendas of local, state, and national press (or news) councils. The National News Council, with a mandate "to serve the public interest in preserving freedom of communication and advancing accurate and fair reporting of news," began operations in 1973. It adjudicates complaints from and against national news media. The Minnesota Press Council, established in 1971, does the same for the media and their audiences of a single state. Delaware has followed suit. The city of Honolulu has a Community-Media Council, and there are councils in Littleton and Eagle Valley, Colorado; Peoria, Illinois; and Windsor, Ontario.

Each provides a form of citizen access to the major organs of public opinion and news dissemination in their jurisdictions. Each recognizes the fact that courts are generally unsympathetic to laws that, by attempting to legislate access, violate editorial autonomy.[1] Press councils are an admission that many problems of press freedom and responsibility cannot satisfactorily be resolved in the courts.

Recommended nearly thirty years ago by the Commission on Freedom of the Press[2] as a means of independent citizen appraisal of media performance, press councils have not received a unanimous welcome. The *New York Times,* for example, stated publicly that it would not cooperate with the National News Council, and there are editors in Minnesota and elsewhere who consider press councils an infringement upon their First Amendment rights.[3]

The grandfather of all such bodies may be Sweden's Press Fair Practices Commission, founded in 1916 to mediate between press and public. Britain's Press Council was established in 1953 in response to a critical report by a Royal Commission on the Press and an unfriendly Labour government. America's first efforts in this direction seem to have been advisory councils of community leaders set up by Raymond Spangler, editor of the Redwood City, California *Tribune,* and by Houstoun Waring, publisher of the Littleton, Colorado *Independent,* in 1946. These were followed in 1950 by a citizens advisory council in Santa Rosa, California established by William Townes, publisher of the Santa Rosa *Press-Democrat,* and supervised by Stanford University's Department of Communication. In 1967, under a grant from the Mellet Fund for a Free and Responsive Press, Stanford supervised experimental community press councils in Bend, Oregon and Redwood City, while Southern Illinois University's School of Journalism shepherded similar projects in Cairo and Sparta, Illinois. At about the same time, temporary race-relations advisory councils were put into operation in Seattle and St. Louis.

Publisher Barry Bingham of the Louisville *Courier-Journal* established an ombudsman for his readers in 1963, and since then, twenty or so newspapers around the country have tried it with varying degrees of success. At least twenty-two countries, communities, and three Canadian provinces—Ontario, Alberta and Quebec—have tried press councils with citizen membership. Councils elsewhere have been destroyed by governmental intervention (for example, Chile, Turkey, South Korea, India, Pakistan, and Ghana); others have served as a substitute for such intervention. Among the survivors are Norway, Finland, Sweden, the United Kingdom, the Netherlands, Israel, New Zealand, Australia and the three Canadian provinces. Press councils without lay participation have functioned in West Germany, Austria, Italy, Switzerland, Denmark, South Africa and Japan.

Mediation is the key function of a press council. A hearing before it can be an intermediate step between a purely informal resolution of a grievance between a reader and an editor and a court action, which in fact is a form of governmental intervention. Often the intermediate step is well worth taking.

Some press councils have broader functions than others. Among these functions are: (1) hearing complaints brought by citizens, community leaders, and government officials against the news media and complaints by reporters against news sources, particularly those in government; (2) studying broader complaints against the media, or accumulations of complaints, about coverage of an election campaign, for example, or questions of access both to information and to the media, or the payment of fees to sources of information, sometimes referred to as "checkbook journalism," or deliberate distortion in news or editorial columns; (3) developing codes or guidelines for the professional conduct of journalists or news sources, such as guidelines for the conduct of a press conference by a public official; (4) entering court cases as a friend of the court, or initiating cases in behalf of the public's interest in news and information; (5) lobbying in legislatures for open meetings and open records laws, and testifying before legislative committees on general principles of press responsibility from the perspective of the public; and (6) developing a community news research capability, preferably in conjunction with an academic institution.[4] The Quebec council intends to deal with the question of concentration of ownership, and it includes radio and television within its purview.

Following procedures of the British Press Council, complaints to the Minnesota Press Council go to a grievance hearing panel whose chairperson writes to the complainant to ascertain whether all other possible means of agreement between the press and complainant have been exhausted. The Council will accept any complaint, no matter how trivial it may appear on the surface, but it does expect the complainant to have tried to settle the problem beforehand with the newspaper or broadcast station.

The hearing panel then seeks a bill of particulars from the complainant and, on the basis of that statement, decides whether the case is a proper one for adjudication. If it is, the Council will ask the complainant to waive all future rights to sue in a court of law so as to avoid placing the news medium in double jeopardy and to protect the Council from being used by a future litigant's attorney in building a case.

Both parties are invited by the grievance panel to present evidence, and the eight-person committee then makes its recommendation to the full Council. All sessions are open to the public. The full Council may solicit additional information. The issue is considered by the full Council, and the Council votes on whether or not to accept the grievance committee's recommendations. If they are accepted, the executive secretary prepares a final report, which may include concurring and dissenting opinions. The report then goes to both parties to the dispute and later to all major media in the state. If the Council rules against the news medium, a news release is sent to the news media of the state, and it is hoped that the particular news medium will publish the Council's ruling. Of more than seventy-three complaints in six years, twenty-six have gone through the full adjudicatory process. The Council's twelve press and twelve public members have never voted as blocs on an

issue brought before the Council. The National News Council, which functions in much the same way, with eighteen members (eight of whom are from the media), completed action in sixty-one cases in its first two years. Only five complaints were upheld. The Minnesota Council has ruled against the media at least as often as it has ruled in their favor.

Both national and state councils are building their own sets of precedents incorporating their best judgments of fairness, accuracy, and balance. The councils possess no sanctions or authority beyond their own reputations and the pressure of publicity. No press organizations are compelled to cooperate with the councils, and some have established their own ombudsmen or other mechanisms for handling complaints or engaging in self-criticism. And the councils do not attempt to critique opinion that is clearly expressed as such, no matter how offensive or dangerous it might appear.

Many problems remain unsolved. Where should press councils go for financial support? Should regional councils be formed, since mass media audiences inevitably span state boundaries? Should there be a central clearing house for information about press councils and their decisions? Are the memberships of councils too elitist? Prominent citizens give a council stature and provide it with efficient management, but do they represent those groups in society most alienated by the print and broadcast media? What proportion of council membership should come from the news media? What proportion from other segments, and which segments, of society? Whose standards of ethical performance are to be applied, and how are they arrived at? Should the National News Council hear complaints against the broadcast media given that those systems are already under the regulatory supervision of the Federal Communications Commission? What alternatives are there to this kind of grievance procedure? And do press councils infringe upon anybody's First Amendment rights?[5]

The usefulness of press councils has not yet been affirmed. A committee evaluating the National News Council estimates that a minimum period of ten years will be required before a sound evaluation can be made. Two researchers report that "although press councils do not apparently infringe on press freedom as some thought they might, the councils do not appear to have improved press responsibility as some others would have liked."[6]

Nevertheless, sustained and systematic criticism, some of it appearing on the pages of the newspaper itself, has at least the potential of increasing reader confidence and press credibility, and it is certainly a better option than expensive and nerve-shattering litigation or angry confrontations between press and public.

Most complaints are eliminated by procedural defects or are settled without having to come to a hearing. More often than not, settlements are facilitated by staff clarification of disputes between the parties or by education of complainants where the press has acted within its First Amendment rights.[7]

The appendices contain examples of the results of completed hearings, and other functions, of the National News Council, the Minnesota Press Council, and the Honolulu Community-Media Council.

The *Columbia Journalism Review* regularly carries summaries of the work of the National News Council.

NOTES

1. *Miami Herald Publishing Co.* v. *Tornillo*, 418 U.S. 241 (1974). See Benno C. Schmidt, Jr., *Freedom of the Press vs. Public Access* (New York and Aspen, Colo.: Praeger and the Aspen Institute Program on Communications & Society, 1976), pp. 246-251.

2. Commission on Freedom of the Press, *A Free and Responsible Press* (Chicago: University of Chicago Press, 1947), pp. 100-102.

3. Ronald P. Kriss, "The National News Council at Age One," *Columbia Journalism Review,* November/December 1974, pp. 31-38.

4. Jim Richstad, "Press Councils: Emerging Forms of Media Criticism and Accountability" unpublished paper for the Association for Education in Journalism Convention, Ottawa, Canada, 17-20 August 1975.

5. See John C. Merrill, *The Imperative of Freedom* (New York: Hastings House, 1974), in which the emerging

social responsibility "theory" of the press first articulated by the Commission on Freedom of the Press in its 1947 report is rejected in favor of personal freedom and autonomy. Merrill's idea reflects the older libertarian "theory" of the press upon which the Constitutional guarantees of freedom of speech and press appear to be based and which attaches no qualifications or conditions to those freedoms. It is Merrill's contention that a press system that becomes responsible to anyone other than itself will, in the end, sacrifice its freedom ultimately to government control. For a brief exposition of the social responsibility "theory" and other essays elaborating on this concept see Theodore Peterson, "Social Responsibility—Theory and Practice," in *The Responsibility of the Press,* ed. Gerald Gross (New York: Simon and Schuster, 1966), pp. 33-49.

6. Erwin Atwood and Kenneth Starck, "Effects of Community Press Councils: Real and Imagined," *Journalism Quarterly* 49 (Summer 1972); 230.

7. *In the Public Interest, 1973-1975* (New York: National News Council, 1975), p. 21.

FURTHER READING

Balk, Alfred. *A Free and Responsive Press.* New York: Twentieth Century Fund, 1973.

Bingham, Barry. "Plan for Local Press Councils," *Columbia Journalism Review 2* (Winter 1964): 45-47.

Brignolo, Donald. *Community Press Councils,* no. 217. Columbia, Mo.: Freedom of Information Center, 1969.

Grimes, Paul. "Honolulu: Trials of a Media Council," *Columbia Journalism Review* 12 (May/June 1973): 59-61.

Koenig, Robert. *Community Press Councils-II,* No. 33. Columbia, Mo.: Freedom of Information Center, November 1974.

Levy, H. Phillip. *The Press Council: History, Procedure and Cases.* London: Macmillan, 1967. (An account of the development and work of the British Press Council.)

Lowenstein, Ralph L. *Press Councils: Idea and Reality.* Columbia, Mo.: Freedom of Information Foundation, 1973.

Murray, George. *The Press and the Public.* Carbondale: Southern Illinois University Press, 1972.

Paul, Noel S. "Why the British Press Council Works," *Columbia Journalism Review* 10 (March/April 1972): 20-26.

Polich, John. "Newspaper Support of Press Councils," *Journalism Quarterly* 52 (Summer 1974): 200.

Report of the Special Committee on Mass Media, vol. 1: The Uncertain Mirror. Ottawa, Canada: Queen's Printer, 1970.

Rivers, William L. "How To Kill a Watchdog," *The Progressive,* February 1973.

Rivers, William L., Blankenburg, William B., Starck, Kenneth, and Reeves, Earl. *Backtalk: Press Councils in America.* San Francisco: Canfield Press, 1972.

Starck, Kenneth. "What Community Press Councils Talk About," *Journalism Quarterly* 47 (Spring 1970): 20-26.

The National News Council, Inc., *In the Public Interest, 1973-1975,* New York: 1975.

APPENDIX A

National News Council
Complaint No. 46
(Filed September 7, 1974)

ACCURACY IN MEDIA
against
JACK ANDERSON

Nature of Complaint: Accuracy in Media complained of a Jack Anderson column (United Features Syndicate) published in the *New York Post* on August 3, 1974, and in many other newspapers on or about that date.

The column asserted that "Students at the International Police Academy, a school run by the State Department to train foreign policemen, have developed some chilling views about torture tactics." In support of this statement it quoted from papers written by five students at the Academy—two from South Vietnam, one from Nepal, one from Colombia and one from Zaire. AIM asserted that the quotations were taken out of context, and misrepresented the attitudes of the students in question on the subject of torture. Mr. Anderson and his associate, Joseph C. Spear, denied this.

Members of the Council staff visited Washington and examined the five papers in full and in detail. They found that the quotations by Anderson did in fact misrepresent the attitudes of the students toward torture as set forth in their papers. In addition, they found that all five papers were written in the years 1965-1967, a fact not mentioned in the Anderson column (which gave the impression that they were reasonably contemporary).

Response of News Organization: In a letter dated December 30, 1974, Mr. Anderson insisted that the statements in his column were supported by sources whose identity he could not reveal, and suggested that members of the Council staff "spend a couple of months talking to Amnesty International and the National Council of Churches," as well as with Sen. James Abourezk and unnamed members of his staff—all of whom, it was suggested, would support Anderson's charges.

Conclusion of the Council: If such support as was alleged by Mr. Anderson exists, it is up to him, not this Council, to develop and publish it. AIM's complaint alleged simply that the five quotations set forth and relied on in the original Anderson column misrepresented the views of the writers; and the complaint is quite correct.

Nor can Mr. Anderson escape responsibility for the misrepresentations by pointing to the second sentence of his column, which stated, "After a lengthy investigation, we found no evidence that the academy actually advocates third-degree methods." In the first place, exculpating the academy itself does not excuse leaving a false implication with respect to the views of the five named students. In the second place, the sentence was simply inconsistent with the general thrust of the column, which Mr. Anderson's own syndicate titled "The Torture Graduates."

In the circumstances, we believe the complaint is justified.

Concurring, COONEY, DILLIARD, FULD, McKAY, OTWELL and RUSHER.

Dated: February 4, 1975

Note: Since adoption of the above conclusion, the Council has learned that the title to the article as prepared by Mr. Anderson's syndicate, was "U.S. Trained Foreign Cops Prefer To Stick To Torture." The title "The Torture Graduates" was placed on the column by the *New York Post*. The Council's conclusion is accordingly amended to reflect these facts. Approved by the full Council at its April 8, 1975 meeting.

National News Council
Complaint No. 75
(Filed January 6, 1976)

MOYERS et al.
against
THE WASHINGTON POST

Nature of Complaint: Twelve participants in a regional seminar on Women In Public Life—sponsored by the LBJ School of Public Affairs and the LBJ Library in Austin, Texas—complained that an article which appeared in *The Washington Post* (11-12-75) about a speech given at that conference by Australian feminist Elizabeth Reid was misleading, giving readers the erroneous impression that she "was advocating women to use their sex to get ahead."

Complainants submitted a transcript of Ms. Reid's speech, summarizing the relevant portion of her remarks as follows:

Elizabeth Reid said women in public life are still confronted by an expectation that they will give sexual favors as a routine lobbying practice—an expectation not applied to their male colleagues, of course. Reid said she had refused to do this in her job as top advisor to the prime minister. She said this had hurt her ability to get through programs or to get good press coverage of them.

The *Post* article, headlined "Women and Sex," began with the statement, "Sex [is] the easiest and most effective route to political

power for women, according to an Australian feminist," and picking up a part of a UPI story, went on to say:

Elizabeth Anne Reid, speaking to a conference on women in public life Monday, said male politicians expect women to act as sex objects.

"I'm sorry about that, but you'll be expected to do it," said Reid, who recently resigned as advisor to the prime minister of Australia.

"If you don't———the press, you won't get good press and if you don't———the cabinet members you won't get your programs.

"If you don't do it, you won't be as effective."

The overflow audience included Lady Bird Johnson, former U.S. District Court Judge Sarah T. Hughes and scores of women presently serving as legislators, mayors and other elected or appointed public officials. Reid drew a standing ovation.

Also provided was a copy of the UPI wire story, dated November 11, 1975, covering that part of Ms. Reid's speech described above. The UPI account was determined to be the source of the edited version which appeared in *The Washington Post* on the following day. Complainants pointed out that the *Post*, while using the UPI story, had "edited out the denial and other material."

The part of the UPI story which was *not* used by the *Post* included the statement "Ms. Reid said refusing sexual advances cost her a bad press and failure of some programs she wanted in Australia."

The following paragraphs in the UPI story were also omitted from the *Post* article:

She said she did make some compromises on appearances, however, that helped her in relations with male politicians.

"The more pleasing the woman is to the eye of the beholder the more likely she is to be listened

to," said Ms. Reid, adding that women politicians had to wear lipstick and nylons to get a receptive audience.

Male officials, she said, do not even listen to suggestions from women wearing jeans and sandals.

"If I turned up as a potential you know what, they at least listened," she said.

The Australian feminist said women should work to put more feminists in positions of power.

"We have to attack the root problem. We have to attack the attitudes, beliefs, myths, cliches about women. These attitudes exist as much in our heads as much as they exist in the heads of men," she said.

The UPI release concluded, "Ms. Reid drew a standing ovation."

Complainants maintain, regarding the *Post's* editing:

This left readers believing that Lady Bird Johnson, former Federal Judge Sarah T. Hughes and other women in the audience were giving Reid a standing ovation for encouraging women to use sex to further their careers. In fact, they were applauding her recommendation that women work harder to permeate all levels of politics and public life to eliminate such sexism.

The twelve participants in the seminar who joined in bringing this complaint include: Judith Moyers, Cathy Bonner, Mary Virginia Busby, Susan Caudill, Sey Chassler, Deborah Leff, Patricia Lindh, Jill Ruckelshaus, Isabelle Shelton, Peggy Simpson, Scott Tagliarino and Susan Tolchin.

Response of News Organization: The Council notified the Executive Editor of *The Washington Post*, Ben Bradlee, of receipt of the complaint on January 4, 1976, and at that time provided him with a copy of the full text of Ms. Reid's speech. In a letter to the Council, dated January 20, regarding this complaint, Mr. Bradlee stated:

Whatever else Ms. Reid said, or whatever impression she meant to leave, she did say "– – –ing. I'm sorry about that, but you'll be expected to do it....I mean that seriously...if you don't – – – the press, you won't get good press, and if you don't – – – your cabinet ministers and their advisers, they won't listen to you."

He concluded by saying, "I don't think the UPI story left the reader with an erroneous impression."

Conclusion of the Council: Taken side by side, *The Washington Post's* article, the UPI release, and the transcript of Ms. Reid's speech show noteworthy discrepancies.

The portion of Ms. Reid's speech which is quoted in both the UPI release and the *Post's* article which says "If you don't do it you won't be as effective" is not evidenced in the transcript. What is in evidence, including what was omitted in the news organizations' quotes, is the following statement:

[Y]ou'll be expected to do it. And if you don't [do it]...the backlash will be quite dramatic. And I mean that seriously, because if you don't – – – the press, you won't get good press, and if you don't – – – your cabinet ministers and their advisers, they won't listen to you, and I'm sorry about the language, but I have lived through it. I didn't. And the stories that went around and the total lack of support were unbelievable....
[B]asically the world's perception of women has to do with that, and though we're in there to combat it, we're then faced with the dilemma that you won't be so effective at combating it if you don't do what it is that has been traditionally expected....

This portion of Ms. Reid's speech was part of a discussion of the political "games" encountered by the author during her career in politics and she concludes her speech with the recommendation that women fight such discriminatory practices. The Council finds persuasive the evidence submitted to it, and presented here, in support of the charge that the *Post* article was edited in such a way as to be misleading. By omitting the closing paragraphs of the UPI release and retaining only the concluding sentence, "Ms. Reid drew a standing ovation," the *Post* article changed the thrust of the speech and misrepresented Ms. Reid's position, *i.e.,* that she had refused sexual advances and strongly urged others to be aware of and to attack this form of sexism. It is this position, as the UPI release indicates, that received a standing ovation from the overflow audience which included Lady Bird Johnson and former federal judge Sarah T. Hughes and not, as the *Post* account would indicate, the view that sex is the easiest and most effective route to political power for women.

Further, we find the response provided by the Executive Editor of *The Washington Post* unsatisfactory, focusing as it does on precisely that part of Ms. Reid's speech which, when quoted out of context in the *Post,* was so misleading. What she conveyed in her speech was quite different from the selected, and abbreviated, quote. We note further that, while stating his opinion regarding the merits of the UPI story, Mr. Bradlee declined to comment in any regard on the comparable merits of the version which appeared in his own paper.

The complaint is found warranted.

Concurring, COONEY, DILLIARD, FULD, GHIGLIONE, GREEN, HEIGHT, McKAY, RENICK, RUSHER and STRAUS.

Dated: March 30, 1976

APPENDIX B

Determination of Minnesota Press Council Determination No. 7 (1973)

In the Matter of the Grievance of the Minnesota Education Association and 32 Minnesota newspapers.

Procedural Summary

A. L. "Bud" Gallop, executive secretary of the Minnesota Education Association, addressed a May 4, 1973 letter to the Minnesota Press Council through its chairman C. Donald Peterson, complaining about what appeared to him to be unethical practices by a number of Minnesota newspapers in handling of a February 20,

1973 news release widely distributed by the Minnesota School Boards Association.

Chairman Peterson brought the letter to the attention of the Press Council at its meeting of May 18, 1973. Due to the unusual nature of the complaint, in that it involved a number of independent newspapers and their separate performances in regard to a common press release, the Press Council directed its chairman to ask the MEA for more detailed information, including a complete list of identified newspapers and their addresses with respect to whom the MEA makes its charges.

In correspondence dated May 30, 1973 the MEA responded with a detailed, documented complaint against 35 Minnesota newspapers, as requested previously by the Press Council. To further satisfy the Press Council requirement that there be a clear exchange of views on a complaint between the grievant and the newspaper involved, the MEA mailed individual letters of complaint and explanation to each of the 35 newspapers during the period of June 6-14, 1973 seeking a response or explanation from each newspaper in regard to its handling of the MSBA release.

By August 3, 1973 nine of the newspapers had responded in varying ways. A letter was sent by Press Council chairman Peterson to the newspapers which had not responded, advising them of an August 23, 1973 hearing on the matter, inviting them to attend the hearing, and urging them to give some explanation of their position in the matter for Press Council consideration.

The Minnesota Press Council held a public hearing on the MEA complaint on August 23.... Peter G. Pafiolis, director of public relations for MEA, presented the MEA complaint complete with copies of the article in question, copies of correspondence with newspapers involved in the complaint, and copies of correspondence with the Minnesota Press Council.... None of the newspapers were represented at the hearing, although they had been extended invitations to attend, as previously cited. However, responses were read from 26 newspapers, including in some instances editorials and news articles on the matter. Nine newspapers were noted as having made no response to either the Press Council or the MEA.

At that time, the MEA said it wished to withdraw complaints against [three newspapers]. The three complaints were dropped. The Press Council then proceeded to consider each newspaper separately. It was noted how and when the information was originally published, what response was made by each newspaper, and what explanation—if any—was given by each newspaper.

Factual Summary

The Minnesota School Boards Association, a voluntary statewide association of independent school boards in Minnesota...distributed a news release dated Feb. 20, 1973, for "immediate" release, concerning pending legislation in the 1973 State Legislature.

According to the usual mailing procedures of the MSBA as explained to the Press Council by its executive secretary, William Wettergren, the release was mailed to all Minnesota newspapers, to school superintendents and to several local school board members throughout the state for the purpose of presenting the MSBA viewpoint on the subject matter. A cover letter accompanied the release as mailed to local school officials, advising them to take the release personally to local newspapers as an additional means of gaining widespread publication.

The press release, in varying forms, then appeared in print in newspapers throughout Minnesota during late February and early March, 1973.

Text of the MSBA release of February 20, 1973 is as follows:

MINNESOTA SCHOOL BOARDS ASSOCIATION

Who should control your schools? Do the people of Minnesota want to give teachers and other public employees of our public school districts the right to strike? Do you want an outside, non-elected arbitrator, who is in no way responsible to the taxpayers of your district, to set school district taxes and the educational and personnel policies of your district?

This is exactly what will happen if bills being discussed by the Minnesota Legislature (House File 295 and Senate File 365) pass during this session.

These bills call for binding arbitration of those matters not agreed upon during negotiations including economic aspects and personnel policies along with educational policies. In short, if teachers and school boards do not agree, the matter goes to binding arbitration for a decision. These bills provide that, if public school boards do not accept the award or decision of an arbitrator or arbitrators, the teachers and other employees of the district have the right to strike.

The provisions of these bills would make it almost impossible for the elected school board members to be responsible for the educational programs of the district, for controlling expenditures of the district and for levying the taxes by officials elected by the public. These bills threaten to end significant participation in the control of Minnesota's public schools by the citizens of the state.

If passed, this legislation would mean that every decision made by an elected school board and its administration could be overridden by an outside arbitrator if the teachers and employees of a school district did not agree with the decision of the board. Citizen participation in the affairs of local government will, for all intents and purposes, be nullified by a person or persons far removed from the local unit of government.

Members of the legislature should be contacted immediately on the threat to local government and citizen participation contained in these two bills.

The Minnesota Education Association, in a May 4, 1973, letter addressed to Press Council chairman C. Donald Peterson, called attention to what it termed "a matter without precedent concerning what appear to be unethical practices in the performances of a number of newspapers relative to the use of material supplied by the Minnesota School Boards Association...."

...The complaint was based on findings in what MEA said was a massive research task, during which it claimed to have inspected state newspapers on file at the Minnesota Historical Society. Papers examined were published during the period of the last weeks of February and early weeks of March, 1973, and research revealed that more than 60 newspapers used the MSBA material, of which more than 30 used it in a questionable manner in the view of the complainant MEA. [There follows a list of thirty-two newspapers that used the release as a news story or an editorial without attribution or identification of source.]

The MEA mailed individual letters of complaint and explanation to each of the above newspapers, and furnished copies of all correspondence to the Press Council for examination. The MEA sought responses or explanations from each of the 32 newspapers cited. The first letters were mailed out by MEA during the period of June 6-14, 1973.

Nine of the newspapers responded to the MEA complaint and inquiry as of Aug. 3, 1973, including three newspapers against whom complaints were withdrawn at the Aug. 23 hearing. The responses varied from publication of subsequent apologies for poor performances, to letters explaining circumstances of publication, to letters attempting to justify procedures used.

Twenty-six newspapers did not respond. They were advised in a subsequent letter sent out by Press Council chairman Peterson that a public hearing on the MEA complaint had been set for 9:30 a.m. on Aug. 23, 1973.... Each of the newspapers were invited to attend, but if they could not be represented it was suggested they give some response to the complaint to assist the Press Council in its deliberations.

By the date of the Aug. 23 hearing, all but nine newspapers had responded either directly to the MEA or the Press Council, or both.

DISCUSSION

As a matter of first concern, the Minnesota Press Council is not considering the subject matter or the viewpoint expressed by the Minnesota School Boards Association in its news release of Feb. 20, 1973. That is not at issue here.

It is clearly within the rights of the MSBA to issue such releases to newspapers, school officials, legislators or anyone else as part of its organizational purpose as an association of independent school boards in the State of Minnesota. More realistically, the MSBA should be considered as a lobbyist and pressure group for an acknowledged public purpose—the status quo or betterment of school board operating rules and regulations, and the protection of school board rights and authority with respect to proposed legislation. An editor can welcome such organized activity by citizens and groups, but he should not neglect to test their objectives and their means. Many such groups are powerful lobbies serving special interests—whether they be the objectives of MSBA, MEA or the countless hundreds of other groups and causes organized as part of our participatory democracy. Many of them can and do block legislation proposed for Minnesota. They have a right to be heard. They have a right to protest. They have a right to opinions and viewpoints. But in a responsive, fair press, they have no right to dominate.

A good editor must make it his business to know something of the history of organized groups, their present strength and leadership, and their strategy and tactics. At the same time, newpapers have an established right to accept or reject any such organizational releases submitted for publication, or to edit such materials. The case before the Minnesota Press Council does not involve access to news columns, nor does it involve libelous or slanderous materials, nor does it involve what the MEA termed "an insidious attempt to subvert the press."

Responses from the challenged newspapers themselves seem to indicate widespread inconsistent and sloppy procedures by many newspapers in the handling of submitted news releases.

The issue squarely before the Press Council is two-fold: (1) Is it good journalism for a newspaper to publish verbatim a news release without giving some information as to the source of the release? and (2) Is it good journalism for a newspaper to publish a news release verbatim as an editorial, without attribution of source?

The objection raised by the Minnesota Education Association in the handling of this news release is not to the content of the release itself, but rather the fact that so many newspapers elected to publish a disputed viewpoint in a number of forms without attributing that viewpoint to the MSBA, or identifying the MSBA as the source of information—thereby helping the reader to evaluate the opinions expressed.

The release obviously presented one viewpoint—the MSBA viewpoint—on the ramifications of pending legislation in the 1973 Minnesota Legislature. However, nowhere in the body of the release was it ever mentioned that it was an MSBA viewpoint. From discussion, the Press Council concluded it was the hope of the MSBA that the release receive widespread publication.

Prepared news releases are a common publicity device used extensively by individuals, groups and organizations in Minnesota today, and probably used as a natural means of access to news columns throughout the history of journalism. It is well known that the better prepared a news release is, the better opportunity and likelihood it will be published. Busy editors and newspaper staff members are often tempted to give copy a cursory markup, rather than close editing to include the source of the release, among other details. Thus, news releases often appear as submitted.

Such public relations and publicity techniques, widespread as they may be, do not excuse or alleviate the need for editors and news staff members to scrutinize copy carefully. Newspapers should jealously guard the credibility of their news columns—and clear identification of news sources wherever possible, and certainly when necessary, is a strong journalistic device for instilling reader confidence.

Mr. Justice Felix Frankfurter put it this way in a 75th anniversary supplement published by the St. Louis *Post-Dispatch* in 1953:

News columns are not only accepted as affording a true narrative of events; through headlines, spacing, repetition and characterization they subtly infuse the reader's mind and largely influence his standards of judgment. It is the news columns that heavily determine the thinking habits of the reading public. It is they that shape the attitude of lazy credulity receptive to fear and prejudice rather than one of critical open-mindedness.

The unconscious, and therefore uncritical, absorption of print is much more powerful than any skeptical alertness which most readers bring to print. To an extent far beyond the public's own realization, public opinion is shaped by the kind, the volume, the quality of news columns. It depends on the quality of news columns, day after day whether the public's judgment is confused instead of enlightened, whether its feelings are debilitated or steadied, its reason deflected or enlisted. Everything, therefore, depends on what news is presented and how the news is presented.

Anticipating the Justice's line of thinking, editor E.P. Scott of the Manchester, England, *Guardian* stated it this way more than four decades ago (underlining is the Press Council's for emphasis):

There may be no actual perversion of the facts; a judicious selection may equally suffice, and this apart from any real malice. That is why the sources of information *are so important and the* responsibility *of the purveyors of the news is so great. That of those who handle and display it is, perhaps, no less. For the important may be shown as unimportant, and the unimportant as important, by devices so simple and innocent as type, headlines or position on the page. It is all a matter of discretion and good faith.*

The MEA complaint, in the opinion of the Press Council, comes down to a matter of discretion and good faith. Should a newspaper publish a controversial story without attribution of sources? Should a newspaper publish verbatim an editorial without any attribution, in such a way that readers believe the editorial was written by the local editor or members of his staff?...

Principles of good journalism suggest that readers should clearly be able to differentiate between objective news stories and editorial opinions. First, the matter of editorials.

Editorials, by their very definition, are slanted writings. They represent the opinion, the viewpoint, of the newspaper—or at least of the editorial writer—on whatever subject is being discussed. Editorials should be clearly labeled as such, and perhaps be established on an Opinion Page for that purpose. While the Press Council favors development of distinct editorial pages in newspapers, it understands that such display is not always possible or feasible. Whether they are signed or unsigned is a side issue—not a part of this determination.

On small weeklies and small city dailies, the owner most often writes the editorials. If he doesn't, readers of the editorials know who does. It is also known to the Press Council that many newspapers publish editorials from other newspapers, other publications, or perhaps even contract for an outside, professionally written editorial service. Such procedure, of course, rests with the control and conscience of the individual newspaper.

As a general guideline, however, the Minnesota Press Council urges that newspapers adopt a consistent policy that published editorials from outside sources, or written by persons other than newspaper staff members, should carry attribution as to their source or author. Such attribution may appear in the text of the editorial or if verbatim publication is made, attribution may be in the form of a credit line at the beginning or the conclusion of copy.

In looking specifically at those charged with publishing the MSBA release as an editorial or personal column, the Press Council is of the opinion that such verbatim, non-attribution-of-source use is a breach of

faith with readers! Any attempt to pass off another's word-for-word statements as one's own is a form of journalistic plagiarism that is deceptive and unfair to readers. We feel such practice is harmful to the reputation and credibility of the newspaper in the long run. Again, it is a matter of discretion and good faith. Readers will likely have little confidence in an editor who is elusive or a newspaper that is evasive in attributing news sources.

Turning to the matter of using the MSBA release as a news story, without attribution or identification of source, the Press Council again points up the need for discretion and good faith in dissemination of news in a fair and forthright manner.

It has been a long acknowledged and established principle of responsible journalism that sources of information be revealed, as a matter of credibility and perhaps as a matter of privilege. For example, when reporting accident stories, a responsible and alert newspaper attributes source of information in such terms as "according to the Sheriff's Department" or "according to police reports" or "as reported by witnesses at the scene." It is a device for telling the reader the source, and hence the reliability, of the information.

The same procedure is true with respect to prepared statements on political issues, speeches by elected officials, statistics released by companies or groups or individuals or government agencies. It may be "according to the Department of Labor" or "as revealed in statistics released today by the County Auditor" or "in the viewpoint of gubernatorial candidate John Smith" and so forth.

In the case at hand, it is not at all unreasonable for a reader to expect its local newspaper to be candid about the source of the MSBA story. Insertion of the term "according to the Minnesota School Boards

Association" would have been desirable. Such attribution is particularly crucial to readers in evaluating stands taken in regard to political issues and controversies surrounding pending legislation. The Press Council reiterates its statement that there is nothing sinister or awkward in pressure groups sending out press releases. And there is no question that the MSBA or the MEA or any other organization has a right to its viewpoint.

From the outset, this has been an unusual case for the Press Council in that we have nearly three dozen independent newspapers under attack for the various ways in which they handled a common news release. It should be mentioned that an equally large group of independent newspapers also used the same release, but with proper attribution of source.

Thus, the Press Council must address itself on a large scale to the general problem of attribution of sources and identification of sources in news stories and editorials published in Minnesota newspapers. Part of this determination is directed at offering guidelines to all newspapers interested in abiding by responsible tenets of journalism.

The remainder of this determination is directed at the specific newspapers, treated separately and individually, involved in this complaint.

DETERMINATION

1. With respect to editorials, newspapers which publish editorials from outside sources, or written by persons other than newspaper staff members, should carry attribution as to their source or author. Such attribution may appear in the text of the editorial, or if verbatim publication is made, attribution may be in the form of a credit line at the beginning or at the conclusion of copy.

2. With respect to news stories, attribution or identification of source is a vital facet of responsible reporting—a yardstick by which readers can better measure the veracity and reliability of the viewpoints expressed. Such attribution is particularly crucial to readers in evaluating stands taken in regard to political issues or pending legislation. News stories should be attributed to sources.

3. With respect to news releases, editors should be alerted as to source and purpose of any such submitted copy, and inform their readers accordingly. Newspapers are encouraged to adopt consistent policies for handling releases, and should insist that all releases submitted for publication be clearly identified as to source.

4. We release this determination to the news media for publication....

APPENDIX C

News Conference Guidelines
Prepared for Honolulu Community-Media Council
1974

The guidelines set forth below are intended to govern both elected and appointed government officials as well as the news media. These guidelines have taken note of the infinite variety of the people, institutions and practices involved in the news gathering and disseminating process and therefore are based upon the assumption that some degree of flexibility is required in order to encompass this variety of individual styles and circumstances. However, the authoritative formulations of the guidelines will serve to indicate when the underlying intent and spirit, if not the letter, of the guidelines are being systematically violated, even though there may appear to be literal compliance with the guidelines.

GUIDELINES

1. A "news conference" is defined as a meeting between one or more elected and/or appointed public officials and representatives of the news media (i.e., of the electronic as well as printed media) for the purpose of disseminating information intended to be received by the general public. If any meeting is qualified as a "news conference", as herein defined, then the label placed on such meeting is insignificant. In these news conferences, representatives of the media should not only receive statements from officials but should also be allowed to ask questions about those statements and other matters of public policy. Such questioning is vital to the two-way communication aspect of the conference, in that it not only elicits responses from the official for the public's knowledge, but also serves the purpose of informing the officials of public opinion and thought.

2. No government official should conduct a news conference without giving reasonable prior notice of the time and place of the news conference by so informing the Honolulu bureaus of the Associated Press and United Press International, and also informing all those accredited media representatives who are formally assigned by their respective employers to regularly cover that particular government official or agency's activities, and who have notified that public office of their assignment.

3. New conferences should be open to all accredited representatives of (a) news publications of general circulation, (b) radio and television broadcasting stations, (c) news and feature syndicates, (d) wire news services, and (e) other agencies recognized to be substantially engaged in gathering and disseminating news. No such accredited representative should be barred from a news conference held by an elected or appointed city, county or state official, provided that such accredited representative is authorized by his employer to participate in news conferences in the course of his work.

4. It is not possible to suggest ideal regularity, frequency, or length of news conference. However, the public interest in matters affecting public welfare indicates the need—which varies from one governmental official to another—for regular and frequent news conferences that permit reasonable opportunities for extensive questioning of the official by representatives of the news media.

5. "Private interviews" of public officials are those meetings, other than the spontaneous and casual encounters of an official with a news media representative, which result in the dissemination of news and in which only the official and a single media representative or a single news agency represented by two or more of its delegates are present. Except in unusual circumstances, these interviews should be initiated only by a representative of the news media. The calling of continuous private interviews, and interviews called by the official, are suspect and should be scrutinized in order to prevent them from becoming instruments which deny equal access of all media to the news.

6. The number of exclusive interviews granted by an official should be dictated by the enterprise of media representatives, and should not be used by either officials or journalists to discriminate or exclude other media. Officials who grant interviews as rewards and withhold them as punishments, or use them in any discriminatory fashion, do not serve the public interest, and in fact prevent the public's receipt of comprehensive news coverage.

7. A representative of the news media should not participate in news conferences or initiate interviews if he is also employed by an individual, group, organization or firm whose interests might reasonably be construed as conflicting with his work in representing a news agency.

8. Responsible executives of news agencies represented in news conferences, interviews, and other news media representative-official contacts that result in news dissemination, should evaluate complaints made by officials and by other citizens. Corrections should be promptly and prominently published or broadcast in all cases of error or unfairness.

9. It is recognized that several forms of media-official contact, in addition to news conferences and exclusive interviews, result in news dissemination. These range from relatively formal sessions such as background briefings to broadcasts in which officials are questioned by the media representatives of several news agencies. However, except in centers of government such as Washington, D.C., where the sheer number of media representatives precludes the presence of all such representatives, such background briefings and similar selective briefings are suspect, especially if used as a subterfuge to avoid equal access of all media. If, after a period of several such contacts, a pattern of exclusion of one or more agencies appears, then these contacts should be condemned as violations of the guidelines laid out herein.

10. Representatives of the news media should substantially adhere to the Code of Ethics adopted by the American Society of Newspaper Editors, that of the Society of Professional Journalists (Sigma Delta Chi) or similar codes of other organizations of print and/or electronic journalists, which set forth standards of responsible performance.

THE CABLE FABLE: WILL IT COME TRUE

Anne W. Branscomb

The cable industry is slowly recovering from what can best be described as the TelePrompTer syndrome. This manifested itself in the crisis of September 1973, when two financial officers of the company blew the whistle at the Securities and Exchange Commission (SEC), precipitating the suspension of trading of TelePrompTer stock on the New York stock exchange for several weeks. The rest of the industry waited in a state of suspended animation.

There were massive dismissals of personnel; all regional offices were closed; program production stopped; management was reorganized; and marketing efforts were reoriented toward increasing subscribers in existing systems rather than expanding services. Franchising operations, which had been brisk and successful, ceased. Personnel assigned to franchising turned to work on rate increases.[1]

The time to make systems "operational" (a euphemism for profitable) had proved far longer than predicted. The projected earnings per share of TelePrompTer stock was 12 cents for 1973 compared with 79 cents per share in 1972.[2] This news predictably precipitated much foreboding within and without the industry. Venture capital became apprehensive. The values of cable stocks dropped phenomenally. Although the entire stock market was unstable during 1973, the cable stocks were the greater losers. Market capitalization decreased from $1,110,129,000 in September of 1972 to $397,650,000 in September of 1973 for eight of the ten largest multiple system operators (MSO's) for whom such statistics are available....

On March 22, 1973, Bill Bresnan, then president of TelePrompTer, speaking to the

Reprinted from "The Cable Fable: Will It Come True?" by Anne W. Branscomb in the Journal of Communication *25:1 (Winter 1975), pp. 44-56. Copyright © 1975 by* Journal of Communications; *reprinted by permission.*

San Francisco Society of Security Analysts in San Francisco, said:

...rather than being light years away from the so-called cable revolution, the CATV industry in 1973 is standing on the threshold. Regardless of future regulatory posture, the CATV industry is destined to grow dramatically over the next several years....How much it will grow is open to speculation. Most observers estimate that by 1980 at least one-half of U.S. households will be wired for cable. Specific estimates vary between 25 million and 45 million homes. A report prepared for the White House Office of Telecommunications Policy estimates the industry's potential total gross revenues for two-way services to reach 99 million by 1980, 3.8 billion by 1984 and upwards of 19 billion by 1989.

Only six months later, the cable industry was in serious trouble. What are the problems and what is the prognosis?

The Cable Industry Was Oversold to Itself, to the Public, and to the Investment Community. What started as a simple extension of antenna capacity to receive or improve television signals became the communications utility of the future, the umbilical cord through which every person would be plugged into the world. A communications revolution of two-way interactive cable, it was predicted, would bring the dawning of a new day of the individualized computer terminal through which all citizens would communicate with their peers, merchants, banks, elected representatives, libraries, investment counselors, and doctors, as well as receive a smorgasbord of specialized choices from the entertainment media.[3]

Cable was a new toy to be teased, tested, and reflected upon. The promise of new markets captivated the investing public, and cable became a glitter stock of the early 1970s. Public officials latched onto the new industry as a means of increasing public resources—or at least of assuring substantial public use of the new channels of abundance. The dreamers dreamed of a great new electronic highway and a "wired nation" in which everyone could communicate with everyone—and a body of credible intellectuals

predicted that 40-60 percent of the nation would be cabled by 1980.[4] Responsible cable operators shook their heads in amazement, while their more apprehensive colleagues pocketed their profits and cable stocks soared ever higher. This was the era of "science fiction" which Ralph Baruch, president of Viacom, calls most damaging to the industry.

Clearly the acceptance of the dream by cable operators was not deliberately deceptive. The price of stock on the market is directly related to the ability to accumulate capital in order to expand. Most of the simple cable systems have been built; the expensive ones in suburbs and small towns, and the large capital expenses, are ahead of the industry. In order to amass the necessary capital there is a tremendous temptation to try to "talk a stock up" in the eyes of the investment community, in order to persuade the bankers that sufficient equity exists to borrow larger amounts of capital to construct new systems.

The Financial Difficulties Which Beset the Cable Industry Are Real Rather than Contrived. These difficulties are not temporary and very unlikely to decrease in severity. Partially they are the result of a general softness in the economy; partially a result of inflationary trends which have increased debt service, construction, and labor costs; partially the result of overselling the immediate potential of the industry to the investment community; and partially the result of rules restricting investment from a large number of potential investors. Very little is due to squandering of resources.

Investors are becoming more sophisticated about the risks inherent in cable investments, as costs have risen and return on capital investment has receded. Furthermore, the trend toward carrier status and possible rate-of-return regulation makes the pot at the end of the rainbow less reachable. Certainly cable operators consider the divorce of carriage from content a device to separate them from their just rewards after building the rainbows—and costs of construction keep climbing upward, rendering the completion of the system less likely with each passing year. The cost of constructing a strand mile of cable has increased from an average of $3,000 or $4,000 during the last decade to about $6,000 today for non-urban overhead installation. Putting the cable underground (as is more often required by franchising authorities and ecological mandates) can cost anywhere from $9,000 to $40,000 or $50,000 per strand mile in congested metropolitan areas.

Debt service has almost doubled in the last few years from 6 percent to more than 11 percent in 1973. Cable operators simply cannot afford to borrow money to build new systems unless they are in marginal television reception areas where the profitability and immediate return on investment is assured. Municipal or public ownership of some kind becomes more attractive both to the smaller communities (which are likely to be left in the interstitial spaces between successful cable operations) and to the larger cities, where the capital costs are high and the amortization of costs projected over too long a period for traditional venture capital to be attracted. The debt service on tax-free municipal bonds is approximately half the cost of conventional bank financing, so more and more cities will likely turn, as Baltimore has, to some mode of municipal financing. Cable companies are said to be attracted to partnerships which relieve them of the burden of arranging for construction capital but keep them in the role of lessee of the facilities or operator under some form of management contract.

The costs of wiring the nation are staggering: $1.2 trillion for a completely switched or dial-access system like the telephone or $123 billion for a traditional tree-branched system. Recent estimates, based upon 86 million families to be served in 1985 utilizing microwave interconnection, arrive at a more realistic figure of $82.5 billion, comparable with the current investment of $67 billion in telephone plant and annual construction commitments of $12.5 billion in the telephone system.

Two questions which do become apparent are: (1) whether or not it makes sense to duplicate transmission facilities at staggering costs when modification of the present nationwide system may achieve the desired results; and (2) how the cable industry, which represents a minuscule 1.8 percent of the $22 billion annual revenues of the communications industry, is expected to accomplish the communications revolution when the giants of the industry—telephone companies, television networks, and television stations—are prohibited from investing in the developing technology of cable.

The Cable Industry Is Primarily a "Piggyback" Operation Which "Has Grown over the Years by Free Loading".[5] Because the industry has developed as a transmitting rather than as a programming service, it has neither the will nor the creativity to produce new kinds of programming and services; nor is the subscriber base yet substantial enough to sustain much original programming designed for cable. The token commitment to program orientation (which became legally binding upon TelePrompTer as a precondition for approval by the FCC of the merger with H and B American in August of 1970)—was the first promise to be broken in the financial crunch of 1973; practically the entire programming production capability was eliminated as an economy move. Cablecasters at the 1974 National Cable Television Association (NCTA) convention concluded that program orientation was losing money and gaining few viewers.

Furthermore, the importation of distant signals to large metropolitan markets has been disappointing as a marketing attraction. The compromise which precipitated the 1972 FCC rules, with their incredibly complex formula for deciding who can import which signals, has not been the great boost to the development of cable in the cities which was ancitipated. Penetration in the New York systems of TelePrompTer and Manhattan Cable remains stationary at less than 30 percent. Furthermore, the non-duplication and syndicated exclusivity rules are so stringent that a careful calculation of the permitted signals in the top 100 markets discloses that there are only 17 markets in which the importation will create attractive marketing potential. In the other markets, the cable system will be importing signals which will be largely blacked out because of existing program contracts in that market; the present attractions—largely sporting events not currently carried on the networks—would be exterminated by sports blackout legislation currently proposed in Congress.

Thus the industry is now relying upon pay cable as the way to salvation. However, despite all the protests to the contrary, there is no reassuring evidence emanating from the cable industry that it will provide a very different source of programming supply than the current broadcasters. Thus the primary advantage of pay cable may be merely the opportunity to pay for the same old movies but without the advertising interruptions—an advantage not to be ignored; but there is no evidence at the moment that the cable industry will produce the imaginative cable services promised by the cable dreamers.

On the other hand, the technology is rapidly being perfected to bring as many as 80 channels to all cable systems via satellite distribution at a modest cost. The predicted current capability, if all the earth reception facilities currently on the drawing boards were in place using existing microwave networks, is only about two million homes.[6] Nonetheless, the cable industry currently has installed coaxial cable in front of more than 12 million homes—the market which the Sloan Commission crudely estimated to be sufficient to support the revolutionary "blue sky" services which would constitute the communications revolution predicted.[7] Thus it is particularly ironic that the crisis in financial capability has come at a time when technical capability is almost within grasp.

The Dream Was Not Dreamed by Those upon Whose Labors the Realization of the Dream Depended.   The projection of potential for the cable industry came largely from the scientists and the social philosophers, not from the pole climbers and television salesmen who put the industry together. The cable industry is not populated by the AT&T's, the IBM's or the ITT's. It is populated by a large number of small-town operators predominantly in rural areas whose sole original purpose was to provide an antenna service to deliver existing television signals to customers unable to obtain an acceptable signal through their own devices.[8] Many of these companies were and still are "mom and pop"-type operations, although the trend is toward amalgamation and the top 12 MSO's serve 50 percent of the cabled homes. Nevertheless, the largest of the MSO's was still operated in 1973 as a large family—which still had difficulty keeping track of its many branches and was yet unable to cope with modern administrative and accounting practices.

It is no quirk of fate that William Bresnan, interim president of TelePrompTer from 1972 to 1974, started his career in cable more than 20 years ago as a pole climber. A business school-trained executive like Amos Hostetter, vice president of Continental Cablevision, seventeenth largest MSO (with only 78,000 subscribers) is a notable exception in the industry. It is difficult for people whose main stock in trade is stringing coaxial cable from pole to pole to conceive of an information retrieval system.

The industry is certainly not unaware of its personnel problems, both administrative and technical. It may be that industry decision-makers are beginning to be more conscious of the management skills required for realizing the growth potential: two new MSO Presidents, Clifford Miner Kirtland, Jr., of Cox Broadcasting Corp., and Lawrence B. Hilford, of Viacom Enterprises, are Harvard MBA's.

Russell Karp, the new president of TelePrompTer, is a graduate of the Yale Law School with financial and managerial experience in the entertainment industry.

The Industry Is Regulated by a Three-Tiered System Which Can Only Be Described as Excessive. Ironically, the cable industry, which fought long and hard to avoid federal regulation as inhibiting the growth of the industry, now finds itself in the anomalous position of seeking federal preemption of regulatory authority in order to get the state and local authorities off its back.

The FCC has considerable doubts about its power to completely preempt cable regulation, although it has recently preempted regulation of leased and pay channels. However, the FCC cannot will away the cities' legitimate legal interest in cable strung over and under the city streets. There is, therefore, substantial doubt that federal preemption would completely exclude local authorities from the regulatory process or that such exclusion would be in the public interest. In the realm of truly local signal service, cable has the potential to provide an avenue of communication which the broadcasting industry has failed to provide and to develop the system of locally oriented program services which the Communications Act envisioned.

One weakness of the present FCC regulations is that they have come too early and with too much detail in the area of local preemption. Although the abuses of the franchising process are too well known to be reiterated, what is not so well known is the inhibitory influence of a standard rule in cutting off the more experimental modes of local ownership and/or regulation which might have developed without the heavy hand of the FCC.

Another weakness is that FCC rules were unfortunately written by regulators uninitiated in the mysteries of cable operations. Even the authors of the regulations often admit that they do not understand what a particular rule means. For example, rules which preceded the new cable rules have been continued without any rationale for their perpetuation. A cable system must provide non-duplication protection to a television station which its subscribers can receive with rabbit ears on a local television antenna. Certainly the system should not be required to provide non-duplication protection for television signals which it is required to carry. All "significantly viewed signals" which systems are required to carry should be treated equitably. The prior system of priorities of protection for Grade A contour signals against Grade B contour signals should be abandoned—but this is only one example of the complexity of the cable rules which defy the average cable system operator's ability to master and which force every system to have competent FCC counsel in order to decipher. It seems doubtful that the single system operator can survive without the economy of cost which can be realized by pooling systems and legal resources. The FCC has recently determined to review and simplify its cable rules by announcing some proposed changes, and the formation of a Cable Television Re-regulation Task Force may signify a more lenient future stance toward cable operations.

Another Problem Implicit in the Present Rules Is that They Have Saddled a New Technology with Too Much Public Responsibility in Its Infancy Before It Has Had Time to Develop the Economic Base Necessary to Sustain Such Public Commitments. The reason the cable industry has been overloaded with public responsibilities is not difficult to discern. The early legislative debates on the Radio Act of 1927 and the Communications Act of 1934 are replete with promises of great public service responsibility of the then nascent radio industry. Each successive technology has been the repository of these hopes, and has failed them. In cable, public-service advocates feel they have finally found a medium that can deliver. The failure of the legislative architects to provide a workable framework for the use of radio for fruitful public debate led public-interest advocates to pursue the imposition of public responsibilities more diligently in the regulations governing cable.

From a financial standpoint, however well motivated the dedicated channels may have been, the promotion of their use and the commitment of financial support for program production must be undertaken with vigor if the new services are to fulfill their promise. Cable operators themselves are the least well equipped—psychologically or financially—to take responsibility for the development of these channels. The dreams of the wide-open, robust, and uninhibited public debate will not be realized by merely setting aside some channels. They will only be realized through the diligent cultivation of those channels by a public which wants to be heard.

State regulatory commissions are adding a third dimension to the regulatory scene which appears superfluous and oppressive. Few lawyers are proficient in the vagaries of state cable regulation, and an ailing cable industry which already must have both local and FCC legal capabilities can hardly be aided by another layer of regulatory forms and filings to meet.

The Massachusetts regulations defy the most diligent MSO to comply. In order to qualify its Massachusetts operations, TelePrompTer had five people working several weeks attempting—not entirely successfully—to provide the information required to file for certification of its Worcester system (which serves less than 1 percent of TelePrompTer's total subscribers). This could not be considered cost-effective by any accounting method which allocated time proportionately to operations involved, a system which TelePrompTer was manifestly not using. A prudent MSO would be well advised to pull out of Massachusetts unless it had very substantial investment and a highly profitable operation.

On the contrary, the New York Cable Commission looks upon itself as a promoter of cable development; to the extent that it pursues this goal diligently, it may, in fact, prove highly catalytic in helping to encourage intrastate interconnections, providing legal and technical expertise which

individual small operators cannot afford. However, New York is an ill-conceived geographic unit to encourage the kind of regional interconnection which would be optimum. The New York metropolitan area should logically coordinate its telecommunications planning and development with New Jersey and Connecticut, not with New York State. Virtually no states, in fact, with the possible exception of California, and Texas, Alaska, and Hawaii, contain within their boundaries the communications complexes which constitute the logical regulatory areas for regional amalgamation. If any regulatory entity is to be interposed between the local governing authority and the FCC, it should be regional—New England, Southwest, metropolitan authority.

However, the time is growing short for changing regulatory patterns. Three state cable commissions are already in existence (Massachusetts, Minnesota, and New York); seven states have some type of Public Utilities Commission-type regulation; eight states have regulatory legislation pending; four others have active study groups, and the remaining 28 are pregnant with possibilities.[9] None of these is likely to be willing to relinquish jurisdiction, once acquired, at the mere bidding of a federal regulatory agency. Judicial determination of the parameters of state and federal jurisdiction is likely to be time-consuming, costly, and inhibiting rather than stimulating to the growth of cable generally.

The draft bill of the Cable Communications Act of 1974 (drafted by the Office of Telecommunications Policy) is an effort to roll back the carpet toward a two-tiered regulatory framework, freeing cable operators of many of the more onerous requirements and severely limiting state or local interference with the free play of the marketplace.

The Cable Industry Is Beset with a Cautious Investment Community, an Overzealous Triumvirate of Government Regulators, an Honest Infusion of Self-Doubt, and a Pessimistic Public. Clearly this is not a time for unbridled optimism about the future of cable *per se*. Neither is it a time for deep depression. There is no reason to believe that the "mom and pop" cable systems are in deep financial difficulties. Indeed, they seem to be plodding along doing what they've always done in the same old way. Even TelePrompTer claims to have weathered its financial crisis with blue skies ready to break overhead. The CATV industry will survive. The question is whether or not it will become the electronic highway of tomorrow.

Ironically, the Wired Nation is a reality. The technology is called the telephone, and it is not at all clear that the blue-sky visions of the cable enthusiasts cannot or should not be realized by the utilization or modernization of the existing plant, in which we already have invested $67 billion.

The home interactive computer terminal is a distant dream. This does not mean, as many doubters predict, that the hardware is the major problem and that cities should wait to franchise cable companies until home terminals are perfected. The problem is economic. What many people do not realize is that the capability to produce television sets existed for several decades before the television industry took off. The patents for an electronically produced facsimile newspaper were registered in 1935, but the facsimile newspaper has not yet found a place in our economy. Whether coaxial cable is the preferred material with which to wire the nation, and whether cable service is to become the ubiquitous communications utility of tomorrow, depends upon the conscious choice of policy and allocation of financial resources—both public and private.

Realization of the cable dream may depend upon the ability to reassess some established principles:

1. Cable should be encouraged to develop in partnership with and not as competitor to existing technologies—broadcasting and telephone companies. Much return capability can be provided by existing telephone lines, and experimentation with services using coaxial cable and the twisted pair technology should be encouraged.

   The fibre optical communications system developed at Bell Labs provides the potential for greater transmission capacity even than coaxial cable. AT&T could provide, perhaps at less cost, the facilities about which we are dreaming: the completely wired, interconnected, two-way switched system.

   AT&T is its own worst enemy, since its current financial investment in the Bell plant of $56 billion militates against a huge investment in fibre optics—and the regulatory climate portends a government unfriendly to a single communications giant providing all communications services, even on a common carrier basis. Apparently, the public lacks the capability to regulate Ma Bell.[10]

   Nonetheless, a public decision must be made at some point: whether to continue discouraging the amalgamation of technological power through vigorous use of the antitrust laws or to regulate diversity of access and content in some more socially productive manner. The sooner policy-makers recognize the interrelatedness and interdependence of the various components of our communications system, the more workable and sensible the solutions to existing problems will become.

2. Prohibitions against cross-investment of one technology in another should be abandoned. Such prohibitions, which are the subject of extensive criticism, not only restrict the availability of investment capital, they align powerful political forces against the new technology which may effectively foreclose the potential for growth.

   The broadcaster and the cablecaster should be natural allies—the broadcaster as the program producer and the cablecaster as the transmitting agency. The broadcaster is most logically the lessee of a cable channel and the cable operator the lessor who merely enhances the broadcaster's signal and increases his ability to reach viewers. But the rule requiring cable systems to originate programming (sustained by the courts and currently under reconsideration by the FCC) is ill advised, because it necessarily puts the cable operator into a competitive situation with broadcasters by forcing him to become a broadcaster too on his cable origination channel. This intensifies the ill will of the broadcaster.

The present animosity between broadcaster and cablecaster is more deeply rooted than the change of two rules could improve. Nonetheless, dropping the program origination requirement and the cross-ownership prohibition surely would be a step in the right direction, placing the two opposing factions into their more natural roles as program producer and program transmitter. However, the cross-ownership rule should be dropped now and not at the 50 percent penetration level proposed by the Office of Telecommunications Policy Report to the President on Cable, since the industry may never make the 50 percent level without the added impetus that cooperative investment would provide.

3. Ownership of the hardware should not result in control of the content. Control of the hardware is not necessarily an evil if control of the transmission is divorced from control of content. This is the major contribution to the cable debate of the OTP cable report. The Massachusetts Cable Commission has shown great insight in emphasizing this particular aspect of the cable development. The FCC, on the contrary, has been extremely unwise in the promulgation of rules which expand rather than restrict operator control of content. The cable operator is by nature a transmission expert, not a programmer, and it better befits his natural skills and inclination to remain in a role in which he feels comfortable.

4. Regulation, if it is to be effective, must be efficient and responsive. This means less state and national, and more regional and local regulation. Regulation of the hardware should be by a national standard, but regulation which affects people's political and sociological habits should be regulated by those units of government which have familiarity with the political and social consequences of regulation. Regulation at all levels should concentrate on the positive rather than the negative aspects of telecommunications development—on technical compatibility, quality of signal delivered, diversity of access to the maximum number of users. Above all, the regulatory apparatus should not be used as a device for inhibiting growth potential by competing technologies. Nor should we be afraid to look at alternatives to the current three tiers of regulation. It may very well be that all three are outmoded by the communications capabilities of the new technology. The optimum boundaries of the information utilities of the future may bear no logical relationship to the political boundaries of today.

5. If the public wants to participate in the message, then the public, or publics, whoever they may be, must be willing to pay the price in time, energy, and allocation of financial resources. This may take the form of a national investment in the hardware (either directly or in the form of matching funds to states or local governments) or of the insurance of loans used to construct systems. Whatever it means, it means money and lots of it, energy in great abundance, and persistence. A new telecommunications system can hardly succeed financially on a piecemeal basis, since the more imaginative uses require substantially full penetration—and the costs are staggering.

Either the existing telecommunications companies must be encouraged to incorporate the new technology or a substantial influx of funds from other sources—either public or private—must be stimulated. It is not unfair to conclude that Henry Ford would never have made it to the moon in his motorcar, and that the building of a nationwide, satellite, microwave, cable-connected system probably won't materialize in the foreseeable future without a conscious public decision to support the experimentation in software as well as a sizeable investment in the construction of the hardware.

Whether the cable fable becomes a reality depends largely upon the desires of public—not private—interests to make it so. It may be a serious public error to exhaust the resources of venture capital stringing the cable, leaving no resources for program development. A wiser public decision may be to install the cable with public funds, thus assuring equal acces to all and amassing the market necessary to attract venture capital into the development of the software.

NOTES

1. Facts and figures cited in this article come from interviews with cable industry officials; from records of Federal Communications Commission proceedings and regulations and other legal sources; and from *Broadcasting, Cable News,* and other industry publications. Readers interested in detailed citations are asked to contact the author.

2. It may be indicative of TelePrompTer's financial and accounting difficulties that these figures are in substantial discrepancy with figures reported later in the year. After adjusting its accounting practices, the company announced that net income for 1972 was only 56 cents, and there was a net loss of 6 cents per share in 1973.

3. See Walter S. Baer, *Interactive Television: Prospects for Two-Way Services on Cable* (Santa Monica, Calif.: Rand Corporation, 1971); and Ralph Lee Smith, *The Wired Nation* (New York: Harper & Row, 1972).

4. Sloan Commission on Cable Communications, *On the Cable: The Television of Abundance* (New York: McGraw-Hill, 1971).

5. Vince Wasilewski, remarks reported in *Television Digest,* 24 December 1973, p. 2.

6. This projection was made for the NCTA Satellite Committee and is based on 50 ground stations reaching existing microwave networks. The cost is estimated at $3.5 million.

7. Sloan Commission, *On the Cable.*

8. See Brenda Maddox, *Beyond Babel: New Directions in Communications* (New York: Simon and Schuster, 1972); and Smith, *Wired Nation.*

9. "CATV Regulation: State by State," *TV Communications,* June 1973, p. 49.

10. See footnote 6. The FCC has only one staff economist to cope with AT&T rate regulations. The cable industry was searching diligently during the summer of 1973 for an expert with sufficient knowledge of AT&T accounting practices to assist in negotiations with the telephone industry on the pole attachment rate increase.

FURTHER READING

Johnson, Nicholas. *How to Talk Back to Your Television Set.* Boston: Little, Brown, 1970.

BUT WHO WILL CRITICIZE THE CRITICS?

James W. Carey

One of the domains of experience shared by members of modern society is our experience of the media of communication, the newspapers particularly. And this is a domain about which there is little debate of significance out in the brightly lit arena where the public lives.

These observations cut against the received opinion of many newspapermen. They feel under constant attack and do not respond kindly to anyone they regard as a critic. But attack is not criticism, and it is the absence of substantial criticism that makes the sporadic attacks on the press by government and others so telling.

Let us now assume that all areas of experience, all institutions of modern society, must be subjected to criticism. This criticism must be based upon precise observation, clear procedure, unemotional language, subject to

By James W. Carey in Journalism Studies Review,
June 1976, pp. 7-11 (an excerpt from "Journalism and Criticism: The Case of an Undeveloped Profession," The Review of Politics 36:2, April 1974, pp. 227-249). Reprinted by permission of the author.

the cooperative correction of others, and occurring in the public forum where all affected by the institution can at least observe and comment on the critical process. Moreover, it must clarify our experience of the institution and scrutinize the values upon which the institution is based. The only things sacred in this process are the rules and procedures by which it is done and the manners necessary to make this a continuing process.

If we assume that the newspaper press is the most general forum in which this process can operate, let us look at an omnibus newspaper like the *New York Times*. In its pages, particularly the Sunday edition, one finds information, analysis, criticism of *every* contemporary institution. It treats art, architecture, literature, education, politics, business, religion, finance, film, and so forth. One institution, however, is curiously exempt from analysis and criticism—the press itself. The *Times* does, of course, deal with books and devotes a daily and Sunday column to television. Aside from the quality and relevance of this, the *Times* is virtually silent about the newspaper: itself in particular, the medium in general. A rise in the wholesale price of newsprint will be reported, but that, we all know, is merely to signal an impending rise in the price of the newspaper itself. The newspaper does not, perhaps it cannot, turn upon itself the factual scrutiny, the critical acumen, the descriptive language, that it regularly devotes to other institutions.

There are a number of responses to this argument that must be anticipated. The first argument heard from many editors, namely, that "we are criticized all the time, that criticism of the press is abundant," simply will not wash. The critical literature in all the fields about which newspapers report, from art through education, to government and science, is enormous and often of quite high quality. For every first-class work of journalistic criticism there are a hundred exemplary works of literary criticism. There is, simply no important critical literature concerning journalism and while the newspaper fosters such literature in *every* other field, it does not foster it in its own domain.

It is often argued that criticism of the press is found in the newspaper because the press reports the statements of its critics and in turn press professionals respond. But this is wholly inadequate. First, it is altogether too sporadic and undisciplined. The criticism awaits some public figure or celebrity becoming exercised and lashing out at what he takes to be unfair treatment. Journalists usually respond in kind and the public then takes its choice among opinions. Moreover, it is usually opinions undisciplined on both sides by fact or substantial analysis, a kind of shouting match that usually talks by the point in question.

Let me anticipate two more responses to the argument that the press is perhaps the least criticized of our important institutions. Editors often point to attempts on the part of some newspapers to create columns about the press or to create a new role within the newspaper, that of ombudsman. I applaud both of these gestures, look upon them as promising, and wish to say nothing that would discourage them. When the first effort is mentioned, the example is usually the *Washington Post* and its column "News Business." The ombudsman is often identified with the pioneering effort of the Louisville *Courier-Journal* and its ombudsman, John Herchenroeder. Similar positions have been created at a number of other newspapers often under a less European title.

Neither of these practices is completely sufficient. The "News Business" column at the *Post* was written by Ben Bagdikian and undoubtedly will be written in the future by a professional newsman. Much as I admire Mr. Bagdikian's work, I hope that he would agree that one needs sustained critical attention from intellectuals, scholars, writers and ordinary citizens *outside* the apparatus of the newspaper, not merely deviant and unusually courageous persons within it.

The ombudsman suffers from the same ailment of being within the newspaper, internal to it rather than outside, and while it does mean that errors are taken seriously, followed up and corrected, and thereby is responsive to the public, it is less than a complete response.

A final defence against criticism is usually expressed as the belief that the public does not, and probably cannot understand newspapers, and that independent critics, because they are not journalists, are not qualified to criticize the press. This is argument by mystification. When a university president rejects criticism directed against him and his institution because journalists are not academics and cannot hope to understand the university, the press quite properly points out that every institution attempts to protect itself by hiding behind special mysteries of the craft, mysteries decipherable only by the initiated, and that the mystery behind the mystery is that there is no mystery at all. Newspapers defend themselves against outside criticism in the same terms they properly reject when offered by the institutions they cover.

But the emergence of a critical community should not be resisted by the press; it should be encouraged. Criticism is not the mark of failure and irrelevance; it is the sign of vigor and importance. In the Soviet Union the arts are not only actively censored but hypercriticized within Soviet bureaucracy. While there is an unfortunate side to this, it does suggest a positive value. In the Soviet Union poetry and literature are taken to be important; the work of artists is taken to be an active part of life, crucial material in the shaping and definition of Russian culture. American artists should be so fortunate. Here they can do anything and not only does the government ignore them, but the general community, when it is not yawning, merely collects their work for status or investment.

The criticism of the press in America, as sporadic, as inadequate, as ill-intended as it often is, is a tribute to the importance of the press in American life, an importance felt not only by government officials but by the community generally. The proper response is not a retreat behind slogans and defensive postures, but the encouragement of an active and critical tradition and an important body of professional critics.

Because such a critical community has not emerged, the press feels itself under greater attack than ever before. The last time this occurred in a sustained way was during the McCarthy era. Then the attack was primarily directed against television, movies and the presumed left-wing press. Today all the media and all newspapers are feeling the criticism, and they react from weakness, as if they are fragile institutions being buffeted about by hostile winds and about to fall before the onslaught. There is some truth in this response but not much. By becoming more professional, in the narrow sense of the self-enchancing, the press is going the way of other professions—teaching, medicine, law, architecture—that can no longer adequately connect with their communities, and whose power and remoteness breed indifference or hostility, a hostility that flashes into the open when touched by an administration spokesman. The answer is not, I think, response in kind but the creation of a tradition of press criticism that will reconnect the newspaper to the community it serves.

But how does a newspaper connect with its community? The most generally accepted method of connection is through the roles of the representative and spectator. Here the newspaper is the eyes and ears of the audience; it goes where the reader cannot go, so that the newspaper is representing the audience at city hall because the audience as an assembled community, a public, cannot be present. It is in this vein that the newspaper takes itself to be representing the public, or more fashionably these days, the people. This is a noble role but, as I have already indicated, it possesses a fatal weakness: the community to be represented has become remarkably dissolved, is in eclipse. The evidence of this eclipse is that the newspaper has little contact of any direct kind, physical or verbal, with this community. In effect, the entire system of communication has become one of address: that is, the people are spoken to, are informed, are often propagandized but in no sense are their own perceptions, understandings, judgments fed back into the process.

A second and more desirable method of connection is through criticism; that is, through the creation of an ongoing process of judgment that sets standards for the production, distribution and consumption of journalism, and in which the community participates in significant ways. There are, at the moment, three modes of criticism: two of them are inadequate and it is the third that I wish to pay major attention.

The first form of criticism is what we might call criticism by standards of public or social responsibility. This is the form of criticism that we have talked about up to this point. It involves the discussion of freedom, rights and objectivity. As a critical process it largely involves various government officials and members of the press who have, at this point, largely succeeded in talking by one another and the public. The weakness of this situation has led to the recommendation for national and local press councils to be the vehicle of assessment of social responsibility.

Are such institutions the answer? I think not. The idea of a press council sounds like a fine idea because it is so British, and I have no doubt that such councils can work in more aristocratic societies where there are men with enough general learning, cultural depth, commitment to the public interest, and leisure to participate in more than pro forma ways. In the United States press councils are likely to become one more bureaucracy.

While the attempt to create a critical tradition of discussion on the public responsibility of the press is perhaps an advance over viewing the press merely as a representative of the people, it is still not an effective answer to the problems we face and, as many journalists and publishers feel, may have its own peculiar dangers and pitfalls.

A second critical tradition to connect the public with the media is that proposed by the social scientists and might be called scientistic criticism. Here the standards for judging the press are not abstract rights, or codes of press performances or press council evaluations of responsibility—all things on which social scientists are rather quiet—but standards derived from scientific studies of the impact of the media upon audiences. The prototype here is the national commissions on violence and pornography where the fitness, rightness, and suitability of the material are judged, not by intrinsic merit or abstract rights, but by the effect the material has on audience attitudes and behaviour. This standard of criticism is simply wrongheaded. Its disastrous results already can be seen in the report of the Commission on Obscenity and Pornography, for the social scientific standards are in a general way destructive of culture. The questions permit no consideration of the quality, truth, or reasonableness of material, and it is obvious that any criticism of the press cannot merely test audience reactions—this would enshrine public opinion into an even more unbearable niche than it now occupies—but must work towards autonomous standards in which the audience participates, but which does not allow the mere criterion of audience appetite to dictate the cultural terms of journalism.

A third tradition of criticism can be termed cultural criticism and defined, first of all, by what it excludes. Cultural criticism is not debate over abstract shibboleths such as the people's right to know, problems of access, protection of reporters' sources or standards of press performance derived from abstract canons. As much as these items may occasionally enter the critical tradition, they do not constitute such a tradition, in any significant measure. By cultural criticism I mean an ongoing process of exchange, of debate between the press and its audience and, in particular, those among the audience most qualified by reason of motive and capacity to enter the critical arena. But what is the substance of this criticism, toward what is it directed?

It is a remarkable fact that each year most of us read more words by a reporter such as Homer Bigart of the *New York Times* than we do of Plato and yet today, 2500 years after Plato wrote, there is more critical work published on Plato every year than there is on Bigart. In fact, there is nothing published on Bigart, here used as an archetypal reporter, yet what he writes provides the critical diet for a major segment of the national "elite" community. I myself have read more words by James Reston than perhaps any other human, living or dead, yet I have never seen his work "reviewed" or criticized except when a few pieces are collected in book form, and then the review is inevitably by a comrade in the press. It is an anomalous fact that all of us consume more words by journalists than any other group, and yet our largest and perhaps most important literary diet is never given close critical scrutiny in any systematic way. In universities we critically review the work of men in every field, devoting thousands of hours to the perceptions, methods and style of obscure 18th-century Romantic poets, yet never consider that journalists, who daily inform our lives, require, for their good and ours, at least the same critical attention. Moreover, unlike other professions, journalists rarely gather to critically review one another's work, to expose its weakness, errors of commission and omission, and its failure to live up to professional let alone public standards. Let me make the judgment general: journalists, of all groups who expose their work to the public, are less critically examined by professional critics, the public or their colleagues. At journalistic gatherings professionals do not critique one another's work; they give one another awards.

Journalism is not only literary art; it is industrial art. The methods, procedures and canons of journalism were developed not only to satisfy the demands of the profession but to meet the needs of industry to turn out a mass-produced commodity. These canons are enshrined in the profession as rules of news selection, judgment, and writing. Yet they are more than mere rules of communication. They are, like the methods of the novelists, determiners of what can be written and in what way. In this sense the techniques of journalism define what is considered to be real: what can be written about and how it can be understood. From the standpoint of the audience, the techniques of journalism determine what the audience can think—the range of what is taken to be real on a given day. If something happens that cannot be packaged by the industrial formula, then, in a fundamental sense, it has not happened, it cannot be brought to the attention of the audience. If something happens that is only rendered in distorted fashion by the canons of journalism, then it is rendered in such distorted fashion, often without correction.

Let me give three examples of the way in which journalism as a stylistic strategy renders a disservice to its audience. The examples are not new or unusual: in fact, they are well known. The first case is the reporting on Viet Nam. Allow me an extended quote from an essay I wrote in 1967:

How does one render the reality that is Viet Nam in intelligible terms? The question is not merely rhetorical, for increasingly the ability of the American people to order and enhance their existence depends on their ability to know what really is going on. But we have this great arrogance about "communications." We treat problems of understanding as exercises in message transmittal. So here we sit shrouded in plastic, film, magnetic tape, photographs and lines of type thinking that two minutes of film or four column inches of canned type adequately render what is happening in Viet Nam, or for that matter anywhere else. In point of fact, the conventions of broadcast and newspaper journalism are just about completely inadequate to "tell" this story. I am not merely caviling about turning the war into an elaborate accounting exercise of hills, tonnage and dead (after all, that is the only measure of hope and progress one has in such a war). But why is this after all a war of accounting exercises? What are the political realities that underscore the day to day events? They are known—dimly of course—and can be found in the pages of more esoteric journals of opinion, and in a half hour conversation with a war correspondent when he is not talking through an inverted pyramid. But this is not a war that affects elites alone nor is it a time when we can all spend after hours with exhausted correspondents. What is sinful is that what is known about the war, and, what is the same thing, the stylistics that can render this knowledge, rarely make their way to the television screen or the newspapers. There the conventions of the craft reduce what is a hurly-burly, disorganized, fluid, non-rectilinear war into something that is straight, balanced, and moving in rectilinear ways. The conventions not only report the war but they endow it, pari passu, *with an order and logic—an order and logic which simply mark the underlying realities. Consequently, for opponents and advocates of the war, as well as those betwixt and between, the war haunts consciousness like a personal neurosis rather than a reality to be understood.*

And to make the case contemporary, one need only look at the ludicrous story to which we have been subject in the last year: the attempt to find and define the last American killed in Viet Nam. The story, so natural to our accepted procedures, merely masked the reality of the war, as if it were a conflict with a beginning, middle and end. Viet Nam might have been a story, but it is not like one of those we read in our youth.

Second, American journalism is still absurdly tied to events and personalities. American journalists are, in general, at a loss for what to do on the days when there isn't any news breaking. We have not learned how to report to the underlife of the country, how to get at the subterranean and frequently glacial movements that provide the meaningful substructure which determines the eruption of events and the emergence of personalities that we now call news. We still do not know how to bring to life the significance of the invisible: a slow shift in Black migration patterns out of the South, the relation between grain sales to the Soviet Union and grain elevators failing in small Illinois towns, the significance of the reduction of the birthrate and the strains

created by radically unequal age cohorts, the relatively rapid embourgeoisment of Blacks—all these "events" which, because they are not tied to personalities or are timeless, escape daily journalism yet constitute the crucial stories determining the American future.

A third example I draw from a colleague, Howard Ziff. The conventions of journalism have led to an increased distance between "the Press and the pace and detail of everyday life." The ordinary events of everyday lives—things which in their meaning and consequence are far from ordinary and insignificant for the audience—have no place in daily journalism. We lack the techniques of investigation and the methods of writing to tell what it feels like to be a Black, or a Pole, or a woman—or, God forbid, a journalist or professor today. This mainstream of overwhelming significant ordinary life—what a literary critic would call the "felt quality" of life—is a main connection between the newspaper and its audience, yet we do not know how to report it well. As a result the newspaper reports a world which increasingly does not connect with the life of its audience in the most fundamental sense that the audience experiences life.

The basic critical act in journalism is public scrutiny of the methods by which journalists define and get what we call news and the conventions by which they deliver it to the public. This criticism must not only be sustained and systematic, as with literary criticism, but it must also occur in the pages of the newspaper itself, in front of the audience that regularly consumes, uses or digests what is presented. Who should do it? In a certain sense, everyone. I have suggested that the newspaper itself must bring this critical community into existence. It must search out and find within its public those laymen who can and are interested in making a critical response to what they see and read daily. Hopefully such people will come from all strata of the public and represent its major segments. But such a community will not come into existence if the press passively awaits its appearance.

The press must recognize that it has a stake in the creation of a critical community and then use its resources to foster it. For it is only through criticism that news and the newspaper can meet the standard set out for it by Robert Park: "The function of news is to orient man and society in an actual world. Insofar as it succeeds it tends to preserve the sanity of the individual and the permanence of society."

THE ACTION/ MOTIVATION PERSPECTIVE FOR EXPLAINING AUDIENCE BEHAVIOR

Denis McQuail and Michael Gurevitch

[The action/motivation perspective of audience behavior] represents a position that many researchers in this field would recognize as at least partly their own, and it may also hold out most promise for future work. The action/motivation perspective can best be explained in terms of phenomenological sociology, especially as developed by Alfred Schultz.[1] His distinction between "conscious behavior" and "unconscious behavior" is echoed by those working in the uses and gratifications field who stress the idea of media use as a rational, goal-directed activity. According to Schutz, "An action is conscious in the sense that, before we carry it out, we have a picture in our mind of what we are going to do. This is the 'projected act'." While

Excerpted from "Explaining Audience Behavior: Three Approaches Considered" by Denis McQuail and Michael Gurevitch in The Uses of Mass Communications *(Vol. III, Sage Annual Reviews of Communication Research), Jay G. Blumler and Elihu Katz, editors (c) 1974, pp. 294-297, 299 by permission of the publisher, Sage Publications, Inc. (Beverly Hills/London).*

not all media use fits this conception of behavior, the researcher working within this perspective would be concerned with situations in which media use appears to be purposeful and in which the actor is able to explain his choices.

Certain assumptions implicit in the action/motivation perspective can be distinguished. First, human action implies freedom of choice, not merely freedom to choose between different courses of action but also freedom to attach different personal meanings to what may seem to be similar actions and experiences. Second, although unconscious motivation may exist, only those actions whose meanings and purposes can be described by the actor are suitable objects of study. Third, the future, particularly the future as perceived by the actor, is emphasized. The future is seen as distinct from the past and present, and neither present nor future is merely a function of the past. The essence of a motivated action, then, is its meaningfulness for and orientation to some future state.

In applying these assumptions to audience behavior, media use is regarded as an act of free choice by an actor who seeks to gain some immediate or delayed future benefits, to be or do what he wishes. The observer or investigator makes no presuppositions about the causes of behavior, on either a personal or a situational level. Although this approach may appear unrealistic, given the extent of social constraints on media use, its adoption may lead to observations, explanations, and insights that would not be produced by more deterministic perspectives. This is not merely a matter of adopting a general scientific open mindedness in advance of specific evidence, but rather one of rejecting explanatory frames of reference that are not those of the actor and that therefore might be alien to him. The primary source of evidence is the actor's own view of what he is doing.

When these assumptions of the action/motivation perspective are translated into methodological rules for studying the experience of the mass media audience, the following guidelines emerge:

1. To find out why viewers, listeners, or readers attend to media, *ask them*. They are likely to have some awareness of their motivation, and in any case their answers are the only relevant explanation of the actions in question.

2. Do not assume that any experience has a *unitary meaning*. Different people will give different accounts of the same media experience and will attribute personal meanings to that experience. Let the respondents provide the components of any explanatory framework.

3. In asking questions, focus on the *anticipated outcomes* of a communication experience. Direct inquiry to the future, not to the past.

4. Concentrate so far as possible on the *communication experience*. The personality, life circumstances, and past experiences of the person, as well as the content of the message, are secondary to the *relationship* between the message and the recipient.

Moreover, the adoption of this approach would tend to confine the investigator to certain types of research problems and to favor techniques that encourage respondents to give subjective accounts of their media experiences. The assumption of conscious choice and action requires finding an audience situation in which this level of awareness is likely to exist. This suggests a concentration on "fans"—either of a particular and established type of content or of an item typical of a genre, or possibly fans of a given medium in general. Established genres are most likely to give rise to clear expectations in prospective audience members, and fans are more likely to have, and to be aware of, motives for exposure than are casual members of the audience who simply "drop in." While we are here more concerned with representing the principles of a research approach, we can find several

examples of uses and gratifications studies that have exemplified this strategy.[2] Of course in a "pure" action/motivation approach fans can only represent themselves. However, some investigators have regarded fans as spokesmen for the less committed or articulate consumers of the same media content, who are then perceived as paler and less distinct versions of the former.

Since this perspective requires that data be collected from the vantage point of the media receiver, descriptive, qualitative, and exploratory procedures are more appropriate than carefully controlled experiments and representative sample surveys. Interviewing in depth and participant observation are techniques well suited to the approach. Studies are likely to be small in scale but detailed and intensive. A significant problem arises in devising techniques to obtain information about an individual's motivation for *future* behavior, since, ideally, motivation for future behavior and past experience should be separated, at least on a conceptual level. The investigator should, at least, aim to avoid obtaining rationalizations of past behavior, unprobed stereotypes, and current popular ideas about the appeal of the content.

The main prescription for data collection from this perspective is that it should explore the source of *meanings* present in media use situations and indicate the frequency of given types of interpretations. In this way, it might be possible to enhance our understanding of certain processes of media reception and to develop something approaching an ideal type for particular media use situations. Although the connection of media behavior with other features of a person's social situation should not be ignored, this connection should be established through the person's own perception rather than by a pattern of correlations. And although generalizations about a wider population and prediction of patterns of behavior for individuals or groups would not be the primary goal, research of this kind might yield statements of expectation about the occurrence of audience use phenomena structured in particular ways.

Given the basic assumptions and modes of research outlined, it would be inappropriate to state formal hypotheses for testing. This is not to suppose, however, that there would be no pattern in the findings. While assuming choices to be freely made, the investigator would also assume them to be rationally and meaningfully related to other acts and experiences in the individual's situation. Thus, patterns might show themselves because individuals sharing a set of situational circumstances are likely to choose, and give meaning to their choices, in similar ways—not because common circumstances *cause* common behavior but because the meanings given to acts of choice *take account of*, and are consistent with, what is involved in those circumstances. In addition, a given kind of content that has attracted a patterned set of associations and expectations may generate characteristic interpretations among its audience members, even though these may also vary according to other features of the individual's experience. Underlying this argument there is a more general hypothesis that audience members' recurrent objectives and aspirations are likely to be linked to some extent with regularities and standardization in content themes. Otherwise, however, this approach requires the least specific hypotheses to guide research designs, and there is no pressure to force its lines of reasoning into a hypothetico-deductive mould.

As we noted at the outset, this perspective has not been consciously adopted as a model for audience studies, and yet much of what has been said will be recognizable to anyone familiar with uses and gratifications research as describing procedures and commonsense assumptions of fieldwork. The theoretical distinctiveness comes from the rejection of interpolated "explanations" based on correlational evidence, the avoidance of any concept of unconscious or latent motivation, the stress on motivation as having a necessary future reference instead of being open to inference by introspection. If data were to be collected and these prescriptions adhered to, one would have a theoretically consistent study of the audience deserving a uses and gratifications label and yet in no way functionalist in concept. ...

...Other approaches appear, in any case, to have a different kind of relevance for policy making. None would help very much to give direct answers to media planners with specific problems. The action/motivation perspective would seem, however, with its stress on the objectives and purposes of self-conscious consumers, best suited to helping to plan for the more well-defined needs of subgroups and minority audiences rather than for the *mass* audience as such. ... To attempt to understand audience behavior in this way could also help to reinforce a non-manipulative, *service* attitude toward the individual audience member which might, in the final analysis, be regarded by many, especially in Western democratic societies, as the raison d'etre of the entire mass communication process....

NOTES

1. Schutz, A. *The Phenomenology of the Social World.* London: Heinemann, 1972.

2. See Herzog, H., "What Do We Really Know About Daytime Serial Listeners?" in Paul Lazarsfeld and F. N. Stanton (eds.), *Radio Research.* New York: Duell, Sloan & Pearce, 1944. Also see Blumler, J. G., Denis McQuail, and J. R. Brown, "The Social Origins of the Gratifications Associated with Television Viewing." Leeds: University of Leeds, 1970.

Index

e

Eagleton, Sen. Thomas, 166
Easton, David, 89, 90
Economies of scale, 263
Edelstein, Alex S., 106, 211-12
Editor & Publisher, 77
Effects of media on children, 47
Electronic News Gathering (ENG), 263
Eliot, T. S., 52
Elite culture, 59
Ellsberg, Daniel, 164, 177
Ellul, Jacques, 150, 152
Elmira, N.Y. Study, 87, 99
Emerson, Thomas, 276
Empirical research, 67
English press, 132-33
Ephemeral Folk Figures: Scarecrows, Harvest Figures, and Snowmen, 54
Epstein, Brian, 56
Epstein, Edward Jay, 125, 148, 208-09
    article by, 161-167
Erie County study, 9, 25, 38, 72, 87, 96, 98, 102
Escapism in media, 11, 52, 114
Ethics, 146, 264, 265, 341, 342
Event-centered news, 142
Experimental studies, 32, 40, 65

f

Fairness Doctrine, 272, 273
Family Life Coordinator, 86
Fallows, James, 208
Fantasy and media, 47
Farm Journal, 25
FBI, 164, 167, 175
Federal Communications Commission, 159, 251-54, 266, 267, 273, 275, 331, 342, 356, 358, 359, 361
Federal Trade Commission, 272
Festinger, Leon, 32, 33, 34, 66, 118
"Fighting Words," 271
First Amendment, *see* Freedom of Speech and Press
Fiske, Marjorie, 61, 111
Flamm, W. H., 333
Folk culture, 54, 58
Foreign Affairs, 150

Foreign language press, 130
Forster, E.M., 284
Fortune, 23
Frankfurter, Felix, 331
Freedman, Jonathan, 66, 108
Freedom of Speech and Press, 262, 265, 270, 327, 335, 342, 343
Freidson, Eliot, 58
Freund, Paul, 275
Freud, Sigmund, 48, 50, 114
Friendly, Fred, 159
Fuller, Buckminster, 264, 301
Functions, of mass communication, 11
Funkhouser, G. Ray, 107
Furu, T., 113

g

Galtung, Johan, 68, 69
Gannett Co., 145, 256
Gans, Herbert, 10
    article by, 61-64
Garvey, Michael Angelo, 295, 296
Gatekeeper, 125, 182
Gaudet, Hazel, 30, 38
Geddes, Patrick, 297, 298
Gertz v. Robert Welch, Inc., 265, 334-335, 340, 69
Gillmor, Donald M.
    articles by, 269-278, 340-354
Ginsberg, Allen, 55
Glazer, Nathan, 62
Gleason, Ralph, 55
Goddard, Morrill, 138
Goodman, Paul, 297
Gosnell, Harold, 30
Graff, Henry, 156
Grateful Dead, The, 55
Gratifications of media, 111, 113
Gratifications, substitute, in media, 48
Great Debates, The, 90
Great Exhibit of 1851, 295
Great Society, The, 55
Greeley, Horace, 15, 25, 131, 134
Greenberg, Clement, 51, 52
Greenstein, Fred, 86, 89, 90
Grotta, Gerald L., 248
Group affiliation, 32
Group ownership, 262, 263
Gruson, Sidney, 320, 321
Gurevitch, Michael, 12, 115, 268, 368
    articles by, 110-121, 368-370

†